The War Outside My Window

The Civil War Diary of
LeRoy Wiley Gresham, 1860 - 1865

edited by

Janet Elizabeth Croon

SB

Savas Beatie

California

Library of Congress Cataloging-in-Publication Data

Names: Croon, Janet Elizabeth, author.
Title: The War Outside My Window: The Civil War Diary of Teenager LeRoy Wiley Gresham, 1860-1865 / Janet Elizabeth Croon, ed.
Other titles: Civil War Diary of teenager LeRoy Wiley Gresham, 1860-1865
Description: El Dorado Hills, California : Savas Beatie, [2018] | Includes index.
Identifiers: LCCN 2018006100| ISBN 9781611213881 (hardcover: alk. paper) | ISBN 9781611213898 (ebk)
Subjects: LCSH: Gresham, LeRoy Wiley, 1847-1865–Diaries. | United States–History–Civil War, 1861-1865–Personal narratives, Confederate. | Teenage boys–Confederate States of America–Diaries. | Teenage boys–Georgia–Diaries. | Tuberculosis–Patients–Diaries. | Plantation life–Georgia–Houston County. | Gresham family. | Macon (Ga.)–History–Civil War, 1861-1865–Personal narratives. | Macon (Ga.)–Social life and customs–19th century. | Macon (Ga.)–Biography.
Classification: LCC E605 .C94 2018 | DDC 973.7/82–dc23
LC record available at https://lccn.loc.gov/2018006100

ISBN (print): 978-1-61121-388-1
ISBN (ebook): 978-1-61121-389-8

First Edition, First Printing

SB

Savas Beatie LLC
989 Governor Drive, Suite 102
El Dorado Hills, CA 95762

Phone: 916-941-6896
(web) www.savasbeatie.com
(E-mail) sales@savasbeatie.com

Savas Beatie titles are available at special discounts for bulk purchases in the United States by corporations, institutions, and other organizations. For more details, please contact Savas Beatie, P.O. Box 4527, El Dorado Hills, CA 95762, or you may e-mail us at sales@savasbeatie.com, or visit our website at www.savasbeatie.com for additional information.

Proudly published, printed, and warehoused in the United States of America.

MIX
Paper from responsible sources
FSC
www.fsc.org   FSC® C011935

To my daughters Allison and Lauren,
and to all of my "other kids," my South Lakes Seahawk students.
May LeRoy inspire you to keep reaching for your best.

And to Dr. Dennis Rasbach,
for tirelessly working to solve the puzzle of LeRoy's fatal disease.
Without his help, this book would not be as impactful
or important as it now is.

LeRoy Wiley Gresham at about 10 years old in 1857.
Library of Congress

Table of Contents

Table of Contents (continued)

PHOTOS AND MAPS

Leroy Wiley Gresham (frontis)

A photo gallery follows page 250

A map gallery follows the *Dramatis Personae*

Saturday night
Macon Jany 10/57~

My dear Mary.

Upon our return this afternoon from Houston I received your very welcome letter and read the readable parts of it to our dear boys who were delighted to hear from you. . . .

It was pretty hard work to keep warm last night, and the wind blew as it only blows on this hill & in our room. Thomas slept with me, & LeRoy on Minnie's couch. He was heard from all night till was late before we had the courage to reach our toilette this morning.

Thomas enjoyed himself finely killing birds in which he was quite successful, and poor Loy seemed happy + cheerful, but was not disposed to take much exercise and remained mostly about the house and yard. He stood the ride home very well to day + sang + laughed nearly all the way, while my heart was aching with pain.

I could think of little else and would often ride with my arms around him—pressing him to me—how little he or any but you knew what I felt. When I lost my hurt boy in your absence—and such a boy—and how to break the news to you myself, I thought the trial severe, but this—who can tell the anguish—I can't write about it + yet I can write about nothing else. Perhaps I was wrong to say I was perfectly miserable. I have yet other blessings left for which I would not be ungrateful. But my poor boy!!

. . . It is time to go to church + will close for today with the assurance of my unchanging love and a promise of another letter soon.

Your devoted H.
J.J.G——

I shall let Loy go to school in the morning, but the Doctors wish to examine him again before giving their advice. I think I should take him North before long.

Publisher's Preface

Until the spring of 2017, I had never heard of LeRoy Wiley Gresham. Odds are you hadn't either.

Jan Croon, a former teacher and friend on social media living and working in northern Virginia, passed on a link to me of a 2012 article by Michael E. Ruane in the *Washington Post* entitled "Invalid boy's diary focus of Library of Congress Civil War exhibit." I receive articles like this almost daily, so I nearly skipped past it. What a mistake that would have been. I clicked the link and started reading. The lengthy story mesmerized me from the first few sentences.

The Library of Congress was featuring a large display of Civil War material to mark its sesquicentennial, among them "Gresham's little-known diary"—a seven-volume account donated by the family in the 1980s. The writer was a nearly bedridden teenage boy from a wealthy slave-holding family in Macon, Georgia. Some years earlier he had badly broken a leg that never fully healed. How he had hurt it was a mystery left unaddressed.

LeRoy (or just "Loy" to his family) spent 1860-1865 recording what he read, heard, observed, thought, felt, and experienced. He was a voracious reader and devoured everything he could get his hands on, including Shakespeare and Charles Dickens. Arithmetic and word problems fascinated him, as did railroads, science, and chess—a game he played at every opportunity. Most of his time outside was spent in a small custom-built wagon, pulled around town by a slave about his own age or his own older brother Thomas. His last diary entry was June 9, 1865. He died eight days later.

By the time I finished reading the article, my fascination with the young lad had changed to one of curiosity. According to the Library of Congress, this remarkable account had yet to be published. The article was five years old, so surely his diaries were now readily available in book form. I searched the Internet and found a second article, this one written two years later in 2014 by the same reporter in the same paper titled "Mary Gresham's grief over invalid son's death echoes from 1865." The focus of this piece was a seven-page private letter written by LeRoy's mother Mary to her sister shortly after LeRoy died. Mary's tender soaring prose included a detailed description of LeRoy's final hours. Her palpable pain at his passing tugs at one's heart strings and is, even now, difficult to read.

I kept searching. To my astonishment, other than tangential references to LeRoy or the Gresham family, there was not a single word about the diaries having been published, or that anyone was even considering doing so. How could this be? I followed the link to the Library of Congress website and spent a couple hours reading from the diaries. Then and there I made my decision and picked up the phone.

"Jan, are you interested in transcribing and annotating LeRoy's journals for publication?" Her reply was an enthusiastic "Yes!" A staff member at the Library of Congress soon confirmed there were no restrictions on publishing, and that to her knowledge, no one else was preparing to publish the diaries.

Marketing director Sarah Keeney and I charted a rather expeditious course of action. Once we signed a contract with Jan, we distributed a press release announcing that Savas Beatie would be publishing the book the following year—an admittedly aggressive schedule. My hope was that the news would flush out other efforts farther along than our own, and so save us an inordinate amount of time and money. It also might discourage anyone who was thinking of transcribing and publishing them. Because of his obvious interest in LeRoy's remarkable story, I emailed a copy of the press release to *Washington Post* reporter Michael Ruane. Michael quickly replied that he was pleased LeRoy's efforts would be published, and to keep him informed as the work progressed. Michael would almost certainly have known if someone else was working on the diaries.

It looked as if the way ahead was clear.

*   *   *

LeRoy Gresham was 12 years old when he began writing in his first journal in 1860. The blank book was a gift from his mother so he could record his experiences with his father, John Gresham, on their upcoming trip to Philadelphia to see a medical specialist about LeRoy's "condition." Apparently his unhealed crushed leg was getting worse. How had he broken it?

Further research uncovered a newspaper account written many decades after the event by Macon native Albert Martin Ayres in which he reminisced about his time growing up in Georgia. It also included a story about an accident that had crushed a young boy's leg and left him a cripple. Ayres' distant recollection placed the event in about 1854, but Gresham family letters and Leroy's own pen date the accident to September 21, 1856. Ayres left a somewhat longer account in a brief memoir:

> The next and last teacher in Macon was Mr. Sylvan Bates. . . . Returning from school one afternoon a crowd of us boys stopped to look at the ruins of old Washington block which had burned the night before. I saw the bricks slowly sliding out at the base of a tall chimney. . . . I was standing at the cellar steps at the time. I shouted to the boys and we ran into the street, spreading out into a fan. The bricks must have disintegrated from the top of the chimney. I found myself on the ground in a cloud of dust and bricks. My head became matted with blood but apparently I wasn't badly hurt. The little boy at my side had his leg all broken up and I think he was crippled until he died. Someone scratching among the bricks found one of my books and decided I must be under the bricks, but I had gotten my other books and gone home rubbing my head.[1]

A collapsed chimney had inflicted the painful and crippling injury that left eight-year-old LeRoy a prisoner within his own young body.

LeRoy and his father made the 1,400-mile round trip by sea from Savannah to Philadelphia to seek an effective treatment. Unfortunately, there was nothing the Northern specialist could do for the young man except prescribe some medicine (presumably for pain) and recommend "extended rest." The disappointed father and son returned to Macon, where LeRoy kept writing. Deep in the heart of Georgia, mostly from reclined positions, he put pen to paper with a vim and often tongue-in-cheek vigor that impresses even now, almost 160 years later.

The youngster soaked in everything around him. He read books and devoured newspapers and magazines. He listened to gossip and discussed and debated important social and military topics with his parents, older brother Thomas, other relatives, and family friends. He recorded his thoughts nearly every day.

His early daily logs began with unpretentious observations about the weather and his sea journey and visits to Philadelphia and New York. LeRoy wrote for the next five years about politics and the secession movement, the long and increasingly destructive Civil War, life in Macon at the center of a socially prominent slave-holding family, his interactions with many of the slaves, and his multitude of hobbies and interests. His straightforward and (usually) well-organized journals are riddled with doodles, math and word problems, charts of chess moves and games, lists of books he read, poetry, religious references, drawings, and even detailed tables recording the weather.

---

1   Iris Margaret Ayres Smale, *Albert Martin Ayres I Memoirs* (LuLu, 2004), 8.

It quickly becomes clear LeRoy's diary became an important part of his life. He wrote about his extended family in Macon, Sparta, and Athens, where his grandmother (who had six living sons who served in the Civil War) resided. LeRoy marveled as Macon, "safe" in a central location in the Deep South, evolved into one of the Confederacy's most important industrial centers. Tens of thousands of Southern troops passed through the important railroad city. Thousands more trained there and left for the front. Union prisoners were confined there. LeRoy witnessed it all.

As the years progressed, so did LeRoy's capacity to reason, analyze, and expound. His ability to handle major events in a concise and crisp manner is surprising for one so young. What began with uncomplicated simple observations evolved into complex and nuanced entries. He learned to take early reports of important military events with a grain of salt, and to question the truth of what he was being told or reading in the papers. Late-war entries reflect disagreements with his father (whom he adored) about the course of the bloody war, and demonstrate his healthy skepticism regarding political pronouncements. His pen occasionally dripped vitriol. He found it easy to mock politicians or generals he disliked, and he often did so with gusto. Despite the depressing nature of his world, most of his entries were penned with a certain irrepressible youthful optimism laced with clever hilarity and grin-inducing charm. Clever Twain-like phrases sprinkled throughout capture his precocious nature.

And then there is the matter of slavery. Human bondage is a stain on humanity; it existed at some point or another in every country in the world, and this one fought a long bloody war—the central feature of these journals—that ended it. Slaves were omnipresent in LeRoy's short life. He was born a rich plantation-owner's son, so slavery to him was the only way of life he ever knew. Unfortunately, he did not elaborate at any depth about the institution. Because he was so young and so sick, and was moving toward adulthood as fast as he was to the grave, it is doubtful he had the requisite time to reach any firm conclusions about the morality and ethics of slavery.

It is important to keep in mind that this is a primary source from another time—a time into which LeRoy was born and raised. It should therefore come as no surprise that he used terms freely that are not socially acceptable today. This says little about LeRoy other than that he was a product of his age, upbringing, and social status. He used words like "darkies" or "nigs" or "negroes" descriptively, not pejoratively. He wrote often about the Gresham slaves by name and detailed their comings and goings and changing relationships with the family as the war progressed. Many entries exhibit an obvious affection or concern, as the situation dictated. He was born and raised with slave-servants in the Macon home. Some, like Frank, had carpentry skills and helped LeRoy build things, while Julia Ann and others cooked much of their food, and Bill and Allen pulled him around town in his wagon. It is difficult to imagine that someone like

LeRoy, living his entire life in proximity with them, would not form some sort of bond under such circumstances. As he matures, he offers a few clues on this subject; I leave it to readers to reach their own conclusions.

The overriding theme of these diaries is the Civil War, but there is something else lurking within these pages, something dark, menacing, and ultimately, horrific that will eventually become clear to readers: The gifted teenager was suffering from much more than a crushed leg that had not healed properly. He was ill, and his condition slowly, if steadily, worsened until his young body finally gave out. What, exactly, had killed LeRoy at such a young age?

For help with a diagnosis, I reached out to Dennis Rasbach, an experienced general surgeon for whom the Civil War is a serious avocation. Intrigued by the challenge, he rolled up his sleeves and began unraveling the mystery. LeRoy's own writings offered more than enough clues. He recorded his many symptoms, his array of treatments (one might charitably describe as pharmaceutical roulette), and his horrendous suffering—often in agonizing detail. Additional medical and historical research, coupled with discussions with other disease experts, confirmed Dr. Rasbach's suspicions: The Macon teenager had been fighting and losing his battle with a fatal disease for several years. It was this very illness that had prompted his father to take his son north to see Dr. Pancoast as the diary opens. In fact, local doctors had diagnosed his disease in early 1857 in news that crushed his loving parents. LeRoy's ill-healed broken leg had nothing to do with his trip north.

LeRoy's parents and doctors (and eventually, and almost certainly, his older brother Thomas) knew exactly what he was suffering from, and that he was terminally ill. For reasons that are their own, no one shared the news with LeRoy, who, unbeknownst to him, was chronicling his own slow and painful descent toward death in tandem with the demise of the Southern Confederacy. Finally, when he was too weak to write, eat, and barely able to speak, he looked up from his deathbed to quietly announce, "Well, Mother, this is the end," to which Mary Gresham asked, "What do you mean, my Son?" His five-word reply broke her heart: "I am dying, ain't I?" LeRoy passed away the next day, just weeks after the Confederacy's final field army surrendered. He was just 17.

In addition to being a publisher, I am a trained historian who has been studying the Civil War for a half-century. To my knowledge, no other male teenage civilian, North or South, left a diary spanning the entire Civil War; certainly one like this has never been published. Most that have found their way into print were penned by soldiers like Confederate Sam Watkins (*Company Aytch: A Sideshow of the Big Show*) and Unionist Elisha Rhodes (*All for the Union: The Civil War Diary and Letters of Elisha Hunt Rhodes*). Others were kept by adults who lived and mingled in high society, like Southern aristocrat Mary Chesnut (*A Diary from Dixie*), wealthy Louisianan Sarah Morgan (*A Confederate Girl's Diary*), and Northern attorney George Templeton Strong (*The Diary of George Templeton Strong*). LeRoy was not a soldier or an adult, and he rarely left home.

When I asked editor Jan Croon whether anything similar to LeRoy's effort came to mind, the former teacher suggested a faint resemblance to *The Diary of Anne Frank*. It is not a perfect comparison, for Anne was persecuted because she was Jewish, and her account is justly venerated as being in a class of its own. Still, there are several parallels worth considering. Both journals were kept by adolescents during wartime, and both were keen observers of societies undergoing radical change. Both were eloquent writers, especially given their age, and each offers readers a detailed record of their daily experiences. There is another similarity, less obvious but deeply influential. Anne and LeRoy both observed their changing worlds at a distance. Anne spent years hiding and writing from the confines of secret rooms to avoid arrest by the Nazis. LeRoy was also confined, though by a physical ailment that kept him nearly immobile, mostly housebound, and largely unable to take part in the society in which he lived. He could not attend school or church, he missed nearly every major local event (including many family affairs), and he could only watch from the rolling confinement of his wagon as his friends played "town ball," an early form of baseball. LeRoy's main threat came not from Nazis, or even from the Union "invaders" who would eventually occupy his home, but from within his own body as it slowly weakened and withered away.

I urge you to read this diary slowly, deliberately, and thoughtfully. It is not a fast-paced piece of literature, and it was almost surely never intended to be read by anyone outside the family. Curb your natural instincts for haste. Introduce yourself to everyone, for you will come across a host of fascinating people who exist no where else but within these pages. Use freely the *Dramatis Personae* to meet them. Understand their relationships. The footnotes offer information to better grasp what LeRoy and his family and relatives were reading in the papers and discussing around the dinner table. Absorb the atmosphere of the Gresham home and consider the palpable angst they felt as the long bloody war turned against them. And never forget John, Mary, Thomas, Minnie, and the slave-servants would have heard LeRoy's bouts of coughing around the clock, and looked on helplessly as their loving son or brother or young master wasted away, knowing all the while he would leave them sooner rather than later.

Now, you too have heard of LeRoy Wiley Gresham. I am confident you will think of him, the other members of the Gresham family, and of the vanishing world of which he wrote, long after you finish this book.

Theodore P. Savas
Publisher

Introduction

Le Roy Wiley Gresham left behind seven separate diaries. The first begins in the middle of 1860, detailing his trip north with his father and later, the rise of the secession crisis, and the breaking apart of the United States. The final volume ends in June 1865 just weeks after the close of the Civil War with his death. Although at first glance his journals appear relatively straightforward, in fact they are layered with a host of complexities. Preparing them for publication was a fascinating process that needs to be understood in order to get the most out of what LeRoy left us.

Publisher Theodore P. Savas and I extensively discussed how to handle a work of this length, depth, and complexity. His advice and suggestions (not to mention his detailed hands-on assistance with the military aspects of LeRoy's writing) have been immeasurably important in the creation of this book.

Transcribing the Diaries

I have worked with archival materials at the Virginia Historical Society in Richmond, the Woodrow Wilson Library in Staunton, Virginia, and elsewhere, and so I was looking forward to seeing LeRoy's journals in person at the Library of Congress. Working with archival documents brings the past to life. Viewing the documents themselves, rather than copies or scans, can reveal details that are otherwise not readily apparent. The Library of Congress, however, had scanned all seven diaries—including the covers— and made them available digitally. I used these digital images to transcribe what LeRoy had written.

The Library of Congress did a remarkable job with this project, and the ability to enlarge the handwriting, zoom in on a particular section, or download a high-resolution page and manipulate it in Photoshop to double-check a particular word or sentence, made my job substantially easier. For example, enlarging some pages revealed faint words or sentences that had been written in pencil. In addition, pens occasionally skip (this was especially true of his mother's handwriting near the end of the journal) and the ink does not get into the paper. Sometimes, however, the nib of the pen left trace amounts, and magnification allowed me to see what my eyes otherwise would not have picked up from the original scan itself.

It was very important to let LeRoy speak in his own voice. This was fairly easy to do because his writing is clear and usually easy to follow—with some caveats. Some of his abbreviations were puzzling or a bit unusual, and it took some time to understand was he was doing and how he was using them. I left most in place and their purpose will quickly become obvious. His punctuation was not always consistent. To enhance readability, I added periods to the end of sentences that lacked them, and inserted occasional commas where needed. Little else was changed, added, or deleted. LeRoy was a remarkably good speller for his age, but he chronically misspelled certain words like Tuesday (Teusday), guard (gaurd), Augusta (Agusta), enlist (inlist) and a handful of others. Despite my chronic "red pen" tendencies, I left them as he wrote them. (Ironically, he does not spell George McClellan's last name correctly until after that Union general was permanently removed from command!)

He often named people or events that will be familiar to Civil War students, but not to readers of other genres. In such cases I used footnotes to clarify his meaning. He also occasionally used words that will cause most modern readers to stumble. Take, for example, "yclept." I typed it just as he spelled it fully expecting my software to underline it in red to denote a misspelling. It did no such thing! I looked up "yclept" and discovered it means "to name or call out." The word was in LeRoy's normal vocabulary, but is no longer in use today. In other instances it made sense to add a word or short phrase in a bracket to clarify his meaning. For example, the addition of "[hallway]" clarifies this sentence: "Minnie and Alice are in the passage [hallway] reading Fairy tales out loud to one another."

The *Dramatis Personae*

The most difficult aspect of preparing LeRoy's diaries for publication was identifying and keeping track of the large number of individuals who bob and weave their way through his life. Some are prominent and famous; most are not. Many family members have the same or very similar names. (LeRoy's extended family entails some 1,700 individuals, although thankfully he doesn't mention them all!) The Greshams lived in a large home at 353 College Street in Macon. John Jones Gresham was prominent in the city and across much of Georgia, so his home was a busy place. LeRoy enjoyed mentioning who came by, when, why, and for how long. The multitude of people who stopped in for breakfast, lunch, dinner, tea, or to chat, play chess, fix things, or remain for an extended stay was part and parcel of Southern culture in the middle of the nineteenth century. Understanding who these people were and how they fit into the landscape of LeRoy's life is important.

Thankfully, my forte is genealogy, which is one of the reasons Ted asked me to act as editor of these diaries. After some discussion Ted suggested I prepare a *Dramatis Personae* (literally "the persons of the drama") to help readers keep everyone straight and (mostly) easy to identify. The *Dramatis Personae* includes a list and short description (together with relevant dates, ranks, and titles) of everyone who lived in the Macon residence (the Gresham family and their slaves/servants); the plantation slaves mentioned by LeRoy; Macon residents; extended family members; and distant relations. Footnotes in the main text, where appropriate or needed, clarify a person's identity, but whenever in doubt please refer to the *Dramatis Personae*. This will slow down the reading a bit, but in the end make for a more rewarding experience.

This stage of the editing process was also consumed with outlining family relationships and determining who belonged to which branch of this close-knit family. LeRoy, of course, knew who "Aunt Sarah" and "Cousin Eliza" were when he wrote their names—but which Sarah or Eliza? For example, Ancestry.com tossed up 56 different Sarahs (among them more than one aunt), and 86 Eliza/Elizabeths. This Southern family and their relations had many similar names (including more than one LeRoy). Maiden names were often used as middle names, and I discovered two separate branches of Wileys involved. I had a teaching colleague named Sally whose given name was Sarah, which turned out to be useful information I readily applied in my exploration through the expansive Gresham family tree. However, it was only through sheer perseverance that I was able to match nicknames like "Jenks" or "Link" to a particular person. (Even now, as we go to press, I am still working to identify the three Knox brothers who have thus far eluded me.) Sorting through the Gresham family was a long, though ultimately satisfying, task.

Individuals mentioned by LeRoy who are not listed in the *Dramatis Personae* are given more extensive treatment in the footnotes. To keep the book accessible and readable for all audiences, and to better keep the focus on LeRoy and his life, we decided to forgo the use of extensive academic-style citations. The vast majority of the information concerning Macon and it residents came from a handful of authoritative sources (see A Note on Sources), and in most cases everything in the notes can be easily explored at depth on the Internet with a few key clicks.

The Editing Process

Once the journals were transcribed and I had finished identifying nearly everyone mentioned in the *Dramatis Personae*, Ted and I decided certain things LeRoy included could be removed to substantially improve readability without losing anything of substance. For example, LeRoy recorded the temperatures three times a day for several years. Although modestly interesting in the short term, over time rows of numbers cease being interesting. LeRoy's daily description of the weather ("cloudy and warm," for example) was sufficient. The temperature becomes an important element of the story when it was oppressively hot or extremely cold; those notations or descriptions were left as he presented them. For example, the Greshams lived in what was considered in those days a mansion, but even wealthy families did not have central heating. As a result, it was not unusual for the temperature inside much of the house to drop to freezing (or lower) in the dead of winter. Other items of little interest, like who delivered a sermon or unimportant visitors passing through the story without impacting LeRoy or an important thread, were removed or at least reduced to keep the focus on the main characters and keep the story moving.

The major theme throughout LeRoy's diary is the Civil War and its effect on the Confederacy and Georgia, the Gresham family and their friends and relatives, and of course, Southern society. We discussed at length how to handle the large number of references to officers, battles, campaigns, maneuvers, and other aspects of the conflict LeRoy found interesting enough to write about. Much of it required some sort of explanation in a footnote. In an effort to balance readability with knowledge and context, we decided to offer enough general information to inform readers what LeRoy was reading and hearing, but in most cases not include detailed citations. Ted's forte is the Civil War, so he graciously helped me identify many of the confusing people and events in this area, and prepare those notes.

The Plantation

Determining the location and name of the Gresham plantation was something of a mystery that needed solving. LeRoy often notes his Father or someone else "left for Houston" or "came up from Houston." My first thought, naturally enough, was that he meant Houston, Texas, but surely that was not right. As it turned out, Houston (pronounced Howston) is a county in Georgia directly south of Macon, which is in Bibb County.

Using Ancestry.com, I discovered that John Gresham owned not one but two plantations. Other information revealed the names of two different agents (overseers), the number of slaves held on each property, and the district in which the property was located within the county. Librarians Susan Clay and Meagan Duever at the University of Georgia map library helped me locate taxation records for Houston County, and we placed the plats on both contemporary and modern maps. Muriel Jackson, at Macon's Washington Library, provided me with helpful maps of antebellum Macon.[2]

John Gresham was one of the largest plantation owners in Georgia. Pineland and Oakwoods totaled 1,715 acres and were adjacent to one another along the western bank of the Ocmulgee River some 40 miles southeast of Macon. Both were accessible by a long day's ride by wagon. It was usually slaves (primarily Howard, and often unaccompanied) who traveled back and forth in this manner with meat, vegetables, and fruit to supply the Macon home. The plantations also provided the family with substantial wealth, mostly from cotton.[3]

The Federal 1860 Census data identified the plantation "agents" (overseers) as Kindred Kemp and Jessup R. Hill, and offered additional information about each man including their immediate families. LeRoy mentions both men several times in his diaries. According to the 1860 Federal Census, 1860 Slave Schedules, and LeRoy's own writings, Hill was in charge of Pineland and 50 slaves living in eight slave cabins, while Kemp oversaw 43 slaves of varying ages living in six slave cabins at Oakwoods. By its very nature, slavery is cruel and inhumane. Unfortunately, no records exist as to how the slaves were treated on the Gresham plantations, or whether the overseers were particularly callous or vicious. The records also do not indicate which of the Houston slaves listed in the *Dramatis Personae* lived and worked on which plantation. Slave Schedules recorded only gender, age, and degree of color (full black, black, and mulatto, for example). However, a careful reading of LeRoy's diaries and various Gresham family letters made it possible to put together a list by name, gender, and approximate age of the slave servants who staffed the Macon home, as well as some intimate information about them (special skills, etc.). I was able to put names to the Slave Schedule descriptions with the exception of the oldest, who was a runaway at the time the census was taken.

---

2   See http://freepages.genealogy.rootsweb.ancestry.com/~ajac/gahouston.htm.

3   Georgia Property Tax Digest, 1793-1793, Houston, 1872-1877, p. 263, Ancestry.com. Most of the land is now covered with housing subdivisions, with only a small portion of the original plantation property left as agricultural land. Later in his journals, LeRoy explains that his father and Thomas occasionally took the Macon & Brunswick Railroad partway to the plantations, finishing the journey by wagon or on horseback.

Examples of LeRoy's Handwriting

We decided to include a variety of cropped images to demonstrate how LeRoy wrote things, including his own name. He had beautiful handwriting and took special care in how he crafted certain letters. These examples of his writing include everything from important points he made to some of his drawings, doodlings, margin notes, and the usual types of things young boys of his age will write when they think no one is looking.

*   *   *

There is so much of value in what LeRoy left behind. As an educator, it was exciting to follow LeRoy's writing as it evolved from an elemental level of comprehension to more advanced levels of synthesis and evaluation. Simultaneously, it was heartbreaking to vicariously experience his decline in health, read of his pain and afflictions, and follow him to the grave on a journey he did not fully understand or even know he was taking until it was nearly at an end. It was also incredibly sad to think of the horrendous life endured by so many of the people he names—slaves who spent most or all of their years on earth toiling in bondage.

In addition to all of the other attributes of his diaries, LeRoy's account demonstrates how people in that era lived, worked, entertained, and cooperated (or didn't) with one another. It was especially fascinating to learn firsthand, over a long period of time, how civilians gathered and processed information and then acted upon it as the only world they knew slowly crumbled into history.

There are many valuable lessons within these pages and something of lasting value for general readers, Civil War and medical history historians, educators, and students. Working to help bring LeRoy and his vanished world to you has been a special pleasure I will long remember.

Janet Elizabeth Croon
Ashburn, Virginia

A Medical Foreword

Historians get excited about personal diaries, which often contain material that would be unavailable in any other context. This certainly is true for the journals of LeRoy Wiley Gresham, an invalid teenager who wrote about his life and troubled times in the South during the Civil War.

What makes his journals especially noteworthy, however, is that throughout the time he was recording his invaluable observations he was also dying, though he did not know it. For five years LeRoy methodically documented his symptoms and the largely ineffective treatments prescribed by his doctors as his vitality slowly ebbed.

The nature of LeRoy's illness and the cause of his death have long been surmised. Until now, however, they have never been scrutinized through the lens of modern medical knowledge. His initial disability was attributed to a childhood accident in 1856 that crushed and crippled his left leg. That injury seemed to set off a cascade of medical troubles. But the variety and inexorable progression of symptoms far exceeded the suffering one would expect from a broken leg. Eventually the process claimed his life.

Medical entries found throughout his journals deal almost exclusively with symptoms—coughing, pain, fever, insomnia, vomiting. This is the focus one would expect from a person experiencing a medical ordeal. He never mentions a specific underlying diagnosis. If the physicians attending him made such a pronouncement, they did not communicate it to their patient. After devoting much thought to this account, I feel confident in concluding—with a high degree of medical certainty—that LeRoy Gresham died of advanced tuberculosis, and that the trauma he suffered from the initial accident was essentially a red herring in the chain of events leading to his premature demise.

Today we understand tuberculosis as an infectious disease caused by a mycobacterium. Specific and effective treatments are available to cure the malady, although a constant battle is being waged against resistant strains. Unfortunately, in LeRoy's day there was no understanding of a "germ theory" of disease, and no specific treatments existed. Almost everyone who developed active tuberculosis died from it sooner or later.

Also known as "consumption," "phthisis," and the "white plague," tuberculosis was a prolific killer in the nineteenth century. In fact, it claimed more lives than any other disease. Many of its victims came from among the young working poor of urban centers. No demographic group was spared, however, and the prevalence of the illness among artists, writers, and musicians led to a peculiar association of tuberculosis with the romantic spirit of the era. Composer Frederic Chopin died of tuberculosis. John Keats, Edgar Allan Poe, Charlotte Brontë, and Fyodor Dostoevsky wrote about it in their poems and novels, and the disease was depicted operatically in Verdi's *La traviata* and Puccini's *La bohème.*

Despite the widespread employment of tuberculosis as a literary and artistic motif, there is a paucity—perhaps even a complete absence—of first-person accounts charting the course of this lethal malady as it progressed over time, before effective treatments became available. Thus my comment earlier about why LeRoy's account is especially noteworthy. His diaries offer an extremely rare chronicle of consumption. They provide a unique window into an affliction that must have been very prevalent among families on both sides of the parallel conflict that was devouring the material and human resources of the nation.

Before opening the pages of this diary, I urge a word of caution. The practice of medicine is a sacred trust. When a patient consults with a physician, it is often a time of vulnerability. Confronted by threats to physical or mental health, he or she concedes temporary but unparalleled access into very private areas. In these personal entries, LeRoy Wiley Gresham recorded the kinds of intimate details he might have shared only with a close family member or trusted physician. He very likely did not intend for us to be privy to these musings. I therefore invite you to enter his sick room in a manner befitting a loving caregiver—quietly and with decorum appropriate to the solemnity of the occasion.

Dennis A. Rasbach, MD, FACS
St. Joseph, Michigan

Dramatis Personae

Inside the Gresham Residence
at 353 College Street, Macon, Georgia

John Jones Gresham (1812-1891). LeRoy's father. Plantation owner, former lawyer and judge, and president of Macon Manufacturing Company ("Macon Factory") at the corner of Lamar and Oglethorpe streets. Elected mayor for two one-year terms (1843, 1847). Before secession, he wrote "there was little hope in the peaceful solution of the slavery question."

The patriarch of the Gresham family was born January 21, 1812, in Burke County, Georgia, to Job and Mary Jones Gresham, who had married in 1807. John was raised on his father's farm near Brier Creek. His early education was accomplished in local rural schools until he reached fourteen, when he went to an academy in Waynesboro and then another academy at Bath (in Richmond County). John entered the sophomore class of Franklin College (later the University of Georgia) in 1830 and completed his degree three years later with first honors.

John studied law in Augusta and was admitted to the Georgia bar in 1834, though he soon discovered that practicing law was not as enjoyable as he had hoped. (By 1857 he was serving as a judge in Macon and was called "Judge" thereafter by most who knew him.) He moved to Macon (Bibb County) in 1836 and married Catherine Elvira Flewellen on October 30, 1839. Unfortunately, she fell sick and died less than six months later on March 20, 1840. Three years later John married Mary E. Baxter. John and Mary had five children. Two sons (Edmund and Edward) died in infancy and LeRoy would die in his teens; only Thomas and Mary ("Minnie") would survive into adulthood and have families of their own.

The Gresham family lived in a large Greek Revival home on College Street in Macon. John made most of his wealth owning and running a pair of plantations collectively called "Houston" (after Houston County) south of Macon and owned a large number of slaves.

In addition to his plantations Judge Gresham engaged in a number of businesses including insurance and textiles. He acquired an interest in the Macon Manufacturing Company in 1850, built a cotton mill in 1851, served as mayor of Macon twice, and would be elected to the Georgia State Senate in 1865. He served as the president of the Breckinridge & Lane Club of Bibb County during the 1860 presidential election and supported the secession of Georgia. John contributed money and supplies to the Confederacy and near the end of the war was conscripted into the Georgia home guard.

Mary Eliza Baxter Gresham (1822-1889). LeRoy's mother. Almost nothing is known of Mary before the Civil War, and virtually nothing after it. She was a leading member of Macon society and deeply involved with the Ladies Soldiers Relief Society and the Wayside Home during the Civil War. Her health was somewhat fragile during the war years (and perhaps before). She lost two small children (Edmund, 1845-1846, and Edward Tracy, 1851-1853) and suffered at least one miscarriage/stillbirth (ca. 1856).

Thomas Baxter Gresham (1844-1933). LeRoy's older brother. Thomas played a large role in LeRoy's short life, and the siblings were very close. Thomas eventually was subject to conscription and served in the Macon Home Guards, as a lieutenant in the Topographical Engineers in the Army of Northern Virginia, and with the 13th Georgia Infantry during the final months of the war, returning to Macon just before it was occupied by Union troops.

LeRoy Wiley Gresham (1847-1865). The diarist. He suffered a severely broken left leg on September 21, 1856, when the chimney of a burned-out building collapsed on him. LeRoy (or "Loy" to his family) began keeping a journal in 1860, and he continued doing so until his death in 1865.

Mary Jones Gresham (1849-1931). LeRoy's younger sister. Mary, with whom LeRoy was also very close, was referred to as "Minnie" or "Min" by her friends and family. She was something of a social butterfly. She attended Wesleyan Female College in Macon.

Slaves / "Servants"

The eight different slave servants who worked in Macon home lived behind the house in three slave homes. The Federal census of slaves did not include the names of the individuals, but did provide their age, gender, and "color." Identifications are based on the content of LeRoy's journals.[4]

Howard, age 35 (mulatto): He was often sent back and forth to the Gresham plantations without white supervision, helped with work on the Macon property, ran errands for the family, and was John Gresham's body servant during Sherman's invasion of Georgia in 1864.

Mary, age 35 (black): The Gresham family cook. Mary included the Gresham children in some memorable kitchen activities, which LeRoy especially enjoyed.

Willis, age 35 (mulatto): Like Howard, he also traveled between the plantations and the Macon home hauling food and other supplies to the family, but there are indications he spent most of his time on one of the plantations, and would die there in 1864.

Eveline, age 35 (black): Mary Gresham's personal maid, and may have served in the same role to Minnie as she grew older. Eveline accompanied Mary Gresham on trips.

Julia Ann, age 20 (black): A maid-servant in the Macon house who often made clothing for the family.

Ella, age 14 (black): Being so young, she was likely an assistant to the others, helping in the kitchen, assisting with the laundry, mending, and cleaning.

Florence, age 3 (black): Julia Ann's daughter. Small children like Florence were not given work to do until about the age of eight when they would learn simple tasks.

Although not included in the household census, there were at least two other slaves who became part of the Macon household. **Allen** was brought up from one of the plantations to be LeRoy's personal valet on September 16, 1861. He assisted LeRoy, pulled him in his wagon, etc. Allen was replaced by **Bill** on February 23, 1865. Their ages are unknown, but it is apparent from the journals that Allen was about LeRoy's age or a bit younger. A servant closer to his own age could learn to handle the more complicated aspects of dressing LeRoy given his injuries while acting as a companion.

---

4 Ancestry.com, 1860 U.S. Federal Census – Slave Schedules [database on-line], Provo, UT, USA: Ancestry.com Operations Inc., 2010:30.

At the "Houston" Plantations

Those identified by LeRoy as "coming up from Houston" are as follows:

Green	Richard	Jake	Chany
Arthur	Big Ben	Francis	Bob
Aunt Peggie	Dave	Peter	Bill
Ralph	Fred	Ben	Abram
Johnson	Sam	Blount	Isaac Scott family
Frank Baxter	Hank	Daniel	Mary
Milo	Ned	Hamp	Frank Jones
Betty and baby	Scip	Nabb	Elbert
Bil	Solomon	Little Ben	Medley
Jim	Old Aunt Hester	Martha	

Macon Friends and Society

Anderson: Judge Clifford Anderson (Major, CSA). Attorney married to Anna L. C. Anderson. Their children in 1860: Sallie (two) and William (one month).

Bates: Sylvanus Bates, prominent Macon school teacher who taught the Gresham children; Children: Robert Bates (11), LeRoy's friend; Olivia (8).

Beal (or **Beall**): Martha Beal, social acquaintance of Mary Gresham. Married to planter Nathan H. Beal (Major, CSA). Children: George Beal (16), LeRoy's friend; Julia (19), married Dr. George G. Griffin (Captain, CSA).

Boudre: Preston S. Boudre was a prominent merchant in Macon, married to Mary E. Boudre. They had one son, Edward (20).

Butler: Rebecca A. Butler appears to be a widow with two sons. John C. Butler (26) was a telegraph operator while Thomas Butler (28) was a cotton merchant.

Campbell: Mary Campbell (12) was a close friend of Minnie; Jim Campbell (20) was a friend of Thomas and LeRoy; their parents were Thomas and Anne Campbell. A Miss Flora Campbell would visit Mary Gresham socially; she was 56 years old at the time of the census and it is not clear if she was related to this family.

Collins: Thomas Collins (16) was a friend of Thomas. His father was banker Robert Collins, married to Eliza C. Collins.

deGraffenried: Mary Holt Marsh deGraffenried (1825-1901), Gresham family friend, married to William Kirkland deGraffenried (1821-1873, Colonel, CSA), prominent Macon citizen. Children: Tscharner Kirkland (1870-1906), Mary Clare (1849-1921), "Minnie's" friend and frequent visitor to the Gresham home. Valedictorian of Wesleyan Female College in 1865. Her last minute switch of valedictorian essay from the one approved to one that "was a glowing defense of the Confederacy" almost led to the closing of the school, as Macon was under Federal control at the time. She was included in a series of articles by John T. Boifeuillet on the 25 "greatest women" (*Atlanta Journal*, Sept. 18, 1925). Mary Clare wrote several articles focusing on the role of women in the workforce throughout her life.

Edwards: James Corson Edwards, a local land agent, and his wife, Elizabeth Griffin Hunt Edwards, were nearby neighbors; their son Richard (14) was a friend of LeRoy; daughter Susie (10) was a friend of Minnie. The couple had six other children.

Emerson: Dr. George W. Emerson was a Macon dentist, residing at the Lanier House Hotel at the time of the 1860 census.

Fitzgerald: Dr. Edward Fitzgerald was one of LeRoy's doctors in Macon. He was married to Louisa M. Fitzgerald.

Freeman: Charles H. Freeman was a member of the Macon Independent Volunteers; his son Scott Freeman was LeRoy's friend.

Green: Harry Green (11) was a friend of LeRoy. His father was physician Dr. James M. Green, married to Sarah V. Green. They had three other children.

Hardeman: Captain Thomas Hardeman was a Georgia politician elected to the U.S. Congress in 1858. During the Civil War, he served as the colonel of the 45th Georgia Infantry and in the Georgia House of Representatives. He was also the commander of the Floyd Rifles, one of Macon's pre-war militia organizations. His wife was Jane Hardeman; they had two small children in 1860.

Huguenin: Julia Emily Fort Huguenin (1826-1863) was a neighbor and close friend of the Gresham family. She was the second wife of planter Edward David Huguenin (1806-1863, Colonel, CSA), the sponsor and military leader of the Huguenin Rifles. Children: daughters Martha (11) and Eliza (9); one son (Edward, 10) born in 1860, and two more daughters (Julia and Dora) born after the 1860 Census.

Johnson: This is another name that has too many possibilities to clearly identify Mrs. Johnson or Miss Annie Johnson. Hardin Johnson of the massive home fire in March 1863 was a railroad clerk in 1860; E.J. Johnson was a jeweler in Macon.

Johnston: William B. Johnston was a local civic leader and a jeweler; his wife, Anne Tracy Johnston, was the sister of LeRoy's Aunt Carrie Baxter. They had a son named Edward who was 5 months old at the time of the 1860 census.

Lamar: John B. Lamar was the wealthiest citizen in Macon, a successful planter, and a highly prominent civic figure, as well as the brother-in-law to General Howell H. Cobb. Lucius M. Lamar was a wealthy planter with a young family. Henry G. Lamar was a Judge of the Supreme Court in Georgia; his son, Leonidas, was killed at First Manassas. These three related families held a great deal of Macon's wealth and influence.

Matthews: Lucy Dicey Matthews was a 55-year-old widow in 1860. Her husband, Isaac Matthews, died earlier that year. She lived near the Greshams in Macon, and possibly on a rented section of the Gresham parcel.

Moughan: William Sanford Moughan was another of Macon's wealthy planters, and one who often entertained. His wife was Parthenia Portia Ramsey Moughan, with whom he had two daughters, Emily and Elizabeth, who were both 10 years of age in 1860.

Nisbet: There were several branches of the Nisbet family in Macon. "Mrs. Judge Nisbet," Amanda Melvina Fitzallen Battle, was an acquaintance of Mary Gresham; she was the wife of Judge Eugenius Nisbet, another very influential civic member of Macon and Georgian society. Their daughter "Deny/Denie" (Eugenia) died at age 16 on May 25, 1861. Her younger sister, Leila, was 13 at the time of the 1860 census. James Taylor Nisbet was another Macon attorney, while Richard H. Nisbet was a Macon physician.

Parker: Virginia Parker was an acquaintance of Mary Gresham; Theodore Parker commanded the Jackson Artillery (Captain, CSA).

Plant: Robert Kenilworth Plant (12) was a friend of LeRoy and an early beau of Minnie. His father was bank agent Jucrease C. Plant, married to Elizabeth Plant. George Plant was 11 at the time of the census; there were two sisters, Mary (14) and Elizabeth (2).

Poe: The Washington Poe family was another very influential family; Salina Shirley Prince Poe was one of the mainstays of the Macon Ladies Soldiers Relief Society and the Macon Wayside Home during the Civil War. Miss Mary Poe was 23 in the 1860 census; her wedding was one that both Gresham parents attended.

Ralston: Aurelia L. Ralston was an acquaintance of Mary Gresham; James A. Ralston was a local planter, but also owned the building that housed a popular local theater ("Ralston's Hall") and was a prominent member of Macon society. They had sons Henry (14), James (12), and Davis (10).

Rowland: Miss Sue (Sadie) Rowland (20) was a frequent visitor of Mary Gresham's and resided with Miss Flora Campbell according to the 1860 census. It is not clear if she was related to one of LeRoy's earliest teachers, Ed Rowland, who committed suicide on November 20, 1861.

Smith: Mr. Robert A. Smith led the Macon Guards (Captain, CSA).

Strohecker: Sarah Ann Williams Strohecker was a social acquaintance of Mary Gresham; her husband, Dr. Edward L. Strohecker, was the postmaster of Macon.

Tracy: (1860-1900). One of John Gresham's first law partners was Edward Dorr Tracy, Sr., who died in 1849. His first marriage produced two sons: Judge Philomon "Phil" Tracy, a prominent civic figure in Macon and a member of the Jackson Artillery (Major, CSA; died at Antietam), and Edward Dorr Tracy, Jr. (General, CSA; killed during the Vicksburg Campaign in 1863 in Mississippi), an attorney in Huntsville, Alabama. Tracy's second marriage produced a son, Campbell Tracy, and two daughters, Harriet (Hattie) and Caroline (Carrie). Carrie's marriage to LeRoy's Uncle John Springs Baxter united the two families.

Whittle: Lewis N. Whittle, a prominent Macon attorney; His wife Sarah was an acquaintance of Mary Gresham and an exceptional chess player (who loved playing LeRoy). The couple enjoyed entertaining. They had three children: Zilla (11), Abner (7), and William (5).

Wills: David Wills was the minister of the First Presbyterian Church which the Gresham family belonged. Wills grew up in Gettysburg, Pennsylvania and eventually became president of Oglethorpe University, 1870-72. He was married to Francis Rebecca Watt Wills, and the couple had five children by 1860: Mary (10), James (8), John (6), Margaret (4), and David P. (1).

Extended Family

Unless otherwise indicated, information about the extended Gresham-Baxter-Wiley-Jones family comes from a family tree generated on Ancestry.com. There are currently 1,700 individuals included on this tree (though some mentioned by LeRoy remain unidentified). Wren Bird, mentioned in Volume 4, is likely the nickname of a member of the Bird branch of the family; "Aunt Morgan" remains a complete mystery. Also not identified are the three Knox brothers from Volumes 6 and 7 (Jimmie, Sam, and Bowie). They are probably from parts of the family that moved to Missouri or Texas. Only the family members whose lives intersected with LeRoy's are mentioned.

The Wiley Family:

Grandma: Mary Ann Wiley Baxter (1798-1869) was LeRoy's maternal grandmother and only surviving grandparent. She resided in Athens, Georgia. Her siblings and their offspring mentioned in LeRoy's journals are outlined below. They are presented (in bold) the same way LeRoy referred to them:

Aunt Eliza: Eliza Jane Wiley Carnes (1795-1880), Grandma's older sister. She had two children and lived in Milledgeville:

Ann Eliza **"Cousin Annie"** Tinsley (1834-1903) married **Cousin Howard** Tinsley (1829-1884). He was elected colonel of his local militia and was in the 4th Regiment, Georgia Infantry as Acting Quartermaster. Annie and Howard had daughters **Lucy** (1856-1882) and **Mary** (1854-1882) and had four boys later; one son, Edward, died in July 1860.

Cousin William Walker Carnes, Jr. (1830-?)

Uncle Jack: Dr. John Barnett "Jack" Wiley, Jr. (1803-1861) was a younger brother of Grandma. He was married to **Aunt Ann** Green Clopton Wiley (1816-1891) and they resided in Macon. They had several children:

Son: **Cousin David** Leroy Wiley (1839-1869).

Son: **Cousin Charles M. Wiley** (1841-1927) was a member of the Macon Rifles; adj. 44th Georgia. He married **Sarah Juliette Reid** (1843-1907).

Daughter: **Cousin Mary** Clopton Wiley Harris (1837-1914) was married to **Charles J. Harris** (Colonel CSA). The couple had 14 children: LeRoy mentions baby **Charlie** who died 1862 and daughter **Effie** (Clara Ophelia), born in 1864.

Daughter: **Cousin Anna** Lamar Wiley (1848-1885) married in 1873.

Daughter: **Cousin Jinnie** Wiley Blount (Eugenia Clopton Wiley, 1843-1936) married her husband, James Henderson Blount (1837-1903) in 1861. **"Cousin James"** served in the war but was discharged. They lost two infant daughters during the war, but had five other children beginning with Joseph G. Blount in 1864.

Son: **Cousin John** Barnett Wiley, Jr. (1854-1920).

Uncle LeRoy: LeRoy M. Wiley (1794-1868). Grandma's oldest brother. He owned a plantation in Alabama along the Flint River. He visits the Gresham family in Macon fairly frequently. Uncle LeRoy is not married and has no children. He has several business interests, including a foundry in Alabama and a railroad ownership interest in New York. He maintained enough of his wealth to pay the educational costs for Minnie and her cousin Sallie Bird in Baltimore after the war.

Aunt Sarah Ann Wiley Hayes (1808-1869). Grandma's youngest sister who also lived in Athens. She was a widow who had seven children, three of whom are mentioned by LeRoy:

Cousin "Teadee": Cousin Sarah C. Hayes (1843-1864) was very close to LeRoy's sister Minnie. She died suddenly during the war without any outward symptoms of illness.

Cousin Sam Hayes (1843-?): While there is no known date of death, he appears in the 1880 Federal Census with his mother Sarah residing with his family.

Cousin George Hayes (1836-1864).

Cousin Sarah Wiley (1825-1907): Cousin Sarah was the daughter of John Wiley (1796-1844), Grandma's brother. She lived in Texas and visited Macon. Her father is not mentioned in the journals.

Cousin Sue Wiley (1833-1902): Susan Louisa Wiley McCay, a daughter of grandmother's brother Thomas Harris Wiley (1797-1865). She came to visit Greshams. Her father is not mentioned in the journals.

The Baxter Family

Uncle Andrew Baxter (1820-1903): Andrew was Mary Gresham's older brother who was living in Texas in 1860. One of his daughters, **Cousin Alice** Baxter (1851-1930), came to visit family in Georgia when she was nine years old.

Uncle Tom and **Aunt Ellen** are LeRoy's mother's brother Thomas Wiley Baxter (1825-1898) and his wife Ellenora Francisca Scott Baxter (1835-1898). The couple had no children.

"Auntie/Aunty": Sarah Catherine Julia "Sallie" Bird (1828-1910) was Mary Gresham's only surviving sister. She was married to **Uncle Edge** (William Edgeworth Bird, 1826-1867, Major, CSA) and lived on their plantation "Granite Farm" in Hancock County outside Sparta, Georgia. Their two children were closest in age to LeRoy and Minnie Gresham:

Son: **Wilson** Edgeworth Bird (1850-1910).
Daughter: Saida **"Sallie"** Bird (1848-1922).

Uncle John: John Springs Baxter (1832-1896, Surgeon 46th Regiment, CSA) was another of Mary Gresham's brothers. He was both a physician and merchant in Macon. He was married to **Aunt Carrie** (Caroline Matilda Tracy, 1836-1861), who was the half-sister of Major Philomon and General Edward Dorr Tracy (see above). They had a young son **Tracy** born in 1860 (whom LeRoy references often). **Cousin Helen** was Carrie's sister-in-law (Ellen Elizabeth Steel Tracy, 1833-1868, married to E. D. Tracy), and her sister was **Cousin Hattie** (Harriet C. Tracy, 1842-1922), both of whom acted as caretakers of **Tracy**, the couple's son mentioned earlier (Tracy Baxter, 1860-1900).

Uncle Link: Eli Leroy Baxter (1834-1862) was another of Mary Gresham's brothers who had migrated to Texas. He graduated from Franklin College (University of Georgia) in 1854. He married **Cousin Mary** Burton. They had one son, but he died soon after birth. After Link's death during the Civil War, Cousin Mary remarried well before the proper amount of grieving time had passed, causing LeRoy to refer to her during a visit as **"Mrs. Betts."**

Uncle Edwin: Edwin Gilmer Baxter (1836-1863) was yet another of Mary Gresham's brothers who went to live in Texas. He also died during the Civil War. He married **Aunt Jule** (Julia Chloe Hardwick Baxter, 1838-1928) who sent Cousin Alice some of Baby Eddie's hair. It is possible that the baby born to the couple in 1860 named Gilmer Baxter was nicknamed "Eddie."

Uncle Richard: Richard Bolling Baxter (1840-1924, Captain, CSA) was Mary Gresham's youngest brother, just seven years older than LeRoy. He joined the Athens Guards (Co. K, 3rd Georgia) in 1861. Uncle Richard was captured and imprisoned at Rock Island, Illinois in 1864.

The Gresham Family

Uncle Edmund: Edmund Byne Gresham (1809-1872), John Gresham's only surviving sibling, lived in Burke County, Georgia. He was married to **Aunt Sarah** (1817-1888) with whom he had several children. Those mentioned by LeRoy are as follows:

Daughter: **Cousin Mollie**: Mary Jane Gresham Green married Jesse Patterson Green (1839-1864) with whom she had three children. Her husband died in service in Florida.

Son: **Cousin Jones**: John Jones Gresham (1845-1910) served in Marsh's Co., 5th Georgia Cavalry, Wheeler's division. He married Ella Ulla Lassiter (1851-1936) after the war.

Son: **Cousin Job**: Job Anderson Gresham (1843-1940) married Anna Lassiter (1856-1939), the sister of his brother's wife. He was enlisted as sergeant in Co. D, 48th Georgia Infantry and was promoted to ordnance sergeant. He was mustered out at Appomattox, Virginia.

Daughter: **Cousin Adeline**: Sarah Adeline Gresham (1841-1927) did not marry.

Aunt Margaret: Margaret Gresham Bright (1821-1893), John Gresham's cousin from Sweet Springs, Missouri. **Cousin Mary** Bright (1843-1877) was her daughter.

Cousin Mary Gresham: A cousin of John Gresham, born ca. 1822. Little more is known about her.

The Jones Family

Aunt Margaret A. Jones (1800-1893) John Gresham's maternal aunt. Her children included:

Son: **Cousin Jenks**: John James "Jenks" Jones (1824-1898) was John Gresham's cousin, one of ten children in the family. He and his wife **"Cousin Eva"** (Evalina Toombs, 1830-1900) had five children, of whom Seaborn and Martha were born during the period covered by LeRoy's journals.

Daughter: **Aunt Sarah**: Sarah Elizabeth Wimberly Jones (1806-1888) married John Gresham's uncle John (1769-1857).

Son: **Cousin Jack**: John Edward Jones (1827-1891) was another cousin of John Gresham. His wife was **"Cousin Bella"** (Arabella O. Dean, 1830-1891), with whom he had six daughters and one son. Their daughter **Hennie** (Henrietta E. Jones, 1854-1889) is mentioned in Volume 4 of LeRoy's journals.

Daughter: **Cousin Eliza**: Elizabeth R. Jones (1833-1866) married **"Cousin Jimmie"** (James J. Snider, 1830-1869) with whom she had eight children, not all of whom reached adulthood. During the bombardment of Savannah, she evacuated inland with the children she had at that time: Madge (**"Maggie"**), **Sallie**, and **George**.

Son: **Cousin George** Jones (1825-1900, Major, CSA) served as a part of Jefferson Davis' military escort to his inauguration. He married **Cousin Kate** (Catherine Lucretia Calhoun, 1835-1911) during the war. They had two children while LeRoy was writing his journals: Enoch and Mary Eugenia. Two more sons were born later.

Son: **Cousin Zeke** was Aunt Sarah's nephew: Ezekiel P. Wimberly (1837-1892).

The Distant Relations

Grandmother Wiley's sister Eliza Jane married William W. Carnes, whose brother Robert married Martha Laird Jones. Their daughter, **Sarah Elizabeth Carnes "Sallie" Wiley** (1827-1902) was a cousin to Mary Gresham and Auntie. She married **Cousin Samuel Harris Wiley** (son of Edwin Wiley and Elizabeth "Eliza" DeWitt). His sister was **Cousin Elizabeth Baldwin Wiley Harris.** This was a totally different branch of the Wiley family, yet they were known to LeRoy and his family as "cousins." One of their ten children was Sarah Bird **"Birdie" Wiley** (1848-1943), known to the Gresham and Bird families.

Map Gallery

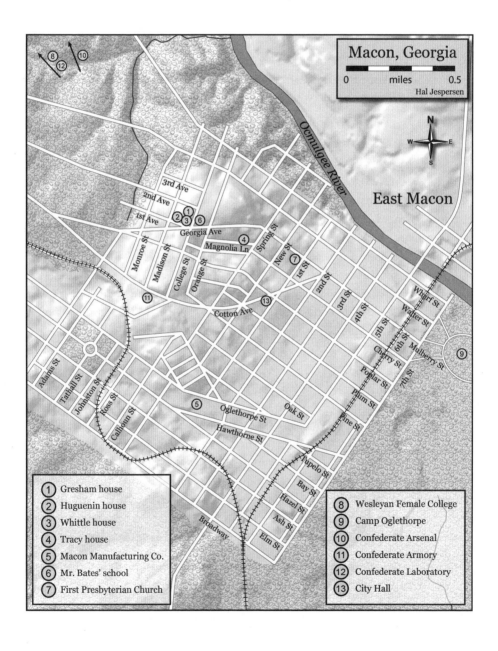

Macon, Georgia

0 — miles — 0.5

Hal Jespersen

East Macon

Ocmulgee River

N
W — E
S

3rd Ave
2nd Ave
1st Ave
Georgia Ave
Magnolia Ln
Spring St
New St
1st St
2nd St
3rd St
4th St
5th St
6th St
7th St
Wharf St
Walter St
Mulberry St
Cherry St
Poplar St
Plum St
Pine St
Monroe St
Madison St
College St
Orange St
Cotton Ave
Adams St
Tattnall St
Johnston St
Ross St
Calhoun St
Oglethorpe St
Oak St
Hawthorne St
Tupelo St
Bay St
Hazel St
Ash St
Elm St
Broadway

1 Gresham house
2 Huguenin house
3 Whittle house
4 Tracy house
5 Macon Manufacturing Co.
6 Mr. Bates' school
7 First Presbyterian Church

8 Wesleyan Female College
9 Camp Oglethorpe
10 Confederate Arsenal
11 Confederate Armory
12 Confederate Laboratory
13 City Hall

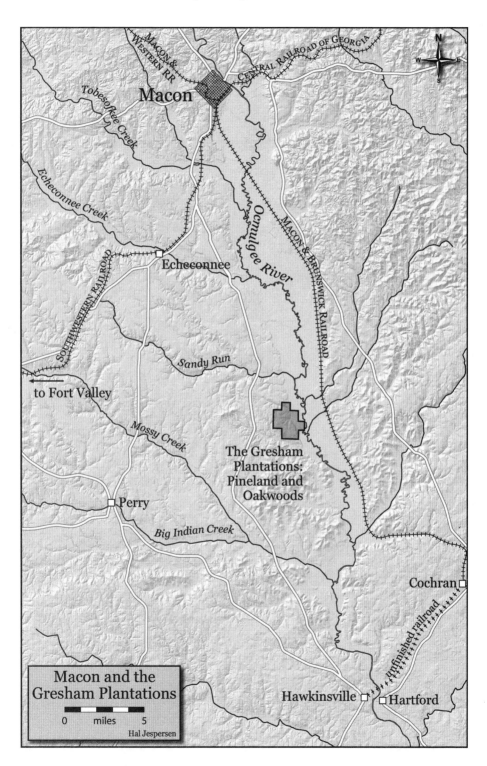

Macon and the Gresham Plantations

0   miles   5

Hal Jespersen

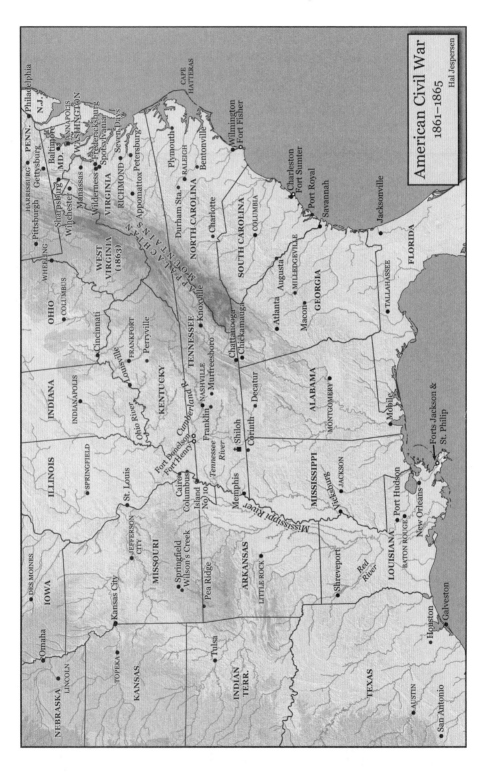

American Civil War
1861–1865

Hal Jespersen

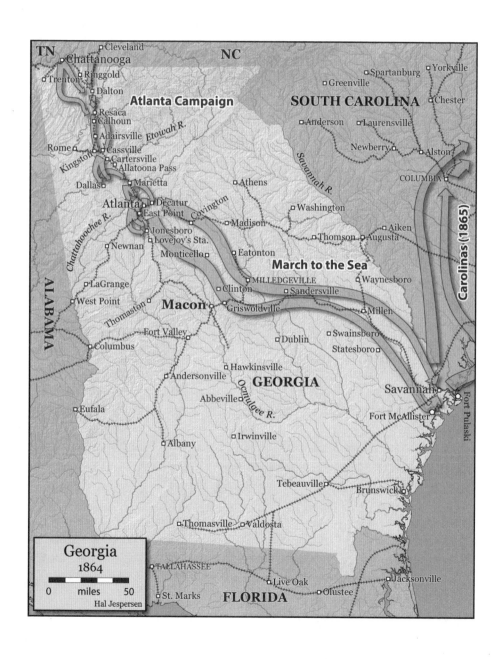

The inside front cover (left) and the first entries (right) in LeRoy's diary.

Volume 1

June 12, 1860 - March 26, 1861

LeRoy Wiley Gresham

Macon, Georgia 1860

Designed and executed by the above

June Teusday, 12th, 1860: Mother has gone to the serving society.

June 14th, 1860 – Thursday: Afternoon 6 oclock. Mizpah — The Lord watch between me & thee when we are absent one from another. Gen[esis] XXXI.49.

[In their own handwriting]:

Your mother

    Mary B. Gresham

Your Sister

    Minnie Gresham

Your Brother

    T. B. Gresham[1]

---

1 The Gresham family was very religious. LeRoy and his father were leaving for Philadelphia to see a specialist about LeRoy's deteriorating physical condition. Traveling long distances at that time was always fraught with peril. He (or perhaps his mother) selected the appropriate verse from Genesis (31:49), and his mother, sister, and brother signed his first journal. Mizpah was a place near Gilead (Jud 11.29) and refers to a pillar of stones set up by Jacob and Laban. The pillar acted as a witness to the bond between the two men.

June 16 Saturday: [Aboard ship from Savannah to Philadelphia] It is a very clear + pleasant morning and the sea is not rough at all. Met and exchanged signals with the steamers *Montgomery* and the *Keystone State*.[2] The rockets were very pretty indeed. [Leroy also wrote in the upper margin that first day:] Nearly all the ladies on board are [claiming to be] sick but very few are.

Sunday June 17: Passed Cape Hatteras early this morning.[3] It is still smooth. We have very good eating and I have not missed a single meal. The coast has been in sight most of the day.

Monday June 18: Arrived safe at Philadelphia and are lodged in the Continental Hotel where we have very good quarters.[4] It is quite warm here. The number of our room is 104. We arrived here at about one oclock.

Teusday June 19: Went over to the Board of Publication rooms this morning and bought *Luyman Hogue*. It is a very nice little book indeed. In the evening, Dr. Pancoast[5] came up + saw me. He gave no decided opinion, but said he found me better than he expected. Father and I went round to the academy of Natural Science. It is a most wonderful place. There are birds and animals of all descriptions. There are also skeletons of all and about 500 skulls all on shelves.

Friday June 22: Dr. Pancoast came to see me again to day and did nothing but prescribe a fourth medicine. I went round to the mint to day and excepting that have layed down most of the time. It is quite warm here.

Saturday June 23rd: Mr. Reese and Mr. Hull arrived last night. I have not been out any but have layed down a most of the time. I can see a fire from the window but it don't seem to be a large one. Dr. Pancoast came to see me again this evening.

Sunday June 24: A bright and pleasant morn. I went to hear Dr. Boardman and he preaches from Mark 6c + 56 verse [Mark 6:56] and Dr. Reese went with us there. Dr.

2   SS *Montgomery*, an 1858 wooden steamer, and SS *Keystone State*, an 1853 side-wheel steamer, were used by the Union during the Civil War. The *Montgomery* collided with another ship and sank off NJ in 1877.

3   Cape Hatteras is a thin strand of barrier islands off North Carolina between the Outer Banks and the mainland. The waters off Hatteras are especially treacherous and known as the Graveyard of the Atlantic.

4   The lavish hotel that once stood at Ninth and Chestnut streets hosted presidents and world leaders. Built in 1860, it was torn down in 1924.

5   Dr. Joseph Pancoast (1805-1882), a prominent Philadelphia surgeon associated with the Jefferson Medical School and Hospital, was known for innovative procedures and was one of the first plastic surgeons. LeRoy broke his leg years earlier (1856), and was diagnosed with tuberculosis ("consumption") a few months later. When the disease moved into his spine in 1860, his father took him north. Dr. Pancoast's proposed treatment correlates with the diagnosis of tuberculosis. LeRoy was not told of any of this. See Dr. Dennis Rasbach, Medical Afterword, pp. 411-422, for more information.

Pancoast came late at night and prescribed issues and lying down for the summer alas all the year.[6]

New York. Monday June 25: Left Philadelphia this morning at 9am and got here to dinner. I saw several Japanese walking about the streets.

Teusday June 26: There was a grand ball up to the Metropolitan given to Japanese last night. Left New York this evening at 4 oclock on the *Florida*.[7] New York Bay is beautiful.

Wednesday June 27: The sea is very smooth indeed and but one man is sick. They do not have as good eating on this boat as they did on the *State of Georgia*.[8] We saw some 15 or 20 whales this morning and one came so near we could see him good; others were spouting at a greater distance. The boat stopped last night for a good while. I believe there was something the matter with the engine. There is not more than a dozen passengers aboard.

Thursday June 28: Met the steam ship *James Adger* and exchanged signal. Saw a great many flying fish and we saw a comet too.

Friday June 29: It is very pleasant. We arrived at Savvanah at 4 oclock this evening after a passage of 72 hours. Stopped at Pulaski House.[9] Ate supper and left at 11 oclock.

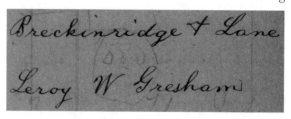

Macon June 30: Arrived safe at 9am. All well.

July 4th Wednes.: Not much of a show here today, I should guess. A sword was presented to Captain Hardeman.[10] Hot as fire. 100 degrees. Breckinridge + Lane[11]

Leroy W. Gresham

6　Dr. Pancoast's prescriptions for LeRoy help us date his illness. "Issues" were a treatment for abscesses, though LeRoy had no idea what had caused them. See footnote 19 for more information.

7　A wooden side wheel steamer built in 1850. Bought by the US Navy in 1861 and commissioned USS *Florida*, she served on blockade duty along the Atlantic coast and in the Gulf of Mexico.

8　*State of Georgia* was the large 1851 side-wheel steamer that had carried LeRoy and his father John from Savannah to Philadelphia. The ship would be used by the U. S. Navy during the Civil War.

9　A popular hotel in Savannah (corner of Bull and St. Julian's streets). The building still exists today.

10　Thomas Hardeman, Jr. was commander of the Floyd Rifles, one of many local Macon companies raised for Confederate service.

11　The "Southern Democratic" ticket for president and vice president during the 1860 election. This suggests the political leanings of the Gresham family.

July 9th 1860 Monday: Thermometer 96 in shade. A curious sentence, Sator arepo tenet operas rotas, a sentence which reads backward and forward the same way. Take the first letter of each word and proceed on the same manner with the rest and it will have the same result. Copied from the *Savvanah Republican.*

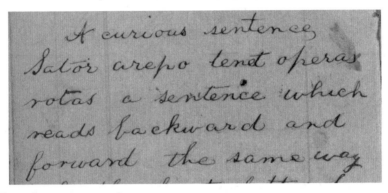

[Several pages torn out.]

Beginning 22nd Sep 60: [LeRoy lists 32 books he had read, including *Memoirs Madame Junot (Duchesse D'Abrantes)* and *The Count of Monte Cristo.*]

Teusday Oct 9 1860: Went down to dentists and had a rousing plug [filling] put in. Also one on the 17 and 18 days of October.

Oct 20, 1860: A drizzly day and Thomas' birthday.[12]

Oct. 23: Father went to Houston.[13]

Oct. 24: Wagon came up bringing Green + Arthur. Mrs. deGraffenried sent me a basket of books.[14] Advice about teeth: In the morning before breakfast brush your teeth first with water only then with powder. Powder should be used at least once a day. Using a brush just before retiring at night is a commendable practice. To brush effectually place the upper and lower teeth together then, using the brush up and down the teeth, between the teeth gums, being not unmindful or fearful of brushing the gums as well as the teeth thereby toughening one and cleansing the other. Your back teeth

---

12 LeRoy's older brother, Thomas Baxter Gresham.

13 Houston (pronounced "Howston") County was where the two Gresham plantations (Oakwoods and Pineland) were located, about 40 miles southeast of Macon. Father and Howard and Milo (slaves) often made the trip by wagon so they could haul food and other supplies to the Gresham home. Sometimes Father and Thomas took the Macon and Brunswick Railroad (chartered in 1856) most of the way and completed the journey by horse or wagon. The line was incomplete when the Civil War began and work on it stopped. After the war it was completed to Hawkinsville.

14 Green and Arthur were two of the Houston County plantation slaves. Mary Marsh deGraffenried was a friend of the Gresham family and a frequent visitor to their home.

need more brushing than the front ones. Wisdom in this respect will be displayed if you show a practical care for the back and front outsides of the rearmost teeth above and below. After each meal a toothpick and silk thread (waxed) should and be used and the mouth rinsed; food is the worst enemy you have.

[No Date]: Always speak truth. Make very few promises and keep them all. Have no very intimate friends and love the few you do have. Never speak lightly of religion. Do not play at any game of hazard. Never get in debt and you will have little trouble in getting rich and when you do get rich spend it in a good way.

Two persons A + B depart together, one from Boston, other Hartford. distance 100 miles after 7 hours meet. A had gone 1½ miles faster than B. How fast went B?

The above may be found in Davies Arithmetic.

November 11, 1860: My birthday and I have just recovered from a spell of sickness. [The remainder of the page is removed.]

1861

January 15, 1861: It has been extremely foggy all day and is rainy and windy tonight. The Convention[15] meets tomorrow. Thomas is reading *The Count of Monte Christo.*

---

15 The Secession Convention in Georgia met January 16 – March 23, 1861 in Milledgeville and voted 208 to 89 to secede from the Union and form its own constitution. The document included specific provisions to protect slavery within the state.

Jan. 2nd: Rainy 3 4 5 6 Clear and pleasant. It feels warm a plenty for a spring morning. My Back does not pain me except when it is being dressed.[16] Two bottles of medicine came by exp[ress] from Dr. Joseph Pancoast.

January 6th 1861: Thomas has got the Rheumatism [inflammation or pain in joints] so bad that he is confined to the house. I also am troubled with a pain in my hip. My Christmas Gifts were: This desk which I am now using; as many fireworks as I wanted, and much big heap of goodies. [Page torn.]

Jan 8 1861: All the [militia] companies are out. There was a coal oil lamp bursted over to Mrs. Edwards and like to have put out Harry's eyes.[17] No one else was injured. Father gone to Houston. Father sold pony today. Adieu.

Jan 17 1861: Father went over to Milledgeville this morning. It is clear and warm. [Practices writing a series of the letter "M."]

January 19, 1861: Father returned from the [Secession] Convention last night.

January 20, 1861: Uncle Edmund came over last night and stayed Sunday with us. Cousin Jack came up last night to see us.[18]

January Monday 21: Today is Father's birthday. The peas were taken out of the issue this morning preparatory to healing up.[19] It is cloudy today.

January 23 Teusday: There was a great celebration on account of Georgia's going out of the Union. The procession passed down by the College where there was a splendid display of fireworks. Every body illuminated, we among the number. The Blind Asylum was very beautiful, also the college.[20] I could not go down town to see all the show but it was described as exceedingly beautiful. As the procession passed Dr. Emerson's balcony, the ladies sung the "Marseilles Hymn." . . .

---

16 LeRoy has not yet described the specific condition of his back, but the dressings were part of the care of the "issues" relating to the treatment of his spinal tuberculosis, as recommended by Dr. Pancoast.

17 Elizabeth Griffin Hunt Edwards was a nearby neighbor. Harry was likely one of her house servants.

18 Paternal uncle Edmund Byne Gresham was the only surviving sibling of LeRoy's father, John Jones Gresham. John Edward Jones, a maternal cousin of LeRoy's father, lived in Macon.

19 Issues and peas had very specific meanings and uses in the treatment of tuberculosis of the spine. An "issue" was a defect—an ulcer or opening—in the skin and deeper tissue, intentionally created by the application of a caustic substance or by an incision to allow decayed and infected matter in the deeper layers surrounding spine to drain out. This relieved the pressure on the spinal cord that was the source of paralysis. Peas (or beans) were compressed inside the ulcer cavity (the "issue") to help keep it open to prevent healing until the paralysis was "cured." As one might expect, this would have been very painful and rather frightening for LeRoy. Dr. Dennis Rasbach, email, March 13, 2018.

20 Wesleyan Female College was the country's first chartered college to award a diploma to a woman (1840). The Georgia Academy for the Education of the Blind opened in July 1851 with four pupils.

January 25 Friday 61: The Jackson Artillery left here today to go down to the coast to repel invaders.[21] Beall Powers was married to a Miss Fosters. It is very cloudy and looks like rain. The Belgian-American direct trade company open their goods today for public sale.[22] My leg and back not improved much and give me a good deal of pain and trouble. It poured down rain all day, day before yesterday, and night.

January 26, 1861: It rained all night last night "but" it is tolerably clear now. My cough is no better. I have not been out on my wagon for two months.[23] . . . Thomas bought me a *Harpers Weekly* with pictures of Forts Sumter and Moultrie.[24]

Sunday Jan 27 1861: A very bright and beautiful day and all the folks have gone to church.[25]

Monday Jan 28 1861: Clear and bright. Howard gone to the plantation.[26]

Teusday Jan 29 1861: Clear and bright.

January 30 Teusday: Father went down to Houston today.

Feb 1 Friday: Slight rain. Father returned home.

Feb 2: Rained a good part of the day very hard and I think there will be a frechet [a flood caused by heavy rain].

Monday Feb 4th 1861: The [Ocmulgee] river here is very high indeed, higher than it has been any time since 1841. Thomas threw a bottle into the river this morning which contained a paper on which was written the date and directing those who found it to send the paper to him. Mother bought me three white handkerchiefs to day.

21 The Jackson Artillery, named in honor of Andrew Jackson, was organized in 1859 and commanded by Capt. Theodore Parker.

22 The exhibition featured decorative and innovative products from Belgium as well as major Southern cities such as Baltimore and Charleston.

23 LeRoy mentions his wagon throughout his journal. It played a large role in his short life. Unfortunately, there are no detailed descriptions of the wagon used to transport him (mostly outside the family home) although a letter written before he began his journals notes that his Uncle Richard built him one as a Christmas gift. LeRoy later discusses its suspension and cushions. He was pulled (he often calls it "rode") by house servants (slaves), friends, and family members.

24 *Harper's Weekly* was a popular political magazine published in New York City from 1857 to 1916.

25 The Gresham family attended the First Presbyterian Church in Macon at First and Mulberry streets. John Gresham was involved in the church leadership.

26 Howard was a Gresham house servant (slave) who traveled between the plantations and the Macon home on a regular basis and usually by himself.

Teusday Feb 5: A clear and bright day. Aunt Eliza came over this morning to make us a visit.[27] She brought me a nice pair of slippers and Mother a tidy. The track of the Brunswick R.R. was washed away in several places by the recent heavy rains. The Southern Congress met yesterday and elected Howell Cobb president [of the Confederate Senate].[28]

Feb 5 1861: Wednesday: Mother and Minnie[29] have gone down to the dentists and Aunt Eliza stays with me. Clear and bright.

Febuary 7, 1861: Clear and bright. Slept very poorly last night. Mother is knitting Aunt Carrie a blanket for the baby.[30] My leg and back are no better but I hope they will improve soon.

Febuary 8th 1861: Got a long letter from Aunty today. Aunt Ann[31] and all the family came over to see us last night. My cough has been a great deal worse in the last two or three days.[32]

[Writes his name vertically in the margin]

Feb 8 1861: Wagon came up last night with 3 or four of the negroes. I went on my wagon to day for the first time in 3 months. Carrie sent the baby [Tracy] up to see us and he looks fat and hearty. Aunt Eliza and Mother have gone to town. Cuffie is a good dog. It looks a good deal like rain but I hope it won't being as tomorrow is Sunday. Mother bought 18 bananas and 12 apples this evening for me for which I am much obliged Mr. Bates has

---

27 Eliza Jane Wiley Carnes, sister of LeRoy's maternal grandmother. Aunt Eliza was LeRoy's great-aunt and lived in Milledgeville, Ga., the state's capital.

28 Howell Cobb, former U.S. secretary of the treasury during the Buchanan presidency and future Confederate general, was a familiar figure in Macon. His sister, Mary Ann, was married to John B. Lamar, the wealthiest resident of Macon.

29 LeRoy's younger sister, Mary Jones Gresham, usually called Minnie or just Min.

30 Caroline Matilda Tracy Baxter (1836-1861), married to one of LeRoy's maternal uncles, Dr. John Springs Baxter (1832-1896). They had one son, Tracy, and resided in Macon.

31 Two different women. "Aunty" or "Auntie" was Sarah Catherine Julia "Sallie" Wiley Bird, LeRoy's maternal aunt (his mother's sister) who lived just outside Sparta, Ga, on Granite Farm. "Aunt Ann" was Ann Green Clopton Wiley, who was married to a brother of LeRoy's maternal grandmother, Dr. John "Jack" B. Wiley, Jr., making them LeRoy's great-aunt and great-uncle. They resided in Macon.

32 In addition to his badly broken leg that didn't fully heal and his low back abbesses, LeRoy suffers from a chronic cough as a result of his tuberculosis. His cough will become more severe as he ages, and accompany other painful and debilitating symptoms he will describe in detail later in his journal.

the mumps in his family school.[33] Six babies were baptized in our church this afternoon. [Page is torn.]

Febuary 9, 1861: [blank]

Febuary 10 1861: The Southern Congress has elected Hon. Jefferson Davis president and Hon. A. H. Stephens vice president of the Southern Confederacy.[34] It is a prime ticket. It is so warm to day that I fear if it continues so long we will have no fruit. To day is communion day and Aunt Eliza staid home with me. Minnie got a letter from Miss Gay and Mother one from Miss Melville.[35]

Febuary 11 Monday 61: It rained all night last night and is very cloudy this morning. Minnie gone and Mother with her to the dentists.

Febuary 12 Tuesday: Clear and bright. Bob Bates[36] has got the mumps and also the Bands and Moughons. Mother sewing and Aunt Eliza knitting a baby blanket. My cough is, I hope, a little better but my leg is not—Mother and Aunt Eliza went over to Mrs. C. Collins to see her flowers.[37]

Febuary 13 Wednesday: Clear and pleasant day.

Febuary 14 Thursday: Valentines day and I got a valentine and sent one. Raining hard. Thomas bought for me a bundle of candy. I got another valentine and I don't know who it's from. Minnie got a heart with an arrow sticking in it.

Feb 15 Friday: Clear + bright. Mother has made some apple float for dinner.

Febuary 16 Saturday 61: Cloudy and exceedingly windy. A great big can of Brandy peaches came over this morning, a present from Aunt Eliza. Elegant they are.

Feb. 17 Sunday: All gone to church + I am lying in the sitting room. Got up to breakfast this morning for the first time in a long time.[38]

---

33 Sylvan Bates was a prominent school teacher in Macon.

34 Jefferson Davis from Mississippi and Alexander Hamilton Stephens from Georgia were both Democrats. Davis served with distinction during the Mexican war, as secretary of war during the Pierce administration, and as a Federal congressman and senator before becoming the Confederacy's first and only president. Stevens served as a Federal congressman and, after the Civil War, as governor of Georgia. The Confederacy's only vice-president, Stephens spent most of the war at his home in Georgia.

35 Minnie's former teachers. By this time Minnie was attending Mr. Bates' school. Prior to LeRoy's accident, his parents considered sending him to Miss Gay's and Miss Melville's school, but came to believe Mr. Bates' would be a better fit for LeRoy.

36 LeRoy's friend.

37 Probably Eliza C. Collins, the wife of banker Robert Collins.

38 LeRoy was ambulatory at this stage and could apparently use crutches, but movement of any distance was always difficult and involved some level of pain or discomfort.

Mr. LeRoy

Febuary 18 Monday: Father left for Montgomery [Ala.] yester night to see the new president [Jefferson Davis] inaugurated.[39] Mother and Aunt Eliza have gone down town shopping. Uncle John came up to see me this evening.[40] Begun digging a well to day.

Teusday Feb 19: Went out on my wagon to watch the men dig the well. Aunt Eliza is knitting me a pair of Polish Boots.[41]

Wednesday Feb 20: It rained very hard last night and is clear and bright this morn. Aunt Ann and Aunt Carrie and Uncle John stayed all day. Went out in my wagon and feel ~~sort~~ a little tired. We got a letter from Grandma saying she was coming home in March.[42] Mother and Aunt Eliza have gone down to see the belgiam auction sale. Thomas a little unwell and stayed at home.

Thursday Feb 21: Father came home last night and says he saw the inauguration. Cousin Howard stayed all night with us. It is clear and cold. Mother bought a half bushel Scalybarks [hickory nuts]. Today morrow is Uncle Andrew's birthday.[43] Aunt Eliza is knitting me a pair of socks. My back is not healed up yet and my leg is no better. The well gets along mighty slow. Thomas still at home. Aunt Eliza has been sick a little today.

Febuary 22 Friday: Washington's birth day. The [militia] companies paraded as usual. Thomas still at home. Warm and balmy day.

Feb Friday 23: Raining off + on all day. Mrs. Johnston and Mr. E. Tracy came over after supper. Mr. Smith stayed all night with us.[44]

Feb 24 Sunday: Bright and clear, and cold. Rained exceedingly hard last night and thundered considerably. My cough is very troublesome last night. . . . Aunt Eliza made some sugar candy yesterday.

---

39 Montgomery, Alabama, was the first capital of the Confederacy.

40 Dr. John Springs Baxter was one of LeRoy's uncles (his mother Mary's younger brother). He was also Aunt Carrie's husband and father to baby Tracy. They lived in Macon.

41 Heavy knit mid-calf slippers.

42 LeRoy's maternal grandmother, Mary Ann Wiley Baxter, who lived in Athens, Ga. She was the only living Gresham grandparent during the Civil War years. Her daughter was LeRoy's mother Mary.

43 The eldest of his maternal uncles (1820-1903). He and his family resided in Cass County, Ga.

44 Anne Clark Tracy Johnston was the wife of William B. Johnston, a local civic leader, and the sister of Aunt Carrie. Edward Dorr Tracy, Aunt Carrie's half-brother, was a local Macon citizen and future Confederate general. Robert A. Smith led the Macon Guards.

Monday 25 Feb: Pretty cold ice this morning. Cousin Helen came up to see Mother.[45] Was sick all night, coughed a great deal. Mrs. Whittle came over to see Mother this evening.[46] Cousin Howard is elected colonel of the militia.[47] Father is pretty bad off with a cold. Thomas is still staying at home.

Feb 26 Teusday: Cloudy and cool. Thomas gone to school this morning. Coughing almost incessantly. Mrs. Parker came to see Mother and Aunt Eliza.[48] The well is almost done, but I have not been out on my wagon for two or three days.

Feb Wednesday 27: Mother and Aunt Eliza gone down town to day. Aunt Eliza gone to spend the rest of the day with [incomplete]. Father started to the plantation, but met the wagon half way and concluded he would come back. Aunt Peggie came up with the wagon.[49]

March 1st 1860: Father and Mother went to Miss Mary Poe's wedding.[50] Mother and Aunt Eliza went to the cemetery. Had Ice cream for supper and it was very nice. It is quite warm.

March 2nd Saturday: Warm as summer time. Aunt Eliza and Mother gone down town. The well is 59 or 60 ft. deep but no water yet. My cough troubles me some though not so much as it has done. My issues have not healed up yet and it is over a month since they started.[51]

Sunday March 3: Mother and Aunt Eliza both stayed at home to day. Uncle John came up to see us.

Monday ~~Feb~~ March 4: Today [Abraham] Lincoln is inaugurated. Aunt Eliza made some more sugar candy. Minnie stayed at home because of a pain in her back and was in bed nearly all day. Aunt Eliza has made some beer which is nice. We received a long

45 Cousin Helen was married to Edward Dorr Tracy.

46 Sarah Whittle, the wife of Lewis N. Whittle, a prominent Macon attorney, and an acquaintance of Mary Gresham.

47 Howard Tinsley, husband of Aunt Eliza's daughter Ann Eliza "Annie" Carnes Tinsley. The family resided in Milledgeville.

48 Virginia Parker, wife of the commander of the Jackson Artillery, Theodore Parker.

49 Aunt Peggie was one of the plantation slaves.

50 Daughter of Washington Poe, a major political figure in Macon. His wife Selina was the president of Macon's Ladies Soldiers Relief Society.

51 As noted earlier, an "issue" was a ulcer or opening in the skin and deeper tissue. In LeRoy's case, it was probably created by an incision to allow the infected matter to drain out. See footnote 19 on page 6.

letter from Grandma to day. It has rained a very little to day in intermittent sprinkles. G[eorge] Beal has got the mumps.[52]

Teusday March 5: Cool and pleasant. Mrs. Huguenin came to see Mother.[53] The Southern congress has adopted a most ugly flag. Old Abe inaugural address came to hand, a poor thing too. Had oysters for dinner.

March 6 Wednesday: Father left for the plantation. Mrs. Ralston came to see Mother.[54]

March 7 Thursday: Cool and pleasant day. Thomas came home from school to day with a headache. Mrs. Huguenin sent over a very nice pone of Rusk [bread]. Mother and Aunt Eliza gone over to Mrs. Huguenin. Eddie came over for them. Mother is making an Afghan + she has put Ella at it who got along quite fast.[55] Aunt Eliza went to see Mrs. Strohecker.[56] Howard went to [the] mill.[57]

March 8 Friday: The newly adopted flag was flying over Woodruff's shop. Thomas at home. I have just finished a book called *Broken Cisterns*. Miss Pink Towns married last night. We had a beautiful serenade from the brass band. The telegraph was printed on Belgian paper today. Aunt Eliza + Mother went down town and bought cots and cords. Father came home this afternoon. All well.

March 9 Saturday: Aunt Eliza went home this morning. Minnie has made me a flag of the Southern Confederacy. There was a high wind and rain last night, and the wind is blowing now. Father came home last night. Miss Hause sent me some of Miss Pink Town's wedding cake. Got a letter from Auntie.

March 10 Sunday: I am reading a book called *Habits of Animals*, my annual dollars worth from the Board of Publication.

March 11 Monday: Clear and pleasant day. Our hyacinths are in full bloom and are beautiful. The well is 70 feet deep and no water yet. George Beal is very sick indeed. Read *Recollections of a Southern Matron*, a very good book.

---

52 George Beal was LeRoy's friend.

53 Julia Emily Fort Huguenin was a close Macon friend of the Gresham family. Her husband was a wealthy prominent citizen.

54 Aurelia Ralston was an occasional visitor to the Gresham home. Her husband James owned Ralston's Hall, which housed one of Macon's local theaters.

55 A 14-year-old Gresham house servant. Ella was learning to knit or crochet.

56 Sarah Ann Strohecker, a social acquaintance of the Gresham family. Her husband, Dr. Edward L. Strohecker, was postmaster of Macon.

57 The Macon Manufacturing Company, where John Gresham served as president.

March 12 Teusday: Adderhold's stable was burned down last night about 10 oclock, a total loss of $5000. 10 horses burned to death.

March 13 Wednesday: Richard Edwards [friend] came over to see me. My back was dressed this morning and it is not healed up yet. Mother and I were out in the yard most of the evening making pickle and beer. Mrs. Butler sent me a bowl of Baked apples and custard.[58] Mrs. Huguenin lent me the Rollo Books[59] and sent me a nice pone of rusk and sweet-wafers. George Beal is better than he was. Mr. Wills came up to see me a little while yesterday.[60] Mrs. Huguenin also lent me a game called Solitaire. It is a regular spring day.

Thursday March 14: Clear and pleasant. I wrote a letter to Aunt Eliza. Father bought a dozen bananas. The wind blew up very cold and to night very cold. Mary has made some very nice gingercakes. Howard came up this evening from the plantation. This evening I have been trying the game of Solataire.

March 15 1860: A pretty cold day, and Thomas stayed home in consequence of being a little unwell.

March 16 Saturday: A very cool and pleasant day. Uncle John's baby [Tracy] came up to see us.[61] My cough very troublesome indeed. Mary's little dog Rollo died from being bitten in a dog row, such as we often have.[62] Foolish.

Sunday March 17: It is very cloudy and looks like rain. I am reading the Rollo books and am very much interested in them. It was very cloudy and towards night it rained pretty hard.

Monday March 18: Cloudy and Damp.

Teusday March 19: Last night about 9 PM it commenced snowing and this morning the ground is covered about an inch thick. It is not cold much either and I went on my wagon and looked at Mother knock it off the flowers. Mr. Bates gave holiday, as well as the rest of the schools and Thomas and Minnie with the a good many other boys and girls went to walk. All the fruit is undoubtedly killed.

12 oclock: All the snow has melted and I hear it running through the gutters now. Our well is 70 feet deep and they have stopped work on it for the present. We have

---

58 Rebecca A. Butler was a family acquaintance.

59 A popular series of 14 children's books written by Jacob Abbott.

60 The minister of the First Presbyterian Church in Macon.

61 Tracy Baxter, a regular visitor to the Gresham house.

62 Mary was the Gresham family's cook-servant.

Sasafrax [sassafras] tea every night at supper. Father brought up some apples. I forgot to state in my diary a few weeks since that Father had bought a new buggy.

March 20 Wednesday: Warm and pleasant. Heavy frost though. I received a letter from Aunt Eliza. My back was dressed this morning and it beginning to heal. Sweet time about it. Mrs. Beal sent me the nicest plate of ice cream yesterday, frozen with snow.[63] Willis came up with the wagon.[64]

March 21 Thursday: George Beal is out again and looks very much worsted. Father brought me a bottle of Sherry wine.[65] I read over *The Conquest of Mexico*. Truly he is a beautiful as well as interesting author and a treat to read him. Thomas is trying to play Money allush [game] and succeeds better than I had any idea he would.

March 22 1861: Heavy frost ruinous to fruit....[66] Minnie went out in the woods after violets. Pop fetched me bag of apple and celery for dinner.

March 23 Saturday: Cloudy and threatening to rain every minute. Thomas killed a poor robin and maybird this morning. Quite warm and no need of a fire but still we are obliged to have it to gaurd against colds. Alas poor Yorrick Lark, Uncle Richard's dog,[67] has gone to the estimable practice of sucking eggs, a suck egg dog who does not despise? Father brought up an American *Almanac*, a very good thing to refer to. An Arkansas paper says they have tasted the bitter fruits of the tree of Union. Prentice, editor *Louisville Journal*, says Eat on and when you come to the core you can see seed.

Secede.

Sunday March 24: Uncle John came up this afternoon to see us all. Read some of Charlotte Elizabeth's works to day. Got a good long letter from Wilson Bird.[68] I have a bad head ache to night and shall go to bed directly. Thomas + Father gone to church. It has been a very bright and beautiful day.

Yours Truly, Leroy

---

63 Martha F. Beall was George Beall's mother and a friend of Mrs. Gresham.

64 Another of the Macon slaves who often made wagon trips to the plantations in Houston County.

65 LeRoy often drank alcohol. It was more common for children to drink in those days, but it will become clear the alcohol was usually taken for medicinal reasons to help him sleep, relieve pain, and as a means to increase his caloric intake.

66 Here, LeRoy doodles with the names and birthdays of one of his aunts and her daughters.

67 Confederate Capt. Richard Bolling Baxter, Mary Gresham's younger brother and LeRoy's youngest maternal uncle, was just seven years older than LeRoy. Richard lived in Athens, Ga.

68 LeRoy's cousin and Auntie's son, Wilson Edgeworth Bird.

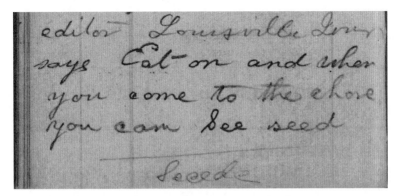

March 25: Very warm and pleasant I have [incomplete]

March 26 Teusday: Very warm and we are sitting without a fire. Aunt Carrie came up to see Mother. Mrs. Butler sent me a nice bowl of baked apples and custard. . . . Thomas shot at a cat and missed her: "a great achievement truly." Alas poor Yorrick. Snow is very rare but we had [some].

Bible Questions

What miracle was wrought to recover a borrowed axe (2 kings 6-6)

How many brothers had David (2 Sum 16-10)

Where is a pen first mentioned in the Bible (Job 19-249 or 17-1)

Who lived in an ivory house (Ahab von [illegible])

Who was buried hundreds of years after his death (Joseph)

What bitter waters were made sweet by the branch of a tree (Jordan)

Who wore the first Andal veil (Rebecca)

Who in battle disguised himself in vain (Ahab)

Whose words brought deep repentance to David (And Nathan said unto David Thou art the man Kings)

Who saw a sight that made his bone to shake (Eliphaz the Temanite Job/4c/4ver)

A nice joke for worthy of Prentice

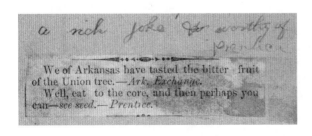

[LeRoy made a long list of most of the books he read from May 1 - August 1861. The list offers a good indication of how much, and how widely, he read.]⁶⁹

Oliver Twist, Dickens

Dombey and Son, Dickens

Georgia Scenes and Characters

Little Nell, Dickens Borrowed

Travels in Mexico, Borrowed

Old Curiosity Shop, Dickens

Ella Clinton, SS book

Violet or the Cross and the Crown

Martin Chuzzlewit, Dickens

Great Change, S.S.

Part *The Life*, S. S. Prentisss

Mission Inquiry to the Jews

Part *Keith on the Phrophecy*

Wide Wide World

Queechy by the same

The Heir of Redclyffe

The Water Witch

Heir of Redclyffe

Lives of Great Men

The Still Hour

69 More information on the books LeRoy was reading: Charles Dickens, *Oliver Twist* (London: Richard Bentley, 1839); Charles Dickens, *Dombey and Son* (London: Bradbury & Evans, 1848); Augustus Baldwin Longstreet, *Georgia Scenes and Characters* (New York: Harper & Brothers, 1850); Charles Dickens, *Little Nell* (serialized 1840-1841, London: Chapman & Hall); Albert M. Gilliam, *Travels in Mexico* (Aberdeen: George Clark & Son, 1847); Charles Dickens, *Old Curiosity Shop* (London: Chapman & Hall, 1841); Martha Farquharson, *Ella Clinton*, (Philadelphia: Presbyterian Board of Publication, 1856); Maria Jane McIntosh, *Violet, or the Cross and Crown*(Boston: John P. Jewett & Co., 1856); Charles Dickens, *Martin Chuzzlewit* (London: Chapman & Hall, 1844); George Redford, *Great Change* (London: Religion Tract Society, 1843); George Lewis Prentiss, ed., *A Memoir of S. S. Prentiss* (New York: Scribner, 1861); Andrew Alexander Bonar, Robert Murray M'Cheyne, *Mission Inquiry to the Jews* (Edinburgh: William Whyte & Co, 1849); Rev. Alexander Keith, *Keith on the Prophecy* (J. Hatchard & Son, 1831, 7th ed.); Susan Warner, *Wide Wide World* (New York: G. P. Putnam, 1850); Susan Warner, *Queechy* (New York: G. P. Putnam, 1852); Charlotte Mary Younge, *The Heir of Redclyffe* (London: John W. Parker, 1853); James Fennimore Cooper, *The Water Witch* (Dresden: Walther, 1830); Charlotte Mary Younge, *Heir of Redclyffe* (London: John W. Parker, 1853); Henry Wadsworth Longfellow, *[Lives of Great Men]* "Psalm of Life" from *The Knickerbocker*, 1839; Austin Phelps, *The Still Hour* (Edinburgh/London: Alexander Strahan/S. Low, 1860).

Volume 2

March 27, 1861 – August 1, 1861

March 27 Wednesday: Hon. Howell Cobb made a political speech last night and Thomas went. Father bought Minnie a beautiful album yesterday and Minnie bought me this book. It is a warm spring day. Rained a good deal last night. Father brought up a bottle of Rockbridge alum water. Not very nice.[1]

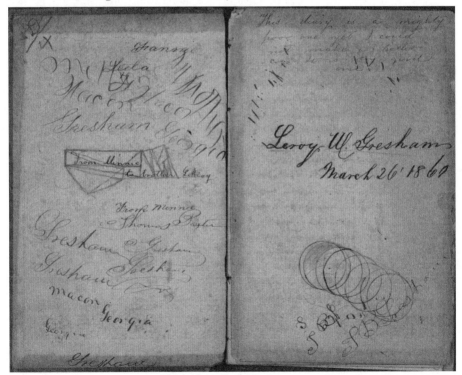

The inside cover of volume 2. *LOC*

1   Mineral water from the Rockbridge Springs in Virginia.

March 28 Thursday 1861: Father left here this morning for Houston. Mother is not very well today and they are putting quicksilver on the beds upstairs.[2] Well 90 feet, no water. Mother went over to see Mrs. Huguenin and Thomas stayed at home with me. Also Mary made some most delightful nondescripts.[3]

Friday March 29 1861: Howard left here this morn for the plantation. Had a bad headache all night and did not sleep well.[4] I went out in the streets and watched the boys play town ball and I was scorer.[5] While I was out it clouded up and the wind blew and waived a few drops and is now very sultry. 1861

Saturday, March 30: Bright and beautiful day. Vegetation has advanced very rapidly and looks very spring like. Howard and Father came back this eve.

Sunday March 31 1861: There is no service in our church on account of the absence of Mr. Wills. My leg don't get any better or any worse; neither does my cough. It is clear and bright and the Mocking birds are singing in the trees. Mary Campbell[6]

Monday April 1st 1861: April fool day . . . 5 or 600 troops came on the [rail] cars[7] here today: 1st regiment.

Teusday April 2 1861: There is 1000 troops in town today and will leave in a few days for Montgomery, [Ala]. Very warm indeed. Thomas and Minnie both stayed to home.

April 3 Wednesday 1861: Coughed nearly all night and coughed nearly all morning. Father and Mother. Thomas and Minnie gone down to the fairground to see the Gov., Joseph Brown, review the troops assembled here for the purpose of electing a colonel and then go just where Mr. Davis orders them, a good many for Pensacola, I reckon.[8] I got a letter from Dr. Pancoast today. Mr. Bates gave holiday this evening only because

---

2 A treatment to prevent bedbugs.

3 A deep-fried cookie dipped in powdered sugar.

4 LeRoy suffered frequent headaches of varying intensity, as he notes throughout his journals. A variety of things can trigger headaches. In his case, the side effects from the wide variety of home remedies and prescribed medicines he was taking (including opium and mercury—a poison) to alleviate his daily chronic back and leg pain and his inability to sleep, took a severe toll on the young man.

5 An early version or precursor to baseball.

6 One of Minnie's best friends and frequent visitor to the Gresham home.

7 Macon was a major training ground for Georgia military units; troops regularly arrived and departed Camp Oglethorpe.

8 Joseph E. Brown was the 42nd governor of Georgia. He opposed many of Jefferson Davis' policies.

he did not have any scholars. There will be a few peaches this year I hope, contrary to my expectations. Father bought me some Hore Hound candy today.⁹

April 4 Thursday 1861: Father bought me some paper with the flag of [the] Southern Confederacy on it. Cloudy day. Cough still troublesome. Father left here this morning for Presbytery.¹⁰ Cousin Howard came up to see us this morning. Every body gone to fair ground again today to see the "<u>troops</u>."

Friday April 5 1861: Dr. Collin's funeral is this morning at 10 oclock, and Mother and Thomas have gone to it. Brown's Infantry left here to day. Cough is troublesome. Wrote to Wilson. Mother gone over to see Mrs. Huguenin.

April 6 Saturday 1861: Today there was to have been a picnic but it looks so bad that I reckon it will be postponed. Eleven oclock: It has brightened up considerably and Thomas and Minnie have gone. It is quite a large affair.

Sunday April 7 1861: Father came home from Eatonton this morn. Mr. Wills came from S[outh] C[arolina] also. Rained in fitful gusts through the night and is drizzling now. My cough is not so troublesome as it was. . . . Reading a book called *The Priest Puritan and Preacher: A History of Ridley Latimer and Etc.* 12 oclock: It has cleared up.

April 8 Monday 1861: Dark and gloomy and you can hear the muttering of distant thunder, like the grumbling of some demon. Quite cool. Cough a good deal better. Raining hard all morning. Mary laid up sick in bed.

April 9 Teusday: Aunt Margaret and Cousin Mary¹¹ came last night at eleven oclock. Bright and clear. Willis came up last night bringing old Aunt Peggie. Father last night brought me up a box of sardines.

April 10 Wednesday: Father, Aunt Margaret and Cousin Mary went to ride. Tom stayed home with me.

April 11 Thursday 1861: All the folks gone down to see Mr. Johnston's house. It is a beautiful day. I found a little knife in the streets. My cough is considerably improved. Aunt and Cousin gone down to Cousin Jack's. The news is very warlike. Lincoln has chartered the *Baltic, Atlantic,* and the *Illinois,* and sent them south. [Lincoln] has notified

9 Horehound was an herbal candy often used as cough suppressant.

10 An annual meeting of Presbyterian elders and ministers in different geographic regions. John Gresham was one of the elders representing Macon.

11 Margaret Gresham Bright, a paternal cousin of LeRoy's father, and her daughter Mary Ann Bright. Both resided in Sweet Springs, Missouri.

Gov. Pickens that he will carry out the laws.[12] Let him try! The port of Charleston is in a perfect state of defense and officers say they can reduce Fort Sumter; War! Thou demon that ravishes fair countries, stay thy mad career. Saw off my leg.[13]

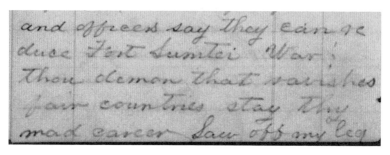

April 12th Friday 1861: The news from is uncertain but warlike. It is reported that Lincoln's men were landing in surf Boats. Gov. Brown has called for 3000 more from Georgia. 12 oclock: The rumor about the surf boats is a fabrication. There is now a report that the firing on Sumter commenced early this morning. True.

April 13th Saturday: War! War! War! The firing on Sumter is still going on. Major Anderson ceased firing last night at 7 oclock.[14] The Batteries have so far stood the majors fire well. None of the Carolinians yet killed. The abolition party in Washington terribly frightened. The telegraph wires are cut by the officers; C.S. [Confederate States] mail also. It is reported that Sumter has surrendered and no one hurt on our side. Tomorrow we will know how much truth is in it. Fired roman candles in honor of it. Another picnic today, not half so large a one as the other. I am firing a salute. After the fight was over four of Anderson's men were killed by the bursting of a gun.

Sund April 14: Mr. Wills and Dr. Mann swapped.[15]

---

12 The Federal government leased steamers *Baltic, Atlantic, Illinois* (and others) as transports to haul troops and supplies to relieve Fort Sumter ("the news is very warlike") at a cost up to $1,500 per day per ship. Once the ships were known to be off the coast, the Confederates opened fire on Sumter. Whether Lincoln was trying to simply resupply a Federal fort, or was maneuvering the South into firing first, is still debated. Francis Wilkinson Pickens was the governor of South Carolina.

13 This is the first of several instances in which LeRoy writes "Saw off my leg." Not only was his left leg mostly useless after the accident, but it also caused him tremendous pain. LeRoy still believed that all of his medical troubles stemmed from his accident, when it fact he was already terminally ill.

14 Maj. Robert Anderson was in command at Fort Sumter when the Confederates opened fire on April 12, 1861.

15 Visiting ministers often assisted Mr. Wills with the twice-Sunday preaching.

April 15 Monday: Despatch says Lincoln has ordered 75000 troops to the south. Jackson Artillery came home today. The Macon Gaurds are ordered to Savvannah [Savannah]. Thomas stayed at home. There is 8 feet water in the well. Father brought me up a bottle of Florida [cane sugar] syrup; very nice indeed. Raining very hard and fast all the evening, and Minnie stayed at home. Thomas went. Back very nearly well.

April 16 Teusday: The Gaurds left here this morning for Savvannah. News very warlike. Virginia wavering about Secession. All the states have been called upon for troops to come southward to Washington, and how much farther no one knows. Major Anderson, it seems, has been allowed to go to New York on parole I suppose. It is a very dark and gloomy state things. Weather in the same condition. Rumor says that a cargo [of] shot and shells have been landed at Fort Pickens on the point to which all eyes are turned.[16] Uncle John came to see me this afternoon. Kentucky and N. Carolina being called upon refuse to send troops to fight the South.

April 17 Wednesday: Very cool; fires feel good. Columbus troops passed through here last night on route for Savvannah. Full account of the surrender of Fort Sumter in the morning papers. 7 or 8 ships are now off Charleston. Cousin Annie and Mary[17] came over this morning. Head ached all day.

April 18 1861 Thursday: The Granite Hall was burned down last night together with Mr. Pradden's store.[18] Mother gone down town and Cousin Annie over to Uncle Jack's. Fort Pickens was reinforced the other night: 1000 men and provisions. Virginia went out [left the Union].

April 19 Friday: Cousin Sue Wiley spent the day with us.[19] Girls and boy all went for flowers.

April 20 Saturday: Put a belladonna plaster on my back last night. Cousin Anna making Mother a pair of slippers.[20] There is a company forming here to be called Home

---

16 Fort Pickens (named after Revolutionary War hero Andrew Pickens) was a US military bastion built in 1834 on Santa Rosa Island in Pensacola harbor, Florida. Today it is part of the Gulf Islands National Seashore and administered by the National Park Service.

17 Annie Carnes and Mary Bright.

18 Four different businesses were displaced by the loss of "one of our best and most beautiful buildings" to an act of arson. *Georgia Journal and Messenger*, April 24, 1861.

19 Susan Louisa Wiley, one of Mary Gresham's maternal cousins and the daughter of her uncle, Thomas Harris Wiley.

20 Anna Lamar Wiley, daughter of Dr. John Barnett "Uncle Jack" Wiley, Jr. and Aunt Ann.

Gaurds.[21] The chair for me from Uncle Leroy[22] came yesterday. General Scott[23] has resigned ("a lie"). Major Anderson is now denounced as a traitor. The north is now aroused and war must ensue in its most awful form; no one can see the end of it all. Mr. Lamar called.[24] Volunteers and Rifles both ordered off.

April 21 Sunday 1861: All the folks went down to see the Volunteers and Rifles go off. Slight frost yesterday.

April 22 Monday: Mrs. Annie Johnston's little baby died yesterday. A very beautiful day, rather cool for the season. Got a letter from Grandma. Says she will be home about May. I hope so.

April 23 Teusday: Cousin Jinnie Wiley was married last night.[25] My cough is some what worse. Mrs. Logan came to see Mother to day. Mrs. Huguenin also. Did not sleep well on acct of the intolerable itching of the Belladonna plaster.

April 24 Wednesday: Mother got her permanent set of teeth. [Cousin] Mary Gresham [Bright] gone to spend the day at Mrs. Parkers. Had a very violent spell of coughing together with vomiting. Very warm indeed; put on summer coat for the first time. Took a little morphine last night and did not sleep well, consequently drowsy all day. Our companies have arrived at Norfolk.

April 25th Thursday: Cousin Annie left for home this morning. Father started to plantation. Slept only with the aid of an opiate. Aunt Carrie sent me some strawberries.

April Friday 26 1861: I am now reading for the second time the grandest of Scott's novels. It is cloudy and warm. [Friends] Robert Kenilworth Plant and Harry Green came to see me today. Got a letter from Aunt saying she had been sick a good while. . . There is no news especially interesting, but there is every prospect of a bloody battle at Norfolk or Fort Pickens or both.

21 Company C of the Macon Volunteers organized in March 1862.

22 Great Uncle Leroy M. Wiley was the eldest brother of LeRoy's maternal grandmother. He lived occasionally in New York City during the war, but owned property in Georgia and Alabama. His business interests included the Great Western Railroad. John Rozier, ed., *The Granite Farm Letters: The Civil War Correspondence of Edgeworth and Sallie Bird* (Univ. of Georgia Press, 1988), 262.

23 Gen. Winfield Scott, a hero of the Mexican War with a long and distinguished military career, was also a candidate for president in 1852 for the Whig party. He was one of Lincoln's initial wartime advisors.

24 Capt. Lucius Lamar was the first captain of the Macon Guards, which would become Company C, 8th Georgia Infantry.

25 Eugenia "Jinnie" Clopton Wiley, cousin of Mary Gresham, married James Henderson Blount.

April Saturday 27 1861: The dwelling house of Mr. D. Ross was destroyed by fire at about 11 oclock last night. Thomas gone a fishing out on Tobesofkee creek. Rained very slightly. Father came back from Houston.

April 28 Sunday: Minnie sick all night. Rained very hard in the night. I was very restless and did not sleep well.

April 29 Monday: Clear and pleasant. Uncle John came up to see us last night. Minnie still unwell and in bed. Slept miserably last night.

April 30 Teusday: Thomas, Mother, and Father gone down to Cousin Jack's to see Aunt Morgan[26] . . . Minnie is better. There is some what of a calm in the news world at present. The riots are rampant in N. York, and it is extremely dangerous for a southern man to be there. The savannah line of steamers have all been pressed into service, the captains offered the alternative to serve or be hung. Troops are passing through here every day for Virginia. Cousin Jinnie went on last night with Mr. Blount, who is a member of the Rifles. A good many schools give holiday all the week although there is to be no celebration. Aunt Carrie sent me a mess of strawberries yesterday which were very welcome indeed. Mrs. Freeman and Scott came to see me and gave me a pair of rabbits ears genus Jackass.[27] Father bought Thomas a gun and to all appearances it is a very nice one. Mr. Bates gave holiday to day for one today.

May 1st Wednesday: Father left for Atlanta last night to attend to some business. It is not warm enough here to put on summer clothes. There is no celebration and I a'int sorry one bit. My leg is in the same condition and I hope it will get no worse. Slept indifferently although I took opium Hyociamus and spirits of lavender.[28] The mumps have gone the rounds but we did not take them this winter. Thomas was down town all the morning on business, but stayed home in eve and had nice time.

May 2 Thursday: There is news this morn of importance. There seems to be every prospect of a bloody battle at Norfolk or Washington. Aunt Carrie some more strawberries sent.

---

26 The identity of "Aunt Morgan" remains a mystery. She may have been an elderly slave who belonged to Cousin Jack.

27 Scott was one of LeRoy's friends. His father, Charles H. Freeman, was a member of the Macon Independent Volunteers.

28 Hyoscyamus Niger (more commonly Henbane or Stinking nightshade) is a poisonous plant. Before the development of anesthetics, surgery and other painful procedures were performed under the influence of alcohol and/or toxic plants. LeRoy was in pain, and given these home remedies to help him sleep. He was experiencing chronic pain and discomfort, though he did not always mention it.

May 3d Friday: Minnie has got the mumps and I slept up stairs in consequence with Father. Thomas stayed home with me. Howard gone down to the plantation. There are no papers now to read, the mail from the north being very irregular except the daily paper.

May 4 Saturday: Richard Edwards came and sat a greater part of the morning with me. Thomas went down town. Tennessee it is supposed has seceded.

Leroy W. Gresham

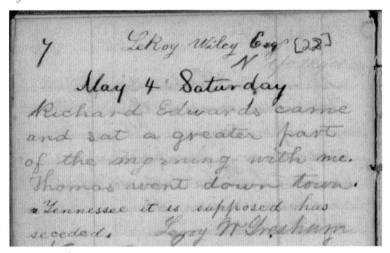

May 5 Sunday: Grandma + Uncle Richard came yesterday and brought a box of oranges. Cousin Jenks came in the evening.[29] It rained most of the day.

May 6 Monday: I have had almost constant headache for the last two or three days. Uncle J[ohn] and Aunt Carrie came up. Cousin Jenks left here. Grandma brought Alice[30] with her from Texas. Uncle Richard saw Gen. Beauregarde[31] in Atlanta. Minnie is getting rapidly over the mumps, and no one else has taken it. It is very windy indeed and warm too. There seems be no news at present of importance. There is a funeral at our church today. A Mr. Sloane ran over by the [train] cars and both legs broken.

29 John James "Jenks" Jones was his father's cousin and the son of Aunt Margaret and Uncle Seaborn Henry Jones.

30 Alice Baxter, younger daughter of LeRoy's oldest maternal uncle, Andrew Baxter. The family resided in Texas.

31 Gen. Pierre G. T. Beauregard was in command at Charleston and had opened fire on Fort Sumter. He was something of a celebrity and widely considered one of the best Southern generals. That view would change in 1862 as he fell into disfavor.

Grandma brought a picture of Uncle Ed's baby and a nice little fellow he is.[32] A great pile of *Journals of Commerce* came to day, having been detained also *The Eclectic* for May.[33]

May 7 Teusday: Grandma sick with a cold. Pretty cool and calm. Uncle Jack came over this morning.[34] Uncle John too. I slept well last night. Minnie very sick and Grandma had a chill. 3 companies arrived here today.

May 8 Wednesday: Very cool and Minnie a great deal better. There [was] a very heavy hail storm down towards Houston. I hope it did not extend down so far. My cough is pretty troublesome. There was a fire here yesterday: Mr. Warren's stable back [of] Dr. Fitzgerald.[35] There was a concert down town last night for the benefit of soldiers. Uncle Jack and Aunt Ann came over. Father bought me some cream crackers. Uncle John's baby was up to see us and looks well. The troops at Norfolk [Va] don't do anything at all worth mentioning.

May 9 Thursday: Uncle Richard left here for Athens, taking Lark with him. No one else besides Minnie has taken the mumps. Bright and clear May Morning. There is now about a regiment down to fair Grounds going to Pensacola [Fla].

Friday May 10: Warm spring day.

Saturday May 11: Grandma left for Sparta. Companies are daily leaving here. I very much fear that if there is a collision at Norfolk we will have the worst of it. There was a bad accident on the South Western railroad yesterday. Some wretch unhung had pryed up the rail in such a manner as to throw the engine and 3 cars down an embankment 25 feet high. There was but a few people hurt: the conductor and others. Minnie is up and looks a good deal worsted. It is very warm and cloudy. I am sleeping up stairs with Father yet. Mr. Edwards is very sick with a large carbuncle on the back of his neck.[36] Uncle LeRoy is still in New York and does not talk about coming out. Kentucky is furnishing troops for the federal government and also for the south. Tennessee comes

---

32 Gilmer Baxter, son of LeRoy's maternal uncle Edwin Gilmer Baxter, born in Texas in February 1860.

33 *The Eclectic*, a "magazine of foreign literature, science, and art" published in New York (1844 to 1898).

34 Dr. John "Jack" Barnett Wiley, Jr. was the next youngest brother of LeRoy's surviving grandmother, and lived in Macon. He and his wife, Aunt Ann, were Cousin Jinnie's parents.

35 Dr. Edward Fitzgerald, one of the doctors who called on the Gresham family.

36 The Richard Edwards family lived near the Gresham home. Susie was Minnie's friend, while Richard Jr. was friends with both LeRoy and his older brother Thomas. A carbuncle is a red, swollen, and painful cluster of boils under the skin caused by a bacterial infection.

forward like a man.[37] The ships sunk at Norfolk are not so much injured as was at first supposed and with some trouble can be made sea worthy.[38] The crew of the *Niagara*, which had been to carry home the Japanese, were astounded when they arrived home late by and found the country in arms against each other.[39] All kinds of provisions are rising, especially tea and coffee, on account of that man Lincoln's blockade on our ports. My cough and leg do not improve in the least and I am rather hopeless about it, however there is no telling how it may turn out in the end.

Sunday May 12th: Very warm—I got a letter from Wilson Bird. Mr. Wills preached to the soldiers at Fair Ground; Mr. Smith preached in the morning.

Monday May 13: The news is of such a character that no just conclusion can be formed.[40] The general opinion is that Alexandria and Harpers Ferry are in some danger. Slept down stairs last night. My back was dressed this morning and it was not in a good condition. It ran a good deal and was very sore. One of them is entirely well.

We got a letter from Uncle LeRoy; he does not speak of coming south. There is no commander in chief at Virginia, and the people write rather gloomily. It is very warm, very seasonable weather too. Had some Ice Lemonade today; lemons is up to a dollar a dozen. Two companies left here last night and such a drum beating for Sunday night never was heard. Rained very hard in the evening. Mr. Edwards is <u>ill</u> with a carbuncle and Susie has got the mumps. Cool + pleasant. I do not read so much as I used to; the newspaper are about the only things. Martha and Eliza H[uguenin] started to Mr. Bates.

Teusday May 14 1861: Cloudy and pleasant day. No news stirring in the paper. Went down town in the carriage and got me some clothes. Quite warm. The Ladies relief

---

37 Note the clever dig LeRoy threw at Kentucky by praising Tennessee. Four slave-holding states never declared secession: Kentucky, Missouri, Maryland, and Delaware. Four others did not vote to secede until after the Confederates fired upon Fort Sumter on April 12, 1861, and until that time were considered border states: Arkansas, North Carolina, Tennessee, and Virginia. West Virginia (which formed from 50 counties of Virginia, many of which had originally voted for secession) became a new state in the Union in 1863 and was widely considered a border state.

38 The Federals sunk ships at the Norfolk Navy Yard on April 20, 1861, to keep them out of Confederate hands. One was the 1855 frigate USS *Merrimack*, which was burned to the waterline. She would soon be raised by the Confederates and rebuilt as the ironclad CSS *Virginia*, which would meet the USS *Monitor* in Hampton Roads the following March in the first battle of iron ships.

39 The USS *Niagra*, a steam frigate built in 1855, carried Japan's first diplomatic mission to the United States from Washington to New York, where LeRoy first saw them, and then home to Japan. She left New York on June 30, 1860, and returned to Boston on April 23, 1861, where her crew learned the country was engaged in a civil war.

40 LeRoy's is growing in his ability to analyze and synthesize information at deeper level. This is not just repetition, but the attempt to reach a conclusion on his own.

society[41] were sending off the clothes to Pensacola: 150 pair pants, 150 pairs socks, fans, +c. I got a drink of soda water for the first time this year. Mr. Edwards about the yard.

May 15 Wednesday 1861: Minnie making lint for the soldiers.[42] Father stayed over to Mr. Edwards till late last night. Minnie is sick in bed with a cold. Wrote to Wilson D. Bird. Richard Edwards lent me a book: *Memoirs of S.S. Prentyes.* My cough shows no sign of improvement. Thomas and George B. went out to Earnest's mill pond.

May 16 Thursday: Uncle Jack's [slave] Chany died yesterday. Mr. Wills came to see me.

May 17 Friday: Father sat up with Mr. Edwards. Howard gone to the plantation. Quite cool. Howell Cobb [is elected] President [of the Provisional Confederate] Congress. Minnie is about again, though her cold holds on. No one else has taken the mumps as yet. It is painfully dull for me these long summer evenings: Father and [others] go off and go to sleep and I can not do that. College caught fire but was immediately put out. Mr. Edwards died this evening. Father bought me *Georgia Scenes* today. It is a great book. It is extremely warm here today. Mother very unwell.

Saturday May 18 1861: Hottest day of the season. There is no news at all to day, and Folks attended Mr. Edward funeral at 5 oclock this evening.

Sunday May 19 1861: A good deal cooler than yesterday Mr. James Griffin of the firm of Hardeman + Griffin died yesterday. I took a ride as far down as Mrs. Clark's yesterday in the buggy. My appetite is very variable indeed. Sometimes better, again worse. For the last two or three days I have not had enough for a cat. Howard returned yesterday from Houston. Got also a letter from Grandma saying she would leave Sparta on Monday (tomorrow). Father brought me a book *Analysis of Rock Bridge Alum Water.* If it does all the book says it must be a great thing.

LeRoy W Gresham

Macon May 20 Monday: Minnie started to school again this morning. Warm and cloudy. Thomas is learning to play "New Orleans Waltz" [on piano] and improves

---

41 Groups like the US Sanitary Commission organized in the North on a national level, but women in the South organized on their own. In Macon, the Soldiers' Relief Society allocated different sewing and knitting tasks to make uniforms and other necessary supplies for the companies raised in Macon, with financial support from businesses, local government, private donations, and fund-raising. The women would later cook for the troops as well. Mary Gresham played an important role in this group.

42 Loose lint was put on a wound before bandaging. Lint was created by scraping cotton or other natural fiber fabrics. It was a common task performed by young girls during the war.

quite fast. Some men came today to fix the balustrade on top of the house. No news at all in the papers this morn, except Arkansas had joined the Confederacy. There is a comet visible now in the handle of the dipper with a good spy glass.[43] Raining very hard as I write at 10 oclock day. 5 oclock evening: We have had two or three showers and a slight hail storm, and it is now quite damp cool and raining. Went on my wagon and was driven in doors. There is no apples on Fall tree, but there are a few leaves.

May 21 Teusday 1861: It is quite cool since the hailstorm. Douglas[44] has accepted a Major Generalship under Lincoln. The papers say so. I am coughing a good deal more than usual this morning. Rained again this afternoon. Mrs. Huguenin is making caps and there are some men making arrangements to begin the manufacture of arms.[45] This looks well for the south. There has been a ship fired in to ~~at~~ in Virginia on York River by the Macon Battalion. The ships were at half-mast all day. I wonder what is the matter.

May 22 Wednesday: Father is gone to Houston. It is really quite cool and I have been out all day. Anointed [my dog] Cuffie with flea powder to day. Senator Douglas has been very ill for the past week or two but is now better. It was the Columbus company in the fight not ours. Bob Bates quite sick. Despatch says North Carolina has seceded unanimously. Kentucky will maintain an armed neutrality if she can. There is very few Chinaberries this year but plenty of peaches. Haven't heard a word from Auntie since Grandmother left here. There are a great many poppies in bloom and they do look beautiful. Went down town with Mother and got soda water.[46]

Your sincere friend, LeRoy W Gresham

---

43 The Great Comet of 1861 (formally C/1861 J1 and 1861 II). This long-period comet was first seen on May 13, 1861, and was visible to the naked eye for about three months. It was one of the eight greatest comets of the 19th century.

44 Stephen A. Douglas, half of the famous Lincoln-Douglas Debates in Illinois in 1858. He was strongly against secession and called it "criminal." He was never offered a position in the army by Lincoln and died of Typhoid fever on June 3, 1861.

45 Women across the South often helped make cartridges and other types of armaments. Macon would soon be a major munitions and logistics hub with an armory, arsenal, and armaments laboratory.

46 After this paragraph, LeRoy practiced signing his name.

Thursday May 23, 1861: Cool day got on winter clothes I have slept a good deal better for the last week and hope to continue to do so. Minnie stayed to tea with Mary Campbell last night—Mary Campbell.[47]

Friday 24 May: Cool and bracing weather. Father returned from Houston.

Le Roy Wiley Gresham

Friday May Saturday 25: Thomas and Minnie gone to the Soldiers Relief concert. Cotton Avenue . . . burned last night. Lincoln's troops have taken possession of Alexandria. Deny Nisbet died suddenly today.[48] . . . Mr. Huguenin called to see M[other].

Sunday May 26 1861: Yesterday was celebrated with ice cream and blackberry pies. Very warm and sultry. Thomas bought two pair shoes. Thermons 89 in passage. Blackberry pie for dinner. Mary Campbell stayed all day with Min yesterday. We got a letter from Granma saying Uncle Richard was to leave for Virginia on Saturday today to join Athens G[uar]ds. My back not well yet; they are putting Jinison Weed salve on it. My back it is not improved in the least although my General Health is remarkably good. Thomas, Father and Mother + Minnie gone to Denie's funeral.

Monday May 27 1861: Very warm indeed. There is no news at all this morning. My appetite is a good deal better lately. Mrs. Huguenin sent me a dove yester morn. Father went off quite unexpectedly to Milledgeville to a meeting of the trustees [at] Oglethorpe [Univ.]. . . . Thomas + G[eorge] Beal went out to Earnest's millpond. Today has been very sultry indeed. I think it very curious that no one besides Minnie took mumps. There is as usual a great deal of diarrhea about, but I happily have not had it at all. Mother and Minnie both been sick with it.

Le Roy W. Gresham

Teusday + Wednesday May 28: Father has returned home, bringing a piece of loadstone and a piece of the floating battery at Charleston.[49] College . . . [Oglethorpe] has broken up on acct of the war. We got a letter from Auntie yesterday. It is very warm in the day but cool in the night and soon in the morning. Mr. Clifford Anderson's little

---

47 Why he wrote Mary's name twice is unknown, though it may reflect that he likes her—which would be emotionally appropriate for a young man his age.

48 Eugenia Amanda Nisbet (age 17) was one of the youngest daughters of Judge Eugenius and Amanda Nisbet. Judge Nisbet was a significant and influential member of Macon and Georgia politics.

49 A naturally magnetized mineral/magnet that can attract iron. LeRoy would have found it fascinating.

baby was buried today. [It] died at Norfolk and was brought home by them. There is nothing of acct from Norfolk. On the taking of Alexandria by the New York Zouaves: Col. Elsworth was shot in the act of pulling down SC [Southern Confederacy] flag by proprietor of one of the hotels.[50] There have been a few spies shot on both sides at Pensacola and Norfolk. The government has at last moved to Richmond from Montgomery, Ala and President Davis has gone on. I hope he will take charge of things in person now. Mr. John B. Lamar of Macon has loaned 600 bales of cotton to the Confederate States, a nice little loan truly.[51] Mr. Johnston has been turning water in his fish pond for some time now. The water has a beutiful slimy appearance. I went down town and got some soda water. . . . Jefferson Davis our noble president, Confederate States.

May 30 Thursday 1861: Very warm and cloudy had awful headache all day and slept in the evening.

May 31 Friday: Very warm. Minnie a little unwell and stayed home. R[obert] Bates is well again. Minnie got a letter from Sallie.[52] "No news." Thomas got a letter from [friend] Thomas Collins. Whortleberry pies for dinner to day, also "snap beans."

Saturday June 1: Summer comes in on a pretty warm day. Mother gone to Soldiers' Relief Society, and Father made Min a member.

Sunday June 2 1861: Warm very. Minnie is very unwell with sore throat. It is reported that they are fighting at Aquia Creek below Washington City [D.C]. Macon now has about 800 men in the field. 6 companies gone and another almost ready to go. There is has been remarkably few deaths among our soldiers: one active at Norfolk and 2wo at Pensacola. One [in] the Clinch rifles died from the bite of an adder [snake]. There is has been a regiment ordered to Virginia from Pensacola, which certainly seems to imply that no attack will be made for the present.

Monday June 3rd 1861: My wagon has gone to the shop to be remodeled entirely.[53] It is very warm indeed. No important news today at all. There is not one single newspaper come now except the *Southern Presbyterian*. My back is very sore indeed now, and I wish

---

50 Union Col. Elmer Ellsworth, commander of the 11th NY Volunteers and a close friend of Lincoln's. He was the first Union officer killed during the war.

51 The Confederacy did not yet have a viable currency, and cotton had an intrinsic value that could be used in many ways to support the war effort.

52 Cousin Saida "Sallie" Baxter Bird, Auntie's daughter and Wilson's sister.

53 We don't have a detailed description of his wagon, and he doesn't tell us what was being done, but likely it was being altered to provide more comfort and perhaps to include a leg brace.

An experiment that surely made LeRoy smile: An entire entry written in cherry juice. The original words are still red. *LOC*

it was well. Musquitos are just coming in vogue and sorry am I. Minnie has gotten entirely over her sore throat it seems. For the last week or two I have been reading *Literary Messenger* in which you will find many interesting stories.[54] Mother has gone to see Mrs. Judge Nisbet. My cough is improved.

Teusday June 4 1861: Warm + sultry.

Wednesday June 5 1861: Lying on front porch. There is no news at all, not even a telegraphic dispatch, an ominous silence I fear. Minnie is entirely well again. There are prayer meetings in our church twice a week for soldiers. My back is not healing hardly at all. I look [at it] but almost fear to do so. My leg is improving. My cough is certainly improved a great deal. Mother bought some cherries today and I am writing with it now. We are wanting rain. Sadly the ground is parched up. It is very cloudy now. I hope it will rain more.

Thursday June 6 1861: Warm, though pleasant. Minnie started to school to day. There have been a great may whortleberries offered for sale here this year. R[obert] Bates and Harry Green came to see me. I miss my wagon a good deal and hope it will not be long before it comes back. Mother got two pair of soldier pants to make up to

---

54 Richmond-based *Southern Literary Messenger* (1834-1864). Its tag line: "Devoted to Every Department of Literature and the Fine Arts." The publication included poetry, fiction, non-fiction, book reviews, etc.

day. The June apples are very mean this year, full of worms. The news came yesterday that Stephen A Douglas had [died]; Peace to his ashes. Very dry, no rain. Mr. Huguenin's baby came over to be seen.

June 7 Friday 1861: We had a very fine shower yesterday evening. It is cloudy and sultry now. I wish I had my wagon away, away, away over yonder.

June 8 Friday 1861: No news, except a few skirmishes of which you can't get the truth. The Lincoln men, if so they may be called, are acting with the most outrageous brutality. There has been a spy in Mannasas Junction hung. The Lincoln men galloped through Fairfax, Virginia, firing right + left among women and children. The northern people stay at home and send the contents of drinking saloons to fight the rebel South. Father brought home the *Richmond Despatch*, full of the accts of the brutality of their men.[55] It is warm and pleasant, hot, and cold. Cold in morning, soon warm at ten oclock, hot then the rest of the day, and pleasant at night. My back was dressed to day and shows few signs of healing. This is certainly a sore of the longest calibre I ever heard of. There are a great many skirmishes, but the bloody fight at Virginia has not yet come. I have been painting Confederate flags all day. The Central City Blues leave to night all. Nothing happens. Mrs. Huguenin's baby was over here yesterday, and [it] drizzled rain and drove them home, then stopped. The spring has been so late this year. Have not taken off undershirts. We have moved up stairs for the summer. . . . Mother went down to a meeting of the Relief Society and brought home a pair of pants to make. There is not near so many letters from Pensacola and Norfolk.

Sunday June 9 1861: . . . I feel truly bad, having had a very annoying and depressing headache all day. Thomas did not go to church on account of Rheumatism in his hip. Have been reading *Juryman Hogue* all day. Mother has been quite unwell and did not go to church. It is quite cool this evening. Thomas went to river with a crowd of little boys and Causey run them and cursed some. The taxes was to day. Grieve not the spirit.

LeRoy Wiley Gresham, Macon

June 10 Monday 10 1861: Thomas at home. Howard gone to plantation. I have not entirely got over my headache yet. Have not heard one word from Sparta in lo these many days. Mother is very unwell with a headache.

Teusday June 11 1861: My headache still continues and is very annoying. Mother still continues very unwell. I miss my wagon much. . . . Not a letter or paper today. 3 PM:

55 Diminishing opponents by demeaning them is nothing new; LeRoy was reading and hearing this.

Thermometer 84, cloudy. My cough has grown suddenly worse again, greatly to my sorrow. Have expectorated a great deal today.

June 12 Wednesday 1861: Woke up with a headache again this morning. Thomas still home. There was a fire last night. I am reading *Travels in Mexico*. I am very sorry my ~~back~~ cough is worse. Howard came back. There is a report that a body of Lincoln men had landed on the coast opposite Tybee [Island, Ga]. Extremely hot in the evening.

June 13 Thursday: Fast day—Slept most bad last night, and feel as if I had been beat this morning.

Friday June 14 1861: Exceedingly hot and sultry. We are in need of rain sadly. I slept most miserably last night. The musquitoes are outrageous, scampering over the bed at a fast rate. I am free from a headache this morning, although I feel very bad. Mrs Beal + Miss Sue Rowland came over to see Mother. Father went over to see Uncle Jack, who is sick. There is no paper today and consequently no news. The Huckleberries and Blackberries are offered here every day in abundance. Thomas has gotten over his Rheum almost but has not gone to school. There is a great many rumors afloat; one is that 4000 Federal troops attacked about 1000 Confederates and were repulsed with a considerable loss, while on our side 1 man was killed and 5 wounded. It has been a good while since we have heard from Grandma. I should like very much to hear, as through her we might know something of Uncle Richard's whereabouts. I do hope to get my wagon tomorrow evening. Thomas got up his kite and brought it in the porch for me to hold. Phillipi, Virginia, was retaken by our troops lately.

Saturday 15 June 1861: I feel very drowsy and bad this morning, having taken a Dover's Powder[56] last night. I also cough a good deal. I will not get my wagon until next week. We got a letter on yester eve from Grandma saying she was well and heard tolerably often from Uncle Richard.

Sunday June 16 1861: Uncle LeRoy got here yesterday evening [from New York], bringing Mother and Minnie such a lot of dresses as the world has never seen. Took a Dover's Powder and slept very badly; it is exceedingly sultry. Uncle Jack is very sick and Father sat up with him. I do not feel quite well yet, still having a lurking headache. My Mother + Uncle LeRoy have gone over to Uncle Jack's. My cough is a little better this morning.

---

56 Dover's Powder, a traditional medicine for colds, fevers, and even dysentery, was a combination of ipecac (which induced vomiting) and opium (for pain) in a syrup base. It was in use up through the 1960s.

Monday June 17 1861: Minnie's birthday. Mother sat up with Uncle Jack. Warm and pleasant. Aunt Eliza came over this morning and brought me a piece of the *Harriet Lane*.[57] I feel tolerably well today. Will not get my wagon to day or tomorrow either, I reckon. There is no news. It is <u>reported</u> that Harpers Ferry has been evacuated.

June 18 Teusday 1861: Uncle Jack is no better. Very warm; we are needing rain sadly. I slept better than usual. Our troops have evacuated Harpers Ferry, burning the bridge, and 70 locomotives. Mr. Bates has commenced to teach till two oclock. There was a fire last night and I believe it is the Arch Street Methodist Church. Father has subscribed [to] the *Richmond Despatch*.

Wednesday June 19 1861: Clear and cool. Father sat up with Uncle Jack. No news. Slept very well indeed for me. The privateer *Savvanah* was captured off Savannah near city.[58] Kozzin Jinnie and Cousin Charlie[59] have come home, having been [advised] of Uncle Jack's illness. My back appears not to be healing at all. Put beeswax and tallow on it this morn, a concoction of Father's. I think my leg is better, and my cough is also improved again I hope. There has been a few watermelons brought to Market. I hope there will be a large crop. There is no rain.

Thursday June 20 1861: Mother sat up with Uncle Jack last night. There are a great many rumors this morning of Battles at one place and another: one at Harpers Ferry another at Newport News. My wagon has come and is very nice. Uncle Jack stays about the same.

June 21 Friday 1861: Exceedingly warm. No news. I went out on my wagon yesterday and it suits me exactly. I am now reading *Dombey and Son* and like it very well. It [wagon] goes through all the gates very easy. I rather think that this is the warmest

---

57 The US revenue steam cutter *Harriet Lane* fired the first naval shot of the Civil War during its attempt to relieve Federal troops at Fort Sumter in April 1861. She ran aground attempting to enter Pamlico Sound through Hatteras Inlet in North Carolina on August 29, 1861, but returned to Federal service and was captured at Galveston (January 1863) and put into Confederate service. How Aunt Eliza was able to obtain a piece from the ship before she ran aground is unknown.

58 The capture of the *Savannah* led to an important legal case that defined part of the war itself. The privateer, authorized by the Confederacy to seize Federal ships, left Charleston on June 2, 1861, captured the brig *Joseph*, and that same day was herself captured. The crew was taken to New York and tried that October for piracy (for which the penalty was death). The Lincoln administration viewed the war as an insurrection and argued the Confederacy had no legal standing. Southern officials threatened to execute Federal prisoners in retaliation, and they were selected and made known by name. The jury, however, deadlocked and the Lincoln administration dropped the charges. The 13 crewmen were regarded as prisoners of war and not pirates and were later exchanged. The Lincoln administration had effectively conceded the rights of belligerency (war) upon those who fought against it at sea.

59 Charles M. Wiley, a staff officer in the 44th Georgia Infantry, was one of Uncle Jack's sons.

days we have had. Aunt Eliza has been trying to persuade me to have my [draining] back burnt with caustic.[60] This is a good deal the hottest day we have had.

June 22 Saturday: It is scorching hot and dry. Father sat up with Uncle Jack. Mary brought me in a few wormy peaches; very nice what there was of them. Had breakfast early and I went on my wagon and gathered June Apples. It is very hot indeed. Mother, Father, and Uncle LeRoy over to Uncle Jack. Corn is suffering badly as well as all other growing things for want of rain. Uncle Jack died this morn. Hot.

Sunday June 23rd 1861: Another scorcher. I have never suffered more in heat in my life than I have in the last two or three days. Father is sick with a headache No one went to church today from our house. . . . Every body gone to Uncle Jack's funeral, leaving me lying in the passage [hall]. The Thermometer at 97: awful. Today equals last summer for heat and certainly for being dry far excels it. The June apple tree has borne plentifully this year and we have enjoyed them mightily, and peaches are coming on slowly. This time last year I was in Philadelphia, the headquarters of abolitionism, lodged in room 104 Continental Hotel. I don't care about going there but I would like to see Dr. Pancoast. I have slept tolerably notwithstanding the awfully hot weather. I wear my calico shirts now and hardly ever put on a coat. It has clouded up; there is no rain there though. Wind blows too.

Monday June 24 1861: It is cooler this morning than yesterday on acct of the blow we had last night. Uncle LeRoy leaves this morning for Alabama. Not one drop of news this morn. I wish my back was well, but I do hate to put caustic on it. Aunt Eliza has gone home. Cloudy, and you can hear thunder. Somebody is having rain, I hope. 5 oclock: A most refreshing shower. Willis came up this evening bringing butter, eggs, +c. Thomas got up his kite and it broke with the strong wind preceding the rain. Thomas saw a bomb [shell] fired at the Sewall's Point battery. There have been two men deserted from Captain Smith's company and went over to Fortress Monroe [in Va]. There were two Yankees who had only been South about 12 months. I have been sleeping with Father and Mother on account of the "skeeters." I had a few ripe peaches today and they were very nice indeed.

June 25th Teusday 1861: Very warm, cloudy.

---

60 Spinal tuberculosis or Pott's Disease, from which LeRoy was suffering, includes local pain and tenderness accompanied by stiff muscles and spasms, abscesses, prominent spinal deformity, drainage, and other symptoms. An abscess slowly develops when the infection spreads to adjacent and soft tissues and ligaments. Aunt Eliza was convinced the only way to get them to heal was to burn or corrode LeRoy's lower back with caustic chemicals.

June 26th Wednesday: We got a letter from Auntie saying Uncle Edge had joined a company and was daily expecting to be ordered away.[61] I hear that there has been fine rains in Houston county.

Monday June 27 1861: Father left for Houston this morning early. Frank Baxter came up last night from Houston and says they have had a good rain down there.[62] We had our first watermelons today and yesterday. I have had a sort of crick in my neck for a day or so. I think I must have taken cold. We had a very fine shower in the night last night. Mr. Bates gives three or four [academic] prizes this year. I have been reading *Oliver Twist* . . . I like it very much. There are a squad of our companies home on furlough. All got big tales to tell. Rain; healthful and refreshing rain. Made doughnuts. Couldn't go on wagon alone though.[63]

June 28th Friday 1861: Was restless all night. It has been cloudy all day. Miss Flora Campbell came to see Mother.[64]

June 29 Saturday: I am very well except that every night I have a right decided fever and consequently sleep bad. Howard has gone to mill. Mother made some beer dowdy. =*LeRoy W Gresham*= My back heals awfully slow. — LeRoy — Father came back today bringing some green apples for pies. Bought some Huckleberries today. There is a dearth of news now. . . .

June 30 Sunday 1861: Wound up the clock. A great achievement truly. See page 107 this book.[65]

July 1st Monday 1861: There was a fire last night and it burnt from Father's store to the Rio Grande. It was hard work to save them. Mother is making Thomas some shirts. Mary Campbell has lent me *Little Nell*, an extract from *Dickens Old Curiosity Shop*. I shall read it first, then the latter. We have bought two or three watermelons this year, all green or half ripe. The *Richs Depatck* [*Richmond Dispatch*] comes now. It is a passably good paper. I took a dose [of] blue mass[66] last eve. There is no preparation for Thu.

61 Maj. William Edgeworth "Edge" Bird was married to Auntie, and the father of LeRoy's cousins Wilson and Sallie. He owned Granite Farm, a plantation in Hancock County near Sparta, Ga.

62 Frank Baxter was a slave with valuable carpentry skills.

63 Even though he often writes as if he goes out and about alone, someone (usually a slave) pulled him.

64 One of Mary Gresham's acquaintants.

65 LeRoy is referring to what he wrote on page 107 of his journal, which appears here on page 47.

66 Blue mass was a mercury-based compound common in the 17th, 18th, and 19th centuries and used to treat several maladies including syphilis, but was more widely recommended as a remedy for tuberculosis,

July 2nd Teusday 1861: Election for the ratification Constitution [of the] state of Georgia. Had a watermelon this eve which was nice. I have been reading [Charles Dickens'] *Old Curiosity Shop* itself today. Old Quilp is the perfect wretch and Nell is a beauty. Thomas got up his kite.

July 3, 1861 Wednesday: There is a large comet visible now.[67] The Tail is very dim but of immense length. It is about half way between the horizon and the Zenith, and the tail points up. It reaches up to the Zenith. It seems in the early part of the evening to be about 2 points North of northwest, and later in the night it gets further north. It is the largest one I ever saw, though not so pretty as the one in the fall of 1859. This time the war seems to have come in advance of the comet. Thomas is drawing.

Thursday 4th July 1861: It is quite cool this morn, and is raining slowly and steadily. Mother went down to see Aunt Carrie and found her quite sick with fever. S[usie] Edwards is slightly sick. It seems to me Macon is uncommonly sickly this year. Sometimes there is two or three funerals a day. Minnie is making one of my shirts herself. Miss Julia Beal was married [to] Dr. George G. Griffin MD. Thomas is reading *Kenilworth*. Cotton planters' convention met today and was addressed by Ex Gov. [Charles S.] Morehead of Kentucky. This is altogether the best rain we have had and it is very cool too. Thermometer has been at 72 and 73° all day. Min is reading *Dombey + Son* and I *Curiosity Shop*, and Tom *Kenilworth*.

July 5 Friday 1861: We have had a beautiful shower this morning and it is now quiet, cool, and clear. Thomas made a kite. Back has not healed at all. I slept in a bed by myself, having slept with Mother for a good while. There are constant reports of skirmishes but no great battle. The last two or 3 days has been delightful indeed. Dressed my back today. 4 oclock: And we have had another shower as fine as the other. Aunt Carrie is some better. Mother, Thomas, Minnie went to the Concert given by the college girls for the Soldiers. I have got a headache.

July 6 Saturday 1861: I have still got a headache, and Mother gone to Soldiers' Relief Society.

July 7 Sunday 1861: Commencement Sunday. There was a very heavy thunderstorm. The thunder was it seems to me the loudest and most constant that I have heard

---

constipation, parasitic infestations, toothache, and even pain from childbirth. In addition to being 1/3 mercury (a poison), it contained 5% licorice, 25% Althaea, 3% glycerol, and 34% rose honey. LeRoy mentions it in passing. Taking new medications and remedies in an effort to relieve his suffering was, by now, becoming commonplace.

67 This is the same comet he had seen previously (The Great Comet of 1861).

in many a day, if ever. Mother went to the Soldiers' Aid Society and brought home 50 caps or rather "Havelocks"[68] and some buttons, thread, + tape for me to assort and tie in bundles. There are authentic reports of a heavy battle. The forces of General Cadwallader, about 8000 men, attacked Col. Jackson with about 800 men and he as I supposed retreated. General Johnson CSA then marched up and met the combined forces of Cadwallader and Patterson and repulsed them three times.[69] There is no report of killed or wounded but necessarily It must have been a bloody one. Readers will bear in mind that this is only the report; I expect it will be greatly modified. However, if it is true, the Macon Gaurds' Capt. Lamar[70] must have been in it. The above may be all fabrication or it may be the truth.[71]

July 8 Monday 1861: Despatches of this morn contradict the statement in regard to Gen. Johnston. Aunt Carrie is really very sick. Did not sleep well at all. Got some Dalley's Pain extractor [liniment] to put on my back today.[72]

Macon July 9 Teusday 1861: Father brought home a piece of a bomb [shell] fired at Sewall's Point.[73] Dressed my back with pain extractor. Heavy shower. I am reading *Martin Chuzzlewit*. Comet in sight and very bright tail, bout 100 yards long. Thomas is upstairs drawing Mrs. Lamar's House.

---

68 A cover for a soldier's kepi/forage cap that draped down the back of the neck to protect the skin from sun and rain. They were uncomfortable and hot, and out of favor by the end of 1861.

69 Union Gen. George Cadwalader. Confederate Gen. Thomas J. Jackson (soon to be known as "Stonewall" Jackson). Gen. Joseph E. Johnston was one of the South's leading generals and would be a household name after First Manassas (July 21, 1861). He waged a war-long feud with President Davis over his rank and other matters, including how best to conduct the war. Patterson is Union Gen. Robert Patterson.

70 Leonidas Lamar, son of Superior Court Judge Henry Lamar of Vineville, Georgia.

71 The fighting mentioned by LeRoy is Falling Waters (or Hoke's Run) fought in Berkeley County, western Virginia, on July 2, 1861, an early episode of the Manassas Campaign and Jackson's real combat. Jackson had orders to delay Patterson's advance after he crossed the Potomac River. He did so, withdrawing slowly. Losses were light (23 killed, wounded, and missing for the Union and about 90 in total for Jackson). LeRoy's skepticism toward early news is increasing as he begins to realize just how often news from the front is unreliable.

72 John and Mary Gresham were willing to try anything to alleviate LeRoy's daily suffering. Dalley's Pain Extractor (composition unknown) was created in 1839 by Cornelius Dalley. It met with little success. He died 1852 and C. V. Clickener, a druggist in New York City, took over the product. In 1855, he published a 24-page booklet praising the remarkable virtues of the ointment, something the Greshams or a doctor read. According to an ad of the era, the "great family ointment" cured burns, piles, corns, bunions, chapped skin, erysipelas, and skin diseases. It cost 25 cents per box.

73 The Battle of Sewell's Point (May 18-21, 1861) was an exchange of fire between Union gunboats *Monticello* and *Thomas Freeborn* against Southern batteries on Sewell's Point in Norfolk County, Virginia.

July 10 Wednesday 1861: [no entry made]

July 11 Thursday 1861: Poor Aunt Carrie's funeral is this morning. The funeral of Mr. W. A. Ross is also this morning. Mr. John Ellis is not expected to live, having been found in his bedroom, lying on the floor, speechless. Mrs. Corbin has a negro boy not expected to live. Mrs. Whittle's baby has scarlet fever. Mrs. Johnson's Adeline has Typhoid fever. Macon is sickly, more sickly that I have ever known it to be. Uncle Edge has been ordered away to the war. Uncle John's little baby is very sick; I hope he will get better. Cousin Helen was here to dinner yesterday.[74] Ralph and Willis came up last night bringing the cow and calf.

Friday July 12 1861: Mr. Ellis's funeral was on yesterday evening. Today the weather is truly delightful. Uncle Edge leaves for the war on the 17th. Mrs. Evans, our neighbor, has Typhoid fever and is very low. My Back is no better. Cuff Cuffie

Saturday July 13, 1861: Pleasant day Thomas and Minnie have gone to a "Levee" at Mr. Moughan's. Mother has gone to sit up with Uncle John's baby. Leaving Father with me. I have been assorting buttons for the Soldiers Society all day and Reading Dickens. We have quit putting Dally on my back now. I am getting along very well except this. I do wish it would heal.

Macon July 14 1861: Quite cool. Mother sat up with the baby. He is a little better. Boregarde [Beauregard] There are reports of a battle or so in Missouri. Do not know about truth. Mr. Wills is sick and there was not service in our church this morning. I am Reading *Keith in the Prophecies*. Miss Hattie Tracy sent me some peaches + a cantelope this evening.[75] The city hands have improved the road in front of our house very much, and are hauling the dirt out of our garden. Brought up a new cow and calf last Wednesday night. {The grass is green, and so am I} The latter part of the above sentence was written by my brother Thomas. I am sorry he has so bad an opinion of himself, however I think as he does. That is a whale.[76]

Macon July 15 1861: Have had a bad headache all day. Uncle John's baby is a good deal brighter. Put black wash on my back.[77] There are reports of a battle in which a Georgia Regiment was engaged. I have sorted a goodly number of buttons today. Thomas Got a headache. We [now] have some fine peaches on our lot. Miss Hattie

74 Ellen Elizabeth Steel Tracy, Aunt Carrie's sister-in-law married to her half-brother Edward D. Tracy.

75 Hattie or Harriet was Aunt Carrie's sister.

76 He is using "whale" to mean "entertaining" or "amusing," as in "We are having a whale of a time."

77 Black Wash consisted of glycerine and black oxide of mercury or nitrate of silver.

Tracy. *L. W. Gresham* is the gifted author of this stupendous work of art Happy is she who reads it. Thomas is reading *Quentin Durward*.

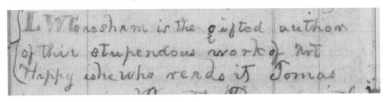

July 16 Teusday 1861: Sorted a large box of buttons today. The baby is better. Report of a battle in which the Confederates were whipped.

July 17 Wednesday 1861: There has evidently been a heavy battle in Missouri. Laurel Hill has been evacuated. The Confederates were pursued by the federals again their advance gaurd engaged the rear gaurd of the Confederate. It is reported that 4 Georgia captains and lieutenants were taken prisoners. The First Georgia regiment was in the engagement. General Garnet has been killed. The enemy lost no man or few. General Garnet had resigned from the United States forces + was undoubtedly a very fine officer.[78]

Have finished *Martin Chuzzlewit*. My back shows no sign of healing and won't till caustic is put on it. Uncle Edge leaves Sparta for the war today. Thomas is writing to Uncle Richard as some gentlemen leave here tonight for Virginia.[79] It sprinkled rain here early this morning soon but not enough to wet the ground. We have on our lot as many peaches as we can eat. We have had a great deal of delightful weather in the last two or three weeks, the thermometer hardly ever reaching 90°F.

July 18 Thursday 1861: Howard left for Houston. The comet has disapeard out of sight. Have been reading *Mission of Inquiry to the Jews*. Grandma to our great surprise + joy arrived here this afternoon. Her visit is entirely unexpected. Uncle Edge is in Atlanta with his regiment and Auntie Sallie + Wilson are with him, and she [Grandma] went down to see them and thought she might as well come down to Macon. She brought a likeness of Uncle Richard which is very striking. It was taken in Virginia and sent to her. Some of the reports are that 4 companies of Georgia Volunteers had been

---

78 The Battle of Corrick's Ford or Rich Mountain (July 13, 1861) along the Cheat River in western Virginia was little more than a skirmish and part of the larger overall operations of the West Virginia Campaign. This fight was the end of a series of clashes between Confederate Gen. Robert S. Garnett and Union Gen. George B. McClellan. Garnett died in the fighting—the first general officer to die in the Civil War.

79 Thomas was handing a letter to someone to hand-deliver to Uncle Richard, which was more reliable and faster than Confederate mail.

taken prisoners [and] Gen. Garnet has certainly been killed. My back was dressed and actually it has healed a little. It is reported that Lincoln men are marching on Alexandria. Cousin Jack sent me a beutiful map of the war. Minnie and Susie Edwards reared down pulling me on my wagon. Uncle John and Father and Mother are making up a box to send to Uncle Richard. It has been cloudy all day and a heavy rain towards Dinner. Miss Hattie Tracy sent me a cantelope. There is a half a dozen men home on furlough, all from Sewall's Point, Va. Scarlet fever still at Mr. Whittle. LeRoy

Friday July 19 1861: Heavy rain about eleven oclock, but is now clear. Thomas is reading *St. Valentines Day*, the fourth of [Sir Walter] Scott's he has read this season. I hope my back will be almost well by the next dressing. Uncle John's baby is decidedly better. I think he will get well. Despatches say that Gen. Bonham had been attacked at Fairfax by 10,000 "Hessians" and that he had repulsed them with a heavy loss on their side, and they had immediately retreated to Alexandria.[80] The *Mission to the Jews* is very interesting, but I must say there is too many quotations, both scriptural and Classic, 10 and eleven on a page. Grandma went over to Aunt Ann's this morning.

Saturday July 20 1861: Slept well. It is said that 900 men were killed (Federals) at "The Battle of Bulls Run" [and] 140 Confederate.[81] Julia Ann is seriously though not dangerously sick. Uncle John came up to see her this morning. It is the 20th July. Appointment Gen. Scotts.[82]

Macon July 21 1861 Sunday: We were yesterday visited by a very heavy shower indeed; cloudy again. Today Julia Ann is much better than she was. Mother has fixed up a box of peaches for Auntie [as] there are no peaches in Hancock. Grandma left here for Athens with the hope that we would soon follow. Rain. Uncle John expects to go if nothing happens and the baby is well enough. No more from Virginia at present.

Macon July 22 1861: Another great battle at Manassas! Sherman's Battery taken! Terrible Slaughter on both sides! The enemy retired from the field. The Fight commenced 4 oclock this morning and continued until about seven. The battle raged

---

80 Gen. Milledge L. Bonham led a brigade in Gen. Beauregard's Southern army in Virginia. LeRoy did not know that the Manassas (Bull Run) Campaign was beginning. On July 18, Gen. Irvin McDowell's Union army had reached Centreville. Part of it had orders to scout Rebel defenses at Blackburn's Ford on Bull Run creek, but not to fight, but they attacked and were beaten back. Bonham's command was nearby, but his men were not involved. LeRoy's use of "Hessians" was a dig at Federal soldiers. Hessians were paid German mercenaries used by King George against the colonists in the Revolutionary War.

81 LeRoy is again referencing the July 18 fight at Blackburn's Ford. Actual casualties were 83 Union killed, wounded, and missing, and 68 Confederates.

82 It is unknown what LeRoy means with this statement.

with terrible force and a heavy loss on both sides. There has evidently been a signal Victory at Bulls Run.[83] President Davis' message is out. It is not only well written, but beautiful in contrast to the boorish effort of Doctor Lincoln, Chief magistrate of United States. Raining very slightly before breakfast this morning. Sad news Gen. F. S. Bartow is killed.[84] Macon Gaurds in the fight. President Davis commanded in person; Beauregarde + Johnson's army both engaged 40 000 to 70 000 on a side. Beauregarde's horse shot from under him. It will be sometime before we can get the truth of it. Dressed my back this morning and its healing though very slowly. General Wise has also gained a signal Victory in western Virginia, killing 150 federals and losing few of his men.[85] Julia Ann is up and about again. Very heavy shower this afternoon. Uncle John, Deo Volente [God willing], leaves for Athens tomorrow. Father comes home but there are no more reliable dispatches. The battles undoubtedly sends a thrill of Anguish to many an anxious heart in the newborn Confederacy. Ave Maria Jose [goodbye].

July 23 Tuesday 1861: Very cloudy. No more news. Mr. Charles Harris came back from Virginia the other day and says Uncle Richard is well, +c. More news: showing the battle of Manassas Junction to be a bloody victory. There is no way of telling the number killed. Mr. Edward Tracy was in the battle. The Macon Gaurds were certainly in it. The federal dispatches are very gloomy saying that Washington is shrouded in gloom and that there are 5000 killed; there is no account of our killed. The bells rung at 12 oclock. Better not holler fore they get out of the woods. There was a large meeting here today to send nurses to the sick. Big meeting in Richmond for the same purpose. Confederate Congress held a meeting thanking God only for the Victory. Our Force engaged was 15000 against 35000 whole force 40000 against 80000. Gloom will go through the south such as patriot hearts can only bear and joy of some will be sadly marred by the loss of friends + kindred. Borrowed *Boat life in Nubia* and *Tent Life in the*

---

83 Confederates named battles after the nearest significant town (Manassas), and Federals after geographic features (Bull Run creek). The Battle of Manassas (Bull Run) was the war's first large-scale combat. Gen. McDowell attempted to flank the Confederates by moving around their left, but they rushed men there and routed McDowell's troops. Southern reinforcements from the Shenandoah Valley under Gen. Joe Johnston arrived by rail just in time to take part in the battle. Gen. Jackson stood "like a stonewall" against Union attacks and earned his famous nickname. Each side had about 18,000 men in the fighting, although nearly double that number (35,700 Federals and 32,000 Confederates) were available. Union losses totaled 2,708 (481 killed, 1,011 wounded, and 1,216 missing); Confederate losses were 1,982 (387 killed, 1,582 wounded, and just 13 missing). The first large battle of the war was over.

84 Col. Francis Stebbins Bartow's brigade included the Macon Guards, part of the 8th Georgia regiment. Bartow was mortally wounded and died the following day. He was the first Confederate brigade commander killed in action.

85 Gen. Henry A. Wise was also the 33rd governor of Virginia. News of a battle was false.

Holy Land. Am reading *Wide, Wide World.* Uncle John left for Athens. Mrs. Dessau is going around getting lint for Soldiers.

Wednesday July 24th 1861: Clear and cool. No more news of <u>our</u> companies. Aunt Eliza arrived here and stayed all night on her way home from Marietta, where she had been on a visit.

Thursday July 25th 1861: Father gone to Houston this morning. Mr. Leonidas Lamar was killed at Mannassas we hear.[86] My back is nearly well and I am very glad. Have finished *The Wide, Wide World.* It is truly a most delightful book. So full of true Christianity + yet so unpretending. The *Richmond Dispatch* has a fine editorial in it today on the "Rout of Gen. Scott's best drilled 'regulars' by our untrained volunteers." Hurrah 2x. Every one seems expecting to hear of the Attack on Sewall's Point. I am hear interrupted by the talented drawing you see before you. "Saw off my leg." I had a headache all the morn and it is much better now. 3 PM: Mother went down town this morn and tried to get me a testament but could not get one in the large metropolis of Macon. I have been putting up buttons for the Relief Society and I am glad I can put in so small a mite for the brave defenders of our homes + fire sides. "Don't nobody read this page if they please."

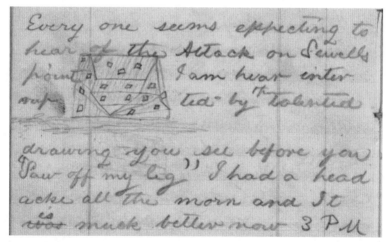

Friday July 26 1861: Clear and pleasant. Susie Edwards stayed all night with Minnie. There is no fresh news. It is said that Gen. Scott's epauletts and Sword were captured which <u>I</u> put down as a lie. Richard E[dwards] [friend] came over to see me yesterday. My back is at last well. There was an alarm of fire last night. It was a kitchen on Cotton

86 Leonidas Lamar served in the Company C (Macon Guards) in the 8th Georgia regiment. He was 27 years old. His body was brought back home for burial in Macon's Rose Hill cemetery.

Avenue. The Confederate captured 20 000 stand of arms in the late battle. Cuff bit Susie Edwards today, a thing I never knew him to do before. R[ichard] Edwards brought me over the extra [paper]. Capt. Edward Tracy is safe and promoted to the rank Major. "Utah Johnson" alias ASJ is in Texas and on his way to Richmond.[87] General Bartow's body is now in Charleston. Some of the Yankee regiments have gone back home, their 3 months being out. I have started *Queechy* by the author of *The Wide, Wide World*. I do not like it so much, however Fleda [a character] wept.

Saturday July 27 1861: Howard brought home my mattress for my wagon.[88] Minnie hemmed a pocket handkerchief for Father. Mr. Robert Toombs has been appointed Brigadier General.[89] R. M. T. Hunter of Virginia has been appointed in his place as Secretary of State, right too.[90] There is a fellow by the name of Melcher taken up and ordered to leave here for uttering treasonable sentiments. Father and Thomas have come back from Houston. Somebody came and stole some of our finest peaches last night.

Sunday July 28 1861: Clear and pleasant.

Monday July 29 1861: Warm and clear Mother has gone down to see Aunt Sarah Jones.[91] No news this morning. We expect if nothing happens to go to Athens this week or next. Liza Huguenin sent me some beautiful pears this morning.[92] There are two new companies formed, The "Lockrane Gaurd" and the "Bloom Infantry." *Queechy* is a very good book but somehow things do not go to suit me. Fleda has too many troubles and takes too much upon herself. *The Wide, Wide World* is much better;

87 Gen. Albert Sidney Johnston led a US army in the Utah War of 1857-1858 against the Mormons. He would cast his lot with the Confederacy, be promoted to full general, and posted in the Western Theater.

88 This is the first indication that the wagon had a cushion or support [a mattress] inside.

89 Gen. Robert A. Toombs, a pre-war attorney who had served in both the House of Representatives and Senate, was the first Confederate secretary of state. He was the only member of Davis' administration to object to the attack on Fort Sumter the past April. As he presciently told Davis: "Mr. President, at this time it is suicide, murder, and will lose us every friend at the North. You will wantonly strike a hornet's nest which extends from mountain to ocean, and legions now quiet will swarm out and sting us to death. It is unnecessary; it puts us in the wrong; it is fatal." Frustrated, Toombs sought a field command and was appointed general.

90 Virginia native Robert M. T. Hunter, an attorney and former US Representative and Senator, took Toombs' place. Hunter later served as a Confederate senator and was pictured on the Confederate $10.00 bill.

91 Sarah Elizabeth Wimberly Jones, maternal aunt of John Gresham, married to his late uncle John Jones. She was visiting from Savannah.

92 One of the Huguenin daughters.

Ellen is a much better character. I sleep most <u>misbrally</u> these nights tho. Beauregard is reported moving on Alexandria. It will take the "Yankee" army a good while to reorganize. Part of the First Georgia Regiment have come back home. They were 4 days, 5 nights in the mountains without food, having been cut off by the enemy. They lost everything but their arms and the clothes upon their backs. Poor fellows; they need help bad.

Teusday July 30 1861: Jerry [a horse] bit Johnson [a slave] on the face this morning making a very bad sore. It is very warm. Aunt Sarah Jones spent the day with us. Frank is making a box to put my wagon in to go to Athens.[93] Our troops captured at Manassas: 500 boxes arms and 500 baggage wagons full of all sorts of Luxuries. No news. . . . We need rain some. Arthur and Milo went back to Houston carrying the cow. I doubt very much whether we will get off Thursday, Mother being so busy and having company too. The sickness in Macon is much better. . .

July 31 Wednesday: <u>A</u> <u>scorcher</u>: <u>83°</u> <u>8</u> <u>in</u> <u>morning</u>. Father bought me a diary yesterday. Johnson says "he "feels <u>right</u> <u>smart</u> this morning." Father packed up the box to go to Uncle Rich. We every year just seem to strike the hottest time to travel to Athens. M[other] + Father sent Uncle Edmund a box [of] peaches. Very warm; a very slight rain about dinner [with] the sun hardly going in. Father is going to carry my wagon to Athens. I have suffered more with heat in the last two, three days than usual, though it has not been as hot as some. Rode down town in the carriage with Mother.

August 1st Thursday: We leave for Athens this morning. It is very warm. There is not news stirring at all. I hope there will be no crowd. Phil Tracy brought up a drum for us to carry to the baby.[94] I do not reckon we will have room this morn. Johnson is a little better. They are going to stop running the night train on the Macon + Western railroad, the stingiest of Roads. Mother is very busy indeed. I expect we will have a hot dusty and disagreeable ride.

Athens Friday August 2: We left Macon yesterday morning and after a hot ride got to Atlanta. The *Asbury Hull* [locomotive engine] brought us up. We then got on the Georgia Road which was as usual crowded to excess. There was soldiers on board and every [one] halloed and waved handkerchiefs at them. When we got to N[orth] Point, had to stay 4 hours in the cars. It rained a little. My wagon is at Atlanta. We found all

---

93 The family is planning their annual trip to Athens, GA., to spend time with Grandma.

94 Philomon Tracy was Aunt Carrie's half-brother. He lost his wife, Caroline M. Rawls Tracy, and only son during in childbirth in 1858.

well here. Mrs. Tracy came as far as Atlanta with us. *Richmond Inquirer* comes here; it is a better sheet than the *Dispatch*, but not so good a paper.[95]

[LeRoy writes out the poems "The Last Leaf," by Oliver Wendell Holmes, and "A Song of Life," by Henry Wadsworth Longfellow, and adds this signature:]

Your most affectionate friend

And counsellor

1860 LeRoy W Gresham

Eighteen things worthy of being improved upon:
    Loud laughter
    Reading when others are talking
    Cutting fingernails in company
    Leaving meeting before its closed
    Whispering in meeting
    Gazing at strangers
    Leaving a stranger without a seat
    A want of reverence for seniors
    Reading aloud without being asked
    Recieving a present without any manifestations of gratitude
    Making yourself conspicuous
    Laughing at the mistakes of others
    Joking others in company
    Correcting older persons than yourself especially parents
    Commencing to talk before others have finished
    Answering questions when put to others
    Commencing to eat as soon as you get to the table
    In not listening to what other people are saying

[LeRoy spends several pages writing stanza's from Sir Walter Scott's "Marmion" (*Canto* VI) and Henry Wadsworth Longfellow's "A Psalm of Life." He then copied the entire long and sad poem "Lament of the Irish Emigrant," by Helen Selina, Lady

---

95 Mrs. Edward Tracy. A "sheet" is one double-sided piece of newsprint, or four pages (two on a side) and two spreads (one on each side). LeRoy seems to be comparing the layout of the *Richmond Inquirer* (which he prefers) to the overall content of both papers (preferring the *Dispatch* over the *Inquirer*). It unusual that one so young not only noticed such things, but had a preference.

Dufferin, writing at the bottom of a page, "This piece was copied into this book for want of something to do."

[This is the point page 107 from his journal begins. Recall he wrote on June 30, "See page 107 of this book." LeRoy was having some fun, adding additional information and commentary to previous entries.]

21st 22 + 23d Days of June will be remembered as three of the longest, hottest, dryest days of the season. . . .

April 13 1861: On this page you will find a few lies and some important disquisitions in reference to the taking of Fort Sumter by the Gallant Beauregarde. Readers will find June 30 1861 a very eventful day. LeRoy[96]

[June 5 and June 6]: The reader will find pages 31-2 of this highly interesting work written in Cherry Juice. He will also find a valuable piece of information on top page 22 [May 22 entry] in relation to an interesting specimen of the canine race.[97]

Remarkable events *May 2* Minnie took the mumps *May 5* Grandma + Uncle R and Alice come from Texas *April 13* Fort Sumter taken *Jan 21* Peas taken out my back *May 14* Mr. Edwards very sick with a carbuncle *April 22nd* Cousin Jinnie Wiley married *April 17* Cousin Annie came over *April 18* Granite Hall burned down *April 27* B. F. Rosses house burned down *April 1* Aunt Margaret and Cousin Mary came up on their way to Bakerly *Feb 18* President Davis inaugurated in Montgomery *May 17* Mr. Edwards died *May 18* Arkansas Admitted *May 25* D Nisbet died *20th May* N Carolina seceded

On the bottom of page 69 [July 17] the reader will find an interesting discussion.

From the 4th July we have had very delightful rains. Grandma says they have had no rain in Athens as yet since the 1st July or the last June.

[After writing two important dates in his journal—"20th July 1861" and "July 20 1861," LeRoy wrote, "Readers will be apt to mind April 14 fraught with interesting matter."]

Saw off my leg.

96 In his original April 13, 1861 entry, LeRoy recorded that the Confederates did not suffer any losses during the battle for Fort Sumter, and that four Union soldiers had been killed. In fact, one Confederate was mortally wounded, and two Union men died during the firing of the 100-gun salute.

97 The "valuable" information: "Anointed [my dog] Cuffie with flea powder to day."

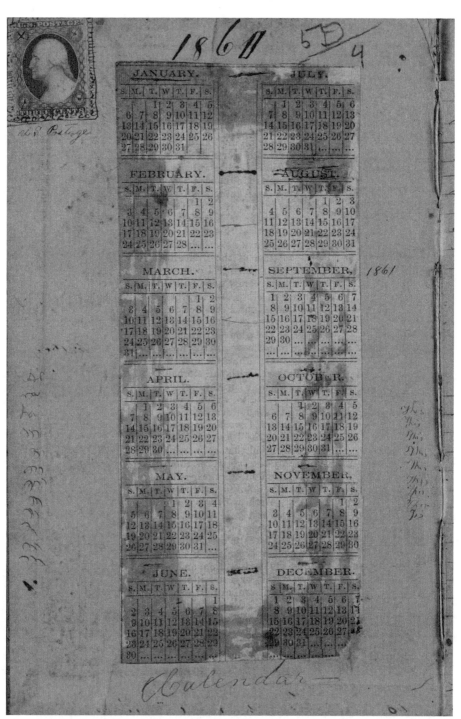

The inside front cover of volume 3.
LOC

Volume 3

August 2, 1861 – December 30, 1861

Le Roy Wiley Gresham, Athens Geo

Le Roy Wiley Gresham

August 3rd 1861

From Father

To Le Roy

Athens Friday August 2 1861: We left Macon yesterday morning and after a very hot and dusty ride arrived at Atlanta. The *Asbury Hull* brought us.[1] We then got on the Georgia RR., which as usual was very crowded. There was some soldiers on board + ladies came down to the cars + threw bouquets and waved hankerchiefs at them. When we got to Union Point, we had to stay 4 hours in the cars. It rained while we were there. My wagon came as far as Atlanta with me. We found all well here. It is very warm indeed. Mrs. Edward Tracy came up as far as Atlanta with us.

It is reported Uncle Richard's regiment (3d) has been ordered to Manassas. Grandma takes the *Richmond Inquirer*. It is a much better sheet than the *Dispatch*. Uncle John's baby is much better. There was an old French lady came to see Grandma today, and entertained us all the evening. Dr. Reese came to see Everybody this evening. Thomas has taken a bad cold and has a cough with it. Had a slight rain here this morn.

Saturday August 3 1861: Rain. Very pleasant day. I slept very badly. Mother was carrying me this morn + stumbled and fell hurting her knee. It did not hurt me at all.

---

1 The Greshams were going to see Grandma for an extended visit. LeRoy has a special interest in locomotive engines (the *Asbury Hull*) because his great-uncle LeRoy M. Wiley holds a large ownership stake in the Great Western Railroad. The locomotive *L. M. Gresham* was the first to pull the "Presidential Special," hauling President-elect Abraham Lincoln from Springfield to the Indiana line as he traveled to Washington, D.C. for his first inauguration.

The fruit is very small and knotty up here – a contrast to that in Macon. Grandma got a likeness of Uncle Link's baby today from Texas.[2] Mr. Johnston called. My wagon has come and I am glad. Aunt Sarah Ann[3] came down to see us.

Sunday August 4 1861: Cloudy. I enjoy my wagon very much. There are so many new places to go. Grapes and cantelopes are very plentiful. I lead just such a life here as I do at home. Minnie has started to Sunday school and is going while she is here. Mammy Dinah[4] came up to see me and is of course hardly able to get about. I heard just before I left home that Mr. Wills had gone to Virginia,[5] and Father says if there is another battle he would go on his own expense as a nurse. Rained a little bit.

Monday August 5 1861: Thomas' cough is not any better; he took paregoric[6] last night. A large bunch of papers came today with a great many different accounts of the battle, but no news. General Patterson has resigned and N. P. Banks[7] has been appointed in his place. There is no account of the Yankee killed but they vary from 600 to 6000. Uncle John, Thomas, and myself shot a parlor pistol at a mark and I almost came up as with Uncle John. Grandma got a letter from Uncle Richard.

Teusday August 6 1861: Cloudy. Presbytery meets here today to dissolve the connections between the north and the south. General Scott says the reason they got whipped at Manassas was that he was forced into battle before he was ready. It is said that every man when he arrived in Washington reported himself the last man in his regiment. The cavalry company is in camp here now, and is going on the 7th in Cobb's Legion. Also a company got here yesterday from Madison. There was a shooting match in Uncle Richard's regiment and he and a captain beat [won]. Thomas' cough is a good

---

2   Eli Leroy "Link" Baxter had moved to Texas with his wife, Maria Burton Baxter. No reference to a child has been found in any genealogical records.

3   Sarah Ann Wiley was one of LeRoy's great-aunts, a sister to his grandmother. Sarah Ann lived in Athens, Ga.

4   Likely one of grandmother's house servants.

5   Many of Macon's civic leaders traveled north to Virginia in general and the Manassas area in particular to help the large number of wounded and the sick, and to deliver supplies gathered by the Macon Ladies Soldiers' Relief Society.

6   Paregoric was an opium-based product widely used to suppress coughing and provide relief from diarrhea.

7   Former Massachusetts governor Nathaniel P. Banks was the first political general appointed by President Lincoln (over the heads of Regular Army officers) because Banks could help bring in recruits and money to the Union cause. Unfortunately for Lincoln, Banks had limited abilities and would lose fights against Thomas "Stonewall" Jackson's small army in the spring of 1862 in the Shenandoah Valley, and in 1864 lead the disastrous Red River Campaign in Louisiana.

deal better. The night are much pleasanter here than in Macon. Mrs. Foster's little baby died this morning. Minnie and Alice pulled me to Aunt Sarah Ann's and while we were there, it rained a little. Colonel Franklin called.

Wednesday August 7 1861: Cloudy. Mrs. Foster's baby was buried today. There is a story in the papers that "A bottle was found near the Hebrides Islands containing a note from someone on board the lost Collins steamer *Pacific*, saying she was surrounded by icebergs and going down?"[8] Thomas Killed a bird with a pistol, hitting him (bird) in the head. Minnie mashed her finger in door. I am reading *The Heir of Radcliffe*. I borrowed it from Aunt Sarah. It is very dry here, although it has rained every day since we came. Generally it is cloudy early in the morning and rains a little and late in the evening again. The Relief Society up here seems to be very active and Grandma is one of the distributors of work. We have not heard from Aunty since we got here. Rained a little—very little.

Thursday August 8 1861: Cloudy and damp. We found a rabbit's nest in the garden with four young ones in it. Brag [a dog] ate one and Thomas shot one with a pistol. They were very pretty. The Macon papers state that there has been heavy rains there since we left. Dr. Hoyt is in the parlor. I slept very badly last night. 11 oclock: Quite a good rain. I woke this morning with a sore throat but do not think it permanent. Athens is a miserable place to get news, there being no telegraph. We have to wait for the papers and very few of them.

Friday August 9 1861: Cloudy and damp. Thomas has gone down town. Minnie got a letter from Susie Edwards saying that Johnston was better. A "leetle" drop of rain. Generals Beauregarde + Johnstons' address to the army is very fine. The northern papers are quarreling about who the responsibility of the defeat rests upon. But I think with *The Constitutionalist* that it rests entirely upon the able Generals Beauregarde + Johnston.

Saturday August 10 1861: Cloudy. Mother rode out to the encampment yesterday evening. There is not one drop of news from Richmond, and General Beauregard has

---

8 SS *Pacific* was a wooden-hulled side-wheel steamer. On January 23, 1856, she departed Liverpool for New York, carrying 45 passengers and 141 crew. The bottle with the message was found in the summer of 1861 on the remote island of Uist in the Hebrides, an archipelago off the west coast of mainland Scotland. It read: "On board the Pacific from Liverpool to N.Y. - Ship going down. Confusion on board —icebergs around us on every side. I know I cannot escape. I write the cause of our loss that friends may not live in suspense. The finder will please get it published. W.M. GRAHAM." William Graham was a British sea captain aboard as a passenger to take command of a ship in New York. See Jim Coogan, "A Message from the Sea," http://www.barnstablepatriot.com/home2/index.php?option=com_content/task=view/id=15011/Itemid=306.

cut off the mail from Manassas. Rained a little. Minnie + Alice have gone to spend the day with Dr. Jones' little girls. Grandma's grapes are very fine and plentiful. I have finished *The Heir of Radcliffe* and like it very well, but not so much as I expected from Aunt Sarah Ann's glowing account. She says she cried over it; Mother did too. I went down in the grass lot once since I have been here + it is a very dirty place. Uncle John cut Tracy's gums today.[9] The mosquitoes have not as <u>yet</u> made their appearance and I am very glad. They are great bothers.

Sunday August 11: Clear and pleasant day. It has rained every day since we have been here, but still it is very [nice] day and pleasant. There are not near so many letters from the soldiers in the papers as there was at first. There is literaly nothing in the Macon papers but what you have seen in others. There has been a meeting called there for the purpose of administering a test oath to the people. Columbus, Georgia has sent 12 companies to the war. General Beauregard has been promoted to the highest office the congress can give him. Rained a little here this evening. Lincoln has appropriated 2 000 000 million dollars for the purpose of arming the Union men in Kentucky and Tennessee. Alfred Ely,[10] a member of the federal congress, was taken prisoner as a spectator at Manassas. I see a piece in the paper proposing to change the flag.[11] I hope they will do no such thing. A writer in *The Telegraph* proposes to erect a monument in Macon to the Guards.

Monday August 12 1861: Rained a little and is quite cool. I have been reading a little in *The Spectator*[12] and find some right interesting pieces in it. Grandma gave me a piece of the flagstaff that was on Fort Sumter in the fight. Mr. Richard Johnston came up to see us and promised to lend me some books. Got a letter from Auntie and she did not say a word about coming up. The papers come, but there is no important news. It is said one of our congressmen (found to be untrue) had been taken prisoner. Our

---

9   This would allow baby Tracy's emerging teeth to get through the gums easier. Fortunately, Uncle John was a doctor.

10 Alfred Ely, a Republican representative from New York, was held in Libby Prison in Richmond for almost six months until his exchange.

11 Beauregard discovered at Manassas that the first Confederate national flag (the "Stars and Bars") was hard to distinguish from the U. S. national flag during battle. He proposed a new flag design, which led to the Confederate battle flag (crossed blue bars with stars on a red background).

12 A British weekly begun in 1828 that dealt with politics, current events, and culture. It is still in publication today.

privateers are doing finely![13] The rain continues all the evening. Towards night it grew cold enough for winter clothes, but I did not have any and took a little cold.

Teusday August 13: Very cloudy, and damp and cool. Last year at just this time there was a storm like this one (the one of yesterday). Grandma sent out a supply of ham and bread for the soldiers' supper. We are sitting by the fire this morning and it is very comfortable indeed. A company came in this evening and Thomas pulled me down to Mrs. Lumpkin's to see them. Grandma has been making large quantities of biscuits for the soldiers. Mr. Tom Cobb[14] went off this morning to the wars. Great quantities of biscuits have been sent in to feed the soldiers. Hams also in abundance. Uncle John's baby rode all round the garden with me on my wagon, a great wonder.

Wednesday August 14: Cool enough for fire. I have got a very bad headache. Father left for Macon at eleven this morning. Grandma making biscuits again.

Thursday August 15 1861: Very cool, cloudy, and damp; have had a fire all the morning. Thomas has gone over to the depot to see the cavalry off. Rained a little. There has been a terrible railroad accident at Mannasas, killing three or four soldiers and wounding many. I am reading *The Water Witch* and think it splendid, one of [James Fenimore] Cooper's best. Mr. Johnson has sent me a basket of books. The baby has been riding in his carriage today and yesterday for the first time since I have been here, and seems a good deal brighter. Georgia has more troops in Virginia that any other state beside Virginia herself. Two weeks today since we left home. Finished *The Water Witch* and am now reading *The Queen of Hearts* by Wilkie Collins. It is a queer collection of stories within a story. It is very thrilling, worthy of the author of *The Woman in White*.

Friday August 16: Very cloudy, and cool and damp. Mary Walton and Lucy Johnson stayed to dinner. Had a fire all the morning. Reading Dickens' Christmas stories: "Cricket on the Hearth." Reports of a heavy battle in Missouri. 800 federalists killed, General Lyon among them.[15] It seems to be true. I hope so at any rate. It is raining slowly all this evening.

---

13 Privateers were privately owned ships authorized by the Confederate government to sink Union vessels and run supplies past the Union blockade.

14 Brother of Howell Cobb, Gen. Thomas R. R. Cobb from Athens would lead Cobb's Legion, and be promoted to general to command a brigade in Gen. Lee's Army of Northern Virginia. He was killed at the Battle of Fredericksburg on December 13, 1862.

15 Wilson's Creek near Springfield, Missouri, on August 10, 1861 was the first major battle west of the Mississippi River. Gen. Nathaniel Lyon was beaten by Confederate forces under Gen. Sterling. Lyon was killed in the fighting.

Saturday August 17 1861: Cold + rainy; Today is a day to keep close in the house. *The Battle of Life* is one of the sweetest stories I ever read. Minnie and Alice are in the passage [hallway] reading Fairy tales out loud to one another. Got a bad headache today. Dispatches of today state that a party of 1700 federalists crossed the Potomac (afterwards found to be a lie) and before they could get back; 300 were killed (a lie) + 1400 taken prisoners by the Confederate troops. The fight (was a lie and fabrication) was at Leesburg. There has been a Juvenile Fair in Macon for the benefit of the soldiers and they, by selling all sorts of knick nacks, raised 700 dollars, a splendid success. Contributions are pouring in to the Society down there. General Lyons' death is confirmed today. A letter today from Auntie says she will leave Hancock Thursday for Athens. Mrs. Johnson sent me *Millechampe* and *Katherine Walton* by Gilmore Simms. It has rained heavily this evening. A rainy day truly.

Sunday August 18 1861: Cloudy, damp. Rained very heavily in the night and is warmer this morning. Grandma is sick with a cold, Mother in bed, and nobody able to go to church. Thomas' cough is very bad although he does not cough very often; when he does it is very disturbing. Uncle J[ohn] gave him some medicine for it.

Monday August 19: Rain, Rain, Rain. Rained all night long and is raining this morning. If it rains much more, we will have a freshet [flood]. I wrote to Father yesterday. Mother got a letter from him this morning saying Johnson and all the rest were well. Uncle LeRoy was there with him. They were flooded with rain down there. Minnie got a letter from Cousin Adeline[16] and Thomas got one from Uncle Richard. All well The Fight at Leesburg was fully <u>confirmed</u> (is a lie). Grandma in bed today and Mother up. General Lyon is surely dead. There has been a very serious accident on the Muscogee Railroad, smashing 3 cars. There was three companies on board; only one or two [soldiers] were killed. The accident was caused by the track washing away. South Western Railroad.

August 20 Teusday: The first clear day in a good long time, and I have been on my wagon nearly all the morning watching the carpenters fixing a new wellhouse on the well. Uncle LeRoy got here this morn from Macon. The Leesburg fight is reported this morning to be a lie. *Katherine Walton* is a very good book. In the Missouri fight it is <u>reported</u> 2000 killed on both sides, a second Mannass truly. It is exceedingly warm today. Grandma is better of her cold. Mrs. Joseph Lumpkin[17] has offered the loan of

---

16 Sarah Adeline Gresham (1841-1927) was a daughter of Uncle Edmund Byne Gresham.

17 Joseph Henry Lumpkin was the first Chief Justice of the Supreme Court of Georgia. His wife, Marion McHenry Grieve Lumpkin, was in Grandma's social circle in Athens.

any books she has to me. She is very kind. A letter from Auntie today. Slight Headache today.

Wednesday August 21: Rained heavily from daylight till eight oclock. Mother sick in bed with a very bad head ache. They New Yorkers have presented the *Journal of Commerce* for sympathy with the South. The *Daily News* and others. That's noble worthy of them. Uncle LeRoy gone to dinner at Aunt Sarah Ann's. Got a long, sweet, nice, elegant, good, newsy, interesting letter from Father. He says there are some fine peaches there and he finds it very lonely at home. I wish he was here. There was a list of all the Georgia regiments in the morning paper and Uncle John copied it off for me; very kind. Minnie got a letter from Mary Campbell. The papers report our killed and wounded in Missouri 1000 and Yankee 2500. All right they are wooled on all sides. Gen. Mclelan[18] has ordered 900 rifled cannon to defend Washington. Uncle Edmund writes that Cousin Job[19] will go to Virginia in the Fall. Thomas wrote to Uncle Richard yesterday. No Macon paper today. Messers Noble + Co. of Rome are engaged in making rifled cannon. Do it boys. Father sent a box with my winter clothes, some peaches + dress.

August Thursday 22: Cloudy. Father sent another box of peaches to us this morning. Uncle LeRoy stayed all night at Aunt Sarah Ann's.

Friday August 23: Rained slowly all night and is raining now at 12 oclock. Aunty arrived here this morning and brought me three bottles of wine (one of Scuppernong[20] champagne and two of wine, one of the wine from Cousin Sallie Wiley[21]), a bullet from Mannassas, also a piece of the celebrated Sherman's battery. She also read out loud numerous interesting and entertaining letters from Uncle Edge describing his Journey to Mannassas and how he was fixed there. He says they are under an iron rule there, but he thinks it all right and that there is great difficulty in getting letters there except by private hands[22] and that such an immense array of men he never saw. If I were to tell all the interesting things he said, All the more interesting as coming him, It would fill these

---

18 Gen. George B. McClellan graduated second in his West Point Class of 1846, performed well in the Mexico War, and served overseas as an observer during the Crimean War. Lincoln put him in charge of military forces in and around Washington.

19 Sgt. Job Anderson Gresham was Uncle Edmund Byne Gresham's son.

20 Champagne made from a type of Muscatine grape grown in the southeastern United States.

21 Sarah Ann Wiley Perkins, who lived in Texas, was the daughter of Grandmother's brother John Wiley.

22 It was faster and often more reliable to give a letter to a person traveling to where the recipient was located than to use the Confederate mail.

pages fast. Aunt says there was 5 or 6 wounded soldiers came down this morning on cars with them.

Wilson is very well; I am glad to have him here. Sallie has grown a great deal. I got a sweet letter from Father this morning. . . . Aunty brought a splendid watermelon with her. She has got a list of all the (15) Uncle Edge's regiment. Thomas readeth all *Kate Walton*. Wilson pulled me all over the lot, it being a new thing. It did not rain in the evening for a change. The piece of the battery was from Mr. Edwards; Mrs. Whitehead the bullet, with her regards.

August 24 Saturday: Cold and raw. Thomas + Wilson pulled me up to the institute this morn and had a nice time. I have got on winter clothes today and they feel very good. Aunt Sarah Ann lent me *Leirs Arundel, or the Railroad of Life*. Says is splendid. The ink on the opposite page Uncle John made himself. Got a letter from Uncle Richard by one of the mess, Mr. Nash. He is well. Mr. Nash brought a piece of the Sawyer Shell at Sewall's Point. Dr. Reise is in the parlor now. Confederate killed in Missouri was 265 (correct). This is General McCullough[23] official dispatch. No news today. Rosa Jones is here to see Minnie + Alice and Sallie. They went up to Aunt Sarah Ann's.

Sabbath August 25: A splendid bracing morning, not cool enough for a fire, but just right in all respects. Dr. Lipscombe is to preach in the Presbyterian Church today. It is a very clear and beautiful day, the first day that I have woke in the morning and found a clear sky. Mother has a headache today very bad. Dr. L preached a good sermon today. They all rode in Mrs. Richardson's carriage to hear him. The sermon was #1.

Monday August 26: Clear and beautiful day. Lieutenant Daniels leaves for the seat of war today, and Grandma sent several things to Uncle Richard by him. I have lost my gold ring today and hardly ever to expect to see it again as I have no Idea where I lost it. The Privateer *Jeff Davis* was lost in an attempt to enter St. Augustine Harbor. All her crew and armament were saved excepting two small guns. I am very sorry for she was one ours most successful and daring ships and did a great deal of damage to Yankee Commerce. There is a good account of Battle of Springfield[24] in the *Constitutionalist* of today. General McCullough is a fine man and officer. Tracy looks like another baby than when I first came up here. He looks so well + bright. Uncle John has got his uniform. He wages war on the bats every evening with a buggy whip. He knocks them

23 Confederate Gen. Ben McCulloch was a former Texas Ranger and Mexican War veteran who fought at Wilson's Creek with Sterling Price. He would be killed at the Battle of Pea Ridge on March 7, 1862, in Arkansas.

24 Battle of Wilson's Creek. See footnote 15.

and we kill them if not already dead. Thomas + Wilson got on the house and threw China berries down the gutter . . . and they made more noise than a little. Mrs. Henry Hull[25] called this morning. I forgot to state that on Saturday Uncle LeRoy left here for Charleston. Mother and Auntie appear in their dark New York brown + white squares muslin and Minnie + Sallie the next. I am upstairs writing this, Wilson on the floor, Thomas on the bed reading *Queen of Hearts.*

Teusday 27 August: Somewhat cloudy but not damp. Got a letter from Mr. ole Edge today. One from Uncle Richard too. He says that cannon are being rifled at the Navy yard. Mr. Ponce's wine is "all good." Thomas and every body else went to tea at Mrs. Hull's. No news except the account of the loss of the *Jeff Davis*.[26] Cotton is 19½ cents in New York and rising rapidly. I would like to have 100 bales there. I wrote to Uncle Edge. Malcolm Johnson came to see me and brought me 3 books called *Worth American Sylva.*

August 28 Wednesday: Cloudy and sultry. Every body gone to Soldiers' Prayer meeting and Mother brought me a large pear and a bottle of extra fine brandy from Mrs. Cobb.[27] Mr. Cobb imported it himself. Aunty brought some very fine peaches. We got a letter from Home. Father speaks of leaving there Friday (and did it too). There was one for Minnie. Uncle John, Tom, + Wilson played "knucks"[28] all the morning in the yard and ring marbles together. Sallie got a letter from Uncle Edge. His Regiment is in Toombs Brigade, and he said that General Toombs had arrived at Mannassas. Stayed in Uncle John's room all the evening and he read aloud some parts of *Hiawatha* and *Japhet in Search of a Father*. It is raining hard now. The books Mrs. Johnson sent to me have some of the best pictures of different kinds of trees I ever saw, and it is very interesting also. Father writes that they are flooded with rain at the plantation, and that

25 Mrs. Anna Maria Thomas Hull was the wife of prominent Athens and Savannah banker Henry Hull.

26 The *Jefferson Davis* (or just *Jeff Davis*) was a former merchant brig equipped as a Confederate privateer. She was trying to reach St. Augustine's harbor in Florida when she ran aground and was lost.

27 Likely Mrs. Mary Ann Lamar Cobb, wife of Howell Cobb.

28 A type of marble game.

the cotton was injured and the fodder was gone. There was one Macon paper came this morning; the first one for a week. We played "20 questions" last night till bedtime.

Thursday August 29: I have been reading *Worth American Sylva*. Got only one paper and no news attall. Thomas ++ Wilson are playing "Hop Scot" in the yard. 4PM: Very heavy rain, accompanied with a sharp storm. General Sydney Johnston is in Arizona territory. Rained all the evening.

Friday August 30: Very cloudy and sultry. Malcolm Johnson came to see me this morn and brought me some books among which was *Footprints of Great Men, The Pleasant Philosopher, Peter the Great*. I have had a bad headacke all day. We got a letter from dear Father and espects to be here tomorrow. And he says Judge Nisbet says if it had not been for the Potomac rising, we would have been across by this time. General Bragg has been ordered to the Potomac, and Brigadier General R.H. Anderson[29] to succeed him. Uncle John brought me a cigar box from town today. He, Tom, + Wilson went round by the bridge to the new cemetery. There has been 3 more companies gone from Macon: the Lochrane Guard, the Rutland Guard (Bibb Greys), and Jackson's Artillery has been ordered away. This makes ten companies from old Macon. How the men of Georgia spring to arms at the call of the president. This war is bringing out the great men and good fast. Father had been to the plantation when he wrote. Minnie + Sallie and Alice stay upstairs playing dolls a great part of the time. Everybody gone to Mrs. Dr. Jones[30] to tea. *Valeo* Gresham.[31]

Saturday August 31: Sunny day. We were all startled and awakened about daylight this morning by an unusually severe shock of earth quake for this country. It shook the windows + bed considerably. I did not wake in time to hear the best of it. There is a rumor in the paper saying a fleet had descended on the North Carolina coast near Cape Hatteras and took some batteries and 400 prisoners.[32] Father got here today to our great joy and reports all right "to him." Sandy Rucker is here to see Wilson, and they have gone to the Mineral spring. Sallie + Alice have gone to spend the day at Mrs. Jones.' It is exceedingly warm + sultry. Mother got a letter from Susan Edwards and

29 Gen. Braxton Bragg; Gen. Richard H. Anderson.

30 It was not uncommon for women married to prominent men to include their husband's title in their own. Mrs. Judge Nisbet is a Macon example.

31 *Valeo* is Latin for "be strong," or "have power," or "be well."

32 The Battle of Hatteras Inlet Batteries (August 28-29, 1861), the first successful implementation of the Union Navy's blockading strategy, captured two small Confederate forts (Hatteras and Clark). Southern losses included nearly 700 captured. The victory gave the Union access and domination over the North Carolina sounds and reduced commerce raiding.

Aunty got one from Uncle Edge. Aunty has made Uncle John a beautiful needlecase[33] to carry to the wars with him. Father says the Musquitoes are bad in Macon, and I am glad they are not so bad here. Wilson is writing up stairs to his Father; Minnie is also writing to Uncle Edge. I rode up to Aunt Sarah Ann's + saw Beauregarde, Davis, and Anderson. I think Beauregarde's a pretty good face, but surely in this case the face is no index to the mind. I sleep with Tom.[34]

Sunday September 1st 1861: Summer <u>months</u> are gone, and fall months are come. The folks have gone to church and left me alone except Grandma. I slept with Thomas and for a wonder slept tolerably well. This is a very delightful day; the air seems to be unusually pure. Father says our Macon Relief Society has been working hard and have nearly done the soldiers' winter clothes. Grandma has been cutting out drawers and shirts for Uncle John and other soldiers. Uncle Richard writes that ducks are getting plentiful at Portsmouth and he wishes for his shotgun.

Monday September 2nd: Clear and pleasant. The children pulled me down to the mineral spring and then up to the Institute Street and down home again. Mother is gone out returning visits. Wilson and Uncle John gone down town. It is decidedly warmer today than it has been in a good while. There is no confirmation of the Hatteras affair. Uncle John is reading *Lewis Amdel*. I do not know whether I will or not Read the "Cricket on the Hearth" over again today. Aunty has got Wilson a flute and he has been playing on his flute (superfluous by one word) all day. Mr. Henry G. Lamar[35] has died since Father left Macon. Mr. Clarke preached here yesterday for the benefit of the hospital at Richmond. Played throwing lights last night until bedtime.[36] Thomas has got a very bad sore on his leg brought on by scratching a bedbug bite.

Teusday September 3d: Minnie and Sallie, Alice +c. have gone to spend the day with Mary Walton Johnson. Late yesterday evening I rode up to Mrs. Rucker's to meet Mother and Auntie who were out visiting. There has a map come out in the Richmond paper of the Battle Ground and the vacinity thereof. Aunty borrowed a map of the Mannassas battle Ground, which Dr Lipscombe drew himself. It is very perfect indeed,

---

33 Also known as a "huswife" or "housewife," the small case carried needles, thread, spare buttons, and often a small pair of scissors.

34 It was not uncommon for children to share beds, and in this case there was probably a lack of beds due to all the visitors at Grandma's house. Even students who were away at boarding school shared beds.

35 Judge Henry Graybill Lamar was an associate justice on the Georgia Supreme Court. It was widely believe he never recovered from the loss of his son Leonidas at First Manassas.

36 How this game was played is unknown.

showing the position of the different Generals and regiments with accuracy and skill. It is also prettily drawn. Aunty got a letter from Uncle Edge. 4 oclock: She + Mother have gone out visiting. The weather has changed and it is the warmest day we have had in a good while. Captain Smith of Uncle Edge's company is dangerously ill at Mannassas. A company left here today from Watkinsville, Clark Co., Captain Vincent [commanding].

Wednesday September 4: Clear and warm. Father is too unwell to come down stairs today on account of a severe cold and general sickness of all over. Aunty read out Uncle Edge's letter and it was long + interesting. He says the two Generals live in very comfortable houses. He says there has been a slight skirmish and a few killed. Captain Camak's company, Mell Rifles,[37] expect to leave tomorrow. Gen. A. S. Johnston has arrived safely at New Orleans with a good many other resigned officers. The Athens Gaurd[38] has been ordered to the coast of North Carolina, Roanoke Island. *The Still Hour* is a very sweet book; Mother got it from Mrs. Cobb.[39] Wilson got a letter from Uncle Edge. Grandma got a letter from Uncle Richard; he seemed to expect an attack from the fleet which took Fort Hatteras. Uncle Edge has been ordered to be ready for a battle (40 rounds cartridges and 3 days provisions). Father has gone up to Aunt Sarah Ann. My dearest Mother and Auntie have gone out visiting also. Wilson is still engaged in writing to Uncle Edge. Uncle Richard says he is keeping the sardines I sent him for a march. He said he had just finished eating a watermelon and sent Grandma some of the seed to plant for his sake, and she gave Mother and Auntie some. Grandma got a letter from Aunt Jule[40] and she sent Alice some of Little baby Eddie's hair. It has been very warm here today and sultry. Mr. Johnston called here also. Mr. George Carleton of the Athens Gaurd, orderly sergeant. He came on as far as the coast with the company.

Thursday September 5: Captain Vincent's Company has arrived in Augusta. Captain Camak's left here, and Wilson and Uncle John went down to see them off. There are full accounts of the Hatteras affair. There seems to have been some treachery about it which is not understood by the newspapers.

---

37 The Mell Rifles was Company D of Cobb's Legion. It was raised in Athens, GA in July 1861 and served with Lee's Army of Northern Virginia until just days before Appomattox, when it surrendered Sayler's Creek.

38 The Athens Guard, part of the 15th GA Infantry, became part of Toombs' brigade of the Army of Northern Virginia.

39 Austin Phelps, *The Still Hour, or Communion with God* (Goould and Lincoln, 1860). It is still in print today.

40 Probably Julia Chloe Hardwick Baxter, wife of Leroy's maternal Uncle Edwin. Baby Eddie may be their son Gilmer, born in 1860 (who may have called "Eddie").

Aunt Sarah Ann came down to see us this morning. Mrs. Hunter is in the parlor now. Wilson is playing on his flute. I did not sleep so well last night on account of the musquitoes. *The Constitutionalist* comes out today in a reduced sheet on account of the high price and scarcity of paper. Thomas' leg is no better and they have put calomel on it to dry it up; Minnie and the rest are going up to Aunt Sarah Ann. Winfield Scott is evidently laid aside since Manassas, and McClelan has succeeded him virtually.[41] Uncle Richard writes that the nights are getting cool in Virginia, and they will soon need warmer clothes. Macon papers seem to have quit coming entirely. Beauregarde's official report of the battle of "Bulls Run" is in the papers today. "Av coorse" it is very interesting. Father is well again.

Friday September 6th 1861: Rain – Rain. It was clear and warm all day yesterday until night when we had a violent storm of rain, and it has been raining this morning and is still cloudy and damp. I rose early this morning and got on my wagon and rode Tracy all over the yard and garden. I have finished *The Still Hour* and like it very much indeed. All the girls are going to Aunt Sarah Ann's this morning. General A. S. Johnston is in Richmond and is next in rank to Adjutant Cooper.[42] There has been a struggle for the possession of an important hill and 300 Yankees killed and very few Confederates. The Yankee prisoners are to be sent to the forts at New Orleans. Dry Dock at Pensacola has been burnt. I am reading *The Words of Jesus*. Munson's Hill.[43]

Saturday September 7: Slight Rains There was another slight shock of earthquake last night, but no one but Aunty felt it who was awake. Hal Linton came up to see Wilson to get him to stay all day with him, but he did not go. Full accounts of the Hatteras affair today: 6 or 700 taken prisoners. Father went out to see Dr. Church today with Dr. Reese. It is exceedingly sultry today and it is very cloudy. There has been a severe skirmish near Manassas, and 400 Yankees killed and some 100 Confederates.[44] Thomas' leg is very sore yet and runs a great deal. Uncle John weighed Tracy Baxter the

---

41 After the defeat at First Manassas, Gen. McClellan was given command of the army at Washington (now the Army of the Potomac). He quickly came into policy conflicts with Winfield Scott, the 74-year-old commanding general of the US Army. McClellan used his political connections to help ease Scott off the stage, and the old general and Mexican War hero formally resigned in November 1861.

42 Adjutant and Inspector General Samuel Cooper was the highest ranking officer in the Confederate Army, though he was a bureaucrat in Richmond and never held a field command.

43 Munson's Hill was held by the Confederates since their victory at Manassas. The hill offered an expansive view of Federal areas in Fairfax County all the way to outskirts of Washington. Many skirmishes took place around Munson's Hill until the Confederates pulled back to Centreville, Virginia, on September 28, 1861.

44 This was a rumor he must have heard or read, for there was no fighting around Manassas.

other day and he brought down 21 pounds. The <u>Confederate</u> Flag is flying in sight of Washington City, the boasted metropolis of Yankeedom! Hurrah! Major Philomon Tracy is now in Macon.

Sunday Septermber 8: Rainy and cloudy and cool: Fall Weather. No one goes to church today. The bell is ringing now. The girls went to hear Bishop Elliott in the evening.

Monday September 9: Cloudy and damp. Thomas and Wilson went up to the horse lot to get some chestnuts, but there is very few there. We expect to leave here today if nought happens to prevent us. Mrs. Richardson's carriage will take us over to the depot. Union Point, Green Co., Georgia: Left Athens this morning and arrived here this evening. The *Agusta* brought us down and it was rather the pleasantest ride I ever took on the Athens Branch. Auntie received a long letter from Uncle Edge just as we left. Wilson came to the depot with us. We have just had an elegant dinner which Grandma provided for us. My wagon is here. There were a good many gentlemen that I knew: Mr. Hull and Mr. Stovall and others. Among the engines I have seen is the *V. K. Stevenson* which brought down the train from Atlanta. The Frieght engines were *Hays*, *Bowdre*, *E. E. Jones*, *Southern*, or *J. W. Davies*. The *New Republic* is a very pretty engine and has a picture of Fort Sumter on it.

Atlanta September 10: Arrived here safely as 12 oclock last night. The *Morris Ketchum* brought us down here. It was decidedly the pleasantest ride I ever took on the Georgia Road. There was no crowd at all. We met two trains: the *C. I. Pollard* and the *U. States*. My wagon is here. Plenty of engines here too. I lay on two chairs out on the porch and looked at them: The *Gazelle*, W + A.P. *Stovall*, A + W. *I. Mclendon*, A + M *Chatham*, A *I. Berry* A + W. W. M. *D'antinac* brought in the Georgia train *Mazeppa* Ws Our train is backing in; it is the *Georgia*.

September 11 Wednes.: Home again! Arrived here safely with a scorching headache. Every body is well. The cars were not crowded until we got to Griffin, where a great many people got on. As we came in to Griffin, we saw the encampment of the regiment assembled there. My dinner was brought to me in the car. The *E. Foote* met us there. Six or seven soldiers got on there and came down to Barnesville. There was one woman who stood in the aisle and palavered about a seat 'till the cars started, but no one rose.[45]

45 LeRoy—an inveterate reader—continues to demonstrate a remarkable vocabulary for his age. A palaver is a long discussion, often between persons of different cultures or levels of sophistication, which matches entirely the type of conversation he witnessed.

When the conductor came, he asked the gentlemen to let this lady have a set and there was 3 or 4 arose. Then she looked like she had conquered a nation. But that will do.

Minnie started to school today. How natural every thing looks. Cuff and Kitty are both well though, Cuff is not in very fine spirits. There is a pile of papers here to read. The mosquitoes are terrible yesterday. As we came through town, it was the militia drill and the town was full of men and all had good guns too. There was more chingquapens[46] to sell on the road than I ever saw before. Mr. Bates' school is, as I hear, doing pretty well. Mr. Mason got his leg broke here yesterday by a horse running away. It is quite warm here today. My wagon is in the yard. No news at all today. Judge Nisbet is a candidate for Governor of Georgia unanimously.

September 12 Thursday: Cuff has not looked well since we came and this morning: he is dead. I almost know he has been poisoned for he was perfectly healthy a week or two ago. I am truly sorry. It is warm and clear. There are a few peaches and one or two or so scuppanong. Another new company has been formed called Thomson Gaurds.[47] This makes eleven companies from Macon. Uncle Edmund arrived here today on his way home from the convention. Cousin Job is going to the coast in a cavalry company soon.

Friday ~~August~~ 13: Clear and warm. *The Telegraph* is out in a hot piece in favor of Judge Nisbet. Father got me *The Words and Mind of Jesus*. Father talks of sending Thomas to college in October. Kentucky has ordered the Confederate troops from her soil. Excepting that there is no news of importance. Georgia has 30 000 in the field. Mrs. Huguenin called to see mother and brought the baby to see me and is very fat and has grown very much. I have never seen anything like the growth of Mother's front yard. It is like a forest of flowers and shrubs.

Saturday September 14: Clear and warm. Richard Edwards came over to see me last night. Mr. Leroy Holt died last night. Thomas is going to Burke[48] with Uncle Edmund if nothing happens to prevent him. It is fully as hot as it was in August. Our Mother has gone down town and Uncle Edmund with her. He will take tea with Cousin Jack and go on down to the depot tonight. Mr. Holt's funeral is this evening at 5 o'cl. Every thing is as quiet as possible at the seat of war, though the two armies are in 3 miles of each other and the pickets are constantly fighting. I wish I could hear some more Uncle Edge's letters.

---

46 Chinquapins are a nut similar to the chestnut, but about half the size.

47 He is likely referring to Thompson's Guards, which would become Company I, 61st Georgia Infantry.

48 Burke County, Georgia, was about 100 miles east of Macon.

Sunday September 15: Clear and pleasant. Thomas left for Burke at 10 oclock last night. Father and Minnie went to church; Mother was too unwell. I lay in her room all the morning. Willie Edwards is staying in Burke's Book store.

September 16 Monday: Clear and warm. I have got a bad cold in the head and do not feel well at all. I am quite lonely without Thomas, and I don't know what I shall do when he goes to College. No news of consequence in the daily. Judge Nisbet has accepted the nomination. Lochrane[49] has been appointed judge in Judge Lamar's place. They say there was frost in Western Virginia two weeks ago. It is hot enough here. I have been pasting in my scrap book all the morning. Mother has been in sick in bed all day. Willis came up tonight bringing Allen to pull me.[50] I have been alone nearly all the evening with Florence.[51]

Tuesday September 17: Clear and hot Mr. Von Briesin[52] called. The Confederate troops have refused to leave Kentucky until the Federals do the same.[53]

Wednesday September 18: Clear + warm. I have recovered entirely from my cold. Mr. Von Briesin gave Min a [piano] lesson today. There has been a ship arrived in Savannah yesterday loaded with rams and munitions of war. The Name has not been found out. She is direct from Europe. It was not allowed to be published. Gen. "Utah" Johnston has taken command of the Army of the West.[54] Miss Julia Griffin and Mrs. Beal called to see Mother. Mother is up again and I am very glad. <u>Very</u> hot.

---

49 Osborne A. Lochrane, an Irish-born jurist whose name was given to the Lochrane Guards, an all-Irish battalion.

50 Allen was one of his father's slaves brought up from one of the plantations to assist LeRoy and also be available to pull him around town in his wagon. Although Allen does not appear in the slave census and we don't know his exact age, by all indications, including clues through the journals, he is about the same age as Leroy (13).

51 The daughter of Julia Ann, one of the household slaves. She was four years old at this time according to the 1860 Slave Schedule. (Slaves were never listed in the Federal census.)

52 Oscar von Briessin was a Prussian-born music teacher.

53 Kentucky was a border state trying desperately to remain neutral. On September 4, 1861, Confederate Gen. Leonidas Polk made a momentous strategic decision (most call it a strategic blunder) and ordered Southern troops to cross into the state and occupy Columbus, KY. Union forces countered the move by also entering the state, effectively removing the large buffer zone the South had enjoyed.

54 Albert S. Johnston was given command of the Western Military Department (commonly referred to as the Western Theater), which at that time was the area west of the Allegheny Mountains (except for coastal regions) all the way to the Mississippi River. The large area west of that great river was called the Trans-Mississippi Theater.

Thursday September 19: Clear and cool. All well. Mr. Brinn[55] called and sat a greater part of the evening with Father. Have not heard from Athens since we left there. The Macon Volunteers have been moved down to within 2 miles of Norfolk. The Jackson Artillery left here for the coast Tuesday night at last. Allen pulls me very well but of course is "green" about town as yet.[56] Very hot in the sun, cool in the shade. Musquitoes truly awful.

Friday September 20: On this day 5 years ago my leg was broken and from that time I have never been altogether well. *Volo Valeo.*[57]

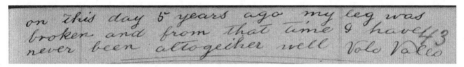

Warm and clear. The garden is beginning to suffer for want of rain. Father brought up some splendid Catawba wine yesterday. He bought it at Mr. Bowdre's. It is fully equal to Mr. Ponce's. Tracy was just a year old day before yesterday. Monday I have got a bad headache and did not rest well at all. Mother is writing to Athens now. There are to be some tableau tonight for the soldiers and Minnie is going. The secratary of war L. P. Walker has resigned and has been appointed Brigadier General Confederate Army.[58]

Saturday September 21 equinox: The moon is passing beautiful every night and it extremely sultry now. There was a dash of rain which did no good + made it hotter. Thomas came home this morning. One Jackson Artillery[man] was killed on the way to Savannah and it was not discovered 'till they arrived there. His remains were brought back and buried here yesterday by the German Artillery.[59] Thomas says Cousin Mary Jane's baby is one of the finest he has seen yet and runs all about and that he had a good

---

55 Richard Brinn was a Macon master carpenter.

56 Allen had apparently spent most or all of his life on one of the Gresham plantations, so specific directions as to where to pull LeRoy would have been necessary until he learned how to get around Macon and was no longer "green."

57 Latin for "stay strong" / "be strong" / "prevail."

58 LeRoy P. Walker, first Confederate secretary of war (replaced by Judah Benjamin). The prewar lawyer had no military training and was unsuited to the position. He resigned on September 10. Davis appointed him general and Walker commanded army garrisons at Mobile and Montgomery before he resigned in March 1862.

59 A Macon unit made up of Germans. The commander, Capt. F. H. Burghard, had been involved in various conflicts in the German states before coming to America. Many of the men were skilled artillerists.

time.[60] Cousin Jones weighs 145 pounds; Cousin Jenks is captain of a company.[61] Thomson Gaurds are ordered away. They are composed mainly of Young America No 3. There is a company now being raised by John B. Lamar and it is called Lamar Infantry.[62] The Tableau folks report the house crowded, some of them were pretty and some ugly. Bob Bates acted. They came home at 11 o'clock. I was left by myself and I read *Barrington's Sketches* 'till bedtime. My amusement now is to shoot bow and arrow and make Allen bring it to me. Minnie wrote to Alice. Thomas brought me a small melon; Hattie sent it to me. After dinner: it is very dark and is raining hard now. Mother went down town [at] 8 oclock. It is raining steadily now. Mother got some swan quill pens. Thomas has a very bad cold. His leg is not well yet. It is very cool and pleasant night.

Sabbath day September 22: Cool and cloudy. Slept very badly last night. . . . Allen is staying with me. There is no service in our church on account of Mr. Wills' absence at Presbytery. Father went to Methodist church at night. . . .

Monday September 23: Very cool. Had a fire for the first time. There are five new companies now here wanting recruits. Ross Volunteers is a bran new one. Received a letter from Wilson and answered it. Thomas wrote to Uncle Edge. Mrs. Johnson and Mrs. Butler called and spent the evening.

Teusday September 24: Cool and bracing weather. Mother is making Thomas some shirts. There is a meeting down town today to nominate somebody for the senate and legislature. Mother went to see Mrs. Holt. Father and myself read out *Barrington's Sketches* 'till bedtime.

September 25th Wednesday: Cool, delightful day. The well diggers are here cleaning out the well. The *Macon Messenger* is out for Nisbet. Mother has gone down town shopping. Governor Brown is out in a "three column piece" apologizing (defending) for his running a third time. There <u>has</u> <u>been</u> (it was supposed) a large fleet left Fort Monroe for the southern coast; it may be Georgia. Father and Minnie went to prayer

---

60 Mary Jane "Polly" Gresham Green, married to Jesse Patterson Green. The baby is likely Jesse Patterson Green III.

61 Cousin Jones was John Jones Gresham, who served in Marsh's Company, 5th Georgia Cavalry, Joe Wheeler's division.

62 Young America No 3 was one of the Macon fire companies. The Lamar Infantry would become Company A, 54th Georgia Infantry. John B. Lamar, a former U.S. congressman, planter, and author, was Howell Cobb's brother-in-law and aide. Lamar was mortally wounded on September 14, 1862 at South Mountain in Maryland trying to rally Cobb's brigade. He died the next day.

meeting. Thomas and myself played backgammon (Russian Game) until bedtime. It is a good deal warmer.

Thursday September 26: Warm and cloudy. Thomas has been sawing off dead limbs this morning, shooting bow, jumping, +c. Mother bought some Macillage.[63] Miss Susan Rowland is very sick with fever. Zilla Whittle has also got chills and (Typhoid) fever. Iola Lamar is very ill with fever.[64] It has been raining slowly since dinner. Have been reading *Visits to European Celebrities*; Mr. Wills loaned it to me.

Friday September 27: Rainy, stormy, and damp. It rained all night accompanied with a very had wind. It is raining very hard and blowing. I hope Lincoln's fleet will have the full benefit of it. This is the equinoctial storm. Ella is sick a little. It is warm and close. Minnie received a letter from Alice. She says Tracy has been very sick. Uncle Edge has been moved to Centreville. 12: It has stopped raining and has faired off cool. No news from the camps. I have come across a picture of Gen. Albert S Johnson in an old *Harpers Weekly*. Kitty has "cotch" a "mice." The Yankee prisoners[65] have been sent to New Orleans and Mr. Wills saw them. George Beal came to me and told me about his visit to Virginia. I do not feel well at all.

Saturday September 25: Cool, splendid weather. Put on undershirts this morning and winter clothes in full. Minnie stayed all night at Mrs. Huguenin's. Col. Huguenin[66] gave the Warrior Rifles a 1000 [dollars] and they changed their name to Huguenin Rifles. No telegraphic news at all. I slept very badly indeed, and coughed a good deal during the night. Mrs. Huguenin called yester'e'en. Father has not yet decided to send Thomas to college, though he will go Monday if he goes. I rode down in the carriage and looked at the [Ocmulgee] river. It is very high indeed. We went to Wood's Factory and to the upper and railroad bridges. We then drove round the trotting track. On the way home we saw the Volunteers, Company B. They are not overly well drilled. Mother went to the meeting [of the] Soldiers Relief Society. The river is as high as it has been since the Harrison freshet. No Richmond papers today. Minnie bought some yarn and is going to knit socks for Soldiers.

---

63 Mucilage is a type of glue.

64 All three girls are the children of family friends.

65 Federal prisoners were initially kept at the fair grounds (Camp Oglethorpe) beginning in the spring of 1862. Enlisted men were later moved, and only officers were kept imprisoned at Macon.

66 Edward D. Huguenin held the honorary title of colonel. He was a successful businessman, planter, and civic participant. Huguenin Rifles would become Company D, 30th Georgia Infantry.

Sabbath day September 29: Cool, bracing, splendid day. Clear as a whistle. Ella is still unable to do duty. Mother gave her quinine today and yesterday. Father got me some Horehound candy for my cough yesterday.[67] The river has fallen a great deal since yesterday when we were down there to see it.

Monday September 30: Cool and pleasant. Thomas went with Howard to the plantation today and carried his gun. There is a dispatch today saying there had been another battle in Lexington, Missouri in which the Yankees were defeated and 5000 prisoners taken. The siege of the batteries lasted 59 hrs. Gen. Price commanded our side, Col. Mulligan on the "Yanks." All their arms and 250,000.00 in specie were taken. This is the "report."[68] The daily comes out today in a reduced sheet: scarcity, paper, hard times. +c, +c. Thomson Gaurds go into camp today.

Teusday October 1st: Cloudy and cool. The (recent heavy) Brunswick rains washed away the Brunswick road for several hundred yards. A man came today and fixed the grate. I wear my Polish boots now a good deal. Butter is now 45 cents a pound [and] shot $4 a bag. Thomas returned this evening and says the cotton is injured a good deal by the storm and the corn by the fresh[et]. He brought two doves, some wheat, potatoes, butter, and other necessaries of life. It rained some on the way as it also did here. A man here by the name Harold who was in Fort Lafayette has got home. Read *The Little Pilgrim* through today. It is a very nice book. Mother went to see Mrs. Beal. George has started to Mr. Bates. The late rain storm seems to have prevailed all over the country.

Wednesday October 2nd: Cloudy and very warm. Governor's election today. Captain Tharpe's[69] company, Huguenin Rifles, left today after voting for "Old Brown." Uncle LeRoy arrived here last night at 9 oclock from Alabama. He is very well. It has been drizzling rain now and then all day. Col. [William H.] Stiles' regiment is to come in this eve from Atlanta.[70] Gen. Wise has been recalled and his command given to Gen.

---

67 A hard candy made from the Horehound plant that tastes like licorice, mint, and root beer. It soothed throats and was believed to suppress coughs.

68 The First Battle of Lexington (Battle of the Hemp Bales or Siege of Lexington) in Missouri (Sept. 12-20, 1861) was a small affair by later standards. Sterling Price led the Missouri State Guard in the Confederate victory over Union forces led by Gen. James A. Mulligan. Losses of killed and wounded were about the same (150) although some 3,000 Union men were taken prisoner. Specie is coin rather than paper currency.

69 Capt. Cicero A. Tharpe led the Huguenin Rifles.

70 Col. William H. Stiles, 4th Georgia Battalion, was born in Savannah and served as a US Congressman. He would also serve as colonel of 60th Georgia Infantry, resign in August of 1864, and die in December

Floyd.[71] Mother has made Allen some aprons. Willie Edwards came to see me last evening. Mother got a letter from auntie today. I am strongly of the opinion that "Brown" [Joseph Brown] will be elected governor and if so it will be a disgrace to Georgia. Uncle "Edge" is now at Fairfax Courthouse. Minnie is hard at work knitting for the soldiers. No particulars have been received of the Lexington affair. The Yankees blame General Fremont[72] greatly for not reinforcing Colonel Mulligan. I read a little in *Pilgrim's Progress*. Dr. Reese is unwell again. The Old Market house was sold yesterday for $450. It is quite warm and "close." Raining at 9'o tonight. Thomas hit a pigeon with a rock.

Thursday October 3d: Damp warm and drizzly. Judge Nisbet is elected in Bibb.[73] The county precincts not heard from in town. Nisbet 618, Brown 219. No other counties heard from. Whittle and Washington [counties]: 631-614. Father bought some apples yester'eve. No news at all. General Price's official [report] says our loss at Lexington was 25 killed and 75 wounded, 3500 [Union] prisoners, 118 officers, 5 cannon, 2 mortars, 3000 stand of muskets, a large number sabres, 750 horses, 100 000 in money. Great seal of state + a great many other (bad grammar) army equipments, +c. Breckinridge has been obliged to cut right out from Kentucky. She's <u>neutral</u>.

Friday October 4th: Foggy, damp, warm morning. I have a very bad headache and did not sleep well at all. The Thomson Gaurds, Number 12 left for the coast last night, and Uncle LeRoy left for Charleston. Martha and Lila Huguenin stay to tea and after tea 'till ten oclock. Uncle LeRoy gave me a perfect oyster shell which he picked up at his Flint River plantation.[74] Monroe County, Spalding, Putnam [all] gone heavily for Brown. He is certainly elected. President Davis visited the camp on the Potomac [River]. The Yankees have taken Munson's Hill and there seems to be no doubt that there will be another great battle. Pasted a good deal in my scrap book today. Mrs. Huguenin is in the parlor now. Mother went down to Soldiers Relief Society this evening. *Vale*.[75]

---

of 1865. For information on many of these men found in this journal who achieved the rank of colonel, see Robert K. Krick, *Lee's Colonels: A Biographical Register of the Field Officers of the Army of Northern Virginia* (Morningside, 1991), 359.

71 Gen. John B. Floyd, former governor of Virginia and US Secretary of War. He is primarily known for having lost Fort Donelson the spring of 1862, for which he was relieved of command.

72 Union Gen. John C. Fremont.

73 Judge Eugenius Aristides Nisbet ran against Joseph Brown for governor of Georgia.

74 While he some spent time during the war in New York, LeRoy M. Wiley spent most of his time on his property in Alabama along the Flint River.

75 Latin for goodbye or farewell.

Saturday October 5: Clear and warm. Mother gone down to Soldiers Society. One company of Stiles regiment came down yesterday eve, and Thomas went down to see it. There is a great big rattlesnake down town at Massenburg and Son and all the boys are going down to see him. It is as warm as August today. Mother went down to Prayermeeting this evening. Gen. Henry R. Jackson was attacked in Western VA and by the Yanks. They were repulsed with heavy loss.[76]

Sabbathday October 6: Clear, warm, beautiful day. There was an alarm of fire late last night. I do not know where the fire was; Father went to the top of the hill to reconoitre. Uncle John is expected home this week. . . . Allen went to church today for the first time and saw the town. Uncle LeRoy got back here today from Charleston. The fire was an old stable on the lot by the Baptist church. *Volo Valeo*

Monday October 7th: Cloudy and warm. The house was entered last night and Father's and Uncle LeRoy's pocket books were stolen with a considerable amount of money. None of the doors were unlocked either. Nothing else was taken. Father and Uncle both left for Houston today. It rained heavily in the night. Gen. Fremont, the papers say, has been superceded Gen. Wool, also by General Mansfield.[77] The Lamar Infantry goes into camp today. Yesterday was an awful day for me.[78] 4 clock: It has been raining pretty hard this evening and it is very warm now. I have been reading *Harpers Weekly* and pasting in Mother's scrap book. Zilla Whittle is going to Mr. Bates and there was two new scholars: Julia Hines and one named Wilbur Rutherford. He has now got his number.[79] Carleton Coles also goes there now. There is to be another tableax here shortly. Thomas and myself played backgammon at night and he beat me

---

76 Battle of Cheat Mountain (October 2, 1861) between Confederate Gen. Henry R. Jackson and Union Gen. Joseph J. Reynolds in what is now West Virginia. Losses from all causes totaled about 90 for each side.

77 Gen. John Ellis Wool was a veteran of the War of 1812; Gen. Joseph Mansfield would be killed at Antietam on September 17, 1862.

78 LeRoy often mentions his physical health only in passing ("Yesterday was an awful day for me") before continuing on to other matters. A close reading of his entries and an understanding that he was suffering from tuberculous spondylitis, as described by Percivall Pott in the early 1700s (see Medical Foreword and Medical Afterword in this book) makes it clear LeRoy suffered considerably more discomfort, and other issues, than he shared with his journal, including but not limited to: headaches (many brought about by the various "medicines" and home remedies routinely served him), fever, severe lower back, chest, and leg pain, pus and fluid drainage from his back abscesses, foggy thinking, chronic coughing, vomiting, general weakness and lethargy, trouble sleeping, appetite issues, and a depressed immune system.

79 Mr. Bates now has enough students to make his school financially viable for another term.

every single time badly. Mrs. President Davis and Mrs. Gen. Johnston were thrown out of a carriage in Richmond and severely injured.[80] Musquitoes are awful indeed.

Tuesday October 8th: Clear, cool, delightful day. Two Richmond papers today. Shot my bow and arrow all the morning. Went down to the schoolhouse before the boys went in this morn and the boys were playing "hundreds."[81] Allen stays in the house with me all the time now, and waits on me very well indeed. Thomas has gone to the tableaux, and Minnie to Mrs. Tracy's to see about her stocking, and Mother and myself are by ourselves in the sitting room. I am very tired tonight having been on my wagon nearly all day. President Davis has returned to Richmond. He was received with great enthusiasm at Fairfax and other military points. I suppose he went a good deal to encourage the troops. Julia Ann is sick in bed. Common.

Wednesday Oct 8: Clear and splendid day. Thomas was very much pleased with the tableaux. I made me a new bow today and it shoots very fine. I can make flies hop around. There is no news of importance today. Col. Wright's 3d Georgia regiment, Roanoke Island, captured on an adjoining Island: 31 live Yanks, 1000 muskets, 6 cannon, tents, provisions, socks, shoes. Our loss was 1 man who fell dead going double-quick. Col. Wright's horse was shot from under him also.[82]

Thursday October 10: Damp, drizzly, dark, cool, uncomfortable fall day. We had breakfast early and Thomas and George B[eal] have gone in a buggy up to Howard's Station hunting. Uncle John arrived yesterday at 5 o bringing a letter from Aunty. All well. Colonel McLaws has been promoted to a Brigadier Generalship, Mr. Ed Tracy to Lieutenant Colonel, J. B. Cumming to Lieutenant Colonel, Lucias Lamar[83] to Major, and so they go. There has been a battle on Santa Rosa Island, and a part of the 5th Georgia was in it. More particulars tomorrow. Father and Uncle LeRoy arrived here today. Father has lost a negro man: Jack. He died quite suddenly. Uncle LeRoy left for Alabama.

---

80 Varina Howell Davis, second wife of Jefferson Davis, and Lydia Johnston, wife of Confederate Gen. Joseph E. Johnston. Whatever injuries they suffered, if any, were not serious.

81 It is unclear how this game is played.

82 Gen. Ambrose R. Wright, a prewar lawyer and politician. Roanoke Island, off North Carolina.

83 Gen. Lafayette McLaws; Col. Joseph. B. Cummings; Col. Lucius Quintus Cincinnatus Lamar II, cousin to James Longstreet.

Friday October 11: Clear, warm, delightful day. Our loss on Santa Rosa was 10 killed and 30 wounded.[84] There is another company forming here: the Napier Artillery [under] Captain Napier.[85] Uncle John came up to see us on last evening and told us how they were in Athens. Auntie left with him for Sparta. Howard has got an old dog out in the yard and we have dubbed him "Jeff Davis." It is raining hard now at 8 oclock. It is raining and it is ruinous to crops. Henry Ralston has come home from the north. General Wise is now very ill in Richmond. Johnson broke in the Gaurd house last night drunk. Beat Father at Backgammon tonight. I have got me + bow and shoot a great deal.

Saturday Oct 12: Clear, cool, bracing day. Thomas has gone hunting with George Beal and I have been on my wagon all the morning. I have been reading *The Woman in White* lately. Mother has gone down town to the Soldiers Society. Thomas brought home 7 or 8 field lark [birds] which is quite good for <u>him</u>. Father has found his pocket book. It was picked up in the street and left at Mr. Ell's store. Minnie had her hair cut off short and looks first-rate. Pasted in my scrap book all the evening. *Volo Valeo*

Sunday Oct 13: Clear, cool, and bracing day. It is as fine weather as I ever saw. Read *Lectures on Daniel* today. Thomas leg is entirely well. It was really a very bad sore indeed for a while. I had an invitation to come down to see Miss Annie Johnston in her new house[86] of which I certainly shall not avail myself. Mother was down to see her yeter'eve. I promised Auntie to write Uncle Edge yet never have done so. Mr. Loyal Coles stayed to tea with us. His accounts of his journeys between the north and south were very interesting and entertaining. He left a paper here printed on the day of the battle of Manassas with glowing accounts of what their grand army was to Heroic chieftain Victory after Victory (no quarter to traitors Invincible Army). Praising "old Scott" for all that's good. "Dick Sabre" or the federal soldier a sensation story. Flaming accounts of large battles alias "Picket shooting."

---

84 The Battle of Santa Rosa Island, Florida (Oct. 9, 1861), was an failed attempt by Gen Richard H. Anderson to capture Federal Fort Pickens commanded by Col. Harvey E. Brown. Losses all cwere 67 Federals killed, wounded, and captured, and 87 Confederates.

85 Napier Artillery became known as the Macon Light Artillery after May 15, 1862 when Capt. Henry Napier (who left for the infantry) was replaced by Capt. Henry N. Ells. The artillery became part of the Phillips Georgia Legion.

86 Known today as the Johnston-Felton-Hay House, built by William Butler Johnston at 934 Georgia Avenue. It was considered by many to be the finest home in Macon. It is now a historic site on the Mercer University campus and open to visitors.

Monday October 14: Clear, cool, and bracing. Commercial Convention meets here today. Cousin Howard came up to tea and [stayed] all night. *Volo Valeo*[87]

Teusday October 15: Clear, cool, splendid day. Thomas gone down to the Convention. Stayed out all the morning on my wagon, shooting my bow and arrow, and went down to school at recess. Cousin Howard stayed all night with us and promised to send me a letter. Dear alias fawn Minnie came home really quite sick with a cold, and did not sleep well at all. She has finished one sock. Thomas bought some ink: Arnold's writing fluid.[88]

Wednesday October 16: Cloudy and warm. Cousin Howard left for Milledgeville. The German Artillery are going to give a concert for the Soldiers. A flag was presented to the Ross Volunteers. The address was delivered by the Rev. David Wills. There was a fire here Teusday night. It was Mrs. Morris' dwelling house. The bells rang for a half an hour. It was near daylight. Bob Beal has got the Whooping cough. The boys all go down by Mrs. Bonds and slide on the pine straw. Tom gone to Convention. Father brought home some sugar cane at dinnertime, and Thomas some maple sugar. I did not go on my wagon in the evening because it was so raw and damp. Gen. H. R. Jackson's official report of the Battle of Greenbrier in the papers today. I have finished *Woman in White*. There was a naval engagement off New Orleans between the Confederate and United fleets, in which the blockading squadron was broken up and one ship was sunk. They had twice the number of guns that we had. It was a complete success. I did not state it earlier because I did'nt believe it.[89] There is an english nobleman and MP visiting the Confederate camps now, Sir James Ferguson.[90] Uncle John came up and stayed to tea with us. He speaks of going off next week. Captain Smith [of the Macon Guards] is here.

Thursday October 17: Rained a good part of the night and is raining heavily now. It is also very warm. No new news at all. Father left for Alabama to go to Uncle LeRoy's

87 Latin meaning: "I am willing, but unable."

88 Arnold's Superior Writing Fluid was a high quality ink produced in London.

89 *The Woman in White* by Wilkie Collins (London, 1859), was considered one of the first "mystery" novels. LeRoy is referring to the Rebel ram *Manassas* and two armed steamers that challenged the Federal blockading squadron off the mouth of the Mississippi River. The USS *Richmond* was rammed and grounded as was the *Vincennes*, but both escaped. The blockade was disrupted for a short time—more of an embarrassment to the Union navy than anything else.

90 Sir James Fergusson, 6th Baronet was a Crimean War veteran and a Member of Parliament. Many foreign observers from different countries visited America during the Civil War, the most well-known being Gen. Sir Arthur James Lyon Fremantle, who wrote the fascinating book *Three Months in the Southern States* (Mobile, 1864).

plantation on a visit. Minnie is walking about the house today. 12 oclock: It has cleared off bright. I have cut my finger and cannot write at all hardly. I put soot on it. Raining heavily tonight. I went on my wagon in the evening a little while. The papers all seem to expect a battle at Fairfax shortly. I can't afford to keep up with Rosencrantz. Lee is "in status quo."[91]

Friday October 18: Damp, misty, disagreeable day. The Convention adjourned last night to meet in Montgomery. Lamar Infantry went off last night to the coast. The Terrell Artillery passed through, also a company from Monroe. I did not sleep well at all. I had a very bad pain in my back and Mother put a mustard plaster on me over which I made a tremendous fuss.[92] I went down to the school house this morning. Our army on the Potomac has fallen back to Manassa and the old 21st battle ground. The concert of the German Artillery was a complete success. Minnie has started to school. I am going to try to keep very quiet today and not get up at all. I expect that's what's the matter with my back now.[93]

Read *Mia and Charlie* through yesterday. It was a very nice book [from the] Presbyterian Sunday School. We got a letter from Grandma. Uncle Ed and Tom[94] have gone to the war in this time. Uncle Link will probably be ordered to New Mexico. She says the 3d regiment has hard time at Roanoke in throwing up breastworks. She had'nt heard from Uncle Richard in a long time. Fitz's panorama[95] shows here tonight for Soldiers Relief Society. Thomas is reading the *Woman in White*. 2 oclock: It is very bright now. My back pains me very bad.

---

91 Gen. William S. Rosecrans and Gen. Robert E. Lee, who was approaching the end of his command of western Virginia forces, were confronting one another without much action in western Virginia (hence the "status quo" comment). Lee would soon be sent to command the Dept. of South Carolina, Georgia, and Florida in November, be called to Richmond, and soon thereafter put in charge of the Virginia army (soon to be named the Army of Northern Virginia) just outside the capital. Lee appears frequently in these notes, and with more biographical depth. Rosecrans would enjoy considerable success in the Western theater at the head of a Federal army until his stunning defeat at Chickamauga in September 1863.

92 A mustard plaster is a poultice (soft, moist mass often heated) of mustard seed powder inside a dressing applied to the skin. The wet mustard powder produces a chemical (allyl isothiocyante) absorbed through the skin, providing warmth. The stimulation of the nerve endings eased pain.

93 LeRoy means he has been too active, and the activity has strained his back.

94 Thomas Wiley Baxter was another of LeRoy's maternal uncles. He was residing in Texas at the time with wife Ellenora.

95 Fitz's Panopticon of the South was a mechanical presentation, included scenes from "The Revolution of 1861," and could be viewed from every point in the room.

Saturday October 19: Cloudy and warm. It rained heavily in the night. I slept none. The pain in my back was very bad; I took a Dover's Powder. Thomas and Minnie went accompanied by Martha and Lila to the panorama. They liked it finely. Thomas has gone hunting with George Beal in the buggy. A regiment passed through last night for the <u>coast</u>; J. Hill Lamar is a Major on the coast.[96] No Telegraphic news at all. *Vale vale* [Farewell, farewell]. I feel very bad and sleepy from the Dover's Powder. 12 oclock: Milo has got here with the wagon. He [got] bogged up in the swamp and was delayed so long that he camped out there all night. I have slept all the morning and have now got a headache. Howard is hauling some plank from the Old stores. Julia Ann and Ella are both sewing on shirts for Uncle John. This is the first morning I have stayed in the house for sickness in a long time. I hope it will be the very last one. Thomas brought home 6 birds. It rained this eve at 3 oclock. I went on wagon a little while. Thomas got a letter from Henry Fears at Roanoke Island, 3d regiment. He described their late battle +c. Rain, Rain.

Sunday October 20: Cloudy and warm. Thomas' birthday. I feel a good deal better. Mother is sick. Took some seltzer water. . . . Minnie brought me a Sunday School book home; *Holiday House* is a very nice little book. It rained a little this evening. The pain in my back is a little better.

Monday October 21: Raining and damp, warm. It rained very hard early this morning. I slept very badly and I took a Dover's Powder. The pain in my back was very bad. No news at all of importance. Breckinridge has entered the army at Bowling Green as a private in the ranks. Started *The Two Gaurdians*. Mother and I played Backgammon tonight. Ike Scott has started to Mr. Bates. The pain in my back is not so bad as last night. Stayed on my wagon all the evening watching Tom clean out his gun. We tried to get some molasses yesterday and there was none to be had in town. I am very sorry too. Mother made some ink today. Father has not come yet.

Tuesday October 22: Cloudy and cool and damp. No New News. The city council is going to issue shin plasters as low at five cents.[97] A great many peach trees are in bloom now. It is a late fall. Our new postage stamp has an engraving of Pres Davis on it and is colored green. Thomas brought home some sugar cane today. Father arrived here at

96 Macon native John Hill Lamar eventually reached the rank of Confederate colonel.

97 Due to extremely high inflation and a shortage of coin (specie), it was difficult to make change for purchases with paper money. Communities like Macon had permission from Richmond to issue their own paper "shinplasters" from five to 50 cents. Unfortunately, they were illegally produced by all kinds of entities, which only increased the problem. Supposedly, one 2-cent shinplaster was redeemable in persimmons. People began to turn to Northern greenbacks (paper dollars) as a reliable, stable currency.

8.26, and Uncle John was playing chess with me and he beat me by a stalemate, a drawn game.

Wednesday October 23: Misty, rainy, damp, and disagreable. A battle is <u>reported</u> to have occurred near Leesburg.[98] Uncle John leaves tomorrow. Susan Edwards Stayed to tea last night. She brought me a book: *Poor and Proud* from the Telegraph office. Father got up this morning with a very bad sick headache. Every dog on the hill has been poisoned almost and poisoned meat has been found on some lots. A company came down from Atlanta this evening. It is a good deal cooler this eve.

Thursday October 24: Clear and cold. The federals crossed the Potomac on Monday at Leesburg and were driven back with terrible loss: 600 prisoners, 1200 stand arms. Our forces were two Mississippi and 2 Virginia regiments. The rout was terrible. Hundreds were shot while struggling in the river. I hope it won't prove to be a hoax.[99] Tracy came up to see us. Brag has a broken leg. Out on my wagon all the morning shooting flies with my bow and arrow. Miss Kate Fort sent Mother some Dahlias. Played chess: Tom beat. Uncle John came up to tea tonight.

Friday October 25: Cloudy and cold. The news from Leesburg is better still: 527 prisoners have arrived in Richmond and more expected. Our side was commanded by Gen. Evans. We drove them into the river at the point of the bayonet. The Ross Volunteers and the German Artillery paraded yesterday. The Ross leave here tonight. Uncle John came up to see us. It rained a little late this eve. Thomas and I made 3 arrows for "Bargat."[100] It is quite cool.

Saturday October 26: Cold, damp, and disagreable. Played chess yesterday: I beat. Got a letter from Grandma, and one from Candace to Laura.[101] In it she says Uncle Richard had been lost on Roanoke Island and was thought to have been dead but turned up in two or three days. Mother went down town this eve to the meeting Soldiers Relief Society. Played chess: I beat Tom. Uncle John did not go last night.

---

98 The Battle of Ball's Bluff (October 21, 1861) outside Leesburg, Virginia, along the Potomac River. Confederates led by Gen. Nathan G. "Shanks" Evans threw back a Union raid across the river led by Gen. Charles P. Stone. The defeat dampened Northern morale, and Stone was imprisoned.

99 The news was not a hoax. Union losses were about 950 killed, wounded, and missing while Confederate losses totaled 155. Many of the Union dead drowned.

100 This is the only time LeRoy uses the word "Bargat," which almost certainly is what he named his bow. A bargate is a medieval city gate, which would have been defended by archers. Once again his extensive reading allows him to demonstrated the depth of his knowledge.

101 Candace is a servant for Auntie; Laura may be one of Grandma's servants. These families allowed their slaves to be openly literate.

Minnie has finished her socks. I am inclined to think the Battle of Leesburg the most brilliant in the war, though the Battle of Oak Hills[102] gained more real advantages. There was a concert here last night given by the ladies and it is to be repeated tonight for the soldiers. Father brought home a bag of apples. It is a good deal warmer this evening. I am very well.

Sabbath October 27: Warm, rainy, misty, damp, and disagreable. Thomas stayed at home because of a sore nose and a bad cold. Rained quite hard last night. Howard has brought "Nuckie" up from the stable since the death of the lamented Cuffie. He is a "sneak." Mother gave me a bookmark. I would like to hear Uncle Edge's description of the retreat from Fairfax. Father brought home 3 or 4 pairs [of] shoes for Minnie, as they are getting very scarce indeed. When Uncle John gets off Grandma will then have 6 sons in the war counting Uncle Edge. That will do certain. It is said that 3 cold days added to the effective force of the Army of the Potomac: 4000 men who had been in the Hospital.[103] I finished *Poor and Proud*. Pretty good.

Monday October 28: Warm and clear. On my wagon nearly all morning. The Yankees have reoccupied Lexington in Missouri. The peach trees are beginning to blossom again and in a few instances there are small peaches. Tried to work out some chess problems, but failed entirely.[104] There had been no frost yet. It is very late indeed. Col. Thomas'[105] address of the 15th is in the papers. It is short and pithy.

Tuesday October 29: Cool, clear, delightful day. Father and Thomas left for Houston this morning early. Yesterday evening I came very near putting Allen's eye with my bow, hitting him on the nose. Minnie is knitting a scarf for Charlie Campbell.[106] It will be very pretty. Zilla Whittle has started to Mr. Bates. The fruits of the Battle of Leesburg are: 725 prisoners, 4 pieces artillery, 1600 stand arms, and a quantity of clothing. 1500 confederates engaged 7000 feds. Our loss killed and wounded 150;

---

102 Another name for the Missouri battle of Wilson's Creek.

103 The Confederate Army of the Potomac (not to be confused with the Union command of the same name) was a short-lived Southern army in northern Virginia early in the war. Its only battle was First Manassas.

104 As will become apparent, LeRoy was consumed with chess, and especially specific opening strategies. He often played several games a day with his brother and father.

105 Confederate Gen. Meriwether "Jeff" Thompson.

106 Jim and Mary Campbell's elder brother.

Federal near 1000. General Baker, United States senator from Oregon, was killed.[107] He was a "red-mouthed abolitionist."

Wednesday October 30: Cool, delightful day. *Telegraph* says Gen. Jeff Thomson[108] engaged the enemy with 1300 men, the Hessians 5000. After some hours hard fighting retreated, with 42 killed and wounded. I hope it is not true. A list of the killed and wounded in the Battle [of] Leesburg is out this morn. It is said 36 steamers left Hampton roads yesterday, destination unknown. Howard has ploughed the rye lot and is going to plant rye therein. Miss Sue Rowland came to see Mother. It is cooler this eve than this morn. I have been engaged in the delightful occupation of shooting flies. Mr. Edward Tracy has been promoted to Lieutenant Col. George Beal has got a coon. He is a very funny fellow. I have a headache tonight. We will have great difficulty in getting coal this winter, I fear. Governor Brown will receive no more men for coast service. Mother wrote to Grandma, +c, +c.

Thursday October 31: Cool, fine, bracing morning. We had frost, though not a heavy one. Mr. Clisby[109] has by some way got hold of a copy of the *Herald* of which his paper is full. I stayed out doors all the morning; I have as yet had no sign of the return of my bad cough. A ship has run the blockade at Mobile loaded with coffee and other valuables. She brings the news of the arrival of the comissioners Mason and Slidell[110] in Havana. Captain Smith came up to see me this morning. It was very kind in him. He asked at the door for me. He is going away tonight and tried to get me to write to him, but I did not promise. Mr. Von Briesin came today; he has had chills and fever. No mail today at all. They are miserably irregular. Brooker's Negro minstrels give another concert tonight for the soldiers. They had a crowded house last night. *Volo Valeo*

---

107 Union Gen. Edward D. Baker was also a sitting U.S. Senator from Oregon and a close personal friend of Abraham Lincoln.

108 The Battle of Fredericktown, Missouri (October 21, 1861). Thompson and his Missouri State Guard (about 1,500 men) advanced against Cols. Joseph B. Plummer and William P. Carlin (about 3,000) and soundly defeated. Federal losses totaled 67, and Confederate 145. LeRoy was using deprecating language by referring to the Union troops as "Hessians," which were paid German troops employed by the British during the American Revolution.

109 Joseph Clisby was the editor of the *Macon Telegraph*.

110 The *Trent* Affair began when the USS *San Jacinto* stopped the British ship *Trent* on the open sea and captured Confederate diplomats James M. Mason and John Slidell, who were on their way to Europe to lobby for diplomatic recognition and support for the Confederacy. A war between the British and the United States was avoided weeks later when the Lincoln administration released the men and issued a formal apology.

Friday November 1st: Damp, bleak, cold, disagreable morning. No news of the Lincoln fleet. Gen.W. H. L. Walker[111] has resigned on acct of bad treatment from the War Department. Captain Trapier[112] has been appointed to the command of the Military Department of Florida. New York City was illuminated in honor of the taking of New Orleans. The German Artillery, Captain F. H. Burghard [commanding] left yesterday morn at 10 for the coast. The number 65 "able bodied men." They marched down on foot. Lieutenant Wilcox, Macon Gaurds, has been promoted to quartermaster of the 8th with the rank of Captain. H. I. Menard to 1st Lieutenant. 12 oclock: Rained all morning tremendous hard and the wind did blow, but it is clear now. 4 oclock: Father and Thomas arrived this eve after dinner, bringing 4 doves [and] 7 squirrels. They got the whole of the morning rain. It commenced raining at 4 and continued steady till night.

Saturday November 2: Cloudy, cold and windy. The coldest day we have had. Overcoats in requisition. Snow in Western Virginia. Minnie started a pair of socks for me. No new news at all. I went on my wagon a while and pulled round by Mr. Moughan. Mr. Von Briesin came. The negro minstrel troope raised by their concerts $300 for the Soldiers. That's first-rate.

Sabbath November 3: Clear, cold, splendid day. I put on my undershirt today. I have got a slight sore throat this morn. Played draughts [checkers] last night: Father beat. Played two games chess & beat. Played three games backgammon: Tom beat. The Yankee papers say it was the *Richmond*[113] which was run into but she was not sunk. Mr. Bates came up to see Father. Mother is gone to church with Father and left us 3 young "uns." The weather is considerably warmer this eve than this morn.

Monday November 4: Clear, cool, splendid day. The federal accounts of the fight at Leesburg acknowledge it to have been a complete rout. Tracy came up to see us today. He looks mighty well. A cavalry company or rather 2 came marching by here today and by the most terrible of efforts [I] got out in time to see the horses' tails. It is reported here that 22 Lincoln men-of-war are off the bar at Savannah. There is a long and very interesting letter from the regular correspondent of the *Richmond Dispatch* giving a description the battle ground at Leesburg. Played two games chess: 1st I beat, 2nd drawn game. Mother went down town and visiting. I have had a bad cold in my head;

---

111 Confederate Gen. William Henry Talbot Walker. The irascible Walker argued with nearly everyone until his death outside Atlanta in the summer of 1864.

112 Confederate Gen. James H. Trapier.

113 USS *Richmond*, a wooden steam sloop.

my throat is a good deal better. I have been reading *Ten Years of Preacher Life*. Father brought me two S[unday] S[chool] Books: *Rainbow in the North, Harp*.

Tuesday November 5: Cool and clear. Mrs. Ralston came over to see Mother. There is a report that Beauregarde is going to resign (canard). I don't believe it. The *Union*,[114] a Yankee ship, was lost on North Carolina shore, and the men and cargo captured and two more on the South Carolina shore. Good.

Wednesday November 6: Cool, windy, exhilerating day. The [Confederate] presidential election. The Lincoln fleet attacked Port Royal, South Carolina and one ship was driven off another run aground. The result has not been ascertained. 500 men went up from Savvannah. Father brought me a splendid overcoat for a birthday present. It is all I could desire. I am greatly delighted, too. Mrs. Huguenin lent me a bound copy of *Punch*.[115] The wit is <u>deep</u>. Certain it is all stuff about Beauregarde going to resign; I thought so. The Macon and Western have changed their time of coming in to 7 in the evening. The Central has changed goes out at 12½ and 8.50. Colonel Wright's 3d regiment will, it's said, be ordered to Richmond. Mr. Wills and lady[116] came to see us. Mother and Min have gone after tea over to Mrs. Huguenin. The cavalry left here yesterday in single file for the coast.

Thursday November 7: Warm, clear, delightful day. No more from Port Royal. The legislature met and elected Warren Aiken, Esq. speaker of the house and Colonel Billups[117] president of the senate. Played chess: I beat and Tom beat also draugts [checkers] and Thomas beat me "<u>awfully</u>." The firing on Port Royal[118] is still going on; the guns are distinctly heard in Savannah. Commodore Tatnall is there with steamers.

Friday November 8: Warm, clear, delightful day. Firing on Port Royal still going on. Stiles' regiment has gone up. Uncle LeRoy arrived here last night. Minnie and Thomas

---

114 In fact, the *Union* was decommissioned as a reconnaissance ship on the Potomac River in December of 1861.

115 A British satirical magazine published weekly beginning in 1841.

116 Mrs. Frances Rebecca Watt Wills.

117 Warren Aiken, Sr.; Col. John "Jack" Billups, whose granddaughter, Tallulah A. Billups, would marry LeRoy's brother Thomas on October 27, 1869.

118 An amphibious battle fought in Port Royal Sound below Charleston, South Carolina, November 3-7, 1861. Union forces under Adm. Samuel F. duPont and infantry under Gen. Thomas W. Sherman (no relation to William T. Sherman) were pitted against a small collection of gunboats under Confederate Commodore Josiah Tattnall, Jr. defending a pair of forts under Gen. Thomas F. Drayton. The Union bombardment captured the forts and with them, a vital coaling and re-supplying station to support Union blockading efforts off Charleston and Savannah.

went to the Negro Minstrels show[119] last night. They thought it first-rate. Howard left for the plantations this morning. Mother and Mrs. Huguenin have gone visiting. Thomas has just come from down town. Our batteries are silenced and our men have retreated to Fort Beaufort.

Saturday November 9: Warm and very windy. Lockett and Bates[120] came and spent the morning with me. No more from Port Royal. Mother is terribly scared. There has been a great battle at Columbus, Kentucky. Our side was commanded by Gen. Pillow. The Yankees by McLernard and Bradford. 8000 men. Our ammunition gave out and we charged with the bayonet and routed them. They threw away all encumberments. The paper says "it is a bloody battle and brilliant victory."[121] A great many women and children came up from Savannah this morn, Aunt Sarah among them; Cousin Eliza comes up tonight.[122] Gov. Brown's message is out today. I have a bad pain in my back and took a Dover's Powder. Bob Lockett hit Allen on the head with a rock today. We had a great deal of fun last night. Mary Campbell stayed to tea. We had a "white horse"[123] to our delight and the terror of Allen, who cried like a baby. I played chess with Uncle LeRoy who beat me because of the above frolic. He left for the plantation this morning. Father bought Thomas a pair of boots.

Sunday November 10: Warm, clear. I feel very sleepy and bad today, having taken a Dover's Powder. The pain in my back is not improved and I am coughing very considerably. Mother got a knit cap from Aunt Margaret. The town is greatly excited about the probable taking of Savannah. Mother and Father went to see Cousin Liza and Aunt Sarah. There is a great panic in Savvannah. People are constantly leaving. The daily commenced coming out on Sunday. Today Thomas wrote to Henry Fears. It rained a little last night. There is a call for a company in the paper from Father and Mr. Bloom. Minnie is gone to singing school. The bank in Savannah has moved up here. Father got me a book called *The Woodcutters and Exiles*.

119 "The Confederate Minstrels" were a popular performing group from South Carolina.

120 LeRoy's friends, both named Robert or "Bob."

121 Gen. U S. Grant moved a 3,000-man Union force by riverboat to the Missouri side of the Mississippi River across from Columbus, KY, to attack a small Confederate outpost. The move triggered the Battle of Belmont (Nov. 7, 1861), Grant's first combat of the war. Confederate Gen. Leonidas Polk had 5,000 in Columbus and dispatched 2,700 under Gen. Gideon Johnson Pillow. Gen. John A. McClernand led two of Grant's brigades. Grant withdrew after a sharp but inconclusive fight.

122 Many people fled areas close to the fighting and became refugees. Aunt Sarah and her daughter, Elizabeth R. "Eliza" Jones Snider, moved from Savannah (on the coast) inland to Macon.

123 The meaning of "white horse" is unknown.

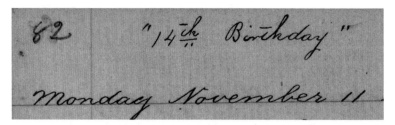

Monday November 11: Warm and cloudy. My 14th birthday: Father, an overcoat; Minnie, a pretty little remembrance and a pair of socks. I feel better this morning. Mr. Brinn came after tea to see Father and Mother. *Valeo*

Teusday November 12: Warm and pleasant. Played chess: Uncle LeRoy beat. He got back from Houston today. Cousin Eliza came to see Mother yesterday. Father has planted rye on some of the beds in the Garden. The Union men of Tennessee have burned several railroad bridges on the East Tennessee + Virginia road. Uncle LeRoy brought up some very curious rocks from Houston. Nothing new; a Yankee fleet still off Port Royal.

Wednesday November 13: Warm and clear. Brown's majority over Nisbet is only 13,975. More news about the burning of the bridges. Thomas and Uncle LeRoy played a game of chess and Tom beat him. Mr. Whitehead stayed to tea with us last night. Gen. R E Lee has been appointed to the coast South of Virginia and is now at Savannah. Thomas and Minnie gone to prayer meeting. Uncle LeRoy played draughts and he beat me twice and I him once. Milo came up.

Thursday November 14: Warm and clear. Uncle LeRoy left for his plantation. Milo went back to Houston. Cousin Eliza and Aunt Sarah have rented with Mrs. Lockett, the house over here back of Mrs. Edwards. Pasted in my scrapbook this morning. Our front yard is very beautiful now and people come and beg for flowers. We got a letter from Aunty. Grandma is in Hancock. She says her yard was pretty too.

Friday November 15: Warm and clear. Fast day; everybody gone to the church. Another steamer loaded with arms, blankets, shoes, +c. has arrived in Savannah. Played chess yesterday: I beat. I feel very well today, and stayed on my wagon all the morning, shooting bow and arrow. It is cooling fast.

Saturday November 16: Clear, cold, and bracing. Mother has been making onion pickles this morning. Uncle Edmund came up to dinner. He is one of the committee to inspect the Blind Asylum. A little schooner has run the blockade in Savvannah loaded with coffee, salt, +c. The steamer had 11000 rifles and more on board. Minnie has finished my socks. I wore my overcoat today for the first time. Father has got only one load of coal this winter, it is so very scarce. George Beal came to see us last eve. Ira Fort came to see me, and Tom yesterday evening; I have not seen him in a long time. The yankee fleet passed Fernandina [Fla] a few days ago. Now for the Gulf ports. Cousin Jack came up and took tea with us tonight, and after tea went over to see Aunt Sarah and Eliza.

Sunday November 17: Clear and cold. Uncle Edmund went back to Milledgeville today. There is no war news. A battle is hourly expected at Manassa. There is great rejoicing in Washington in about the Fight at Port Royal. It is supposed 6 or 7 large ships of the armada had been lost. The French ship of war *Prony* has been lost on the North Carolina coast and in trying to save her, a CSN ship was lost. Several Federal steamers passed but did not try to help the *Prony*.[124] Her men have gone to Richmond. Fast day was very generally observed. There was no service in our church. Played chess last night: a stalemate the Result. Gen. Mclellan is now in General Scott's place, he having resigned some time ago. . . . I got a letter from Uncle John and he says he saw Morphy in Richmond and other great men.[125]

Monday November 18: Clear, cool, and bracing. Kitty cotch mice. The sad news of the capture of our commissioners Mason + Slidell. The steamer from Havana was boarded by the US Steamer *San Jacinto* and they [were] taken off. Ira Fort came over to see us. Our men surprised a party of federals at Guyandotte, Virginia and out of 150 feds, only 50 escaped.[126] Played chess: I beat Tom + Ira played + Tom beat. Gen. Fremont has been supersided by Gen. Hunter.[127]

Teusday November 19: Clear + cold. Mother got a letter from Aunty and Grandma. There is a dispatch today of a battle at Springfield[128] between the Yankees and McCollough[129] and Price. Played chess: Thomas beat me. Cousin Liza's three Children (Maggie, Sallie, George)[130] came over to see us today. I have a headache this evening. The state of Georgia has now over 30 000 men in the field. I have been reading *Uncle*

124 The French corvette *Prony* ran aground off Ocracoke Inlet, North Carolina. Bad weather made assistance nearly impossible, and the ship was a total loss. No Confederate ship was lost.

125 Paul Charles Morphy was a renowned 21-year-old American chess player who beat the leading European chess players of his time. He was considered the unofficial world chess champion from 1858-1862. Morphy came from a prominent New Orleans family, and had applied to P. G. T. Beauregard for a position on his staff, on which he may have briefly served.

126 Now part of West Virginia, Confederates left the Union-held town with prisoners; Union troops burned much of the town.

127 Union Gen. David Hunter.

128 The evacuation of Springfield after Hunter replaced Fremont.

129 Confederate Gen. Ben McCullough.

130 Madge Waldron Snider, Sally Wimberly Snider, and George John Snider.

Jack the Faulskiller today. There are some very contradictory dispatches about a battle at Pikesville, Kentucky.[131] The Federals claim a victory and we do the same. Mother wrote to Aunty. There was a heavy frost here this morn. Both Milo and Arch with cotton came up tonight. Jim Campbell has promised to come up some night very soon and play chess with me.

Wednesday November 20: Cold, dark, cloudy, and Rained a little. We have been burning off the asparagus beds and leaves in the lower yard this morning. Toombs and Hill[132] are elected senators. General H. R. Jackson has been made a Major General by Gov. Brown. Mr. Ed Rowland, my old teacher, shot himself lately in Alabama. The Yankee papers report the South Carolinians eagerly flocking to the support of the stars + stripes at Port Royal. Their killed 8 and 23 wounded. Cousin Lisa, Aunt Sarah, + Ira[133] came to dinner today. Maggie stayed all night with us.

Thursday November 21: Cold and damp. Every body gone to Mr. Ed Rowland's funeral. He committed suicide.[134] The affair at Pikesville, Kentucky is a small, but glorious victory. On our side, 300 rebels were commanded by a gallant Captain Jack May. The enemy lost some 400. Our side none.[135] Some of the papers think that the capture of Mason + Slidell is an insult to England; others do not. Played two games of chess: I beat and Tom beat. After that, we went out and he cut wood and I made arrows. Father and Mother have gone out to spend the eve at Colonel Huguenin. Started a letter to Uncle John.

Friday November 22: Damp, tolerably cool, and awfully foggy. I write to Uncle John. President Davis' message is out and it is in his beautiful style. Father says it is a splendid

131 Battle of Ivy Mountain (Nov. 7, 1861). Federals under Gens. William "Bull" Nelson and Joshua W. Sill pushed Confederate forces under Gen. John S. Williams from their recruiting mission in southeastern Kentucky back into Abingdon in southwestern Virginia. Casualties were light on both sides. Encounters like this one would soon be considered minor skirmishes and no longer considered newsworthy.

132 Benjamin H. Hill.

133 Ira Fort, one of LeRoy's friends.

134 Edward Roland was LeRoy's public school teacher before his left leg was crushed by the falling chimney in the 1856 accident. No other information on the circumstances of his death has been found. Mr. Bates taught older kids. A pair of women taught Minnie, but LeRoy's father did not think his son would do well with them.

135 Col. Andrew Jackson "Jack" May, 5th Kentucky Infantry. The affair was a clear Union victory, despite what LeRoy believed, heard, or read, with Union losses about 30 from all causes, and Confederate losses about 75.

paper.[136] Played chess: I beat. Thomas has been playing Tivole for one strait hour.[137] Colonel Thomas, the hero of the *St. Nicholas*, is now crazy.[138]

Saturday November 23: Cold, clear, splendid day. . . . Mother gone over to see Mrs. Huguenin's baby, who is sick. All the Huguenins came over last night. Blind Tom, the musical prodigy, is now here and shows in the city hall.[139] The Confederate minstrels show [is] here tonight for the soldiers. It is reported Fort Pickens has opened on our batteries. General Sherman of the Yankee fleet has issued a proclamation calling on all loyal citizens to come to the support of the stars and stripes. Only one man has gone over, one Chapman who delivered up his cotton and negroes. Minnie has made a kaleidascope out of the melodeon, which is really pretty.[140] They are really firing on Fort Pickens. Brought on accidentally.

Sunday November 24: Cold, clear. The firing at Pensacola was brought on by Fort Pickens firing opening on a Confederate steamer, to which Gen. Bragg replied. Father brought me *The Life of Caroline Smelt*, a real girl in Agusta, Georgia. Gave Allen a pair of shoes today. . . . Floyd has fallen back and always is.[141] He is now at Raliegh Court House. Read a little in Hannah More's works today. Our rye looks very green and pretty now. Mother went over to see Mrs. Huguenin's baby, who is still sick. Minnie went to singing school and found it a failure as it was last Sunday. Governor Brown's

---

136 Davis' address to the Congress of the Confederate States, November 18, 1861.

137 A marble game played on a game board.

138 Col. Richard Thomas, who adopted the last name "Zarvona" after spending time fighting with Garibaldi in Italy, was an 1851 West Point dropout who formed a company of Zouaves that would eventually become Company H of the 47th Virginia Infantry. Thomas earned undying fame by becoming "a French lady" when, with the assistance of Virginia government officials, he boarded the steamer *St. Nicholas* in Baltimore disguised as "Madame le Forte." He and his accomplices overtook the ship and used it to capture the brig USS *Monticello* and schooners *Mary Pierce* and *Margaret*. The *St. Nicholas* was renamed the CSS *Richmond*.

139 The remarkable story of Thomas "Blind Tom" Wiggins (1849-1908), also known as Thomas Greene Bethune or Thomas Wiggens Bethune, began in 1859 when his mother was sold to a new owner and her baby (Tom) was included for free because he was blind and not considered worth anything. His new owner let him roam the mansion, where he listened to his children playing piano. Tom taught himself how to play by age four. He played for President Buchanan in the White House in 1860, and became an internationally recognized musical savant, known as "the eighth wonder of the world" and "the greatest musical prodigy of the age." He is widely recognized as the most celebrated black concert artist of the 19th century. One of Tom's feats was the ability to play three songs at once—two of which were "Yankee Doodle" and "Dixie." He was one of Mark Twain's favorites. Tom died of a stroke in New Jersey in 1908. His burial place remains something of a mystery.

140 A melodeon is type of button accordion.

141 A reference to Gen. Floyd, an officer so inept even at a 14-year-old boy could discern it.

men are all over the state siezing [sacks of] salt at 5,00 for which the merchants paid 10,00 and says that is enough. He siezed two or three lots here one was Mr. J.B. Ross's.[142]

Monday November 25: Cold, clear. Heavy frost. The firing at Pensacola still continues. 7 men killed in Brown's Infantry. Heavy firing all day Saturday. Fort Pickens' fire is very rapid and wild. Brown's Infantry is in the most exposed position. Every body is anxious to hear.

Teusday November 26: Cold, clear, splendid day. A very heavy frost. There was no firing on Fort Pickens all day yesterday, nor Sunday. 6 bodies were brought up last night + buried today. One man was buried by the military and fire companies. All this, and no decisive results gained, poor fellow. But let us hope Captain Bragg knows.[143] A despatch came for Loren Dickinson's father and Mother saying he had been shot and it was feared the ball had entered his lungs.[144] Nothing more was said. Thomas and I played a game of chess and I beat; yesterday he beat me bad twice.

Wednesday November 27: Cloudy + cool. Jim Campbell and Mary came up and he played chess with me. He is a real first-rate player and beat me bad one game. He beats Uncle LeRoy. I went down town in the carriage yesterday and got me a pair of gloves. We moved downstairs Monday night. Mother and Father pronounced Blind Tom a perfect wonder. Played 2 games chess today: I beat both. Tracy came up to see us today. Mother heard from Aunty yesterday. Bragg in his official dispatch says he crippled two of the enemy's ships [at Pensacola]. Mother is now writing to Uncle John. A battle is hourly expected every where. A tremendous flotilla has been prepared and is now ready to come down the Mississippi. Meanwhile Mclelan will advance on Centreville [northern Virginia], and the ocean fleet will attack some other point. The Yankee papers heartily endorse the "seizure of the rebel commissioners [Mason and Slidell]." The Canadian papers are down on it, say that "the meanest government would resent it." Mr. Clisby says he is tired looking to England. Some Yankee ships came and shelled Tybee Island [Georgia] for the space of two hours, and finding no one, there took

142 Governor Brown was seizing (impressing) important commodities for the use of the state's military forces. Salt was $2.00 a sack before the war, and as high as $125.00 one year after LeRoy penned this entry. Salt was integral in the preservation of meat for many families.

143 Confederate Gen. Braxton Bragg was in charge at Pensacola. He was widely known during the Mexican War for his skill and discipline as a Regular Army captain. LeRoy is referring to him in that capacity.

144 Loren Dickinson was a Macon local serving in Company C, Georgia 2nd Battalion Infantry. Although his wound was serious, it was not fatal. He survived the war.

possession of it and will make batteries there, I suppose. . . . Capt. Lafayette Lamar[145] of the 15th died lately at Centreville. I saw a CS postage stamp yesterday. It does tolerably well. They have taken 40 or 50 of those bridge burners in East Tennessee. I rubbed Kitty's back and [it] cracked and sparkled.

Thursday November 28: Foggy, warm, + disagreable. I slept in the dressing room.[146] Father left for Milledgeville this morning to look around. Howard returned today and brought me a potato almost as big as my head. There was a large funeral procession today: 4 men of Browns Infantry buried. Mr. Wills made a sort of funeral oration to a large audience at the City Hall.[147] First the brass band and the soldiers, then the large express wagon with the bodies covered with a Confederate flag. Mr. Bates gave holiday [to the students]. I did not know anything about it until I heard the band. There was a large crowd of boys along + I dropped my bow and lost it. The regiment on the Potomac have raised the war flag. Gen. W.H.T. Walker has been made a Brigadier by Gov. Brown. The enemy are advancing on Centreville and Evansport, fortifying as they go. There are also preparation for an advance in Kentucky. Missouri is now numbered among the Confederate States of America.[148] It is really warm tonight. Howard brought up some flour tonight.

Friday November 29: Warm and very cloudy. Got a letter from Wilson. Blind Tom shows again tonight and tomorrow even. Mother wrote to Aunty. I made me a new bow. It rained heavily at dinner time today and cleared off this eve. Played chess and Tom beat me by an oversight; I lost my queen. No news at all. My new bow is nearly as good as the old one.

Saturday November 30: Cold + windy. Father returned last night. It rained tremendous last night. Father brought me a fawn from Cousin Howard.

Sunday ~~Nov~~ December 1st: Cold + clear. I went to see Blind Tom on yesterday and was perfectly astounded at his skill. He played *Home Sweet Home* according to the Hoyle FC;[149] his 3 tunes at once was fine and I am glad I went. My fawn was quite stiff in the joints this morning. The city hall is a much better looking building than I thought it

145 Capt. Lamar died November 17, 1861, in Warrenton, Virginia.

146 A separate room off the downstairs master bedroom.

147 More than 1,000 citizens attended the service for the seven Macon soldiers killed, apparently in the fighting around Pensacola.

148 The Southern Congress admitted the state of Missouri to the Confederacy on November 28, 1861. It was little more than a symbolic gesture.

149 It is unknown what he means by Hoyle FC.

would be.[150] Allen knocked a bird out of the tree and hurt him a little and he got loose again. There is no news today of any consequence. Played a game of chess yesterday and I beat Jim. I have been sleeping very well lately + my cough does not return as I expected. I wish I was in Dixie land.

Monday December 2: Dark, rainy, and warm; rained off and on all day. My poor little fawn is dead and we do not know what was the matter with him. I am mighty sorry. I have had a very bad headache all day. Played chess: I beat. 3 dispatches today. Minnie did not go to school. Tremendous rains.

Teusday December 3: Cold, raw, and cloudy. Got a headache still. Father bought me a splendid new diary with 222 pages in it. Read General Thomson's report of the Battle of Fredricktown. Blind Tom made 236 dollars while he was here. Mother in bed all day. She finished some drawers for me last week. Father brought home some Macon-made envelopes.

Wednesday December 4: Cold + clear. Heavy frost. There has been an accident on the Central road; the track was torn up about 20 yards on level ground [and] 3 cars smashed. Nobody killed. They've hung 2 traitors in East Tennessee, a great wonder. It looks like we never hang anybody that deserves it.

Thursday December 5: Cool, clear day. The Confederate steamer *Nashville* has arrived in Europe, at Southampton [England].

Friday December 6: Cool, clear day. Thomas and Allen pulled me out to Mrs. Clarke's to get some forked sticks to make an ash hopper.[151] Howard left for the plantation today. I have got a pain behind my shoulder today. Judge Nisbet has resigned his seat in the provisional congress. Minnie has done a pair of socks for Thomas. The Yankees at Port Royal are very quiet indeed. Thomas and I played chess yesterday: I beat.

---

150 LeRoy's father was instrumental in the construction of the City Hall prior to the outbreak of the war.

151 A device used to funnel or strain lye out of ashes to make soap.

Saturday December 7: Warm and cloudy. To my great surprise and delight I woke up last night about one oclock and found Grandma, Wilson, + Alice. They came over to Milledgeville to bring Alice to meet a Mr. Ross who is going to carry her to Texas. I was mighty glad that Wilson came over. Some of Uncle Richard's letters were read aloud and they were very interesting indeed. He gave an account of the Chickamacormica affair and the capture of the *Fanny*.[152] Wilson pulls me all around the yard. Wilson + Thomas took a game of Backgammon. A schooner has ran the blockade at Sav[annah] loaded with coffee. The Yanks have got about 20 or 30 old whalers loaded with stone which they intend to sink on the bars of the principal southern harbors, most of them at Savvanah. Great fight on the Potomac so on. Mrs. Tracy[153] sent up a letter tonight from Uncle John. He has got into winter quarters and is very comfortable. Uncle Richard says he has got to be quite a cook now from necessity. Howard returned from the plantation.

Sunday Dec. 8: Wilson and Grandma stayed home with me. It is cloudy and warm and I think it will rain soon. Wilson and Grandma are writing to Aunty. Grandma brought me a roll of tobacco from Eliza and a very fine apple also. A synopsis of Lincoln's message is out and it is not very warlike.[154] Grandma has been very unwell ever since she got here, but is a little better today. I believe Montgomery and his Kansas Jail hawkers[155] have been captured. It is reported that Price is marching on St. Louis. Henry Heath has been made a Major General over General Price.[156] Father got a copy of the 2nd days' proceedings of the General assembly and Dr. Palmer's opening sermon. It is the daily *Southern Presbyterian* temporarily. Mr. Evans preached in our church today, Mr. Wills being absent at the Gen. Assembly. Howard brout up a few sausages yesterday. Alice expects to leave tomorrow night. 2 Richmond papers came today. I feel just as well as I can today. It is a little cooler today than it was yesterday, and it rained a little. A ship load of coffee got into Savvannah lately.

---

152 A trio of Confederate ships surrounded and captured the gunboat *Fanny* on October 1, 1861. The new CSS *Fanny* was used in an attempt to take a Union encampment at Chicamacomico, the lighthouse at Hatteras Inlet, and destroy it and the Union forts there. The effort failed.

153 Probably Aunt Carrie's mother, Rebecca Caroline Campbell Tracy.

154 LeRoy is referring to Lincoln's Annual Message to Congress, delivered December 3, 1861.

155 "Jail hawkers" is a play on words. Union Col. James Montgomery was a "Jayhawker," a name for guerrillas or militant bands who battled with pro-slavery citizens of Missouri during the "Bleeding Kansas" years before the Civil War.

156 Confederate Gen. Henry "Harry" Heth.

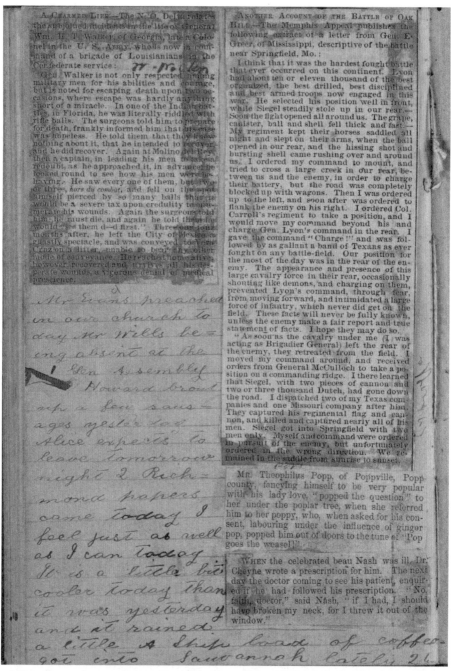

LeRoy devoured newspapers and inserted many columns into his journals. They give modern readers a good sense of some of the news he was receiving. *LOC*

Monday December 8 9:[157] Clear and warm. All the children played "hide the swich" this morning.[158] Mother and Grandma went down town this morning. Abe Lincoln's message is out this morn in full. He says the cause of the Union is steadily advancing southward. All of us went down to the graveyard this evening and went all over it.[159] And we stayed down there all the evening. Alice leaves for Texas tonight. It is as warm as summer today.

Teusday December 9 10: Clear + warm. Mother and Grandma have gone to the graveyard. Wilson pulled me over to Uncle Jack's this morning. Alice left for Texas last night at one. We have been shooting arrows all this morning. W.C.M. Dunson a member of the Macon Gaurds is dead. Gov. Brown is out in a message of two columns about nothing. My mother and Grandma went down town and G'ma brought us more apples, oranges, candy, + than a little. Tracy came up to see us this afternoon.

Wednesday December 11 1861: Wilson and Thomas pulled me over to the railroad to see the train pass by. Wilson and Grandma have gone over to Aunt Ann's. 20th Georgia regiment to dinner. Mother got a letter from Aunt. A fight is expected on the Potomac.

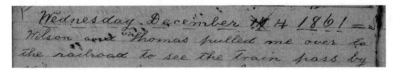

Thursday December 12: Cold and cloudy. Winter again. Wilson and Allen pulled me all around the hill, and I drove them. We went down to the schoolhouse and watched the boys play "socket." Tracy came up to see us today. It turned cold so suddenly last night. Thomas was a little sick and Mother slept up stairs with him. My leg pained me all night and I did not sleep well at all. Auntie sent me one of Alexander's letters with a conversation between a Georgian and a Yankee.[160] The "intelligent" Georgian is

157 Note: The entries beginning with December 9 through the 15th were written on previously blank pages. They have been reproduced here chronologically to improve readability.

158 "Hide the Switch" was a game popular with slave children. It involved one of them hiding a switch, or thin branch and the others seeking it. The one who found it would chase the others and try to whip them with it. It could be seen as an attempt to psychologically come to terms with the constant fear of the lash and ever-present authority of the white master.

159 Rose Hill Cemetery in Macon, where many Confederate soldiers and dignitaries were eventually buried.

160 Likely Col. Alexander S. Reid. His daughter Sarah Juliette Reid married Cousin Charlie Wiley, making them distant relations.

supposed to have been Uncle Edge. Mother bought a great big hat, big enough to cover a common sized house. Yesterday I came across the prettiest couple of moves, problems in chess I ever saw. Aunty in her letter of yesterday said that Uncle had just seen Generals Beauregarde, Johns[t]on, and Smith, and he looked at them for 5 minutes.[161]

"I loathe that low vice curiosity and the overcurious are not over wise"

My Friends

Take this to heart

He who prieth into secrets will surely come to trouble.

Do not look any farther in this book than this

Do not

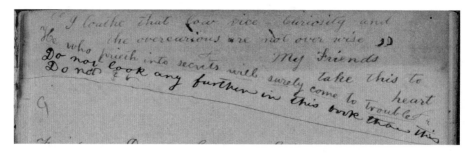

Friday December 13: Clear and cold. I have got a distressing headache and I took a Dover's Powder last night. Grandma and Wilson left for Athens this morning. Tracy came up to tell them all Good bye.

Leroy Wiley Gresham, 1861

I have had a very pleasant time and have been perfectly well until today. There is awful news this morn. Charleston has been visited by a most terrible fire. 1 Third [1/3] of the business part of town was utterly destroyed. The Catholic cathedral, St. Andrews, and the theatre were burnt together with a large number of dwelling houses. The loss must be immense. The fire was started, I have not a doubt by some "Southern

---

161 It is important to realize that most people did not know what famous politicians and generals looked like, except for the occasional likeness of a woodcut in a newspaper or magazine. In this instance, Uncle Edge was fortunate enough to see these generals in person at Centreville.

Yankee."[162] It by far worse news than the capture of Beaufort or Hatteras. Wilson and Minnie after supper last night took a game of chess. It was long and well contested on Wilson's part: Min beat.

Saturday December 14 1861: Cool, clear day. We have been popping coal this morn like "40" [pieces]. No news from Charleston. I wrote to Auntie. I feel better today. Thomas and I took a game: I beat. Got a letter from Uncle John today. Mother went down town this eve. Tom + I took a game: he beat me horrid. Uncle John says there are a great many rumors in camp. He says no more furloughs will be granted. He had got my letter now.

Sunday December 15: Cool, clear. General peace has not been superseded. There are reports of a battle in Western Virginia. The 12th Georgia Col. Johnston[163] was attacked by 5000 Yanks with the usual result. There has been meetings in Agusta and Richmond to help Charleston. Congress has advanced 250 000 dollars. Yesterday was the Mayor's election. The same ticket [Methvin Thomson] was re elected. There is going to be a Christmas tree here for the benefit of the sick soldiers. Minnie stayed all day at Mrs. Campbell's yesterday and she brought home some beautiful oranges raised in southwestern Georgia. I have been reading a Sunday school book called *The Happy Home*. Father heard down town yesterday that Uncle Edmond and Cousin Adeline were both sick with the measles in Milledgeville. Willis came up last night bringing a supply of sausage meat, spare ribs, and backbones. They have killed 15 hogs. The pain in my side has left me entirely. It is said the fire in Charleston burnt almost from one [end] clear to the other one.

Monday December 16: Cold and clear. Father and Thomas both left for Houston. Mother has gone down town. I have been engaged in shooting my bow all the morning. Willis also left for Houston. Minnie is knitting Father a pair of socks. I am reading *Flora or Self-deception* PSS.[164] Mother bought Allen a very nice pair of pants today. There was a funeral over to Mr. Ralston's this eve, a baby negro.

---

162 Exactly how what came to be called The Great Fire of 1861 began remains unknown, but the flames were seen six miles out to sea by Union sailors and 14 miles away by Confederate soldiers. A large swath of the city was destroyed, including many prominent landmarks.

163 Battle of Camp Allegheny, or Allegheny Mountain, in western Virginia (December 13, 1861. A small force under Confederate Gen. Edward Johnson camped on the mountain was attacked by a similar-sized force under Union Gen. Robert H. Milroy. Johnson repulsed the attack and earned the nickname "Allegheny."

164 A Presbyterian Sunday School book.

Teusday December 17: Cool, clear, delightful day. The legislature has appropriated $100 000 for Charleston. I made me 4 nice arrows this morning. No more [news] from the 12th regiment. General Price has not been superseded.

Wednesday December 18: Cool and clear. The nights and the days are both beautiful now. Mother has gone down [to] the dentist. The fire had been troubling me greatly by popping all over the room. My couch cover has been ruined and there is a hole in the piano cover. The 12th Georgia lost in the late engagement about 20 men and the 8th Virginia regiment 80. There is stirring news from England, if it is true: the dispatch on receiving the news about Mason + Slidell. There was a mass meeting and resolutions passed demanding [their] reparation. The Yankees are very mad. It is said our Government will move all Southern troops away from West Virginia and let Virginia troops fight it out. 4 Georgia companies have moved to Charleston. I saw Richard Edwards yesterday for the first time in a long while. Mother sent Uncle John's cap to Mr. Joel Branham[165] who leaves tonight. . . . While Father is gone we read a story aloud nearly every night.

Thursday December 19: Cool, Clear, splendid day. Old Sam came today and drawed out 3 curbs. There came very near being a serious accident here. Just as the first curb was nearly out of the well dragging one man nearly in the well by his foot, [it] was caught by the falling windlass, which was all that saved his life. Johnson was knocked down. Nobody hurt but Sam whose finger was badly cut.

There is great news! Our commissioners [Mason and Slidell] are demanded by England. Lord Lyon has instructions to demand his passports if the demand is not immediately complied with. The Queen[166] has issued a proclamation forbidding powder or any of the ingredients to be exported. Captain Wilkes[167] in his report apologizes for not siezing the steamer herself. Congressman Ely has been exchanged for Hon. C.J. Faulkner.[168] General Hunter is reported to have been superceded by

---

165 Dr. Joel Branham was an influential member of Macon civic life, joining John Jones Gresham in the Georgia Hospital Relief Society in August 1861.

166 Victoria was queen of England from June 20, 1837 until her death in 1901.

167 Later an admiral, Charles Wilkes was the commander of the USS *San Jacinto*, the ship that intercepted the HMS *Trent*, from which he seized Confederate diplomats Mason and Slidell.

168 Charles James Faulkner, a former congressman from Virginia, had been arrested for attempting to negotiate the purchase of arms from France. He negotiated his own exchange for Congressman Ely and then enlisted in the Confederate Army.

General Halleck.[169] "Yankee" Father and Tom arrived this eve with a full gamebag: 7 squirrels, 3 wild "dux," 4 partridges, +c +c.

Friday December 20: Cloudy and warm. Great news! Minister Adams has demanded his passports.[170] War with England is thought to be inevitable! Mr. Faulkner is in Norfolk. The 3d regiment has been moved back to Norfolk. The Yankees have certainly got their hand full. A fight is hourly expected in Kentucky!! Father bought Thomas an elegant new knife! Cotton is 42 cents [a lb.] in New York! Father was advanced 15 cents [a lb.]![171] Thomas has got a very bad cold. I got a letter from Wilson yesterday, giving a description of his journey to Athens. The wagon came up bringing up Betty, her baby, and a boy "Bil."[172] Uncle LeRoy came this evening at nine oclock.

Saturday December 21st 1861: Warm, clear, delightful. I went round on Bond's hill to see the funeral procession of Mr. Bloom. It was in Mr. Johnston's house. Colonel J.E. Jones commanded the military. Sam does not get along well at all. He has not gone one curb down. They were too large. The news about Minister Adams is contradicted.

Sunday December 22: Cold, damp. Rained in the night pretty hard. I took a Dover's Powder on account of my leg. There is an account of a small fight on the Potomac.[173] Our side was repulsed with 30 killed + as many wounded. No more from Mason and Slidell. The coals popped so tremendously we moved into Mother's room. Dr. Fitzgerald came to see Betty yesterday and put a plaster on her and gave her some med.

Monday December 23: Cold + clear windy day. Thomas and I commenced a match of seven games in chess. No 1: He beat as Uncle left for Ala. this morn. Sam finished here today. It has been a bad job. Mother has gone down town this evening. Dr. came to see Betty today. Mother is making Allen a pair of pants. Both Armies have virtually evacuated Western Virginia. It rained a good deal last night. Father bought some oranges yesterday. A coal popped out, burnt a hole in Mother's beautiful quilt, in her apron, on the couch, burnt the pillow, turned a corner, and set Mother's workbasket on

169 Union Gen. Henry W. Halleck would serve in the Western Theater before being brought to Washington to serve as Lincoln's general-in-chief of the Union armies.

170 Charles Francis Adams, the U.S. Minister to the Court of St. James, was the son of President John Quincy Adams and the grandson of President John Adams.

171 At the beginning of the Civil War, cotton was about .10 per pound. Later in the war it would rise as high as $1.89 per pound.

172 Slaves from the Houston plantations.

173 Gen. James Ewell Brown (Jeb) Stuart fought Federals at the Battle of Dranesville, Virginia (Dec. 20, 1861). Both Stuart and Union Gen. Edward O. C. Ord ran into one another while foraging, precipitating a two-hour inconclusive fight.

fire. Burnt the carpet. Burnt my hand. Burnt Mother's hand. Burnt everything it could. It is a perfect nuisance. Minnie has gone down to Mrs. Dessan's to help about the Christmas tree. She carried 4 bookmarks down. Cousin Anna Wiley came to see us today. The water in the well is pretty clear. Milo and Arch both came up last night with a load of cotton. Mother lent Cousin Anna *Vernon Grove*. Mother went down town on a shopping expedition. There is a party of children over to Mrs. Whittle's tonight. Took a game of chess: I beat No. 2.

Tuesday December 24: This is Christmas Eve my 14th year!: Lucy Cox promised to lend me *Jack Hinton*. Thomas has got a very bad cold. There is a list of the killed and wounded in the late fight on the Potomac. There was a member of the Lochrane Gaurds; he arrived here today, came home + died.

Christmas Day 1861: Cold + clear. A heavy frost. My Christmas presents are *The War of the Roses* and a Book on chess, 2 packs of poppers, +c. Minnie Went to a party at Mrs. Whittle's last night. We had an egg nog also. Thomas got *The Dictionary of Poetical Quotations*. Minnie got a knife from Thomas and a thimble case. Both Thomas + I got a book mark from Minnie. My new diary was also one of my presents. A coal popped out and broke a glass, notwithstanding we had a piece of wire over the fireplace. Santa Claus brought Allen a snake who wags his head. And he is awful scared at it. Mother has gone down town to help about the Christmas. Allen's Christmas present was a pair of pants. I caught everybody on the lot.[174] Mr. Boardman has lost a child with scarlet fever. Minnie got an elegant hymn book. Took a game of chess: I beat. Jim came up bringing meat. Tonight is the Christmas tree. The new year comes crowding in with its many changes. How different we are situated from what we were a year ago!

December 26 Thursday 1861: Cool, clear, delightful day. Mother brought me some cake from the Christmas Tree. Mother has got the Rheumatism in her hands and feet. No paper. Today I popped both packs of poppers.

December 27 Friday 1861: Cool, clear, splendid day. Prince Albert[175] is dead of Gastric fever. Mother wrote to Auntie and Uncle John. My book on chess is very fine indeed. It has got a heap of games in it too. Mrs. Abner Lockett called to see Mother this morn. A battle is imminent in Kentucky. I bought myself some fire crackers and they don't half of them pop. They are not worth anything. I hear that [it] is feared that Loren Dickenson will be permanently disabled. The news from England has vanished

---

174 Meaning he received more presents than anyone. Poppers has a tiny explosive charge inside, and could be thrown against a hard surface to ignite with a sharp pop.

175 Albert of Saxe-Coburg and Gotha, Prince Consort to Queen Victoria, died of typhoid fever.

into the thin air. There is no decided news yet received from England. I have never in my life seen a prettier Christmas than this one has been.

Saturday December 28 1861: Cool, clear, delightful day. Tom put up an ashhopper today. I popped the last of my fire crackers today. The Ladies are going to have a New Year's supper for the poor.

Sunday December 29 1861: Cool, clear, splendid day. Paul Morphy's games are elegant.

Monday December 30 1861: Cool, clear, splendid day. Took a game of chess. Some body has stolen my silver dollar out of Mother's room. *The War of the Roses* is very interesting. Cousin Anna has lent me a book of Eastern Travel. Aderholds + Smiths have both come home on a furlough of 30 days. They have reinlisted for the war. The Lincolnites have determined to surrender Mason + Slidell on the demand of the Queen.

Teusday December 30: (miserably written) Cool, clear, delightful day. I have never in my life seen such pretty weather. The sun was eclipsed this morning about half. Mary Campbell came up to see Minnie and brought Rusty. He is very smart indeed. Thomas' knife has come to light in Ella's room, [j]ust where every stolen thing is found. Thomas and I took a splendid game of chess: the Queen's Gambit, and it was drawn. Minnie has started a fifth pair of socks for Uncle LeRoy. Jim Campbell promised to come up and take a game of chess. Folks went to new year's supper.

Wednesday December 31: No Entry

The inside front cover of Volume 4. LeRoy went back and created a
general index of his major Civil War-related entries.

Volume 4

January 1, 1862 – December 31, 1862

LeRoy Wiley Gresham Macon

A Christmas present from his Father, 1861

January 1, 1862: The New Year comes in with a clear cool day. All the folks went to the Supper last night and Thomas stayed home with me. Mr. Emmett Johnson is to be buried here today. Mother had gone down now to help give the supper out to the poor. Tracy came up to see us yesterday. Played a game of chess: Tom beat me. Thomas wrote to Uncle Richard today.[1] Mrs. Vardell, Mrs. Ralston's sister, died very suddenly here yesterday.

Thursday January 2nd 1862: Warm and cloudy. Took a game of chess: Tom beat me. "Ginco Piano" opening.[2] Mary, Wills + Olivia Bates spent the morning here. It is rumored that they are firing on Fort Pickens. The fort commenced first. There are also reports of fighting between Savvannah and Charleston. Finished *The War of Roses*. The weather today is as warm as in spring. Uncle Richard has got back to Portsmouth again and Uncle John is opposite.

Friday January 3d 1862: Foggy, warm. Got a letter from Uncle John this morning by Cousin Charlie. The Lincoln government will give up Mason and Slidell; this is settled.

---

1   Uncle Richard (Dick), Mary Gresham's brother, was only seven years older than LeRoy.

2   A way of beginning a game of chess.

I have got a bad pain in my side today. Mother got some ripe strawberries out of the garden yesterday. They are a rarity certain. After firing one day at Pickens they have stopped again no loss on our side. The enemy attempted a landing on the main land at Port Royal and were repulsed with 15 killed on our side. Their loss is not mentioned. Father took Minnie out to the factory[3] this eve and showed her round; she has never been to a factory before in her life.

Saturday January 4th 1862: Clear, warm, spring like day. I took a Dover's Powder and my leg hurts me now. I went down to Mr. Bates and stayed all the morning.[4] I have been reading a little in Shakespeare today and yesterday and like it tolerable. Played two games of chess: I beat one and Tom one yesterday. It is so warm today that we have been sitting without a fire. General Floyd's army is now at Bowling Green.[5]

Sunday January 5th 1862: Dark, rainy, and warm. It rained very heavily all night. Took a Dover's Powder. Communion day. . . Mother is sick in bed and it is too wet for Minnie to go. My leg is much better. Tracy came up to see us yesterday and he can nearly walk alone. Tom Collins is home on a furlough. [Gun]powder is about 2 or 3 dollars a pound in Norfolk. Reading *Pioneers + Preachers* today. The War flag is a red field with a large blue cross in the centre, Stars in the cross equal to the number of states, and a yellow fringe around the whole.[6] . . . I wrote to Uncle John.

Monday January 6th 1862: Quite cold, clear. Mother still in bed sick. Howard and Thomas left for the plantation this morning. The Holidays are o'er and Minnie has started to school. A coal popped out and burnt a large hole in my mattress and the carpet. Mr. Holmes (a return soldier), a son of Mr. Billy Holmes, shot a man in town in a gambling saloon. Captain Bartlett of the Huguenin Rifles attempted to shoot Mr. Isaac Scott the other day. Father got a letter today announcing the safe arrival of Alice in Texas.

Tuesday January 7th 1862: Cold, clear day. I went down to the schoolhouse at recess. Mason and Slidell have sailed for Europe. I have been reading *El Fanèdis* today. General Price has abandoned Missouri and retreated to Arkansas for the present. Howard returned from Houston bringing 16 turkeys and Frank Baxter.

3 John Gresham was the president of the Macon Manufacturing Company, a cotton mill located at the corner of Lamar and Oglethorpe streets (also known as the Macon Factory).

4 LeRoy liked the teacher very much, and obviously wished he could attend his school.

5 The Confederate capital of Kentucky.

6 LeRoy is describing the Army of Northern Virginia's battle flag, adopted to reduce confusion between the Stars and Bars and the Stars and Stripes experienced at First Manassas.

Wednesday January 8 1862: Cold, cloudy day. Father and I took a game of chess with odds of Queen and rook. Frank is making a mantelpiece for Julia Ann's house.[7] Today is the celebration of the Battle of New Orleans.[8] Battles of more importance are before us now! Arch came up this evening bringing backbones and spare ribs also a letter from Thomas in which he says he will not return before Friday. It is raining very considerable. Mr. Kemp[9] had killed 28 hogs whose average was 220 pounds, Pretty good! We sold 15 turkeys today. I wrote to Thomas today.

Thursday January 9th 1862: Cool, foggy, disagreable day. I have got a pain in my back and have had for several days. Mr. Bates has got a new scholar; her name is Jessie Burgess. Father and I played two games of chess out of the book. Minnie got a letter from Cousin Teadee[10] and Mother one from Grandma. General Pillow has resigned. Colonel Johnson of the 12th regiment has been made a Brigadier General; also Adjutant Wayne, who declined.[11]

Friday January 10th 1862: I went down to the schoolhouse at recess. Julia Ann is sick. Father was sick all night with earache. Commenced reading *Temper* today. It is a very nice book. This warm weather is very bad on meat.[12] Dr. Fitzgerald came to see Betty today and prescribed a course of treatment for her, and will not come again unless sent for.[13] Oglethorpe University has 7 students. Mr. Clisby noted our strawberries today. I gave Allen my coat which I wore last winter. General McLellan who had been very sick is now recovering.[14] Father and I took a game of chess and it was drawn. Father had a lot of chances to mate me in one. Minnie stayed to tea with Mary Campbell and I am promised to come up.

7 Frank, one of family's skilled slaves, is making the mantel for one of the slave homes on the Macon property. Many male slaves learned specialized skills such as carpentry or blacksmithing, while female slaves learned about sewing or child care. They were occasionally hired out to others, and sometimes allowed to keep part of the proceeds.

8 The final battle of the War of 1812.

9 Kindred Kemp was one of the Gresham overseers at the Oakwoods plantation. He had a wife and three small children.

10 Sarah C. Hayes, daughter of grandmother's sister Sarah Ann Wiley Hayes, living in Athens, Georgia.

11 Gen. Edward Johnson. He would end up with a division and be captured at Spotsylvania on May 12, 1864.

12 Because there was no refrigeration, people relied on cold temperatures to keep meat fresh, which was why they also often salted or smoked meats.

13 Betty was a plantation slave. Dr. Edward Fitzgerald was a Macon physician.

14 He had contracted typhoid fever.

Saturday January 11th 1862: Foggy damp and warm. I rode down town and went to the Brunswick depot for Thomas, who did not come. Father and I took a real elegant game of chess and he did beat me fairly: checkmated me. There is a good deal of Scarlet Fever in town now. Captain Smith of Brown's Infantry is a Lieutenant Colonel. We sat out on the colonade this eve, it being warm enough.

Sunday January 12th 1862: Warm as summer. Clear and bright. The daily will hereafter be published on Monday. I wish it would turn cold on account of the meat. The wind is blowing as if it would shake down the house. Cousin Howard stayed to dinner with us. The "Governor's Horse Guard" from Western Virginia came down today on their way to South Georgia.

Monday January 13th 1862: Warm as summer. I did sleep most miserably last night. Jim Campbell came up to night and played two games of chess. The first game we played I beat him. The opening was the "Ginco Piano." I checked his Queen and Rook with a KT. I don't think he tried his best. The next game was much longer. Jim declined the gambit this time. We were left with K and Rook and 3 Pawns K + R + 5 pawns. He queened a pawn and I gave it up. He brought his chessboard which is beautiful.

Teusday January 14th 1862: Cool, cloudy day. My leg is drawn up a good deal this morning. A coal popped out and set Mothers work basket on fire this morn.[15] I think that the Confederate States will be recognized before long. Jim Campbell sat up with Tom Collins who is <u>very</u> sick. Gen Mclellan is still very sick. 11 o'clock Raining slowly and it is turning <u>very</u> cold. Father and I played chess at odds of a Queen—drawn game. Father brought up some old blank books today for waste paper.

Wednesday January 15th 1862: Rained all night and it is cold and cloudy this morning. Adjutant Wayne has declined the Brigadier Generalship. Minnie and I played chess at odds of a Queen: I beat. I gave Jim Campbell a [mathematics] problem to work out and he sent it back with a full solution today. I wonder that Thomas did not come home today. I went down to the schoolhouse this eve. It is raining now at bedtime.

Thursday January 16th 1862: Cold, clear, beautiful day. Father left for the plantation this morn. He was quite unwell all day yesterday with earache, cold, +c. Mother got a letter from Aunty in which she says Uncle Edge is going to try and get a furlough very soon.[16] I tried to work out some chess problems this morn but it was a failure. Colonel

---

15 LeRoy treats the episodes of popping coals rather casually, but popping coals were extremely dangerous and often caused serious fire damage.

16 William Edgeworth Bird of the Athens Guards, 15th GA Infantry.

Jackson of 5th regiment has been made a brigadier General.[17] General Humphrey Marshall with 2000 men met the enemy 8000 strong near Prestonburg, Kentucky and after had fighting defeated them with loss of 25 killed, 15 wounded; Yankee loss 200 killed. After the battle he retreated.[18] Thomas returned home from Houston this evening by the railroad, and I am very glad.

Friday January 17th 1862: Cool, damp, and cloudy. Minnie being somewhat unwell did not go to school today. Thomas and I played chess. He beat me. Rained pretty hard before day this morn. There is a large naval expedition fitting out at Fort Munroe for the south. Its commander is General Burnsides.[19] I have had a distressing pain in my hip point. I wonder whether I am going to have hip disease. I read some in *The Lofty and the Lowly*. I wish very much I could hear from Dr. Pancoast to know whether or not I am getting well.[20]

Saturday January 18th 1862: Warm and foggy. I slept very miserably last night on acct. of the terrible pain in my hip and back. Minnie was also sick. I had to take a Dover's Powder before I could rest at all. The *Telegraph* says that old Cameron[21] has resigned and gone to Russia. General Johnston has ordered away from Centreville all the newspaper correspondents. Snow a foot deep at Centreville. I hope this pain in my leg is rheumatism. Father got a letter from Cousin George Jones[22] at the seat of war and he inclosed a map of Manassa and vacinity which he says is very correct. Thomas and I took a game of chess: "Mucio gambit." It was an acknowledged drawn game though when played out, I beat. Mother and Minnie gone to town. Father returned home.

Sunday January 19 1861: Warm and damp. I slept under the influence of a Dover's Powder tolerably well, though suffering a good deal. Minnie was unwell all night and had some fever. Father rubbed my back with liniment last night. The weather is bad on meat again. This day a year ago Georgia seceded from the Union. Long may she wave!

17 Gen. John K. Jackson.

18 The Battle of Middle Creek (January 9, 1862), a sharp skirmish in eastern Kentucky involving the withdrawal of a small force under Confederate Gen. Humphrey Marshall away from a similar sized command (2,100) under future US president Gen. James A. Garfield. Losses were minor on both sides.

19 Fort Monroe was a large stone fortress on the tip of the Virginia peninsula; Union Gen. Ambrose E. Burnside.

20 His 1860 visit with Dr. Pancoast in Philadelphia was brief, but LeRoy liked and trusted him. He also fervently hoped for good news and an an improvement in his health, neither of which would come.

21 Simon Cameron was Lincoln's secretary of war until January 14, 1862, after which he became ambassador to Russia for a short time.

22 Maj. George Jones was a maternal cousin of LeRoy's father.

Monday January 20th 1862: Warm + clear. Sitting without a fire. Spent a night of pain and took a Dover's Powder. My leg is no better. Ex-president Tyler[23] is dead. Captain Lockett of the Bibb Cavalry has resigned and J.G. Holt elected to fill the vacancy.[24] The great Burnside expedition has appeared off Hatteras and it is thought will take Roanoke Island. Thomas got a letter from Uncle Richard and he is in winter quarters. Father and I played chess and he beat me badly, an oversight of mine. Minnie is going into *Virgil*.[25]

Teusday January 21st 1862: Warm and clear. Last night at about 10 o'clock the wind blew very hard and it rained a little. I spent a better night and my leg does not hurt me as bad. Mr. Parks, Minnie's new music teacher, came today and gave her a lesson. . . . Finished *Lofty and the Lowly*. It is a very fine book and ends beautifully. Mr. Amos Benton was buried here today. Mr. Bates has a new scholar named Cochrane. Father and Thomas played chess with Queen odds and Father beat him bad.

Wednesday January 22nd 1862: Cool cloudy day. My leg is nearly well. Tom and I played chess: Muzio Gambit. He beat me bad. The soldiers passed by here today on their way from the cemetery. The number of the Federal steamers off Hatteras continues to increase and their numbers are now immense. Major General Van dorn[26] has been transferred to Missouri and Arkansas and General Ewell[27] has promoted to Major General. It is turning cold with appearance of rain. There is a large fire in situ over the river.

Thursday January 23d 1862: It rained steadily all night and has rained all the morning. Uncle LeRoy arrived here last night. He is well. He killed largely at both his plantations on Monday week.[28] The fire last consumed a large two story house over the river belonging to Mr. Burt. It was non-occupied at the time. Loss was $1500. I commenced studying arithmetic with Thomas as my teacher yesterday. I commenced at Federal

---

23 John Tyler, the 10th president of the US.

24 Legislation passed by the Confederate government allowed enlisted men to elect their own line officers (colonels and below).

25 Virgil, considered one of the greatest Roman poets, was the author of *Aeneid*, which is almost certainly what Minnie was reading.

26 Gen. Earl Van Dorn was transferred to command the Confederate Trans-Mississippi District west of the Mississippi River.

27 Gen. Richard S. Ewell began serving under Gen. Thomas "Stonewall" Jackson in the Shenandoah Valley, and would rise to prominence in Gen. Lee's Army of Northern Virginia.

28 Likely hogs or other livestock used for meat.

numbers. The soldier who was buried here yesterday was named Maynard of CC Blues[29] and was killed in action at Alleghany. 9PM: It has rained hard all day and has turned very cold. Uncle LeRoy and I played two games of chess. The first time he replied to K.Kt.to B.3 with P.to K.B 4.3 and I won his R by Q. To KR.5 and so on.[30] The next time I won his Queen by getting it before his King and beat him eventually. Tom and him played and he beat. Thomas and him played draughts. He beat Tom two games and Tom beat one game. Minnie has finished Uncle LeRoy's socks and gave them to him.

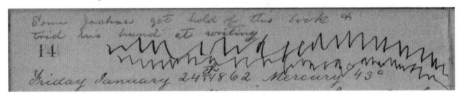

Friday January 24th 1862: Cool and cloudy. Bad news: General Crittenden has sustained a disastrous defeat. General Zollicoffer killed and our army in full retreat.[31] This is the Yankee account. Thomas and Uncle LeRoy played 5 games of chess: Uncle beat the first, 2nd Thomas beat [in a] mean game. The 3rd game was well contested on both sides Tom beat. 4th: Poor game. Thomas checked and won both of his Rks with a Kt. 5th: Thomas penned his Queen and won eventually. . . .

LeRoy's wrote (above) in the margin: "Some Jackass got hold of this book and tried his hand at writing." There is nothing else on this page except for the large scribble, as shown. He would not have referred to Thomas or Minnie as a "Jackass," and a slave-servant would never have done this. The culprit was likely 2-year-old Tracy.

29 Central City Blues.

30 K.Kt.to B.3 and other similar notations are movements of chess pieces, with K being a knight, B a Bishop, and so on.

31 The Battle of Mill Springs (Jan. 19, 1862) in eastern Kentucky. 5,900 Confederates under Gens. George B. Crittenden and Felix K. Zollicoffer were beaten by 4,500 Union troops under Gen. George H. Thomas, ending an early-war Southern offensive. Southern losses were 530 killed, wounded, and missing, with Union casualties less than half that at 250. Zollicoffer was killed.

Saturday January 25th 1862: Clear, cool, beautiful day. Zollicoffer's death and the defeat of the army is confirmed! General Crittenden was wounded! 2 to 300 killed on our side! 500 "Yanks"! The enemy repulsed 3 times and driven to their intrenchments. The Confederates being outflanked are compelled to retreat and cross the Cumberland under a heavy fire! We lost all our horses, tents, and eleven guns! Our forces numbered 6000! Yankees about 14 000! The battle occured near Preston & Somerset, Kentucky. Mother and Minnie went down town. Tom and I played chess: he beat. Tom and Uncle played draughts. It is turning cold.

Sunday January 26th 1862: Clear, cold, beautiful day. Uncle LeRoy left for Sparta last night. Read some in *My Juvenile Days* by "Mary Howitt." General MClelan is now ready and there will be a general advance, a dying but terrible effort [to] "crush out the rebellion." The last *Presbyterian*[32] is a very fine number. Mother's new oil clock[33] which came last week from Charleston is very beautiful. Tracy came up to see us yesterday and is learning to walk fast.

Monday January 27th 1862: Cool, clear day. Howard and Betty, Julia Ann, Bil + co. left for Houston this morn. Thomas and I played chess, 2 games: I beat. He beat. I went down to the schoolhouse this eve. I saw Tom Collins this eve and he is very pale. Jim Campbell sent a [math] problem up for me to work out which Thomas did in a few moments.[34]

Tuesday January 28th 1862: Foggy, damp day. Jim Campbell came up last night and played two games of chess. I beat him first and he beat me. I gave him some problems to work out. The Yankee vessels have got up between Fort Pulaski and Savannah. They are in the little inlets and not in the river, but they can fire on passing ships. The city is not in danger. Jim sent me one of my problems with the solution. I worked out two problems myself this morn. Howard returned this eve with Julia Ann. Both overseers killed hogs: Mr. Kemp on Saturday, Hill[35] on Monday. Willis also came up bringing meat of all kinds + turkeys, chickens, +c. Father and Tom took game of chess last night: Pa beat.

32 The *Presbyterian Magazine* was published in Philadelphia from 1808-1860, and began again in 1863.

33 A glass vessel with a gauged frame indicating time as the oil burned. Given his interests and the way his mind worked, this is the type of device LeRoy would have especially enjoyed.

34 Because he was not attending school, exchanging math problems was a substitute for learning the subject, which LeRoy viewed as an exciting challenge rather than a boring chore.

35 Jessup Riley Hill was the overseer for the Pineland plantation. Like Kemp, he also had a wife and three small children.

Wednesday January 29th 1862: Warm, clear day. I slept very bad. General Beauregarde has accepted the command at Columbus, Kentucky and is second only to General Johnson. It is said that the reason of the defeat in Kentucky was that General Crittenden was drunk as a beast. Sam Virgin lent me *The Crusades and Crusaders*.

Thursday January 30th 1862: Warm as summer. Rained in the night. Mother was sick all night and is in bed this morn. Thomas went in to see Jim Campbell and played two games of chess. Thomas beat one and Jim one. They also worked out several enigmas.[36] The Napier Artillery went off last night to Savannah. Thomas is reading *The Gamblers Wife*. Rained hard. Worked out a math problem today.

Friday January 31st 1862: Warm and rainy. Jessie Burgess stayed to tea and all night with us. There is no school today. Mr. Bates is sick, and Mary Campbell came to see Minnie, and it rained so hard and steady that she could not get home and had to stay to dinner. No more news from Savannah. Played two games of chess: I beat one and Thomas one. Worked out two problems.

Saturday January 31st 1862 1st day of February: Rained steadily all night. It is said that 45 vessels of Burnside's armada were lost in the late storm on the coast. General Beauregarde's official report of Manassas is out. Colonel Extor of the 13th is dead.[37] Cousin Howard came up stayed to tea and went home tonight.

Sunday February 2nd 1862: Cool, clear day. Minnie received a letter from Sallie to day. Uncle LeRoy was there. They had heard from Uncle Edge and he had failed in trying to get a furlough. Read some in *Rome Scenes* today. A soldier was buried here this evening.

Monday February 3d 1862: Cool, cloudy day. Rained hard all night. Jim sent up three problems: 2 two move and 1 move, also the solution to one we sent him, which was not correct. It was so raw and damp today that Mr. Bates taught till two o'clock. I have got the old pain in my side today and I am very sorry. I never saw as much rainy weather in my life. Minnie is knitting a pair of socks for Uncle Edge. Finished the *Crusaders* today. It is a very good book. Mother has a bad cough and cold which annoys her very much.

Tuesday February 4th 1862: Cloudy, damp, and rain. Rained in the night. Father rubbed my back with liniment and it feels a good deal better this morn. Mother's cough troubled her so much that she had to take a Dover's Powder. There was a shooting

---

36 These could have been anything from crossword puzzles to coded messages to solve.

37 Col. Walton Ector, 13th Georgia Infantry, returned to Georgia to recover his health, and died in Greenville.

affray. Mr. Phil Lamar was dangerously if not fatally shot by his overseer, a Mr. Sawyer. Highly Important! News from Europe! England and France have determined on "Armed intervention." Father and Thomas played chess last night and Father beat. Colonel Williams[38] of the Georgia Regulars is dead. Jim Campbell sent us a two more problems today, which we solved in no time. This eve it was very clear and pleasant and I went down to the school.

Wednesday February 5th 1862: Cool and cloudy. Jim came up and played two games of chess, both of which he easily won. I gave him a problem also. Mother is sick in bed. Jim lent me his book on chess this morning. It is a very good work.

February Thursday 6th 1862: Warm and cloudy. Howard went to mill yesterday morning early and returned at night. Father and Thomas played chess last night, and Father beat. Thomas and I played today: I beat. Thomas went out in the garden and dug at the roots of peach trees. Jim sent the solution to that problem today. Took him 2 hours and a ½. Worked our two problems today. Mother got a letter from Grandma today. Uncle Edge, to their great joy, is at home on furlough. He left camp perfectly well but was taken sick in Richmond where he was delayed a day. His furlough is 30 days. I cut a piece out of an old paper and Father gave it to Mr. Clisby; it came out today.[39] Played chess with Father and he beat me. It has started to rain now at 6 o'clock.

Friday February 7th 1862: Rained hard all night long. There has been a skirmish in Kentucky; a company of ours attacked and whipped some "Yanks," killing a captain and seven men. Raining hard and steady. 3 o'clock: The news of the capture Fort Henry[40] on the Tennessee River came today; "no particulars." Worked out a problem. Mother still in bed coughing badly.

Saturday February 8th 1862: Cloudy with rain. Rained hard all night; the river must rise very high. Thomas went down to Mrs. Campbell's to play chess last night and played 3 games of which he beat one. I also played a game with Father and beat him. We played today and I beat Thomas. Mother is up again today. It is quite warm. No more news from Fort Henry. Mr. Bates has a new scholar named Jim Graybill.

---

38 Charles J. Williams, 1st Georgia Infantry.

39 Newspapers often printed articles from other papers. LeRoy had submitted one to be reprinted in the *Daily Telegraph*. Mr. Clisby was its editor.

40 Fort Henry was a poorly designed position on the Tennessee River held by Confederates under Gen. Lloyd Tilghman. The flooded fort was shelled by Union warships. Tilghman surrendered with a small number of men while others retreated to eight miles to Fort Donelson on the Cumberland River. Fort Henry's fall was the first major Western Theater victory for the Union, and for Gen. Ulysses S. Grant.

Sabbath day February 9th 1862: Cloudy and cool. Read some in *Memoirs of Lady Colquhoun*. We weighted Kitty yesterday and 7¼ pounds was the amount. General Pillow has withdrawn his resignation. The Burnside fleet has shelled and taken Roanoke Island, also 1000 of our men together with the General.[41] This was of course to be expected with such a force; only one or 2 of their ships were lost. An attack on Columbus is daily expected. The enemy in and about Tybee are "in statu quo." The C.S.S. *Sumter* is at Cady and is all right. The *Nashville* is at Southampton with a federal war steamer who is waiting to take her.

Monday February 10th 1862: Cold, clear, day. Bad news! The yankees have taken all our men on Roanoke. Their gunboats have come down the Tennessee as far as Tuscumbia, Alabama. I am very much afraid that they will take Norfolk. They have certainly got the upper hand of us now. General Pillow is in command at Fort Donelson, Tennessee. It <u>does</u> seem to me that nothing but bad news comes nowadays. Yesterday I "Got things mixed." It was at Fort Henry that General Tilghman and 100 men were taken. 5 oclock: Played chess: Tom Beat. Queen's Gambit. Worked a problem too. Went down to the schoolhouse. Mother went down town. Mrs. Towns called to see Mother today. They have been planting potatoes all day. Howell Cobb is in town. Played chess with Father: I beat, he beat.

Teusday February 11th 1862: Cold, clear day. Father left for Houston. In the late battle on Roanoke, 200 of our men were killed. Yankee loss supposed to be much greater. The yankees are landing on Skidaway and Warsaw Island and it is supposed that there will be an attack on the city at an early hour. General Beauregarde is at Columbus, Kentucky. There is a company of "six months" men now forming here named "The Gresham Rifles." Howard is to day hauling wood from the railroad.

Wednesday February 12th 1862: Moderately warm day. Uncle LeRoy arrived here ~~today~~ last night at bedtime. There has been a number of gunboats burnt by our own men on the Tennessee; only one fell into the Yankees hands. All our gunboats were taken at Roanoke. Our entire loss there was 1700 men in killed + prisoners. Played chess – Drawn. Sent home Jim's book. A good many Virginia regiments are reinlisting; if they don't there will be a draught [draft]. General Bonham[42] has resigned. France is

---

41 A Federal naval force of some 60 ships commanded by Flag Officer Louis M. Goldsborough overwhelmed a small fleet under Capt. William F. Lynch just below the Virginia border during the early stages of a large amphibious operation known as Burnside's Expedition. Gen. Henry A. Wise was ill, leaving Souther forces under Col. Henry M. Shaw, who surrendered 2,500 men and many artillery pieces (otherwise, casualties for both sides were relatively light).

42 Gen. Milledge L. Bonham resigned his commission to serve as governor of South Carolina.

very mad about the stone fleet at Charleston, and protests against it.[43] There has just been a fine gunboat launched at Mobile named *Morgan*.[44] General Wise is very ill in North Carolina. Elizabeth City was burned by the inhabitants on the approach by the Yankees. The 4th regiment, it is thought, will reinlist.

Thursday February 13th 1862: Clear, warm, sunny day. Uncle LeRoy left for his plantation. Mother walked down town to day. Richard[45] came today to take down the book case and all the books were taken into the back parlor. "Bohemian," the correspondent of the *Dispatch* was taken at Roanoke.[46] The 4th Georgia passed through Atlanta on their way to Florence, Alabama. I am just to Fractions in my Arithmetic. Father returned home this eve. Played chess and was badly beat. Tracy came up to see us and was very sweet. He walks very well.

Friday February 14th 1862: Warm and cloudy day. St. Valentine's Day. Colonel Howell Cobb has been made a Brigadier General. Governor Brown called for 12 regiments and if not responded to, it will be followed by a draughtft. The enemy attacked Fort Donelson[47] on yesterday and fired all day with their boats and on land but were repulsed with loss. It is thought that the attack will be renewed. Howard finished hauling wood today. I got a Valentine from Father; Minnie got a Valentine too.

Saturday February 15th 1862: Raw, cold day. Mother [and Minnie] left here last night for Sparta. Father went as far as Gordon with her, where Cousin Howard met her. Father returned home by 10 oclock. Thomas and I played chess until about ten oclock. It is now bachelor's hall about here. Willis came up with the wagon, Big Ben also last night. The whole town is exercised on the subject of being draughtfted. The "Gresham Rifles" has 40 men in the war. There is also a company just starting: "Lewis

---

43 Ships filled with stones and sunk by the Union navy to block shipping channels into and out of Charleston, which made it harder for Southern blockade-runners to trade with foreign countries.

44 A partially armored gunboat with 10 guns.

45 One of the Gresham slaves who specialized in carpentry.

46 The pseudonym of Dr. William G. Shepardson, who wrote for the *Richmond Daily Dispatch*. Correspondents were often combatants as well as active journalists.

47 The Battle of Fort Donelson (Feb. 12-16, 1862) was a decisive Union victory. The strong fortification on the bluffs overlooking the Cumberland River was attacked by a Federal army under Grant and naval flotilla under Adm. Andrew Foote. The Confederates, under Floyd, Pillow and Gen. Simon B. Buckner, had been advised to abandon the position, but did not before being surrounded. A Southern attack (Feb. 15) broke open the Union right, but Grant restored his lines before a retreat could be made. Floyd and Pillow evacuated to save themselves, leaving Buckner to surrender more than 12,000 men on Feb. 16. The loss of Forts Henry and Donelson were major Southern defeats that opened two major river arteries into the Confederate heartland.

Volunteers" [under] Captain Hardy Nary [for] 6 months [service]. There has been meetings in all the churches for the last 2 or 3 days for the country and soldiers. Rained in the evening every day since Thursday. The enemy have been trying to shell out Fort Donaldson; I reckon there will be news tomorrow. Father and I played chess and he beat. They have finished the bookcase + it now "sits" in the sitting room.

Sunday February 16th 1862: Cold, damp, and cloudy. 8PM: It has been raining slowly all day. Read some in *Faggots for the Fireside*. It is said that the steamer *Victory* has arrived in New Orleans with 12,000 stands of arms. 4PM: Misty and damp.

Monday February 17th 1862: Cold, damp, raw. Had very considerable sore throat through the night and this morning. We were fighting all day at Fort Donelson and had whipped them, taking 1000 prisoners and were driving them back with cold steel, +c and so on. This morning there comes a dispatch from Chattanooga stating that the enemy had taken Fort Donelson. Generals Pillow, Floyd, Buckner with their commands are prisoners, and that Nashville is in their power: Kentucky and Tennessee both gone, 12,000 of our men are prisoners. All the government stores in Nashville lost, and amid all this Savannah is in imminent danger. So is Weldon [North Carolina], the key to all the railroads that run to Virginia. It's perfectly awful! I wrote a letter to Mother today. It is reported that the enemy had shelled Bowling Green and on account of some movement of the enemy. General Johnson [Johnston] had evacuated it. It commenced raining this eve at 3 and rained hard until now, 9 oclock. Father and Uncle LeRoy took a game of chess: odds queen. Father mated Uncle LeRoy and I played 7 game of backgammon: I 4, He 3. Thomas and Uncle LeRoy played 7 games of draughts: Thomas beat 3 games.

Tuesday February 18, 1862: Cloudy, damp, and rainy. Rained the whole night and until nine AM. Thomas is writing to Mother. Some people don't believe that news about Fort Donelson. There has been a dispatch saying that Nashville has not surrendered and do not know about Donelson. Commenced to rain at ten AM, and has rained very hard until 9 PM. A rainy day truly. We received a short letter from Mother. She got along very well and was met in Sparta by the family. My sore throat is entirely well.

Wednesday February 19th 1862: Very warm and very foggy early in the morn, but very bright towards midday. Uncle LeRoy left here this morning. Bad news! Fort Donelson is certainly taken and I don't know how many men. It is reported General Buckner taken. But nobody knows. The river is taken. But nobody knows. The [Ocmulgee] river is tremendous and I am going to see it. Rained hard and late in the evening.

Thursday February 20th 1862: Cold and cloudy. I went down yesterday after dinner in the buggy to see the river and it was a sight certain, as high Father says as in the

Harrison freshet. The Brunswick train tried to come up and they had to stay in the bridge all night, the road being washed away before + behind. Nothing certain from Tennessee, i.e. It is rumored that our loss in Killed + wounded is 9 or 10,000; Yankees much more. General Buckner and the remnant of his gallant band had cut their way through to Nashville where, it is said, General Johnston will make a stand. It seems impossible to get the straight story.[48]

Friday February 21st 1862: Cloudy, cold day. General Buckner is captured. Floyd + Pillow escaped. Our loss in killed 200, 800 wounded. I have caught a bad cold in my head which worries me considerably. Snuf-Snuff. President Davis has proclaimed Friday the 28th a day of fasting, and Governor Brown the 8th of March.[49] Played chess last night with Father, who beat me. We got two letters from Mother: one to me + one to Father. All well. Aunty thinks she will go on to Virginia and take Wilson. Mother is much depressed about the bad news. It has rained there as much as it did here. Thomas wrote a letter to Minnie.

Saturday February 22nd 1862 AD: Warm, clear, delightful day. I took some pepper tea last night and my cold is a great deal better. The freshet at Columbus did a good deal of damage. Washed away a bridge, broke the canal, and damaged the Factories. Today President Davis is inaugurated for 6 years.[50] Today the "Great Rebel" George Washington was born.[51] The 5th Georgia Regiment is at Knoxville. The 3d is at Elizabeth City, North Carolina. General Magruder[52] will take command of Weldon. General Beauregarde is sick in Tennessee. Captain R. Smith is going to try and raise a regiment. A fight is reported between General Price and the enemy in Missouri near Arkansas, killing 700 Yankees and losing himself 100. The enemy in North Carolina are occupying themselves burning towns. Father is writing to Mother. There was a fire

48 LeRoy, who once believed everything he heard and read, has come to realize initial news reports are often wildly in error.

49 It was not uncommon for President Davis to set aside a day of fasting, and for Governor Brown to make it a different day for Georgia. Brown disliked Davis and objected to the centralization of power in Richmond.

50 Davis had been serving since February of 1861 as the provisional president of the Confederacy, and was elected to a full six-year term on November 6, 1861. He was inaugurated in Richmond on February 22, 1862.

51 Many Southerners identified with Virginia native George Washington, and believed they were fighting a second American Revolution.

52 Confederate Gen. John B. Magruder.

over the river today, consuming a meat house (500 hogs' meat) in it. It made a very black smoke. I have commenced to take Iron pills again.

Sunday February 23d 1862: Warm, clear, very beautiful day. Read a little in Dr. Olin's *Travels in the East*. I received a letter from Mother; also Father one from Mother <u>and</u> Minnie. My cold, through the influence of pepper tea and a little care, has left me. The Macon Volunteers have determined to go on "their own hook" to Savvannah for a few days. The "Gresham Rifles" are near full. Mother will leave Sparta on Teusday or Wednesday stopping a day in Milledgeville.

Monday February 24th 1862: Cool, clear, and very windy. No news from Tennessee. Major Lucius Lamar has been elected Colonel of the 8th Regiment of Georgia Volunteers. Towards night it turned very cold. General [Albert S.] Johnston's army is at Murfreesboro, 20 miles from Nashville. Father wrote to Mother.

Teusday Wednesday 25th February 1862: Cold, clear day. Thomas snapped his gun at a robin – robin flew. Nashville is certainly in the possession of the federals who declare that they will trouble no one who does not trouble them.[53] Major Hardeman, 2nd Battalion, advertises to raise a regiment. The Napier Artillery at Savannah now number 96 men. The fight at Donaldson was the bloodiest ever on America. Our total loss was 23 Company regiments [of] infantry + 2 batteries artillery. There was an alarm of fire yesterday at dinnertime which proved to be a Factory hand's house. Fire originated in a spark on the roof. Played two games of chess: I beat.

Wednesday February 26th 1862: Cold and dark; rained steadily all the morn. Despatch say the Yankees have <u>not</u> occupied Nashville <u>yet</u>. "Gresham Rifles" went into camp last night and Father and Mr. Holmes went around to get blankets for them. Uncle Edge's furlough is out today. Fort Pulaski[54] is entirely cut off from the city and the men can only hold out as long as their provisions do. Uncle Link is in Missouri in Colonel Look's regiment. Have had a bad pain in my head all the eve and have coughed a good deal. There's a company forming here called Whittle Gaurds.[55]

Thursday February 27th 1862: Clear, warm, bright. 12 AM: We are suddenly awakened by a knock at the door and found that Mother and Minnie had arrived safe both tolerably well – Minnie has had a sore throat and has not recovered yet. My

53 The important railroad and manufacturing center of Nashville fell on February 25, 1862. The Confederates never reoccupied the city.

54 Fort Pulaski defending Savannah was named for Polish officer and Revolutionary War hero Kazimierz Pulaski (1745-1779), also known as the "father of the American cavalry."

55 The Whittle Guards would become Company D, 10th Georgia Infantry Battalion.

Mother brought me a little book carved out of a stone from the Spring Battle field of Manassa Plains. Cousin Sam Wiley[56] made it. Father got a letter from Uncle John [via] Cousin Jinnie Blount, who has got back home. President Davis' inaugural is out. Howard left for Houston. Minnie brought home some beautiful moss from the cooks. Mother has entertained us this morning with the accounts of what she had done. Tracy came up to see us and looked very well and walked all over the yard.

Friday February 28th 1862: Warm, clear, delightful day. Fast day appointed by President Davis. Mother too unwell to go to church. . . The boys are shooting robins today all around here. Thomas has not killed any. No news of importance. Howard came back; he brought some turkey. Betty's baby is dead and she is sinking fast.

Spring Saturday March 1st 1862: Warm clear day Coissin Mary Jane has got another baby, a boy too.[57]

Sabbath day March 2nd 1862: Cloudy and warm. Father too unwell to go to church. . . . Mother brought two beautiful hens from Sparta of the Java breed. "Old Abe" has lost a son lately.[58] Cousin Job has joined a volunteer company for the war. I had the last of my Catawba wine today and I am very sorry.[59] Read *Corolinn: A Tale of Persia* today, and it is very interesting. *The Literary Messenger*.[60]

Monday March 3d 1862: Rained very hard indeed in the night and is still cloudy. General Pillow's official report of the Battle of Fort Donaldson is out. The C.S. *Nashville* has arrived in Beaufort, North Carolina with a cargo worth 3,000,000. The blockaders fired 22 times at her. The *Sumter* is still around Gibraltar burning Yankee ships.[61] Mother went to Miss Helen Franklin's funeral this even. A very high wind has prevailed all day Very cold and cloudy.

---

56 Samuel Harris Wiley, from a different branch of the Wiley family, had married a distant cousin of LeRoy's mother. He was the husband of his grandma's niece, Sarah Elizabeth Carnes.

57 Walter Gresham Green, son of Cousin Mary Jane Gresham Green and Jesse Patterson Green.

58 William Wallace "Willie" Lincoln probably died from typhoid fever.

59 Catawba, a red American grape variety used for wine and juices, grown from Maryland down through the Carolinas.

60 The story was serialized in the magazine.

61 CSS *Nashville* was a former mail steamer captured in Charleston at the beginning of the war and converted into a Confederate commerce raider. CSS *Sumter* was a merchant steamship built in Philadelphia before the war, purchased by the Confederate government, and converted into an armed commerce raider.

Teusday March 4th 1862: Cold, clear day. Rather the coldest day of the season. This is draughtft day. Richmond, Norfolk, and Portsmouth have been declared under martial law by President Davis. Governor Brown issued a proclamation ordering the siezure of every still used for making whiskey from grain. A good many other states have done the same.[62] All our men were released on Parole at Roanoke, "Bohemian" included. Generals Buckner and Tilghman have gone to Fort Warsaw. The "Queen Sisters," a southern [musical] company, are here now. Frank Nisbet has been very sick for two or three days. Thomas shot a robin for my dinner. 3 PM: I went down to the fairground this morning to see the great show. A whole regiment of militia, Colonel Jones commanding. The regiment was drawn up and then a call was made for volunteers to fill up the Gresham Rifles and Whittle Guard. After much screwing + twisting and bounty offering by private citizens, the required number was finally raised. "Glorious old Bibb [County]." Hurrah.

Wednesday March 5th 1862: Cold, clear, and very windy. I did sleep most miserably. Minnie and Thomas went to the "Queen Sisters" and stayed 'till twelve PM. And I was awake when they came home. I made a bow yesterday and it is very mean. No daily today on account of the draft. Cousin Eliza came up last night form Savannah. She sent us some oysters today. Father came home to dinner to day with a bad headache. Mother went down to see Cousin Helen who is just from Virginia. Thomas shot an old black cat who has been serenading us for a long time.

Thursday March 6th 1862: Cold, windy, cloudy day. I slept very bad and got up at eleven AM. A coal popped out and burnt a hole in a picture by getting up behind it. The federals have at last occupied Nashville and are trying their best to conciliate the rebels and encourage the union men. We surrendered 26 regiments at Donelson. General A.S. Johnston is falling back on Alabama.

Friday March 7th 1862: Very cold + clear. All tender things killed. Cousin George Jones stayed to tea with us last night. He gave Minnie a heart carved out of a piece of wood from Manassa. Today is state fast day. An attack is daily expected at Norfolk, for which I fear we are not prepared to resist. Captain Robert Smith is here.

Saturday March 8th 1862: Cold + clear. Thick ice. I have got my old pain in the back and hip. Had to take Dover's Powder. Rubbed my back with liniment. Beauregarde has evacuated Columbus, Kentucky. There are three thousand sick soldiers in Atlanta and they are trying to get some down here. There was but one county in the state that was

---

62 Grain was required to feed civilians and soldiers, so its use for alcohol was officially prohibited.

drafted and that was Chatham.[63] All other counties responded nobly. The war on the distilleries is going to do a deal of good. Tracy came up to see us this evening and is fat + rosy. Mrs. Holt, Jr. and Sr. called to see Mother. 5 P.M.: The weather has moderated very much. It's quite warm.

Sunday March 9th 1862: Cool, clear, splendid day. Read some in *Chambers Papers for the People*. The pain in my back is gone, and I am well again. Father bought me a new supply of Catawba wine. Yesterday Father brought me *Life of Major General Burn*.

Monday March 10th 1862: Warm and cloudy. There has been a great naval victory near Newport News. The ironclad steamer *Merrimac* went down and was attacked by the frigates *Cumberland* and *Congress*. The *Cumberland*, she sunk. It was said that *Congress* also sank, but it was not known certain. The next morning she was attacked by the steamer *Minnesota*, which being badly damaged by the *Merrimac*, was compelled to run ashore, where she was at last accounts.[64] In turning a corner this morn very unexpectedly on my wagon [while being pulled], I was thrown off and received a severe jolt which did not hurt me at all at the time, but which I fear will be of no good to me.

Tuesday March 11th 1862: Cool + cloudy. I went down to see the "Gresham Rifles" go off.[65] They are strong, good looking men. The "Whittle Gaurd" also went off. They had not got their uniforms. The companies go to Griffin, where there is a rendezvous. There were also a great many men of the 1st Georgia Regiment down there. It disbanded at Augusta a few days ago. I saw Captain Rogers of the C.C. Blues. The frigate *Congress* was not sunk, but surrendered, and was burned by our men. We lost (it is reported) 9 killed, 12 wounded; 3 Yankee schooners captured! The Ericsson battery engaged the *Merrimac* at a distance of 40 yards! The *Merrimac* ran aground when shot + shell was poured into her, but without effect! After getting off she ran into the Ericsson, which fled. The loss of the enemy was awful.[66] Mother is making hospital

---

63 The county in which Savannah is located.

64 The Battle of Hampton Roads. The screw frigate USS *Merrimack* was burned in Norfolk, raised by the Confederates, rebuilt as an ironclad, and christened CSS *Virginia* on February 17, 1862. Among the first of its kind in the world, it is unusual LeRoy did not mention her earlier. The *Virginia* (also still often called *Merrimack*) sailed into Hampton Roads on March 8 and sank the USS *Cumberland* and USS *Congress*, and the USS *Minnesota* grounded. Darkness ended the fighting.

65 LeRoy is proud of this company, which bears his family's name and monetary sponsorship.

66 The "Ericsson" is a reference to the USS *Monitor*, a John Ericsson-designed ironclad with a revolving turret that arrived in Hampton Roads the evening of March 8 and engaged the CSS *Virginia* the next day. The *Monitor* inflicted some damage on the *Virginia*, though both ships eventually withdrew for different reasons, ending the first battle of iron ships in a technical draw. LeRoy's follow-up news about the USS

sheets to go to Atlanta. Thomas played chess with me and I beat. Played with Father also. Georgia has responded to the call for 12,000 men nobly. Hurrah. 22,000.

Wednesday March 12th 1862: Cool, cloudy day. Mother gone to a meeting of the Soldiers Relief Society. Companies are passing through every day; 2 or 3 today.[67] We took 4 gunboats at Norfolk, Virginia. General Beauregarde has taken command of the army of Mississippi. Generals Polk and Bragg will be connected with him in the command.[68] Martial law is proclaimed in Memphis. President Davis has suspended Generals Floyd + Pillow for their conduct at Fort Donelson. I am reading *Nemesis*. It is "said" General Loring has been ordered to North Carolina and General Pemberton[69] to South Carolina and Georgia. The *Merrimac* was very slightly damaged in the late affair. Rained hard for an hour or two on this eve. Made a "bow" today – got a letter from Auntie today, who had arrived safe and was lodged in a private house 6 miles from Manassa. Has had a "conversation" with Mrs. Gen. Johnston at the Spottswood [Hotel] in Richmond. Met Cousin George on the way. Grandma is still in Sparta with Sallie. Glorious. "Old Bibb."

Thursday March 13th 1862: Cool, cloudy day. Father left for Marietta. Two trains of soldiers went out on the M.+W.R.R., heavily loaded. I received a Norfolk paper today from Uncle John, with accts of the fight in it. He witnessed the whole from Sewall's Point. Most of our men were killed under a flag of truce while saving the crew of the sinking *Congress*. "A mean Yankee trick"! Hancock [County] was called upon for 40 men and responded with 96! "Good for Hancock." 5 P.M.: Commenced to rain and rained 'till near light. Thomas killed 4 robins. There are vague reports of a heavy battle, or rather a series of battles in Benton County, Arkansas. Our forces, 30,000. Men are under VanDorn, McCullough, Price, Mcintosh + Slack. Our loss is very heavy including Generals McCulloch and McIntosh. General Price wounded. The result is not ascertained.[70]

Congress was incorrect. She was burned by hot shot fired from the *Virginia* the previous day. Confederate losses totaled 95 from all causes, while Union losses were 369 and two valuable frigates lost.

67 Macon was a major rail hub used to shuttle troops to various points of the Confederacy.

68 Gen. Bragg moved north from Pensacola, FL with reinforcements for the Confederate army gathering in northern Mississippi.

69 Gen. William W. Loring; Gen. John C. Pemberton.

70 The Battle of Pea Ridge (March 7-8, 1862) in Arkansas. Confederate generals Price and Van Dorn were beaten by Gens. Samuel Ryan Curtis and Franz Sigel. Confederate Gens. James M. McIntosh, William Y. Slack, and Ben McCulloch. The important victory kept the Rebels out of Missouri and opened up a large swath of Arkansas to Union forces.

Friday March 14th 1862: Warm, cloudy day. The chagrin of the "Yankees" about the "terrible" *Merrimac* is unfounded. "Old Abe" even going so far as to shed crocodile tears over the destruction of two of their best ships. More news from Arkansas. We whipped on the 7 ~~8th~~. On the 8th, we fell back 13 miles. On the 8th by a flank movement had cut off his baggage and completely surrounded him. Finished *Nemesis*. Rained hard at 6.P.M.

Saturday March 15th 1862: Warm, windy, and clear. Mother got a letter from Grandma, with one from Uncle Richard enclosed. He is in six miles of Elizabeth City. Commissioner Yancey[71] has arrived in New Orleans. The "Vandals"[72] have occupied Fernandina, Florida, Brunswick, St, Mary's, Florida. Nearly all the citizens had left. I expect they'll be sorely disappointed in the booty they find in the "Land of Flowers." Wrote in M.L.C's album.[73] Father arrived here at 12 A.M. Rained very hard in the night last night.

Sabbath day March 16th 1862: Cold and cloudy. Our forces have evacuated Centreville and the enemy have occupied it. We have also left Leesburg and Winchester. Our men have nearly all left Pensacola and the enemy may take it at any time. There is a general drawing in of our lines. Floyd's Brigade is at Chattanooga. There has not been much Union sentiment displayed in Nashville as yet. The "Army of Columbus" is now at Island No. 10! A very strong point on the Mississippi near New Madrid. A fight is expected, at the latter place, daily. A steamer with powder and arms has arrived in Charleston. Frank Nisbet is still very ill indeed. Read *The Farmers Daughter* through today. It is very good.

Monday March 17th 1862: Warm, bright, beautiful day. Thomas killed 9 robins and 5 maybirds in 6 shots. Cousin Eliza and Aunt Sarah called. She has got another baby.[74] Mr. Wills also called: "Dave" is in jail, having been run away over a week.[75] Captain

---

71 William L. Yancey was a distant relative of the Greshams through his Uncle Edgeworth Bird. Yancey was a staunch supporter of slavery and secession and worked for Davis' administration as a diplomat. He had been in England attempting to court British support for the Confederacy and passed through New Orleans on his way back to Richmond.

72 LeRoy's use of the word "Vandals"—a migratory war-like Germanic tribe or group of tribes—evidences how widely read he was by such a young age.

73 Likely Mary Campbell. Writing in someone's autograph album was an honor bestowed by its owner.

74 Gertrude Snider, born in Macon on January 8, 1862.

75 Dave was returned to the Greshams. How or whether he was punished is unknown.

Smith and Major Hardeman are elected Colonels at Griffin.[76] I shot a robin this eve. My head aches very bad. No decided news from Missouri. It is uncertain which side whipped. The fight was <u>very</u> bloody.

Teusday March 18th 1862: Warm, clear, delightful day. Father left for Houston to day. Howard went down too, to carry "Dave." Have got a pain in my back and shoulders. "Voila"! Thomas killed 2 robins and a thrush with his bow. We have bird pies for dinner "Robins thick"! Hoppy. New Bern, North Carolina is taken.[77] Our men made a slight effort to hold it. General Johnston is in Huntsville with his army. President Davis is on his way west. New Madrid is evacuated which <u>greatly</u> endangers Island No. 10 and consequently Memphis.[78] Read *The Wide, Wide, World* today. Minnie is on her 8th pair of socks.[79]

Wednesday March 19th 1862: Cloudy and warm. I received a long letter from Aunty today. She is at Gordonsville, [Va]. Uncle Edge was at Culpeper, 40 miles off. Uncle John's letter to mother gives nothing new. Pain in my back better today. General R.E. Lee has been made commander-in-chief of the Confederacy.[80] Commenced to rain at 11A.M. and continued to do so until night. Read *Only a Pauper*, a Sunday School Book. It is very good.[81]

Thursday March 20th 1862: Rained hard all night and is raining now. Warm. Howard returned from Houston thoroughly wet. He was in the rain all day yesterday. Mr. Cook, a member of the "Gresham Rifles," was buried here day before yesterday. Minnie wrote to Cousin "Teadee." About dinner-time it cleared off, and the wind blew hard.

---

76 Smith of the 44th Georgia, and Hardeman of the 45th Georgia.

77 The Battle of New Bern (March 14, 1862) was part of the Burnside Expedition. Poorly trained militia units led by Gen. Lawrence O'Bryan Branch were defeated by Burnside's troops. New Bern remained under Federal control for the remainder of the Civil War.

78 Battle of Island Number Ten (Feb. 28-April 8, 1862) was fought near New Madrid near the Kentucky bend of the Mississippi River where a strong Confederate position blocked Union access south down the river. The loss of New Madrid (and then Island No. 10 on April 7), opened the river south to just above Memphis.

79 Knitting socks and other items for Confederate soldiers was considered an appropriate contribution for a young lady of Minnie's age and societal position. The daughters of Robert E. Lee also regularly knitted socks.

80 Lee was President Davis' military advisor, not the Confederacy's commander-in-chief.

81 LeRoy tends to read the PSS (Presbyterian Sunday School) books on Sundays while the family attends church services; this was on a Wednesday.

General C.W. Randolph is now secratary of war.[82] Commenced to Read *Castle Avon* today.

Friday March 21st 1862: Cold + windy. The steamer *Minnesota* was so badly damaged that she could not be kept up, and after being dismantled, sunk. Frank Nisbet is recovering. Our loss at New Bern was about 500; Yankees nearly double. We do not play chess at all now, Tom being disgusted with it.[83] Father returned home this even by the upper road. The river is very high like September 1861. Cousin George Jones made us a short visit this eve on his way to Manassa. The "Jackson Artillery" is home again. Thomas has gone to a concert given for the benefit of the Ladies Gunboat.[84]

Saturday March 22nd 1862: Windy, cold, and cloudy. The *Minnesota* is "alive" and "kickin." A "reliable gentleman" said she was sunk. I passed a most uncomfortable night in consequence of a pain in my hip. Thomas, who, by the way, thinks nothing of hitting a wad at the distance of 30 feet every time, killed a robin today with my bow. The concert was a decided success, a house full. Cousin Charlie is at home. Finished *Castle Avon*; Charlie is an unnatural character. At ¼ past 11A.M, it sleeted for about the space of one minute. It is <u>very</u> cold indeed <u>now</u>.

Sabbath day March 23d 1862: It is cold and cloudy, and it drizzled a little in the morn. At 7:50 it commenced to snow and continued to do so about 10 minutes. There was no service today, Mrs. Wills being sick. I have had my old troublesome enemy, the pain in hip and back, in full force today, and yesterday. Last night I took a Dover's Powder which gave me a quiet night and made me feel sleepy and bad today. Read *Clara Stanley*.

Monday March 24, 1862: Cold, cloudy day. Rubbed my back with liniment last night and took some brandy in going to bed, but did not go to sleep, and had to take a Dover's Powder. Today I am worse still. A <u>constant</u>, never <u>ceasing</u>, pain. No sleep at night, no rest in the day. It hailed very hard yesterday at 6 P.M. for a ¼ of an hour. I enjoyed eating it very much and ran about a good deal which made my leg worse.[85]

82 The youngest grandson of Thomas Jefferson, Gen. George Wythe Randolph, was tapped as secretary of war when Judah P. Benjamin became Davis' secretary of state.

83 Why Thomas was "disgusted" with chess is unknown. His refusal to play greatly disappointed LeRoy, who relied upon mental stimulation to make up for what he could not accomplish physically.

84 The proceeds of the concert went to support the Ladies Soldiers Relief Society project, which at that time was raising money to construct the ironclad CSS *Georgia* in Savannah. The ladies also held raffles and sales of their jewelry, paintings, silver-plate, and other precious items to raise some $5,000.

85 A hail storm was an uncommon event. LeRoy could not run, so his use of the word "ran" should not be taken literally. He spent nearly all of his time lying down or reclined, but would very occasionally move about on his own or on crutches. Being a young boy, he naturally tried to do more than he could or

"Brown's Infantry" is at home. A greater part will reinlist. Beaufort, North Carolina is virtually in Yankee hands. Consequently the *Nashville* put to sea. She was fired at 40 times. The 2nd Georgia Battery is at Goldsboro. There is vague rumors of the Yankees bombarding Island No. 10 for four days, but without success. The contributions of brass for cannon goes bravely on.[86] Father is planting elms on the side walk. Mother is making Father's shirts. Received a letter from Grandma today. C.M. Wiley [is] Adj. 44th Georgia.[87] Willis came up from Houston tonight, bringing 12 hams. I lay on the floor in the eve, feeling stupid + sleepy.[88]

Teusday March 25th 1862: Clear cool beautiful day, or at least every body says so. My hand trembles very bad and I am hardly able to write. I am a great deal easier today for which I am very thankful. I took a "Dover" and had my back rubbed. Slept until about 11½ A.M. at which fashionable hour I arose and partook of breakfast. I took one of Dr. Spencer's celebrated pills today. Also some Seltzer. "Georgia Cadets," a boy company, is just formed here. No Union sentiment in Nashville yet. Father and Thomas went to Milledgeville for Thomas to be examined and entered into College.[89] Jim Campbell came up to play chess with me, but my leg was too bad. It grows much worse toward night. Thomas shot a good many robins today. Went out a little while. Tracy came up to see us, and Mother was gone down town. 10 P.M.: Father and Thomas just got back. They were about a minute too late. Just as they came in sight the train left.

Wednesday March 26th 1862: Windy + warm. Slept bad. Took a Dover's Powder and a Spencer's pill. This morn, I took two more pills and a dose of Seltzer. Tom killed 2 robins with his bow. The sitting room is completely dismantled: the carpet up, the pictures down, and we are in Mother's room. Mother is in bed. Commodore Tattnall has been appointed to the command of the *Virginia*.[90] Mother sent down some brass for cannon today.

---

should. Three years after his 1856 injury, for example, his father wrote his mother that he had to warn LeRoy not to try and slide on the ice like the other boys.

86 Civilians began collecting brass bells from churches and plantation fields (the City Hall bell was exempt because it was needed to raise fire alarms). Macon's women collected 120 pounds of brass household utensils, but it was not used because zinc was in most household brass items.

87 This is the same Cousin Charlie mentioned earlier in the entry for Saturday, March 22, 1862.

88 "Stupid" (or groggy) is a reference to how the various medicines and home remedies he was taking made him feel.

89 Oglethorpe College in Milledgeville.

90 Josiah Tattnall, Jr. assumed command of CSS *Virginia* following the Battle of Hampton Roads.

Thursday March 27th 1862: Clear + warm. Took a Dover's Powder last night. Father and Thomas went to Milledgeville last night. The enemy are still firing on Island No. 10, and our side are confident of holding it. 2 Yankee boats sunk. At New Bern, the Yankees raised the white flag twice but we didn't see it and run. We killed 1500. Our Killed 500. My leg still hurts me some.

Friday March 28th 1862: Clear + warm. Father and Thomas got home safe last night at 12 oclock. Thomas entered third term Sophomore very easy. I slept very poor last night. My leg gave me a great deal of pain, although I took a Dover's Powder. General Stonewall Jackson has had a fight near Winchester[91] and was compelled to retreat: Our force 9000; Yankees 18000. Our loss 150 to 400 Yankee. "Enormous." The river at Island No. 10 is rising so fast that it is thought we will not be able to hold it long. Cousin Eliza sent a jar of preserves yesterday which were splendid. Father put a Belladonna plaster on my back this eve.[92] Mother in bed. Thomas wrote a letter to Grandma today.

Saturday March 29th 1862: Warm, spring day. Spent a better night with the usual remedy and feel better today. Fred came today and helped to put down the oilcloth[93] and it looks very nice too. Mother up a little this eve. Plaster is very comfortable. Put all the books in the bookcase today which helps things considerably. Old Abe has taken command of the army. Minnie spent the eve at Cousin Eliza's. Read *Eclectic Magazine* all the evening. Have not got my lesson for over a week on account of sickness.

Sabbath day March 30th 1862: Warm, clear. Mother too unwell to go to church. I slept very bad. My plaster itched all night so I had to take a Dover's Powder. It itches now. Read *Wings + Stings*. Very warm. Took the plaster off tonight and it had drawn very much indeed.

Monday March 31st 1862: Warm spring day. Went out a little while today. Howard left for Houston. Tracy came up to see us and was very smart and pretty. He is learning to talk. It has been a regular warm summer day. My back is better though it keeps me constantly scratching. Thomas cut off the hedge. Sat after tea with all the windows open.

Macon Tuesday April 1st 1862: Warm and clear. The waste house of the Factory, a building of little value, was consumed by fire last night at bedtime. Annie Johnson

---

91 The First Battle of Kernstown (March 23, 1862) was a rare tactical defeat for Gen. Stonewall Jackson, but an overall strategic victory that set the 1862 Shenandoah Valley Campaign into motion.

92 Belladonna is a poisonous plant, its leaves and root used to make medicine since ancient times. Atropine, derived from Belladonna, is effective at relaxing muscle spasms.

93 Painted oilcloth was often used to protect a floor and was often as elaborate as carpeting.

came to see Mother yesterday. Read *Deerstalkers* today. "You're an April fool, reader." Mother gone down to see Aunt Sarah.

Wednesday April 2nd 1862: Warm and cloudy. Mr. and Mrs. Pitzer got here from Sparta at 12 oclock last night. Some kind of barefooted rogue came and took nearly all the chickens in the coop. Howard did not come home until near 8 oclock last night, having driven slow on account of Duke's being a little ailing. There was a man shot down town yesterday on Mulberry St. The murderer, Ware by name, was arrested. Both men were from Twiggs Co. Mrs. Whitehead sent me a beautiful boquet by Mr. Pitzer. Mr. Mickle and Dr. Patterson of Griffin dined here. Dr. Safford called to see Mr. Pitzer. As I write at 4 in the evening . . . Mother and Mrs. Pitzer are down town. The trees begin to show Spring.

Thursday April 3d 1862: Warm + cloudy. Commenced to rain yesterday evening at dark and rained all night till 12 noon. Presbytery[94] did not meet, on account of the rain, until this morn. Mr. Bates and Mr. Reid came up after tea. Dr. Patterson and Mr. Mickle left for Columbus after supper. Drs. Wilson and Talmage came to dinner today. Mother and Mrs. Pitzer have gone to Presbytery this evening. Hardeman + Smith's regiments are ordered to Goldsboro, North Carolina. Captain John Morgan,[95] the rebel Scout of Tennessee, is now making a great show by his bravery and daring in taking any straggling parties of the enemy venturing to go in their very midst. The other day he captured a train of cars. There is still a lurking pain in my hip which worries me at night very much.

Friday April 4th 1862: Warm + cloudy. Rained so hard last night that the ladies did not go out to hear Dr. Beman.[96] Thomas and I played backgammon after tea. Mother being very unwell went to bed early. Mother bought a bottle of ink yesterday. The pain in my hip has returned and I had to take a Dover's Powder last night. Mr. Byne came here to stay yesterday eve. Mr. Reid is moderator of the Presbytery. Grandma sent the book Thomas wrote for by Mr. Newton. Mrs. Pitzer and M[other] went to Presbytery

94 The annual Georgia Presbytery meetings were held in Macon in 1862; many of the visitors during this time were participants.

95 Gen. John Hunt Morgan, who would gain lasting fame as a Southern cavalry commander.

96 Rev. Carlisle Pollock Beman, D.D. was also a distant relation.

this morn. In the evening, Mrs. Pitzer went out to the cemetery. I have been sick since and took a little brandy and had a poultice put on me.

Saturday Apr 5th 1862: Warm and clear. I was quite sick all night and not able to get up today at all. Pain in my hip very bad. Dr. Beman went home today. I slept with mother last night and Tom [slept] in the back-parlor. Dr. Wilson[97] preached last night! There was also a very large prayermeeting in the church at 4 P.M. Mrs. P.S. Holt called to see Mrs. Pitzer. Tracy came up early this morning to see Dr. Beman. Thomas writes this for me this afternoon and mother has gone to church.

Sabbath day April 6th 1862: Rained very hard early in the morn but cleared off bright and warm before church time. Dr. Axson[98] preaches. It is communion, too. Mr. Kaughman preached last night in the church. Mr. Houston in the day. I write this lying in Mother's bed and in a very awkward position. I slept a great deal better last night than I have done in a good while before. I was suffering the most terrible pain when I took the Dover's Powder, and it gave me relief almost instantaneous. I took a Blue Pill last night, and am in terror of a dose of <u>oil</u>.[99] Mr. Pitzer addressed the Methodist Sunday School today and Dr. Wilson preaches in the church. Mr. Byne went home last night; at 9 Mr. Lane called. Mr. and Mrs. Pitzer went to tea at Judge Nisbet's. Mr. Pitzer preached in our church in the evening and Dr. Wilson at night. Took Blue mass again.

Monday April 7th 1862: Warm + clear. Slept tolerable. Took Citrate of Magnesia. I have eaten literally nothing since Saturday but tea and feel very weak. A battle is pending at Yorktown.[100] The two armies are so near together that there has been some heavy skirmishing. There will be reinforcements sent from the Army of the Rappahannock. I received a long letter from Auntie today, and she seemed to think Toombs and several other brigades would go to Goldsboro. Colonel Thomas of the 15th had resigned and Major Mcintosh is now colonel. The bells rang long and loud this morn on the receipt of a dispatch saying there had been a great battle near Corinth

---

97 Future president Woodrow Wilson's father, the Rev. Joseph Ruggles Wilson of Augusta, Georgia, who was instrumental in the split of the southern Presbyterian church from that of the North.

98 Rev. Isaac Stockton Keith Axson of Savannah, grandfather of Woodrow Wilson's first wife, Ellen Louise Axson. He performed their wedding (along with Wilson's father) in Savannah.

99 Castor oil, which was used as a laxative and the bane of children for generations. LeRoy's lack of activity, together with the opium in Dover's Powder, would have made him constipated.

100 Gen. George B. McClellan opened the Peninsula Campaign by shifting the Union Army of the Potomac by sea to the tip of the Virginia peninsula in mid-March. His objective was to move quickly inland and capture Richmond before the Confederates in northern Virginia could react. Yorktown, however, was heavily fortified and the first major obstacle McClellan faced, together with bad roads made worse by heavy rains.

and a glorious victory. This is "Jubus"?[101] The Yankee General Shields lost an arm in the late "Battle of Winchester."[102]

Battle at Corinth

Tuesday April 8th 1862: Warm and clear; Great and Glorious Victory! The whole Federal army in full retreat and the Confederates in hot pursuit! General Prentiss is a prisoner! General Grant was the commander of the Federals! Our commander General Sydney Johnston fell leading our men to victory! A glorious death! The fight raged all day Sunday; 2000 prisoners sent to the rear. Loss awful on both sides. We attacked the enemy in strong position. General Buell not in the fight. This is a very great victory. We took nearly all the artillery. The men were Alabamians, Missisipians, and Lousianians.[103] Dr. Fitzgerald came to see me and prescribed some stuff for me to take 3 times a day. Last night I dressed and came into the sitting room to bid Mrs. and Mr. Pitzer and Dr. Wilson Goodbye. I am up and feel tolerable. Colonel Goulding is dead.[104] The Battle of Corinth was at a little place called Shiloh church.[105] It

101 Doubtful or skeptical.

102 Gen. James Shields' arm was broken, but not amputated. He was the only person to serve as U.S. Senator for three different states (Illinois, Minnesota, and Missouri).

103 The Battle of Shiloh (Apr. 6-7, 1862) in southern Tennessee just north of Corinth, Miss. Gen. A. S. Johnston led the Confederate Army of Mississippi north from Corinth in a surprise attack against Gen. Grant's Army of the Tennessee camped along the Tennessee River near Shiloh Church. The attack was initially very successful, inflicted heavy casualties, and drove back much of the Union army. Johnston was killed early in the action, however, and Gen. Beauregard assumed command. He relayed premature news of a great victory to Richmond that evening. The Union Army of the Ohio under Gen. Don Carlos Buell reached the field that night, and Grant assumed the offensive the next morning, driving the Southern army off the battlefield in a stunning turnabout. LeRoy is referencing Union Gen. Benjamin M. Prentiss, who was captured at Shiloh. Combined losses exceeded 24,000 men. The bloody and hard-fought battle shocked the entire nation, and everyone now realized the war would be long and costly.

104 Edwin Ross Goulding, 9th Georgia Infantry, from Talbottom, Ga., died of disease at Orange Court House, Va., April 4, 1862. LeRoy had a particular interest in the fate of Georgia soldiers.

105 He is referencing the Battle of Shiloh, which was called by several names.

commenced to rain at about 8 oclock and has rained very hard until 8 P.M. Thomas was packed + ready to start to Milledgeville but was detained by the rain. My leg pains me just enough to keep me awake at night. We are still sitting without a fire.

Wednesday April 9th 1862: Clear, bright, pleasant day. Rained in perfect torrents the whole night, accompanied by very heavy thunder + lightning. Cousin Sallie Wiley[106] got here this morn. She was on her way to Columbus. They left here last night and the track washed away before them. On trying to come back, they found the track had washed away behind. She brought her little girl along with her. Her name is Birdie.[107] I received a letter from Wilson. I commenced to take my medicine today.

Thursday April 10th 1862: Cool + clear. The wind blew very hard yesterday, and before night it turned coldish. Thomas went off to College last night. I will miss him a great deal. There is no more reliable news from Corinth. Beauregard, it is thought, has retreated on the receipt of large reinforcements by the enemy. The Yankees have commenced to bombard Fort Pulaski. Mother and Cousin Sallie have rode out to the cemetery. I have had a head ache and felt dull and stupid all day. I slept very bad last night. I wrote to Aunty today.

Friday April 11th 1862: Cool and cloudy. Not much of importance occurred in the long, dull, painful day. I lay in bed all day. Cousin Sallie sat in Mother's room. There are no reliable dispatches from Corinth. The firing on Pulaski is still going on.

Saturday April 12th 1862: Cloudy + warm. Slept bad. Had to take a small Dover's Powder. I am out of bed today. Nothing in the world seemed to agree with me. I threw up yesterday morn. I have not had a bit of appetite; I do believe I've got regular Dyspepsia [indigestion]. Cousin Sallie left here this morn for Columbus via Atlanta + Lagrange. The Southwestern road will not be in running order for a week or two. Fort Pulaski has surrendered. It is reported that there has been a fight at Corinth between Buell and our men. Our loss 5000; Federal 20000 including Generals Buell + Wallace.[108] They were completely routed and driven to their gunboats. Surrender? numbers of prisoners taken. The iron Ram *Virginia* has gone out again.[109] We have just

---

106 Cousin Sarah Elizabeth "Sallie" Carnes was married to Samuel Harris Wiley. They are both distant cousins to both the Gresham and the Bird families.

107 Sarah Bird "Birdie" Wiley, one of the ten children in the family.

108 Gen. Lewis "Lew" Wallace. This news was the result of rumors, for there was no fighting yet around Corinth.

109 The CSS *Virginia* steamed back into Hampton Roads in search of a fight with the USS *Monitor*, but the Union commander declined to risk his ironclad and no battle ensued.

got a letter from Thomas, and there was a wash on the road before him which occasioned some delay in getting there. His umbrella was stolen at Gordon. He is getting along very well indeed. I have stopped taking my medicine.[110]

Sunday April 13th 1862: Damp and ugly all the morning, and about eleven oclock it commenced to rain and is raining steadily now. My leg hurts me a good deal in the night, and is pretty bad now. I wrote to Thomas last night. I read the *Robby Family* P.S.S. this morning. The enemy 17,000 strong are at Huntsville, [Alabama]. It looks <u>very</u> much as if they would come everywhere soon. My appetite is a "<u>leetle</u>" better today, always fluctuating.

Monday April 14th 1862: Rain! Rain! All night long. Warm and cloudy. 2 to 300 sick soldiers are coming up here from Savannah and they have rented the Floyd house as a hospital.[111] Last night they sent around bedticks to be made and Mother got up early this morning and made 4 of them. The wire had just jumped up and knocked two of the shades of the chandelier off and smash, they came down to the floor.[112] Sent off two dailies to Thomas this morn. No school today. The Volunteers are going off tonight to Savannah. While the [train] passengers were out at breakfast up on the State road, a party of Federals numbering 20 men run off with the engine and 3 cars. 17 have been captured.[113] Mother was taken sick at dinner and soon after Father was taken with the colic [abdominal pain] and wanted brandy, but the closet key could not be found until he was so bad off that he had to take laudanum.[114] Mother was sick all night. Run ahead of time.

Teusday April 15th 1862: Warm and cloudy. Slept tolerably, but was annoyed by my cough. The Macon Volunteers, Company B, left for Savannah last night. Mr. Polhill's

---

110 We do not know what Dr. Fitzgerald prescribed for LeRoy, but it obviously made him so sick that he stopped taking it.

111 Dr. William Henry Doughty, a physician from Augusta, Georgia, was named head physician at Floyd House Hospital.

112 A bedtick is a homemade bag filled with straw or feathers to serve as a mattress. Wire was often used to give the mattress its form.

113 The "Great Locomotive Chase" or "Andrews' Raid" was one of the more colorful events of the Civil War. Civilian scout James J. Andrews led a handful of Union soldiers behind enemy lines to Atlanta, where they stole a train and steamed toward Chattanooga intent on damaging the railroad as they moved north. Confederates pursued them for 87 miles on the Western and Atlantic RR before Andrews and his men scattered. All were eventually caught. Andrews and seven others were hanged for espionage.

114 Laudanum, a combination of 10% powdered opium, or the equivalent of 1% morphine, was a potent narcotic used for pain.

and Branham's schools are both stopped.[115] Wrote a long letter to Thomas. Suffered with a headache nearly all day. Coughing very bad.

Wednesday April 16th 1862: Warm, clear. Suffered terribly with headache all night and all day today. It is aggravated by my cough which has returned as bad as in my worst days; expectorating all the time. When I cough it feels as if my head would come open. I lay perfectly quiet all day but it is as bad as possible. My leg is a good deal better today Cousin Jinnie and Mr. Blount called yesterday. I am not able to write hardly at all.

Thursday April 17th 1862: Warm and clear. Suffered with headache all night and have still got it. I took a Dover's Powder and I counted the strokes of the hour from nine till four. The 2nd Georgia Battery arrived here early this morn. The fight with General Buell at Corinth [Shiloh] the second day was drawn. The Yankees say <u>their</u> loss was 20 000 and ours 38,000, about as many as we had in the field. General Wallace is dead. General Gladden C.S.A. has died of his wounds.[116] General Bragg is made a full General. General Grant would not let us bury our dead, saying that he had already done it. The conscription act has passed: every man between 18 and 35 is bound to go and by October. Thomas will be one of them.[117] 2 soldiers died yesterday at the Floyd house. No school scholars [as they are] all down town. Teusday night Minnie went to the concert with Robert Plant.[118] Uncle John came up after tea and told us of what he had seen and heard: A description of the *Virginia* vs. the *Monitor* and the whole fight [is out].

Friday April 18th 1862: Warm, clear, delightful day. Got a letter from Thomas. Howard left for Houston. I took an anodyne.[119] My head was very bad and still pains me. Cough <u>bad.</u> Slept very heavily. Nose bled several times. There has been a small

---

115 There is no explanation given as to why the two schools closed.

116 Gen. Adley H. Gladden. In fact, the second day at Shiloh (April 7) was a Union victory and the Rebels were driven off the field.

117 The Confederacy passed the first conscription law in American history on April 16, 1862, drafting men ages 18-35 for a three-year term. Men subject to the draft (there were many types of exemptions) could hire substitutes.

118 One of Minnie's earliest suitors.

119 An anodyne (a common medical term before the 20th century) is a substance used to reduce pain or discomfort. Today we refer to them as analgesics or painkillers. Because so many things could be an anodyne (from a narcotic to an herb), it is impossible to know what he was taking without more information.

fight at Yorktown between General Cobb's brigade[120] and the enemy, which last were repulsed; nearly all of General Johnston's army is on the peninsula. Toombs' brigade has gone down there.

Saturday April 19th 1862: Warm and cloudy. Pain in my head still very bad. I can not explain it at all. Cousin Howard Tinsley came up to dinner + tea yesterday. Howard came home this even and brought some chickens. Betty is very low. We heard from Thomas to~yesterday~ and he is getting along finely [in Milledgeville]. Macon Volunteers, Company B, returned home to day after a campaign of less than a week. Minnie's bureau got here safely today and it is a little beauty. Minnie is delighted with it too.

Sabbath day April 20th 1862 A.D.: Warm and cloudy. Took an anodyne pill and slept until 10 oclock. My head is better today, though it ached all night. Rained a little. My cough is pretty bad, and I take a gargle for it. Father rubbed my throat last night. Commenced to rain about dark and rained until we went to bed. It is also a little cooler. There is no news of importance in the papers.

Monday April 21st 1862: Windy + cool. Slept tolerable [but my] cough, very hard. Mr. Branham's school will start again soon. No news. Island 10 is taken with all the men and guns. It looks very much as if we would be overun.[121] Minnie's bureau is up and looks beautiful. Aunty is in Richmond now, and I reckon will leave there before long. Minnie got a letter from Sallie and she is at Mrs. Richardson's and Grandma at Mrs. Delony's. The Ross Volunteers have come home. My cough has troubled me all day. If it was'nt for that I'd be pretty well. . . . Governor Brown has turned over the state troops to the government and General [Henry] Jackson, having resigned, Savannah is in a state of utter confusion and can be taken without any trouble.

Tuesday April 22nd 1862: Cold and windy. Did not sleep well. Father went to the plantation in the morn. There has been a fight at Elizabeth City[122] and the 3d Georgia Regiment was in it. The 3d and another regiment attacked the enemy, but there being a larger number of them than they thought was obliged to retreat to a "strong position." I

---

120 Gen. Howell Cobb's brigade. Essentially, the armies that had once faced one another in northern Virginia after First Manassas in July 1861 were now confronting one another on the Virginia peninsula. Heavy rains, bad roads, and strong fieldworks slowed the Union advance.

121 This is LeRoy's second passing reference as to how vulnerable the South appeared to be to determined Union offensive efforts.

122 The Battle of South Mills (part of Burnside's Expedition) was an attempt to cut off Norfolk's naval yard via Elizabeth City and South Mills in NC. Gen. Ambrose R. Wright repulsed Union forces led by Gen. Jesse L. Reno, who retreated to New Bern.

got a letter from Thomas. There are a great many soldiers riding out every evening in buggies and carriages.

Wednesday April 23d 1862: Warm and bright spring day. Slept well. Went down town in the carriage with Mother and looked at the Floyd Rifles. They are splendidly drilled. I never saw any soldiers drill with as much ease and grace and I would have enjoyed it much more if the horses had not been frightened at the rattle of the muskets.[123] The Volunteers shot for a prize this morn. Wrote a letter to Thomas today.

Thursday April 24th 1862, A.D.: Warm, clear, bright, spring day. Uncle LeRoy got here last night just as we had finished tea. The South Western road has just commenced to run again. The enemy have been shelling Fort Jackson, New Orleans for two or three days but the fort still holds out.[124] The postage on letters is raised to ten cents. My cough is better today. Father came home from Houston this eve. Uncle LeRoy and I played backgammon + draughts nearly all the evening. I backgammoned him once. Uncle John came up after tea and we spent a very pleasant evening altogether.

Friday April 25th 1862: Warm + cloudy. No News. Brigadier General Breckinridge is made a Major General; General Hindman[125] ditto. General G.B. Crittenden has resigned. General Seigel[126] U.S.A. is dead. We received news from Grandma yesterday. She is in a bad state. Fell senseless in a room by herself and remained so until found; she does not know how long. Dr. Reese is thought to be dying. Has not spoken for 3 or 4 days. Captain I. Harvey Hull, Irish. Vol., 5th Georgia Regiment, is a prisoner. Commenced to rain at 6 in the evening.

Saturday April 26th 1862: Cloudy early in in the morning, and raining slowly towards noon. Rained heavily in the night. Thomas got here last night; Uncle LeRoy left here this morn for his plantation. Slept well. New Orleans is in Yankee hands taken by the gunboats. This is the plain unvarnished fact. The enemy are shelling Fort

---

123 The Gresham carriage horses were not used to the sound of gunfire and they became difficult to control.

124 The Battle of Forts Jackson and St. Philip took place over ten days beginning on April 18, 1862. The Union assault plan included bombardment and then slipping past the installations to essentially leave them useless. Adm. David G. Farragut did exactly that. His fleet then sailed upriver and captured New Orleans on April 29. Gen. Benjamin Butler governed the city under martial law.

125 Gen. Thomas C. Hindman, Jr.

126 Gen. Franz Sigel, a political general of German descent, was still very much alive.

Pillow.[127] Minnie has got a present of a little black puppy from G. Plant, esq.[128] 5 oclock: It has turned quite cool.

Sunday April 27th 1862: Cool, raw, disagreeable day. . . . I read *A Ray of Light*. Could not rest well last night on acct of a sort of soreness of the muscles of the abdomen, which hurt me very bad when I coughed. At 1 oclock. Father got up and gave me a pill. I have enjoyed Thomas' visit home <u>very</u> much and am very sorry he will have to go back so soon.[129]

Monday April 28th 1862: Cloudy and raw. Thomas left last night to my sorrow. The U.S. Gunboats arrived opposite New Orleans and demanded a surrender, which was refused by General Lovell who evacuated the city, burning as much cotton as he could.[130] Memphis and in fact all our river and seaport cities are as good as gone. "Gipsey," Minnie's dog, is doing very well but misses his "Mamma" at night <u>very</u> much. . . .

Tuesday April 29th 1862: Cool and cloudy, with dashes of sunshine. The weather has been dark and cloudy for two or three days. Howard went to Houston this morn. The Gunboats are at New Orleans and the authorities are making terms. Forts Jackson and St. Philips are still in our hands and the boats ran by them. They threaten to shell the city if our flag is not hauled down and so on. Uncle John came up after tea to bid us all Goodbye. He is gone by Agusta to Athens, where he'll stay two days and push on after his company at Petersburgh, Virginia.

Wednesday April 30th 1862: Cloudy and warm. Mr. Bates was taken sick soon after school took in and is quite sick now. There is a long account of the fight of the 3d Georgia at South Mills in the paper this morn. We got a letter from Grandma yesterday, with one from Aunty enclosed. She fell back from Richmond to Charlotte, North Carolina.[131] Rained hard from 4 oclock till night.

127 Located on the Mississippi River about four miles below Plum Point Bend.

128 George H. Plant, Robert's younger brother. Their father, Jucrease C. Plant, was a bank trustee in Macon.

129 LeRoy and Thomas were very close. In fact, Thomas would name his only son after his younger brother.

130 Gen. Mansfield Lovell would be loudly criticized for his failure to prevent the city's loss. In fact, he did not have enough men or guns to defend it. He was given an infantry division in Mississippi, but relieved because of his "poor" performance at New Orleans. He demanded a court of inquiry that met in April 1863 and cleared him. However, he did not get another assignment for the rest of the war.

131 Uncle Edge and Auntie had a very loving relationship, and she wanted to be as close to him as possible in case anything happened. The armies were moving up the peninsula toward Richmond, so

Thursday May 1st 1862: Rained in the night very hard. Rained slowly all the morn until noon, when it began to pour down and continued to do so until 3 oclock. Fort Macon, after making a pretty good fight, surrendered on condition that the garrison be released which was done.[132] The Floyd Rifles + Macon Volunteers, Company A, left last night with full ranks. The City Light Gaurd + the Spalding Grays went the night before. My cough is annoying beyond measure. I had to take an Anodyne for it last night. This is a very cool May Day.

Friday May 2nd 1862: Warm, bright, beautiful day. Stayed on my wagon all the morn. Got a letter yesterday from Grandma with one from Uncle Richard enclosed telling about the fight. Mother is sick in bed. I slept very badly last night. Took an Anodyne pill. Mr. Bates is recovering. No news. The Pulaski prisoners are in New York. "Gipsey" cries all the time to get into the house. He is improving. My cough is constant and annoys me very much. I have quit coffee + tea.

Saturday May 3d 1862: Clear, cool, beautiful day. Slept tolerable. No News. We are, in my opinion, being overrun. New Orleans is gone. They have attacked Cumberland Gap, [Kentucky], which will be taken of <u>course</u>. Bought some strawberries. 900 prisoners are daily expected here. Yesterday eve about 6 oclock it clouded up very black and rained hard after night. Received a letter from Grandma and one from Thomas. There are only 3 students who sleep on the campus. Strawberries for dining.

Sunday May 4th 1862: Beautiful bright day. . . . Got a letter from Uncle John in Athens. ~~Leaves~~ft on yesterday for the war. Mother still in bed. It is 5 years ago since I first lay down. It will soon be two since I laid down this time, and I often wonder whether I am going to get well again. My back is in a great deal worse condition than it was the other time. I [wish] there were a Doctor that "could tell" me something.[133] Forts Jackson + Philips [on the] Mississippi River have fallen and all our ships are sunk.

Monday May 5th 1862: Cool and cloudy. 700 Yankee prisoners are at the <u>Fairground</u>[134] <u>and I don't see how they'll be accommodated. LeRoy H. Washington</u> has got home from New Orleans and tells a big story: 10 gunboats of ours sunk and as many Yankee ones. A large amount of cotton, sugar, molasses, +c were destroyed. Commenced to rain at 2oc + rained hard for an hour.

Tuesday May 6th 1862: Cool, warm, sunny day. Commenced to rain yesterday eve at half past five, and rained very hard until dark. I went out and watched the boys play town ball. In the evening went down town and saw the Yankee prisoners. Some were drilling, others cooking, some playing ball.[135] Some were very dirty, others looked well. There are over 300 sick. The fair ground is full. Got a letter from Thomas.

Wednesday May 7th 1862: Cool, clear, sunny day. Sitting by a fire. The Napier Artillery is encamped at the Academy and they are a fine company, finely equipped in every way. They came up on the hill this eve and we saw them at a distance. Cousin George Jones came to see us this eve. He is just from Yorktown, which place is "evacuated" by our men. Norfolk is evacuated also, it is thought. The hostile armies are about 4 miles apart at Corinth [Mississippi] and must fight. Our army is reinforced by Price and Vandorn.

Thursday May 8th 1862: Warm and bright. Mrs. Judge Nisbet sent me a plate of cakes. Went out before school and watched the boys play. Father went over to Milledgeville this eve. I got a puppy today, but I find he is a female and I'll have to tell Dwight Roberts that I can't keep him. "Gipsey" is also a "female." The Yankees have appeared before Mobile, [Ala.] and I suppose will take it without trouble.

Friday May 9th 1862: Cool + clear. General Johnston has had a fight on the peninsular. While our forces were falling back, the enemy attacked our rear gaurd in force and was driven back. Our forces were under Longstreet, Stuart, + Early. The enemy's loss was heavy, including 900 prisoners and ten pieces artillery. Our loss 500. General [Jubal] Early is reported wounded. General Anderson killed.[132] Howard left for Houston taking Frank. Ten more prisoners arrived here today. Give my puppy away to a boy.

Saturday May 10th 1862: Cool in the house and hot out of doors. Father returned home last night at 1 oclock. He saw Thomas, who was well. My puppy, like a bad penny, came back this morn. The fighting at Corinth[133] is begun by Beauregarde's attacking the enemy. Stonewall Jackson is also fighting the enemy.[134] The press broke down last night and the daily came out in a little slip this morning.

Sabbath day May 11th 1862: Warm, clear day. The Central City Blues were in Jackson's fight. Had 4 killed 6 wounded, one mortally. All the other companies in the

---

132 The Battle of Williamsburg (May 5, 1862). Johnston's Confederates evacuated Yorktown and Union troops struck them in the rear during the retreat toward Richmond. The fighting was sharp but inconclusive, and Johnston pulled his army back to the outskirts of the capital. Losses in killed, wounded, and captured were 1,682 for the Confederates and about 2,300 for the Union. Gen. R. H. Anderson was not killed at Williamsburg.

133 After Shiloh, Union forces under Gen. Henry Halleck slowly made their way south toward the important rail junction at Corinth, Miss, where Gen. Beauregard's Confederate army was recovering from the Shiloh disaster.

134 The Battle of McDowell (May 8, 1862) in the Shenandoah Valley was an early battle in what would come to be known as Jackson's 1862 Shenandoah Valley Campaign. Stonewall Jackson's small command of 10,000 repulsed an attack by a smaller Union force under Gen. Robert Schenk.

regiment suffered more or less. ~~Capt~~ Reid of Putnam, Captain Furlow of Americus, Captain McMillan were killed. A dispatch from Beauregard [in MS] says he has driven back the enemy several miles. Howard returned yesterday. Had bad luck. Wagon got stuck twice; Duke broke the singletree.[135] . . . Mr. Wills preached to the prisoners.

Monday May 12th 1862: Warm and cloudy. Father got a letter from Thomas saying he would be home tonight or tomorrow night, being left entirely alone on the campus. Mr. Damour died here this morning. Mr. Harris has succeeded in raising his company, which goes into camp in a few days. Major Butts is elected Colonel 2nd Georgia Regiment and Mr. George Jones Captain Macon Volunteers.

Tuesday May 13th 1862: Cool and clear. Thomas arrived last night and is well. My back hurt me last night and I had to take a pill. Cough troublesome. The enemy at Corinth did not give General Beauregard a battle, but retired on his approach. Norfolk is evacuated. The *Virginia* blown up [and] our forces retired to Weldon.[136] G.W. Ross is Major [of the] 2nd Battalion. Everybody gone down town. Pain in my back too bad for me to go. Finished *The Conquest of Peru*.

Wednesday May 14th 1862: Warm and clear. Put on summer pants for the first time. Mother brought home two coats for me to try, but neither fit. I was so sore last night I took a pill and feel better today. About 5 P.M. it clouded up and looked like it would pour down. The wind blew very hard and raised clouds of sand. It rained very little + so it was a Simoon.[137]

Thursday May 15th 1862: Warm and cloudy early in the day, clearing up at noon. The gunboats are in the James River 35 miles from Richmond and 12 from Petersburg. Felt very weak and sore on going to bed last night aggravated by a continual hacking cough and took an anodyne pill as I have done for 4 nights past. Slept a greater part of the morn. Had a nice mess of strawberries for dinner. It rained a little in the night. Cough very hard and dry. Father bought me a new Marseilles coat.[138]

---

135 A singletree is the bar between the horse and wagon to which the traces were attached; Duke is one of the Gresham draft horses.

136 With Norfolk in Union hands, the CSS *Virginia* no longer had a home port. She drew too much water to get over the sandbar and up the James River, so the Confederates burned the ironclad.

137 A Simoon is a dry wind that blows sand in the Sahara. His use of the word demonstrates how widely he had read.

138 Marseilles cloth is very similar to matelassé, a complex type of woven fabric with a three-dimensional design formed on it by placing cording beneath two types of woven threads.

Friday May 16th 1862: Cool and clear. A day of special prayer appointed by President Davis. Service in all the churches. Aunt Eliza arrived here to supper and Cousin William[139] too. Cough <u>very</u> bad. Richard Edwards[140] came to see me this eve. Tracy came to see us this eve and is very well.

Saturday May 17th 1862: Cool and clear. Went to sleep at 3.A.M. Took an anodyne. Coughed all night. Did not get up to breakfast. Father bought me some quinine pills to stop the fever I have every eve.[141] Rained a little about sundown. Cousin Anna called to see Mother and Aunt Eliza.

Sunday May 18th 1862: Warm and clear. Rylander's Battalion is in town. Jackson Artillery went off last night. Cough little better. Cousin William left this morning. Rained in the night. Mary made me crackers.

Monday May 19th 1862: Cool and pleasant. Spent a very bad night. Cough annoying beyond measure. Pain in my back very bad. All my nice cough medicine is gone and I can get no more. One or more prisoners are buried here every day.[142] Two or three generally go in the procession. Aunt Eliza went out and got me quite a nice mess of straw + Raspberries. My delectable "pup" has arrived and has barely found his legs as yet.

Tuesday May 20th 1862: Pleasant day. Took a Dover's Powder. Aunt Eliza gone to spend the day at Aunt Ann's. They are taking up all the carpets up stairs and cleaning up. The Yankee boats are making their way to Richmond. Some of the *Monitor's* crew came ashore and were captured. L.P. Walker, Brigadier General, is captured.[143] Mother took dinner with Aunt Ann and they sent me some of the "goodies." Tracy came up to see Aunt Eliza this evening.

Wednesday May 21st 1862: Warm + clear. Thomas left for Houston early this morn. Aunt Eliza has got a puppy here and she is going to carry him home. Had to take a Dover's Powder to stop my cough. Had a violent coughing spell this morn. Went to sleep at 3 A.M. Today is Miss Katherine Clark's wedding day.

---

139 William Walker Carnes, Jr.

140 Richard Edwards was a friend of LeRoy's, and, according to the 1860 census, 14 years old.

141 This is the first time LeRoy mentions he is spiking a fever "every eve." He has many more ailments than he records.

142 As many as 1,400 prisoners would be in housed in Camp Oglethorpe by the summer of 1862, with as many as 500 requesting medical care daily. Mortality rates rose to as many as seven per day later.

143 LeRoy Pope Walker, the first Confederate secretary of state, was not captured. It is unclear why LeRoy thought so.

Thursday May 22nd 1862: Warm and clear. Our men under Heath [Heth] and Marshall have routed the Yankee army in Southwestern Virginia, and taken 1800 prisoners.[144] Dr. White of Milledgeville called to see me today. He examined my back thoroughly and prescribed for my cough. He says I must take iron too. Minnie is going to the dentists this eve. My cough is a little better. Thomas arrived home late this evening. Got a letter from Uncle John on the margin of a newspaper. He is elected surgeon. The 3d Georgia Regiment is ordered to Petersburgh, [Virginia].

Friday May 23d 1862: Warm and clear. Slept tolerable. Gipsey cried all night. Dr. White came to see me again today, and washed my throat with a solution of caustic. He recommended Porter for me.[145] There is a man in Milledgeville who makes my cough medicine. "Remus," Aunt Eliza's pup, is very smart and bright. Mine is not yet got any sense. Very heavy rain with loud thunder. Thomson Gaurds left Last night. Dr. Church is dead. He had a painful illness. Got a letter from Grandma. Mother + Aunt went down town and was caught in the rain.

Saturday May 24th 1862: Warm + cloudy. Aunt Eliza left here last night. I commenced to take my new medicine today. It has no taste hardly, and I don't think I'll mind it. Father brought home *Irving's Works*: Mother's anniversary present. Perfectly beautiful![146] It has been raining very heavily all the evening with heavy thunder.

Sabbath day May 25th 1862: Cool, damp, and unseasonable. Rained nearly all the morning and no one went to church. Sat by a fire in Mother's room. Mr. Wills' baby is very ill. Hennie Jones,[147] Cousin Jack's little girl, has Scarlet fever. Maggie Snyder also has it.[148] I have named my dog "Price" after the great Partisan [Sterling Price] and he (my dog) is very weakly. My cough [indecipherable] throat is a little better for a time.

144 Giles Court House (May 10, 1862), in southwestern Virginia. Gens. Heth and Marshall repulsed a small force of Federals who were part of a larger operation trying to move into Eastern Tennessee.

145 The exact nature of "solution of caustic" is unknown, but it was likely some sort of antiseptic throat gargle. "Porter" was dark beer, which some believed had medicinal properties.

146 A six-volume set of Washington Irving's collected works published in 1860 by the International Book Company of New York. The books had maroon embossed leather covers with gilt titling on the spines, with tissue paper placed over the pictures.

147 Henrietta E. "Hennie" Jones.

148 Madge Waldron Snider, one of Cousin Eliza's daughters.

Monday May 26th 1862: Chilly and cloudy. General Jackson has again met the enemy and routed them.[149] They are skirmishing within 7 miles of Richmond. All the prisoners left here Saturday except about 100.

Tuesday May 27th 1862: Cool and clear. There is a big rumor out to day. General Jackson has taken Winchester and 3 or 4,000 prisoners.[150] <u>Four</u> ships have got into Charleston with arms + munitions. One is a Confederate war steamer. I have slept well the last two or 3 nights having had scarcely any fever. My cough is better. Minnie had a bad tooth pulled today. Reading in Irving's *Sketchbook* and it's beautiful.

Wednesday May 28th 1862: Warm and pleasant. General Jackson's victory is confirmed by an official dispatch. On Friday, Banks' army was routed at Front Royal! On Sunday again at Winchester. A large amount of stores are taken. There is very heavy skirmishing around Richmond![151] At Corinth all's quiet. Father has a very bad cold and is nearly sick. Hennie and Jack both very sick. Maggie, better. Scarlet fever is very prevalent over town. Cousin Eliza is here. Cousin Jimmie[152] has got a discharge. Mrs. Wills' baby has Erysiphelus.[153] Got a letter from <u>Aunt</u> Eliza today and she and "Remus" got home safe + sound. Slept well. "Tom" is reading *Life of Columbus*; Minnie *Philip the Second*. I have had a slow headache all day. My new couch came home this even.

Thursday May 29th 1862: Warm + clear. Slept miserably and feel sore all over today. Howard left for Houston. Mother gone to the Soldiers Relief Society. Dr. White sent over my medicine today. To our joy Grandma and Sallie arrived here this morning at 12 A.M. Wrote to Aunt Eliza. Sallie + Minnie gone to see Tracy. Finished the *Sketchbook*. Touched my throat with "Nitrate of Silver."[154]

149 The Battle of Front Royal (May 23, 1862) in the Shenandoah Valley.

150 First Battle of Winchester (May 25, 1862). Stonewall Jackson defeated Nathaniel Banks' Union command and had by this time cleared most of the enemy forces out of the Valley. The name "Stonewall" was becoming a household word, and the authorities in Washington were growing alarmed by the Southern victories in the Valley.

151 Battle of Hanover Court House (May 27, 1862) north of Richmond was part of Gen. McClellan's deliberate approach toward the Southern capital. An ill-considered Confederate attack was repulsed.

152 James English Snider, Maggie's father, was discharged from the military for health reasons.

153 Erysipelas is an acute skin rash/lesions of the upper layer of skin, often with a high temperature and chills. Today it is easily treated with antibiotics, but in the 19th century it could be fatal.

154 Nitrate of silver was used as a disinfectant and had antimicrobial properties.

Friday May 30th 1862: Warm + clear. Read over some of Uncle Edge's letter and he is now Captain. The former Captain is Major. Mother has just made a cover to my couch and I am now lying on it. This is the warmest day we have had yet. Thomas went down to hear the boys speak. I had a fine mess of strawberries and raspberries out of our garden. The 2nd Georgia Battalion has moved from Wilmington to Petersburgh, Virginia.

Saturday May 31st 1862: Warm and hot. Commenced reading *Crayon Miscellany* by Irving. Slept well – took a dose of my new medicine and it is - - - "nasty." Mother is making starch.[155] Thomas went in the river first time yesterday. Howard got back yesterday and brought some plums. Sallie and Minnie pulled me around on Bond's hill. Grandma is sick this morning.

Summer Sabbath day June 1st 1862: Very warm day the first day of summer. The hottest day yet. Rumors of a heavy battle at Richmond. General Jackson is reported marching into Maryland. The "bloody" 3d Georgia Regiment is in Richmond. The 2nd Battalion is on its way. It is reported and believed our army at Corinth is falling back. This long, long! evening every body sleeping, and I alone in my glory. The musquitoes are here, though not thick. Slept tolerable. Grandma still very unwell indeed. 6 PM: Furious fighting at Richmond.

Monday June 2nd 1862: Warm and clear. Grandma still in bed sick. There was a great battle near Richmond Saturday though not a general engagement. There are no particulars except that we had driven them back a mile and a half, inch by inch! After hard fighting, had taken 3 batteries of artillery! Our wounded were coming in by hundreds. General Hatton Killed! Cam Tracy wounded! On Sunday General McClellan commanded in person. Our troops were enthusiastic, cheered by the presence of General Lee + President Davis! Carnage was terrible on both sides! The battle is not decided, but I am almost certain that our gallant troops gained a glorious victory!![156] Dr. Fitzgerald came to see Grandma this eve. Rained a little about 3 P.M. and heavily in the night with thunder and lightning. Mrs. Tracy leaves for Virginia tonight.

---

155 Boiled cornstarch used in ironing. One use example for its use was in keeping a woman's petticoats stiff.

156 The Battle of Seven Pines (Fair Oaks), May 31-June 1, 1862). Gen. Joe Johnston attacked McClellan's Union army, which was divided by a swollen river just east of Richmond. The attack plan was too difficult for a young army to pull off and it fell apart amidst heavy fighting. President Davis and his military advisor, Gen. Robert E. Lee, rode out to observe the fighting. Johnston was severely wounded near the end of the day. The inconclusive battle raged the next day. Davis used Johnston's injury to to appoint Lee to command the army, which Lee named the Army of Northern Virginia. Gen. Robert H. Hatton was killed; Lt. Campbell Tracy was the brother of Aunt Carrie and served in the 6th Ga. Inf. Regt.

Tuesday June 3d 1862: Cool, dark, and cloudy with drizzling rain. Rained heavily early in the night. Uncle LeRoy arrived here last night. Grandma is no better. Colonel Lomax[157] was killed in the late battle. Mrs. Tracy is not going on. They stopped fighting Sunday. A drawn battle! My cough is Troublesome. It has rained all day. I have just got over a terrible coughing spell which completed exhausted me. Dr. Fitzgerald cauterized my throat.[158]

Wednesday June 4th 1862: Cool and cloudy. Grandma better. Mother sick in bed. Reading [Irving's] *The Conquest of Granada*. Uncle LeRoy left for Alabama this morn. All quiet at Richmond. Dr. came to see Grandma. My cough is very, very, bad.[159] Miss Annie Johnston called. Uncle Leroy played backgammon last night and got beat. Mother has been very sick all day. The enrolling officer of the conscription is in town.[160]

Thursday June 5th 1862: Warm and clear. Mother is a good deal better. Finished *The Conquest of Granada* and think it splendid. Corinth [Mississippi] is evacuated by our forces.[161] No mail or news from Richmond. Had a fine mess of strawberries for dinner.

Friday June 6th 1862: Cool and rainy. Grandma down stairs. Mother up. Thomas left for the plantation early this morn. It is reported that General Stonewall is moving on Washington.[162] The fight at Richmond must have been a terribly bloody one but there is no news of it. It rained steadily all the morning until dinner. General Johnston is reported wounded in the late bloody engagement. The enemy are landing in force in

---

157 Confederate Col. Tennant Lomax from Eufaula, Ala., shared his premonition of death with Gen. John B. Gordon, who noted it in his memoirs. Many newspapers ran the story.

158 LeRoy mentions this so casually it is hard to know what to make of it. He did not mention bleeding problems, or how his throat was cauterized, so the exact procedure and why it was undertaken is something of a mystery.

159 LeRoy's ongoing coughing fits were the result of pulmonary tuberculosis, a disease that a large majority of the people contracted in that era. Most, however, had the immune system and vitality to keep it in check (passive) so that it never became active.

160 Conscription in Macon proved more complicated than in many other Southern cities because so many men had already joined a unit (23 companies thus far) and many more were given exemptions to perform specialized jobs within the growing arsenal and armory industries.

161 Following Shiloh, Union forces slowly advanced south against Corinth, where Beauregard's army had withdrawn to regroup. The important rail center (which Sec. of War Walker had called "the vertebrae of the Confederacy") was under threat and quasi-siege from the end of April. Heavily outnumbered, Beauregard finally withdrew on May 29. It was a major strategic defeat for the South.

162 Jackson, who had been active in the Shenandoah Valley, was rumored to be everywhere and viewed as a real threat by the Lincoln administration.

the rear of the forts at Charleston. Memphis is as good as gone. Fort Pillow abandoned.[163]

Saturday June 7th 1862: Warm and clear. Sallie and Minnie went to the tableaux last night with Miss Irene Hazlehurst. Thomas returned this morn early from Houston, and brought plums, blackberries, hams, +c. Mother made Walnut Catsup today.[164] Received a letter from Aunty and she was very anxious about Uncle Edge. The musquitoes are quite bad. Reading [Irving's] *Ferdinand + Isabella*. They are expecting an attack at Charleston every hour. "Hackneyed."[165]

Sabbath day June 8th 1862: Warm and clear. Tracy came up to see us this morn. Slept up stairs last night for the first time. Mother did not go out today. Got a letter from Dr. White giving directions about medicines. Had blackberries for dinner. Read *Sacred Mountains*. . . . Long lists of killed + wounded in the late battle. The 6th and 23rd Georgia suffered severely, as well as many other Georgia Regiments. Cousin Job is at Richmond in the 49th Georgia [under] Colonel [Andrew J.] Lane.

Monday June 9th 1862: Cool and cloudy. Rained hard in the night, and the wind did it blow. Uncle LeRoy arrived here last night. Long lists of killed + wounded are out. Lincoln has called for 200 000 more troops. Mother is sick in bed. Sallie gone to the dentist. Father bought 2 dozen bottles of Porter today. 2 Federal Generals Were killed at Richmond.[166] Beat Uncle LeRoy playing draughts.

Teusday June 10th 1862: Cool and clear. It was really cold last night. Good news! Glorious Old Stonewall Jackson is again victorious! General Shields attacked him and was gallantly repulsed. Fremont attacked General Ewell and was completely routed! Our army in pursuit and pressing him hard! Generals Stewart and Elzey wounded. General Turner Ashby killed! General Jackson is a hero.[167] Sallie went to the dentist

---

163 On June 6, a Union fleet moved south and crushed a small enemy flotilla, nearly eradicating the Confederate presence on the Mississippi River. Memphis surrendered a few hours later.

164 Walnut catsup was popular in the 19th century. It was a sauce or paste mixture made with green walnuts soaked in vinegar, onion, and spices.

165 LeRoy had heard and read so often that Charleston was about to be attacked that the news was now stale, or "hackneyed."

166 No Union generals were killed in the fighting.

167 The decisive battles of Cross Keys and Port Republic (June 8 and 9, 1862) ended Jackson's Valley Campaign by driving Union forces from the Valley. This, in turn, allowed Jackson's army to move east in time to participate in Lee's planned attack against McClellan outside Richmond in what would come to be known as the Seven Days' Battles. Confederate Gens. George H. Steuart and Arnold Elzey Jones, Jr. were wounded; Gen. Turner Ashby had served as Jackson's cavalry commander.

again. Commenced *Alhambra*. Cough better. Mother is engaged in making some more starch today.

Wednesday June 11th 1862: Cool and clear. General Jackson's victory is confirmed. He captured a regiment and 6 pieces of artillery. The fight was at Port Republic. Sallie gone to dentist. Uncle John has resigned his position as Surgeon 2nd Georgia Battalion, and taken a surgeon's place in the 3d Georgia Hospital.

Thursday June 12th 1862: Warm and clear. Grandma, Sallie, Uncle LeRoy, Laura,[168] Tracy, +c left for Athens. My cough continues better. General Kirby Smith[169] is at Chattanooga and the Yankees are threatening the city.

Friday June 13th 1862: Warm and clear. There has been a fight at Charleston ending in a partial repulse of our troops. 47th Georgia bore the brunt of the fight. Their loss 65 killed, wounded, +c.[170] On Wednesday night from 11 to 1 oclock the moon was totally eclipsed. The yanks have taken a company of the 12th Georgia prisoners. Cousin Howard arrived here at supper. Reading over *The White Chief.*

Saturday June 14th 1862: Warm + clear. Put up mosquito nets. Cousin Howard left this morn. We have got some honey at last. Father took the trouble to send out to the man's house to get it. It is very nice – "Rumor" says Lord Lyons[171] has gone to England. Had blackberry pie for dinner + jam. Cousin Jinnie Blount has got a little daughter.[172]

Sunday June 15th 1862: Warm and clear. Mr. Goulding preached. Thomas went to the Catholic church, as the bishop is here and he had never been before. Today we had the first ripe peach of the season and we all had a taste. Read *Historical Geography of the Bible*. Had a bad coughing spell today. Went to sleep this evening and took a good nap. The 3d Georgia is in the advance of Richmond and will probably be in the thickest of the fight when it comes. The enemy acknowledge themselves licked by Jackson.

Monday June 16th 1862: Windy, cool, and cloudy. Father left for Houston early this morn. Rained slowly for over an hour this eve. I have been annoyed by a continual hacking cough all the evening. I took some of my cough medicine, but it did'nt seem to

168 Laura was one of Grandmother's servants.

169 Confederate Gen. Edmund Kirby Smith.

170 A small fight on James Island, a precursor to the Battle of Secessionville (June 16, 1862).

171 Richard Bickerton Pernell Lyons was Queen Victoria's ambassador to America during the Civil War.

172 The baby was named Jane.

do any good. Finished *Wood Rangers*. Thomas brought up a bottle of wine from Aunt Eliza, which Cousin Howard brought over.

Teusday June 17th 1862: Warm and cloudy, cool. Minnie's birthday. We bought 6 quarts berries to make jam. There <u>was</u> a very good crop of apples on the tree near the kitchen, but they have nearly all dropped. The enemy are in possession of Memphis at last. General Stuart made a reconnoissance in force at Richmond lately + burnt 3 gunboats, riddled a train, burnt 100 wagons, and turned with 160 prisoners + 300 mules, losing only one man.[173] Rained slowly at 5 oclock. Read in *Robinson Crusoe* nearly all the evening. Slight pain in my hip.

Wednesday June 18th 1862: Cool and cloudy. I coughed so bad last night that I could not sleep so I got up and got in bed with Thomas. He came back from the tableau about 11½ oclock. I took the new medicine twice but it did no good. A little after supper, Mother was taken sick, fainted and fell, was very sick all night. My cough is no better, and I can't do it any good. C.J. Harris is major. His regiment [under] Colonel Brown is down at the trotting track. General Beauregard is reported to be on his way to Richmond. There has been another fight at Charleston: We whipped.[174] Uncle LeRoy arrived here to dinner from Athens. He brings a letter from Uncle Richard and Sallie. Campbell Tracy is at home. Uncle Edge is camped right on the battle field. Kentucky rollers [bourbon balls] and some very nice onions came by Uncle LeRoy. There had been very heavy hail at and near Athens. Mother is about again. Took a good nap in the evening. Had a very nice mess of strawberries for supper.

Thursday June 19th 1862: Warm + clear. Minnie went to the dentist. Father returned home this morn at 11 AM. He brought some fine apples and chickens. Commenced *Bonneville's Adventures*. The Queen Sisters are here. Put on summer again today; wore winter coat since Sunday. "Price" is still very weakly. Thomas gone to the show. Lightning constant at bedtime.

Friday June 20th 1862: Cool and clear. Uncle LeRoy left for Alabama. 5 Yankees have escaped down town.[175] "Gipsey" has come to be a regular suck egg! And has killed

---

173 Stuart's "Ride Around McClellan" (June 12-15, 1862). Gen. James Ewell Brown (Jeb) Stuart, Lee's cavalry commander, took a sizable portion of his cavalry and rode around McClellan's army east of Richmond to gather information. The man lost was Capt. William Latane, whose death inspired a renowned poem and a painting, the lithograph of which was found in many Southern homes.

174 The Battle of Secessionville (June 16, 1862) was the only direct Union attempt to capture Charleston, South Carolina by land. Gen. Nathan "Shanks" Evans and Col. Thomas Gresham Lamar repulsed a Union attack by Gen. Henry Washington Benham.

175 They arrived at Fortress Monroe in Virginia at the end of June.

a chicken. Had apple pie for dinner. Bought 12 quarts blackberries. Commenced to take Dr. White's medicine today. 1 Yankee was killed in the attempt to escape from the fairgrounds last night. We've got a tree near full of ripe peaches. We also have some ripe figs. My cough is a little better although it troubles me some yet. A negro boy was drowned up at the shoals the other day. There is a long account of General Stuart's affair in the paper today.

Saturday June 21st 1862: Cool and clear. Minnie and Thomas went to the Queen Sisters last night and stayed till 12 AM. They were very well pleased. Commenced to read *Tales of a Traveler*. Mother went down town and got the cloth to make me a coat. The escaped prisoners are on their way to the coast of Georgia, C.S.A.

Sabbath day June 22nd 1862: Warm and clear. Colonel Jack Brown's [Georgia] regiment is encamped down at the trotting track and he is commander of this district. Mr. Wills' baby is still very ill indeed.

Monday June 23rd 1862: Warm + clear. The warmest day of the season. Poor little Alfred Edwards[176] had both hips broken by a fall from a tree. Dr. Brasham set them. Jerry[177] took a notion to run away this eve and ran from Mrs. Edwards towards the stable. Have had a headache all the evening and do not feel well.

Tuesday June 24th 1862: Warm + clear. No news. Howard left for Houston. The hot day of the season. Bought 12 quarts blackberries. Read *The Little Savage*. General Johnston is improving. Got a letter from Aunt Eliza in a box containing 2 beautiful mats. LeRoy Washington is in jail for attacking Colonel Brown. There was a terrible "clapper clawing" fight here the other day between Miss Kitts and a virago.[178]

Wednesday June 25th 1862: Hot, dry day. The poor corn suffers for rain. Last night at bed time the thermometer was 87?. Thomas went to the Queen Sisters. I had a little fever last night and did not go to sleep till after 12. Commenced *Wolfort's Roost*. Hotter still. Howard returned this evening with apples +c. Betty is dead at last after an illness from which there was no hope of recovery. The report about General Beauregard

---

176 Alfred was Richard's younger brother, age 11.

177 One of the Gresham's draft horses.

178 Exactly what LeRoy was referring to is something of a mystery. A "virago" is a loud, overbearing woman. Perhaps it was his playful way of noting an actual cat fight between Kitty (Miss Kitts) and another cat.

going to Richmond is false. It is said we've blown up a Yankee ship, killing 183 out 185 in Arkansas.[179]

Thursday June 26th 1862: Warm and clear. I was really sick this morning before I got up. We got some fine figs today. Had a peach pie. Mother went over to see Aunt Ann, who is sick. The ground is parched and dry and we long for rain.

Friday June 27th 1862: Warm and clear. 4 oclock: clouded up and rained a little. Commenced *The Pirate*. It is reported that the great fight at Richmond (The 3d Georgia will be in the hot part) has begun.

Saturday June 28th 1862: Warm and cloudy. Rained in the night. The fight at Richmond has begun on our left wing. General Stonewall Jackson is there. We have driven the enemy back several miles. Taken his entrenchments. Cousin Charlie + Captain Smith are slightly wounded. It is said that we gained a glorious victory so far.[180] Brigadier General Ed Johnston has had his leg amputated from a wound received at the Battle of McDowell.[181] Aunt Ann is sick in bed. Alfred Edwards is getting along very well. Mr. Bates gave holiday yesterday. Wrote to Sallie, and Minnie got a letter from her. Tracy has the mumps. Had a very fine shower at 5P.M.

Sunday June 29th 1862: Warm and clear. It clouded up towards 12 oclock and rained a little. Mr. Wills being absent, Mr. Goulding preached. Rumors of a glorious victory at Richmond, 3600 prisoners! I hope it is true. Harry Bond is very ill with Scarlet fever. Mr. Friarson, who lately bought Dr. Cor's house, is dead. There is a prayermeeting this eve in our church. Read *Donaldson Manor*. Cousin Jimmie Snyder has bought Mrs. Martin's old house. I have not as yet taken off undershirts. Captain [Col.] Robert Smith is dead of his wounds. Lieutenant Colonel Phil Tracy was wounded in the cheek and thigh.

179 The ironclad gunboat USS *Mound City* was engaged in an incident in which a shot pierced its steam drum and scalded the majority of the crew; only 25 men escaped uninjured. The *Mound City's* commander, Adm. Augustus H. Kilty lost his left arm.

180 The Seven Days' Battles (June 25 – July 1) was Lee's attempt to destroy McClellan's Army of the Potomac north of the Chickahominy River, or at least drive it away and end the threat to Richmond. Like Johnston's Seven Pines plans, Lee's plans were also too complex. Jackson was present, having been called up from the Shenandoah Valley to fall upon the exposed Union right flank. Oak Grove (June 25) was a minor Union offensive against the Confederate right south of the river and was thrown back. Beaver Dam Creek or Mechanicsville (June 26) was the first major Confederate attack. Jackson arrived late and Gen. Ambrose P. Hill attacked without him and was bloodily repulsed. Gaines' Mill (June 27), the first and only tactical Rebel victory of the campaign, was a large-scale assault that pierced the Union V Corps line under Gen. Fitz-John Porter and sent his men retreating across the Chickahominy River.

181 Edward "Allegheny" Johnson was wounded in the ankle at McDowell on May 8, 1862. His leg was not amputated, but he walked with a limp for the rest of his life.

Monday June 30th 1862: Warm + clear. Rained in the night. Slept Elegantly. The Battle of Richmond! Utter discomfiture of McClellans army – 3600 prisoners, 3 Generals captured. Old "Stonewall" in his rear! Great excitement in Richmond! Major Wheat killed. The battle is not decided but it is thought will be renewed with greater fury than ever. The 7th and 8th Georgia charged a battery and <u>captured it</u> (a mistake; they did not succeed) with heavy loss. Colonel Lamar wounded + a prisoner. Colonel Newton 4th Georgia Killed. Macon Gaurds: 1 killed, 1 wounded. Colonel Hardeman's regiment: 10 killed, 32 wounded. This is the largest battle of the war. 700 000 men on a side.[182] Got a letter from Richmond (I meant to say Grandma) with one from Uncle Richard enclosed. He and Uncle Edge are near to each other. Thomas has quite a bad boil on his cheek. Read *Win and Wear*. My cough is very bad. Gypsey killed a chicken.

Tuesday July 1st 1862: Warm and clear More News. Colonel Lamar is in Richmond.

Colonel Newton is not dead. If dispatches are to be relied on, We have whipped the Yankees so bad that they will not get over it in a hurry. We have taken 6,000 prisoners (folly though) I reckon. Mclelan is driven into the swamp with our troops close on his heels. They was compelled to destroy an immense amount of stores. We have taken 8 or 10 batteries, artillery with terrible loss. If this be true, it is Glorious news. Clouded up in the eve and rained a little. My cough troublesome. Read *Children of the New Forest*. Uncle Richard and Uncle Edge will be in the fight. Minnie stayed all day at Mrs. Campbell's. 6 oclock: a most splendid shower.

---

182 The Seven Days' Battles continued, with more news pouring in. The Macon Guards were engaged at Oak Grove (June 25), while Col. Hardeman's 35th Georgia took part in Beaver Dam Creek and Gaines' Mill. Lamar was wounded and captured in the Battle of Garnett's and Goldings' Farm (June 27) south of the Chickahominy. The armies were large, but not as large as LeRoy heard or imagined. Lee's was about 92,000 (the largest Confederate army assembled during the war), while McClellan's was about 115,000.

Wednesday July 2nd 1862: Cloudy and rain. More hard fighting at Richmond in and about White Oak swamp. After very hard fighting, we had driven the enemy back two miles. Loss immense on both sides. We captured Generals McCall and Mead.[183] The battle not yet decided. Magruder's division was after the enemy. There has been 5 or 6 distinct fights before Richmond since Thursday. Commenced to rain at 10 AM and rained slowly for an hour. Mother finished my coat. Colonel Hardeman is wounded. 3 Gresham Rifles killed. (wounded) Cannon were fired here this evening. Rained at 5 oclock; not much though.

Thursday July 3d 1862: Warm and cloudy. Rained quite hard from daylight until 7 oclock. The decisive fight at Richmond has yet to be fought! We have got Mclelan so he will have to fight. He has a strong position and the taking of that position decides the series of bloody battles which have been fought before Richmond this week. No General killed on our side. Our loss must be immense. (This paragraph is altogether a mistake) The British war steamer *Racer* is lying at the Charleston wharves. Read *The Lost Will* through. More news! The Yankees have abandoned their strong position and fell back. The gunboats are shelling portion of our men. The fighting was desperate beyond measure.[184]

Friday July 4th 1862: Cloudy and cool. The news is somewhat uncertain. Colonel Doles [of the] 4th wounded. Colonel Mcintosh [of the] 15th, leg shot off. Colonel Johnston [of the] 18th killed. General Sumner U.S.A. surrounded and a prisoner. General Hooker is [indecipherable] mortally wounded.[185] I slept very badly and feel sore in all my bones this morning. Mother bought Minnie a little umbrella. The 4th of July 1862 will be rendered a memorable day in Macon by the sad and solemn ceremony of Colonel [Robert A.] Smith's funeral. I rode round on Mrs. Bond's hill to see the procession. If all the carriages had been in the procession it would have been immensely long. The Rangers first, M.L. Artillery next, Colonel Brown's regiment, Rylander's Battalion, Rifles and Volunteers C.B. The express wagon draped and

183 Gen. George A. McCall was captured in the fighting at Glendale (June 30); Gen. George G. Meade, who would one day lead the Army of the Potomac, was not captured.

184 After shoving McClellan nearly all the way back to the James River, Lee launched a final ill-advised assault on July 1 at Malvern Hill, which was bloodily repulsed, ending the Seven Days' Battles. Lee's aggressive tactics worked, and Richmond was no long under direct threat. His losses were heavy at 20,000 killed, wounded, and captured; McClellan's totaled about 16,000.

185 Gen. Edwin V. "Bull" Sumner was not captured, and Gen. Joseph Hooker, who would also one day command the Army of the Potomac, was not mortally wounded.

decorated was the hearse. Officers, Militia, Odd fellows,[186] Private carriages +c. Mr. Lane came over to the funeral and came to see us after tea.

Saturday July 5th 1862: Cool + cloudy. Harry Bond's funeral is this morning. 5pm: Have got a slight pain in my hip from my ride. . . . The Yanks are shelling Vicksburg and Gen Vandorn has resolved to defend it to the last extremity.[187]

Sabbath day July 6th 1862: Bright and cool. Every body is anxious about Richmond, afraid McClelan will be reinforced. The gunboats are in the James + furiously shelling the shores. There is a good deal of talk about France, intervention, +c. This is communion day. Read *Donaldson Manor*. We are anxious about Uncle Richard, the 3d [Ga.] having been in a heavy fight and suffered severely. Captain John Sturgis of Burke killed.

Monday July 7th 1862: Clear and pleasant. There was an alarm of fire yesterday at 11 AM aroused by a small house catching fire. It was soon extinguished. News uncertain. Do'nt know the position of Mclelan. Father cut my hair. Price barked for the first time. Examination is going on at the College. Junior and Sophomore today. Reading *The Life of Washington* and like it very well.

Tuesday July 8th 1862: Hot and clear. Commencement at the College. No news of importance. Mclelan is supposed to be largely reinforced and will never give up. Father bought a half peck [1/8 of a bushel] of fine soft peaches and I tell you we made 'm fly. Mother went to the prayer meeting. General Vandorn is "<u>reported</u>" to have taken Baton Rouge, Lousiana with 1500 prisoners.[188] The musquitoes are a little worse than usual. We would have had several Trees full of ripe peaches had they not been stolen. Captain Rube Nisbet was wounded in <u>the</u> fight.

Wednesday July 9th 1862: Warm and cloudy. Father and Howard left early this morning for Houston, taking both horses. Heard from Uncle John: Uncle Dick was sick in camp and he had sent a carriage for him. Last day of commencement. Miss Cater

---

186 The Independent Order of Odd Fellows was a fraternal organization from England founded in the U.S. in 1819.

187 Vicksburg, Miss, a major river port and fortified city on the Mississippi River, was also a critical link to the distant Trans-Mississippi Theater to the west, and a vital stronghold that helped keep the river open for Confederate traffic. Adm. Farragut had steamed upriver from New Orleans and demanded the Vicksburg's surrender, which its commander, Gen. Earl Van Dorn, rejected.

188 There was no fighting there at this time. The attempt to take Baton Rouge would come nearly a month later on August 5, when some 3,000 Confederates under Gen. John C. Breckinridge attacked and were narrowly repulsed.

(a mistake) took the 1st Honor. Rained a little before dinner. Took off my undershirts to try it.[189]

Thursday July 10th 1862: Cloudy and sultry. Armies at Richmond "in status quo." General Robinson [Beverly Robertson], successor to Ashby, has taken Moorfield, Northwest Virginia, with 80 prisoners, commissary stores, 100 Enfield rifles, +c. Received a letter from Grandma with one from Aunty enclosed. Tracy has had Scarlett fever; Sallie is very sick with it, has been for a week. Candace has scarlet fever. Violet[190] has been very ill. Aunty has seen Uncle Edge. Uncle Richard is sick with dysentery. Auntie was on the battle field and describes the suffering and heroism of our men with a graphic pen. The noble 3d Georgia regiment suffered awfully in charging a battery. Father got here at 8½ oclock after we had given him out, bringing 14 chickens. 2 bushels [of] apples, 2 water melons. +c. We had a very hard rain from 5 to 6 with very heavy thunder and they were in it.

Friday July 11th 1862: Warm + clear. Clouded up in the eve and rained tremendous hard for an hour or so. We ate today the two first watermelons of the season: one was white and the other red meat. I could not enjoy mine on account of my harassing and violent cough. It is my <u>chief</u> trouble and wears me away. I am reading with great interest *Washingtons Life*. "Précsis's" is as much of a fool as ever and very stumpy and stunted.[191]

Saturday July 12th 1862: Warm and cloudy Cousin Charlie is home. LEROY Mr. Wells called. Mother went down town and got me a cap, but it was too big. It is rumored that General Huger is suspended.[192]

Sabbath day July 13th 1862: Warm and clear. Received a letter from Sallie, who is convalescing. Tracy is over the Scarlet Fever but his ears run yet. I have been reading *Capt. Russell's watchword* today. Received a note from Uncle J. Yesterday. We are just now having enough of peaches to eat without stint. Mr. Goulding preached at night. Had a watermelon No 2. They are very high: 50 cents to $1.

Monday July 14th 1862: Warm and clear. Since yesterday morning my cough has not annoyed me at all. General Bragg is now in command of the Army of Mississippi,

189 LeRoy was easily chilled, and it was now warm enough for him to be comfortable without his undershirts.

190 Candace was one of the Bird family's servants; Violet was one of Grandmother's.

191 This was one of several war correspondents who published under a pseudonym; LeRoy was critiquing his reports.

192 Confederate Gen. Benjamin Huger was relieved of command on July 12 and assigned to the Trans-Mississippi Theater.

General. Beauregarde having been relieved on acct of sickness. "Old Scott" A.T. is now secretary of war to Lincoln.[193] Father bought me a nice new cap today. 4 Richmond papers came today. Had a fine watermelon. Milo came up from the plantation and brought 8 fine ones. The papers say we have taken upwards of 25000 muskets at Richmond and about 50 pieces artillery.

Tuesday July 15th 1862: Hot and clear. Read *The Boat Club*. Suffered more with the heat than I have this summer. Eat two melons. Father left for Richmond right after supper.

Wednesday July 16th 1862: Terribly hot. Suffered with heat badly last night and as I write at 5.P.M. I am stinging all over with the heat notwithstanding we have just eaten a nice melon. Got a letter from Aunty. She was sitting in a private house and Uncle Richard was near her + glad to be so comfortable. The "perspiration" pours off me and drops on the book. Mother in bed sick.

Thursday July 17th 1862: Hot + clear. Thomas bought 10 sacks salt for $160. Judge Nisbet sent me a translation of Virgil [*Aeneid*]. Thomas and Mother wrote to Father jointly. Mother in bed still. There is great excitement in New York about the money market. Cousin Annie Tinsley has a baby boy.[194]

Friday July 18th 1862: Hot! Hot! Too hot to sleep last night "at all, at all." Wrote to Father and Minnie did too. At two PM there was a slight shower and the sun shone hotter afterwards; clouded up again at 5. I am very much interested in *The Life of Washington*. General Magruder is transferred to East Tennessee. It is said he was drunk at Richmond. Gallant Old Stonewall is a full General. 22 cannon arrived here yesterday. They ran the blockade in the *Nashville*. About half of Clinton was burnt up Wednesday night. Minnie is invited to Mrs. Whittle's tonight to a sort of tableaux or something.

Saturday July 19th 1862: Weather continues fiery hot night + day. Minnie went to a large party at Mrs. Whittle's last night and out to the camp of the Artillery today. The heat is so terrible I can hardly write and it is bad on me. The match factory was burned down last night. It was a small wooden building on Woodruff's factory lot. Got a letter from Mr. R. Johnston, 4 pages fools cap, closely written.[195]

---

193 LeRoy seems to be referring to Gen. Winfield Scott, but if so this is incorrect. Edwin Stanton remained Lincoln's secretary of war for the duration.

194 James N. Tinsley. Annie was a cousin of LeRoy's mother.

195 Foolscap is legal-sized writing paper.

Sabbath day July 20th 1862: Awful hot! My cough, yesterday, returned and this morning my breast has a strange soreness in it and I have been coughing badly. My leg is all drawn up and I am unwell. Mrs. H-g-n [Huguenin] called yesterday and brought me gingercakes. Hon. Philomon Tracy is in town. Last night we let a melon down the well and this even when we ate it was diliciously cool and nice. Right after eating I had a bad coughing spell. Read *All Aboard*, a sequel to *The Boat Club*. I got a long and interesting letter from Auntie. Mother is up again and went to church and they all suffered with the terrible heat. There are no signs of rain. The Ram *Arkansas* is doing good service out of Vicksburg. The Yankees still continue to shell Vicksburg.[196]

Monday July 21st 1862: Scorching hot. My breast was sore enough all night and is no better today. The Confederates under Colonel Forrest have taken Murfreesboro after a sharp fight with 1200 prisoners, among whom was General Crittenden.[197] Our loss 16 killed Yankee 2 or 300. We burned 500,000 in stores and retreated. Today is the Anniversary of "The Battle of Manassa."

Tuesday July 22nd 1862: The fiery weather still continues. Recieved a very interesting letter from Father. He arrived safe on Friday and saw all our folks. General Jackson is <u>not</u> a full General. Bought two melons, and they were both green. Thomas wrote to Uncle Dick. Cough bad as ever and I can hardly eat with any comfort. Mother went down town this eve. Dr. Jimmy Le Corte is dead. Colonel Morgan with 1500 picked men is in Tennessee.

Wednesday July 23rd 1862: The weather is absolutely awful: 5PM 90?. Finished *The Life of Washington* and I think it the best biography I ever read, and very instructive.[198] Ate melon.

Thursday July 24th 1862: The heat continues and is debilitating beyond measure. IF we do not have rain before long everything will burn up for certain. Colonel Morgan is in the heart of Kentucky. Has been through Frankfort and Lexington and in 50 miles of

---

196 The ironclad CSS *Arkansas* steamed down the Yazoo River on her maiden voyage and into the Mississippi River, battling through the Union fleet in spectacular fashion to reach Vicksburg. Hundreds of soldiers and civilians lined the riverbank watching her arrival.

197 Gen. Nathan Bedford Forrest; Gen. Thomas T. Crittenden was in command of the Union forces, but he was not captured.

198 Washington Iriving, *The Life of Washington* (GP Putnam & Co., 1855).

Cincinnatti. Captured large amounts all kinds of things.[199] Ate a very fine melon. Mother went down town late in the evening.

Friday July 25th 1862: Weather terribly hot. Last night I suffered very much and could not sleep. Howard left for Houston and took both horses and the buggy. Morgan has taken Newburg, Indiana. Minnie has yesterday and today been engaged in making emory.[200]

Saturday July 26th 1862: No sign of rain and the heat as oppressive as ever. Howard got back this morning soon after breakfast. Minnie got a letter from Father. He sees all the kin. Had got my letter. We ate a melon out of the garden and it was ripe but wilted. Cousin Eliza and Aunt Sarah called yesterday. She has been quite sick. The Ralstons left for Montvale. This is Mother's birthday. Minnie is unwell and lying down.

Sabbath day July 27th 1862: A little cooler today. No one but Thomas at church today. Minnie in bed. I am lying on the back porch writing this. . . . Today has been a wonderful relief from the terrible heat of the past ten days, though a hot day itself. We got a letter from Uncle Edmund saying he had sent us some melons +c. We will send to the depot tomorrow. We are suffering for rain.

Monday July 28th 1862: Very warm and dry. Mother got a long and interesting letter from Father. He had visited the field of battle and rode 50 miles on horseback.[201] The reports: Uncle Dick convalescing slowly, Uncle Edge was in on a furlough. I wrote to Aunty today. The Macon Light Artillery left this eve at 7 oclock for the war. Read the *Young Maroones* through.

Tuesday July 29th 1862: Sultry and <u>hot</u>. O! that it would rain. Every thing is burning up. Halleck is commander in chief USA. General Stuart CSA is promoted to be Major General [of] cavalry. After dinner we were greatly refreshed by a hard shower. Minnie and Susy gone down town in the carriage. We got a letter from Grandma; Sallie has been sick. Tracy is well. Mrs. Edwards came to see Mother, and lent me a book. Alfred [Edwards] is sitting up and had had the splints taken off his legs. Reading *The Heir of the West* [by] Wayland.

---

199 Cavalryman Col. John Hunt Morgan with 900 men was making his first Kentucky raid, launched July 4, 1862.

200 A dark mineral used to polish metals often found in pincushions to sharpen needles and pins and keep them rust-free. Needles were made outside the South. Emory helped keep them in use much longer.

201 John Gresham was in Richmond, and visited the battlefields east of the capital.

Wednesday July 30th 1862: Very hot and dry. We were not looking for Father and were greatly surprised when he arrived. We all got up and talked a long time. Father brought me a "Map of Virginia" and Thomas a very good book, *The First Year of the War*. He also gave me two epaulets: one he picked up in McClellan's tent + the other on the field. Wilson sent me two yankee bullets and Aunty two Yankee papers full of lies. One was *Evening Express* and the other the *New York Times*. Thomas received a letter from Uncle Richard, who is now getting better. Mother got one from Aunty. Father visited the battle fields with Lieutenant Rowland + Captain Plane[202] and rode 30 miles on a horse. Fannie Payne stayed all day with Minnie. Uncle Edmund's melons, 24 in number, arrived here. 3 or 4 were sour. They are fine though not so fine as usual.

Thursday July 31st 1862: Hot as fire. Beautiful rain at dinner time, a nice season. Cousin Jenks came to dinner. Ate two melons and sent two or three to the neighbors. Read in *First Year of the War* and find it very interesting indeed. Liza Huguenin has measles. It looks very much as if we would have a hard rain tomorrow. After breakfast Read *Sophie DePrenty, or The Sword of Truth*.

Friday July August 1st 1862: Rainy, cool. Tremendous rain before and after breakfast. Good for corn. Our cavalry made a "brilliant dash and captured Summerville, Northwest Virginia and took 63 prisoners and burned a large amount of stores and +c."[203] Rained nearly all the morn and tremendous in the evening. Ate 4 melons. Father bought some nice tinley Peaches. Commenced to read *Ellen Middleton*. Pasted in my scrap book in morn. One year ago we left here for Athens.

Saturday August 2nd 1862: Raining slowly, surely, steadily, and as I listen to it I am glad for many a poor man's sake whose only hope is his corn crop.[204] The latest northern news is Mclelan is "falling through;" they have inaugurated the most brutal system of warfare ever known and intend to carry it out to the letter. General Jackson has returned to the Valley of Virginia to oppose General Pope.[205] A great part of

---

202 William Fisher Plane was the husband of Carolyn H. Jemison, a maternal cousin of LeRoy's father. He would be mortally wounded and captured at Sharpsburg on September 17, 1862.

203 The cavalry raid overnight on July 25, 1862, in Summersville (now WV) was undertaken by a Confederate team of local "Moccasin Raiders" from the area.

204 LeRoy is showing concern for the poorer farmers of Georgia who have only their current crops to rely upon for survival. Plans were in place for the wealthier planters and producers of Georgia to take care of the indigent and the families of soldiers.

205 With McClellan's Army of the Potomac pinned against the James River, Lee began shifting Jackson and some of his troops north into central Virginia (not the Valley) to ward off the newly formed Army of Virginia under Gen. John Pope, which was moving south from Washington against him.

Bragg's army is at Chattanooga, and he is there himself to oppose General Buell. The Yankees have given up Vicksburg as a "hard case" after a terrible bombardment of nearly a month killing 30 men at our batteries and damaging the town . . . . Two or 3 men got in a boat at Petersburg . . . and went right into the midst of the Yankee fleet and burned a transport, taking her captain prisoner. Stopped raining towards noon and commenced again at 5PM slowly and steady. Kittie had a hard fit and we thought at first it would kill her but she recovered entirely. Finished *Ellen Middleton*. It is a strange book and I am sorry I read it. Macon has 2 companies in the field.

Sunday, August 3d 1862: Cloudy and cool. Yesterday we received the sad news of Poor Uncle Link's death at Guntown.[206] Miss Sallie Bird still continues sick. . . . 3PM: Commenced to rain steadily and continued to do so nearly all the evening. . . . Read *Patient waiting no loss*.

Monday August 4th 1862: Cloudy and pleasant. The Yankee General Pope is surpassing Butler in outrageous brutality to private citizens.[207] From 12M to 3PM: It rained as hard as I ever saw; it was tremendous. Father bought us some nice plumstone peaches; ate the last of Uncle Edmund's melons. Commenced to read *Ivors* [by] Miss Sewell.

Tuesday August 5th 1862: Pleasant day. General Cooper has ordered that Pope and his officers when captured be not considered prisoners of war subject to exchange, and that they be placed in close confinement. General A.P. Hill's[208] division has gone to reinforce General Jackson; the Yankees are fast bringing this war to be one of mutual extermination and murder.[209] Cousin Eliza and Aunt Sarah came to see Mother.

Wednesday August 6th 1862: Very warm and clear. Foreign news of vital importance! France is on the "eve" of "recognition"![210] Slight rain in the PM. We received two fine

---

206 Eli Leroy "Link" Baxter was one of LeRoy's uncles. He died in Confederate service at Guntown, Mississippi.

207 Gen. Pope issued orders aimed at punishing Southern civilians. Gen. Lee labeled him a "miscreant."

208 Gen. Ambrose P. Hill, no relation to Confederate Gen. D. H. Hill.

209 In April 1861 few people believed the war would last more than a battle or two. By now it was obvious it would be long and exceptionally destructive. Lincoln would not let the South leave, so LeRoy blamed the Yankees for "bringing this war" to the point of "mutual extermination and murder."

210 Many Southerners put their hope in foreign recognition by England and France, but there was little chance either was going to recognize the Confederacy. At the war's outset, the Confederacy made a major miscalculation by withholding its cotton from Europe to force recognition. The decision hurt the Southern economy, and Europe had large stores of cotton and acquired more from foreign sources. There was also little evidence the South could actually win, so backing a losing effort was not appealing.

melons and a box of peaches from Cousin Jenks. Minnie dined with Susie Edwards. Wrote a letter to Mr. Johnston. Finished *Ivors*. It ends badly and is too much drawn out. The "ball" is "imminent" between Jackson + Pope; so says "P.W.A."[211] My cough is better today more tomorrow. Leg "in statu quo."

Thursday August 7th 1862: Thomas bought me "A connected acct of 'The Great Battles before Richmond' taken from the press." General Breckinridge has taken Baton Rouge. Colonel Edward Tracy is in town on his way to Chattanooga. Mother rec'd a letter from Uncle Dick and he is going to camp in a day or two. George Beal came over last night and sat 'till bedtime. Mrs. PHD Tracy[212] called. This has been a regular "August" day and the sun is awfully hot.

Friday August 8th 1862: Awfully hot. Gen. Breckinridge took Baton Rouge and then had to fall back. Our loss equal to theirs. General Clark[213] mortally wounded. Generals Buckner, Tilghman, Pettigrew,[214] Colonel Rasson, are in Richmond. A large steamer was captured while attempting to run the blockade at Savannah. Bought a melon. It was half rind. Got a letter from Cousin Susan[215] and Uncle LeRoy is well. Different intensity with the heat. No comfort in such weather.

Saturday August 9th 1862: Awful hot. Last night was terrible not a breath of air stirring. I suffer very much with the heat. Read *Peter the Whaler*. Aunt Ann called. Ate a very fine melon and put the other down the well. Father and Minnie took a ride on horseback before breakfast. Minnie went to a "candy pulling" at Mrs. Huguenin's and spent the day.

Sunday August 10th 1862: Terribly hot. Another scorcher! I do not remember ever suffering so much with the heat before. We have retaken "Malvern's Hill." When the

---

That fall, Lincoln passed the Emancipation Proclamation, which broadened the Union goals of the war to include the eradication of slavery. Thereafter, England and France could never intervene on behalf of the Confederacy because it would show support for slavery, something they had already abolished.

211 Pseudonym for Peter Wellington Alexander, a war correspondent writing for the *Savannah Republican* and *Richmond Times Dispatch*.

212 Caroline Walker Tracy, the second wife of Major Philomon Tracy.

213 Gen. Charles Clark was not mortally wounded, and served as governor of Mississippi from 1863-1865.

214 Gen. James J. Pettigrew.

215 Susan Louisa Wiley McCay was the daughter of Grandmother's brother, Thomas Harris Wiley. Susan and her husband, Robert Thorton McCay, lived in New Jersey in 1860. Uncle LeRoy Wiley had business interests in New York, and had likely taken a trip there from his Alabama plantation, somehow making it through the blockade or by obtaining a pass to allow him through the lines.

Yankees took it the other day they took Marion Stovall prisoner. The Yanks attacked the Ram *Arkansas* at Vicksburg, and after fighting gallantly, we abandoned her and "blew" her up.[216] Mr. Goulding preached, Mr. Wills being absent. Ate a cool nice melon. Read *Frank Netherton*.

Monday August 11th 1862: Hot! Hot! Hot! Hot! Hot! as fire all night and fiery again today. The Mercury [at] 8PM [was] 90°. I was very restless all night and today; my leg is so drawn up I can hardly put my foot to the floor. Gen. Jackson has captured 1 Brig. Gen., 27 officers, 300 men of Pope's army! General Winder[217] killed on our side. The enemy were totally defeated. Mr. Johns Maulsby, Killed in an affray with Mr. Dudley on Saturday, was buried by the "Partisan Rangers." Dudley was also mortally wounded.

Tuesday August 12th 1862: Hot and clear. My leg hurts me very bad. Ate a melon which was two thirds rind. The 12th and 45th [Georgia regiments] were in Jackson's fight. At Baton Rouge, two Generals killed and 2 mortally wounded. There has been a fight at Tazewell, East Tennessee in which the Yankees were routed. Only 1 or 2 regiments engaged on other side. Read *Mary Bunyan*. Minnie went to a large party at Mrs. Whittle's.

Wednesday August 13th 1862: Awfully hot. At 4PM there was a very slight shower and then the sun is out again with tenfold power. Bought me some Red Ink. [Minnie's friend] Jessie Burgess spent the day here. Father left for Houston very early this morn. I have a stigh [sty] upon my eye. My back pained me all night and gave me no rest hardly. General McCook U.S.A is reported killed by guerillas.

Thursday August 14th 1862: Very hot and clear. Spent a miserable restless night and woke more tired than when I went to bed. Susie Edwards leaves this morn for Knoxville. General Jackson's official dispatch announces another victory. The 12th Georgia had 8 killed and 27 wounded. Lincoln has called for 600,000 men to be drafted. Yesterday after supper it clouded up and the wind blew but no rain. At 11 AM It rained a very little and then turned off. Hotter "now" [than] fire. Father came back from Houston. Milo and Sam also came.

---

216 The ironclad CSS *Arkansas* was ordered to leave Vicksburg to support an attack on Baton Rouge. Her engines failed, and when Union ships approached, her crew burned her on August 6, 1862.

217 Jackson moved north and was attacked at Cedar Mountain (August 9) by Gen. Nathaniel Banks' Union troops from Gen. Pope's Army of Virginia. Jackson was nearly routed, but reinforcements and a counterattack broke Banks' lines. The commander of the Stonewall Brigade, Gen. Charles Winder, was killed. Jackson's losses were 1,340 killed, wounded, and captured, while Banks' casualties totaled 2,350.

Friday August 15th 1862: Very warm, though a little cooler than it has been. Milo went back [to Houston] carrying the mules. They are very pretty little ones. 45 chickens + 6 melons were brought up. 5PM: It is raining hard and has been for an hr. I hope it will be cooler. Sent my mattress down to be "fixed." Minnie went to a party at Mr. Cole's last night. My cough worries me very much today and yesterday. Jackson's [Cedar Mountain] fight was a large one 10 to 15 000 on a side. A good victory too!

Saturday August 16th 1862: Rather pleasant to what it has been lately. Cousin Howard stayed all night with us. Cousin Annie's baby is called Jimmie Nichols.[218] Ate a melon and then I coughed awfully. My cough is not improved a bit as yet. Received a letter from Auntie. Minnie went to a party at Mrs. Huguenin's last night.[219] Got my mattress and it does very well. "Price" is getting to be a very good dog. Father bought a peck of peaches. My leg gets no better at all.

Sunday August 17th 1862: Clear delightful day. Mr. Goulding preached; Mother did not go to church. Slept well last night. Took a good nap today. Ate two melons.

Monday August 18th 1862: Deliciously cool and beautiful day. General [Simon] Buckner is made a Major General. [John Hunt] Morgan has gone to Kentucky again. Father bought 2 pecks peaches. My leg is very badly drawn up and does not get any better. We have figs in great abundance now, more than we can eat. Minnie and Thomas went to ride before breakfast. Congress meets today.[220]

Tuesday August 19th 1862: Pleasant day. Slept very well. Father got me some iron pills. Mclellan's army has gone [by water] to reinforce Pope, and Uncle Edge's regiment has gone to Jackson. Captain Nisbet is Colonel [of the] 3d Georgia Regiment. Minnie had a party of girls to spend the morning with her; what with dancing + they spent a very pleasant one. Mother went down town.

Wednesday August 20th 1862: Raining slowly. Minnie went to a large party at Mr. J.B. Ross' last night. Hank is making some bedposts to the front (a bust) room bed. The Queen of England has made a speech which is a deathblow to recognition. Read a fine story in *The Eclectic*: "A marvelous identity." Got two or 3 ripe scuppanongs [grapes] out of the garden. "Gipsey" barks loud and shrill every night and I want to wring his

---

218 James Nichols Tinsley, born June 30, 1862 and the fourth of the Tinsley children, lived to 1942.

219 Minnie Gresham was not old enough to be introduced into adult society or eligible for marriage (what people at the time termed "on the carpet" and would generally not be until she finished college after the war). The chaperoned entertainments she attended helped instruct young people in proper behavior and expected etiquette in formal social settings.

220 The Second Session of the First Confederate Congress met August 18-October 13, 1862.

neck. "Price" grows in favor daily and is learning to make "Gip" shinny on his own side. Mr. Wills has come back!!!

Thursday August 21st 1862: Cloudy and pleasant. Nearly all our army [of Northern Virginia] has gone to Gordonsville. I went over to see Alfred Edwards. He is nearly well. We are on our last tree of peaches. My leg hurts me some and continues to be badly drawn up. I am trying Iron Pills because I can't get any other medicine.[221] We are wanting rain sadly. Mother went down town and bought Minnie a Gold belt buckle. O Ho! Ho!

Friday August 22nd 1862: Very warm. Commenced to rain and there was a pretty good shower. No news is allowed to come from the army at all. General Lee is in command at Gordonsville. The Yankees acknowledge a loss in the "Battle of Cedar Run" [Mountain] of 1500, while our own was probably 800. It was a hard battle and the Old 12th [Georgia] bore a prominent part in it and it is enough to say "she sustained her reputation." Pope's army is carrying out to the letter his brutal and outrageous plan of warfare.

Saturday August 23rd 1862: Rained in the night, and is raining slowly this morn. Uncle LeRoy arrived last night to supper. President's message out. Took some porter [beer] on going to bed and slept better than usual. Howard sick in bed. From before 11am till sometime after dinner there was <u>very</u> heavy rains! Coming down nicely. Uncle LeRoy left for Milledgeville.

Sabbath August 24th 1862: Warm and cloudy. Rained very hard in the night. Minnie has a very bad cold. Uncle LeRoy returned today. Slept better last night and my leg does not hurt me or my cough trouble me either. Mr. Wills preached today. 12M: . . . It's two melons, the last of summer I reckon. Rained heavily at dinner and slower in the PM. Read *Dream Life* by McMarvel. Father got me *Anna*, a P.S.S. book. There is no signs of an early battle between Lee + Pope.

Monday August 25th 1862: Cloudy and cool. General Pope is retreating. He crossed the Rappahannock and left a rear gaurd of 150 men to burn the bridge, but our [side] captured the whole of them. Also two engines which they were to go off on. Uncle

---

221 LeRoy's tuberculosis, which is eating away his lower vertebrae and discs (tuberculous spondylitis, also called Pott's Disease), is causing great pain and nerve damage that is drawing up his limb. Medicines of all types were becoming harder to obtain because of the blockade, and most that were available were being used to treat thousands of ill and wounded soldiers.

LeRoy left. There is a very small comet visible now in the north.[222] We have a few ripe scuppernongs [grapes] in our garden. We have not heard from Grandma in a long time and feel a little anxious.

Tuesday August 26th 1862: Pleasant + cloudy. Rained while the sun shone; not enough to make me go in the house. Received a letter from Grandma. Aunty is sick in Richmond. Wren Bird[223] is dead! Poor Fellow. The 3d Georgia + 2nd Battalion have "gone to Stonewall." All our peaches are gone. Someone cleaned the tree last night. Father bought some, also some nice sweet potatoes. Uncle Eli[224] has gone home from Texas. The Yanks are still prowling around Vicksburg. Our men have occupied Baton Rouge.[225]

Wednesday August 27th 1862: Somewhat cloudy. Mother left at 9AM for Athens taking only Eveline along with her. She was very reluctant to go but said she felt she ought to go to Grandma. I feel sorry to see her start by herself in these troublous times. Cousin Sallie Wiley's brother stayed all night with us.[226] My cough has been bothering me a good deal. The comet which is visible is getting larger and more distinct. It is in the northwest. Very slight rain at dinnertime. Pasted all the eve in my scrapbook. Thomas has gone to the Brunswick depot to get butter.

Thursday August 28th 1862: Warm and clear. Leila Nisbet came to see Minnie!!! The comet's tail is about 6 feet long and is very plainly visible. Ate a watermelon out of our garden and it was a very nice one. The Partisan Rangers[227] are camped out by Mrs. Clark's. The news is that Pope is retreating and there has been really heavy fighting of which there are no authentic accts. In one fight where our passage across the river was disputed there was 150 killed + wounded on our side while the Yankee loss was supposed to be much greater. Major General Stuart surprised and routed 5000 Yanks,

---

222 He was probably viewing the Comet Swift-Tuttle, which was discovered in July independently by Lewis Swift and Horace Parnell Tuttle. It was the "parent body" of the Perseid meteor shower and appears about every 133 years.

223 Unable to identify this person.

224 Eli Harris Baxter, Sr. was a brother of LeRoy's grandmother. He lived in Houston, Texas.

225 The Confederate effort to take Baton Rouge failed, but Southern troops occupied and were building powerful earthworks at Port Hudson, south of Vicksburg in Louisiana, to help control the flow of traffic on the Mississippi River.

226 She had three brothers: James Louis, Stephen Jacob, and Charles Wiley, all of whom were from Texas.

227 48th Georgia Infantry.

capturing immense amounts [of] stores, 367 prisoners, officers, General Pope's equipments, 50 000 in specie and lost 2 killed 5 wounded.[228]

Friday August 29th 1862: Warm and cloudy. Robert Plant and Mary Campbell came up after tea last night and we had a very pleasant time. When I first got in bed I slept very well but woke up and had an exhausting fit of coughing which kept me awake a long time. Morgan has had quite a fight. The enemy 800 strong and we 1200. The enemy were badly beaten with a loss of 300 prisoners among whom was General Dick Johnston.[229] Our loss some 25 to 120. No more from Pope. He is "skedaddling" toward Manassas so fast he left his wounded behind. It is terribly sultry.

Saturday August 30th 1862: Hot and cloudy. Slept most miserably. It was <u>so</u> hot. I drank Porter before getting in bed but was never more restless in my life. Slept with Father too. The comet is very dim and nearly out of sight. Minnie got a letter from Sallie and she says her mother is expected daily. Uncle John left Richmond for Charleston to be surgeon of Colquitt's 46th Georgia, and I suppose Auntie will come with him.[230] Thomas is writing to Mother. Father received a letter from Mother and she was safe in Athens. The "Daily" did not come today. The news from the Rappahannock is as good as none, it is so vague + uncertain. Rumors of a heavy battle. Mr. Spahr came and mended the piano. 5½ PM: a storm of wind + heavy rain.

Sabbath day August 31st 1862: Cloudy and warm. Rained hard in the night. I have got another stigh [sty] <u>upon</u> my eye and I put some pain extractor on it. . . . There is to be a meeting beginning Wednesday night and continuing the rest of the week. Rained a little in the eve. My eye hurts me very much, and I have a headache. Wrote to Mother. This item just fills this page.

Monday September 1st 1862: Autumn comes in drizzly, damp, morning. My eye hurts me very badly. Rained in the night. Cleared off at 1½ M. I got a letter from Mother. Tracy is awful fat. Dr. Hoyt has had a hemorrhage and is very low indeed. The comet has disappeared. We have got the Federals hemmed in at Cumberland gap and expect to "bug" them daily. Our forces have occupied Manassas and it is hoped we will defeat General Pope. No telegraphic news comes. There was a grand parade and review here

228 Word is beginning to filter through the media of the Second Manassas Campaign. Minor actions were fought along the Rappahannock River from August 22-25, with the major fighting to come on August 28-30. Stuart's affair was at Catlett's Station (August 22).

229 Gen. Richard W. Johnson had been sent to push John Hunt Morgan out of Tennessee, but was instead defeated and captured.

230 Gen. Alfred H. Colquitt led a brigade in Lee's Virginia army and was distantly related to the Gresham family through marriage.

yesterday by order of General Mercer.[231] It is a great pity that no more appropriate day than Sunday could be found for such a show. My cough worries me at times during the day. Alfred Edwards is walking on crutches. My leg is "all" drawn up.[232] At 4 oclock it commenced to rain + continued to do so for an hour. Mary Campbell came to see Minnie this evening.

Tuesday September 2nd 1862: Cloudy and warm. Mary stayed all night with Minnie. Glorious news! If true. Our army has gained a signal victory over the combined forces of Pope and Mclellan in the Plains of Manassas.[233] Each wing of the army repulsed with valor the attacked's made on them separately. The battle was on the 27th and 28th. The news is not very satisfactory and the anxiety will be very great to hear more. Mrs. Bates sent me some scuppernongs. Minnie received a letter from Mother. Putting down Carpets up stairs.

Wednesday September 3d 1862: Clear and "wary" pleasant. News confirmed! The Yankees attacked one wing of our army under Longstreet [Jackson] on the 28th and were gallantly repulsed. The next day, the 29th, they attacked the other wing under Jackson and with a like result. On the 30th was the grand engagement which resulted in a glorious victory for us. The Yanks claim a victory. Minnie has gone to spend the day with Fannie Payne. Thomas got a letter from Mother and made me a cross bow. Cousin Eliza has the measles in her family.

Thursday September 4th 1862: Cool and pleasant. Slept miserable. Father got a letter from Mother. Most glorious news! Kirby Smith is victorious! The enemy 15,000 strong under General Munson were completely routed in 3 fights. General Miller killed. 3000 prisoners, among whom was General Munson + staff. General Bull Nelson wounded and it is thought that a large portion of his army would be captured!! This victory will

---

231 Gen. Hugh W. Mercer.

232 There is a tinge of frustration and even envy in LeRoy's statement. Like himself, Alfred had also been seriously injured, but while he was getting better and could now easily use crutches, LeRoy was never able to easily use crutches, and his condition was slowly but steadily deteriorating.

233 The fighting that comprised Second Manassas (Second Bull Run) took place on August 28-30, 1862 between Lee's Army of Northern Virginia and John Pope's Army of Virginia. Jackson's wing had marched around Pope and destroyed supplies at Manassas Junction. On the 27th, Jackson attacked a portion of the Union army, revealing his position. Pope spent the 28th attacking Jackson's position, but was repulsed. James Longstreet's wing (with Lee) arrived on the field and on the 29th, Longstreet attacked a surprised Pope and drove his army off the field in a complete rout. Lee's losses were about 7,300 killed, wounded, and captured, while Pope's exceeded 14,000.

help greatly to deliver Tennessee.[234] From Virginia the news is more and more encouraging. Pope's Army is badly beaten. We have taken immense numbers of Prisoners. Our cavalry in one dash took 2000 without firing a gun. O it does ones very heart good to hear such news.

Friday September 5th 1862: Cool, clear, delightful day. Partisan Rangers leave today for Tennessee. . . . More confirmation of the glorious news. Our arms are again triumphant on the spot already immortal from "The Battle of 21st July 1861." Pope admits a loss in one battle of 8000. Generals Ewell, Trimble[235] + others severely wounded. Our men took thousands of prisoners, numerous batteries, stands of colors. The Feds lost 5 men to our 1. I took a ride in the carriage round by the C.S. Armory[236] and then way out by Brown's regiment. I saw them on dress parade and they looked firstrate. I saw Colonel Brown + Cousin Charlie. After staying as long as I wanted to, we came home and I do not feel at all worse for my ride. The anxiety to hear the news is intense.

Saturday September 6th 1862: Real September day. One week ago, our army was in an awful fight and yet no news is allowed to come. We receive full Yankee accts but none of our own. No casualties – the Colonel Bowdre wounded. General Ewell leg off. We took Manasas: 11 engines, 50 000 lbs. bacon, and large amounts of other stores. Great panic in Washington! There are numerous rumors of Pope's + Mclelland death. At 12 oclock Mother arrived safe [from Athens] and sound and brought me all the presents from Grandma. 1st a beautiful sponge cake which we cut and ate in honor of Mother's return. And also a nice jar of jam, 1 of Raspberry Jelly and some other Jelly, and a nice measure and lastly some elegant Romanites [apples] + grapes. Mother brought one or two peaches which are the last I expect to see. The news or really none makes us think the victory has not been complete and anxiety is felt about the army. Mr. Mickle came down with Mother to assist at the meeting.

---

234 To generate support for the Confederate cause and force Union troops to withdraw from Tennessee, Gen. Bragg's Rebel Army of Mississippi moved from Tennessee into Kentucky in August, and a second Confederate column under Gen. E. Kirby Smith did likewise from Knoxville, Tenn. Smith won a stunning victory at Richmond, Ky, on August 29-30 against Gen. William "Bull" Nelson. Smith's losses were just 450 killed and wounded against Nelson's 5,400, including 4,300 captured. Gen. Nelson was wounded, and Gen. Mahlon D. Manson (not Munson) was captured. There was no Gen. Miller involved.

235 Gen. Isaac R. Trimble.

236 LeRoy visited the temporary armory, which was operating out of the leased Depot of the Macon & Western Rail Road. The facility was for producing various armaments, and especially rifled-muskets. The permanent building would be constructed elsewhere in 1863.

Sabbath day September 7th 1862: Warm and clear. . . . Ate onions for dinner and am now in misery from the smell. Generals Bohlen and Kearney U.S.A. are killed, 5 or 6 others reported. Wilcox and Early CS[A] wounded, Taliaferro "ditto". Generals Jenkins + Fields ditto.[237]

Monday September 8th 1862: Warm and cloudy. No news except casualties. The Colonel [of the] 7th Georgia killed, Lieutenant Colonel [of the] 8th wounded. Pope is retreated to Alexandria. We took 10 000 prisoners, 20 pieces Artillery. Had sponge cake and jam for dinner. Mr. Bates' [school] opened today. Mother covered this [journal] and my bible [in brown paper]. A house in the neighborhood of Findley's foundry was burned last night at bedtime. The light was plainly visible from the upstairs window. I enjoy my apples very much indeed. Mother has gone down town. General Beauregarde has been assigned to the command in Charleston. General Joseph Johnston has entirely recovered [from Seven Pines wound].

Tuesday September 9th 1862: Warm and clear. Father and Thomas left early for the plantation. There are was a lunar rain bow last night round the moon + it was really pretty. It promises rain.[238] Received letter from Sallie Bird with a telegram from Auntie enclosed dated the 5th stating Uncle Edge was wounded. Shoulder bone broken in the desperate combat of 30th. She herself had been ill but was out of danger. Uncle Edge had not arrived in Richmond. Uncle Dick was not engaged at all [at Second Manassas]. We gave "Gipsey" away to a man at the livery stable. Adieu, "Gip" Adieu!

Wednesday September 10th 1862: Warm and clear. Stirring news from the West! Kirby Smith has taken Covington + Newport and demanded the surrender of Cincinatti![239] "Old Stonewall" is reported to be threatening Washington via Leesburg with 40000 men! General Stevens U.S.A killed. Captain M.R. Rogers is home, wounded in the knee. The 1st Georgia Regiment went in [at Second Manassas] with 170 men and 18 only escaped unhurt. Reading *Grantley Manor*. Hot as summer today + musquitoes <u>very</u> <u>bad</u> in the <u>daytime</u>. Father returned this eve. He left Jerry and brought back Duke. Scarlet fever at the plantation.

---

237 Gen. Henry Bohlen, a foreign-born Union general, was killed along the Rappahannock River prior to Second Manassas. Union Gens. Isaac I. Stevens and Philip Kearny were both killed at the Battle of Ox Hill (Chantilly) on September 1, 1862, a battle following the Rebel victory at Second Manassas. Of the Confederate generals noted, William B. Taliaferro, Micah Jenkins, and Charles Field were severely wounded, but Cadmus M. Wilcox and Jubal Early were not.

238 A lunar rainbow or "moonbow" is created the same way that a rainbow is, only with light from the moon refracting water droplets in the atmosphere.

239 Cincinnati was never in serious danger.

Thursday September 11th, 1862: Hot day for Sep. Bragg's army is pushing for Nashville; Huntsville is evacuated. Alabama relieved. Rained very hard with heavy and constant thunder in the night. J.A.C.K.S.O.N and L.O.N.G.S.T.R.E.E.T. are in Maryland; General Lee is at Leesburg. We are giving the Yanks "jessie." We Will burn Washington I hope. General Lee has been hurt by his horse. Wrist sprained and a bone broken. He will still do his duty.[240] Rained a little a 3PM: Received a telegram today from Auntie today telling Father to come on and then another countermanding it saying Uncle Edge was better. She herself is sick. He has not arrived in Richmond yet.

Friday September 12th 1862: Hot and clear. The waste house of the factory was burned again night before last at about 10 PM. Cause – "spontaneous combustion." Frank is making a windlass to the well. Mr. Goulding is going to teach school. The weather is debilitating beyond measure. Father bought me an elegant little measure [ruler]. My leg grows more and more crooked and I can bearly put it to the floor.[241]

Saturday September 13th 1862: Warm and clear. My Dr. Pancoast is division surgeon of Old Kearney's division and the "piece" said was going to embalm his body. To see anything <u>about</u> him (Dr P., not Kearney) makes me want to <u>see</u> <u>him</u> more than ever.[242] Minnie stayed all night with Mary Campbell. Thomas went to a regular ball at Mrs. Whittle's and stayed till 1AM. Thomas made me a crossbow. Our army is at Frederick, Maryland. Mother is in bed sick[243] We are needing rain very much and it is terrible hot for season.

240 Following his Second Manassas victory, Gen. Lee decided to carry the war north of the Potomac River and began crossing on September 4 1862. "Jessie" may have been a reference to the Jessie Scouts—Union troops who infiltrated CSA units and spied and scouted independently from a regular command. Shortly after Second Manassas Lee was holding the reins of his horse Traveller when the animal spooked and pulled him to the ground, breaking bones and injuring both hands. He spent most of his time in Maryland riding in an ambulance.

241 LeRoy's leg contractions have worsened because of his spinal nerve damage, and he can no longer straighten it sufficiently to touch the floor.

242 It is worth noting once more how much faith LeRoy placed in Dr. Pancoast, the Philadelphia physician he and his father had visited in 1860, and how little faith he had in most others. Of course, what he did not know was that there was nothing anyone could do for him.

243 It is unclear if LeRoy's mother had a chronic condition or if she had a weak overall constitution. If her issues were gynecological, it would make sense for LeRoy to not write about them, or even know about them in any detail as such things would not have been discussed with a young son.

Sabbath September 14th 1862: Sultry and cloudy. . . . Father brought me *Magdala and Bethany*. Mother in bed. Cousin Mary Harris' baby named Charlie[244] died yesterday at 4 o'clock and the funeral is today. It died very suddenly. Josephine Ralston's child had spasms last night and there was a great racket over there till after 11PM. Ate a very good melon, the last of the season. Rained in the eve pretty hard. Major General Pope is transferred to St. Paul, Minnesota, and is succeeded by McClelan "alias" 2.[245] No service at night on account of the hard rain.

Monday September 15th 1862: Coolish and rainish. Rained off and on all night and all the morning. Mother still sick. Received a letter from Grandma + Wilson enclosed. Cousin Sam Hayes is severely wounded in head.[246] No more from Uncle Edge. Mr. Tom Beman, a son of Dr. Beman, is killed. Father is suffering very much with toothache and his face is swollen. My cough has been better for a week. We killed in the late battle 6 Yankee Generals and wounded 3 or 4 more.

Teusday September 16th 1862: Warm and cloudy. Cousin Eliza + Aunt Sarah called. My leg is very bad and the skin and muscles are very sore indeed, so that when I stretch out the pain is bad.[247] Father's lip is badly swollen. Mr. L.P. Strong's funeral was this morning. All our army is in Maryland. General Smith is in Lexington, Kentucky. I stayed in Mother's room with her all the morn.

Wednesday September 17th 1862: Warm and clear. Minnie and Thomas went to "a dance" at Mrs. Moughan's last night. My leg is very bad; kept me awake nearly all night. Mother gone to town. Our army is in 12 miles of Baltimore, subsisting on the country.

Thursday September 18th 1862: Warm and clear. Thanksgiving day for our victories. Thomas has a boil on his face + did not go to Church. . . . Reading *Home Scenes* lent me by Mary Campbell. I feel sore and tired today beyond measure and slept very little after tea. Had an exhausting fit of coughing, a little worse than I ever remember to have had before.

Friday September 19th 1862: Warm and clear. Slept pretty quiet after taking some Porter and cough medicine, and feel a drop better now. Mother got a letter from Uncle Edge. He is in Richmond and doing well. Auntie is slowly recovering. Has been very ill

244 Charles Wiley Harris was the son of Charles J. Harris and Mary Clopton Wiley, a sister of Cousin Jinnie. They resided in Macon.

245 After his thrashing at Second Manassas, Pope was relieved and McClellan (having returned from the Virginia peninsula) was ordered to reorganize the shattered Union armies.

246 Sam was the son of Aunt Sarah Ann Wiley and brother to "TeaDee" Wiley in Athens. He survived.

247 This is typical of atrophied leg muscles, coupled with nerve and bone damage.

indeed. Also a letter from Sallie and Grandma, Cousin Sam Hayes' wound is slight. Mr. Nealy died last night. Conflicting rumors of a two days fight against heavy odds in Maryland. Stonewall has taken 8000 Yanks at Harpers Ferry. Very uneasy about the army.[248]

Saturday September 20th 1862: Coolish and cloudy. Rained in the night. "Rob" Plant called on Minnie last night, who was in bed fast asleep. The capture of 8000 prisoners is confirmed. Meagre accts of a big battle in Maryland on Sunday + Monday: Hill + Longstreet against 50,000 yanks. Loss <u>very</u> heavy on both sides. Dr. Scherzer called to see me. Father called on him for the reason there's no one else.[249] He examined and listened as the other doctors did, and presented 2 medicines and a salve, fresh air, +c. He is foreign in his manner. Mary made Gingercakes.

Sunday September 21st 1862: Cool and cloudy. Thomas' boil is so big he can't go to church. It is right by his eye.... Drizzled "off and on" through the day. Cough very bad at intervals. Florence is 6 years old, and 6 long years have rolled by since my leg was broken. Then began my troubles.

Monday September 22nd 1862: Cloudy and cool. Commenced to take Dr. Scherzer's medicine No. 1 + 2 alternately, 4 times a day. News of a terrific battle in Maryland at Sharpesville![250] When the fight ceased the "advantage" was on our side. It was reported that next day the fight was resumed and we drove them back Five miles! Generals Stark, Manning + Branche killed![251] 2 Jones' Ripley and Lawton wounded! This was on

248 Gen. Lee divided his army into several parts, some of which surrounded the Union garrison at Harpers Ferry. McClellan discovered that Lee's army was divided and drove through the gaps of the South Mountain range on Sept. 14. The battle there ended at nightfall with the Confederates in full retreat. Harpers Ferry fell the next day to Stonewall Jackson with 12,500 men and significant armaments. Lee's army, however, was dangerously divided and his campaign in complete turmoil.

249 Dr. Scherzer was a local Macon physician and native of one of the German states. He does not appear in the 1860 census for Macon. We do not know what he prescribed, though Leroy later refers to one medicine as a powder.

250 The Battle of Sharpsburg or Antietam (Sept. 17, 1862) was the bloodiest one-day battle in American history. Lee took up a position behind Antietam Creek near Sharpsburg, Maryland, where McClellan attacked him. Lee's lines barely held. McClellan did not attack the following day, and on the evening of September 18-19 Lee retreated into Virginia. Some 10,300 Confederates were killed, wounded, or captures, and Union losses totaled 12,400. Confederate Gen. Ambrose Ransom Wright of Georgia was among the wounded. It was a small tactical victory for Lee, but a decisive strategic victory for McClellan that ended the threat to Maryland and provided Lincoln with the "victory" he needed to announce the intention of implementing the Emancipation Proclamation.

251 Gens. William E. Starke and Lawrence O. Branch were killed, but Col. Van H. Manning was wounded. "2 Jones" (Gen. John R. Jones and Col. Robert H. Jones), Roswell Ripley, and Alexander Lawton.

Wednesday 17th Sep; General D.H. Hill's fight was Sunday + Monday 14-15th. Cumberland Gap is evacuated! General W.W. Loring after incessant fighting has taken Charleston, Virginia + the Saltworks.[252] Major General Stonewall Jackson has taken Harpers Ferry with <u>11000</u> prisoners, 73 cannon, 200 wagons! Our loss (a lie) 3 killed, 43 wounded! Mother went to see Cousin Mary Harris.[253] Every one is anxious beyond measure to hear more from the fight. All concur in thinking our army in a very critical state. Mother got a letter from Grandma with one from Uncle Dick [Richard] enclosed.

Tuesday September 23rd 1862: Cool and cloudy. Thomas left for Houston. No news! Reports of recrossing into Virginia. I am afraid we have been whipped. . . . My cough is "sorter" "so so."

Wednesday September 24th 1862: Warm and cloudy. In the late Battle of Sharpsburg, both sides claim a victory. Our object was to hold MClellan in check while we took Harpers Ferry and we succeeded perfectly in doing that. The Battle was the most terrific of the war. General A. R. Wright wounded. Yankee General Reno killed. Price + Rosencrans Have had a "fout" at Iuka who drove them back + then retreated. General Jackson is reported to have routed the Yanks 10000 strong at Sheppardstown since the big [Sharpsburg] battle.[254] Howard returned, and reports 3 or 4 cases of Scarlet fever [at the plantations].

Thursday September 25th 1862: "Very" delightful day. Reports of casualties come thick and even when we gain a <u>victory</u> the names of so many brave men killed is sad indeed! Major General Anderson badly wounded – Generals Armstead, Ransom, + Toombs wounded, also Brigadier General Anderson.[255] 11 in all mentioned. Our army it is said has crossed into Virginia. The Yankees are in a perfect Jubilee; wild with joy over the victory! Report all our Generals from Lee down, killed or captured with their commands!! Our side report a loss of 5000 while the Yankees report it as 40 000!!!!

---

252 Now in West Virginia, the Battle of Charleston (Sept. 13, 1862) was a short-lived success when Gen. Loring forced the Union troops out of Charleston and over the Kanawha River.

253 Mary Clopton Wiley Harris was a cousin of LeRoy's mother, Cousin Jinnie's sister and baby Charlie's mother.

254 The Battle of Shepherdstown (Sept. 19, 1862). Federal forces under Gen. Fitz John Porter attempted to pursue Lee's retreating army across the Potomac and were sharply beaten back. Union Gen. Jesse Reno was killed at South Mountain on the 14th. The Battle of Iuka, as noted by Leroy, was the beginning fight of the Iuka-Corinth Campaign in northern Mississippi, where Union Gen. William Rosecrans stopped an advance by Confederate Gen. Sterling Price.

255 Gens. Robert Toombs, Richard H. Anderson, and George B. Anderson were wounded (the latter mortally), but Robert Ransom and Lewis Armistead were not injured.

Thomas got me a nice letter of "Personne's" [256] about the Manassas fight, Aug 30th 1862. On Wed 17th we had 862 against 150 000!! O—i Mother in bed. I am in back piazza on my mattress. Father bought Thomas a pair of shoes, regular "stompers," for 8 Dollars. Captain J.G. Rodgers of the C.C. Blues is killed. Mrs. Tracy left for Athens to get Tracy and bring him home again. The report of Colonel J.B. Lamar's death is discredited. . . . Miss Susie Rowlands sent me some shrimps.

Friday September 26th 1862: Warm + clear. Ate a "pile" of shrimps and had the night-horse [diarrhea] in consequence. The list of killed + wounded is sad beyond measure. Captain Reuben Nisbet is reported killed. Colonel Newton [of the] 6th Georgia, Colonel Holmes [of the] 2nd + Colonel William [of the] 18th Georgia, ditto. Colonel Cumming [of the] 10th Georgia killed and Major Tracy[257] wounded. Colonel [Robert H.] Jones [of the] 22nd wounded. Sheppardstown victory by Jackson is confirmed. Enemy routed! 5000 prisoners! Colonel Smith? [of the] 27th Georgia Killed. To every one's regret, the death of Colonel John B. Lamar[258] is confirmed.

Saturday September 27th 1862: Very cool + cloudy. Stayed down at Mrs. Barnes' corner on my wagon nearly all ~~day~~ morning. "Rumor" says our army is still in Maryland pursuing McClellan, though I ca'nt credit it. The news from Kentucky is very cheering. I think Bragg will take Louisville, while General Smith is in possession of a large part of the state. Received a letter from Uncle John. He has been made "full surgeon" of 46th Georgia. My cough is about the same. Have fits of it once or twice a day. Drizzled a little.

Sabbath day September 28th 1862: Cool and rainy. We are sitting this morning by the first fire of the season, and it feels really comfortable. Slept well and my cough has not worried me any. Mr. Stump Rowland is slightly wounded; Major Tracy is a prisoner. We heard this evening of the death of Cousin Jinnie Blount's baby. It died out at Mr. Blount's.[259] [Two lines are scratched out and illegible.]

Monday September 29th 1862: Warm and clear a little mist early in the morn – clear at 10AM. Tracy arrived last night; Mrs. T[racy] [came] after him and brought us a box of

---

256 "Personne" was a pseudonym for Felix Gregory deFontaine, a correspondent for the *Charleston Courier*.

257 Lt. Col. James M. Newton (6th Georgia) and Lt. Col. William R. Holmes (2nd Georgia). There was no Col. William in the 18th Georgia; Maj. Philemon Tracy.

258 Col. Levi B. Smith (27th Georgia). Col. John B. Lamar was mortally wounded at South Mountain on Sept. 14 and died the next day.

259 No record of this child has been found, which was not uncommon with infant deaths.

elegant apples from Grandma. Uncle Rich wounded in hand. Uncle Edge is on his way home. Uncle John's regiment (46th Georgia) ordered to Richmond. Dr. Scherzer called; ordered my medicine to be taken every 2 hrs. 3 Dispatches today. 0 in them. My back hurts me today, though my cough is quiet for a wonder.

Teusday September 30th 1862: Warm and clear. Pain in my back and leg very bad all night and my good leg is a little affected.[260] Took Porter on going to bed. Dispatches state that Major Phil Tracy has died of his wounds. Cousin Howard stayed to tea + all night. The Thomson Gaurds had out of 10 men 8 killed + wounded. The Yellow fever is raging in Wilmington as an epidemic. The last battle in Maryland is the most tremendous of the war. We must at the very least have lost 8000 men in all. Father subscribed for *The Constitutionalist* and the first No. [issue] came today. Mother has gone down town. Tracy came up to see us yesterday. He is fat beyond comprehension and talks incessantly.[261] . . . My appetite to day is so very funny. I could eat – nothing at all. A letter from Colonel Hardeman states the death of Captain William Plane. All our kin thus far that have been heard from are either killed or wounded. Tomorrow is October. Tom is reading *Mahomet*.[262]

Wednesday October 1st 1862: Warm + clear. Slept miserable and feel bad in proportion today. Took some Porter on retiring which had the delightful effect of making me sick at the stomach. Coughed at intervals in the night and today. Everybody (so to speak) seems to have been hurt at Sharpsburg. The "Troop Artillery" of Athens and 900 of "Cobb's" Legion reported prisoners. Our loss must amount to 9000 in all. "Personna" has a splendid acct of the fight this morning. Mary is sick + Julia Ann cooks.

Thursday October 2nd 1862: Warm as August. Ira Fort came to see us today. Mr. Plane was shot in the abdomen. Father went to Houston. I was very restless all night. Mr. Spahr gave Min a lesson today. Cough bad in night. Mother went down to see Miss Annie Johnston. The lying Yankees state their loss at Sharpsburg at 10,000; without doubt it was 22,000.

---

260 This is LeRoy's first reference to the leg that was not severely injured in the 1856 chimney collapse. It is not until now that we learn his right leg was not injured in the accident.

261 Frequent visits by little Tracy, whose mother had died and whose father (John Springs Baxter) was away at war, is one of the ways family ties kept people close. Tracy is growing up with his older cousins and aunts and uncles he has known since birth.

262 Captain Plane, Phil Tracy, Uncle Edge, Uncle Richard, Cousin Sam Hayes are all kin mentioned by LeRoy who had been wounded in the recent fighting from Second Manassas to Sharpsburg. Thomas is reading *Mahomet*, a five-act tragedy by French playwright and philosopher Voltaire.

Friday October 3d 1862: Mild October is very hot so far. Last night Mother was awakened by the slam of a door and she arose + called Thomas to make a reconnaissance. They made a suitable noise to scare the robbers and on coming down the house had been entered + the rogues fled. Still Later Intelligence! The house was entered via Mother's room + they went in the pantry + took sugar, coffee, soap, + horror of horrors! My wine. In their hasty exit they dropped 7 bars of soap + part of the coffee. Of course false keys were used. Uncle Dick's little finger (left) was shattered [at Sharpsburg] and amputated. I pasted in my scrap-book all the morn. My back is better but cough only "so so." I am reading *The Life of Mahomet*. Cousin Mary Harris had gone to Richmond. Father returned this eve.

Saturday September [October] 4th 1862: Hot as summer. I feel "out of sorts" and have put Sep. instead of October, and took medicine No 1 instead of No 2. My cough is bad I had one hard spell yesterday and 2 today and it makes me so weak – Father and Mother went to see Cousin Helen. The News – From [the] Army [of] Northern Virginia is dubious in the extreme, as is that from Kentucky. The army is stated to be strong as prior to the battle.[263] Our loss will not amount to 6000 (Official). Gold is 28 in N.Y. Lincoln has declared slaves of rebels free.[264] . . . About 18 girls and 5 boys came + stayed all the morn and romped + played, and I looked at them from the dining room.

Sunday October 5th 1862: Warm and clear. . . . Read *The Angel of the Iceberg* all the morning. Captain Walker is Colonel [of the] 3d Georgia Regiment. It lost 72 men in the fight. Father rec'd today a letter dated Lynchburg from Uncle Richard begging him to come on; that he was in a miserable place, in a tent, and his hand 3 times worse than when the gun burst.[265] The Yellow fever still rages in Wilmington. Read *Working Man's Friend*. Cough is very annoying. Hot as summer.

Monday October 6th 1862: Warm and clear. Occupied myself with coughing instead of sleeping, and my leg is worse drawn up than ever. General Bull Nelson U.S.A. is

---

263 This was in fact true. Many thousands of Lee's men were either too exhausted to enter Maryland, or simply refused to cross the Potomac. The return of lightly wounded men, coupled with the return of many stragglers, swelled the ranks of the Army of Northern Virginia.

264 LeRoy is referring to Lincoln's Emancipation Proclamation. It is interesting how casually he wrote about it. Lincoln took advantage of Lee's defeat in Maryland to warn the Southern states on September 22 that he would order the freedom of all slaves in any state that did not end its rebellion against the Union by January 1, 1863. None would, so the actual order became official that day. Although it had no practical effect (he had no way of "freeing" these slaves), the proclamation made their freedom a major war aim. By doing so, he made it impossible for Europe to enter on the side of the Confederacy.

265 This explains how Uncle Richard shattered his little finger.

dead.[266] Commenced to take Dr. Scherzer's powder for my cough.[267] They have no taste whatever. The Yanks are crossing the Potomac at Harpers Ferry.

Teusday October 7th 1862: Warm and clear. Father left for Richmond last night to look after Uncle Richard. I slept very well last night. The News – is Price + Van Dorn have had a fight at Corinth and drove back the enemy.[268] Our army is stated that to be in a better condition than ever before. A battle is imminent in Kentucky between Bragg + Buell, 21 miles from Louisville. Nauseating rumors of "Recognition" area afloat. Mother went down town. My cough comes and goes; is better and again worse and then better again.

Wednesday October 8th 1862: Warm and clear. Van Dorn, after having driven back the enemy two days, is defeated. The Yankees receiving heavy reinforcements overwhelmed us and at last accounts were still pursuing us. The slaughter is stated as terrible. Mother is down town. Aunty + Uncle Edge are in Sparta. It is rumored that a fight between Lee + McClellan is pending. Dubious? Mother wrote to Father, and Thomas is gone to "Harry McCarthy" show.[269] The Yankees acknowledge a loss of 12, 000 in the "Battle of Sharpsburg." The weather is hot enough for July and Musquitoes are plentiful day and night.

---

266 Nelson was shot by during an argument by fellow Union Gen. Jefferson C. Davis, who was released from arrest and restored to duty because of the need for experienced officers.

267 The origin and composition of this remedy remains unknown.

268 Battle of Corinth (Oct. 3-4, 1862). Union Gen. Rosecrans defeated the combined forces under Earl Van Dorn and Sterling Price in northern Mississippi.

269 Composer of the highly popular Southern song "The Bonnie Blue Flag."

Thursday October 9th 1862: Warm and cloudy. College has opened and it is said with a large attendance. The News from Corinth is a little better. Our forces were flanked by 20000 men and retreated and made a stand. We repulsed them and then went on. Our loss some 5000 including 2 or 3 Gens. The enemy were strongly intrenched but their loss as usual was reckoned as greater. Read *The Pastors Daughter*.

Friday October 10th 1862: Warm and cloudy. We are wanting rain very much to cool the air. The weather is very debilitating. Dr. Scherzer called. Read *Arabian Nights* all the morn. Last night my leg + back pained me so bad I was unable to sleep with comfort. My cough does not improve. Howard went to [the] mill yesterday. Thomas wrote to Father. There have been numerous attempts at Robbery around town and from that I infer that burglars are about.

Saturday October 11th 1862: Warm and cloudy. Commenced to rain 11½ AM . . . all day. Cousin William Carnes stayed to dinner. There was a big negro "ball" at Mrs. Whittle's last night.[274] Took Porter and my leg hurt me all night. In the day though no actual pain; there is a sense of uneasiness and weariness about it which is very annoying.

Sunday October 12th 1862: Rain! Rain! Rain!! When I went to bed it was raining and it continued to come down in torrents, I may say buckets full all night. About breakfast the very floodgates of heaven (hyperbole) seemed turned loose. . . . "Gipsey" came back this morn. Rained until about noon and then was dark and cloudy. We are sitting by a fire, the first of the season. Read *Rest for the Wary*. My leg is if possible worse drawn up than I ever saw it. It has ached like a tooth +c; no position is easy.

Monday October 13th 1862: Cool fall day. Drizzly! Got a fire. Slept in snatches. Minnie was in bed yesterday with sore eyes. She is up today but unable to go to school. We heard from Uncle Richard through Grandma yesterday. His middle finger is amputated. Also from Father through Cousin Helen. She received a telegram saying Captain Plane died without doubt on the battlefield. . . . Dr. Scherzer called + brought me a supply of Powders. Mr. Spahr is very sick. Aunty is very weak and she fell out the back door and hurt her back. 2 *Dispatches* came. A cavalry force of Yankees crossed the river, when our cavalry under Brig. [Fitzhugh] Lee, "Smote them hip and thigh" and scattered them like "chaff before the wind." General Lee has issued congratulatory ordered to his troops. The loss at "Sharpsburg" – 5000 Yankee 18999 – 5 from 18 – leaves 9000 in our favor. Gold is 26 in N.Y. My cough isnotsoobstreperousasusual.

Le Roy

---

274 Mrs. Whittle, a Macon resident, entertained all levels of society, including slaves and free blacks.

Tuesday October 14 1862: Very bracing and delightful day. Howard left for Houston. (By the By, this pen is wretched + the ink on a par.) We were very much rejoiced to hear that Captain Rube Nisbet is still alive at Hagarstown, Maryland. Cousin Charlie came to see us all. He leaves for Virginia tonight. He wrote in Minnie's album. Mr. Blount went on to see about his brother and found he has been dead 2 weeks. How sad is war! Rumors of a battle (from the north) in Kentucky. 2000 Feds killed 4 Generals. As a victory is not claimed, I hope [we] are gained one. Ate the last of Grandma's apples. My leg is better. Started *D. Copperfield, Esq.* . . . . Congress! For the good of the country has ad'jd [adjourned] – a miserable attempt at a flag was adopted.[275]

Wednesday October 15th 1862: Cool + Clear. 3PM: Drizzling. By a fire all day. Cough and leg middling. A battle of importance has been fought near Perryville, Kentucky.[276] Yankee accts but none of our own from 4 to 5 + 25000 Yankees killed {I do hope to hear of a victory for our arms.} General Stuart with 3000 men crossed the Potomac, made a raid up into Pennsylvania, captured + burnt army stores, Prisoners, horses, +c. [277] Recrossed the river cutting through a division of Feds with the loss of a man. Received letter from Father who is well and would go to Lynchburg in the morn.

Thursday October 16th 1862: Tolerable cool. Fine. No confirmation of news from Kentucky! It's distressing indeed, indeed. Slept tol'ble [tolerable]. Mother in bed. Rather warm for a fire and too cold without one. I've been reading *Copperfield* and am very mad with him now for getting drunk. Hav'nt heard from Tracy since he came home. The disease has appeared among the hogs at our plantation and it will be a terrible calamity if it gets bad. Mrs. Judge Nisbet called. The Ladies Gunboat at Charleston, the *Palmetto State*, is done. Also Gunboat called *Chicora*.[278] Thomas went to auction today.

Friday October 17th 1862: Cool and clear. Thomas washed the groundpeas [peanuts] and put them in the sun. The tardy news of the fight in Kentucky is received at last and

275 The second national flag of the Confederate States was known as the "Stainless Banner," and was put in use on May 1, 1863, replacing the initial "Stars and Bars." It had a smaller version of the Army of Northern Virginia battle flag in the upper left field.

276 The Battle of Perrysville (October 7, 1862) in Kentucky between Confederate Gen. Braxton Bragg's Army of Mississippi and Union Gen. Don C. Buell's Army of the Ohio. The battle was a tactical draw. By this time it was obvious Kentuckians were not going to rise en masse to the Confederate banner, and Bragg retreated back into Tennessee, ending the Kentucky Campaign.

277 Jeb Stuart's Chambersburg Raid, the second time he rode completely around McClellan's army, capturing horses and other supplies while gathering intelligence. His troops also collected civilian officials who were used to exchange for captured Confederate civilians.

278 The *Palmetto State* and *Chicora* were ironclads in Charleston harbor similar to the CSS *Virginia*.

is a little misty. 5 or 6 Fed. Generals "hors de combat" [injured]. The fight commenced on Monday 6th Oct. at Perryville. General [William] Hardee commanded the left, [Simon] Buckner the centre. Marshall + Morgan, the right. 1st day we took 1500 prisoners + slaughtered the Yankees! The fight was resumed next day with still greater slaughter!!! The enemy driven 12 miles. Our loss comparatively small! We took 40 cannon. The Yanks claim a victory!!! General J. Crittenden is a prisoner!! (Horrid pen) I Hope we have gained a victory!!![279] "Dave" is in jail, been run away 2 weeks.[280] Mother in bed. Cough – troublesome. Lay in Mother's room all day. The 3d Georgia Cavalry is reported captured in Kentucky. I do wish we could hear from Father oftener. I begin to want to see him badly. 6PM: Father arrived here this eve at 5PM, and how surprised we were! He came via East Tennessee.

Saturday October 18th 1862: Cool and clear. I was on my wagon out in the street when Father came + was the first one to see him. Uncle Richard is at home – Father brought some beautiful apples. He brought some elegant cloth to make Thomas and I some pants. The cars were jammed all the way. Mother in bed. Slept well. Cough miserable and I am now exhausted by a hard fit of it. It distresses me beyond measure.

Sabbath day October 19th 1862: Was cool +c, clear. . . . Read *Great Change*. Last night we, Thomas and I, were astonished and delighted by two beautiful presents. Mine an elegantly bound set of books called Lodge's *Portraits*,[281] and Thomas' a splendid *Shakespeare* in 4 Volumes, just like Irving. They are intended to embrace Birthday, Christmas, +c, +c. News of yesterday confirmed in a very unintelligible telegram. General Polk came very near being captured.

Monday October 20th 1862: Cool clear day. Thomas' 18th birthday! Coughed incessantly all the morn. Aunt Ann + John[282] called. Got a letter from Grandma. Uncle Dick had arrived. She describes Aunty as in a low condition. Received also a letter from Father in Lynchburg. Rather late! Mrs. Huguenin has a baby. Got a fire – My medicine is out. Milo came up.

279 Gen. Hardee commanded the left wing and Gen. Leonidas Polk the right. Marshall and Morgan were not present. Bragg's command was small, and he unknowingly attacked a significantly larger enemy at Perryville. The fighting occurred on one day, October 8. 1862.

280 The frequency of slaves attempting to escape was increasing, especially after the preliminary Emancipation Proclamation was announced.

281 Edmund Lodge, *Portraits of Illustrious Personages of Great Britain* (London, 1821).

282 John Barnett Wiley, Jr. was the youngest son of LeRoy's late Uncle Jack.

Teusday October 21 1862: Cool and cloudy. Cough incessantly all night and all the morn. If my cough is not stopped it will wear me out. It depresses me beyond measure. Dr. Scherzer's medicine is a farce! General Bragg is falling back. The fight at Perryville was not a large affair. We did not take many prisoners. McClellan is advancing. Milo went back. Mother went down town. My cough + leg have been awful today. Thomas + Minnie's shoes came from Athens and are very fine. They are presents from Grandma.

Wednesday October 22nd 1862: Cool and clear. Thomas went down on the railroad to Houston. Took an anodyne pill last night. Cough not quite as bad – Leg not painful. Dr. Scherzer called +c, put 3 or 4 drops of stuff in one tumbler of water + 3 or 4 in another, and then to take a table-spoonful every hour. Went out to look at the boys play townball. General Lee is falling back! Bragg is retreating! Mrs. Huguenin sent me a "whop pen" pomegranate. I ate it.

Thursday October 23d 1862: Cool, magnificent day. About in full winter [dress], undershirt included for the first time. Cough so bad had to take morphine on retiring. Stayed on wagon till 11AM. Father cut my hair. Father bought some tea at $8 a lb. Our loss at Perryville was 2500, Yankee 5000. [James S.] Jackson + [William R.] Terrill U.S.A. killed. Finished *David C., Esq.* and it's a splendid book too! Jackson, Longstreet, Hardee, Pemberton, Holmes + others are [made] Lieutenant Generals.

Friday October 24th 1862: Normal, clear, cool, beautiful, Autumn October day. My leg pained me and my cough worried me <u>last night</u> and this morn my <u>right</u> leg, my only good leg, is slightly contracted. If it gets worse then may I truly exclaim, "I am on my last legs."[283] There are two spots one on each side of the spine on the large muscle, about as big as a silver dollar which are very tender + and pain me when I cough, from the pulling I suppose. The "Hiccough" is "sufficit" to say intolerable. My only relief from the cough is in the "Syrup of Lettuce." {"*Finis*."}[284] The Vandals have made an attempt to reach the S+C.R.R., +c and succeeded once but were eventually repulsed. The *C.S. "290"* Capt. Semmes[285] is making a star among Yankees ships, having destroyed 14 in short time, principally whalers. All men between up to 40 are called out.

283 Despite all his pain and discomfort, LeRoy never lost his rather amazing sense of humor.

284 This information also confirms LeRoy had contracted tuberculosis. The large spots he describes are infection spreading from his lower lungs into his back tissue. "Syrup of Lettuce" is a home remedy for coughs and bronchial ailments, made from boiling lettuce and sugar in water to make syrup. "*Finis*" is Latin for "the end." Exactly why Leroy wrote that word is unknown. He never suggests that he knew he had tuberculosis, but he may have begun to realize he was not going to ever fully recover.

285 Confederate Adm. Raphael Semmes, captain of the Confederate raider CSS *Alabama*, hull # 290.

All quiet on the lines of the A.N.Va. [Army of Northern Virginia]. I cut an apple every day and enjoy them very much. . . .

Saturday October 25th 1862: Warmer + cloudy. My cough is miserable – wearsome – harassing – and gives me little rest night or day. It is worse when I lay on my left side. Our loss at Pokehistailandhewillgo[286] was 15 killed 40 wounded, while the "abolitionists" was 200 in killed + wounded. Without a fire today. Reading *Friends + Neighbors*, S.S. authors. Rather monotonous. Thomas returned + brought butter.

Sunday October 26th 1862: Joy cold – very high wind – rained a little in the night. We feel the cold very much – in short "it is Joy." . . . We sat in Mother's room all day. . . . Cough a little more quiet + my rest better though I say it with fear + trembling lest it should start now. Read some in *The Wicklyffites*. This just fills out this page exactly.

Monday October 27th 1862: Cold and clear. Not quite freezing. No important news. Slept well. Green and Ned came up bringing Jerry.[287] Mother went visiting. Howard cut down the blackjack [black oak] tree by the smokehouse. Wonder of Wonders! Tracy came to see us. He is as pretty as he can be. . . . Cough comparatively quiet.

Tuesday October 28th 1862: Cold and cloudy. Cough quiet. No news except the disgusting repetition "France, England + Belgium are on the 'eve' of recognition." This is "reliable." Mother gone to town there bought some sugar cane and Father did too.

Wednesday October 29th 1862: Warmer + clear. Cough obstreperous in the early morning then quiet all day. Read letter from Aunt Eliza. "Nary apple." I got a letter from Grandma with one from <u>Uncle</u> Ed enclosed. Uncle Richard's hand is not doing as well as it might. Howard and Ned both hauling our wood from the railroad and Thomas piled ten cords. It is crooked enough but it is <u>all</u> hickory and will burn well. We have been using coal since Monday and it has been behaving beautifully too. I stayed on my wagon till dinner and got pretty tired. Father has a bad cold and then his tooth is so sore his mouth is all swollen up. Literally no news. There is a long obituary of Captain Plane in the paper today. Mary parched some ground peas.

Thursday October 30th 1862: Cool + bracing. Howard + Green hauling wood. There is about 14 or 15 cords in all. Coughed a little in the early morn. Slight frost. Snow in Tennessee, so says Cousin Howard (who called here about half an hour on his way home from there). Mother went to town. Stayed out till 11AM. My medicines out.

---

286 Leroy's spelling (poke his tail and he will go) is a play on words for the Second Battle of Pocotaligo (October 22, 1862), a failed attempt to cut the Charleston and Savannah Railroad in South Carolina.

287 Ned and Green are slaves from the Houston plantations. Jerry is a draft horse.

Brigadier General Wright is in town and on being serenaded made an address. Brigadier General Cobb is here also. No news. "Muigleb has recognized the C.S.A." Note this.[288]

Friday October 31st 1862: Coolish and clearish. Ned and Frank went to Houston, leaving Green behind for a day or two. The C.S.A. are not recognized but "France + England are in accord." This is nauseating; I might use a stronger term. . . . Reading *Sparing to Spend*. T.S. Author. The Smallpox has appeared in several regiments of the Virginia Army, the 7th + 1st Georgia among them. General Bragg has been ordered to report at Richmond. Lieutenant General Pemberton has superceded Van Dorn. General [Joe] Johnston has no command.

Saturday {October} November 1st 1862: Warm and cloudy. Stayed out till 11.45 AM. Tracy came up before we broke fast and stayed till 10AM. He was very affable + sweet. Sowed the ryelot in rye at $6 a bushel. Father's ears ached him very bad + he is nearly sick today.

Sunday November 2nd 1862: Warm and cloudy. . . . Had a bad spell of coughing and threw up my breakfast. Read *Wycliffites*. Eat Sugar cane. Eat Peanuts.

Monday November 3d 1862: Warm and clear. Thomas left today for College. I had a most miserable fit of coughing, sick stomach, throwing up, +c. The U.S. General Buell is reported superceded by Rosencrantz.

Tuesday November 4th 1862: Warm in the early morn, but very much cooler towards evening. Watched Johnson burning leaves and Green cutting wood all the morn. Mother went down town and bought 6 oranges, price $2 a dozen. Colonel Huguenin has been very sick for some time. Rumors of Recognition are rife. Colonel Hardeman has resigned. General Cobb's brigade is ordered to Georgia soon.

Wednesday November 5th 1862: Cool and cloudy. Pasted in my scrap-book all the morning. Coughed all night so that what sleep I got was troubled, and after I came down had a hard fit of coughing. I always feel depressed when I cough so. The wagon

---

288 "Muigleb" is "Belgium" spelled backward.

came last night with Arch + Milo bringing the hams and middlings of a nice fat pig and fresh butter. The Yankees have sent [General] Halleck out west again. General McClellan made military advisor to Lincoln and succeeded by Hooker. This is a very material change.[289] "Recognition abroad" is the topic of the day. . . . Mother and Minnie are both knitting socks and Mother gets on very well.[290]

Thursday November 6th 1862: Cold and windy. Rain in the night. My cough was distressing in the night and would not let me sleep at all. Father sick in the night. Father brought home some nankin[291] knitting cotton. Did not go on my wagon but a little while in the eve. ~~Thomas~~ Received a letter from Tom. He found all his things stolen on his arrival, and started to come back. He boards at Mrs. Tucker's.

Friday November 7th 1862: Cold and cloudy. Took a morphine pill and my cough did not worry me quite so much. There had been a large fire in Agusta consuming $500 000 worth of property, 6000 bales cotton.[292] Father bought some sugar cane yesterday. Reading Lodge's *Portraits*. Dr. Scherzer called and made prescriptions. Moved down stairs this day and took possession of winter quarters.

Saturday November 8th 1862: Coldest day yet. There was frost + ice both. Tracy came up to see us. Father brought home a shanghai[293] coat for me to try on and it fits me very well. The man came + took down the grate yesterday. My syrup of Lettuce came from Milledgeville also and it tastes altogether different from the other. I took a pill yesternight but my cough would worry me in the night. I put on my boots this morn and hardly had strength to do it. Old Governor Brown has out two messages one for the special purpose of abusing President Davis, the conscript act, and the government

---

289 Gen. Halleck did not return out West but remained in Washington. Leroy's mention of McClellan is curious. Lincoln made the decision to sack McClellan on November 5 for his failure to aggressively pursue and defeat Lee after Antietam. It was not made official (and public) until November 9. His replacement was not Gen. Joe Hooker, but Gen. Ambrose Burnside.

290 It sounds as if this was a new skill for Mother, possibly learning the steps in knitting socks from Minnie, who has made several pair.

291 Nankeen is a pale yellow cotton cloth or yarn, originally manufactured at Nanking, China, in the early 19th century from yellow cotton. Southern cotton was dyed this color by the time of the Civil War. The Macon Manufacturing Company factory produced this yarn and fabric.

292 Despite declarations they would only grow enough cotton to provide clothing for themselves and their servants, planters largely ignored them and planted most of their acreage with cash crops like cotton and tobacco, instead of grains worth less on the open market, but which could be consumed by soldiers and civilians.

293 A type of paletot jacket straight cut in front and fitted in the back. Father brought a sample for LeRoy to try on before the coat was cut out.

in general and calls on Georgia to "kick up a row." His long message is 1 mile + 1 go long. Dispatches of today "squelch the resignation question." Mother and Minnie went down town and bought knitting needles. The Army of Northern Virginia has fallen back to the Rapidan, leaving Stonewall [Jackson] in the Valley.

Sunday November 9th 1862: A most glorious and enchanting day, a heavy frost + Ice. I slept a while last night and then woke up + coughed a while then went to sleep again and woke up and coughed again and took some medicine. And so on alternately till morning when my Master became as quiet as a lamb. I can not venture to poke my nose out from under the cover lest I should offend him. My leg continues as crooked as ever but hardly ever pains me. I hardly dare to hope it will ever be straight again. Mary made some gingercakes yesterday. The Federal General Mitchell is dead.[294] I am not disconsolate. General Beauregarde has ordered all noncombatents out of Charleston. Minnie and Father went to church at night and Mother read aloud to me from a book called *Golden Grains*.

Monday November 11th [sic] 1862: Cool and clear. Frost a plenty. Had a bad coughing spell about midnight. Mr. Bates has 32 scholars. I received a letter from Thomas who is very lonely + homesick. Our paper is completely taken up with governor's interminable message, +c. Legislative proceedings. The good Old *Presbyterian* [newspaper] again comes with a full sheet. . . . Dr. Schenger called. Milo came up bringing some huge potatoes. My leg is very painful to night. Uncle LeRoy arrived. The mumps have taken his place + at different times he has had 150 cases and lost 8.

11th Nov. 1862 Teusday: Rather warmer. My 15th Birthday. It is 38 months since I laid down and nearly 6 long years since this disease started and today it is worse and I [am] weaker than ever before![295] My present is *Lodge's Portraits*. Uncle LeRoy and Father left for Milledgeville at noon. Father took some cakes, groundpeas, Potatoes, and a substitute to Thomas.[296] I had to take morphine last night for my leg pained me more than it has since the time of Presbytery. I read some in *Golden Grains* T.S.A. My leg is

294 Gen. Ormsby M. Mitchel died of Yellow Fever in Hilton Head, SC, on Oct. 30, 1862.

295 This is the first and only time he refers to his condition as a "disease," but there is no indication he knew he had tuberculosis, or that anyone told him. We know with certainty that he did not know he was fatally ill. It may be a passing general reference to encompass his chronic coughing, fevers, and infections, but should not be read as an indication he knew of the true seriousness of his illness.

296 "Substitute" was another man willing to take Thomas' place in the army so he could avoid service and continue in college. The Confederate Conscription Act provided that men could hire substitutes to serve in their place from "persons not liable for duty," which usually meant men older or younger than draft age or foreigners. The provision was based on English tradition that concluded men who could afford to hire a substitute were more useful to society and the war effort by remaining outside the army.

> 11th Nov—1862 Tuesday
> Rather warmer. 8 am 44 3 PM 60°
> My 15th Birthday. It is 28 months
> since I laid down and nearly 6 long
> years since this disease started and
> today it is worse and I weaker
> than ever before!

worse drawn up than ever before. . . . We were all shocked + indignant on hearing that Uncle Link's wife was married again to a Baptist minister.[297] The news came through a letter from her. Governor Brown in a letter to President Davis Declares: "That no more conscripts shall be enrolled and releases all those who have been conscribed from their engagements." With the Good old State of Georgia afloat on the broad Sea of rebellion and Governor Brown at the helm, what will become our poor government + us? . . .

Wednesday November 12th 1862: Too warm for a fire and very chilly without one. Sat in Mother's room all the morning so as to let the sitting-room hearth, which had been painted, dry. Uncle Leroy popped in on us between the 1st and 2nd bells. The Supreme Court has declared the conscript act constitutional.[298] Our army is skirmishing with the enemy at Orange Court House, Virginia. My cough has worried me today a great deal. I have had 3 bad spells and my new medicine has no effect. My leg aches like a tooth and I am out of sorts generally. Mother and Minnie have gone to Poor Little Mary Nisbet's funeral. She died after a short spell of pneumonia. I have coughed if <u>possible</u> more than I ever did before in one day. Mother and Uncle LeRoy played backgammon after supper. Minnie started a pair of socks for me, and Mother and Ella are also knitting. It is rumored that a fight is imminent on the Potomac. I don't have much hope, if any, that my cough will be better.

Thursday November 13th 1862: Half cold, half hot. Coughed a good deal. I am about in the same condition now as I was the 1st winter I was sick. That is, I can hardly get along at night without anodyne. Father came back last night, reports Tom well, and

297 Maria Burton Baxter's husband had not been deceased a year before she remarried. It was expected that widows would mourn for two and a half years, so marrying less than a year later would have been rather scandalous behavior.

298 Governor Brown questioned the constitutionality of conscription laws. The Georgia Supreme Court found the law constitutional in the November 1862 case *Jeffers v. Fair*.

says the boys enjoyed the groundpeas very much. Mother taken Thomas' room for Minnie on account of proximity to us. 9PM: coughing constantly.

Friday November 14th 1862: Warmish + cloudy. Uncle LeRoy left for Flint River. Took an anodyne and my cough was quiet in the night. There is a whole lot of stuff about Recognition in the daily and rumors of the supercession of McClellan by General Burnside. Father bought the cloth for my coat. I went down by the schoolhouse and listened to the boys speak.[299] My cough has been as (bad) possible all day.

Saturday November 15th 1862: Warm and cloudy. Stayed on my wagon till 1½ oclock and made a penstaff.[300] Father read a very interesting letter from a niece of President Davis intercepted by the Yankees. + published in the *N.Y. Herald*. Its date is May 7th. I coughed in the night and the muscles on the side of the spine very sore indeed. There are indistinct rumors of an important fight between Jackson + the Yanks. Governor Brown is out in a message No. 4 on about the enemy on the coast. General J.E. Johnston is sick in Richmond, yet General [Howell] Cobb has been appointed to the command in Southwestern Georgia. Kirby Smith at Chattannooga. I can hardly write at all for the position in which I lie makes me cough badly. Brigadier General Edward Tracy called and I went in to see him. He came to bring his family away from Huntsville and leaves tomorrow for Chattanooga to report to General Smith.

Sunday November 16th 1862: Cool dark + cloudy. Put on my new shanghai suit for the 1st time. There is a deal of talk about McClellan's removal. It has every appearance of truth and Burnside is named as his successor – "So must it be." I do not cough "much" early in the night but about midnight it starts and then there is no more rest for me until I cough up the p[h]legm. I am sadly anxious about this for fear it will (if it is not already) seriously injur[e] my lungs and thinking about this often makes me very cross + irritable as well as low spirited. I am grieved to say my cough medicine is a bust.[301]

Monday November 17th 1862: Cool and cloudy. Minnie received a letter from Thomas in which he said he'd be here at Synod.[302] Mother and I both wrote to him today. I took an anodyne last night + did not cough any. Mother got a letter from Grandma. Uncle Dick is in Sparta. She [Grandma] is sick. The talk is McClellan's

---

299 Oral recitation of lessons was an important part of education practice during the 19th century.

300 A pen staff is the wooden portion into which an ink nib is placed. LeRoy had been complaining about the condition of his pen, and decided to make one of his own.

301 Coughing, with sputum, back pain, abscesses, etc., are symptoms associated with active pulmonary tuberculosis.

302 An ecclesiastical meeting of several presbyteries, which in 1862 was held in Macon.

removal. Did not stay on my wagon long because it was so cool + raw. Father brought home some nankin cloth and it is nice. Mother made me a wagon cover out of it. Wrote to Brother.

Tuesday November 18th 1862: Warm and cloudy. Father left for Houston, though it was very foggy and looked very much like rain. Mother is in bed and I am in her room today. Read "Shakspeare." The boys are getting tired of townball. I did not go on my wagon till in the evening because it drizzled rain every now + then. Mrs. Strohecker sent me some dinner pudding. Father bought 4 lemons + I drank some lemonade. There are a great many Florida oranges in town. . . . My cough has been a little more manageable today. My right leg continues badly drawn up (I meant to say my left) but don't hurt.

Wednesday November 19th 1862: Warm and cloudy. Slept very bad on account of my cough and the room being so hot. Took a pill. General Randolph, Secretary of War, has resigned on account of some difference with the President, and General G.W. Smith appointed pro tem. Governor Johnston is elected senator.[303] Got a letter from Thomas. He will be home tomorrow. The Yankees are trying to retake Fredericksburg [Va]. Minnie slept downstairs with Mother. The wagon came bringing Green + Dan, 7 turkeys, 7 hams, walnuts, Groundpeas, potatoes, +c, +c. Father came about 8 oclock with a bad headache. Frank sent me a couple of partridges.

Thursday November 20th 1862: Cool and clear. Rained tremendidous at about 11 oclock at night. Wagon went back this morn. . . . My grey roundabout came home and it is splendid and will do me good service.[304] I read a letter from Uncle John and [got] some relics from the Battle fields around Charleston. My cough is a little quiet. Thomas came over this morn. Commenced on a new bag of coffee + flour. Mr. Baker came at night to stay. Synod opened tonight + Minnie went.

Friday November 21st 1862: Cold and clear. Prof. Smith stayed all night. For a wonder I did not cough any in the night. Mother is quite unwell + hardly able to be up. Colonels Cobb, Doles, +c have been made brigadiers.[305] It is rumored that General Joseph E. Johnston has superceded Bragg. A fight is looked for at Corinth or Murfreesboro. At the latter place we have a very good army. Affairs about

---

303 Herschel V. Johnson, Georgia governor from 1853-1857, was elected to the Second Confederate Congress.

304 A short jacket, close-cut and without tails.

305 Cols. Thomas R. R. Cobb (nominated but not confirmed before his death on Dec. 13, 1862) and George P. Doles (a native of Milledgeville, Georgia).

Fredericksburg and Suffolk look very threatening. Mr. Seddons is Secretary of War.[306] Dr. Wilson, Jr. preached last night. Mr. Mallard tonight. Synod opened + elected Dr. Higgins moderator. Mr. Baker, Mr. Pitzer who got here last night. Mr. Houston, Mr. Palmer, stayed to dinner and we got through about 4 oclock. Mr. Pitzer has a very bad sty on his eye. He smoked his pipe vigorously after meals. Mr. Simpson came to tea + to stay and talked very pleasantly after supper. Mother got a letter from Aunty saying Uncle Richard would be here tomorrow and she was convalescing. Mr. Mallard preaches tonight. Dr. Scherzer called and prescribed some more of his little old powders. Mr. Bates taught till 1 oclock. Prof. Woodrow,[307] Mr. Parker, and Mr. Pitzer are staying with us.

Saturday November 22nd 1862: Cold and clear. Uncle Richard arrived here + we were all delighted to see him. He looks very well and his hand is nearly healed up. Mr. Baker preaches today. Minnie was sick all night with a cold + sore throat + the Dr. came to see her today. Mr. Hendee and Mr. Clisby dined here. My cough is comparatively quiet. Mr. Pitzer has been challenging to a game of chess tonight. Synod adjourned and there will be addresses delivered on the state of the country. There was called a meeting of Hopewell, Pennyslvania to receive Mr. Pitzer.

Sunday Nov 23d 1862: Cool and clear. Minnie was really very sick with sore throat, had a high fever. . . . Mr. Pitzer is hardly able to go out on account of his eye. Got a letter from Grandma. No news. Mr. Rogers of Atlanta stayed to tea yesterday. Mr. Pitzer and I spent the eve together, his eye being so bad he did not go down to hear Dr. Lanneare; Dr. Leyburn is to preach tonight. Mr. Ladson to the darkeys. Uncle Richard + Tom went to a baptizing. He interesting us by fighting his battles over again and telling incidents +c. I have neglected my diary and medicine very much while the Synod has been here.

Monday Nov 24th 1862: Clear + cold. Ice. All the ministers left for home. Mr. Pitzer wrote in Minnie's album. Tracy came up to see Uncle Dick. The Yanks are trying their best on Fredericksburg. Min is well. My cough is comparatively quiet.

Tuesday November 25th 1862: Warmer, cloudy. Thomas left for Milledgeville, taking a trunk full of goobers [peanuts]. Min is knitting nankin socks. . . . Mother bought two pitchers, 6 bowls, +c. Minnie is well again.

306 James A. Seddon was the fourth Confederate secretary of war.

307 This is possibly Rev. Dr. Thomas Woodrow, the maternal grandfather of future president Woodrow Wilson.

Wednesday November 26th 1862: Cold and clear. Mother went down town. Colonel Huguenin is quite ill. M.E. Conference meet in the City Hall. Min started to school. My cough is a little "Under the weather." "Price" [LeRoy's dog] is very playful and is already attached to Uncle Richard. "No news." Long rigermarole about Fredericksburg. The wagon came up last night with Ben + Sip, and returned today. Rained in the night some. The wagon came up [with] Green and Solomon. Towards night; it turned very cold. Uncle Richard went to see Aunt Ann. Wrote to Uncle John, Ike Bowers.

Thursday November 27th 1862: Cold + clear! Tremendous frost! Ice. Green and Howard are hauling wood from SWRR depot. Mother gone to a meeting Soldiers Relief Society. Tracy came up + I went out in the garden + we had a heap of fun playing with Bragg + Price. Uncle Dick's birthday. Towards dark it was icy cold. Dr. Scherzer called and I am inclined to think it will be about the last. Wrote a letter to Thomas + Mother got one from home.

Friday November 28th 1862: Cold and frosty. Uncle Richard left for Athens. Mother gave him an inkstand and a nankin shirt. I am mighty sorry he had to go away so soon. Father bought some sugarcane. Read *Reveries of a Bachelor*. Mrs. Bowie came to beg coffee. The <u>Grand</u> army of Abolitionists are advancing via Fredericksburg and another via Suffolk.[308] They expect to be in Richmond in ten days. The *Alabama No. 290* continues to destroy Yankee ships. Mr. Lem Cherry who was a candidate for Mayor has come down in favor of O.G. Sparks,[309] who will be elected. Mrs. Weed's baby called. My cough is a little worse. I slept splendidly last night. I am the Boomerang.

Saturday November 29th 1862: Cold and clear. Green + Solomon went home. I gave Green some nankin to make some pants. Uncle Edmund + Cousin Maria Betts arrived here this morning.[310] Mother went to Soldiers Relief Society. General Joseph E. Johnston is ere this at the seat of war in the West. A fight is looked for at Holly springs [Mississippi]. Uncle Edmund showed me a letter from Cousin Job. A rumor is out that General [A.R.] Wright has been promoted, but I doubt it. I expected Dr. White to see me today but he did not come. Cough a little quieter. Had potatoe custard for dinner.

---

308 LeRoy may be poking fun at Gen. Burnside's reorganization of the Union Army of the Potomac into three "Grand Divisions."

309 Ovid Garten Sparks had been mayor from 1858-1860, and would be again in 1863.

310 Uncle Link Baxter's remarried widow Maria Burton Baxter (see Nov. 11, 1862 entry). LeRoy mostly now refers to her as "Mrs. Betts" rather than as "Cousin." The family probably welcomed her, but with some distance given the unconventional and socially unacceptable circumstances of her remarriage.

Cousin 'Liza + Aunt Sarah came to see Mrs. Betts; another week has passed away. Uncle LeRoy came.

Sunday Nov 30th 1862: Good, clear, splendid day. Mrs. Betts + Uncle LeRoy stayed home. Dr. Green, a refugee from Nashville + member of the Conference, preached in our church and the congregation was very large. His subject was the "The Prodigal son;" all the pulpits were occupied by the Methodists. Cousin Eliza sent me some bavarian cream + jelly and it was so rich I could not eat much of it. Uncle Edmund stayed to tea with Cousin Jimmy. We lent Old Jerry to them; one of their horses having run away + broke the wagon.

Winter Monday December 1st 1862: Pleasant day. Uncle Edmund left. Cousin Maria spends the day at Cousin Liza's. I did not sleep well. My old cough worried me. Uncle LeRoy and I took some good games of Backgammon: I beat him 4 + he 2, and then he and Mother played. There was a nig by name of Robert Anderson murdered on the suburbs Sat night [indecipherable].

Tuesday Dec. 2nd 1862: Cool + cloudy. Spent a most doleful miserable night. I coughed all the morning long as well as all night long. The two spots on either side of my spine were as sore as any thing could be. I am inclined to think that there is a matter gathered down there. It has the feeling of a very tender bruise.[311] Cousin Maria left for Alabama, and Uncle LeRoy for Marietta. Ella gave me two apples.

Wednesday December 3d 1862: Rained hard all the morning. Took a pill and did not cough any in the night. My cough is in full force. Dr. White being in town, Father got him to see me. He said there was a decided tendency to abscess and prescribed Iodine to scatter the matter. He prescribed the same hyperphosphites as before. Said it was a misfortune I had allowed my leg to become drawn up by holding it in a constrained position. Father was fortunate in getting a bottle of Hyperphosphite already prepared at Zeilins [store].[312] He rather encouraged me to sit up. This is about the sum of what he said. France has made intervention proposals to Russia and England, but they both refused for the present. This is official: I have dismissed Dr. Scherzer. 148 of "3d Georgia" have died + been killed since April. Father bought me 3 gallons of Dr. Bowen's catawba wine. I hope the rogues won't take it. Father + Min stayed at home in the eve.

---

311 More abscesses were forming on his lower back, the result of spinal tuberculosis (Pott's Disease).

312 Hyperphosphite was calcium and iron salts incorporated in medicine tonics in the belief they provided replacement materials for damaged nervous tissue.

Thursday December 4th 1862: Cool + Raw. Slept well and took ½ of a pill. Did not cough much. Julia Ann went to a reception given to Desdemona.[313] Had sausages for breakfast! Father painted the tender places on my back with Iodine and it made 'em black and caused them to Itch. Mother has gone to a meeting of the Soldiers Relief Society. The Abolitionists at Fredericksburg have been completely outgeneralled and foiled in all their plans by General Lee. They expected confidently to have taken that city with but little resistance on our part and then "on to Richmond." There is a rumor out, and it has the appearance of truth, that we have another warship out called the *"606"* or the *Retribution*.[314] Commenced to rain at dinner and rained all the eve. I got a letter from Thomas. He has a bad cold. Got a letter from Grandma and Uncle Dick had arrived. Grandma is still very unwell. Minnie is knitting stockings for herself, her 18th pair in all. Uncle Leroy arrived.

Friday December 5th 1862: Cool, raw day. Rained hard all night and it is dark and foggy this morn. It was a terrible night on the army in Virginia. Took ½ of a pill. My cough was quiet. 5PM: It is blowing off very cold. Mother and Uncle LeRoy played backgammon nearly all the eve.

Saturday December 6th 1862: Coldest day yet. At 9 oclock it was 32° and it must have been much lower than that early in the morn. Took ½ of a pill. Uncle LeRoy left for Alabama. Governor. Brown's agent was in town yesterday seizing all the goods, principally woolen, in town.[315] Mrs. Dessau called. [Pianist] "Blind Tom" is here. The ground was frozen for the first time. Father bought me a fig ham and some apples for the family. Mother + Minnie went to hear Blind Tom at 12 oclock. The Iodine made my back sting like smoke last night. Tomorrow it will be bitter cold. A synopsis of the Royal ape's [Lincoln] message is out and it is not any great shakes.

Sabbath day December 7th 1862: A still clear cold day. Mother bought me a bottle of "Spalding's Blue."[316] Dr. White encouraged me try and straiten my leg but in my opinion it is hopelessly contracted. The muscle seems to have become too short. Mr.

---

313 It was not uncommon for slave owners to give receptions for slave marriages if the slave was particularly valued for their service to the family. Slave "marriages" were not considered legally binding unions, but they were allowed to promote stability. Julia Ann may have been an invited guest to a friend's "wedding."

314 The only ship of that name in Confederate service was a tugboat.

315 LeRoy is referring to impressment agents sent to collect agricultural supplies, a policy that had a negative impact on the economy.

316 No reference to this has been located.

Singleton, the teacher of the Free school,[317] has had smallpox but I hear of no more cases. It is [in] spots all about the country.

Monday December 8th 1862: Cold and clear. Coldest day yet. Thick Ice. Coughed badly in the night. Mr. Tom Ross, Confederate Marshal [impressment agent], was murdered by some desperadoes in Marietta Saturday. My leg is miserable. Old Abe's message is out in full and it is a miserable thing.[318] It is so cold that it is impossible to warm the room or yourself.[319] It is too cold to write. My cough is wearing me out.

Tuesday December 9th 1862: Cold, clear, bracing. I took a ½ pill and my cough started 2 or 3 times in the night, but we checked it by drinking a little water. Milo and Arthur came up and brought a timely supply of spare ribs, backbones, sausage meat +c. We had a sparerib for supper last night and I really enjoyed it very much. Mr. Kemp killed 10 hogs + Mr. Hill none. Frank sent me six partridges. Colonel Huguenin is very ill – has had partial paralysis. Two or three English papers as well as the whole French press are denouncing Earl Russell.[320] Father bought 4 apples and gave 30 cents for them. When I cough much it makes me sore. I have just coughed enough to annoy me today. Mother has gone to town. I mended some broken things with "Diamond Cement." ...

Wednesday December 10th 1862: Cold and clear. Spent a bad night, notwithstanding I took a ½ of a pill 1/24 of a grain of Morphine. I coughed a great deal. I am getting more and more hopeless about this cough. I think it more closely connected with my lungs than my back. I get very down about it sometimes, and think it will never get any better. My leg is no better. I do not say this in a complaining or `whining spirit [2 lines scratched out]. Sic transit Gloria mundi, sultem lumpem, ad sunden O Pelika![321] Minnie's shoes from Milledgeville came yesterday. There is, I am happy to say, a dearth of news. We are anxious to hear from Thomas.

Thursday December 11th 1862: Cold and clear. Took ½ of a grain of Morphia. My cough is very hard to control. Fred knocked a screech owl out of the tree by the gate.

---

317 Macon's Free School was for children who could not afford tuition to the private schools, such as the one Mr. Bates ran. Tuition was paid through an endowment that had been in place for some time. John Gresham was occasionally on the Board of Trustees for the school.

318 Lincoln's second Annual Message to Congress, Dec. 1, 1862, in which he introduced the ideas of gradual emancipation and voluntary resettlement of emancipated slaves.

319 Antebellum homes like the Gresham's did not have central heating, so only a few rooms on the main level were heated with fireplaces.

320 John Russell, 1st Earl Russell, was England's foreign minister during the Civil War.

321 *Sic transit Gloria mundi* is Latin for "Thus passes the glory of the world."

Father found two ingredients of my medicine: Hyperphosphites of Lime + Soda. Colonel John Morgan has had a fight near Hartsville in which he killed + wounded 200 + took 1500 prisoners. Our loss 125.[322] Snow 3 inches deep at Fredericksburg. . . . Mrs. Butler sent me some splendid baked apples and custard!! I read very little nowadays. I have tried a little chess but find my self incomparatively dull. My cough . . . My cough wearies me, uses me up.

Friday December 12th 1862: Cold + clear. The wagon came up last night with hog meat. Peter + his wife Hetty, Medley, Jim came up. Mr. Hill killed 60-70 hogs, all we had. Chany's child Dinah[323] is dead. "Old Beck," a mule, is dead. We are all invited to dine at Cousin Liza's. No news at all. Mrs. Edwards called + loaned me two books: *Parlor Stories*. Went to spend the day at Cousin Eliza's and enjoyed myself very well. . . . We had a fine dinner: Jelly, Cake, Pudding, Bavarian Cream +c. Julia Ann went and waited on me at dinner[324] and for a wonder I did not cough any. I was glad. We received a letter from Grandma. Mrs. Stevens was burnt out and lost every rag of clothing and did not save a thing. A negro girl has confessed having done it. Uncle Dick got his hand hurt and both hands badly burnt. Cousin Jimmie[325] loaned me two books: *History of Cuba*.

Saturday Dec 13th 1862: Warmer. Tracy came up early in the morn; Mother out visiting. The Yanks tried 3 times to cross the river at Fredericksburg [Virginia] but were repulsed with heavy loss. I slept remarkably well did not cough + did not take a pill.

Sunday December 14th 1862: Warm and clear. . . . Father painted my back with "Iodine" and [it] itched so bad I like to run mad, and today the skin peels off and it is right raw. I put lard on it. Read *Parlor Stories*. Mr. Sparks got 366 votes, Mr. J.L. Jones is beaten by Lem Cherry, a vagabond. President Davis is in Knoxville [Tennessee]. Got a letter from Grandma. My leg is drawn up as far as it can be. Poor General Tom Cobb is killed in the recent affair at Fredericksburg. The Abolition vandals have bombarded

---

322 The Battle of Hartsville (December 7, 1862), was the beginning of the Stones River Campaign in north-central Tennessee outside Nashville. Morgan took a crossing on the Cumberland River from the Union troops and captured Union commander Col Absalom B. Moore along with about 2,000 other prisoners at a loss of 139.

323 Chany was one of the male plantation slaves; his daughter Dinah had died, although LeRoy does not give a cause.

324 LeRoy was likely unable to sit at the table with the others and so needed assistance.

325 James English Snider was married to Cousin Eliza.

and burned about half the town. Their efforts to cross have so far failed.[326] Mr. R. McKay is in town just from Yankeedom; been in prison 2 months. Father has gone to see him.

Monday December 15th 1862: Warm, windy, clear. Slept most miserably. My back itched worse than anything I ever conceived of. It was intolerable. We tried everything to allay it. I have not coughed any in two days. General Cobb's body in Richmond. General Gregg + General Hood killed.[327] The battle raged from 9 to 7 Saturday. General Lee's official [report] says we repulsed them at every point but lost many good men. The enemy have occupied the town. Our loss 3000. The Yanks heavier. They are fighting in North Carolina and skirmishing at Charleston. Fighting in Mississippi! There seems to be a general move forwards. The tug of war is upon us. Rylander's Battallion left today.

Tuesday December 16th 1862: Cold and clear. There was rain in the night and the wind blew a perfect hurricane. The news is misty. There is a heavy fight going on at Kinston, North Carolina.[328] The Yanks, it is said, are 20000 in number. General "Leesburg" Evans is in command of the Confederates. The Yanks took Fredericksburg by surprise crossed in the night. Cobb's brigade whipped 5 times their number; the fight is not decided. Read *Tom Brown's School Days*.

Wednesday December 17th 1862: Cold and clear. Thick Ice. Splendid on meat. Mother down town. Minnie is very busy preparing for a Christmas tree which she + the Huguenins are going to have. I recon it will burst up before the time comes. Our loss in the late fight in Virginia is 1800 while that of the 'litionists [abolitionalists] was 3-times as many. The Yanks are heavily reinforced. In North Carolina, they have got possession of the Wilmington road. 15 US officers are on the way here to be confined

---

326 The Battle of Fredericksburg (December 11-15, 1862) between Burnside's Army of the Potomac and Lee's Army of Northern Virginia. The Union forces set pontoon bridges across the river under a heavy fire, bombarded the historic down with artillery, and fought a tough street-by-street battle on Dec. 11-12. On Dec. 13 Burnside attacked both the Confederate right (held by Jackson) and the left (held by Longstreet) and was repulsed with heavy loss. Georgian Tom Cobb, of Cobb's Legion, was holding the famous stone wall on Marye's Heights when he was mortally wounded. Union losses totaled 12,600, with Confederate losses about 4,200. Fredericksburg was a decisive Southern victory.

327 Gen. Maxcy Gregg was mortally wounded, but Gen. John B. Hood was not injured.

328 The Battle of Kinston (December 14, 1862) was an attempt to gain control of the Wilmington and Weldon Railroad at nearby Goldsborough, North Carolina. Federals led by Gen. John G. Foster pushed back Confederates led by Gen. Nathan "Shanks" Evans. LeRoy's use of "Leesburg" harkens back to Evans' victory at Ball's Bluff near Leesburg, VA, a year earlier.

in the jail as hostages for the murder of some men. My cough is not so obstreperous. "Rogers Company" [of the] "Gresham Rifles" lost 1 killed, 4 wounded.

Thursday December 18th 1862: Cold and clear. Thick ice. Heavy frost, +c. Father and Howard both gone to Houston. The Yankee army is again on the north of the river Rappahannock. Their loss is 8000! President Davis is in Atlanta. He will be through here on his return. Cough quiet; the spots on my back are very tender indeed. Mother sick and laid on my couch all the afternoon and I on the floor reading *Lodges Portraits*. I am the boomerang said the [incomplete].

Friday December 19th 1862: The coldest day according to my feeling yet. The frost was like a snow. The news from Fredericksburg improves the better you get acquainted. The Yanks are rather down about it. They talk of 20000 men lost! In official circles in Richmond, they are believed to have lost 15000!!! The news from North Carolina is dubious: We have repulsed them! The fighting was furious on David Evert's farm!!!!!!!!!![329] A battle is pending in Tennessee. Howard returned. Killed hogs today.

Saturday December 20th 1862: Clear + cold. Anniversary of the secession of South Carolina. Thomas and Mr. Sayre[330] arrived this morn. No additional news. The Wilmington + Weldon R.R. is cut and no newspapers from Virginia can come. I think we are getting the worst of it in North Carolina. Mother is sick, though not in bed. Tom and Mr. Sayre rode out in the carriage to look at the town. I coughed and threw up my breakfast and have felt sick all day. [General] Buckner has gone to take command in Mobile and vacinity. Father returned from Houston + Willis came up with a supply of ribs + backbones. They killed 14 hogs. Mr. Sayre went on to Agusta at night. . . .

Sabbath day December 21st 1862: Cold and clear. Willis returned. No news. Coughed a good deal in the night. Had to take some Painkiller to kill a belly ache I had. Mr. Lane preached the funeral of Rev. Mr. Matthews of Florida who himself preached in our church 2 Sundays ago. Mr. Wills has been unwell, Mrs. Wills is sick, all the children and negroes are sick. Mother is still unwell. I hope it will continue cold on account of the meat. Sic transit Ra![331]

Monday December 22nd 1862: This is Monday and it is a clear cold day. I slept well. I did not cough until today. I have been really sick from eating too many ribs. "The 5th Grand On to Richmond" via North Carolina to Suffolk has begun! The abolitionists

329 It is unclear why this was so significant to LeRoy, or the location of this farm.

330 One of Thomas' college friends.

331 Sic transit Ra is Latin for (roughly), "Worldly things are fleeting."

are concentrating all their available force there and in my opinion "the" battle of the war has yet to be fought. I hope General Lee will frustrate their plans as completely as he has done here tofore, for then all will be well. "Saw off my leg." My leg is worse than ever today. I have finished my scrap-book and I am sorry, for I cannot get another. Minnie put on her Milledgeville shoes. Thomas and I played two games of chess. Mother went over to Colonel Huguenin's. He is worse + very ill indeed. . . .

Tuesday December 23d 1862: Clear + cool. The wagon came up with our new cow and calf. Willis, Elbert, Sam + Hetty came. . . . The spots on my back are tender beyond description. General Lee's report of the Great Battle of Fredericksburg is out. Our loss is 1800. There are rumors of a battle in Arkansas in which our loss was 950, Yankees 1000. It is stated that the enemy was defeated. Our forces were under Hindman.[332] Mr. Polhill's exhibition to which Minnie went last night was a tolerable affair. H. + A. Edwards + E. Huguenin spoke.[333] Uncle Leroy arrived and brought me a jug of whiskey, and after tea we had a glorious eggnog. I rode down town for the first time in over 6 months and found the town as lively as possible in anticipation of Christmas. When I came home I was sorer than 13 boils but that didn't do it.

Christmas Eve Wednesday Dec 24th 1862: Cloudy and rather warm. Uncle LeRoy left for Houston. The news, if true is encouraging. Seward has resigned and the Yankee cabinet broken up. Halleck dismissed. Burnside on the eve of resignation. If this be true they are having a good time generally.[334] Their groans over The Recent Thrashing are pleasant to hear. . . . Played two games of chess.

Christmas! December 25th 1862: Cool and foggy. Today is Christmas! We did not hang up our stocking last night at all. Minnie got some beautiful poetry books, as she did not have any when we got ours in October. I got a diary exactly like this one and I was might glad too. Minnie made me a beautiful blue cravat, and one for Tom just like it. I gave Howard a necktie and Min made Johnston and Allen one. Julia Ann gave me a nice apple. I gave Minnie a chain. It does not seem a drop like Christmas. Not a fire-cracker is heard to break. The stillness of the air; all the folks have gone down town. Thomas and Minnie to the Catholic church and Mother to see about the tree. My

332 The Battle of Prairie Grove (December 7, 1862), in northwestern Arkansas. Gen. Hindman was attempting to take advantage of a divided enemy advancing into Arkansas under Gens. James Blunt and Francis Herron. After some success, Hindman was forced to retreat and the Union took control of northwestern Arkansas.

333 Another local school teacher, like Mr. Bates.

334 The only element of truth is that Burnside's position with the army teetered on resignation or removal.

<u>back</u> is evidently worse. The abscess on the left side is decided as to be plainly felt and there is a sharp pain in it when I cough. I am anxious about it as I can be. After ~~tea~~ dinner, Cousin Jimmie Snyder + Cousin Jack came and stayed all the eve. I have coughed a great deal and that two hard fits of it. The resignation of Old Seward is confirmed and it is stated there is to be a "change in their war policy." In my own opinion, McClellan is to be reinstated. The wagon came up with Dan + Ralph, Martha and Dinah. I write this alone with Ella, while all our folks have [left] to Christmas trees and supper, alias Frolic for the Soldiers. Mother + Father both think it a bust. I close this record with the earnest hope that ere another Christmas is gone we may have peace and prosperity! So note it to be and another earnest wish that ere that, the crisis of my disease may have passed and I may be released from the constant confinement of a horizontal position! God grant it may be so! Captain Menard of the Gaurds was buried today. Also old Aunt Charlotte Wakeman. No daily [paper] until Monday – Van Dorn is stated to have made a dash on Holly Springs capturing supplies, prisoners and cutting of General Grant's communication.[335]

Friday December 26th 1862: Warmer and cloudy. The Christmas tree was a perfect jam and squeeze, and the supper a game of "grab and every man for himself." Mother brought me a pitcher of syllabub and a towel of goodies and I enjoyed them very much.[336] I coughed all night and this morning too. Christmas is gone! Mother is making Jelly.

Saturday December 27th 1862: Rainy and warm. Commenced to rain about daylight and rained all day. Cousins Jimmie, Jack, Bella[337] + Liza dined here. Had a nice dinner. Jellie, turkey, Duck, Custard, Pudding, +c. Uncle Richard arrived at 3PM well and hearty. Took a Morphine pill and feel awfully stupid today. Uncle Richard says General Cobb's funeral was tremendously large and Mr. Porter [and] Dr. Hoyt conducted the service. Grandma is tolerable well. It was a sad Christmas there.

Sunday Dec 28th 1862: Cool and clear. . . . Had a good dinner. Cough in the night. Took Morphine. Saw the *Illustrated News* with a picture of General Evans. Christmas holidays are o'er.

---

335 Gen. Van Dorn's cavalry raid on Holly Springs, Mississippi (December 20, 1862) struck deep in Grant's rear and destroyed a large quantity of supplies, thwarting Grant's first attempt to capture Vicksburg.

336 An English sweet frothy dessert drink made of milk or cream plus wine or cider, sweetened and flavored.

337 Cousin Jack's wife was Arabella O. Dean Jones, or "Cousin Bella."

Monday December 29th 1862: Cool and clear. Slept under the influence of morphine. The News – is cheering Van Dorn and Morgan it is said are threatening Memphis and kicking up a row generally. I received a beautiful Christmas gift from Mrs. Dessau, a book called *Great Truths from Great Authors*. Cousin Jimmie sent me P.WA.'s "account" of Fredericksburg. Mother went down town in the eve. The Yanks attacked Vicksburg and are repulsed with loss. Old Butler has been superceded by Banks. It is said that there will be a fight at Murfreesboro soon! . . .

Tuesday December 30th 1862: Cool and cloudy. Mother sick in the night. Uncle Richard left at 12 noon for Athens via Sparta. Received a letter from Auntie. She is well; Uncle Edge was preparing to leave and would make prodigious efforts to take Macon on his way. I got up last night and had a midnight coughing spell. Father bought me a new medicine a Syrup of HyperPhosphate, a sort of chemical food recommended by the celebrated Dr. Jackson of Philadelphia. It will do to take until I can get a supply of Dr. White's medicine, as mine is nearly out. I wish I could get me a scrapbook, as it is a great source of pleasure to me. There was a collision down at Millen + Captain Menard's body did not arrive at the time appointed. It is turning cold now after supper. Heavy fighting at Vicksburg; enemy repulsed with slaughter.[338]

Wednesday December 31st 1862: Cold and windy. . . . It is reported that heavy fighting on both wings of our army had commenced at Murfreesboro.[339] Rosencratz demanded a surrender of the town and General Bragg invited him to come and take it. I hope we will whip them. Cousin Eliza sent me some Jelly and Bavarian cream and it has made me sick. The enemy at Vicksburg have been repulsed 4 distinct times. Received a letter from Uncle John on the edge of a newspaper. He was in Wilmington but was preparing to return to Charleston then with his regiment.

December 25th 1863: I am no better than I was a year ago: 2 sores running constantly.[340]

Jan. 2nd 1863: The *Daily* did not come out yesterday. We have a very aristocratic Old Cat and she (as we call her though he is a fine old gent) is called "Kitty." Her name

338 The Battle of Chickasaw Bluffs (Dec. 29, 1862). Union troops under Gen. William T. Sherman assaulted entrenched Confederates north of Vicksburg, Miss and were beaten back. Union losses totaled about 1,800 men, and the Confederates about 200.

339 The Battle of Stones River (Dec. 31, 1862 – Jan. 2, 1863). LeRoy could not have known this the same day the fighting began, so apparently a rumor reached him that turned out to be true.

340 LeRoy often randomly used free space at the end of his journals, which he appears to have done here with his Dec. 25, 1863 entry and the following Jan. 2, 1863 entry, which is more of a story than a typical journal entry.

is Boy. She was presented to my sister Minnie and is nominally owned by her but she has entirely transferred her affections to me of late. He or Her rather is very hypocritical in her demonstrations of affection to her Mistress and in the morning before breakfast.[341]

When she is practicing he jumps on to a chair then on to the piano + walks along the keys into her lap. He was born about May 1857 and consequently will be 6 years old his next birthday. When he first arrived there was a little terrier dog here whose name was Joe Pancoast and everyone prophesied an irrepressible conflict between them.[342] However after Joe had had a few good whippings, he let him have his own way in every thing and Kitty reigned supreme. He never fails to resent any indignity such as being swept over by a frock by spitting, snarling and running into a corner. Her "master" however bears them with great patience as the common lot of every one who lies upon the floor. He is never crestfallen except when an Uncle of ours comes to see us. He has to cats an unconquerable aversion and when he finds her in a chair he slaps her a somerset. All the time he is here she lurks about under the piano or bookcase.

The shadows of age are beginning to creep over him and he cannot eat bones as of yore so we give him biscuit crumbs. He cannot last many more months tho' excepting the failure of his teeth he is as vigorous as ever. He has fits at long intervals and I suppose one day they will carry him off. I have touched lightly on Kitty's faults for they are few; far fewer than ordinary Kitties. When she dies I'll have some gloves out of her (her mistress says I shan't) skin + bury her in the ryelot.

Pudden Kittie

341 LeRoy explains in a later entry dated June 6, 1864, that "Kitty" was a male cat named "Boy," but the family always referred to the cat as a "she." Why they did that is something he never explains.

342 This is the only time LeRoy mentions the terrier, named after his favorite doctor, Philadelphia-based Joseph Pancoast.

1863   1862   1848. U.S.   1863 s.12

ECLIPSES FOR 1863.—Grier's almanac, for 1863, gives the following list of eclipses for the present year: There will be four eclipses, as follows:

I. The first will be of the sun, on the 17th of May at 11 h. 15 m., A. M.; invisible in Ameririca.

II. The second will be a total eclipse of the moon, on the 1st day of June, partially visible. It will begin at 4 h. 17 m. 33 sec., P. M.; and will end at 7 h. 33 m. 16 sec., P. M. The moon will rise at Augusta with 7 2·10 digits eclipsed on her western limb. The beginning of total darkness will be at 5 h. 24 m. 36 sec., P. M., and the end of total darkness at 6 h. 31 m. 18 sec., P. M. The duration of visibility will be 6 h. 37 m. 16 sec.

III. The third will be of the sun, on the 11th of November, at 2 h. 36 m., A. M., invisible in America.

IV. The fourth will be of the moon, on the 25th day of November, visible, and nearly total throughout the continent of America. It will begin at Augusta, at 1 h. 57 m. 14 sec., A. M., the middle of the eclipse will be at 3 h. 37 m. 53 sec. A. M.; the Ecliptic Opposition, 3 h. 43 m. 21 sec.; and the end of the Eclipse at 5 h. 18 m. 32 sec. A. M. Its duration will be 3 h. 21 m. 18 sec. The number of digits eclipsed will be 11½ on the moon's half limb. At the greatest observation, about 1 24 part of the moon's diameter will remain uneclipsed.

The inside-front of Volume 5.
LOC

Volume 5

January 1, 1863 – December 31, 1863

LeRoy Wiley Gresham

Macon, Georgia

Lines for an Album

If all these names which crowd they book,

Are stars within they mental sky,

To which thine eyes will fondly look

As future years steal safely by,

Be mine of tis thine evening hour.

The first to give its willing ray!

Then morning lures with sweeter power

Be mine the last to fade away.

Thursday January 1st 1863: The New Year comes in with a clear cold day. 1863 is upon us with it's many new associations, it's hopes, it's fears, it's trials, and pleasures. It opens too auspiciously for the success of our arms. The News is that a great battle is going on at Murfreesboro and that both wings of the army were engaged. I was very sick all night. I had a pain which beginning in my stomach, finally went round to my back. I took whisky, Painkiller, and Morphine and applied an iron to my side but nothing did any good and it wore off towards day. There were two alarms of fire in the night. It was a kitchen. Arch came up with 75 bushels of groundpeas. I have been very stupid all day from the effects of the Morphine. Had an eggnog. Mary Campbell spent the day with us. A Happy New Year!

Friday January 2nd 1863: Cold and clear. Black frost. Slept miserably. Got pain in my breast + shoulder and feel sore all over. The Great Battle of Murfreesboro has been fought and won! We have captured 4000 prisoners Taken 2 Gens and killed 4! Our loss is heavy but that of the Yanks is heavier. Gen Rains killed. Col Black, 4th Georgia killed.[1] Mother has gone to town. Willis came up with spare ribs, backbones and 3 partridges. [Overseer Kindred] Kemp killed 20 hogs.

Saturday January 3d 1863: Cloudy and cool. No later news from Tennessee. From all accounts Murfreesboro was a very bloody victory. 12 Noon: Glorious news! Gen Bragg telegraphs to Gen Beauregard! God has granted us a glorious victory and a happy New Year! Rosencrans is retreating and our forces are in pursuit! Gen [Joe] Wheeler, CSA made the entire circuit of their army. Gen Huger is in town. . . . I did not sleep but very little and feel sore all over. My medicine, the Hyph. Potassae, has come from Charleston, and Mr. Massenburg will make it when Dr. White sends the recipe.

Sunday January 4th 1863: Commenced raining at about day and rained till after breakfast: then stopped. Rained at 11 and brightened up at 12 noon. Communion day. Took ½ pill last night and feel a bit better today. The *Daily* came out today dated Monday; *Constitutionalist* comes in an enlarged sheet. The price of both is raised to 10 dollars. . . . The Yanks have left Vicksburg. Beast [Ben] Butler is superceded by [Nathaniel] Banks. My cough has worried me a good deal today. Read *The Chapel at St Mary's*. Towards night it cleared off and I went out on my wagon a little while.

Monday January 5th 1863: Cool and clear. Coughed in the night a great deal. Our wagon came up with Dave + George, Scip + Medley to go to Savannah and they leave tonight.[2] Wayne, Mrs. Wardlaw's boy, is along. The News is not so good from the West. The Yanks are heavily reinforced and stronger than before the fight. Father bought Tom some grey breeches. Marbles in fashion at school.

---

1 The Battle of Murfreesboro or Stones River (December 31, 1862-January 2, 1863) in central Tennessee between Gen. Braxton Bragg's Confederate Army of Tennessee (formerly Army of Mississippi) and Gen. William Rosecrans' Union Army of the Cumberland. Bragg attacked and nearly routed Rosecrans on the first day, but his attacks on January 2 were beaten back with heavy loss. Bragg's retreat boosted Union morale and dashed hopes for Confederate control of much of Tennessee. Union losses were about 13,000, wand Confederates losses 11,800. Four generals were killed: Confederates James E. Rains and Roger Hanson, and Unionists Edward Kirk and Joshua Sill. Col. William T. Black led the 5th Georgia Infantry.

2 John Gresham sent these slaves in compliance with state laws to work on fortifications around Savannah after the fall of Fort Pulaski to Union forces.

Tuesday January 6th 1863: Commenced to rain before day, and the wind blew and it poured down till after breakfast. Took ½ pill. . . . Our army has fallen back to Tullahoma! Murfreesboro was not near as good a victory as we thought. Our loss was 5000. The Yanks 15000. It is reported that the [ironclad USS] *Monitor* with all on board is sunk and the *Galena* damaged.[3] Col Huguenin is very, very, low.[4] My leg is, if possible, worse than ever.

Wednesday January 7th 1863: Freezing cold. I spent a very bad night. Had two exhausting fits of coughing. I dislike the idea of taking Morphine so much, but it is the only thing that arrests the cough. We were very much surprised to see Cousin Jones this morning.[5] The retreat of our gallant army seems to have a depressing effect on every one. We took 4000 prisoners, 5000 arms, 24 cannon. Their loss was 3 to our 1, but still their heavy reinforcements spoilt all and our army was compelled to retreat. Morgan took all Rosencrans' wagons. Mother bought some candy. It is 2.25 lbs. Mother is altering my shirt collars and making them smaller which will be a vast improvement. She is also making Thomas some. The Confederate Steamer *Alabama* is the bugbear of Yankee commerce. She has just captured the California Stmr. *Ariel* with a valuable cargo.

Thursday January 8th 1863: Cold and clear. I was compelled to take a dose of Morphine last night. My breast hurts me when I cough. Mother has gone down to distribute cloth to the poor.[6] Our loss is thought to be 10000 in the late battle. It was an awful affair and nothing gained. Cousin Jones and Tom took tea at Cousin Jack's. Recd a letter from Uncle John on the margin of a *Courier* in which is a splendid letter from "Personne" descriptive of the N. Ca. fights. Big dance at Mrs. Whittle's tonight!

Friday January 9th 1863: Cool and clear. Had a miserable coughing spell in the night. It is stated that we have captured the *Harriet Lane* + blowed up another Yankee steamer

---

3   The USS *Monitor* and 16 of her crew were lost in a storm off Cape Hatteras, NC, on December 31, 1862. The wreck was discovered in 1973 and her guns, revolving gun turret, engine, and other relics can be seen at the Mariners' Museum in Newport News, Va. The USS *Galena* was not involved and remained at Newport News, Virginia.

4   Edward David Huguenin, a friend of the Gresham's, could not serve in the military because of his poor health. The rich plantation owner equipped an entire company that adopted his name (Huguenin Rifles). It was one of at least 17 companies raised or based out of Macon. Edward's title of colonel was honorary.

5   John Jones Gresham, one of Uncle Edmund's sons.

6   Probably nankin cloth from the Gresham's Macon Manufacturing Company.

at Galveston.[7] The 1st 2 numbers of the *Richmond Examiner* came; Father sent on the subscription nearly two weeks ago.

Saturday January 10th 1863: Cool and raw. Hard shower at 12 noon: My cough was so bad I took ½ pill. Cousin Jones left for home. Minnie put on her nankin factory dress and it really looks pretty. The *Monitor* is no doubt gone to the bottom and her consort the *Passaic* put in at Beaufort in a sinking condition. Hurrah for that. Uncle LeRoy arrived last night at 9PM. Gen Bragg says our loss [at Murfreesboro] is 9000!

Sunday January 11th 1863: Cool and foggy. Did not cough in the night. The Yanks are making immense preparations to capture Vicksburg and to cut the Wilmington + W.R.R [in North Carolina]. 81 transports of troops came down the Mississippi the other day. Uncle LeRoy left at 9am for Flint River and returned at dark with a "nig"....

Monday January 12th 1863: Chilly and damp. Slept tolerably. Uncle LeRoy went to Milledgeville to carry that "nig" to Aunt Eliza.[8] Wrote to Uncle John. The 1st No. of the *Fireside* [paper] came. It does pretty well, considering. There are 3 new cases of smallpox in town and there is great danger of it's spreading.

Tuesday January 13th 1863: Clear and cool. The tender spot on the left side of my back was very painful all night + hurt me when I coughed. This morning it feels like it would burst. The papers says a portion of our forces have reoccupied Murfreesboro. I lay all the evening in my night gown because my back was so tender I could not stand the rubbing of my coat. Dr. Fitzgerald vaccinated Father + Allen [for small pox]. Father wrote to Uncle John for my scrap book.

Wednesday January 14th 1863: My back hurt me so that I took Morphine. Dr. White came to see me. He tied a bandage round my back to support it and did very little else. It feels very comfortable. Father went to Houston. The 1st Ga Regulars arrived here Monday night, and the ladies are going to give them a dinner. They are 230 strong. The wind was blowing a gale all the eve. France + England are going to remain neutral!!!!!

Thursday January 15th 1863: Warm and windy. The winds has been blowing hard all day. The regulars marched down to the depot to a dinner and I saw them as they passed

---

7   The Battle of Galveston (January 1, 1863), a successful land-sea endeavor led by Gen. John B. Magruder to expel Union forces from Galveston, TX. The Union revenue cutter *Harriet Lane* was captured, and the USS *Westfield* destroyed.

8   Uncle LeRoy and Aunt Eliza are siblings of Grandma's; Uncle LeRoy is taking a slave to her as a new servant. This is one of the few times LeRoy uses the abbreviation "nig."

the college. Commenced raining about dinner and rained till after tea. Sent an enigma to the *Fireside*.[9] My cough has been quiet all day.

Friday January 16th 1863: Slept finely until near day when I had a slight nightsweat which made me very uncomfortable. The Yankees have attacked the Forts at Wilmington.[10] A few flakes of snow fell before breakfast. "Gipsey" is here nearly every day, and is as mean and sneaking as ever. The Small pox continues to spread; 2 cases among the Regulars. In Richmond it is frightful.

Saturday January 17th 1863: Icy cold. Coldest day of the year. Slept tolerable. Tom got his new pants. Willis came up with hog-meat. Father returned nearly froze. Received a letter from Grandma. She will be down after the 20th when Uncle R[ichard] leaves. I have had nightsweats for 2 or 3 night past and they make me feel so bad. I take whisky every day now. My cough is miserable at night. My leg is drawn up so I cannot put it [within] a foot of the floor.

Sunday January 18th 1863: Clear and cold. Sick all night and am hardly able to write now for my cough is never ceasing. My back hurt me very bad all night. The spots on each side are as sore as possible. I feel like I would never get well. Mother and Tom put on the bandage again and it adds some to my comfort.

Monday January 19th 1863: Cloudy and cold. Anniversary of Georgia's secession! Willis left. Thomas returned to College. . . . President Davis' message is over 5 columns and he gives England + France "fits." The Pews were rented today.[11] I took a pill last night. The 9 oclock bell rings at 7 and no negro assemblages are allowed till the small-pox gets better.[12]

Tuesday January 20th 1863: Rained hard and fast all night and till 10 oclock when the sun came out clear and bright. I took a ½ pill and feel some better. My back feels just like it had been bruised. Gen Wheeler has taken 4 transports on the Cumberland [River] loaded with provisions which he destroyed. Captured 400 prisoners and destroyed gunboat besides. It is reported that things are coming to a crisis again around Fredericksburg but I think a battle is to be fought before long in N. Ca. [Governor]

9 LeRoy submitted a riddle or word puzzle for the paper, which was popular in that era.

10 Wilmington, NC, was the most important Southern port on the Atlantic coast, its defenses centered on massive Fort Fisher.

11 Pews were rented each year to raise funds for the church. The better the seat, the higher the rent.

12 Many thought small pox was carried by slaves, so limiting gatherings would control outbreaks.

Brown is out in a proclamation against deserters + stragglers.[13] There seems to be a good deal of dissatisfaction with Gen Bragg. The "Charge of Breckinridge" [at Murfreesboro] was a 2nd "Malvern Hill" and the whole affair is a second "Shiloh." Uncle LeRoy arrived after supper from Flint River and after tea we had a fine eggnog.

Wednesday January 21st 1863: Very cold and cloudy. Took an anodyne. My cough begins as soon as I lay down at night and unless I do something to stop it, keeps me awake all night long. My back is more tender than I can express. I write with Mother's gold pen. Mother invited to dinner: Cousin Eliza, Cousin Jimmy, Cousin Sarah Margaret[14] + Aunt Sarah. I enjoyed the syllabub, apple float cake, +c hugely. The 1st ham of the season was cooked. Father's Birthday.

Thursday January 22nd 1863: Slept tolerably. My back is like a boil. Mother gone to a meeting of Soldiers Relief Society. Commenced to take my new medicine "The Syrup of the Hypophosphite of Soda, Lime + Potassa." and it is nasty and stinks. It has name enough to cure anything. Father left for Savannah at 9 PM.

Friday January 23d 1863: Clear and cool. Slept very well. Mother had some liquid Morphine made for me. . . . There seems to be a lull in the news world. The two armies before Murfreesboro are recovering from the shock of the late battle. It is said that another attempt to cross at Fredericksburg will soon be made.[15] Affairs are threatening in N. Ca., The Yankee ships got after the *Alabama* when she sank the iron clad *Hatteras*. The *Nashville* under another name ran out of the Ogeechee River the other day where she had been lying for some months. The C.S. Steamer *Florida* is also on the "deep blue sea."[16] Mrs. Huguenin sent me a big lemon. Minnie has gone and to stay all night with Cousin Eliza, and Mother and I are all alone. The *Fireside* came today + it is pretty tolerable poor. The *Examiner* is not as good as The *Dispatch*.

Saturday January 24th 1863: Clear beautiful day, so springlike! Father arrived at 9 oclock. Cousin Eliza sent me some goodies, syllabub, cake, Jelly, ham + salad, and I enjoyed it hugely. Father brought some oysters. Col Morgan dashed into Murfreesboro

13 Problems with stragglers and deserters abounded across the South, harbored by Unionists in northwestern Georgia.

14 Sarah M. "Sallie" Jones, Cousin "Jenks" Jones' sister.

15 In fact, Union Gen. Burnside's "Mud March" began on January 20, 1863, in an attempt to cross the Rappahannock and flank Lee's army. Bad weather ended it two days later, and ended Burnside's career as head of the Potomac army.

16 The USS *Hatteras* was a side-wheel steamer, not an ironclad. She was sunk by the CSS *Alabama* on January 11, 1863 off Galveston. The former Union ship *Nashville* was now the privateer *Rattlesnake*. The double-funneled steam and sail CSS *Florida* was an English-built commerce raider.

and took 20 wagons + 200 prisoners. After capturing the transports, Wheeler + Forrest swam the Cumberland and destroyed a depot + a $1000,000 of stores. He also took another big transport. Recognition is all the talk now. It is <u>too</u> great a "bust." The Yankees say that they have taken Arkansas Post + 7000 prisoners.[17] <u>We</u> have no account of it. I <u>hope</u> it is not so. I slept very well. Father brought 4 quarts of oysters from Savannah and we had them for dinner + supper. I stayed out on my wagon till time to wash. The spots on my back are about the same; I have a bandage on them all the time.

Sunday January 25th 1863: Foggy and raw. Slept very well. I got a long letter from Uncle Jno [John] at Wilmington. It is thought there will be a fight there. Mother also recd one from Thomas yesterday. Father <u>tried</u> to get me a scrap-book in Savvannah. I wish I had one.

Monday January 26th 1863: Foggy and every appearance of rain. The Abolitionists are going to try Vicksburg a 3d time. 61 gunboats and all of Grant's army will unite in the effort. Gen Joe Johnston is in command.[18] I slept well, as I have done for 5 nights past. Wrote to Aunty. It has been foggy all day. Minnie set down on Kitty. A C.S. bearer of dispatches has been captured and the correspondence of Mason + Slidell with the Sec. of War [was] published in the Yankee papers. Some of it was quite important. This item just does fill out this page [of my journal].

Tuesday January 27th 1863: Rained hard in the night and it is very cloudy now. Slept tolerable. No News. A fight is imminent in N. Ca., at Fredericksburg, and Vicksburg. Mrs. Huguenin sent me some Jelly last night. Cousin 'Liza [sent] some custard pie and dried fruit pie, which last was splendid. I finished today the 8th and last [volume] of *Lodge's Portraits*. Min received a letter from Sallie. Uncle E[dge] has gone. Arch arrived loaded with peas + peanuts. Every body gone to take tea at Cousin Jack's notwithstanding the drizzling rain. It has cleared off very cold and the wind is blowing. It has been drizzling every now and then all the afternoon. Gold in New York is 147-8 and if all the papers say is so they are in about as bad a condition about their currency as we are about ours. Col Huguenin is in very low state: no better no worse.

17 The Battle of Arkansas Post (January 9-11, 1863) was a Union effort at the mouth of the Arkansas River during the Vicksburg Campaign. The fort fell with nearly 4,800 Rebels captured, but it had little effect on the overall campaign to take Vicksburg.

18 These winter efforts were called "Grant's Bayou Operations," which sought to use or construct canals or alternative water routes to get troops within striking distance of Vicksburg without having to run ships down the Mississippi directly in front of the enemy batteries. Gen. Joseph E Johnston was appointed to command the sprawling Confederate Department of the West in November 1862. It was Gen. John Pemberton who was in direct command at Vicksburg.

Wednesday January 28th 1863: Bitter cold. Commenced to snow at 7½ PM last night and snow lightly for an hour. Today it is about an inch thick on wood but none on the ground. I ate a plenty. The folks came home in the midst of it. Cousin Bella sent me syllabub + cake and Jelly. The snow has not melted a bit.

Thursday January 29th 1863: Clear and cold. The snow did not melt until towards noon. Mother went to Soldiers Relief Society. Grandma "arriv" at 5PM and she brought a lot of goodies: An elegant cake, some little cakes, Jelly cake candy. She also brought me a spittoon. My back is very sore indeed. Hattie Tracy[19] called. Borrowed *My Novel*. The Yanks attacked Genesis Point on the Ogeechee and were repulsed. Nobody hurt.[20] Cousins Eliza + Sarah Margaret called.

Friday January 30th 1863: Spent a most terrible night of pain, although I took Morphine. I feel very bad today. The abscess on my back is very sore. I did not get up till after breakfast. Cousin Sallie stayed all night. My leg is drawn up awfully. Went on my wagon in the eve and was taken with a violent pain in my hip and suffered very much all the time till after tea.

Saturday January 31st 1863: Last night after tea I was taken with the same pain, only tenfold worse and it was terrible. I took a heavy dose of Dover's Powder and another Morphine. I cough until late in the night and every time it felt like it would kill me. My left leg did not hurt me a drop. I have lain perfectly still all day not daring to move a peg lest it start the pain again.

Sunday February 1st 1863: Warm and cloudy. I took a dose of Morphine. I did not cough till near day. I made an effort and put on my pants and was rolled into the sitting room.[21] My hip and shoulder are sore from lying on them, and I cannot lay on my other side because I cough all the time. The abscess I wish would come to a point. It has rained all the afternoon very slowly. The C.S. Gunboats *Chicora* + *Palmetto State* run out of Charleston the other day and sunk two of the blockading fleet, and dispersed the rest.[22] Our boats and men escaped without a scratch. Gen Wheeler has taken some

---

19 Harriet Charlotte Tracy (one of Aunt Carrie's sisters) lived in Macon and had probably taken over raising little Tracy.

20 The First Battle of Fort McAllister (January 27-March 3, 1863) began with the ironclad USS *Montauk* shelling the fort's earthworks. The Rebels reported the death of Maj. John B. Gallie. The fort would be attacked seven times during the war, and not fall until approached from behind by Gen. Sherman in the March to the Sea in December 1864.

21 LeRoy may have had a chair or small sofa with wheels for use in the house.

22 Two ironclad gunboats purchased by various Ladies' societies, including Macon's Ladies Soldiers Relief Society. The ironclads steamed out before dawn on Jan. 31, 1863 and temporarily dispersed the

more transports on the Cumberland. Gen Burnside is seceded by Hooker.[23] Kirby Smith is ordered to Texas. . . .

Monday February 2nd 1863: Sick, Sick, Slept under Morphine. Laid very quiet all day. I wrote in here today for every day since the 28th from memory and pencil notes. I have not been able to write before at all. I don't expect to have any comfort till this abscess is lanced. Took Citrate Magnesia. It is a long ways the worst turn I ever had. . . .

Tuesday February 3d 1863: Cold and clear. Coughed all night. It rained and stormed in the night. Cousin Annie arrived. Did not get up to breakfast. My leg is better and so is the abscess. Aunt Ann is sick. Miss Sue Rowland called. Julia Ann is in bed. Fighting at Vicksburg. The smallpox is over by Mrs. Lamar's. Mother bought me a gold pen. I was taken with a swimming in the head after tea.

Wednesday February 4th 1863: Very cold indeed. Took Morphine. Did not cough. Dr. White called. Expressed himself satisfied with the action of the bandage + prescribed a liniment. The Yanks are working on the canal at Vicksburg. The swimming in my head still continues, when I sit up. I have not taken my medicine since I was taken worse. 3 oclock: Was taken sick after dinner and threw up. . . . Cousin Annie's little baby [James] is very good. Bridget nurses it.[24] Every prospect of snow.

Thursday February 5th 1863: Rained and sleeted all night and this morning every thing is covered and perfectly white. Took Morph. Grandma made me a bandage that laces up + it is a great deal better than the other.[25] My cough is pretty bad. Gen Joe Johnston has assumed command of the Army of Middle Tennessee.[26] Maggie Snyder sent me some candy. Put out some cream to freeze but it didn't. The trees look beautiful. The Yankees look like they were going to attack Charleston soon. Min stayed home. Mother froze a little ice-cream in a fruit-can for me and it was beautiful. All the trees are bent down so as to nearly to break. Had Oysters for dinner. Cousin Jimmie

---

Union blockading squadron before withdrawing back into Charleston harbor, leading the Davis administration to claim the blockade had been broken. The Union ships quickly returned to station.

23 Union Gen. Burnside was sacked and replaced by Gen. Joseph Hooker to lead the Army of the Potomac.

24 Apparently, an Irish wet-nurse was hired to care for the baby.

25 Grandma made LeRoy a back support or corset. In the mid-nineteenth century, "general supportive measures" (corsets) and rest were standard treatments for tuberculosis of the spine before the era of antituberculous chemotherapy.

26 As noted earlier, Johnston commanded the entire department, but did not assume command of the Bragg's Army of Tennessee. It is curious LeRoy has not yet used the army's name, although it was one of the two prominent Confederate field armies.

brought them from Savannah. Father has the Rheumatism in his shoulder. I have been more comfortable today than I have in some time, although I have coughed a good deal. The abscess is very tender. There is a new Daily started here by L.F.W. Andrews called *The Confederate*. Every body was invited to Cousin Eliza's but it was so bad they could not go. Since I have had the laced bandage I have been a great deal more comfortable.

Friday February 6th 1863: Snow still on the ground. Snowed a little in the night. I went out on my wagon the first time since the 30th and rode round on the snow. I slept very well and without an opiate. No news. Rubbed with Dr. White's liniment. . . . Gen Stevenson is in command at Vicksburg.[27] Father found an old scrapbook down at his office. Wrote to Uncle John. Ate elegant ice cream, frozen with snow.

Saturday February 7th 1863: Slept well. Thomas came over with some crackers from Aunt Eliza. The snow is melting today + everything is dripping. [My dog] "Price" sucked 2 eggs. Every body except Tom dined at Cousin Eliza's. My back hurts me whenever I set up. Every night nearly I have a sweat. Father got me a bottle of brandy to take for it. Had ice cream at supper. Cousin Eliza sent me lot of goodies.

Sunday February 8th 1863: Slept well in the early part of the night, but towards day the abscess pained me a good deal + this morning it is red + inflamed. Grandma stayed at home with me. No important news. I do wish this concern would either break or go away. Spring is coming!! . . .

Monday February 9th 1863: Warmer a great deal. Abscess exceedingly inflamed + painful beyond measure. I am strongly inclined to think that it will have to be lanced. Lay in bed all day. Had fever toward night. Coughed very hard and it hurt my back awfully. Mother + Cousin Annie went down town. Bought osnabergs [fabric] to make drawers, silk to make me [a] cravat, and Morphine pills to make me sleep. Took Morph last night.

Tuesday February 10th 1863: Slept quietly under the influence of a pill. Ate 3 eggs to break my fast. I got out on my couch about 12 noon. I lay writing now in Mother's room and it is warm enough to sit without a fire. Grandma heard from Uncle John. There is a large fleet at Port Royal and it is thought Savannah or Charleston will be attacked at an early day. Howard left for Houston. Navy ship sunk off Charleston. Mr. Harris' stable was burned this PM. . . . My back got to be so terribly painful that Dr. Fitzgerald was sent for. He came after tea + prescribed a poultice. The pain I suffer

27 Gen. Carter L. Stevenson, Jr. was sent from Bragg's army to reinforce Vicksburg. Gen. Pemberton remained in command.

when I cough from the jolting of the abscess is worse than I can describe and I dread to lance it. It is red just like a boil and as tender too.

Wednesday February 11th 1863: Took 1/12 grain Morph and then 1/12 in fluid form. I coughed incessantly last night till ten oclock and every time it looked like I could stand it no longer. Had a poultice of flaxseed put on which feels very nasty. Grandma, Mother, and Father were out in the front yard gardening all the P.M. Towards night had an exhausting fit of coughing. Cousin Annie has gone to stay all day + till tomorrow. [I am] sick in bed. I do not relish any thing but beef tea [broth] + ice cream.

Thursday February 12th 1863: Warm a plenty to go without a fire. Took 1/8 grain Morph which had the effect of keeping me wide awake till near day though perfectly quiet and unconcerned whether I slept or not. Took [Citrate] Magnesia before breakfast. I do not have any ease and will not till this thing is opened. The Dr. came at dinner to lance it but I was not ready and so he came again at 4½ and all that time I had the pleasure of anticipating it. It hurt me a good deal and when I strained as if to cough the matter gushed out and it ran a great deal. After it quit running, Dr. Fitzgerald put a tent in to keep it open and then a poultice. Received a long letter from Auntie and Grandma, one from Uncle R[ichard] dated Fredericksburg. He [is an adjutant's] clerk. Howard returned. Aunt Ann sent me cake and preserves. Ate Ice cream.

Friday February 13th 1863: Clear and warm. Took 1/8 grain Morph. The poultice was taken off at dinner time and soon this morn, and it had ran a great deal both times. Laid on my left side all day so as to let it run. My cough has not worried me. Cousin Liza sent gingercakes. I am lying looking out of the window in Mother's room.

Saturday February 14th 1863: Valentine's day. Took ½ pill. Took off the poultice and put on a greasy cloth. Rolled into the sitting room. It is quite warm. Mother is knitting a glove. Lincoln is going to raise an army of 150000 contrabands.[28] Kentucky growls over the negro [Emancipation] proclamation. Our cavalry have been defeated at Fort Donelson with loss of 100. Forrest, Wheeler, + Wharton were compelled to retire.[29] Cousin Annie left for home today. I sweat heavily every night and have until yesterday had fever in the evening. Had beef tea.

Sunday February 15th 1863: Cool and pleasant. . . . I would have slept very well but for the heavy + exhausting night sweat which took away my comfort. Got into bed with Father. Took brandy. The Dr. came to see me last night. As proof conclusive that this concern would have bursted, another hole beside the one the lancet made has broken. It ran "right smart" this morn. I ate 5 cakes which Mrs. Judge Nisbet sent me. French mediation for the 20th time is again on the tapes. It is stated that the "frenchey Emperair" has made proposals of mediation to both government the commissioners to meet at Montreal to settle terms. It was the "*290*" [*Alabama*] that sunk the *Hatteras*. Received a letter from Aunty; Uncle Edge is Brigade Q.M.[30] 3 new cases of smallpox in town one of which was at the wayside home.[31] All have been removed to the pesthouse.[32] Min received a letter from Tom yesterday.... My back ran a great deal when it was dressed at night. I take brandy 3 times per diem.

Monday February 16th 1863: Slept well, that is for <u>me</u>. It is cloudy and has rained some Grandma "made" me a nankin doublegown.[33] Mother is very unwell and we sit in her room today. . . . Ever since I have been sick, Allen has been vagabandizing.[34] The relief I experience since the abscess was lanced is inexpressible. Howard is hauling wood from the S.W.R.R.

28 Recruitment for United States Colored Troops (USCT) regiments began after the establishment of the Emancipation Proclamation on January 1, 1863. General Order No. 143 did not take effect until May, but open recruitment began at the start of the year.

29 The Battle of Dover or Second Fort Donelson (February 3, 1863) was Joe Wheeler's failed Confederate attack against the Federal garrison at Dover, Tenn. Wharton was Gen. Gabriel C. Wharton.

30 Quartermaster, responsible for managing all supplies used by his brigade.

31 Wayside Homes were temporary hospitals for soldiers in transit to their units from military hospitals or coming from home after recovery and were often staffed by local female volunteers.

32 A local sanatorium used to isolate small pox and other contagious diseases.

33 A heavy reversible dressing gown.

34 Allen did not have a lot to do and/or was not doing all he was told to do. This was an issue for slaveholding families as the war dragged on, especially after the Emancipation Proclamation spread.

Tuesday February 17th 1863: Cool and cloudy. Slept tolerable. The 46th [Ga. Inf.] is in Charleston again. French mediation is a bust. My cough is quiet. My back has not hurt me any. Tracy came up. . . . The Yankees at Vicksburg are deserting by the 100. Wrote to Thomas. Father brought some apples home at dinner. "Nab" came home this morning from the war.[35] . . .

Wednesday February 18 1863: Cloudy and cool. Slept well. Minnie was right sick all night and is in bed yet. Price is as mean a suckegg as ever was. Gen Beauregard has issued a soul stirring proclamation calling upon Georgians + Carolinians to rally to Charleston + Savannah. A combined attack by land and water is anticipated soon. Mrs. Lipscomb was married last night and sent me goodies: apples cake + syllabub. Cousin Eliza sent Pie Pudding + Syllabub. Had Fritters + beef tea for dinner. Father sold groundpeas for 2 dollars a bushel. Trouble seems to be brewing between France + Yankeedom. Our little boats at Galveston have taken a Yankee gunboat without the loss of a man. The first number of *The Daily Confederate* came out today and it looks very well. Rained very hard in the night.

Thursday February 19 1863: Cloudy and cool. Abscess itched a great deal in the night. No news. Grandma is making my drawers. The *Alabama* + the *Florida* continue to cut up shines + burn up Yankee ships by the dozen. Min is up. I am so glad my cough is better, that I don't know what to do. Received 2 papers from Uncle John, one with a long English account of the F[redericks]burgh fight. Letter from Uncle John. "Nary scrapbook." Mother + Grandma out visiting. Bought cake + candy for me.

Friday February 20th 1863: Clear beautiful day. Woke up about two oclock with a bad pain in my stomach and nought would relive it. It must certainly have some connection with my back. About day Father got up and looked out and saw a fire down town. When he got to it nearly the whole square around the livery stables was in flames. The 2 stables burnt down. Mr. Bloom's office. Mr. Wrigley's house + Mr. Nathan Weed's establishment for making axes plows +c were all entirely consumed. A large number of carriages and horses, some of the latter very valuable, were all lost.[36] We did not hear the firebells at all and would not have known it at all but the negroes told us when they came in to open the house. Mr. Bloom's fine mare was lost. More anon

---

35 Slaves were also impressed for labor with the armies.

36 This was one of the most destructive fires in Macon's history. Hayden and Goolsby, who owned the stables, were only insured for one-third of their loss; Weed lost his steam engine and all his stock.

[soon]. Our forces have captured the *Queen of the West* at Vicksburg.[37] Had Beef tea. Mother and Grandma out visiting again. Gip came back. Abscess ran a great deal last night + today at noon. The papers are full of mediation and the correspondence of Old Seward, Dayton, Count Mercier + Drougn De'l Huys.[38]

Saturday February 21st 1863: Cool and cloudy. Took ½ pill. I am suffering very much with weakness in my back. I can hardly sit up at all. Aunt Ann continues quite sick. Heard from Aunty and she speaks of coming over to Macon. Had a shad [fish] for dinner. Price 3,50 Also a partridge and beef tea. It is rumored that Longstreet's "corp de army" is ordered south. Recd relics of the boat *I.P. Smith*, captured on the Stono River.

Sunday Feb 22nd 1863: Cloudy + warm Rained in torrents and the wind blew a hurricane last night. . . . General G.W. Smith has resigned on account of being overslaughed.[39] Heard from Uncle Richard. ("Allen is a fool."). . . . My back is better. I am not so weak as I was yesterday + day before.

Monday February 23d 1863: Cold and clear. Slept good. Howard left for Houston, taking Allen with him.[40] I put on my coat for the 1st time since the abscess was opened. Ice this morn. I got a letter from Thomas. Made nondescripts. An attempt to set fire to Mr. Lanier's house last night, but was discovered in time to put it out.

Tuesday February 24th 1863: Clear and cold. Willis came up last night, bringing a hind quarter of beef and we had splendid steak for breakfast. 500 of Bragg's army are here en route for the coast; yet strange to say Rosencrans is reported advancing. Gov Brown has ordered out the militia officers. The attack in Charleston is postponed on account of disagreements among the Yankees. Wrote to Thomas and sent 2 papers.

Wednesday February 25th 1863: Cloudy and cool. Mother was very sick all yesterday and last night. I slept with Father, and she in my bed. Grandma dressed my back. The Yankees have passed a conscript law calling out all between 20 + 45 at Lincoln's

---

37 On February 14, the Union Queen of the West was crippled by gunfire from Fort DeRussy, a Confederate bastion in Louisiana defending the Red River Valley, and captured.

38 William Henry Seward (US Sec. of State); William L. Dayton (U.S. Ambassador to France); Edouard Henri Mercier (French Ambassador to the US); Edouard Drouyn de Lhuys (French Minister of Foreign Affairs).

39 Gen. Gustavus W. Smith resigned his commission as a major general to serve as an aide to Gen. Beauregard at Charleston for the rest of the year.

40 Allen was getting himself into trouble at the Gresham home, and John Gresham sent him back to work on the plantation.

discretion. They have erected a battery at Vicksburg, on the opposite shore, which commands a part of the town. My cough is quiet. I have a constant craving for something nice.

Macon Thursday Feb 26th 1863: Clear and warm. Slept well and enjoyed my breakfast very much. Mother up again. France is on the "eve" of Recognition. No other news. Warm enough to go without a fire. Read *Grace Hale*. The wind has been blowing hard all day. Mr. Carhart had bought Mr. Ross' house for 50 000 dollars.

Friday February 27th 1863: Rained nearly all night and rains still. . . . My back does not give me any pain or trouble, and is a decided improvement on the cough. The C.S. gunboat *Dr. Badly* has taken the Yankee ironclad *Indianola* at Vicksburg with a loss on our side of 5 men.[41] A tremendous fleet is gathered at Port Royal [N.Ca.]. . . .

Saturday February 28th 1863: Rained in the night and is raining this morn. Winter gives us a weeping farewell, for it has continued raining steadily. Father received a letter from Thomas. The *Fireside* came today. The attack on Charleston is indefinitely postponed. Made nondescripts.

Spring March 1st 1863: Cloudy. Clear and bright. Woke up in the night with a bad pain in my back and side. Suffered a great deal and laid in bed till noon. It is a strange pain. . . . Father spent the morning with Colonel Huguenin. Longstreet and D. H. Hill have assumed command of the Dep [of] N/ Ca. + S. Va.[42] The "Ankeys" have destroyed the *Nashville*.[43] Things are culminating at Vicksburg and there will have to be an awful fight there and at Charleston. It is rumored (but no one credits it) that the U.S.S. *Brooklyn* has been captured by our forces at Galveston. Mother and Grandma went to see Aunt Ann who is sick. Minnie went down + took a class in the "Collinsville Sunday School." Father and Minnie went to church and said Mr. Wills gave them a fine sermon.

Monday March 2nd 1863: Clear and delightful day. Slept well. Mother and Grandma went out shopping. Aunt Ann sent me some nice fresh butter. M[other] + G[randma] bought me candy, baker's bread, apples [at] 2 for 20 cents, celery, two little cakes. In the

---

41 The USS *Indianola* was rammed and run aground by the CSS *Webb* (and the now-CSS *Queen of the West*) on February 24, 1863. It is unknown where LeRoy saw or heard the name he wrote.

42 Gen. James Longstreet was detached from Lee's Army of Northern Virginia with two divisions in mid-February of 1863 and assumed temporary command of the Departments of North Carolina and Southern Virginia. He was given a variety of conflicting objectives that ended that April with the failed "siege" of Union-held Suffolk, Va.

43 Renamed CSS *Rattlesnake*, she was run aground outside Fort McAllister and destroyed by the USS *Montauk*.

eve [they] went to the cemetery and down town. Mother bought a trowel. Tracy was with them and they rode out to see the [Ga] Regulars.

Tuesday March 3d 1863: Clear and warm. Slept well. Father sat up with Colonel Huguenin. . . . Lincoln is Military Dictator of Yankeedom + has unlimited means + money. The consequence is there is before us a long war.[44] Gold is 200, in New York 172. The English and French will wait and give them a last chance to crush the rebellion.

Wednesday March 4th 1863: Clear and cold. Father went to Houston. Took ½ pill. I felt so sore + weak. Did not get up till about ten AM. The attack on Fort McAllister was commenced at 8.30 yestermorn and continued without intermission till night. On our side 2 men wounded and 1 gun dismounted. Mother bought a bottle of brandy for 10 dollars. Dictator Lincoln commences his 3d year of power today. 1610 1611 1612.[45]

Thursday March 5th 1863: Clear and cold. . . .[Gen] Van Dorn has made another brilliant dash taking Franklin, Tenn with 2600 prisoners. Our loss heavy; Yankees 1000. The Bombardment at Fort McAllister continued all night when the enemy withdrew.[46] Made nondescripts. Back running [draining] very freely.

Friday March 6th 1863: Cloudy and cold. Thomas arrived. Mr. Bowdre sent Mother a fine lemon, the largest I ever saw. Cousin Eliza sent me cake + custard. We have blown up the *Indianola* to prevent the Yanks from recapturing her. . . . I spent a very restless night and feel very weak. Mrs. Huguenin is sick in bed + Col Huguenin hardly alive, yet no one knows how long he may linger. *The Field Fireside* is a poor stick. George Beal called to see me. Col Huguenin died at about dinner time. How much suffering he has endured! Father returned from Houston and brought me 18 partridges. Went to bed feeling sore + tired and my hips both aching me. Large party at the Bowdres'.

Saturday March 7th 1863: Did not sleep well at all. Thomas went to Mr. Bowdres' last night and says it was a splendid supper and brilliant assemblage. It is raining this morn. The *Indianola* is not blowed up, only a gun bursted. The ironclads have left Genesis Point [Fort McAllister]. Mrs. Bowdre sent me some of the wedding cake. Went

44 LeRoy had good insight into what it took to pursue and wage war, knew the North had more resources, and was beginning to realize (if not yet voice) that winning the war was becoming unlikely.

45 The widely-read LeRoy may be equating the first three years of Lincoln's administration with the first three years of Jamestown (founded 1607, with fortifications and more erected 1610), implying the Confederacy is to Jamestown as the United States is to the "imperial" reign of James I.

46 Van Dorn's action at the Battle of Thompson's Station in Tennessee was on March 5; it is interesting LeRoy learned of it so quickly. The attack against Fort McAllister was another failure.

out on my wagon. Thomas is vaccinated and it is taking. Col H[uguenin]'s funeral was at 3½ oclock. Rained at 10 am hard. "Price" is a nasty egg-sucker!!!

Sunday March 8th 1863: Warm and clear. Felt so bad and my legs ached me so that I took a pill. I did not get up till 10½. Had lemonade. I eat a partridge for dinner. My back runs a great deal. Mother did not go to church. Went out on my wagon in the P.M. and rode around the garden.

Monday March 9th 1863: Cloudy and warm. Took ½ pill. Father bought 2 pr shoes for Thomas at 12 doll[ars] apiece. Mrs. Bowdre send Mother some wedding cake. Thomas left at 12 oclock. He wore Father's watch. General Toombs has resigned.[47]

Tuesday March 10th 1863: Warm and cloudy Took ½ pill. Both hips ached all night + whenever I move they pain me. My back is as weak as anything can be and I can't sit up without pain. The abscess runs a great deal + I feel weaker every day. Dr. Fitzgerald called. Mr. Gustin's stable was burned down at daylight. A ship arrives in Charleston every week and sometimes 2 + 3. Uncle Leroy arrived after tea. It has been very dark + glowering all the evening.

Wednesday March 11th 1863: Sick. Bright and clear. Rained very hard in the night. I slept but little. Took 1/12 grain Morph. But the pain and soreness in my joints was so bad I could not rest. Uncle LeRoy left for Marietta. I got 2 glasses [mirrors] + looked at my back. Literally "No news." Mother went down town. Suffered a great deal during the eve.

Thursday March 12th 1863: Clear and cool. Slept tolerable. Minnie is sick with a cold. My leg is better. Took 1/12 grain Morphia. Mr. Hardin Johnson's house was burned last night and the family barely escaped with their lives. It was set on fire in 3 places. . . . The Hyacinths are beautiful.

Friday March 13th 1863: Clear and cool. Minnie's eyes are sore that she stayed in bed. I slept pretty well and my leg did not hurt me a bit till I got up. It is my right leg and my only dependence. Father slept upstairs. Burnside has taken command in So. Ca. [War correspondent] "P.W.A." says the attack on Charleston will be made about the 18th when the spring tides are highest.

Saturday March 14th 1863: Clear and warm. Took a pill. My leg ached me all night. I coughed too, a horrid little hacking cough, and that kept me awake. Uncle LeRoy got

---

47 Unable to get a promotion, Toombs resigned his commission in March 1863 and began a relentless campaign against President Davis and his administration. He openly opposed conscription, the suspension of *habeas corpus*, and other official actions. Newspapers editorialized that his actions bordered on treason.

here yesterday and left today. Cousin Eliza and Aunt Sarah called. Cousin Eliza has been quite sick as has Sallie + George.

Sunday March 15th 1863: Cloudy and warm. Slept – none Took 1/12 grain Morph. My leg is no better. Slept all the morn. Mr. Freeman's stable was burned in broad daylight yesterday + about day. . . . "The Republic," +c were burned. 50 bags cotton were destroyed. The "Bombardment" of Vicksburg is begun again. My back ran a great deal today.

Monday March 16th 1863: Cloudy and warm. Took 1/12 grain Morphine. I slept heavily till 11 oclock. I started taking "The Syrup of the Iodine of Iron" the other day, but I don't like it much.[48] The fruit trees are in bloom. The Hyacinths are superb. My hips both ache me from lying on them. Father bought me Jelly Cake. "My back runs hugely." Mr. Deloache's house was fired to day.

Wednesday March 17th 1863: Cloudy and warm. Took Morphine. Literal I have no rest except when I am asleep, for my hips are so sore that I cannot lay on them hardly at all. I feel more discouraged, less hopeful, about getting well than I ever did before. I am weaker and more helpless than I ever was. My hip, when it is not actually paining me, has a weary feeling which makes me want to move. I sleep very little at night. Mother has made 2 little pillows to put under my back. Willis came up with Frank, butter, +c. Mother is in bed today. The Yankees have been gallantly repulsed at Port Hudson with the loss of the USS *Mississippi*.[49] Made nondescripts.

Wednesday March 18th 1863: Clear and warm. Father's Savannah negroes all arrived [returned] here today. Dave has had Measles. George looks awfully: has had measles + mumps and now Dysentery. All except him went down [to Houston] in the wagon today.[50] Wrote a long letter to Thomas.

Thursday March 19th 1863: Cloudy, balmy, spring day and Nature is clothing herself in a garment of flowers. This is the day set for the attack of Charleston but as Burnside has not yet arrived at Port Royal, it may be delayed some time. The enemy attempted to cross the Rappahannock in small force but were compelled to retire. Our loss 250.

---

48 Used as a medication and dietary supplement since the early 19th Century. The medicine (which would soon change to pills for LeRoy) had side effects including headaches, allergic reactions, and depression.

49 The USS *Mississippi* was last in a line of ships, and when she grounded was heavily damaged by fire from the Port Hudson batteries. When fire threatened the magazine, her captain abandoned ship before she blew up. Future admiral George Dewey (1837-1917) served as the ship's executive officer.

50 George remained in Macon to be nursed back to health before being sent on to the plantation.

Enemy's "heavy."[51] At Tullahoma [Tenn.] a fight is "imminent." Fredericksburg ditto. Port Hudson is also menaced by land + water.

Friday March 20th 1863: Cloudy and cold. It rained in the night. Mother still in bed. The Regulars leave at 9 A.M. for Fla. Father bought me a little black walnut table. Slept well. No news. Gen D.H. Hill has had a fight near Newbern, N. C. and as we get no particulars, I reckon we were licked.[52] The Yanks have carried a lot of darkies to Florida where they are colorizing and arming them for a most diabolical purpose.[53]

Saturday March 21st 1863: Cold and cloudy. Rained hard nearly all night and it is a miserable day. The Federals have evacuated Murfreesboro and some grand movement is evidently on foot. I did not go to sleep till very late last night. Mother is still sick in bed. Marked kerchiefs for Mother.[54] Minnie wrote to Thomas. I am very thankful to say I feel a "great" deal stronger and am able to set up and eat and write. I hope I am thankful for it. Had tea and fritters for dinner.

Sunday March 22nd 1863: Cloudy, raw, damp, ugly, cold. Slept miserably. Rumors that the Feds are crossing the Rappahannock are rife. I have had a dull headache all day and am not as well as I was yesterday. . . . My appetite is miserably puny. Heard from Aunty. Grandma is sick with a cold + Sallie too. . . . Cleared a bit toward evening.

Monday March 23d 1863: Cloudy, ugly day. Slept well. Howard went to Houston taking George + Frank. I stayed on my wagon nearly all the morning looking at Mother tie up the grapevines. Father bought me a cover for my table with a chessboard on it. Toward 12 oclock it grew very warm but continued cloudy. The *Fireside* of the 14th came. Willis came up.

Tuesday March 24th 1863: Rained in torrents the livelong night. "Dave" is sick. I did not sleep any till near day. Fred has mended my chess box elegantly for me. No news. The prospect before us is as gloomy as it can be. The Yankees seem determined to

---

51 The fight Kelly's Ford (March 17, 1863) occurred when Union cavalry crossed to engage Southern horsemen. It is famous today because of the death of the young and "gallant" Southern artilleryman John Pelham of Alabama. Union losses totaled 78, and Confederate 133.

52 Confederate Gen. D. H. Hill would fight a battle for Washington, NC in late March and early April, but there was no fighting around New Bern, NC at this time.

53 Arming blacks was a very sensitive issue for many Southerners, all of whom feared violent uprisings like the bloody 1831 revolt led by Nat Turner that killed some 60 people, and the attempt of John Brown in 1859 to incite slaves to violence with his raid at Harpers Ferry, Va.

54 Handkerchiefs could be marked with pencil or a seamstress's pen to embroider initials or place decorative designs, which could be found in popular ladies' magazines like *Peterson's* or *Godey's Ladies Book*.

starve us out and unless large provision crops are planted, they have a fair chance of doing it.[55] Rained like rip from 7 oclock till bedtime.

Wednesday March 25th 1863: Clear and warm. Rained very hard in the night. Willis came back last night with Howard in tow. The wagon broke down in Echeconnee [south of Macon] and the horses ran away with the fore-wheels, but fortunately Willis stopped them. The harness was broke badly. Fred sawed my table off and put rollers on it.[56] No news at all. Slept tolerably. Father made Minnie a present of a beautiful "What Not."[57] . . . The wind blows cold. I hope it'll not hurt fruit.

Thursday March 26th 1863: Clear bright beautiful day. The News is from the West is cheering. The Yanks opposite Vicksburg have been completely drowned out and compelled to move higher up. Our Victory at Port Hudson was indeed glorious. The [USS] *Mississippi* burned. The [USS] *Richmond* riddled. The [USS] *Hartford* and the [USS] *Monongahela* passed the battery badly damaged.[58] Two boats attempted to run our batteries at Vicksburg when one was sunk and the other riddled. [Grant's] Yazoo pass affair is a failure. Gen Joe Johnston is at Tullahoma. Our men are ready and anxious for the attack on Charleston. 150 ships are at Port Royal. I am taking Iodide of Iron pills. Thomas and Mr. Sayre arrived at 4½ PM. The latter left after tea. I rode down town [in my wagon] but it hurt my back. Bought letter paper. Aunt Ann is very sick—does not improve at all.

Friday March 27th 1863: Clear and bright. Day of Fasting and prayer appointed by President Davis + everybody has gone to church. Father has a very bad cold. Thomas brought me some speeches. A [blockade-running] ship runs in every day at Charleston. My back ran a great deal of bloody-looking matter last night and is very sore now. The 1st no. of *The Republican* came yesterday. *The Constitutionalist* is out this month. Prayer meeting in the evening.

Saturday March 28th 1863: Windy and cool. Rained very hard before breakfast. Father was quite sick all night. I slept well. My back is not as sore as it was. [My dog]

---

55 LeRoy was correct. The Confederate government wanted planters to plant grains like corn to feed the army and the civilian population instead cash crops like cotton and tobacco.

56 This made the table more useful for LeRoy, who could then take it with him throughout the house.

57 A piece of furniture popular in the 19th Century consisting of slender uprights or pillars supporting shelves to hold china, ornaments, or "what not."

58 On March 17, 1863, Union Adm. Farragut launched a night attack similar in tactics to the one he used against New Orleans. Some ships made it upriver, but others were destroyed or driven back; the Confederates rightly considered it a victory.

Price continues to suck eggs and I have issued orders for his removal. I cut off some of his hair as a memento. Cousin Helen is here on her way to Maryland in search of Capt Plane's body[59]. . . . Mother gone to prayer meeting Father has suffered a good deal today. . . .

Sunday March 29th 1863: Cloudy and warm. Rained very hard about half the night. Father is a little better now but was sick all night and couldn't go to church. Communion day. "Price" has gone. I hated it too. . . . The folks came home at 4½ PM.

Monday March 30th 1863: Miserable, drizzly, cold day. Father took a Dover's Powder last night and did not get up at all. We sat in Mother's room. Cousin Helen + Liza called. Made gingercakes. Forrest has taken 800 prisoners, destroyed stores, took wagons +c. I am more comfortable than usual. I am hopeless about my leg and try to be content if I am without pain.

Tuesday March 31st 1863: Cloudy in the early morn, but clear and windy toward night. After tea last night it rained hard. Thomas + Howard went to the plantation. My back ran a great deal at the last dressing. Father is sitting up and his cold is better. Mother went to Prayer meeting. We are hard run for wood and had to cut down that tree in the rye lot. Wood is 6 + 7 dollars for a 1 horseload.

Wednesday March 32nd 1863: Clear and cold. Father better. Slept tolerable. There is an April fool in the daily about a big snake on the ruins of the livery stable. Mrs. Clisby loaned *Parton's Life of Jackson* to me. Burnside has gone West.[60] My [good] right leg hurts me and it is slightly contracted. I don't feel well a bit. Thomas arrived with butter and eggs. Reports Dave well. Brought me a hickory stick.

Thursday April 2nd 1863: Clear and windy. Father better; Thomas has a boil on his leg. The women made a descent in a mob on Rosenwald's store and took 3 pieces calico. Today about 50 more started but were dispersed by the police.[61] No War news. I feel a little better today. We were very anxious about frost last night, but it did not come at last. Made molasses candy and had a splendid pulling. Julia Ann, Mary, and Thomas done the work.

---

59 Plane had been killed at Sharpsburg (Antietam) in Maryland on Sept. 17, 1862.

60 Union Gen. Burnside was sent to the Department of the Ohio after being replaced by Gen. Hooker as commander of the Army of the Potomac.

61 As the war dragged on, poor women desperate for supplies became more common across the South. The most famous "mob" event was the Bread Riots in Richmond, Va., the same day as LeRoy's entry. Public complaints that the Macon Manufacturing Co. was pricing its fabrics for the benefit of wealthier Maconites began shortly thereafter.

Friday April 3d 1863: Clear and warm. Dreamed about 'lasses candy. Mrs. H[uguenin] sent me some chicory coffee. No news. Father bought a cooking stove for $136, 100 lbs. sugar at 80 cents. The wind has blown a perfect hurricane all the P.M. Father is suffering with pain in his back. Bought Mucillage at $1,50. Father bought me 3 birds. May the fruit escape – *Parton's Life of Jackson* is too hard for me. My back runs as much as ever.

Saturday April 4th 1863: Clear and cool. No news at all. Thomas has got 3 "biles" [boils]. No Frost. Min made Jellie. Uncle Edmund came over from Milledgeville. Stayed on my wagon a good deal today. Got a long letter from Auntie, and she is not going to Athens. Father put a pitch plaster on his back. *The Constitutionalist* half sheet [entry ends here].

Sunday April 5th 1863: Clear and cool. The Daily comes out in a half sheet on account of the destruction of the Path Papermill. Thomas' boil kept him home. Gen [Henry L.] Benning has taken Toombs' brigade + Uncle Edge is Q.M. [Quartermaster] My back has grown very sore since dinner. The abscess ran very little the last two times it was dressed.

Monday April 6th 1863: Anniversary of the "Battle of Shiloh." Lay in bed all day feeling very miserable from the consciousness that another abscess has started to form just opposite the other one. It is as sore as possible. I am glad my cough is not bad. Minnie caught cold yesterday in church and lies sick in Mother's bed with sore eyes. Important movements are on foot at Charleston which the press "are not at liberty" to make public!

Tuesday April 7th 1863: Clear and beautiful day. Took a Morphine pill. Minnie on a pallet in the back parlor. The Dr. called to see me. Confirmed our opinion as to an abscess. Prescribed Poulticing; I had one on yesterday. Abscess runs very little. Ate the last of the molasses candy. I do dread more than I can tell another abscess. Mother is bad off with Rheumatism in her knee; Father with Rheumatism in back. Rumors are rife of all sorts, from Charleston.

Wednesday April 8th 1863: Clear and warm. In bed. Abscess ran very little. Father's back is very bad. Thomas rubbed it. The "Ball" has opened at Charleston! Seven Monitors and the iron-clad Ironsides opened on Ft. Sumter at 3 P.M. yesterday. The firing was deliberate but terrific. Their fire was concentrated on Sumter. The *Keokuk* is reported sunk and the *Ironsides* disabled! In the fort 1 man killed + 5 wounded. 6000 men are landing to join in the attack. The bombardment ceased at 5½ PM.[62] Minnie is well.

Thursday April 9th 1863: Cloudy and warm. Slept well. Father in bed. Mother down town. A dispatch from Gen Beauregard confirms the sinking of the *Keokuk*. 7 ironclads are still inside the bar. No renewal of the attack. Abscess has quit running. Mrs. Huguenin sent me some nice steak. Mr. Ralston bought Mrs. Franklin's lot for 48000$.

Friday April 10th 1863: Cool and clear. All quiet at Charleston. The Yankee machine to clean out torpedoes is captured. Ironclads still in the bar. We have taken another gunboat in some inlet. Rumor of a fight in Ky, in which we were licked. Affairs at Vicksburg are promising. The Yanks are apparently moving. Gold fell to 149½ from 154 on the supposed capture of Charleston. Father does not appear to be any better. He has pains all over the lower part of his back + hip. Rubbed his back with a liniment of Dr. Fitzgerald's prescription. My abscess does not run and the other one does not increase. I am afraid I'll have a long and painful siege before it opens. It is very tender. Aunt Ann no better. 2 pounds [of] candy arrived. Mother sent to Savannah by Cousin Jimmy for it. Willis came up. Mr. Sayre arrived.

Saturday April 11th 1863: Took 1/12 grain Morphine. I feel very bad. Abscess just runs enough to keep the new one back but not enough to carry it off. I slept nearly all the eve. They tried to make molasses candy but busted. . . . All the fruit is killed in Athens. Uncle Ed's health is improving. Uncle Leroy is in Arkansas.

Sunday April 12th 1863: Spent a miserable night of pain and feel tired to day. I wish this abscess would form. Father unable to get out. It is cloudy + warm. I can't wear my pants at all. My appetite is miserable.

Monday April 13th 1863: Cloudy and warm. Tom and Mr. Sayre left at daylight. I feel a little better. The abscess ran a little more and the sore place on the other side don't increase in size but is still tender. The ironclads have left Charleston + some gone north, others south. Aunt Ann is still very sick. Little George Snider is very ill. Cousin Eliza has chills. Cousin Bella is quite sick, and nearly all the kin are down. Mother is gone to see them. Father is better but his back is still weak. Julia Ann is in bed today with cold + fever.

---

62 The First Battle of Charleston Harbor (April 7, 1863). Federal naval forces under Union Adm. Samuel DuPont (including seven ironclad monitors) attacked land fortifications defended by Gen. Beauregard. Union officials believed heavily armored ships could move in close and reduce masonry forts. The effort failed. The *Keokuk*, an experimental Union ironclad, was hit 90 times, withdrew, and sank the next day.

I have got badly mixed. The part in brackets [parentheses] should be dated the 15th; the other is right.

Tuesday April 14th 1863: Dark and gloomy. Rained last night I am troubled with a bad cold and snuffle continually. Rumors of a defeat of the Feds in N. Ca. and of Van dorn at Franklin, Tenn. He attacked the Yankees with 7000 cavalry when they retreated, but advanced heavily reinforced.[63] When after a bloody fight of 6 hours, we retreated. George Snider is better. Olivia Bates[64] is ill with pneumonia, which disease is very prevalent now. Mrs. Irby who lives at the bottom of our lot had smallpox and she + all her family were removed to the pest house in short order. (Father's back got worse from over-exercise down town this morning + he suffered a great deal all the eve.) My cold is worse and I feel pretty bad I will take a small Dover's Powder tonight. Received a letter from Tom. The fruit is unhurt over there [at Milledgeville]. (The Annual parade of the fire-companies takes place this evening.) Rained very hard from 5PM till night.

Wednesday April 15th 1863: Cloudy and cool. Minnie went down town and got some little books. Took a Dover last night and am in bed today. Father suffering.

Thursday April 16th 1863: Clear and windy. Father suffered so much in the night that he was compelled to take a Dover. Mother is sick today. I am well of my cold. O[livia] Bates no better. Grant and Rosencrantz will no doubt join forces and Burnside with 20000 men will join them and then what will Gen Johnston do? Retreat? It don't look promising certain.[65] Aunt Eliza arrived.

Friday April 17th 1863: Clear and warm. Father suffered a great deal in the night, and is unable to sit up. . . . Dr. Fitzgerald called to see Father this morning.

Saturday April 18th 1863: Clear and beautiful spring day. 8 gunboats have run the gauntlet at Vicksburg. 2 were disabled and 1 burnt.[66] Father took a Dover and is taking Quinine today. Seems to be a little better. . . . Minnie and Aunt Eliza went to the cemetery.

---

63 This First Battle of Franklin (April 10, 1863) was a minor action between cavalry under Confederate Gen. Earl Van Dorn and Union troopers under Gen. Gordon Granger.

64 Sister of Bob Bates.

65 LeRoy's Union configurations would not come to pass, but his deep concern for holding Vicksburg was justified.

66 The early stages of the final effort to capture Vicksburg were underway. On April 16, Union Adm. Porter sent seven gunboats and empty troop transports with supplies past the Vicksburg batteries, which could not depress their guns enough to hit anything but the top of his ships.

Sabbathday April 19th 1863: Clear and warm. The news is poor. A yankee account states that the *Queen of the West* has been retaken. The Yanks have built batteries opposite Vicksburg and have opened on the city. My back run a great deal today. The tender spot continues about the same. . . . Mr. Bates + Lt Col Harris called to see Father. Mother was taken with a terrible headache and did not get relieved till a mustard plaster was applied.

Monday April 20th 1863: Warm and clear. My back pains me today. The coming abscess is very prominent and will have to be lanced. Father is down town. Aunt Ann was taken worse today. George Snider is very bad off. Olivia Bates is better. The "Situation" in the West + Tennessee is considered very critical. The ironclads were seriously damaged at Charleston, and I don't think the attack will come again soon at least in that <u>shape</u>.

Tuesday April 21st 1863: Cloudy and warm. My back has hurt me all day. The abscess on the right side has risen again. Father's back is very weak. The abscess runs perhaps more than it ever did. Dr. White has been over to see Aunt Ann and his prescriptions have given her relief. She sent me some nice Jam + preserves. Toward night the pain grew very bad and no position was easy to me.

Wednesday April 22nd 1863: Cloudy and cool. Took Morphine and my back was so very painful; we applied a poultice. I slept nearly all day. Mother has gone to see George Snider + also down town. She bought some nice flaxseed, a cake, some soap. Washington, N. Ca., Williamsburg, + Suffolk, Virginia are invested by our forces. Hill, Longstreet, + Wise are in command at the points named. The Yanks are gradually coming round to acknowledge a disgraceful defeat at Charleston. Uncle John sent me "Personne's" acct of the fight there. Better than P.W.A.'s.

Thursday April 23d 1863: Cloudy and warm. Took Morphine. Put a nice flaxseed poultice on my back and the sore ran a great deal. The rising has decreased in size. I am anxious for it to form and be done with it. I have not been out of bed; my back + legs ache so. George Snider no better.

Friday April 24th 1863: Clear and warm – Slept well. Lay in bed all day. . . . Cousin Charlie is home. They brought me a nice mess of strawberries. George Snider is very ill yet, no better. I have had fever for a week past every evening. The Abscess runs immensely! My appetite very poor.

Saturday April 25th 1863: Clear and cool. On Mother's colonnade [porch]. Mother and Aunt E[liza] went down town. Cousin Mary Harris sent me the <u>nicest</u> mess of strawberries, and I enjoyed them hugely. Mrs. Hugeunin sent me some crackers + cakes. My back ran a great deal in the morn and then ran so tremendously it had to be dressed in the middle of the day. Aunt Eliza left for Milledgeville at 7.40. We had supper before dark. We are needing rain very bad indeed here.

Sunday April 26th 1863: Clear and beautiful day. . . . Another case of smallpox has occurred in Collinsville.

Monday April 27th 1863: Cloudy and warm. Rained a little in the night and it clouded up + rained very nicely about dark. Cousin Eliza sent me sponge cake, custard, strawberries + turkey. Strawberries are 1 dollar a quart. I rode out on my wagon into the vegetable garden the 1st time in a month + every thing looks green + beautiful. Received an interesting letter from Thomas. He got the best circular [argument] in the class. Mother recd a letter from Mrs. McKay in relation to Uncle Link. A rumor had been circulating in Athens that he was not dead. It all originated in a letter from Aunt Jule to her Aunt, Mrs. Jackson, saying there had been rumor of the sort in Texas.

Tuesday April 28th 1863: Damp and cool. Drizzled rain. The rising on my back was very sore all night. Sometimes it looks like it would open + then it subsides again. Father started to Houston but was stopped by a beautiful rain. My back runs so much that we can't keep it from getting on my clothes. The rising hurts like a boil.

Wednesday April 29th 1863: Clear windy + warm. Father went to Houston. Minnie stayed all night with Mary Campbell and went to hear Dr. Leyburn lecture on Palestine. George Snider is convalescing. Cousin Jack's children have whooping cough. My back runs hugely. It seems to me the flies are worse than I ever saw them. There is no comfort in lying down. Mary got a nice little mess of strawberries out of the garden.

Thursday April 30th 1863: Clear and cool. Howard left for Houston. Gunboats, tugs +c +c pass Vicksburg now without any difficulty. The clerk of the House of Rep. was shot the other day in a street fight with an assistant. Mr. Bates gave [school] holiday yesterday for the rest of the week. Thomas arrived after tea to our great surprise + joy. Miss Delie Dessau + Robert Atkinson were married last night.

Friday ~~April~~ May 1st 1863: Bright, beautiful mayday, and Minnie is gone to a Pic Nic given by Mr. Gouding's scholars. Mrs. Dessau sent me wedding cake: Silver and spice. I went out on my wagon and stayed a long time. It is rumored that "Fighting Joe" [Hooker] is crossing the river. Heavy skirmishing. Great battle imminent.[67] Father and Howard arrived from Houston. 4 picnics today.

---

67 The rumor was true. Hooker's Army of the Potomac was moving in northern Virginia in the early stages of the Chancellorsville Campaign.

Saturday May 2nd 1863: Clear and pleasant. Last night after supper it commenced to rain but soon increased to be a storm. About 10¼ it commenced hailing and such a storm I never heard. The stones were about as large as a marble. It has beat off many a peach + the China trees are badly cut up. It sounded like it would break every window pane. There is sad, sad news today. Gen E.D. Tracy is killed. The enemy were bombarding Grand Gulf all day. He was killed in a fight near there. Vicksburg is considered to be in a great deal of danger. Yankee cavalry are all around it. But we hope for the best.[68] A bloody struggle is pending at Fredericksburg. The Yanks have crossed in two columns above + below; I hope we will "rout" 'em. Mother sat up with Mrs. Tracy. The clock came back this evening looking bran new + pretty.

Sabbath May 3d 1863: Bright and clear. . . . The rising [abscess] is very prominent + hurts a good deal. There has been an engagement on the Rappahannock.[69] One brigade engaged on our side. A heavy engagement occurred at Grand Gulf or rather 7 miles below. Loss heavy on both sides. The Yanks penetrated within 120 miles of Mobile. Read *Beechcraft*. Rained very hard before service and again after dinner. Thomas left at dusk. . . .

Monday May 4th 1863: Rained tremendous hard while we were eating breakfast and again at 4, accompanied by hail. I took Morphine. Abscess was poulticed all night and again today. Dr. Fitzgerald lanced it at 4½ oclock and it hurt a great deal because it was not as ready to open as the other was, and the cut had to be made deeper. I lay in bed all day dreading it and I could not eat till it was done. I do hope it may benefit me. I took a glass of wine previous to having it opened. Father brought me a copy of the NY *Illustrated News*. The fruit is very seriously damaged by the hail! Thousands of peaches are knocked off and a large portion of those left are so bruised that they will rot + drop. Took a pill at about 7 oclock.

---

68 The Battle of Grand Gulf (April 29, 1863) rebuffed a potential landing of Union Gen. Grant's troops by repulsing Adm. Porter's fleet. Grant simply moved down the Mississippi and crossed at Bruinsburg on April 29-30 and began marching inland. Tracy, a 29-year-old Confederate general from Macon—the half-brother to LeRoy's late Aunt Carrie—was killed the next day leading Georgia and Alabama troops in the fighting at Port Gibson on May 1. His body was returned to Macon and buried in Rose Hill Cemetery.

69 Chancellorsville Campaign (Apr. 30–May 6, 1863). Hooker moved most of his Union Army of the Potomac upriver and crossed the Rapidan beyond Gen. Lee's left, leaving the balance of his command at Fredericksburg as a decoy. Lee divided his army and sent Stonewall Jackson on a flank march that rolled up Hooker's right flank, and then turned and beat back a Union attack from Fredericksburg. Jackson was wounded by friendly fire and would die one week later. After another heavy day of fighting Hooker retreated back over the Rapidan River. Union losses totaled 17,300, and Confederate about 13,300.

Teusday May 5th 1863: Clear and warm. Suffered a great deal till after midnight when Mother + Father got up, removed the poultice + dressed my back. After that I was a great deal more comfortable. The news is that a great fight has been fought at Fredericksburg. Gen Lee telegraphs "that Almighty God had given us another victory. Stonewall Jackson + A.P. Hill wounded. General Paxton killed. Heath wounded.[70] I am so sorry about Gen Jackson. Hooker flanked us or rather turned our position and in doing so got himself into a bad position. Jackson as usual got into his rear and two of Longstreet's divisions in front. The fight lasted two days. Hooker at last accts was retreating across the river. 1600 Yankee cavalry penetrated to within 2 miles of Rome [Ga.] but were repulsed by armed citizens and afterwards taken prisoner by Forrest. Forrest has been fighting 5 days + nights.[71] Yankee cavalry are all over Mississippi. They have torn up the RR within 8 miles of Richmond. The new Flag is the "Battleflag for the Union." White field without bars. O Horrid.[72] Rained gently from teatime till 9 oclock. I went on my wagon a little while, but got chilled + came in. Wrote to Thomas. Mother has been very unwell for a day or two + Father fixes my back.

Wednesday May 5th 1863: Clear + cool. Slept well. Back [abscess] no. 1 ran lots; No 2 none, so we put a poultice on that till dinnertime. It does not run any and it looks like it would heal up. Gen Lee says the Battle occurred at Chancellorsville. Gen Jackson's left arm has been amputated below the shoulder. Gen [John] Sedgwick attempted to come up in our rear [at Fredericksburg] but was handsomely repulsed by [Gen] McLaws and afterwards driven across the river by Gen Lee himself. Mother has gone down town. It is a great bother to dress my back and takes 2 to do it.

Thursday May 6th 1863: Cold and unseasonable. Stuck pretty close to a fire all day. Mrs. Clisby loaned me *The Brain*, Wyandotte + L.E. Landon's works. My back has healed up again. It itched so last night that I could hardly stand it. Susy E[dwards] has come.

Friday May 7th 1863: Cod and windy. Back running very little. George Snider is still very low indeed. No news. List of killed + wounded in the Macon Volunteers. 1700 nasty, stinkin' Yankee raiders have arrived in Atlanta. The Yanks made a raid and came

70 Jackson was mortally wounded, A. P. Hill and Harry Heth wounded, and Elisha F. Paxton killed.

71 Streight's Raid (April 19–May 3, 1863) in northern Alabama, which was mounted on army mules, was poorly planned and ended in complete defeat at Cedar Bluff, Ala., not far from Rome, Ga.

72 The "Stainless Banner," adopted May 1, 1863, consisted of a white field with a small resemblance of the Battle Flag of the Army of Northern Virginia in the upper left corner.

within sight of Richmond.[73] No authentic account of the Battle of Chancellorsville. The Yankee loss was 3 to our 1, "mostly foreigners."[74] It was a very bloody fight.

Saturday May 9th 1863: Very cool. Slept well. The bloody fight is over. Hooker is repulsed, but Stonewall Jackson, the pride and the glory of the people, is disabled and worst of all by his own command. He and his staff rode out unknown to the men to reconnoiter and, being taken for Yankees, was fired upon; 1 of his staff killed, 1 wounded. 1 ball shattered the Gen's left arm and another passed through his right hand. 9 men were wounded in the Macon Volunteers, only 1 killed out right . . . Uncle John passed through Atlanta on his way to the west. 5000 men have gone from Savannah to Miss. Gen Tracy was not killed instantly but mortally wounded. Back runs but little. Went in my wagon and stayed nearly all the eve. Made nondescripts.

Sunday May 10th 1863: Clear and cool. Put on white breeches. My abscess on the right ran a little. Lincoln has called out 5000000 men! Our loss at Chancellorsville was 8 or 10000. I don't think the Yankees lost less than 30000 for we took 8000 prisoners. The Yankees are very proud of their escape. The attack was well planned. A terrible storm prevented pursuit. I hope Gen Lee will cross the river himself as soon as the 28 regiments whose term is out leave for home. The army of Tennessee is reported on the advance?? Nary time. Gen Lee has issued congratulatory orders and this is a day of thanksgiving in the army. Gen Van Dorn has been murdered by a Dr. Peters out west. A personal affair entirely.[75]

Monday May 11th 1863: Clear + pleasant. Had strawberries for dinner. Finished Wyandotte. Brave, gallant Stonewall Jackson is dead. He, the pride of the nation, is gone. Dearly was the victory won at such a price. He died from the combined effect of his wounds + an attack of pneumonia. As a commander, it may be said that he never committed an error![76] The Yankee loss was enormous? They already admit a defeat, but plume themselves on their escape. I never in my life saw peaches so defective wormy + rotten everywhere the hail hit them. I doubt if there is enough on the lot for us to eat. LWG

---

73 LeRoy is referring to Union Gen. George Stoneman's Raid (Apr. 13–May 10, 1863) preceding the Chancellorsville Campaign. Its intent was to cut Lee's supply line and force his retreat. The effort failed.

74 Jackson's surprise attack fell mostly upon Gen. O. O. Howard's Union XI Corps, comprised predominantly of Germans.

75 Dr. James B. Peters killed Van Dorn on May 7, 1863, for having an affair with his wife. No charges were brought against Peters.

76 Jackson's arm was amputated, but he developed pneumonia and died on May 10, 1863.

Tuesday May 12th 1863: Clear and pleasant. The news is Vallandingham[77] is in jail. I got a letter from Grandma and a package by express with Longfellow + note paper. We took 53 cannon at Chancellorsville and from 30 to 50000 muskets. Uncle Richard is sick with Dysentery in the army.

Wednesday May 13th 1863: Clear and warm. Slept well. Lt Col Charles J. Harris has been made commandant of conscripts here . . . . Mrs. Edward Tracy is very sick. George Snider is very low. New abscess ran a little. The [draining] matter is very thin indeed. Another attack on Charleston is anticipated before long. Borrowed Undine + Santram from Mary Campbell. Mrs. Huguenin came to see Mother and Mother went to see her.

Thursday May 14th 1863: Cloudy and warm. Mother is gone down town. Cousin Sam Hayes is severely wounded in the head. Minnie is sick in bed. We were badly "chawed" and beaten at Port Gibson. Our force was 4000 while the enemys was about 20000. Our boys held from sunrise till dark killing 4000 and losing 1000, but had to give back at last crossing Bayou St. Pierre and burning the bridge; all our badly wounded and dead were left in the hands of the enemy. The enemy are now entrenching at Grand Gulf. Gen Tracy fell into their hands it is supposed. Drizzled a little. Minister Adams has notified Earl Russell that the departure of the Emperor of China's warships from England will be considered a "Declaration of War!" Now we'll see a backdown by J. Bull at which [Secretary] Seward would blush.[78]

Friday May 15th 1863: Cousin Mary Wiley and Effie[79] came to see us. Mother is making my couch a nankin cover. Gen Joseph E Johnston has gone to Jackson. Brig Gen [Robert] Rodes has been made Major Gen for gallant conduct in the late fights. Gen [Ambrose] Wright also took a prominent part and did his duty well. The 2nd [Ga.] batt[alion] was tried for the 1st time. Had strawberries for dinner. Howard left for Houston.

May 16th Saturday 1863: Drizzly and cool. My crutches came last night. I am very, very weak and can-not take many steps. Minnie has gone with Robert Plant to a picnic

---

77 Ohio politician Clement L. Vallandigham was the leader of the "Copperheads," an anti-war Democrat movement designed to weaken the Lincoln administration. Lincoln eventually exiled him to the Confederacy.

78 "John Bull" is the British symbolic equivalent to "Uncle Sam." It is unclear what else LeRoy was referring to regarding Chinese warships.

79 Cousin Mary Wiley Harris, whose son Charlie had died in 1862. She had a daughter, Mary Euphemia "Effie" Harris, the eldest of the couple's eventual 14 children.

at Benton. Vicksburg is in great danger; Jackson [Miss.] is reported taken.[80] I feel weak + bad today. Howard returned home and brought me a rabbit from Pig Pen. Read *Cleve Hall*. It is very interesting.

Sunday May 17th 1863: Clear and warm. Mr. Wills preached on the 7th commandment and a fine sermon. . . Mother in bed and we stayed in her room all day. My rabbit got loose last night + I reckon the cat caught it for it was found bit to death.

Monday May 18th 1863: Clear and pleasant. Jackson, Miss. is in the enemy's hands and gloomy forebodings are entertained for Vicksburg. Gen Joe Johnston was cut off this side. We fought all day. The 46th Ga. was in the fight. Gloomy times certain. I am quite unwell. Took paregoric last night.[81] Had strawberries for dinner. Went on my wagon and stayed a good long time. Father bought me a nice linen coat. My Back has hurt me all day and itchd very bad. Received letter from Thomas.

Tuesday May 19th 1863: Clear and pleasant. The news from the west is bad. The Yanks after sacking Jackson have evacuated it marching towards Vicksburg. Gen Johnston with 9000 men fought 20000 all day and then being overpowered fell back to Canton. Port Hudson has been attacked! Heavy firing; no other particulars. [Union Gen.] Halleck has gone down to overlook Hooker. Gen [Lloyd] Tilghman is killed. Had dewberries for dinner. Mother in bed yet. Uncle Edge has resigned.[82] The itching of my back at times is intolerable. If the Yanks ain't working us now, you may take my hat. All looks threatening and dark around us. I wish Gen Pemberton was in Guinea or anywhere else but in the place he is. Minnie lost a ring. Hooker's loss in Stragglers, deserters, killed, and wounded is not estimated at less than 40000. They acknowledge officially only 17000. Our loss was about 9000. They captured about 1500 of our men.

Wednesday May 20th 1863: Clear and cool. Took Morphia. The itching of my back was beyond endurance. There has been a very heavy battle between Jackson + Vicksburg.[83] Our loss 3000; theirs 6000. We were compelled to fall back to our ditches [defenses]. Gen Loring was cut off from the rest. I don't understand the status at all at

---

80 Vicksburg was indeed in "great danger." Grant continued inland, fighting and winning Port Gibson and Raymond. He captured Mississippi's capital at Jackson on May 14. Confederate Gen. Johnston had orders to assume command of all Confederate troops in Mississippi. At Jackson, he could do little more than hold off a Union advance as long as possible and evacuate the city.

81 Paregoric, which contained opium, was found in many households in 19th century. It was widely used to combat diarrhea and as a cough medicine.

82 Edgeworth Bird's resigned to become brigade quartermaster, effective March 30, 1863.

83 The Siege of Vicksburg (May 18-July 4, 1863).

all.[84] A great many men have left Savannah and Charleston, + I am afraid the Yanks will make a land attack.

Thursday May 21st 1863: Clear and cool. Here it is the middle of May and no weather; yet when summer clothes were comfortable the highest the thermometer had been yet is 76°. Aunt Ann called. Mother is up. New abscess runs the most now. Got Strawberries for dinner. Rumors bad and good from the west.

~~Thursday~~ *Friday May 22nd 1863*: The news is poor. Vicksburg is closely invested and will probably fall. The news is unsatisfactory in the extreme. Thomas arrived in the evening. Ate a wormy ripe plum, the first of the season.

Sat. ~~Friday~~ *May 23d 1863*: Clear and pleasant. Mary Campbell stayed all night and we had a very nice time after tea. Not a drop of news. It is rumored + O! I hope its so that Gen Johnston has put Old Pemberton under arrest and taken away his sword. . . . I never saw anything to equal the anxiety about the condition of things in the West. If General Grant does take Vicksburg, he must do it in short order.

Sunday May 24 1863: Clear and warm Vicksburg had not fallen at last accts and the condition, though extremely critical, was not at all desperate, and I am strongly in hopes that Grant will yet meet with a stunning defeat. He it is stated was repulsed in 3 attacks on Vicksburg and "Jo Johnston" is pushing in his rear and constantly receiving reinforcements.[85] Cousin Eliza sent me two crabs and some very fine shrimps. There is to be a prayer meeting to pray for our army in the Mississippi Valley in particular.

Monday May 25th 1863: Clear and warm. Had strawberries, custard, + cake, for dinner. No news. The anxiety about our army out West and doubt is freely expressed of Pemberton's loyalty.[86] Minnie stayed at home, Howard left for Houston. Finished *Columbus' Life and Voyages* and begun *Life of Peter Parley*. Went to sleep in the evening. Thomas left for another 3 week [college] term. Recd relic from battlefield sent by Uncle Dick: a fancy roll of the Burnside Gaurds, a company of the 124th Pa.

---

84 Gen. John Pemberton commanded at Vicksburg. He gathered a significant army outside the city at Champion Hill, where he was soundly defeated on May 16 by Grant. Gen. Lloyd Tilghman was killed there; Gen. W. W. Loring's command was cut off and retreated in a different direction. Pemberton's survivors fell back into Vicksburg's defenses and the city was taken under siege.

85 Gen. Grant launched two direct infantry attacks against Vicksburg's strong earthworks (May 19 and 22); both were bloodily repulsed. Richmond authorities pressed Johnston to attack Grant's rear or do something to help break the siege, but he did little other than call for Pemberton to evacuate.

86 Pemberton was a native of Pennsylvania, so his poor record in the field made many suspect his loyalty to the Confederate cause.

Tuesday May 26th 1863: Cloudy and cool. The news is a drop more encouraging from Vicksburg. The Yanks have been repulsed 6 times and with very heavy loss. Grant says he has taken the first line of entrenchments. Johnson is fortifying at Jackson. [Gen. John C.] Breckinridge + [Braxton] Bragg have come to an open rupture and the former has called a court of inquiry.[87] [Joe] Brown is announced for a 4th term [for governor] and there will be no opposition. Howard returned with Allen. Rained a little and blew a good deal. . . . Mrs. Hug[uenin] sent me honey, butter and sug berries.

Wednesday May 27th 1863: Rainy morning. Vallandigham has been sent to our lines as an exile but Gen Bragg has refused to receive him till he hears from headquarters. Mr. Bates has taken a spasmodic notion to teach till two oclock. No news from the west. 3 picket C.S. Reg[iment]s were surprised and licked in N.C. The rainiest day I have seen in a long time. It rained so steady Father could not go to town till 4 oclock. Read in *Penny Magazine*.

Thursday May 28th 1863: Rainy morning. Vicksburg holds out gallantly. . . . Wrote to Uncle Richard + Thomas. Had Raspberries. Mother sick. Nearly cold enough for a fire. Minnie did not go to school. I thought it rained hard in the morn, but from one oclock till bedtime it literally poured + the wind blew.

Friday May 29th 1863: Rained all night at intervals and till 10½ AM. I don't ever remember to have seen such a hard rain before. About 20 feet of the college wall was washed away and a man killed under it. The situation is gloomy in the extreme. Vicksburg is one. It is said that the Yanks have lost heavier than in any previous battle. Rotten Yankees are piled up in such numbers before our intrenchments that the effluvia [smell] is awful. Tar is burnt to prevent sickness. ~~Grant is er~~ [Gen.] Banks is crossing the Mississippi to aid Grant. Farragut is bombarding Port Hudson. Gunboats have passed Vicksburg going up. They'll take it certain. No news of Gen Johnston. Father has no hope of our holding out longer than a week. It is awful.

Saturday May 30th 1863: Clear and warm. Nothing definite from the west. Grant's loss must be enormous. Pemberton's address to the army is received. I can but hope. Grant can get any amount of reinforcements + supplies. Yazoo River and all our river batteries are in their hands. Our Warrenton batteries also. Up to the 27th, our men were cheerful and hopeful. On the 27th, The Feds made a grand attack + were repulsed with loss. The recent rain washed over two or three houses. Mr. McEvoy's stable was washed over too.

---

87 The "rupture" stemmed from Bragg's accusation that Breckinridge was drunk at Murfreesboro and bungled his attack on January 2, 1863, an assault Breckinridge had vehemently opposed making.

Sunday May 30th 1863: Clear and pleasant. Mr. Wills preached on the 9th commandment... No news. People seem to take it as a matter of course that Vicksburg is gone. Ewell and A.P. Hill are Lt Gens.[88] Read *Dr. Alexander.* Hooker is "changing his base" of operations in the peninsular.

Summer June 1st Monday 1863: Clear + warm. It has rained every day since Tuesday. Yesterday there was a heavy shower. Cousin Charlie called yester eve. John Wiley[89] is very sick. Two pigeons are trying to build a nests in the well house. Mother went down town. I rode down to Mr. Foster's on my wagon. The moon rose partially eclipsed this eve. This is the 1st real warm day.

Tuesday June 2nd 1863: Clear and warm. The news is on the whole encouraging. Vicksburg holds out heroically! Gen Grant demanded a surrender, but Pemberton replied that he would die in the trenches. There are some heavy rumors. One is that the enemy made a grand assault and were mown down by thousands, nearly all of them killed or captured. The Yankees say we rolled shells down the hill at them causing immense havoc. One thing is certain there has been an attack and a repulse but as to the slaughter there is a great deal of doubt about that. Our loss is comparatively small. Port Hudson is invested. I wish all the reliable reports we have heard could be true. If Vicksburg does pass this fiery ordeal in safety, how thankful we ought to be! There was a very heavy storm of rain in the eve at 5 oclock. Read *Merikand or Selfsacrifice.* The college girls have formed a company and drill regularly. I rode out on my wagon and it made me feel so sore that I did not sleep hardly at all. It is rumored and credited that Lee's army is in motion. Had strawberries for dinner.

Wednesday June 3d 1863: Warm and clear. Rained an hour or so in the eve, not very hard. . . . I have no appetite for several days and have not [felt] well at all. Dr. Harrison died last night of pneumonia.[90] . . . I get along well enough with my back but my leg will never be straight...

Thursday June 4th 1863: A very beautiful delightful day. Father left early for the plantation. Got a letter from Thomas last night. "P.W.A." has a long account of the Fredericksburg fight, rather too stale. Something is evidently to "Riy" on the Rappahannock, but as to whether it our army or the Yanks no one knows. Vicksburg is

---

88 The death of Stonewall Jackson convinced Gen. Lee to reorganize his army from two corps to three. James Longstreet continued at the head of his corps, Richard Ewell was promoted to lead Jackson's former corps, and A. P. Hill was given a newly created corps.

89 Nine-year old John Barnett Wiley, Jr. was Cousin Charlie's younger brother.

90 Dr. Harrison was a local Macon doctor.

still ours. Grant is <u>heavily</u> <u>reinforced</u>. Pemberton's address to his troops is a defense of himself, not a harangue to the troops. The Yanks have had it captured twice. George Snider is very low. Mrs. Judge Holt called. John Wiley is very ill with inflammatory Rheumatism. Higgelty pigglety pop! O La.

Friday June 5th 1863: Cloudy in the morn till about 10 AM when it began to drop rain and continued raining till after dinner. The "Situation" is on the whole encouraging. If there is any truth in the mass of stuff by Telegraph today, Grant may yet skedadle. It says [Gen] Banks has been handsomely thrashed by Gen Gardner near to Port Hudson and that Kirby Smith is opposite ready to cross.[91] Gen Johnston is on the move to cut off Grant. Grant is moving to prevent it and a great fight is pending on the Yazoo. The stench of rotten Yanks can be smelt 6 miles off. Pemberton calls on Grant to bury them. Contrabands were put in the front of the fight on every occasion. It is rumored Rosencrans is falling back [in Tenn]. Have had a fire all day nearly; winter clothes on too. George Beal came to see me. I eat June apples every eve and they are very nice + ripe.

Saturday June 6th 1863: Rained nearly all night and it is still cloudy. Read *The Laird of Norlan*. Banks was not in the fight at Port Hudson. Sherman commanded and was killed.[92] Out of a regiment of 900 "nigs" only 100 escaped. "Bully for <u>that</u>." A great fight is ere this going on between Johnston + Grant. "Terrific firing heard," and it must be them. Now we must wait patiently for news, but if we don't lick them – well. Minnie has stopped school for this year. Father arrived at dinnertime sick and weary. He brought some apples for pies and about half-bushel of plums. Mrs. Strohecker sent me some nice potatoe custard. Sent plums to all the neighbors. Of all the messes I ever saw this western news beats. I still stick to what I ever said, that Vicksburg would be yet delivered + Grant would yet be defeated. My strawberries + a little bottle of May cherries arrived from Athens.

Sunday June 7th 1863: Clear and warm. . . . Had strawberries for dinner. Cherry preserves I mean, and they were real splendid. Read commentaries on Mark all the morn. No news. Rumors of an advance in Tennessee are afloat. Wrote to Grandma. Prayer meeting for Vicksburg in the eve.

91 Confederate Gen. Franklin K. Gardner was in command of the Port Hudson defenses on the Mississippi River below Vicksburg in northern Louisiana, which were being invested by an army under Union Gen. Nathaniel Banks.

92 The rumor was untrue. Gen. Sherman led a corps in Grant's army in the Vicksburg operation. African-American troops played a large role in Vicksburg operations and suffered significant losses.

Monday June 8th 1863: Clear and cool. Bought Whortleberries at 50 cents a quart. My back runs a great deal now. Willis came up bringing Dewberries.... Henry can walk 50 yards and is a great deal better. John Wiley is out and looks badly.... No news. Gen W.H.T. Walker is a Maj Gen. Had the first apple pie of the season and enjoyed it very much. Received a letter from Uncle Richard. He is in A. P. Hill's 3d army corps.

Tuesday June 8th 1863: Cloudy and warm. It is rumored that Bragg is advancing but is thought they are only feeling one another. Made Jam. Mrs. Nisbet sent me tea cakes and strawberries. Making Allen aprons. Not a rumor from Vicksburg. The affair at Port Hudson was a small affair. My back runs hugely. nellaisakcap Tnarg lliw ylniatrec eb dekcil. [Allen is a pack. Grant will certainly be licked.]

Wednesday June 10th 1863: Cloudy rained a little. Uncle Sam is cleaning out the well. Tracy is playing ninepins with Florence on the floor and slamming the balls about. The news from Vicksburg is encouraging. The Yanks acknowledge a loss of 50,000! 30000 wounded. Rumors state K.I.R.B.Y. S.M.I.T.H. has taken Milliken's Bend + 10,000 men. This is not so. PEMBERTON says he can hold Vicksburg indefinitely. Grant is building parallel lines of fortifications. His loss is immense.

Thursday June 11th 1863: Cloudy and nearly cool enough for a fire. It is unseasonable for June. Mrs. Huguenin sent me some dinner. Mother is sick in bed. Clouded up very dark at dinner and rained hard. Well, if things do not look gloomy at Vicksburg, there a'int no snakes. Grant has called for 50000 reinforcements and he will get them. Alas! We have none to send without exposing an important point. So as it has come to a question of reinforcements, we are gone... Father thinks it. It is a gloomy prospect. There are some wild rumors too. One is that you can walk on dead yankees for 10 acres and not touch the earth. Another says that the blood is shoe deep!! The slain are 60 + 70,000. Ours 600. Another says Pemberton boasts he can hold Vicksburg indefinitely and tells Johnston to take his time. The Yanky exaggeration's are equally wild.[93] They say Pemberton has been hung by our men.... I did not sleep well. I had such a binding pain across the chest and I think it comes from overexertion. My leg distresses me greatly and worse than all, folks say it's my own fault, I can straiten it if I

93 LeRoy enjoys comparing Northern and Southern media reports. He was fairly quick to realize that both sides exaggerate, misreport, and use propaganda to lift the morale of their readers.

would try.[94] Well ~~ . . . Friedapplesaregoodandsoispig. There has been a heavy cavalry fight on the Rappahannock. Gen Lee says "Gen Stuart after a 'severe contest' of 12 hrs. drove the Yanks 'across the river.'" I reckon it was a hard fight.[95]

Friday June 12th 1863: Clear and warm. The pain in my breast is better. Got a letter from Thomas saying he had not received the money sent on Monday, or he would have been here yesterday. Gen Lee is moving but in what direction no one knows.[96] Our loss was 400 in the late cavalry fight. We got the new stove up and it is very nice. The *Field and Fireside* came this day.

Saturday June 13th 1863: Clear and warm. No news. Thomas got home at 4.32. Howard killed a coach-whip snake at the stable. Mrs. Beal called. Minnie went down to Mr. Wills' and got *The Life of Whitfield*. Father bought 25 lbs. of flour at 30 cents per lb.

Sunday June 14th 1863: Clear and pleasant. No News at all. Went to bed feeling dizzy and my head aches now. Prayer meeting for Vicksburg in our church. Tracy Baxter, Georgia, + Suzy Tracy came to see us and the last 2 are beautiful.[97] . . . Today Zilla Whittle brought Minnie a puppy with a brown head and a black spot on his tail. Minnie would not have him because he was white, and so I took him and named him "General Forrest." He is fat as a butterball + more lively than Price.

94 LeRoy is understandably indignant because he is physically unable to straighten his leg because of nerve damage in his lower spine.

95 Brandy Station, Virginia (June 9, 1863), where Union troopers surprised Confederate Gen. Jeb Stuart's men. The combat was a swirling day-long bloody affair that cost the Union 900 men to 520 Confederates. The Union cavalry retreated, but the battle marked a turning point for Union horsemen.

96 Gen. Lee's Army of Northern Virginia was in the initially stages of the Gettysburg Campaign, moving west away from Fredericksburg toward the Shenandoah Valley on its way north.

97 Susan Campbell Tracy and Georgia Eliza Tracy were the daughters of the late Gen. Edward Dorr Tracy and Cousin Helen.

Monday June 15th 1863: Clear and warm. Woke up with headache. Took a blue pill. Father bought me a scrapbook at Mr. Burke's and it is a very nice one. Mrs. Huguenin called.

June 16th 1863: Clear and warm. All of Thomas' class came over last night: Messrs. Askew, Bothwell, Smythe, + Sayre. After tea Mr. Sayre + Pitts came round and we had a nice time. Mr. Smythe played on the Piano and Sung *"Lary Obrien"* + *The Barber*. It was splendid and I never laughed so in my life. Messrs. Sayre + Smythe left at 7 on the CRR. I did not sleep well at all. I had a pain in my head + right hip but feel very well today. This is decidedly the warmest day we've had, indeed the only hot day. Father is very desponding, almost hopeless about Vicksburg, though I see no reason to be more so than usual.

June 17th Wednesday 1863: Minnie's 14th birthday. Thomas gave her *Jack Hopeton, or The Adventures of a Georgian*. I am tolerable. My back ran a great deal of dark bloody looking matter last night. Last night was the 1st time it was warm enough to sleep with out cover. The Mosquitoes are right bad and we'll have to move upstairs shortly. We heard Sunday, Mr. Jim Campbell was wounded. Today heard that he was shot through the liver. It must be a dangerous wound. Early's division has stormed the entrenchments at Winchester and in the language of Gen Lee, God has again crowned the Valor of our troops with success.[98] "Forrest" has come to stay for good and is a very nice little dog. The news from the West is good, if true. General E.K. Smith has taken Milliken's bend. Father says the safety of Vicksburg depends upon him.[99]

Thursday June 18th 1863: Rained hard at 8½ AM. Did not sleep well on acct of the unceasing yells of "Forrest." Mr. Askew left at 5 oclock. Received a letter from Aunty + Wilson. They are going to call Sallie "Sada" [Saida][100] and "Granite Farm" "Vorcleuse." The news is Ewell has captured Milroy's army [at Winchester]. General Ed Johnson took 2000 coming to Milroy's relief. Gen Stuart was completely surprised in the Fight at Brandy station + it was only the gallant behavior of our men that saved him from a

---

98 The Second Battle of Winchester (June 13-15, 1863), an important Confederate victory by Gen. Ewell's Corps in northern Shenandoah Valley, cleared the way to the Potomac River and beyond into Maryland and Pennsylvania.

99 Battle of Milliken's Bend (June 7, 1863) was a Confederate attack in Louisiana against a Union supply depot guarded by U.S. Colored Troops. The attack was beaten off. Gen. Kirby Smith, who was on the far side of the Mississippi River, was not involved. To a degree John Gresham was right. Without help from the Trans-Mississippi Theater, Vicksburg was doomed. No help would be forthcoming.

100 "Saida" was Sallie Bird's given name.

disastrous defeat. Not a word from the "Hill City" [Vicksburg]. A big lie from Port Hudson about "27 repulses."

Friday June 19th 1863: Clear and delightful day. Peaches are getting ripe fast. Jack Ross, Jr. was killed in a late fight at Monticello, Ky.[101] No word of encouragement from Vicksburg. The Yanks have evacuated the Stafford hills and gone somewhere, towards Manassas it is supposed. Our cavalry are pursuing. Weighed "Forrest:" the amount was 2 pounds and 15 ounces. He is quite lively and playful. Gen Forrest has been shot and wounded in the leg by a captain. Father drilled with the Bibb County Hussars. Took a bait of red (not ripe) peaches. Mother was sick in bed all day. The mosquitoes are very annoying. The highest thermometer I have seen has been 89?. It rained very hard at 12 noon.

Saturday June 20th 1863: Clear and warm. Ewell's victory at "Winchester" is confirmed. 7000 prisoners + 3000 horses. It is rumored that our army is pushing into Maryland. The Yankees are under the influence of a grand scare or "uprisings." Lincoln calls for 100000 6 months men and the Gov[ernor]s are calling too. Our loss at Brandy Station was 483; Yanks twice that. "Forrest's" mother carried him home last night. Captain Findlay's Ordnance Gaurd passed by here. Mother is sick in bed. . . .

Sunday June 21st 1863: Cloudy and warm. . . . Rained slowly all the P.M. Our army it is rumored is "en route" to Mld [Maryland].

Monday June 22nd 1863: Cool and cloudy. Rained in the night and is nearly cool enough for a fire. Slept upstairs for the first time last night. O how I could like to have wrung "Forrest's" neck. He yelped without a pause the whole night. My right leg pains me a little. Took good bait of peaches.

Tuesday June 23rd 1863: Cool and clear. Fires comfortable early in the morn. Tracy "called." Put Forrest in the washhouse, where he cried to his heart's content. The June apples are love to the sight and pleasant to the taste. The Yanks have made a cavalry raid into E. Tenn. and after burning a factory and damaging the R.R. were repulsed by the 54th Va. at Knoxville – General Ewell is in Mld. Hooker is near Bull run and "Manassas Plains." Where the grand collision will occur or whither Gen Lee intends to fight, no one knows. I can't see what object we can have in entering Maryland except to get provision or attract attention from Vicksburg.[102] I feel confident that our army can

101 Identity unknown, but likely a Macon or area native known by the Gresham family.

102 If LeRoy reached these conclusions on his own, he was in sync with Richmond authorities who believed Lee's move north would draw off the Union army from Virginia, allow Lee's men to gather supplies, and perhaps force Gen. Grant to withdraw men away from Vicksburg.

whip Hooker's anywhere – Blackberries do not fall below 25 cents a quart. Mother in bed yet.

Wednesday June 24th 1863: Clear and cool. Father and Minnie left early this morn for Burke [County]. Ellen Edwards and Chris Findlay were married last night and went off on the train for Savvannah. The news came yesterday of a grand assault Saturday which resulted in a disastrous defeat upon Vicksburg. (What grammar!) Another report today says an attack was made Wednesday with like result. Don't believe neither.

Thursday June 25th 1863: Clear and warm. Did not sleep well. Peaches are getting ripe but they are watery and mean on acct of so much rain. The movements of Gen Lee are shrouded in complete mystery as are Gen Johnston's [in Mississippi]. Hooker is over the Potomac and the fight will be in Mld. Rubbed "Forrest" with flea powder. They look as if they'd kill him.

Friday June 26th 1863: Clear and hot. Last night was the warmest of the season. "Forrest" weighs 3 lbs. + upwards. No news. Terrific firing at Vicksburg. We had a serenade last night. An accordion, triangle, + singing. Feel sore + tired. Commenced 1st Vol[unteer]s. Parton's *Jackson*. The *Examiner* is out. Willie Edwards came over and sat a little while. Gen Longstreet has crossed the Potomac at Leesburg; Ewell at Harpers Ferry. A.P. Hill is behind. James Campbell is doing well. Rained hard at 11.

Saturday June 27th 1863: Clear and warm. Last night it was very warm and I had some of "Forrest's" fleas on me. Lay on the floor all the morn in the back parlor. Mrs. Butler sent me sweet wafers + cherry preserves. Got letter from Father. They've got along very well. No news of any kind. Ate ½ apple pie, cherry preserves, peaches, wafers, +c, +c.

Sunday June 28th 1863: Cloudy and cool; rained at 8AM a little. Took off my undershirts yesterday eve. My back runs steadily sometimes more, then again less. The Handkerchief tied 'round me is hot. I reckon there will be a tremendous fight in Tennessee in a day or two. Rosencrantz has already driven in our advance-guard. Grant is bombarding Vicksburg by sea + land and apprehensions are felt by some as to the result. Prayermeeting for the country and army this PM.

Monday June 29th 1863: Clear and warm. Rained a little about dark and the wind blew. Read *The Raids + Romance of Morgan + His Men* by Miss Sallie R. Ford and it is splendid. An utter dearth of news. Nothing from the West or Virginia. Mother is very unwell. "Forrest" grows and thrives but I think he is a "fice."[103] My back has not run

---

103 A less common variant of "feist," which means small dog.

much the last week. Mother is reading *Great Expectations* and thinks it strange + unnatural.

Tuesday June 30th 1863: Clear and warm. Mother came home in the rain and was very sick all night. Thomas slept with her. She is a little better today. "Forrest" was taken ill in the night with the belly acke, I reckon. Gave him a dose of oil. The Yanks have made a raid around Richmond, kicked up a dust! Captured Gen W.H. Lee + left.[104] Richmond is menaced by a large force via the Peninsula. Confident is felt as to our ability to repulse them. No General engagement is anticipated in Tennessee. 2 [rail] car-loads of wounded in the late skirmish have come down to Chatt[anooga]. Commencement day at the college. Thomas had to dress my back. The "new un" [abscess] has not run a drop in a day and night. I hope it'll heal up.

Wednesday July 1st 1863: Clear and warm weather. Mother was sent for yesterday by Cousin Eliza and when she got there found little George so low that his life was despaired of. Early this morn she went again but when she got there the poor suffering little fellow was at rest. What a long and painful illness has his been. His last symptoms were dropsical [swollen with fluid] and the doctors Boone and Hammond tapped him.[105] A dwelling house was burned down last night about 2½ AM. "Forrest" is a great deal better today.

Thursday July 2nd 1863: Cloudy and hot. Father arrived at 5½ AM. Minnie is going to stay [in Burke] a little longer. He brought a newsy and interesting letter from Minnie, also a "Map of the Seat of War in Mississippi." Gen Ewell is reported in "Harrisburg" [Pa.]! Battle imminent in Tenn. "Vicksburg is gone," some people say; others think it not so bad as that.

Friday July 3d 1863: Cloudy and warm. Rained briskly about dinner time. Cousin Eliza sent me cake + apples. Read *A Voice from St. Helena* by Dr. O'Meara, a sad acct of Napoleon's exile there. I have felt inexpressibly weary all day, and have had a slight pain in my leg too. Rosencrans, it is said, has flanked our right and Bragg is retreating. Before

104 Gen. W. F. "Rooney" Lee, Gen. Robert E. Lee's son, was injured at Brandy Station and recovering at his wife's family home outside of Ashland, Va., when he was taken prisoner. Rooney and his wife Charlotte had two children, both of whom died in infancy. Because he was wounded and captured, Rooney never saw his wife again. She died on December 26, 1863.

105 John R. Boone and Dudley W. Hammond were both Macon physicians.

he is done I reckon we'll be at Chattanooga again.[106] D.H. Hill is in Richmond and Gen Dix is advancing on the city.[107]

Saturday July 4th 1863: Hot and clear. Well! Well! This is the glorious but "played out" 4th and the only celebration is [editor] Mr. Clisby takes a holiday. 3 years ago I laid down and it has not done me any good. My left leg is worse drawn up than ever. Father brought me some pills: "Dr. Blanchard's Iodide of Iron." I commenced to take them. Do not feel very well today. Made Jam. Not a splash of news from anywhere. We have had roasting ears [corn] since the 30th Ult.[108] Tomatoes will not be ripe in a week yet. Squashes, "cow" cumbers, potatoes, Beans, Beats, +c are more abundant than usual. Father is desponding about Vicksburg.

Sunday July 5th 1863: Very hot. . . . Communion Day. Bragg's retreat to Chattanooga is confirmed. Banks has got licked at Port Hudson.

Monday July 6th 1863: Very hot until toward noon when a beautiful rain fell—a nice season and after that it was cool and pleasant enough. Father was taken sick at dinner, a tendency to cholera-morbus [gastroenteritis] Mother thought. Mother went to bed with violent sick stomack, and I with a pain in the side. Made Mary dip "Forrestia" [dog] with a solution of walnut leaves [for fleas]. Wrote to Minnie and Recd a letter from her. Uncle LeRoy arrived here from Athens this morn. He is just from Charleston. Brought a *New York Herald* with him. Thomas and he are playing backgammon.

Tuesday July 7th 1863: Hot enough to please me. The news is all Northern, Viz. a Battle has been fought at Gettysburg, Pa. between the Yanks under Meade and the Confeds under Lt Gens Longstreet and Hill in which the "Anks" acknowledge that they were worsted. Mr. Clisby thinks it was not a large affair. There will however probably be a big fight as both sides are concentrating their forces.

The most sanguinary battle of the war has been fought at Gettysburg, Pa. Barksdale, Kemper, Garnett, Armistead, Semmes Killed. Hood, Trimble, Pickett, Pender—Hampton, Anderson, Robinson, Jenkins, Jones, Heth, Scales, Pettigrew +c. 50 field officers besides these disabled; our whole loss probably 15000 in killed,

---

106 The Tullahoma Campaign (June 24 - July 3, 1863) was a brilliant operation of maneuver. Rosecrans outflanked Bragg and forced him out of Middle Tennessee. Just as LeRoy presciently predicted, Bragg fell back all the way back to Chattanooga without fighting a significant battle. The operation was mostly overshadowed by grim news from Gettysburg and Vicksburg.

107 The news was false. Union Gen. John Dix was too old for field command and never led an army.

108 "30th ult." means the 30th of the preceding month, or June 30.

Text from the July 7, 1863, entry on the Battle of Gettysburg, written on a loose blue sheet of paper with a dragonfly's wing he had pressed into place between the journal pages. LOC

wounded, and prisoners, certainly not less for nearly all our wounded, who were not able to move or be carried, were left behind. General Lee's army is crossing the Potomac at Williamsport where a severe fight is probably going on with our rear guard. The Potomac is very high and our men are crossing in flats. The loss is appalling and for nothing too. What a host of men have been slain at just such an affair; at Shiloh, Murfreesboro + Sharpsburg! Our army went into Maryland declaring themselves invincible and with an utter contempt for the foe they had so often whipped. Mr. Sam Campbell is missing. Every officer in the [Macon] Volunteers was disabled. Cleveland Franklin was wounded in both legs.[109]

General Hooker has been superceded by Gen "G.G. Meade" a "brave and accomplished officer" which is a capital thing for us. Gens Wadsworth + Reynolds U.S.A. are reported killed. Our army is reported as living "in clover." When a town is entered, a contribution of supplies is levied. Gen Ewell forbids all individual interference with private property. When our cavalry comes across fine horses, they take them and put their jaded ones in their place. The only news we get is that "our army is kicking up a big dust."[110] It is also stated that McGruder [Magruder] is opposite N[ew] Orleans and that we have taken a place above N.O. with heavy siege guns commanding the river; "in short" we are going to take N.O. A cheering bit of

---

109 Union Gen. George Meade replaced Gen. Hooker at the head of the Army of the Potomac on June 27, just three days before meeting Gen. Lee's Army of Northern Virginia at Gettysburg (July 1-3, 1863). The massive battle was the largest of the war and a clear Confederate defeat. Casualties for both armies combined approached 50,000 killed, wounded, and captured/missing. The Southern officers LeRoy named who were killed or mortally wounded included: Gens. William Barksdale (mw), Richard B. Garnett (k), Lewis Armistead (mw), Paul J. Semmes (k), Dorsey Pender (mw), and James J. Pettigrew (mw, July 14). Other prominent officers noted included: James Kemper (w), John B. Hood (w), Wade Hampton (w), John M. Jones (w), Alfred M. Scales (w). George E. Pickett was not injured. Several Union generals were also killed, including John F. Reynolds, commander of the I Corps.

110 The continued entry confirms the confusing and often contradictory nature of the news coming out of Pennsylvania.

"contraband news too delicate for the public palate" has been received from Vicksburg. Port Hudson has been attacked and the enemy awfully licked. I give all this as I heard it and anybody may credit it that wants to do so.[111]

Wednesday July 8th 1863: Cloudy and warm. Slept well. Great and glorious news! Grand defeat of the Yankees. 40000 prisoners. All of both sides engaged. The Yankees massed their forces and attacked Gen [A.P.] Hill in the centre. He fell back and the enemy following our wings under Longstreet and Ewell closed on them, and thus completely defeated them, killing it is said Gens Meade, Wadsworth, Reynolds, Barlow, + Meredith. The prisoners refused to be paroled and Pickett's division was guarding them to Martinsburg. Our loss it is supposed is tremendous. Vicksburg is taken. The news is believed at Jackson. There has been a fight of 3 hours duration at Edwards Station, Miss. + the Yankees licked. The Gens were [Peter] Osterhaus USA + [W. W.] Loring. Gen Johnston is moving; I think it is time. He ought to have attacked Grant without fail; if he takes N.O. however it'll do. I hope that Gen Lee will take Washington. I cannot believe that heroic little Vicksburg is actually gone, but "lack-a-day." I reckon it is so. Gen Dick Taylor has taken a strong position on the other side of Mississippi with 7000 prisoners, 7000 muskets, 2500000 commissary, + 2Ms stores.

Thursday July 9th 1863: Clear and warm. An official dispatch says – "Vicksburg capitulated on the 4th inst. The men were immediately paroled; the officers retaining their side arms + baggage." The cause of the surrender was famine. General Grant had a boatload of provisions brought for our poor men. We had only 7000 effective men.[112] The "Victory" in Pa. grows beautifully less. "Nary 40000." We lost 4000 though. Thomas shot "Forrest" today, a sad and cruel act for which I am very sorry. I don't want any more puppies. He was so sick he could barely stand. Mr. More staid to tea with us and told us many interesting stories about N.Orleans. On Tuesday night the Brown house was fired + put out. On Wed. morn the Lanier house was fired and after considerable trouble extinguished. Today about 10 or 11AM the alarm was again sounded that it was on fire in the garret. The incendiary had fired it with paper saturated with turpentine. After incredible efforts the gallant firemen succeeded in extinguishing

---

111 Once again LeRoy is justifiably skeptical. In fact, none of it was true.

112 This news was true. The civilians of Vicksburg and its Confederate army had been surrounded and besieged for 47 days and were starving when Gen. Pemberton surrendered 29,500 men to Gen. Grant on July 4. The Confederates were paroled (which meant they agreed not to take up arms again unless properly exchanged). It was one of the most complete victories of the war, and, coupled with the defeat at Gettysburg the day before, a double blow from which the Confederacy could not recover.

it. Every particle of furniture was pitched out from the hotel and the stores around a piled in an incongruous mass in the street.[113] Cousin Eliza sent me some "turnovers."

Friday July 10th 1863: Clear and hot. My back has been weak as a baby's for two or 3 days and my leg hurts me a little. The *Examiner* came. Gens Heth, Pender, Hood, Anderson, Pettigrew + Semmes wounded. Armistead, Barksdale killed, + 50 other field officers killed + wounded in the late terrible battle [Gettysburg].

Saturday July 11th 1863: Hottest day yet. Thomas left for Burke – Slept poorly. My leg and side hurt me very bad. Grant is advancing on Jackson [Miss.]. Heavy battle pending. Fighting is in progress at Charleston. Yanks have taken Morris Island batteries. Extreme anxiety is felt about Md. Lee has fallen back. Ammunition out. [Gen] Dan Sickles U.S.A. lost a leg [at Gettysburg]. The Yanks loss was enormous but I fear ours was "enormouser." . . .

Sunday July 12th 1863: Clear and hot as pepper. Nothing from Jackson or Charleston. Capt Ballard + Lt Hodgkins, Macon Gaurds, killed. Major Ross wounded and a prisoner and it is rumored that the whole Batt[alion] are prisoners. The 48th [Ga.] cut to pieces. Col Gibson wounded. We did not get the best of it, or Gen Lee's dispatch would be made public. I am hopeless about my leg; it is drawn so bad. Father is too.

Monday July 13th 1863: Cloudy and hot. We are quite lonely now; two out of our family is a gap indeed. I wish I had something to do, now the days are so long + I get so tired. Gen Semmes is dead. Col Jack Brown of the 69th shot in both legs. One reg[imen]t in Wright's brig[ade] went in with a col, Lt col, + 6 cap[tain]s and came out with under a second Lt.

Tuesday July 14th 1863: Cloudy with every appearance of rain. Sent to market and got tomatoes and Whortle-berries. "Huckles" [huckleberries] have not been offered here for sale but once this year. I am sore + tired today. Gen Lee is at Hagerstown and another fight is probable. Our loss at Gettysburg is estimated at 10 or 15000. Father bought a watermelon at $1,20 and it was "gourdy" + wilted at that, but it was the first of the season and so we managed to "worry down a little."

Wednesday July 15th 1863: Cloudy and warm. The news is The Battle of Fort Wagoner was a bloody affair for the Yankees. Their charge was determined + brave but they were compelled to retire. Their loss was 500 in killed and consequently their whole

---

113 The Lanier House was the premier hotel in Macon. A rash of arson was striking Macon and other Southern cities.

loss must have been 2 or 3000, though some say their whole force was not 2000![114] The casualties from Maryland sadden all hearts. Capt Jones of Volunteers [was] wounded + a prisoner. Lt Campbell missing (Nearly all our wounded must have been taken prisoners.) Port Hudson is taken – O. Massy Me![115] Mother bought whortle-berries at 50 cents.

Thursday July 16th 1863: Warm and clear. Did not sleep well. A little old Dog got into the yard and squealed + hollered the whole night at intervals and dogs run cows in the alley, and then my leg hurt me very bad at first. The times are gloomy beyond all precedent. Father thinks that Charleston is in great danger: Morris Island, save Battery Wagner, is in Yankee possession. Fighting has been going on for 6 days at Jackson. Lee's army is recrossing the Potomac in flats, the river being too high to ford. A soldier of 1812 came to beg here. We have too many of our own soldiers to take care of now. My back run tremendously yesterday.

Friday July 17th 1863: Cloudy and warm. Dr. Patterson arrived at 1AM. Mother was very sick all night, and today I did not sleep but very little last night on acct of my leg +c. President Davis calls on all men up to 45 to enlist. Had cantelope for supper. Heard from Grandma. Old Aunt Sarah is very ill and not expected to live. Aunt Sarah Ann has gone to Thomas Co. to live.

Saturday July 18th 1863: Clear and warm. Minnie and Thomas arrived from Burke. Brought 4 watermelons. Gen Johnston has evacuated Jackson. Lee is once more on Va. soil.[116] Mother in bed today. My leg pains me more than usual today and I feel very sore all over. Nothing from Charleston.

Sunday July 19th 1863: Clear and warm. . . . The Bombardment at the Battery Wagner still continues. The people are all gloomy beyond precedent here. No response to the draft is being made at all. A big rumpus has occurred in New York about the conscription.[117] I did not get up to breakfast this morning; my back felt so bad. My back

---

114 The First Battle of Fort Wagner (July 10-11, 1863) on Morris Island at Charleston. Union losses were 339, and Confederate just a dozen.

115 With Vicksburg lost, Gen. Gardner surrendered 6,500 men at Port Hudson, La., a stronghold on the Mississippi River, to Gen. Nathaniel Banks on July 9, 1863. The loss of Port Hudson effectively put the entire Mississippi River under Union control.

116 The Army of Northern Virginia re-crossed the Potomac River on July 14, 1863.

117 New York City Draft Riots (July 13-July 16, 1863) during conscription registration. The level of violence was so bad that some troops who had been at Gettysburg were moved to New York to quell the rioting and killing. Many of the rioters were Irish fearing competition for work from newly freed blacks who did not have to register for the draft, which led to a race riot and about 120 black deaths.

runs profusely. I cannot keep it off my clothes. Prayermeeting for the country this eve. Willis came up last night.

Monday July 20th 1863: Clear and warm. Minnie in bed with sore eyes and a cold. Thomas has a cold too. My back runs hugely. Father and Dr. Patterson left for Milledgeville. . . .

Tuesday July 21st 1863: Anniversary of the first Great Battle of the war. Sunday was the anniversary of Bull Run [First Manassas] and most gloriously celebrated too by a bloody repulse of the Yanks at Charleston. At dark 10 reg[iment]s attempted to storm Fort Wagner and were repulsed with a loss of 1500. Our loss 25 killed, 100 wounded. Fighting ceased at 11 P.M.[118] "Cam" Tracy has got home from Vicksburg. Jim Campbell has arrived! [and] is better. Min still sick. I had the mare last night.[119] Cousin Jack is quite sick. D.H. Hill has been made a Lt Gen and sent to Bragg to take Lt Gen Hardee's place, who is ordered to Gen Johnston. Took an elegant ride way out to the Armory [and] Arsenal[120] + Father arrived from Milledgeville.

Wednesday July 22nd 1863: Clear and warm. Last night was the hottest of the season. I do not feel any worse for my ride have just finished eating a fine melon. "P.W.A." says our loss in the Battle of Gettysburg was near 16,000. Oliver Poe is not expected to live. He is very ill. Mother is making me drawers. Rioting continues in New York yet. The "Bombardment of Fort Wagner" has been the "most terrific of the War." 5 monitors, 7 wooden vessels were engaged.

Thursday July 23d 1863: Cloudy and warm. Rained toward night. Rode down to Mrs. Raines' corner. Mother in bed part of the day. We killed some 2000 Yankees at Charleston. We are fortifying Atlanta. Meade is across the Potomac in Pursuit of Lee. This riot in New York has been quelled and everything is quiet.

Friday July 24th 1863: Clear and warm. Awful hot. Pasted in my scrapbook all the morn. Mother in bed. Morgan is ere this captured. He is in Indiana + cut off by the rise

118 Union troops under Gen. Quincy Gillmore stormed Fort Wagner at Charleston on July 18, 1863. A Northern attack led by Col. Robert Gould Shaw's 54th Massachusetts (US Colored Troops) was bloodily repulsed. Shaw was buried with his men. The valor of these troops led to the recruitment of more African Americans. The attack and the men were featured in the movie *Glory*.

119 In British informal usage, a "mare" was "a very unpleasant experience." In other words, LeRoy had a night filled with pain and discomfort.

120 The Macon Armory under Lt. Col. James H. Burton. The Macon Arsenal consisted of several buildings rented in the general area of Third Street and included a warehouse on Cherry Street owned by James J. Snider (aka Cousin Jimmie, Eliza's husband).

of the river; his men being captured in squads. Alas![121] Pemberton is as grand a sneak as lives. He could have held Vicksburg a month longer; but surrendered "to stop the effusion of blood." He confesses this himself. O mercy.

Saturday July 25th 1863: Cloudy and warm. Drizzled hard in the early morn. The dastardly foe have utterly destroyed Jackson and fell back towards Vicksburg. My own opinion is that they will send large reinforcements to Tennessee. The Bombardment continues at Charleston. We have more peaches than we can eat now and they are rotting badly. Rained in the eve while we were washing, and it is quite cool too. Father arrived.

Sunday July 26th 1863: Cloudy and warm. Morgan and his men are in a "cul-de-sac." Nearly all his men are captured and he, with a squad, escaped. Cousin Charlie stayed to tea with us. Jack Beal's "co" is ordered away. . . . Mr. Wills has gone to the army. Father arrived yesterday from Houston sick with Rheumatism. He brought some cider and it was splendid too. Mother's birthday.

Monday July 27th 1863: Cloudy and cool. Real Athens morning. Rode over to Mrs. Huguenin's and looked at the puppies +c, and am now as tired as I can be from the jolting. Read Waverly. Milo came up with flour, +c. Lee's army is again at Culpeper [Va.] and Meade at Centreville pushing for Fredericksburg. Recognition is again the go. The Bombardment of Battery Wagner continues unceasingly.

Tuesday July 28th 1863: Cloudy and pleasant. Minnie left for the Indian Springs in company with Aunt Ann. Major Gen Bowen of Grand Gulf renown is dead.[122] The Yanks are much chagrined at Lee's escape.[123] The Vicksburg prisoners are passing through daily, + curse Old Pemberton with a hearty goodwill. Commenced *Guy Mannering*. Cousin Jinnie and Mrs. Nelson have babies.[124] Back runs but little. Commenced raining at dinner, slacked a little, and it raining now at 5PM. Bought a watermelon.

---

121 About 700 of Gen. John Hunt Morgan's Confederate cavalry were captured on July 19, 1863 trying to cross the Ohio River at Buffington Island to get into western Virginia. Morgan and 200 others would be captured near Salineville, OH, on July 26.

122 Gen. John S. Bowen, who played a major role in the defense of Vicksburg, caught dysentery during the siege and died on July 13. 1863.

123 Lee's retreat from Pennsylvania was blocked by the swollen Potomac River, where he built massive fortifications to protect his army. Meade's Federals pinned him there, but Lee escaped before Meade attacked, which both angered and frustrated President Lincoln.

124 No record of these children has been located.

Wednesday July 29th 1863: Cloudy and cool. Rained near all night. Morgan is campaigning over Ohio. Part of his men escaped into Va. Wright's Brigade was attacked in one of the gaps around Manassas by 8000 Yanks, and compelled to fall back suffering heavily, and inflicting a heavy loss on the enemy.[125] It is rumored that Grant is sending men [from Miss.] to Meade. The fruit is rotting badly and in a week it'll all be gone. Lt G.C. Beal's company of siege artillery, Captain Cotten com[man]ding, left this morn for the seat of War in Fla. Auntie is in Athens. Cousin Annie has gone on to Va. to see Cousin H[elen].

Thursday July 30th 1863: Clear and pleasant. Nothing new—a feeling of anxiety is prevalent about the fate of Charleston, though there is no stated cause for it. The enemy it is stated are "tightening their grasp on Morris Ild [Island]," the Key to Sumter – Yet General B[eauregard] has recalled the women +c which indicates a confidence in his ability to hold the city itself. The morbid appetite for news is so great that the public cannot brook silence and so it is fed on the most enormous lies. Gen Lee's whereabouts are not known. Gen Johnston is quiet. Grant is sending off large numbers of men to some point, + Bragg has hung two spies! Foreign recognition, intervention, +c are all the talk, and some say it will come in 2 months. *Nota Benes*.[126] We shall see what we shall see. The French have established themselves in Mexico and they may try their hand. The Hon. W.L. Yancey is dead.[127] Capt Semmes of the immortal *Alabama* has taken command of the *Georgia*, a fine, 16 gun ship. Capt Maury has command of the *Virginia*. Hurrah! C.S.A.[128] Had a nice batch of grapes out of the garden . . . ate a moderate sized watermelon with a thick rind + it cost 2 dollars. My Cantelopes rot as fast as they get ripe. We've not had one.

---

125 Battle of Manassas Gap or Wapping Heights (July 23, 1863) during final days of the long retreat into central Virginia. The defense of the pass was important, and helped allow the rest of Lee's Army of Northern Virginia to move to safety.

126 Latin for "note well" or "pay attention."

127 William Lowndes Yancey, former US Congressman, Confederate diplomat, and member of the Confederate Senate, was a strong proponent of secession. He died of kidney disease July 27, 1863. He was distantly related to the Gresham family.

128 Cdr. Matthew Fontaine Maury. In fact. Semmes remained at sea with the raider *Alabama*. CSS *Georgia* was a new and barely seaworthy ironclad in Savannah. The new CSS *Virginia II* (not to be confused with the CSS *Virginia*, was launched that June on the James River at Richmond to protect the Confederate capital. Ironically, Semmes would command the *Virginia II* during the closing months of the Civil War.

July 31st 1863 Friday: Warm and clear. Morgan is captured at last near Lisbon, O[hio] by a Yankee named Shackelford.[129] It was inevitable. . . . We gathered about a half bushel of Siberian crabs. Wound up the clock and it won't run. Gen Lee calls on all able men to return to the army. President D[avis] proclaims the 21st Aug. a fast day.

August 1st 1863 Saturday: Clear and warm. Slept miserably. My old abscess hurt me very bad. Mother unwell. Cousin Eliza sent Ma some large yellow tomatoes. Arch came up yester'eve with flour, 12 watermelons, +c. Read a "highflown, overwrought, real yellowback" novel: *The Conspirators of New Orleans: or the Night of the Battle* loaned me by [friend] Willie Edwards. . . . Have felt bad all day.

August Sabbath 2nd: Early in the morn it was steaming hot + toward evening it clouded up, rained a little, but still continued steaming. . . . Slept badly, did not get up till after breakfast. The Bombardment at Charleston is continued + heavy. Recognition is "squelched" for the present. My leg is hopeless. Father tries to straiten it, rubs it, tries to cheer me, but It will never be straight.

Monday August 3d 1863: Clear and very hot. Read *The Black Dwarf.* Thomas' company organized; J.E. Jones, Branham, Semmes, + Wood were elected officers.[130] No news. Peaches are going very fast. Sent Miss Talulah Snider figs.[131] The Jews are selling out to leave for a season to shirk the draft.[132] A gambler was knocked down + robbed on Bridge Row and 5 men are up on suspicion. Considerable excitement was manifested in town about it, and a disposition to exercise mob law was apparent. It was also rumored that Gen Lee had resigned. I do not, cannot, think that this will prove true. The *Field + Fireside* came today, illustrated with two "engravings," one of Stonewall Jackson which is hideously ugly. 6PM: Those men who were taken up have

---

129 The capture of Gen. John Hunt Morgan and some of his men on July 26, 1863, near Salineville, OH, was the farthest north any uniformed Confederates would ever reach. On Nov. 27, Morgan and six others would escape from the Ohio Penitentiary by digging a tunnel and return to Confederate service. Morgan would be killed Sept. 4, 1864, in Tennessee.

130 Thomas volunteered for service as 4th Sergeant in the Bibb Volunteer Guard (see LeRoy's Aug. 10, 1863 entry). Several militia units were formed in Macon at this time, including the Macon Manufacturing Guard on August 2, 1863. John Gresham was one of the organizers of this recruitment effort to enlist 400 new men.

131 Georgia Tallulah Snider, Cousin Jimmie's younger sister.

132 This is LeRoy's only reference to Jews in his entire journal and it is likely he is simply reflecting what he read in a newspaper. Generally speaking, anti-Semitism was rampant in the North, but much less so in the Confederacy; Southern Jews played a prominent role in the Davis administration and in the armed forces.

been sent over to Milledgeville to the penitentiary. General [Sterling] Price has resigned.

Tuesday August 4th 1863: Hot and clear. Slept very badly and did not get up 'till after breakfast. My back felt so bad. The report about Lee originated with "Hermes" of the [Charleston] *Mercury*.[133] Some sharp words have passed [between] him + Mr. Davis about the Gettysburg campaign. Commenced [reading] *Old Mortality*.

Wednesday August 5th 1863: Very hot + clear. Slept badly had some fever, I think, and feel sore and tired today. We ate a watermelon in the morn and one in the even + both times when I tried to eat, I coughed so I had to quit. Gen S.D. Lee of the Vicksburg garrison has been made a Maj Gen.[134] . . .

Thursday the 6th August 1863: Very hot and clear. Meade is reported over the Rappahannock. Like *Old Mortality* very well. Feel better today. Slept better too. Pasted heavily in my scrapbook. 10 companies are ready here for home defense, 5 for state service. Cousin Jack has Billious fever.[135] 500000 flies perambulate over me and my couch as I write.

Friday 7th August 1863: Warm and clear. Shower at noon. Minnie arrived at 1 P.M. Commenced *Cosette*. [Col.] Scott's [Louisiana] cavalry is reported captured in Ky. Gen Lee's orders and the President's address are stirring appeals to absent soldiers to return to their com[man]ds in this hour of trial + declaring pardon to deserters who shall return. . . .

Saturday Aug 8th 1863: Clear and awful hot. Dr. Patterson stayed all night. Father bought a peck-o-peaches. Mrs. Ralston sent us home grapes.

Sunday August 9th 1863: Anniversary of the Battle of Cedar Run. Very hot. I suffer a good deal with heat. The peaches are entirely gone. There is a lull in the storm of battle and I reckon the Yanks are concentrating their men for some purpose. All hopes of recognition or intervention have been overthrown by the reception of Gettysburg + Vicksburg. Julia Ann + Fred have gone over to Jones to see Old Aunt Hester.[136] The

---

133 The pseudonym for George William Bagby, the Richmond correspondent for the *Charleston Mercury*. Lee had, in fact, written to Jefferson Davis asking to resign in favor of a "younger and more able man," but his request was denied.

134 Gen. Stephen Dill Lee (no relation to Robert E. Lee) would play a major role in the late-war fighting.

135 Bilious fever caused nausea and vomiting in combination with fever and diarrhea.

136 "Old Aunt Hester" is an elderly slave.

Mercury was 84° at 8 oclock and at 3 it rose to 91½° and it was terribly oppressively hot. Not a sound break on the heated air save the buzzing of the big green flies.

Monday August 10th 1863: The heat is intense and the heavens shine like brass. I sink under it and long for a "Mountain home." Last night I lay and sweltered till 1 oclock and past I may here record the somewhat remarkable fact that before yesterday the Mercury had not risen as high as 90° this year. Today it was 90° and a little over. Finished *Cosette*. Commenced *Antiquary*. "Jake" is here runaway.[137] Thomas is 4th Sergeant in the Bibb Volunteer guard [Co. B, 2nd Georgia Battalion]. Milo + Arch came up with 20 melons.

Tuesday August 11th 1863: Hot. Hot. Hot. Hot. Hot. Hot. Hot. Hot. Thermometer at 90° nearly all day. Suffered much last night with heat. Band played at the gate + Old Ralston drove them off. [Gen. Nathan] Evan's Brig[ade] and some others of [Joe] Johnston's army have passed through to Savannah.

Wednesday August 12th 1863: Clear and very hot. Not a breeze is wafted across the sultry earth. . . . Mr. Goulding sent me a copy of the *Young Marooners*, CS edition. Made envelopes.

Thursday August 13th 1863: Very warm and clear. Not a particle of news from any quarter. Rumor says Gen Hood had been appointed Commander of Cavalry in the Army of Northern Virginia with Gens Hampton and Stuart under him, and that Gen S.D. Lee has been made comdr [commander of] cavalry in the Southwest. This has been a long, hot, dry, dull, evening. It is too hot for Army movements. The two armies of Lee and Meade occupy nearly the same position as they did in June [in central Va].

Friday August 14th 1863: Very hot and dry. Rained a little in the eve but the sun barely went in. I have read 5 of Scott's novels this summer: 1st *Waverly*, 2nd *Guy Mannering* (2nd time), 3d *Black Dwarf* (2nd time), and *Old Mortality*, 4th *Untiquary*. Min is in the depths of *Ivanhoe* and wants to know who the "Black ke–" is. Thomas has read

---

137 Jake was likely a plantation slave who ended up at the Macon residence, or had escaped and been caught and brought to the family like Dave had been.

Bride of Lammermoor, Legend of Montrose, Anne of Gierstien, + *Red Gauntlet.* He is in ecstasies over *Anne of Gierstein.* [138]

Saturday August 15th 1863: Clear and hot. Such a quiet time has not been known in a long time in the news world, and I hope it'll stay so. Though the storm of War has lulled for a season; it may be only to burst upon us with double fury! Arch and Milo came up and brought 10 melons but the soldiers stole 6 of them.

Sunday August 16th 1863: Cloudy and cool. Rained a little early in the morn, cleared up at noon, and rained after dark. The Day Mosquitoes are terrible.

Monday August 18th 1863: Cloudy and warm. Fred has made me a nice box to put my papers in.[139] I forgot to put down in the right place that Thursday night a Deaf + Dumb beau called to see Minnie. She made his acquaintance in Burke [County]. He stayed all night and Minnie and Tom talked on their fingers to him and wrote on his slate. His name is Holdridge Chidester and he is Johnny Greenwood's teacher. Cadmus M. Wilcox has been made Maj Gen.

Tuesday August 18th 1863: Cloudy and warm. Rained at 12, 8, and 5, but not enough to wet the ground. The Yanks are shelling Sumter and have mounted heavy guns in reach of it. No damage done as yet, but timid people doubt the result. I am reading *Heart of Midlothian.* Mother, Min, and Susy E[dwards] have gone to prayermeeting.

Wednesday August 19th 1863: Clear and cool. Delightful fall day. It is rumored from different sources that the *Alabama, Florida, Georgia,* + *Mississippi* had one or "tother" sunk the *Vanderbilt* or the *Vanderbilt* had sunk one of them. I do not believe it. The Bombardment of Charleston, fiercer and more furious than ever before commenced Monday, continued all day and was resumed Tuesday, which is the last news. The Fort was considerably pitted. The Ironsides, 6 monitors, 6 gunboats participated. Poor Charleston; her time of trial is at hand. It is supposed some Yankee of note had turned the corner [died] as the fleet had retired at ½ mast. I got a letter from Aunty with "Mother and Poet," a piece by Mrs. Browning.

Thursday August 20th 1863: Clear and quite warm. The firing continued all day Tuesday, stopped at night, and was resumed Wed morn. On Battery Wagner, the firing makes no impression. Many think the Fort is bound to fall but I hope not. Some rumors of a break in the fort were in town. Father bought some cake. Mother has gone

---

138 Sir Walter Scott was one of the most popular authors in the South during the antebellum period.

139 Fred is another of the slaves from Houston with carpentry skills. He made and fixed many items for LeRoy, including his chess box, table, wagon, and more. Whether he did this of his own accord or because he was asked or forced to, is unknown. There was definitely an affinity between the two.

visiting. Mr. Rice came yesterday, releathered, tuned, +c the piano, and it sounds a great deal better. Read *Highland Widow* and *The Surgeon's Daughter* and the latter is very good.

Friday August 21st 1863: Cloudy and warm. This is a day of National fasting and prayer proclaimed by Prest Davis.[140] We had butter, bread, + tea for dinner. . . . Col Aiken has taken command of this post.[141] The *Gibraltar*, alias *Sumter*, has arrived at Wilmington. The enemy continued to pound away on Sumter all day Wednesday and their shots were beginning to tell! In other words, they are going to batter it down. Its fate is sealed. Battery Wagner is too hard a nut for them to crack. Meade has fallen back to the Potomac. Read *Tapestried Chamber*. Cousin Howard Tinsley stayed to tea with us. He is from Va. Uncle Dick has been transferred to Benning's Brigade. The rumor of the appointment of Gen Hood to the Cavalry of A.N.Va. is not so. Prayermeeting in the evening.

Saturday August 22nd Anno Domini 1863:[142] Clear and warm. The Bombardment of Charleston continues. The 200 pound Parrot guns on Morris Island have hit the Fort 3,400 times up to Thursday, when fire was still kept up, though not so heavy as it was on account of the fire of our James Island Batteries. All the guns on one side are disabled. The Monitors do not take a very active part. Am Reading *Legend of Montrose*.

Sunday August 23d 1863: Clear and exceedingly hot. . . . The Baptist Association is here. As I write a 6PM the band is playing for Findley's company and I think it an outrage.[143] Two walls of Poor old Sumter are in ruins and the others crumbling. The flag flies on the heap. The Bombardment is unceasing. Long range guns have thrown 8 shells into the city from a distance of 4 miles. The forts, + some think the city, are gone. The Yanks shelled Chattanooga [for] two days + killed 2 women. Cousin Helen is at Cousin Eliza's. Sick. The Flag staff at Sumter has been shot away 6 times.

Monday August 24th 1863: Clear and warm. Mother made some soap.[144] Mr. Tom Whittaker took dinner here. Fort Sumter is a mass of untenable ruins. Col Rhett is

---

140 Fasting and prayer days were taken very seriously. Although it was a Friday, businesses were closed and the streets mostly deserted except for people going to and from church.

141 Col. David W. Aiken was made Post Commandant at Macon after the severe wounds he sustained at Antietam and Gettysburg.

142 *Anno Domini* is the full Latin form of A.D.

143 The "outrage" is a band playing on the Sabbath, something LeRoy finds irreligious.

144 Making soap was labor intensive and included boiling ingredients such as lye, lime, ashes, "clean" grease, etc. If his mother was making it, it means soap was not as readily available for purchase in Macon as it once had been.

wounded. My own opinion is that Wagner will be evacuated in a day or two. The citizens + women are leaving in crowds. [Union Gen Quincy] Gillmore says if the Fort + Islands are not given up, he'll shell the city. My back never gives me any trouble now and I never notice it in my diary. It is dressed regularly as "pigs tracks" every morn + eve. Hereafter every Sunday I will tell how it has been through the week.

Tuesday August 25th 1863: Cloudy and warm. Dropped rain. Father started to Houston but returned on hearing the Tobesoffkee Bridge was down. Read *Darrell Markham, or the Captain of the Vulture*. "Hafalutin"! Mother went down town. My wagon went to the shop yesterday to have the springs raised a little and came back this morning.

Wednesday August 26th 1863: Cloudy and warm. Cousin Jack is elected Major by 5 votes of the Battalion over Hardeman. Charleston has not been shelled yet. 2 boats have been taken in the Rappahannock. Alfred Edwards "got" up his kite and I held it a long time. Tom is reading *What Will He Do with It*.[145] My Back has been very comfortable all day. Cousin Zeke[146] left here for the seat of war in Mississippi.

Thursday August 27th 1863: Cloudy all day. Quite autumnal. Another assault on Battery Wagner has been made. The exact result is not known. The Bombardment continues. Ft. S[umter] is to be held with the Bt [Batteries]. Father and Thomas left for Houston. The impressing agent was up on the hill and took some horses.[147] Reading *Monastery*. Have had on a winter coat all day. Was out with Alfred Edwards nearly all the morning flying his kite.

Friday August 28th 1863: Cloudy misty + cool. Slept most miserably on acct [of] a pain in my breast caused by riding too much on my wagon, and I do not feel much better today. Gen Floyd is dead.[148] Major Beal's, Mr. Ralston's, Judge Holt's + co. horses were taken yesterday. Mother is sick. Had on winter coat all day. My leg hurts me very bad. Arch came up this eve. Father came too with a big basket of apples.

---

145 An 1857 novel by popular English novelist and politician Edward George Earle Lytton Bulwer-Lytton. He came up with famous phrase, "The pen is mightier than the sword."

146 Ezekiel P. Wimberly was Aunt Sarah's nephew.

147 Impressment agents were sent across the Confederacy to collect 10% of a farm's or plantation's produce. Many agents took much more, and occasionally took everything. An agent for Mitchell County, Ga., attempted to confiscate every hog in the county for the army.

148 Gen. John B. Floyd, former US Sec. of War, Virginia governor, and utterly inept Confederate general, fell ill and died in Virginia.

Saturday August 29th 1863: Clear and warm. Father and Tom arrived last night and I was in bed. I took an anodyne as I was sick and in pain. They had to run the blockade to get to town. Howard has gone to Houston after Duke [draft horse]. Our horses are bound to "go up" "certin shore."[149] The apples Father brought are little round red ones, very nice + sweet. My leg hurts me some today, my good leg, too.

Sunday August 30th 1863: Clear and ere cool. A real fall morning. Howard came back from Houston with Duke. Cousin George Jones stayed to tea with us. Mr. Wills preached!

Monday August 31st 1863: Cool and cloudy. It is rumored that Burnside with 16000 men is in Knoxville, [Tenn]. Walker's Div[ision] has gone to Bragg and Gen J[ohnston] himself. Gen Theophilus Holmes, it is said, is dead. The Confederacy is bound to go up [lose].

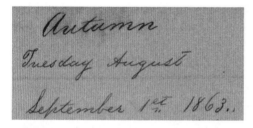

Autumn. Tuesday August September 1st 1863: Cool and Cloudy. Mobile, Knoxville, Chattanooga, and Cumberland Gap are evacuated. That's misery in a nutshell. Gen Johnston is in Chattanooga. The Yanks are in possession of our rifle-pits in 200 yards of [Fort] Wagner. Col Gillmer has been made Maj Gen and put in command at Charleston. The steamer *Sumter* has been sunk by a mistake of one of our batteries. Sumter is to be held.

September 2nd 1863: Clear delightful day. Finley's Co., on receipt of orders, left immediately on the 10AM train. No news at all. Mr. W.B. Johnston sent me 5 splendid pears.

Thursday Sep 3d 1863: Clear and cool. Slept miserably. The Monitors made another big attack at Charleston, but without accomplishing anything at all. This was on the night of the 1st. The firing was the heaviest ever heard on the continent. We have been engaged in "fixing" palmetto to plait.[150] I am reading *Lord Nigel* and do not like it at all. Thomas went to hear Negro Minstrels last night.

149 LeRoy believes the Gresham's horses will be impressed by the army. At the start of the war, only draft horses were bought by the Confederate government to pull wagons and artillery pieces; officers and cavalrymen were responsible for providing their own mounts.

150 Palmetto, a frequent substitute for straw, was twisted into plaits (braids) to make many things like hats and shoes.

John Jones Gresham, circa 1840. LeRoy (inset) bore a striking resemblance to his father.
Library of Congress and 1842 Inn

John Jones Gresham in front of his newly built mansion on College Street in Macon, Georgia, circa 1842. *1842 Inn*

Mary Baxter Gresham on the front porch of her Macon home. This undated postwar image is the only known photo of LeRoy's beloved mother.

1842 Inn

John Jones Gresham on the front porch of his Macon home in an undated postwar image. Although the rocking chair is the same one Mary was sitting on for her portrait (see above), it is clear the photos were not taken in the same sitting.

1842 Inn

LeRoy's younger sister Mary Jones Gresham in an undated postwar image. Mary was usually called "Minnie" or "Min" by family and friends.

1842 Inn

Four Gresham generations. Seated on the right is the only known photo of Thomas Gresham (LeRoy's beloved older brother). On Thomas' left is his son, LeRoy Gresham (named after his brother). Thomas' grandson, Francis Rhett Gresham, is holding his son, who was also named LeRoy Gresham. *Library of Congress and 1842 Inn*

(Left) Thomas Wiley Baxter, Mary Gresham's brother, served in the 13th Texas Volunteers and survived the war and died in 1898. *Lamar Williams*

J. W. Baxter

(Above) John Springs Baxter, surgeon, 46th Georgia Infantry. John, also one of Mary Gresham's brothers, was known to play a lot of what LeRoy called "town ball" (an early form of baseball), in Macon. He also survived the war and died in 1896. *Lamar Williams*

(Left) Richard Bolling Baxter was Mary Gresham's youngest brother, just seven years older than LeRoy. He joined the Athens Guards (Co. K, 3rd Georgia) in 1861, reached the rank of captain, and was captured and imprisoned at Rock Island, Illinois in 1864. He survived the war and lived until 1924. *Lamar Williams*

LeRoy's tombstone in Rose Hill Cemetery, Macon, Georgia. The epitaph written by his parents and carved into LeRoy's tombstone, reads as follows:

"In life this dear child was the light of the home circle, lovely and endearing by nature he was purified by suffering, sanctified by grace and rests now in the bosom of his Savior. Blessed are the pure in heart for they shall see God."

1842 Inn

The Gresham family plot in the Rose Hill Cemetery, Macon, Georgia. From left to right: John Gresham, Mary Gresham, LeRoy Gresham, Edward Tracy Gresham (infant), Edmund Gresham (infant), and Tallulah "Lula" Billups, Thomas' first wife. Susan Jane Harris Billups, Tallulah's mother, is buried in the front corner. *1842 Inn*

Tuesday July 15th 1862
Hot and clear. Mercury 8 A.M 81° 3. P.M. 88 5.P.M. 88°
Read The "Boat Club" Suffered more
with the heat than I have this summer
Eat two melons. Father left for Richmond
right after supper.

Wednesday July 16th 1862
Terribly hot. Suffered with heat badly
last night and as I write at 5.P.M. I am
stinging all over with the heat not=
withstanding we have just eaten a nice
melon. Mercury at 8 a.m. 82° 3 P.M 89° 5 P.M 89°
Got a letter from Aunty. She was sitting
in a private house and Uncle Richard
was near her & glad to be so comfortable
The "perspiration" pours off me and
drops on the book. Mother in bed sick

A very personal page from LeRoy's diary. On a scorching day in July 1862, he wrote that, "notwithstanding we have just eaten a nice melon . . . perspiration pours off me and drops on the book." More than 150 years later, the smudges are still clearly visible on the page—the remains of the teenager's unsuccessful efforts to wipe the droplets away. *Library of Congress*

Friday September 4th 1863: Clear and warm. Slept better. All quiet at Charleston. An immense 600 pound gun has been mounted on the Battery where it will do no good at all. Its range is 4 or 5 miles though. Gen Price has thrashed the enemy on White River in Arkansas capturing 4 reg[imen]ts. The day mosquitoes are awful and their bites are exceedingly poisonous. The days of soup are nearly over and I am very sorry. Tom persueth *What Will He Do with It*. Arch and Milo both came up; Francis is dead. She had been sick some time.[151]

Saturday September 5th 1863: Clear and warm. Lt Col Aderhold has been cashiered for stealing and encouraging desertion.[152] Lt Jewett became Captain of the Bibb Volunteer Guard.

Sunday September 6th 1863: Clear and warm in the morn, but had a nice little shower, the first in 2 months. It was much needed for the dust was intolerable. Thomas did not go to church on acct of Rheumatism in his hip. Friday witnessed another furious attack on Wagner and Gregg. Firing began at daylight and lasted till dark. Sumter, after a terrific bombardment of 20 days, is still proudly silent, defying the foe. 7551 shots have been hurled at it, of which 6,030 hit the fort. The Flag has been shot away 14 times. 1,500,000 lbs. of iron has been expended. 300000 lbs. powder has been burned, which last would cost not less than 120000 dollars and all this to reduce a fort which if taken, can never be occupied, and if it could be occupied, would not be a key to Charleston. There has been few casualties in Fort Sumter. The Yankees have advanced this "sap" [protective barrier] to within 150 yards of Wagner and I reckon they'll take it soon. A battle is not thought to be imminent in Tennessee, though a slight skirmish may bring on a general engagement at any minute. George B[eal] came around after tea and sat awhile.

Monday September 7th 1863: Clear and hot. Thomas is pretty bad off with Rheumatism; had to take Dover's Powder last night. Mary Campbell called to see Minnie this morn.

Tuesday September 8th 1863: Hot and clear. All signs of Sunday's shower are gone and the heat is oppressive and enervating. Up to 9 oclock Sunday storms of shot and shell had for 32 long hours been poured into Batteries Gregg + Wagner without ceasing. The noise of the cannonade was tremendous. This was continued all day on the 6th, and far into the night. An assault on Gregg was repulsed and the enemy

---

151 Francis was one of the plantation slaves. Her age or what she died from are unknown.

152 Macon native Jacob W. Aderhold, who had organized Company A, 1st Battalion GA Infantry, would later claim he served through the end of the war.

severely punished. At 8 oclock Sunday night the enemy, having advanced up to Wagner, both batteries were silently evacuated the men brought off and the guns spiked.[153] A demand was made for Sumter. General B[eauregard] replied come and take it. At 7 last night they were furiously bombarding it. Major Jones' battalion has been detailed to guard the armory, arsenal, +c here! Cousin Jack is sick. Thomas took a big "Dover" last night and is a drop better today. I am perusing *Peveril of the Peak*.

Wednesday Sep 9th 1863: Very hot and dry. Thomas still complaining. His "sojer" clothes have come home and look fine. Milo and Arch came up with new potatoes, apples. Since the evacuation of Wagner, the Monitors have directed their fire against Moultrie, and we have been firing on Gregg. 2 Monitors went out in tow. Do not like *Peveril of Peak* at all. There are 3 candidates for Governor: Brown of course, Mr. Furlow, and Mr. Josh Hill.[154] There was a serenade at Mrs. Edwards and the singing was a burlesque. Minnie is making a hat. There is a great deal of excitement at the North because some ironclad CS Steamers are [said to be] on the way to Charleston.

Thursday September 10th 1863: Clear and warm. I suffer much from heat + it is more depressing on our account of the drought. Father bought me a pair of winter breeches like Tom's suit. The news from glorious Old Sumter is soulstirring. The Yanks attempted to board it from 40 barges and were gallantly repulsed! Our men fighting with brickbats and muskets. Major Elliot is in command.[155] Moultrie +c played on them all the time. Thomas is better. Bought 5 quarts scuppernongs [grapes] from Mr. Bates at 40 cents.

Friday September 11th 1863: Clear and warm. All quiet in Charleston! [156] Many a heart yearns to hear the result of the Grand game that is going on in upper Georgia, a game where states are the stake. [Rosecrans'] Army of the Cumberland and [Bragg's] Army of Tennessee are in motion and a grand battle is about to be fought on the soil of Georgia. All hope and pray that we may win the fight. Cousin Bella sent me custard and cake; Mrs. Whittle some beer. Father's suit has come home. It is of beautiful grey army cloth and a present from Mr. Callaway. Both wagons came up.

153 Driving something into the touch-hole of a cannon to render it unable to fire.

154 Timothy Matthews Furlow and Joshua Hill.

155 Second Battle of Fort Sumter (Sept. 8, 1863). The harbor fort was stormed by boat; Confederate infantry stationed there repulsed the attack with heavy losses. Maj. Stephen Elliott, Jr., was a future Confederate general whose serious wounds would kill him shortly after the war.

156 The Siege of Charleston, or the Second Battle of Charleston Harbor, ended Sept. 7, 1863.

Saturday September 12th 1863: Clear and hot. It was terribly hot last night. No sign of rain. Both of our overseers are ordered into camp and Father is going down [to Houston].[157] Cousin Howard came to see us before breakfast. Lee is sending men to Bragg, probably 20000 men.[158] The enemy are perfectly quiet at Charleston. Our batteries are bombarding them. Thomas went to town. Since Sunday he has lost 6 pounds. There is no immediate prospect of a fight above unless General Bragg attacks Rosencratz.

Sunday September 13th 1863: Clear and terribly hot. I have got a very bad cold. My back felt sore and tired. There is "0" from upper Georgia. [Henry] Benning's Brigade passed through Atlanta. In Raleigh, they mobbed the *Raleigh Standard* office. Our Batteries are pounding away at Charleston; the Yanks are quiet. Father is very much afraid that Bragg has been flanked + outgeneralled.[159]

Monday 14th September: Clear and hot enough to please the most fastidious. Father left for Houston. The Substitute cavalry left for Atlanta. Negroes on the horses. The men on the railroad. Gen Bragg is at Dalton [Ga.]; Walker's div[ision] near Rome, [Ga.]. Next thing he will be in Atlanta. East Tenn. is gone and that it self, without upper Geo[rgia], is enough to pay for the whole campaign. I think we have been awfully chawed.[160]

Tuesday 15th September 1863: Clear, dry. There was a large house burned in the southwest Part of town about 11 oclock last night and another on Cotton Avenue yesterday morn. We lost E. Tenn. without a blow. We have evacuated Chattanooga. We have lost the Gibraltar of the South. We have lost Upper Georgia. Have we, or will we, gain any advantage commensurate with this great loss? 0 from Charleston. 3 monitors left. All quiet. I am reading *What Will He Do with It*. Studied Arithmetic all the morning. Mr. Bates has 24 scholars. Findley's Company came back yesterday. Thomas was out all night gaurding the P[ost] O[ffice]. About 6 oclock PM, the stable + carriage house on Dr. Strohecker's lot were found to be on fire. I went round by Mrs. Huguenin's and had a fine view.

157 Overseers Hill and Kemp had been conscripted by the Confederate Army, and John Gresham was organizing their replacements. Kemp served in the 8th Georgia State Guard.

158 In fact, the rumor was true. Gen. Lee had detached Gen. James Longstreet and much of his corps for a 775-mile rail trip to north Georgia, where the first men arrived on September 17. Their presence would help win the Battle of Chickamauga (Sept. 18-20, 1863).

159 The Chickamauga Campaign (Aug. 21 - Sept. 20, 1863) was underway. Rosecrans fooled Bragg and crossed the Tennessee River beyond his left, forcing Bragg to give up the key city of Chattanooga.

160 Chewed, or worked over.

Wednesday September 16th 1863: Minnie invited Miss Jessie Burgess and Mary Campbell and Jim to come to tea last. Jessie + Mary stayed all night and they had a fine frolic after they went up to bed. There was another cavalry affair on the Rappahannock + we worsted. Fell back of course. Nothing reliable from above. A strong impression prevails among the people that we have been outgeneralled. The papers, as they ever are before a disaster, are confident. Mother is in bed. Father arrived at noon from Houston. The Sparks Gaurd are here on a 48 hours furlough. "Pasted" all the eve. My back [abscess] has now run out all over me.

Thursday September 17th 1863: Cloudy and cool. No news is allowed to come from Bragg's army. The "Yanks" are quiet at Charleston, but working like beavers. Rumor says Gen Lee has gone to Tennessee. The Monster gun at Charleston has bursted like all our attempts. Mother down town.

Friday September 18th 1863: Cloudy and cool. Slept badly. Everybody gloomy about Bragg.[161] All quiet at Charleston. Milo came up with a big load of fodder. Mr. Kemp has gone to Atlanta.

Saturday September 19th 1863: Last night it turned quite cool. Mr. Flinn stayed all night with us. I received today by express a nice pair of homespun pants and a very kind letter saying that they were a present from Grandma.[162] She also said that Uncles Edge and Richard were there for one day run by to see them and they were all happy I know. Poor Grandma. I grieve for her. Today we heard the sad, sad news of dear Uncle Ed's death on the 21st July at 1 oclock in Henderson, Texas.[163]

Sunday Sep 20th 1863: Clear and cool. Out in winter clothes in full. Things look a little more cheering in upper Georgia. The body of the enemy no longer pollute our "sacred soil." Gen Bragg's address says, "We have been largely reinforced and with the help of God will whip the enemy in his fancied security." My back runs a great deal and annoys me by running on my clothes. For a day or so it has been very sore indeed.

---

161 Expectations from Gen. Lee's army in Virginia were always high before a fight, but Gen. Bragg had yet to win a decisive battle, so the populace was less enthusiastic when combat approached the Army of Tennessee.

162 Homespun is exactly what it sounds like: pants made from raw cotton or wool fabric spun into yarn. By this time in the war, wearing homespun was synonymous with patriotism. The 1862 song "The Homespun Dress" (sung to the tune of "The Bonnie Blue Flag") extolled the virtues of homespun; the Palmetto hat was mentioned in the lyrics.

163 Edwin Gilmer Baxter (1836-1863, Sgt. Major, Co. F. 13th Texas Infantry) was the second of his grandmother's six sons to die in the Civil War; another son, Moses Wiley Baxter, lived only three months in 1816.

Monday Sep 21st 1863: Clear, bright, splendid fall day. Cousin Jenks Jones is here and coming to tea. Finished *What Will He Do with It*. My back feels very weak + bad. Cousin Eliza and Aunt Sarah called. Our army is in motion above and a grand battle is being fought.

Tuesday September 22nd 1863: Clear and cool. Probably as large a battle as any of the war is now going on in Upper Ga.[164] Commencing Saturday morning, it continued all day Sunday without any decisive result. The right and left wings of the enemy were driven back, the center standing firm. Our loss lamentably heavy, 5000 it is said. Gens Preston Smith, Wofford, killed. Wounded Maj Gen Hood, leg off; Gen Gregg, Gen Benning in the breast slightly, Gens Walker and Walthall reported killed. Maj Gen Cleburn also wounded. Gen Bragg says, "We hold the field but the enemy still confronts us. We have 20 pieces artillery and 2500 prisoners." The anxiety is intense. My own opinion is that it is another Murfreesboro. Loss frightful and no results! But I hope for the best.[165]

Wednesday Sep 23d 1863: Clear and cool. Father went to Houston yester eve. The News from the Great Battle of Chickamauga is good. We have driven them from every position. The Fight continued all day Monday. Gen Hood is dead. Walker not hurt, nor Wofford. Cap[tain] Sparks Gaurd killed. Gens Helm + Deshler killed. Gen Bragg says "the victory is complete, the cavalry are pursuing. They have retreated on Chattanooga leaving their dead + wounded." With the blessing of God we have accomplished great results, +c. Big fire down town last night: 4 or 5 houses burnt, carpenter shop, 3 houses + blacksmith shop. Down by Findley's Foundry. . . .

Thursday September 24th 1863: Clear cool. Mother made biscuit and sent to sick soldiers. Bragg is pursuing. We are in Chattanooga. Our Loss 15000. The Yanks thought that Bragg would not attack. There was no fighting Monday, only skirmishing.

---

164 The Battle of Chickamauga (Sept. 18-20, 1863).

165 Chickamauga was one of the largest and bloodiest battles of the war. It was also the only clear-cut Southern victory in the Western Theater during the entire conflict. The first evening was skirmishing and light fighting, but the second day (19th) consisted of heavy attacks and counterattacks, most in wooded terrain. The last day (20th) Bragg's attack punched through Rosecrans' line and drove much of the Union army off the field and into Chattanooga. As usual, the early information on who was killed and wounded was not always accurate. The dead Confederate generals included Preston Smith, James Deshler, and Benjamin Helms. John Bell Hood was wounded in the upper thigh and his leg amputated. The Union lost one general killed (William Lytle). Union losses totaled more than 16,000, and Confederates more than 18,000.

The grand fight was Sunday the 20th. Bragg attacked at sunrise Sat. So says "P.W.A." Colquitt of the 46th [Ga.] killed.[166]

Friday September 25th 1863: Clear and cool. Father suffered with his ears very much all night. Gen Benning was struck by a spent ball and not hurt. Our army is in Chattanooga. Rosencrans is across. He was badly defeated. A great many sick soldiers are here. The city hall, Academy, +c. have been taken.[167] We took 50 fine pieces artillery and many prisoners in the "Battle of Chickamauga."

Saturday September 26th 1863: Clear and cool. Things do not look well above. Rosencrans is still in Chattanooga, reinforced by Burnside and fortifying. Our forces 4 miles this side. A fight is imminent in Va. Father's ear very bad indeed. I study Arithmetic a little now, but have no one to teach me.

September 27th 1863: Clear and cool. . . . Rosecrans is certainly in Chattanooga, and our forces are around the city. His loss is 30000. Ours 7000 to 10000. I think we ought to bag him. O massy.

Monday September 28th 1863: Clear and cool. Delightful day. Rosencrans is in a "cul de sac"!!!! Mother has a very bad cold. Father went to College to make arrangements for Minnie to start.[168] Made an envelope pattern. It is not yet settled whether Gen Hood is dead or alive. Major George W. Ross was interred with military honors this evening. The Order of Procession was as follows: Findley's Company, Macon Batt[alion] + Fireman G[uar]d, the whole under Major Jones. The express wagon was draped with green leaves + mourning. On the corners of the wagon the old plumes of the Rifles were stuck. Very few vehicles along; some discharged men of the 2nd Batt[alion] followed in the procession.[169]

Tuesday September 29th 1863: Clear and cool. No News. "Rosey" is in an impregnable position [in Chattanooga]. Our only methods are either to "charge his position" or "endanger his base" with our cavalry. Among the many wild and

---

166 Col. Peyton Holt Colquitt was distantly related to LeRoy through his Jones relations (paternal grandmother).

167 Chattanooga would remain in Union hands throughout the rest of war. An influx of Chickamauga wounded flooded Macon. Many buildings were used as hospitals, including the City Hall, the Blind Academy (renamed the Ocmulgee Hospital), the Floyd House, a permanent Wayside House, the Stout Hospital (formerly the Brown House), and several others.

168 Wesleyan Female College in Macon. Education was extremely important to the Greshams.

169 Macon native Maj. Ross was mortally wounded July 2, 1863, at Gettysburg leading the 2nd Georgia Battalion (Wright's brigade) and died on Aug. 2. His body was shipped back and buried in Rose Hill Cemetery.

extravagant rumors the only reasonable [one] is that Johnston's [Bragg's] cavalry under Stephen D. Lee have got behind Rosey. Let us believe and take comfort, and we may yet "hurl him in utter rout back to Nashville." Thomas was on Gaurd at the armory last night. The Batt[alion] is ordered into camp Saturday.

Wednesday September 30th 1863: Cloudy and cool. Thomas left for Houston, Father suffering greatly with a rising [ache] in his ear. Mrs. Huguenin had her leg broke by jumping from her carriage. Minnie is at the College being examined. Father bought 3 lemons. No News. Gen Hood is not dead, though in a critical condition with his leg.

Thursday October 1st 1863: Cloudy and warm. Commenced to rain, slowly, beautifully, sweetly, for the 1st time since 1st Aug. Cousin Annie is over at Aunt Ann's! Called to see us today. Brought me some apples. No news at all. Mrs. Edwards is moving. Made 19 envelopes. Father's ears are better. Thomas came back from Houston thoroughly wet.

Friday October 2nd 1863: Cloudy and cool. Rode over to Aunt Ann's and stayed till noon. The Yankees commenced to fire on Sumter again Monday. Ira Fort stayed to dinner. Mother in bed. Cousin Helen and Cousin Eliza called to see Mother. The storm of wind and rain continued till 10 or 11 oclock last night, and did a good deal of damage in the way of blowing down fences. The fence of the Orchard was blown down and a calf got in and perambulated [wandered around]. A tree in front was also blown down.

Saturday September October 3d 1863: Cloudy and cool. Thomas goes into camp today out on the Columbus Road. Nothing from the Front or Charleston. Meade's army has been very much depleted to reinforce Rosencrans, and there is no prospect of an engagement unless Gen Lee attacks. The CS Steamer *Florida* is at Brest in France and rumor says may be detained there for good. The Yanks have not heard of the *Vanderbilt* in a long time. May we not hope that they will never find her?[170] Minnie was admitted into the Junior Class at College.

Sunday September Oct 4th 1863: Clear and cool. Father passed a terrible night with his ears, and is unable to attend service. Rosencrans is perfectly safe at Chattanooga. Mary Campbell, Miss Jinnie Lamar, and Ben Smith joined the church today.

Monday October 5th 1863: Clear and cool. The weather is quite cold for the season and winter-clothes are comfortable. Rosencrans has been reinforced and in unassailable. Meanwhile Bragg has taken this emergency to quarrel with his officers:

---

170 The commerce raider CSS *Florida* was in the dock at Brest, France, from Aug. 23, 1863 to Feb. 12, 1864. The USS *Vanderbuilt* was a heavily armed warship at sea hunting Confederate ships.

Polk, Forrest, and Hindman [are] all under arrest.[171] Received a letter from Aunty. Howard had arrived in Athens. Cousin Annie called. My good leg aches like a tooth.

Tuesday October 6th 1863: Clear and cold for the season. Cousin Annie came to dinner. Thomas came round after tea. There is no news.

Wednesday Oct 7th 1863: Clear and cool. Bragg has commenced to shell Chattanooga. It is generally conceded that he will be in Central Ga. this winter. Some folks declare he is losing his reason. Lee's official account [of] the Pennsylvania campaign is in the daily and it is as unsatisfactory as it well can be. This day decides whether Brown is Governor for life or not.[172] It is believed Furlow + Hill will be terribly beaten. Father votes for Furlow. Misted a little.

Thursday October 8th 1863: Clear and cold. Howard arrived. The impressors took our horses. Father sent them down but they were not received. Mrs. Huguenin is in a critical state. There is no news from any quarter. On the 6th at daybreak, we attacked the *Ironsides* and damaged her, alarming the whole Yankee fleet.[173]

Friday October 9th 1863: Clear and cool. Thomas stayed to dinner. Mother and Cousin Annie went down town. The Vote in Macon is Hill 376, Brown 388, Furlow 179. Brown is undoubtedly reelected. . . . Agusta, Atlanta, + Savannah went largely for Brown, Columbus for Hill + Furlow. Hill beat Furlow in his own county, and runs a much better race.

Saturday October 10th 1863: Clear splendid day. Brown is our King for two more years.[174] President Davis has passed through Atlanta on his way to the "front" accompanied by Gens Longstreet, Pemberton, Breckinridge, Cobb + Gov. Brown. I

---

171 Union reinforcements were sent to the vital rail and manufacturing center of Chattanooga soon after the Chickamauga defeat, and Union Gen. U. S. Grant was promoted to lead the new Military Division of the Mississippi and take command. Gen. Bragg, meanwhile, was busy quarreling with many of his officers, some of whom had disobeyed his orders at Chickamauga or were openly conspiring to undermine his authority.

172 Joe Brown was ending his third term as Georgia's governor. No other governor had won a fourth term.

173 The CSS *David*, a steam-driven semi-submersible, attacked the wooden-hulled ironclad CSS *New Ironsides* off Charleston on October 5, 1863. The damage was minor and she remained on station.

174 LeRoy is almost surely repeating what his father (an anti-Brown man) was saying. Brown was virulently against President Davis and his policies and ran Georgia more like an independent nation than one of many states within a confederation.

have a bad pain in my breast; every time I swallow it hurts me.[175] I am perusing *Parton's Jackson*. Cousin Annie dined with us. She goes home [to Milledgeville] tonight. Every bell in town has been taken down + broken to pieces to make cannon, an altogether useless proceeding. Mrs. Huguenin is no better – is delirious – and in a critical state. Our Bell is not taken on account of the City clock.

Sunday October 11th 1863: Clear and cool. No news at all. . . . Father killed a snake 7 inches long behind Julia Ann's house.

Monday October 12th 1863: Clear and cool. An Old cow has learned how to get into our back gate, and we had to put a hook on it to keep her out. Major Jones' Battalion broke up camp this morning. G. C. Beal called after tea.

Tuesday October 13th 1863: Cloudy and cool. Pres[ident] Davis reviewed Bragg's army and looked at the Yankees [in Chattanooga]. The army vote is heavy for Brown. Mother sat up with Mrs. Huguenin. Willis came up last night. Rode down town and out by Tom's camp yesterday evening. Rained very hard this evening and there is a prospect of more.

Wednesday Oct 14th 63: Cloudy and damp. Rained hard and blew harder last night. Drizzled now and then all the morn. President Davis has dismissed the Consuls. Lee has pursued Meade across the Rappahannock and is pressing him to a fight. Our Cavalry has taken a number of prisoners.[176] Things are quiet on the "Front." Uncle LeRoy arrived after tea. Looks feebly. Has been down with a sore leg for 2 months; limps a good deal.[177]

Thursday October 15th 1863: Cloudy early in the morn. Clear towards ten oclock. Uncle LeRoy left for Milledgeville + Savannah. My back hurts me and feels very weak indeed. Mrs. Huguenin is no better. Mother went down town; brought home Minnie's Palmetto hat and it looks very nice indeed.[178] Did not sleep well at all last night.

---

175 LeRoy has a lung infection (pockets of infection) that could have been pneumonia, but by this time he was also suffering from consumption (also known as tuberculosis). He was never told he had the disease, though given his symptoms and the remedies prescribed, his doctors and parents knew.

176 The early stages of the Bristoe Campaign (Oct. 13-Nov. 7, 1863), in which Lee moved north in an effort to flank Meade's Army of the Potomac and bring him to battle.

177 LeRoy never explains why Uncle LeRoy's leg has been sore. With his own leg issues, he would probably have been sympathetic.

178 Minnie likely created the hat by sewing the braided Palmetto and taking it to a milliner to have it shaped. Any further decoration (lace, ribbon, flowers) would have been done by Minnie at home.

Friday October 16th 1863: Clear and cool. Father left for Houston. Passed a restless night. [Joe] Wheeler is operating on Rosencrans rear! Has captured 700 wagons! Captured McMinnville with 530 prisoners, commissary stores, arms, +c, +c, destroyed railroad bridge over Stone River! Took Shelbyville with a large amount of stores which were burned. "Important movements" are on foot in Tenn.[179]

Saturday October 17th 1863: Clear and warmer than it was. Rumors of a heavy fight in Va. Wrote to Grandma. Mrs. Huguenin is worse. I suppose her leg will have to be taken off. Watched Thomas cleaning his musket nearly all the evening. Miss Susie Rowland loaned me Bulwer's Novels. I have been very unwell for two or 3 days, no appetite. The weather is much warmer.

Sunday October 18th 1863: Clear and warm. Father got home from Houston at 11 oclock this morning. He went to Perry, [Ga.] and could not get home yesterday. . . .

Monday October 19th 1863: Clear and cool no news. The Fight in Va. seems to have been a heavy cavalry engagement. We took 700 prisoners with their horses. Mrs. Huguenin is better – but her leg will have to be taken off. Longstreet is reported to be crossing the Tenn [River]. Pres[iden]t Davis has gone west. Lee is hot after Meade.[180]

Tuesday October 20th 1863: Clear and cool. Thomas' birthday. He left on the railroad for Houston. Mother sat up with Mrs. Huguenin. Gen D.H. Hill has been relieved from command, Gen Breckinridge commanding his corps. [Gen] Forrest has resigned his command. President Davis has issued a polished and beautiful address to the Army of Tennessee. He says in a speech at Selma that a "crushing victory" over Rosey "would practically end the war." If he would just bring Gen Joe and put him in command, we might we might achieve that Victory, but under Bragg, never! It is said that the enemy is ready to open on Charleston. Since the 1st we have fired on them unceasingly. The

---

179 Wheeler's October 1863 Raid into southeastern Tennessee. Although cavalryman Joe Wheeler captured hundreds of wagons and caused some disruption, he exhausted his cavalry and was roughly handled while returning to northern Georgia.

180 Cavalry battles (part of the Bristoe Campaign) were fought in northern Virginia on Oct. 13 and 14, at Auburn, and on Oct. 19 at Buckland Station. The main infantry fighting was on Oct. 14, when a rash advance without proper reconnaissance by A. P. Hill led to something approaching a large-scale ambush and heavy losses including the death of Gen. Carnot Posey and the wounding of two other generals. After the battle, Hill and Gen. Lee rode the field. Lee interrupted Hill's explanation and shot back, "Well, general, bury these poor men and let us say no more about it."

Yanks are advancing in Mississippi. Eggs are 25 cents – apiece! Butter 5 dollars per lb. Bacon 3 doll[ar]s. As the croakers say, "What is the country coming to?"[181]

Wednesday October 21st 1863: Clear and warm. Uncle LeRoy arrived from Charleston. There is no news. I am reading *The Last Days of Pompeii*. The Bombardment on our part at Charleston continues steadily. The Yanks work like beavers.

Thursday October 22nd 1863: Clear and warm. Made envelopes all the morn. Uncle LeRoy left before breakfast. There is no news. Received a letter from Auntie. Without a fire today for the 1st time in a week or more.

Friday October 23d 1863: Cloudy and warm. Mother in bed all day. Mrs. H[uguenin] no better. Put on my new blue-gray pants; they fit tolerably. There is no news. The storm of war is lulled and the combatants pant in breathless silence. Father bought apples. Sam Virgin sent me some very nice late peaches. Thomas returned on the R.R. this P.M. Finished *Pompeii* + it is grand and splendid in its conception, and beautiful in its style.[182] Stayed on my wagon till 11AM reading. Meade seems to have escaped Lee. He is safe in his works around Centreville and Manassas.[183]

Saturday October 24th 1863: Cloudy and cool. Rained hard in the night. Mrs. Lamar's dog howled dismally last night and kept me awake. . . . Willis came up last eve + brought squirrels, ¼ beef, 20 hams. There is no news. Father bought me *The 2nd Year of the War*. Mrs. Nisbet sent me 3 beautiful apples. Father bought a dozen splendid ones. Willis brought up honey.

Sunday Oct 25th 1863: Cloudy and cool. . . . Lincoln has called for 300,000 Volunteers. I hope he will not get them. Gen R. H. Anderson is made a Maj Gen. Forrest resigned but President Davis would not accept it, but assigned him to a separate command, a thing which he has long desired.

181 Inflation was skyrocketing across the South and Confederate paper money was falling in value. It was now obvious the South was losing, and the blockade was becoming more effective. This made it harder for the South to export cotton and tobacco and import badly needed supplies.

182 LeRoy's reading skills have substantially increased over the three years he has been journaling. In addition to the story, he also has an eye for construction and style. He developed exceptional analytical skills without any formal schooling.

183 The "Buckland Races" took place on Oct. 19, 1863, while Lee was retreating from the Centreville area; Jeb Stuart's cavalry lured the pursuing Union cavalry under Gen. Judson Kilpatrick into an ambush. The Federal troopers were chased at least five miles down the Warrenton Turnpike toward Manassas.

Monday October 26th 1863: Clear and cool. Meade and Lee have settled down once more. No news. Grant has superceded Rosencrans.[184] My back runs immensely. The President is in Mobile. I hope he'll come here. The Amputation of Mrs. Huguenin's leg was performed this P.M. by Drs. Hammond, Boone, + Fitzgerald

Tuesday October 27th 1863: Clear and cool. The Dastardly foe have opened from Gregg + Wagoner on us at Charleston. We reply briskly. Made me a new bandage [for my back]. Gen Thomas is commander of Rosey's army with Grant as supervisor. Father bought some apples. There is nearly 12000 prisoners confined in Richmond.[185] Thomas went hunting + killed 2 doves, which I enjoyed eating very much. Thomas tied a rope to two trees in the yard and him + Allen cut antics [played] on it. Mrs. H[uguenin] is very low.

Wednesday October 28th 1863: Clear and cool. The Monitors and batteries continue to fire on us mostly at Sumter. 630 shots were fired at her. 4 shots were fired into the city. The Gun burst on the 5th trial. Our Batteries reply. Nothing worth noting occurs in the dull routine of my daily life.

Thursday October 29th 1863: Clear and cool. Put on undershirts. Went down to the depot to see President Davis and was most awfully "chawed" by his not coming. He [was] to be here on a special train this evening. Mother is sick in bed. 4 monitors and the land batteries continue to fire at Charleston, principally at Sumter. 84 out of 679 shots missed. Only a few shots were fired at Sullivan [Fort Moultrie]. Our Batteries fire briskly and accurately. Brought home my puppy. He has brown spots.

Friday October 30th 1863: Cloudy and cool. Thomas has had one of his periodical attacks of Rheumatism coming on for a day or two, and he is now suffering a good deal. I have named my "pipperlopper" [puppy] "Bruno." He is lively enough, quite intelligent, and comes when called. The Bombardment of Ft. Sumter is terrific. 779 shots were fired at it and only 80 missed. Our batteries fire with good effect. Lt Gen Hardee and Lt Gen Polk have swapped places. Mrs. Lamar's dog howled dismally by the space of 3 hours last night and "curses not loud but deep" were muttered upon him. Mother and Minnie slept down stairs last night.

---

184 U. S. Grant fired Gen. Rosecrans in Chattanooga (which was partially encircled by Bragg's Army of Tennessee), put Gen. George Thomas in his place at the head of the Army of the Cumberland, and arrived to assume command in person.

185 Union prisoners were housed in many places in Richmond during the war, including Belle Isle (an island in the James River that by 1863 housed some 10,000 enlisted men), and the notorious Libby Prison, a converted tobacco warehouse used for holding officers.

Saturday October 31st 1863: Cloudy and warm. Thomas bad off with Rheumatism. The Bombardment of Sumter is terrific – from Gregg [and] Wagner. It is the heaviest ever known. Their fire is directed at the Sea face. From Sundown Wednesday to sundown again, 1215 shots were fired at it. Yesterday about 4.30 we went to the depot to see the President. Before 5 a large crowd had gathered and a few minutes past five he arrived on a special train. We were quite near the phaeton,[186] which was drawn by a neat pair of mules, and had a good opportunity of seeing him as he bowed and smiled to the people. As the phaeton moved off, there was a push to get into line but soon all were racing to get to the Lanier House. After the lapse of a few minutes he appeared on the upper porch and addressed the People for about 15 minutes. His [voice] was fine and mellow and his speech, well delivered and beautiful. Loud cheers interrupted him occasionally. All the college gals went down + shook hands with him: Minnie among others. He left on a special train for Savannah a little before 8 P.M.[187] Rained a little last night.

Sunday November 1st 1863: Cloudy and cool. I've changed "Bruno's" name to "Wheeler." He barked twice. Thomas' leg is better. The Yanks are trying to get possession of Lookout Mountain + fighting has been going on. Hood's old Division, now [Gen. Micah] Jenkins was principally engaged against 2 corps of Yanks and lost largely in killed + captured.[188] The Furious Bombardment of Sumter goes on; the Sea wall fell in and killed 12 or 13 men. Wheeler barked at the turkeys. He weighs 5 pounds and 2 oz. Mother went over to Mrs. Huguenin's and found her better. The First number of the Tri-weekly *Charleston Courier* came Saturday. Therefore the subscription commenced on the 29th.

Monday November 2nd 1863: Cloudy and warm. My other grey pants are done. Mrs. Huguenin is better.

Tuesday November 3d 1863: Cloudy and warm. The Bombardment of Sumter is fast and furious. 4 shots per minute. Received a letter from Auntie enclosing a piece of Poetry for me. Harry and Al Prentice came to see me. Cousin David Wiley arrived here night before last from the North via Memphis.[189] Reading *Johnny McKay*. Father

---

186 A small 4-wheeled carriage drawn by horses or mules.

187 For a more detailed description of Davis' visit to Macon, see Iobst, *Civil War Macon*, 283.

188 The Battle of Wauhatchie (Oct. 28-29, 1863), one of the very few nighttime combats during the war. Confederates (primarily Jenkins' division drawn from Lookout Mountain) attacked a Union force near the Tennessee River. It was a bungled affair and the Rebels were driven back with loss.

189 David Leroy Wiley, a brother of Cousin Jinnie and son of Aunt Ann.

brought up two vests for me to try on but they didn't fit. Thomas bought some splendid gray cloth to make him one. Mother borrowed *A Gallery of Indians* from Mrs. Whittle for me to look at, and they are splendid. The engravings are beautifully colored. Gen [George] Thomas is settled quietly in Chattanooga for the winter.

Wednesday November 4th 1863: Clear and cool. Father went to Houston. The Bombardment of Sumter continues. The President is inspecting the works at Charleston. Mother sat till 12 oclock last night with Mrs. Huguenin. I'm reading *The Parlor Library*, loaned me by Mrs. Watkins.

Thursday November 5th 1863: Cloudy and warm. The Firing continues at Charleston: furiously. There is no news. My back has run but little for a day or so.

Friday November 6th 1863: Clear and warm. The wind blew this morning and the leaves are falling in showers. Thus far there has not been a killing frost here: a thing somewhat rare. My Puppy "Wheeler" sleepeth under the steps. Father returned from Houston. Mr. Kemp is at home on a short furlough.

Saturday November 7th 1863: There is no news. The firing on Sumter has slackened. The Legislature met Thursday and elected [former general] A.R. Wright President of the Senate and [Thomas] Hardeman Speaker of the House.[190] Mrs. Huguenin is better. Mrs. Whittle sent me two oranges. . . .

Sunday November 8th 1863: Clear and cool. The Paper did not come. The impression is Bragg will "fall back." . . . Went out on my wagon and ate Hickory nuts. The wind blows very hard this evening. My Back has run very little for two or three days, and has been very sore too. Gen Hood is able to sit up a little. Vague intimations are thrown out that [Gen] Wheeler is on another raid.

Monday November 9th 1863: First cold day of the season. Thomas left on the B.R.R. for Houston.[191] Commenced *Rienzi, or the Last of the Tribunes* by E. Bulwer Lytton.

Tuesday November 10th 1863: Clear and cold. Ice thick as a window-pane: the first of the season. Collards, peppers, Tomatoes frozen. Green + Howard are planting Rye. My back is very sore. The Gov's message is very long. The fire on Sumter slackens. Our men in East Tenn. have captured 840 Yanks, 60 wagons, +c, a thousand mules. Commenced my new scrapbook today.

---

190 Both men also held CSA commissions as general and colonel, respectively.

191 The Macon and Brunswick line, chartered in 1856, ran southeast out of Macon. It was incomplete when the Civil War began and work on it was stopped, though it ran most of the way to the plantations in Houston County. It was finished after the war to Hawkinsville. This is one of the few times LeRoy mentions anyone using the railroad, rather than a horse or wagon, to travel to the plantations.

Wednesday November 11th 1863: Clear and cold. Heavy frost and Ice. Slept down stairs for the first time. This is my 16th birthday.[192] The Barrel of Apples have arrived. Green left for home [at the Houston plantations]. The Fire on Sumter has nearly ceased.

Thursday November 12th 1863: Clear and cool. Auntie and [Cousin] Wilson arrived at 5.30 this morning. Aunty and Mother went down town, and Wilson and I had a good talk. The Fire on Sumter continues. Gens Buckner and Cheatham have left Bragg's army; Hood has been appointed to Hill's Corps.[193] Tracy called to see us.

Friday November 13th 1863: Cloudy and warm. . . . Wrote in Sallie's Album. Thomas and Green arrived from Houston bringing 4 partridges, squirrels, +++c.

Saturday November 14th 1863: Cloudy and warm. Thick fog early in the morning. Susie and Georgia Tracy came to see us and stayed to Dinner, and behaved very pretty. After dinner Thomas, Wilson, Aunty, and I rode out by the Armory, arsenal, and had a fine time. Weighed "Wheeler" and he has gained from 6 ¾ to 8 lbs. since last Saturday. Slept up stairs in the back room with Wilson and Thomas. It is the 1st time I've slept away from Father and Mother both in a good while. The fire on Sumter is 2 per minute. A calcium light is thrown over the harbor every night. Minnie gave me her herbarium for a scrapbook.[194]

Sunday Nov 15th 1863: Clear, beautiful day. I have sat up more in the last week than I have in 3 years before and I hope no bad effects will result from it. Wilson did not go to church. He has a boil on his side. After supper, Mother and Aunty sung some hymns and it was almost as good as church.

Monday 16th Nov 1863: Clear and cold. Greased my wagon. Went down town in the P.M. Aunty went to the dentists. We all went to Cousin Jimmie Snider's and weighed. I weighed 63 pounds; Wilson 71. Took my measure for some crutches. Mother and Aunt bought candy. Mother gave hers to sick soldiers. Came home and Allen and Thomas "kicked up didoes" [tricks] on the rope.

Tuesday November 17th 1863: Cloudy and cool. My back hurt me last night. Slept well though. The Bombardment of Sumter continues heavily. The monitors engaged. Gen

---

192 This is the first birthday that passed without LeRoy noting any fanfare or receiving any gifts.

193 Gen. Ben F. Cheatham. Gen. Hood would recover from his leg amputation and lead a corps, but not until early 1864.

194 A book used for the collection of plants. In this case, it was probably begun to collect dried varieties of flowers.

Hood is in Richmond. Aunt Ann spent the morn. Cousins Eliza + Helen called. "There is nought new under the sun." Aunty and Wilson are gone, and it seems like a dream that they've been here. "Wheeler" looked very doleful after Wilson's departure.

Wednesday Nov 18th 1863: Clear and cool. The "Pegging away" at Sumter continues. The French have siezed our rams and prohibited the exportation of arms to us. "Go it ye cripples." England + France are as thick as two dogs in a hominy pot on the Ram subject.[195] The Corps of Longstreet is at Loudon [Tenn.] pushing "Burnside to the Wall." Important movements are on foot, +c, +c. Lee + Meade are coquetting with each other to the ghastly tune of 50 or 60 men a day, but it is thought both are afraid to give battle.[196] Mother bought *Aurora Floyd, a Novel* – by M.E. Braddon.

Thursday November 19th 1863: Clear and warm. Passed a bad night: had an awful headache and pain in my hip and considerable fever. Longstreet and Wheeler are "over the river." Thomas left for Milledgeville early this morning. Commenced *Aurora Floyd*.

Friday November 20th 1863: Cloudy and warm. Mr. Kemp and his nephew, Lt Walker of Co. D, 18th La. Reg[iment], stayed all night with us and left this morning for the Army. Longstreet is in Knoxville! If that's <u>so</u>, its good news. Generals Cheatham, Buckner, Polk, D.H. Hill, Forrest, [and] Hindman have been ordered away from the Army of Tennessee since Chickamauga. Breckinridge, Hardee, and Longstreet are the corps commanders now. I have been quite unwell for a day or two. Greene left for Home today. Mrs. Huguenin is able to sit up. LeWGr

Saturday November 21st 1863: Cloudy and warm. Commenced to rain at noon and is raining now [at] 3PM. An assault on Sumter was attempted the other night and frustrated by the vigilant garrison. Thomas was elected Lieutenant today [of his company] over Mr. Mallory.

195 LeRoy is referring to The Laird Ram Crisis in England. Two powerful iron-hulled warships were secretly funded and built at Birkenhead, England for the Confederacy. Because of the danger they posed to the Union navy in general, and the Union blockade of Southern ports in particular, diplomatic pressure was brought to bear and the British government seized the ships. They were eventually commissioned into the Royal Navy.

196 Longstreet and his troops from Virginia were sent from Bragg's Army of Tennessee at Chattanooga into East Tennessee in a failed effort to capture Knoxville, which was under the command of Union Gen. Ambrose Burnside. In Virginia, Lee and Meade continued to view one another across the Rapidan River, with the pressure growing on Meade to bring Lee to battle before winter made it impossible.

Sunday November 22nd 1863: Cloudy and warm. . . . The Yanks continue to batter away at Charleston + shell the city occasionally. Nisbet's Foundry blew up Friday.[197] It is not certainly known whether Knoxville is ours or not: as it is uncertain, I am safe in saying that it is not.

Monday November 23rd 1863: Cloudy and cool. Thomas went to Baker this morning. Pasted in scrap-book. The Mosqsuitoes were so bad that Father + Mother slept up stairs last night.

Tuesday Nov 24th 1863: Raining slowly when we got up this morning. There is no news. We have Knoxville invested. But when we invest a place, there is always a place left for the enemy to get out; therefore Burnside is in no danger. The impression prevails, generally, that Grant will fight in 8 or 10 days. I don't see how it is to be done unless he attacks us or Bragg falls back. Mother slept in Thomas' room with me last night. Mrs. H[uguenin] is worse today.

Wednesday Nov 25th 1863: Cloudy early in the morning but clear in the PM. Green and Howard are hauling wood from the S.W.R.R. [Southwestern Railroad]. Green came from Houston yesterday + brought about a half bushel of hickory nuts, eggs, butter, wheat, +c. P.W.A. telegraphs that "the enemy have advanced their lines + there has been heavy skirmishing at Chattanooga. Whether they will attack us in our works is uncertain: but a battle in some shape is imminent." Burnside is entrenched at Knoxville. Mrs. Huguenin is much worse + but little hope is entertained of her recovery. We slept down stairs last night and the mosquitoes were very bad. Mother read out *Aurora Floyd* till bedtime. The [Charleston] *Courier* has suspended for a day or two.

Thursday November 26th 1863: Clear and cold. Bragg dispatches that we have had a struggle for Lookout [Mountain at Chattanooga]. The sad tale is soon told. "The enemy have taken Lookout: Lookout – that position we looked on so hopefully as impregnable against assault any way has been captured by assault. Our left gave way in 'considerable' disorder while the right stood firm." The Army is falling back to Chickamauga and of course large numbers will have been taken prisoners. Longstreet is cut off![198] Robert Carter arrived from Athens this morning with a letter for me from

197 Thomas C. Nisbet, Sr. was a relation of Judge Eugenius Nisbet and his brother and law partner James A. Nisbet. The Nisbet foundry, along the Macon & Western RR, manufactured machinery and castings and offered engines and boilers for sale.

198 The Battle for Lookout Mountain (November 24, 1863) was the first major offensive action by Gen. Grant against Bragg's extended lines above Chattanooga. Joe Hooker's Federals captured the lightly

Aunty, enclosing one from Uncle Edge. Burnside is reported captured. The upshot of it all is: Winter Quarters in Chattanooga.

Friday November 27th 1863: Cloudy and cold. The fire on Sumter "has abated." Uncle LeRoy arrived here last night from Montgomery. His foot is very bad. P.W.A. says "with the enemy in the valley of Lookout, the mountain was untenable." Gen Hardee commanded the right; Breckinridge the left. The Centre gave way, then the left, but the right under Hardee repelled every attack. Our army is at Chickamauga now.[199] Mother bought 1 dozen oranges + 1 dozen lemons at $3 per Dozen. Wrote to Aunty. Received two pieces poetry from her. Am reading *Anne of Geierstein*.

Saturday November 28th 1863: Cloudy and very damp. The walls and every piece of furniture are dripping with moisture. After dinner it commenced to rain hard + fast. Uncle LeRoy left at Daybreak this morning. There is nought from the "Front." Though rumor says our loss in prisoners is large. Gen Bragg is at Ringgold, Ga. The forces on Lookout were cut off and had to run like wrath. No casualties reported. Nothing from E. Tenn. Father stayed at home all day. Headache in the morn; rain in the eve.

Sunday November 29th 1863: Cloudy and cool. Mrs. Huguenin's life is despaired of. Julia Ann has been in bed since Friday; got up today. Grant is pressing Bragg and we are retreating. A Battle is "imminent" in Northern Va. The Firing at Charleston, through steady, has lost interest. My back has run but very little for a day or so and I have coughed a little at night. How soon the cough would return would the issue to stop! "Wheeler" is a fine dog if he does pull the chickens off the roost at night: that is from under the house.

Monday November 30th 1863: Clear and cold. The mercury in our passage [hallway] was 31°. Out on the stoop at 9AM it was 22°. It must have been 19° earlier. Mother was sent for last night to see Mrs. Huguenin die: but she still lingers. Mother sat up there. This is a real "slinger." The Frost is two inches high. Thick ice in the water-bucket. The times look very dark. Bragg will lose Georgia as he has Tenn. But one paper in the state

---

defended mountain that formed Bragg's left flank and put Hooker's men in a position to launch more attacks against Missionary Ridge the following day.

199 The Battle of Missionary Ridge (November 25, 1863). In an attack that was never ordered, Gen. Thomas' Union men assaulted up the slope of Missionary Ridge and broke apart Bragg's army, which fled in one of the worst routs of the entire war. Gallant defensive efforts by part of his army allowed for most of the rest to escape into north Georgia. Bragg's losses approached 7,000 (some 4,000 captured), with heavy losses in baggage and artillery; Union losses were about 5,000. The decisive victory relieved Chattanooga, which was never again threatened by the Rebels. It also brought the war permanently onto Georgia soil—and closer to Macon.

is in favor of him, viz. *The Atlanta Register.* Mrs. Huguenin died at 12.20, just 2 months from the day she was hurt.

Tuesday Dec~~November~~ 1st 1863: Clear and cold. Our army is in Dalton and on this side. It is supposed that it will be here if Bragg remains in command. It is said that a number of men refused to fight under him. O President D[avis].[200] Mrs. Huguenin's body was carried to Milledgeville and Mother and F[ather] are down there now. A division of Army in Va. under [Edward] Johnson fought 2 corps all day Friday (26th) in Orange County + losing 500 men without gaining a thing. It is a horrible thing how the lives of so many good and brave men are thus frittered away without any commensurate damages to the foe.[201] They have many more coming by every ship from Europe, and do not feel the loss of men as we do. Longstreet is shelling Knoxville, [Tenn.].

Wednesday December 2nd 1863: Clear and cold. Father left for Houston. Our calf was slaughtered yesterday and we kept the hind-quarters and sold the rest. It is very nice indeed. P.W.A.'s description of the Battle of "Missionary Ridge" is very gloomy. Our army is in Dalton, Gen Cleburn comdg. [commanding]. Our rear gaurd had a fight beyond Dalton, taking 800 prisoners and killing 1500 of the enemy and driving them back.[202] Our loss is small. Longstreet is in Knoxville and has captured the garrison it is said. Cousin E[liza] + Aunt S[arah] called.

Thursday December 3d 1863: Clear and cold. It is said that Bragg has been relieved of the Command of the A.T., at his own request.[203] No one else appointed as yet. *Courier* came today. Suspended a week to get out of reach of stray shells. Recd a letter from Aunty. Sallie has been ill. Cousin Eliza sent me oysters + cake. We are invited there to night. I don't see how I can go. I have been reading *Castle Dangerous* + *Tales of a Grandfather.* Nothing from E. Tenn. 'though the impression still prevails that "Knoxville is ours." I do not think it's so or that it will ever be. Burnside will be relieved.

---

200 Leroy is lamenting the fact that President Davis had visited the army and left Bragg in command.

201 The battle LeRoy is referencing was Payne's Farm (Nov. 27, 1863), an accidental encounter between Ed Johnson's division and Union Gen. William H. French's III Corps of the Army of the Potomac. Although often overlooked, it was a short but bloody combat that saved Gen. Lee's army from being flanked. The Confederates pulled back a few miles behind Mine Run Creek.

202 Gen. Patrick Cleburne led the rear guard action at Ringgold Gap (Nov. 27, 1863) that allowed the Confederate army's wagons and artillery to escape after the disaster at Missionary Ridge.

203 Gen. Bragg offered to resign on Nov. 29, and President Davis immediately accepted.

Friday December 4th 1863: Clear and cold. Ice + and a tremendous frost. For the past 3 mornings there have been the biggest frosts of the war. We all went round to Cousin Eliza's to an oyster supper and enjoyed ourselves finely. Miss Florence + Miss Tallulah Snider and Mrs. S[nider] were there and Cousin Jack.[204] We came home at 8 oclock. Lt Gen Hardee is in command of the Army of Tenn. Gen Johnston is <u>the</u> man for that place. Meade has fallen back without giving battle. I am mightly glad.[205]

Saturday December 5th 1863: Clear and cold; heavy frost + ice. Father and Thomas both came home. T[homas] brought 20 stalks of sugar cane. Milo came up. Minnie stayed all night at Cousin Eliza's. Morgan has made his escape to Canada.[206] Longstreet has raised the siege of Knoxville – cut out to Va. What a misfortune that the movement was ever made! Mother is sick. Grant is fortifying at Chickamauga. Hardee is ensconced in + around Dalton. I wish we could stay so all the winter. The Southern people are more patient and can better afford to wait than those of the North. Time will surely bring Independence if it does bring Poverty.

Sunday December 6th 1863: Clear and cool. Put on the 1st one of my new shirts made of Macon Mills.[207] The others are not done yet + Mother made this one first to let me try the collar off the shirt. We lost 38 pieces artillery at Mission Ridge + Lookout, so says P.W.A. . . . The Command of the Army of Tennessee has not yet been decided upon, though Rumor says it will be conferred upon Joseph E. Johnston.

Monday December 7th 1863: Clear and quite cold. Ice. Nothing new to relate + there is nothing new under the sun in fact. Piece of cloth came from Athens. . . . Ira Fort came up to stay all night with us.

---

204 Margaret T. Waldron Snider was Cousin Eliza's mother-in-law; Georgia Tallulah and Mary Florence were her youngest two daughters.

205 Gen. William Hardee was given temporary command, but refused permanent command. LeRoy is likely repeating what his father believed—that Joe Johnston should get the position. Meade and Lee faced off at Mine Run, but the former decided the Confederate defenses were too strong and called off a planned attack. The armies in Virginia and Georgia went into winter quarters.

206 John Hunt Morgan and six officers captured during Morgan's Raid in Ohio escaped from the state penitentiary on November 27, jumped from a train they had boarded, and crossed the Ohio River into Kentucky with the assistance of Confederate sympathizers. Morgan reached home shortly after the death of his infant daughter, who was born on the day of his escape.

207 Macon Manufacturing Company owned by LeRoy's father. Its 130 workers produced shirting and cotton fabric for the Confederacy at a rate of 4,000 yards per day. Gresham had finagled exemptions for many of his skilled mill workers. By 1863, however, it was becoming harder to get fabric for clothing and keep his workers out of the army.

Tuesday December 8th 1863: Cloudy and cold. Ira left for Mississippi. Longstreet has left Burnside, on account of the heavy reinforcements going to him, and gone to Bristol, Tenn.[208] Congress met yesterday. Arch came up last night. Mr. Hill, [overseer] who has been quite ill, is getting about again.

Wednesday December 9th 1863: Cloudy early in the morn. The message of President recommends the putting of men with "states" in the Army. There is only a synopsis by telegraph and the beauty of the language is not shown.

Thursday December 10th 1863: Clear + cool. Day of fasting + prayer recommended by Gov B[rown] + sanctioned by the legislature. There are many rumors of an appointment of some one to the Army "above," but no one is settled on. General Johnston is my candidate. The press favor him. An Atlanta paper states that he has been already appointed, but it is doubtful.

Friday December 11th 1863: Clear and warm. Thomas and I play chess a good deal now. Mother gone to Soldiers Relief Society.

Saturday December 12th 1863: Cloudy and damp. Election for Mayor today: S. Collins vs. W.K. deGraffenreid.[209] Longstreet is retreating safely. My Back has been running a great deal in the past day or two. 9 minutes past 11 + it has commenced to rain.

December 13th 1863: Very foggy and warm. Grant is making a large movement of some sort: he has retreated into Chattanooga and is moving to attack some other print. S[tephen] Collins is Mayor by 63 majority. Sam [one of the plantation slaves]came up yesterday to see about sending negroes to the coast again. Father is too unwell to go to church + no one went but Thomas. It is rumored that Morgan escaped into Virginia + not to Canada. I hope it is true. The "Blind Asylum" and the "Free School Academy" have been taken as Hospitals.

December 14th 1863: Rained sweetly and musically after we went to bed last night, and it cold + windy this AM. Thomas had a "tack" of the "Rheumatis" in the back + Mother in her little finger. I took a cold last night + am bad off for a dose of "Peach [brandy]."

208 Gen. James Longstreet's Knoxville Campaign was a failure, and he pulled back and went into winter quarters in East Tennessee.

209 Stephen Collins and William Kirkland DeGraffenried. DeGraffenried was father of one of Minnie's good friends, Clare.

Tuesday December 15th 1863: Clear and beautiful frosty morn. A synopsis of Lincoln's message is out and it offers us rebels under the rank of Colonel a pardon. President Davis' message is as usual in the "sprucest English." It recommends nothing very strongly. George Beal came round to see us last night after tea. Mother has got a little dog and it is perhaps the ugliest thing. Thomas beats me all the time at Chess.

Wednesday December 16th: Cloudy and cool. My cold is no better. The last apple of the barrel is gone. Rained off and on nearly all the P.M. Thomas and I out in the back piazza, he cutting up lead to make duckshot. Grant is reported retreating or sending away a part of his forces to Meade.

Thursday Dec 17th 1863: Rainy and warm. Rained very hard all the night. Did not rest well at all. Played the following "Game of Chess" after tea last night Thomas having the Blacks + the move + I the white: Father acting as secretary:[210]

[See next image of LeRoy's chess moves]

The turning point in the game was 11th Q to K. B. 3d was easily superior + getting R out of play finely if that was white's intention = desperate.

3 P.M. It has rained steadily since this morning. A rainy day truly. Thomas has been engaged all the morn in hammering at some lead. P.W.A. has an account of the campaign in Northern Georgia.

Friday December 18th 1863: Clear and cold. It turned very cold in the night. Cousin Charlie Wiley was married on the 15th in Eatonton.[211] Minnie received an invitation from Cousin George inviting her + Thomas to his wedding in Montgomery on the 6th of Jan. The Happy Lady is Miss Kate Calhoun.[212] Congress has passed a law stopping substitution. Eveline went to Milledgeville this P.M.[213] Mary has a beautiful little Kitty, the most playful one I ever saw. . . . I do not sleep well that is I do not go to sleep 'till late. Mother is reading *No Name* by Wilkie Collins.

---

210 At this point LeRoy divides his page into two columns, one fo the black moves and another for the white moves, and entitles the game "The Muzio Gambit," a very aggressive chess strategy that involves the white player sacrificing a knight for a heavy attack with his bishop, queen, and castled king. He meticulously fills the equivalent of two pages with each specific move, followed by a short commentary.

211 His bride was Miss Sarah Juliette Reid.

212 Catherine Lucretia Calhoun.

213 One of the Gresham house servants in Macon.

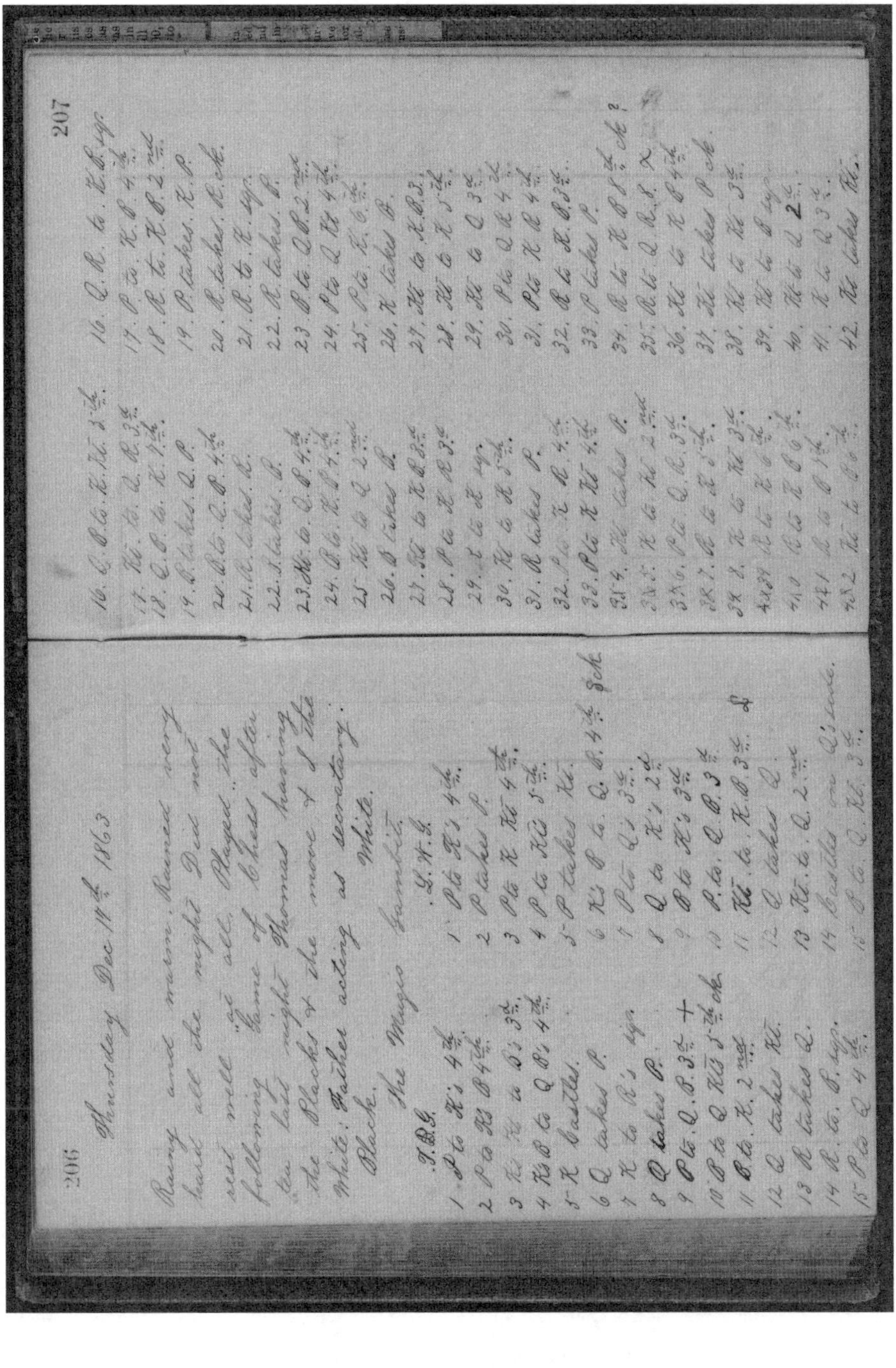

206

Thursday Dec 17th 1863

Rainy and warm. Rained very hard all the night Did not rest well at all. Played the following Game of Chess after ten last night Thomas having the Blacks & the move & I the White: Father acting as secratary:

Black.	White.
The Mugio Gambit.	
T.B.G.	L.W.G.
1 P to K's 4th.	1 P to K's 4th.
2 P to K's B 4th.	2 P takes P.
3 K's Kt to B's 3d.	3 P to K Kt 4th.
4 K's B to Q B's 4th.	4 P to Kt's 5th.
5 K Castles.	5 P takes Kt.
6 Q takes P.	6 K's B to Q. B. 4th ch
7 K to R's sq.	7 P to Q's 3d.
8 Q takes P.	8 Q to K's 2d.
9 P to Q. B. 3d. +	9 B to K's 3d.
10 B to Q Kt's 5th ch	10 P. to. Q. B. 3d.
11 B. to. K. 2nd.	11 Kt. to. K. B. 3d.
12 Q takes Kt.	12 Q takes Q.
13 R takes Q.	13 Kt. to. Q. 2nd.
14 R. to. B. sq.	14 Castles on Q's side.
15 P to Q 4th.	15 B to. Q. Kt. 3d.

207

16. Q. B. to. K. Kt. 5th.	16. Q. R. to. K. B. sq.
17. Kt. to. Q. R. 3d.	17. P. to. K. B. 4th.
18. Q. B. to. K. 7th.	18. R. to. K. B. 2nd.
19. B. takes. Q. P.	19. P. takes. K. P.
20. B. to. Q. B. 4th.	20. R. takes. R. ch.
21. R. takes. R.	21. R. to. K. sq.
22. B. takes. P.	22. R. takes. B.
23. Kt. to. Q. B. 4th.	23. B. to. Q B. 2nd.
24. B. to. K. B. 4th.	24. P to Q Kt 4th.
25 Kt to Q 2nd.	25. P to. K. 6th.
26. B takes B.	26. K takes B.
27. Kt to K B 3d.	27. Kt to K. B. 3.
28. P to K R 3d.	28. Kt to K 5th.
29. K to K sq.	29. Kt to Q 3d.
30. Kt to K 5th.	30. P to Q R 4th.
31. R takes P.	31. P to K R 4th.
32. P to K R 4th.	32. R to K. B. 3d.
33. P to K Kt 4th.	33. P takes P.
34. Kt takes P.	34. R to K B 8th ch ?
35. K to Kt 2nd.	35. R. to. Q. R. 8. x
36. P to. Q. R. 3d.	36. Kt to K B 4th.
37. R to K 5th.	37. Kt takes P ch.
38. K to Kt 3d.	38. Kt to Kt 3d.
39. R to K 6th.	39. Kt to B sq.
40. B to K B 6th.	40. Kt to Q 2d.
41. R to B 7th.	41. K to Q 3d.
42. Kt to B 6th.	42. Kt takes Kt.

Saturday December 19th 1863: Clear and <u>real</u> cold. Green came up to bring word that the over-seer pro tem at Pineland had been conscribed + would have to leave.[214] Macon is the gate city of creation. There's <u>nothing</u> new. Generals Cheatham and Hindman are the corps commanders of Hardee's Army, the latter superseding Breckinridge. Lincoln's message is another one of his shambling "get out" documents. Willis came up with spare-ribs + Backbones, the first of the season. Mother and Thomas + Father went to a grand dining at Aunt Ann's + it was the general verdict that they like to have froze. Aunt Ann sent me some cake, syllabub, custard, jelly, + preserves and they were <u>good</u> too.

Sunday December 20th 1863: The coldest day of the year. Mercury 18½ in the porch 11AM; in the passage 35°. General Joseph E. Johnston has been appointed to the Army of Tennessee. This is reliable. Every thing is frozen light. Cousin's Jimmie + Jack came to see us after dinner. Since about 9 A.M. my leg has been paining me steadily. Susie E[dwards] stayed all night here.

Monday Dec 21st 1863: Cold and clear. Father + Willis left for Houston. The pain in my leg was so bad that I had to take a Dover's Powder. "Christmas is coming!"

Tuesday December 22nd 1863: Moderating. No news at all. Evelina returned last night + is laid up this morning. I suffered a good deal last night, did not sleep well + could not get up to breakfast. The pain is much worse at night.

Wednesday December 23d 1863: Clear and pleasant day. My leg was very bad + I took a little Morphia. Quiet reigns supreme from the Potomac to the Mississippi. My back is very weak. Today College broke up. This evening Mother went down to the Wayside Home. She bought a 75 dollar pair of gaiters.[215]

Thursday December 24th 1863: Clear and cold. General Morgan passed through Columbia, So. Ca. There's no other news. My Vest, a Christmas gift from Father, came home today and it is very nice. "Personne" [anonymous correspondent] has a splendid acct of [Longstreet's] E. Tenn. Campaign. I slept well last night and have entirely recovered from the pain in my leg + Back. Pasted nearly all the morning in my scrapbook. Got a letter from Grandma in Hancock. They were delayed in Athens by

---

214 John Gresham had hired a temporary overseer for one of the two Houston plantations because Hill—the overseer running Pineland—was going into the army or had already done so. As noted in the Dec. 8 entry, Arch reported "Mr. Hill" was getting better. He may have had health issues that kept him out of the army for a while, but he was eventually conscripted.

215 Overshoes made of leather or cloth that go from the instep to above the ankle, occasionally as high as the knee. They are intended to protect the shoe and keep the opening of the shoe clear of dirt.

the serious illness of Sallie. This is Christmas Eve. My vest cost 15 dollars, thrice as much in cost than I ever had before. And then when my pictures of the Generals[216] come, I will have had a nice present from Father + Mother. Mother made about a dontknowhowmany pickles today. Father arrived this PM and the wagon with Peter, Ben, Blount,[217] + Arthur, who have come up to look around.

Friday December 25th 1863: This is Christmas! Clear + Cold. My pictures did not come and I have given them out. Mother had a pound cake baked. Thomas had an eggnog at Dr. Emerson's. There is no news. This is a sad Christmas to many. The Ladies went down + gave a dinner to the Soldiers at Wood's furniture shop. Had a nice eggnog after tea.

Saturday December 26th 1863: Christmas is over. Cloudy and cool.

Sunday December 27th 1863: Cloudy and drizzly and warm. No one but Father went to church. Played Chess after tea last night with odds of a Queen with Father and got charred. The pictures of the Generals were so high we determined not to get them, being 2 dollars apiece. Father bought 2 ducks at 7 dollars yesterday.

Monday December 28th 1863: Cloudy and quite warm. Rained slowly most of the night. Nothing occurs to break or mar the even tenor of our daily life. Father is more despondent about the country than I ever saw him before. Grant is going to lie still until May, when with a column of 150000 men, he is going to take Lynchburg, [Va.]. Meanwhile he with the main Army, like "ye celebrated torrent from ye Appenines," is going to swoop down on Agusta + Atlanta, take Charleston in the rear + end the Rebellion in a Blaze of Glory.[218] 125 shells thrown into Charleston was Old Gillmore's Christmas. Not much harm done. A Change of Programme is evidently about to be made by the Yanks + an attack on Savannah is confidently looked for before many days more, probably next week.

Tuesday December 29th 1863: Cool and clear. Thomas left per BRR [Brunswick RR] for Houston. Gen J.E. Johnston arrived and assumed command "above" on the 27th ult. The new Georgia Militia Bill embraces all over 16; consequently I am in it. Minnie wrote to Sallie. Father and I took an elegant game of chess last eve. 13000 men are

216 LeRoy is referring to a collection of *cartes de visite*s, reproducible images pasted onto a cardboard backing. These images were very popular with citizens both North and South.

217 Peter, Ben, and Blount were plantation slaves.

218 Demonstrating his knowledge of classical history, LeRoy is making a reference to Hannibal's war against Rome, when he used the Appenines mountain range in Italy to military advantage.

reported landing on the coast below Savannah. Major Gen Gilmer C.S.A. is in command on our side.[219] What Whim Led White Whit . . .

Wednesday December 30th 1863: Clear + Cool Heavy frost. I am reading *Nicholas Nickleby*. Commenced to rain in the PM slowly and quite hard after tea. Mother walked down to the Wayside Home and was there nearly all the evening. Susie Edwards came to stay to tea. Made cruller + they were mighty nice!

Thursday December 31st 1863: Rained hard, all night long + has continued to pour down all the morning. Father did not go to town. Susy stayed all night. A law has passed both houses of the Congress to put all who have substitutes in the Army. The Year goes out weeping, weeping we might well think—over the blood that has been shed and the fiery trials this poor Country has been called upon to undergo. Many anxious hearts wonder this day if by the time another Christmas comes those loved ones far away in the camps will be home again. "I hope the war will be over," is the wish and prayer breathed by the whole Confederate people. Father has been at home today. Gen H.R. Jackson has called out all the state troops under his command to go to Savannah for this emergency. I think it will be awful cold in the morning.

[The remainder of the volume includes a large number of clippings, probably obtained during the time LeRoy was unable to obtain a scrapbook.]

---

219 Gen. Jeremy F. Gilmer was Chief of the Engineer Bureau, and not in command on the coast.

The outside back of Volume 5, filled with LeRoy's doodling, his signature, and his own drawing of a Confederate battle flag. *LOC*

The front of Volume 6.
LOC

Volume 6

January 1, 1864 – January 8, 1865

January 1st 1864 Friday: Clear, windy and very cold. The Mercury at half past 10 oclock was 22°. Had splendid syllabub for dinner yesterday. The Macon Battallion is ordered to prepare to go to Savannah on next Tuesday. Thomas came back from Houston this evening nearly frozen. It has been bitter cold all day + the wind cuts like a knife. Frank Baxter came up on the wagon. The creeks were all tremendous high. Echeconnee [Creek] was running over the bridge. Tobasafkee [Creek] over the causeway. Sandy-run [stream] was nearly over the backs of the mules. The ground has not thawed today. Father could not get a diary at a reasonable price so I had to take this old book from Father's office.

Saturday January 2nd 18634: Cold still and bitter cold. At Day the Mercury on the back porch stood at 7° + at Breakfast time 11° at noon 29°. In the passage at 4.P.M. it stood at 27°. This is the coldest weather we've had in 4 or 5 years. The water froze in all the rooms. Minnie put out a cup of milk and it froze hard to the bottom. Last night it being New Year and very cold too we had a glorious eggnogg. The Macon companies are getting ready to go into camp Tuesday so as to be in readiness to leave on short notice. The Yankees are going to try the James Island "on to Charleston." Meade + Lee, Grant + Johnston have gone into winter quarters, consequently all is quiet along the lines.

Sunday January 3d 18634: Cold and clear Mercury 22° at 8½. Put out 3 cups of milk and they froze elegant. No news. Communion day. My Back is not running much at all. Father bought a uniform for Thomas yesterday at 500 dollars.

Monday January 4th 1864: Cloudy and drizzly. Mercury 40° in the house. Pasted in my scrapbook all the morning. Frank Baxter left for Sparta. Cousin David Wiley stayed to tea with us last night. I do not think he is much changed. We all received invitations to Cousin George's Wedding on the 6th. Green came up with ribs and Backbones. Thomas' uniform is beautiful. I am afraid I am going to have pain in my leg again but I hope with a night's rest I will be better.

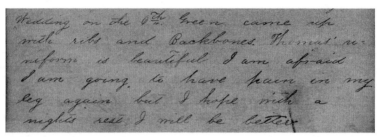

Tuesday January 5th 1864: Rained from day 'till 11 AM. Gen Forrest has been promoted to a Maj Gen. The M[acon] B[attalion] goes into camp today. Two or three regiments [of] state troops have passed through here on the way to Savannah. Mr. Kemp's among them. I am better of that pain in my leg today. "I am the boomerang" said the Wild Man!

Wednesday January 6th 1863: It has drizzled rain—a cold searching rain—all the morning and as I write at 3 P.M. it looks like it would blow off cold. The order for the Battalion to leave is countermanded. They are in camp at the Fair Ground. Thomas had rather go to Savannah than go into camp here. No news. . . . Green + Daniel came up.

January 7th: We went to bed last night expecting to find it clear but it still is very gloomy—has rained all the morning. Every body but me has gone to Cousin Eliza's to a family dining, given to cousin George and his bride. It is miserable weather for dinings. Major Scherck[1] is here from Johnston's Army to attend to the packing and forwarding of 25,000 lbs, of bacon sold to the Army at $1 per lb. This makes 50000 lbs. they have sold. They gather it up by exchanging cloth for it.[2] No news. Daniel returned to Houston, leaving Green. My back is very weak and hurts me when I sit up. Gen Hardee has again taken command of his "Old Corps." It is rumored that Wilmington is to be attacked + not Charleston.

Friday January 8th 1864: The sun rose under a cloud + a few scattering snow flakes fell + it looked like it would be a very bad day, but toward 11 oclock it cleared off +

---

1   Maj. Isaac Scherck was on Gen. Thomas Hindman's staff and later with Gen. Hood's headquarters.

2   The Macon Manufacturing Company was attempting to work within a highly inflationary economy by using a barter system. John Gresham would trade a yard of cloth for a pound of bacon, which he would then sell to the Army of Tennessee for $1.00 per lb. He also donated 5,000 pounds of bacon to the poor in Bibb County.

turned very cold. Cousin George + Cousin Kate, Cousin Jimmie + Cousin Eliza, Miss Eugenia Calhoun, Misses Florence + Tallulah Snider, and Aunt Sarah dined with us today. We had enough coal to make a nice fire in the parlor. We are all invited to tea tonight at Cousin Jack's and to dine at Mrs. Snider's tomorrow. There is a story now coming out in the *Daily Telegraph* called "Nellie Norton, or Southern Slavery + the Bible" by Mr. Goulding. It is supposed an attempt to prove the divine origin of slavery.[3]

Saturday January 9th 1864: Clear and very cold. Nobody is going to Mrs. Snider's. Every body went to Cousin Jack's to tea last evening. Mercury 18°.

Sunday January 10th 1864: Cloudy and cold. Sleeted a little twice in the day. Major Scherck + Mr. Herritt stayed to tea with us last night and we had a very pleasant evening. Mr. Herritt is one of Morgan's men + was with him in his raid into Ohio. Major Scherck is commissary of Hindman's Corps. He is a Pole and lived in Miss. before the war. . . . Mr. Goulding is not the author of "Nellie Norton." Morgan is in Richmond + on his arrival he had a grand reception. Mother is sick. No news.

Monday January 11th 1864: Cloudy + Cold. The Metre [thermometer] froze last night for the second time this winter. Mercury 28°. Mother is sick in bed. Wood is 20 dollars for a 2 horse load. Ours is out. There is but little probability that the Battallion will be ordered off at all as the term of service is out in February. Commenced to rain at 3 and rained the rest of the P.M. Aunt Ann called. Received letters from Grandma and Sallie. Aunty is very sick.

Tuesday January 12th 1864: Cloudy. Drizzled rain in the A.M. Thomas came to dinner. Miss Lou Upshaw [Minnie's friend] stayed all night with Minnie. Mother sick. We [are] in her room. Father started to Houston but concluded not to go. Sent on the money (8 dollars) to take the *Whig* for 3 months.

Wednesday January 13th 1864: Miserable drizzly day. Father left for Houston. "The Attack on Wilmington" has begun. The severity + discomfort of the weather for 10 days past had been without a precedent. I think the Yankees have, in Wilmington, struck the weakest and one of the most important points in the Country and if they are as pertinacious as they were at Charleston, they will take it.[4]

---

3   One of LeRoy few references regarding the overall concept of one human owning another. His entry implies skepticism (unlike many in the South) that slavery was divinely ordained or could be proven.

4   LeRoy has developed a solid grasp of the war effort and the valuable geographic points within the Confederacy. The news, however, was false. There was no effort at that time to take Wilmington.

Thursday January 14th 1864: Cloudy + "drizzly." Rained in the night. Thomas stayed all night here. Nought now. It has not rained though. The air is damp + the ground sloppy. The Yankees are shelling Charleston. I suppose to attract attention from other points. Nothing from Wilmington at all.

Friday Jan. 15th 1864: Cloudy and warm. When we went to bed, the moon + stars were shining so bright, we thought sure this morning would be bright + clear; but the heavens are still of "leaden hue," mayhap a shade brighter than yesterday. It will clear off, for even as I write, the clouds do break + scatter. Mother has walked down town. Congress has been in secret session for two or three days, on the currency + taxes. There are no movements of any sort in the Army. Nought from Wilmington. 160 shells thrown into Charleston. Mother bought 3 dresses; a calico costing 80 dollars for Minnie; and one for her costing an even 100; another purple dress, a sort of worsted + silk. Mary bought 2 oranges + gave them to me.

Saturday, Jan'y 16th 1864: Clear, bright, lovely day. Old Sol, after strenuous efforts, has dispersed the clouds, and it is cold + dry. Thomas stayed all night with us. There is no news. I read *The 12th Night, or What You Will* in Shakespeare. Congress is still in secret session, has not matured anything yet. Father returned from Houston. They Killed 20 hogs with an average weight of 155 lbs. Read *2 Gents of Verona*.

Sunday Jan 17th 1864: Clear + Balmy day. The Yankees are going to raise 1000000 men to liberate their prisoners in Richmond. This is their latest sensation. W.M. Thackeray is dead.[5] Bob Martin was stabbed + killed down town Friday evening about dark. It occurred near the State Bank.[6]

Monday January 18th 1864: Cloudy and cool. Drizzled a little in the A.M. Father took dinner at the Camp today. Thomas' company gave [the] dinner. Cut down that Black Jack by Julia Ann's door. The wagon came up with Kemp, Jake, Frank, + Dave to go to Savannah, but they got here too late for the cars. Brought 2 bags of flour, spare-ribs, and back-bones.

Tuesday January 19th 1864: Clear and cold. Sleeted a little last night after supper. The wagon returned home with the darkeys. Am reading *Philip Rollo, or the Scottish Musketeers: A Tale of the Danish Wars*. Slightly "blood + thunder." Cousin Eliza + Aunt Sarah called. Thomas' term of service is out in February + unless Father can get a place for him, he'll have to go [into the Confederate army as] a private.

---

5 Renowned British author and satirist William Makepeace Thackeray.

6 Bob Martin was a local Macon man. Such violent incidents, together with robbery and arson, were becoming more common as soldiers and civilians from across the South arrived in Macon.

Wednesday January 20th 1864: Clear and cool. Father was taken sick before breakfast and had to have Dr. Hall see him. In the evening I rode down to the Camp to see the dress parade. We had a good time and I supped with the Major Jones. Charleston is shelled steadily. There's no news. Made gingercakes.

Thursday January 21st 1864: Clear and beautiful day. Fathers Birth-Day. Father received a letter from Gen Joseph Johnston about the Bacon the Factory sent the Army. Our horses were sent down to get exemption papers today. Congress seems to be in complete quandary as to what is to be done on the currency + taxes. The Yankees are eclipsing all their efforts to get an army, so as to be able to take Richmond and Atlanta early next spring.

Friday January 22nd 1864: Clear and frosty morning. No news. A few troops (Bates' Brigade) have reinlisted for the war in the Army "above." Mobile it is feared will be attacked. Read *Sword + Gown* by the Author of *Guy Livingstone*, a book with bad morals. Macon is said to be [did not complete]. Went out in the P.M. + trimmed the Scuppernong vine. While out there Father dropped his ring and did not miss it till night.

Saturday January 23d 1864: Clear and cool. Allen found Father's ring. Arch returned to Houston. This has been a lovely day, as balmy as spring. There is not a bit of news and everything is comparatively quiet. Charleston is being shelled, + little or no damage is occasioned.

Sunday January 24th 1864: Clear and bright. Col J. H. Lamar joined our church. Mrs. Fears was buried today. Jake + Ned are here: runaway.

Monday January 25th 1864: Clear and bright. Thomas + Mother to have his deguareotype taken, have gone down town.[7] Mother had a China tree set out in front of the storeroom. Congress, which every one thought would do something for the currency seems to be in complete perplexity on the subject.

Tuesday Jan 26th 1864: Clear and cool. Thomas did not have his Ambrotype taken yesterday + goes again today. . . . Father left for Houston. Made molasses candy. Went out + had the trees trimmed + peas planted.

Wednesday Jan 27th 1864: Clear and warm. This warm weather has set the scuppernong vines to bleeding + the buds to swelling. Thomas slept here last night. I

7   The daguerreotype, named for Louis-Jacques-Mandé Daguerre (1787-1851), was a method for fixing an image to a chemically treated copper surface. By the late 1850s, the daguerreotype was generally replaced by the ambrotype or tintype. These reversed images of the subject, who had to remain still for the length of time needed to correctly expose the image, were not reproducible.

went down to camp at noon + stayed all the evening. Dined with Cousin Jack: had sponge cake + wine sauce for dinner. I took my wagon + rode out to see dress parade.

Thursday Jan 28th 1864: Clear and warm. Spent a bad night: had pain in my hip. There is no war news, but the best of news is the reinlisting of our troops I have a pain in my hip, which gives me some trouble. The Battalion is to go out of camp at the end of the week. Mother went to the S[oldiers] R[elief] Society this evening.

Friday January 29th 1864: Clear and warm. Took an anodyne pill last night, and did not go to sleep till two oclock. I have suffered a great deal today: the pain is just like Rheumatism, and worse than all is in my strait leg. Read *Marius* [the] IIId No. of Victor Hugo's *Les Misérables*.[8] Father arrived on the RR from Houston + Willis by the wagon, bringing the 1st new hams.

Saturday Jan 30th 1864: The pain in my hip has been very bad all day. I took a Dover's Powder last night and got along pretty well. In the PM we all went into the vegetable garden to trim the peach trees. The Macon Battalion, Major Jones Cmdg [Commanding], went out of camp and was disbanded.

Sunday Jan 31st 1864: Cloudy and warm. My leg just hurt me bad enough to keep me awake last night, and still aches a little. The cavalry of Longstreet's army seems to be the only thing in activity now, and it captures + whips the Yankees sometimes + gets whipped sometimes. The Senate has passed a sweeping Military Bill + if made a law will "wake snakes" certain. It raises the conscript age to 50 and greatly reduces exemptions.

Monday February 1st 1864: Cloudy and warm. Took a Dover's Powder. My leg hurt me very bad. It is much worse at night. Mother and Thomas out trimming + cutting down trees in the front yard. Cut down 4 evergreen + a magnolia.

Tuesday February 2nd 1864: Clear and bright. Stayed out the major part of the morning looking at Howard planting potatoes. The grape-vine is bleeding sadly and we don't know how to stop it. My leg is a good deal better today.

Wednesday Feb 3d 1864: Clear and cold. Turned cold in the night and there is ice today. Father's darkeys left for Savannah the other night. P.W.A [is] in town. There is no news.

---

8   LeRoy is referring to the third volume of Hugo's five-volume *Les Misérables*.

Thursday February 4th 1864: Clear and cool. Mr. Kemp arrived from Savannah this morning, the "State Gaurd" having disbanded. Green arrived with the last hog meat of the season + 6 partridges for me. Made me two nice envelope patterns, and made 29 envelopes for Father.[9] Received a long letter from Grandma, saying that she would leave last Tuesday for Athens. . . . Aunty is still in bed. Lee's Army is coming up to the scratch nobly, and many regiments are reinlisting. Mother bought a pan for my back + a dishpan, the one costing 46 and the other $16. Mr. Bates has got about 40 scholars and I don't know hardly any of them even by sight. Minnie is trying to play graces under Thomas' tutelage.[10] Every body down town and I alone occupying myself looking for my scissors which have been lost since Sunday.

Friday February 5th 1864: Foggy early in the morning; bright towards 10 A.M. Half filled the Mucillage bottle. Mother and Thomas threw graces 800 times. Lincoln has called for 500000 men! The present lull in the war is the most impressive time ever known in history. The North is gathering her gigantic legions to hurl them against us in the early spring. Meanwhile we are collecting our energies as best we may to meet them. If we fail none will live to see peace dawn again. If we succeed + the North rallies from the shock, the war again is interminable: but if she fails to come to time, a bright and glorious future awaits us. These are my own opinions. I have an abiding Faith that we will yet be a free people.

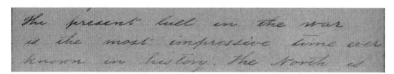

Saturday February 6th 1864: Cloudy and cool. Minnie and Thomas went to a party at Mr. Ralston's last night and stayed until 4 this morning. The Yankees under [Gen.] Sherman are moving from Vicksburg to take Mobile.[11] Congress is coming to a conclusion on the three great bills: the tax, Currency, + Military. There was a little

9 It is unclear whether he is engaged in making envelopes because it is becoming difficult to find them, it is something to keep LeRoy busy, or both.

10 Graces, a game dating back to before the American Revolution, involved two people, each holding two sticks, tossing a hoop adorned with ribbons back and forth using only sticks to do so.

11 The Meridian Campaign (February 3-28, 1864), something of a prelude to Sherman's March to the Sea later that same year. This combined infantry and cavalry march across central Mississippi inflicted substantial damage upon the area around Meridian, which Sherman reached on February 14. His cavalry, however, was defeated and Sherman withdrew.

engagement near Newburn [New Bern] the other [day] in which we licked a party of Yankees and 280 prisoners. Made Gingercakes.

Sunday February 7th 1864: Turned cold again yesterday evening. No news. A great many reports of the evacuation of Knoxville are afloat, but they are not credited. The small-pox is raging there among the Federals. It seems to me that as I grow older, the weary, monotonous life I lead seems more burdensome. If I just had some regular employment, I could get along better: sleeping + eating embrace all my time. "Nabb" [a plantation slave] arrived yesterday. Got a bag of Graham Flour yesterday. The most conflicting accounts of the condition and "morale" of our army at Dalton are rife. One says "There is not 5000 fit for duty," another declares "that the men were never in better spirits." All croakers believe the 1st: good and true men, the last.

Monday February 8th 1864: Clear and cold. Occupied myself all the morning doing nothing and am much fatigued thereby. Wrote to "Blackmar + Bro." about pictures of Generals. The *Richmond Whig*, which we sent for, a month ago, has not come and we have given it up. To send money by mail, nowaday's, is a bad business. *The Daily Confederate* is a very good paper now, Dr. L.F.W. Andrews having sold it to a Mr. H.G. Flash. Cousin David Wiley was sent up to his company, at Rome, under arrest for overstaying his furlough. Poor Dear Uncle Dick! Today we heard the sad news of his having been taken prisoner in a foraging expedition: surrounded by a party of 92 Yankees in a log house himself, and the small detail of men with him had no alternative but to surrender. Green came up with peas and Goobers. Sallie, Wilson, + Grandma have left for Athens. *The Field and Fireside* has improved of late, having changed proprietors.

Tuesday February 9th 1864: Clear and cool. Pasted in my scrapbook. Read *The House on the Rock*.

Wednesday Feb 10th 1864: Clear and cold. At 11 A.M. rode down town to Mr. Peruff's, and Thomas sat for his Photograph. Went out in the Streets and witnessed a fight: Emmett Cochrane vs. Jimmie Burton. Saw my new cousin Julia Wiley, for the 1st time.[12] Maj Butler from Dalton is here to get more Bacon. Mother bought a round comb for Minnie and gave 20 dollars for it.

Thursday Feb 11th 1864: Clear and cool. Thomas left for Athens. He has been detailed as clerk in the enrolling office there. We were all sorry to see him go, for he will in some shape or other be away for many a long day to come. We feel glad to think he is

12 Sarah Juliette Reid, Cousin Charlie's new bride.

going to Athens where he can be with Grandma. I am reading *St. Denis*. The Military Bill has passed. It is rather muddy as in the telegrams, but it retains all the men who are in service between 18 + 45 for the war, and the exemptions are few. It's not a law yet. The President has issued an address to the Army in which in which he says that "while we are strengthening, the enemy are growing weaker"? The Yankees have apparently commenced an attack by land on Charleston, via James Island. Father unable to go down town, in the P.M. in consequence of a severe headache. I stayed out, from 4 P.M. till dark, looking at them planting potatoes.

Friday Feb 12th 1863/4: Clear and cool. Father sat up with Colonel deGraffenried last night, who is very sick. The Yankees under Sherman are advancing with boldness, and leave occupied Brandon, Miss., our forces under Polk falling back, for some deep strategetical purpose, the upshot of which, is to be the capture or rout of Sherman. We will see. The Yankees landed at Jacksonville, Fla. the other day, and are advancing into the interior. A rumor says they have been repulsed by Gen Finnegan.[13]

Sunday February 14th 1863/4: Clear and pleasant. Wednesday, Congress adjourns and yet the three principal measures not matured. Minnie got enough dough-nuts. Cousin 'Zeke is wounded and Ira [Fort] missing in the recent fighting in Miss. Cousin Helen is here to see about it. Read *The Boys Own Guide*. Mobile is threatened by Gen Banks, who has landed at Pascagoula. This is St. Valentines day.

Monday February 15th 1864: Cloudy and cool. Father left on the R.R. for Houston. The wind blew a gale after 11 oclock and it rained quite hard in the evening. I read *Millers Schools and Schoolmasters* all day. My back feels weak and bad enough.

Tuesday February 16th 1864: Clear and windy. Cousin Addie and Cousin Sallie Margaret arrived this morning. Mother received a letter from Tom saying he had arrived safe minus his haversack. Sherman is pushing all before him in Mississippi. I had the Rheumatism in my leg last night. It is blowing off very cold.

Wednesday February 17th 1864: Very cold indeed. Cousin Helen and Aunt Sarah dined with us. My throat is miserably sore and I feel badly. This is the first bad sore-throat I ever had. Rubbed with liniment. Howard fell off his chair in a sort of fit, probably caused by rush of blood to his head, and was insensible some time. Cousin Eliza's horses are impressed. The Tax, Currency and Military Bill have passed and are

---

13 Union troops were marching inland from Jacksonville, Fla, an area that provided substantial provisions to the Confederate cause. Gen. Joseph Finegan was in command of the Southern forces.

sufficiently sweeping.[14] All between 17 + 50 are to be Soldiers. Thomas' photograph came home and I am so disappointed in it. It is a failure. (Man that is born of woman is of few day + pall.)[15]

Thursday February 18th 1864: Bitter cold and Cloudy. A few scattering snowflakes fell about dusk. My throat continues very sore. Every body is frightened at the Currency bill: several stores closed.

Friday February 19th 1864: Bitter cold. Throat a little better. I Received a letter from Thomas and from Uncle Edge. Mother + Cousins have gone to Cousin Eliza's. We have been outgeneralled in Mississippi completely and the march of Sherman has been a triumphal one. Wrote to Tom.

Saturday February 20th 1864: Very Cold. Mercury 27° in the passage [hallway] yesterday, it 16° in some parts of town. Every body except Minnie went down town. No News: but the hateful mystery in Miss. is enough.

Sunday February 21st 1864: Cloudy and moderately cold. Cousin Adaline sick and not able to get out of bed. We made the table walk last night [a parlor game] and had a good deal of fun with it. My throat is well and my cold has settled in my head. Uncle LeRoy arrived from Flint River. For the last 4 days we have paid 15 dollars a load for wood. Pretty decent tax that for the privilege of keeping warm.

Monday February 22nd 1864: Cloudy and cool. Cousins Addie + Sallie spend today with Cousin Eliza. "Tis' years since we last met."

Tuesday February 23d 1864: Clear and pleasant. Our forces under Gen Finnegan gave the Yankees a whipping near Lake City, Fla. on the 20th. They were routed with heavy loss. Our loss 200. We took 5 pieces of Artillery + a large number of small arms.[16] Hardee's Corps has gone to reinforce Polk and a large battle in Ala. may yet be fought. Grant is in Huntsville and it is thought will try to march down and form a junction with Sherman. Longstreet is reported to be moving [in East Tenn.].

Wednesday February 24th 1864: Clear and pleasant. Cousin Ada, Cousin Sallie, + Uncle LeRoy left at daybreak, and we are alone once more. I have been engaged in

14 The State Income Tax Act increased the levy rates for taxation, while the Currency bill gave a 1/3 discount to all paper notes of $5.00 or more.

15 LeRoy is quoting Job, Ch. 14:1 of the King James version of the Bible. He shortened the passage. His notation "+ pall" is a reference to the heavy cloth that covers a coffin.

16 The Battle of Olustee or Ocean Pond (Feb. 20, 1864). Southern reinforcements from Charleston arrived to repulse Gen. Truman Seymour's Union advance from Jacksonville. Confederate losses totaled 946, and Union losses about double that. It was the largest fight of the war in Florida.

reading *Lady Audley's Secret*, by the author of *Aurora Floyd*, and think it very interesting: yet I do not admire that style of book, a mystery from A to Z. Robert Audley was a good fellow and I wish there had been no "Clara" and that he had married "Alicia." "My Lady" is a finely drawn character. I wonder if in every day life there are not women and men who have no Robert Audley to hunt them down, who carry some such dismal secrets to their graves and are thought to be models. Thackeray thought so, but he was a cynic.[17]

Thursday February 25th 1864: Clear and bright. The Honey Peach and the Plum trees are in bloom. The Address of Congress, just published as a model in its way. "The Battle of Ocean Bend [Pond]" Florida was a large affair. The Yankees were 10000 strong. [Gen] Thomas is moving on Johnston and a fight is imminent. From the Potomac to the Rio Grande, the Yankees are advancing. We Received notice from Thomas today saying that he would have to go to the Army and it saddens our heart to think of it. Am reading *Things + Men in Europe* loaned to me by Mr. Wills. Planted Chufas.[18] This has been a very balmy, beautiful spring day.

Friday February 26th 1864: Clear and pleasant day. A battle seems to be imminent in Upper Ga: there has been heavy skirmishing. Sherman is going to occupy Mississippi permanently. Gen Bragg is assigned to duty in Richmond as 2nd in Comd [Command] to the President. Howard left in the buggy for Houston. We are fighting at Dalton [in northern Ga.].[19]

Saturday February 27th 1864: Clear and cool. Sherman is retreating: the enemy are falling back to Chattanooga. After skirmishing + feeling our position, they concluded not to give battle. I am reading *The Cruise of the Betsy* [by] Miller. Allen in bed today with a cold. There had been no *Republican* for 10 days with 1 exception, and I do not know what is the matter.

Sunday February 28th 1864: Clear and beautiful day. Father has subscribed to the *Memphis Appeal* and the *Richmond Whig* but neither have come, so uncertain is the mail. Read *Life of Goldsmith*, [by] Irving. Julia Ann in bed with tooth ache. The yankees have retired from Dalton, but it is thought will return soon. Gen Hood has gone to Dalton to take command of Hindman's Corps. I have had a cold for two weeks and it is hard

17 LeRoy's ability to apply the fictional plot to actual life demonstrates his intellectual growth.

18 A plant that produces a tuber, or nut. Also called chufa sedge or nut grass, it was used to feed hogs and turkeys.

19 The First Battle of Dalton (Feb. 22 and 27, 1864) was a demonstration in northern Georgia by Union Gen. Thomas against Johnston's Confederate defenses. Thomas withdrew after a series of skirmishes.

for me to get rid of it. . . . Mr. Douglas,' Miss Sloane's Husband, funeral was preached in our church yester eve. General Hindman has resigned overslaughed by Hood.

Monday Feb 29th 1864: Clear and cool. Made envelopes. My cold hangs on to me yet. I have had it three weeks. I cough a good deal at night. Mother is making Father some Macon Mills shirts. The 1st No. of the *Memphis Appeal* came today, dated the 28th. [Cost is] 2 Months. 8 doll[ars].

Tuesday March 1st 1864: Cloudy, and warm enough to be without a fire. Took a Dover's Powder for my cold, but it is no better. Allen seems to have chills and fever. Mother got a letter from Thomas saying that Captain Blackshear's orders had been countermanded + for the present he would not leave Athens. I wrote him today. . . . Rained nearly all the evening, and it is raining now at 8PM. No *Republican* for two weeks! Strange! The retreat and disappointment of Sherman is owing to the bravery and daring of Forrest, who fought and routed the cooperating column of cavalry, although they were 3 to his 1.[20] All honor to him! Father reading the *Appeal*; Mother— *Lady Audley's Secret*; I writing on the Floor, and Minnie in Mother's room studying.

Wednesday March 2nd 1864: Cloudy: blew off cold in the night. Maj Gen [James] Patton Anderson has been assigned as commander of our troops in Fla. My cold and cough continue to annoy me, and do not get any better. The *Savannah Republican* came again today. Longstreet is reported on the move; where, no one knows. Maj Gen Patton Anderson + [Gen. William] Bates just made.

Thursday March 3d 1864: Clear and cool. Stayed on my wagon nearly all the morning, watching Howard plant cucumbers. The Peach trees are advancing rapidly, nearly half of them are in bloom. There is no news + people, Father says, are busily engaged in funding money to pay the [increase in] taxes. I received a letter from Thomas today. Yesterday evening I received a letter from Cousin Annie, by Mrs. Fort, and with it the pictures of the Confederate Gens as a present from Cousin Howard. Mother has a sore-throat. Allen is up and at his post again. My cold has settled down into a cough and it annoys me a great deal at night.

Friday March 4th 1864: Cloudy and cool. No news. My cough worried me a good deal in the night. Some Yankee raiders came in 6 miles of Richmond the other day.[21]

---

20 Forrest defeated Smith at the Battle of Okolona, Miss., on February 22, 1864.

21 The Kilpatrick-Dahlgren Raid was a failed attempt by Union Gen. Judson Kilpatrick and Col. Ulric Dahlgren to get into Richmond and free prisoners there. Dahlgren was killed, and papers found on his body indicated another purpose of the raid was to burn the city and assassinate Jefferson Davis and his cabinet.

Stayed on my wagon this evening looking at Howard work in the garden. Milo came up with a quarter of beef, groundpeas, turkeys, +c. Sherman is near Jackson again: he accomplished nothing but the destruction of some property and the humiliation of a few defenceless women and old men. The Bombardment of Fort Powell, Mobile, continues, but without results. Commenced to read *First impressions of* England and its People by Hugh Miller, loaned to me by Mr. Wills.

Saturday March 5th 1864: Clear and cool. Rained a very little toward day. There is news of another fight in Fla., the cavalry being principally engaged. No particulars. Mother got a letter from Thomas. Father sold 73 bushels of groundpeas at 8 dollars. Genl Buckner has been appointed to Hood's old division. Made Gingercakes.

Sunday March 6th 1864: Clear and splendid day. Mrs. Mitchell sent me *The Life of Capt. King*, a tract by Dr. Stiles. The Yankees have raised the siege of Charleston. Both sides are concentrating in Florida. General Beauregard is at Lake City.[22] . . .

Monday March 7th 1864: Clear in the morn, cloudy toward dark. Wrote to Cousin Howard acknowledging the pictures C.S. Gens. Made envelope pattern. Saw to the planting of Cantelopes. The Hyacinths are in bloom and look very pretty. Pasted in my scrapbook. Mother has a bad cough.

Tuesday March 8th 1864: Clear and bright. It was drizzling rain when we retired to our "nocturnal repositories" and looked like it would rain today. Father left for Houston. Recd a letter from Thomas to Father. I have had a dull headache all day and if it does not improve tomorrow I must take some medicine for it. My cold is no better.

Wednesday March 9th 1864: Cloudy and warm. My head still aching. Cousin Eliza had a baby, a girl.[23] No news. Mother and I have both got coughs and we cough all day + night. Macon is funding 500000 per diem. The Old White hen came off with 8 chickens. Another hen, named "Cora" commenced to set. Took Blue Mass.

Thursday March 10th 1864: Cleared up at 10 A.M. Rained a great part of the night. Just after breakfast it poured down. I wrote to Thomas. My head is better. Did not sleep well. Today the windows are open + we sit without fires. Mother in bed. Mr. C.W. Howard lectures in the Presbyterian Church tonight on Women of the 2nd Revolution.[24]

---

22 The Union siege of Charleston was not raised, and Gen. Beauregard remained in command there.

23 Anna D. Snider.

24 Many Southerners considered the Civil War to be a "Second War of Independence."

Friday March 11th 1864: Cloudy and warm. Rained in the night. Father arrived just as we were eating supper last night from Houston. Brought me 6 partridges. Mother up but she still coughs badly. *Whig* of the 7th came, the first no. [of the] 3 m[onth] subscription.

Saturday March 12th 1864: Clear and pleasant. Mother was quite sick all night. Gov Brown's message is more hostile than ever to the Confederate Government + will do a great deal of harm no doubt, and rejoice the hearts of the Yankees. Minnie wrote to Thomas, and Father wrote and enclosed a letter from Gen W.H.T. Walker offering Thomas the position of clerk to his Adjutant General. Uncle John offers a place with Gen [States Rights] Gist, so he has his choice of the two.

Sunday March 13th 1864: Clear and cool. Mother unable to go to church. My cold is well: it hung on a long time though. . . .

Monday March 14th 1864: Cloudy and cool. I received a letter from Thomas dated Decatur, Ga where he had come to bring a deserter. The deserter jumped off the train, while the car was going full speed. Two soldiers from the Hospital came here this evening and walking in without ringing the bell informed Mother that they had come to take supper with her: but supper was not ready and so they had to go away without it.

March 15th Tuesday 64: Clear and cool. Mr. Kent McKay stayed to tea with us last night. It is turning cooler fast. . . . Mother has gone to prayermeeting. Recognition ghosts again stalk abroad, and France will recognize us through the Mexicans. I do not think this has the least foundation and its origin is in the fertile brain of the Yankees. Maximilian, the Emperor of the Mexicans, is on his way to Mexico. The new disease "Spotted Fever" is increasing and there has been a good many deaths. 6 or 7000 Yankees are now located in a pen near Americus and they escape in numbers + are roaming through the country.[25]

Macon March 16th 1864:

My Dear Sir:

The weather here turned quite cold in the night and there was ice which makes us fear for our fruit to night if it is not already injured. Our wagon came up last evening with supplies from the plantation. Cousin Jenks Jones

---

25 Camp Sumter, more infamously known as Andersonville, was about eight miles northeast of Americus, Ga.

took tea with us last night: is here attending court. Ira Fort is not a prisoner; has come in. Cousin Zeke is safe, slightly wounded in hand.

Thursday March 17th 1864: Clear and bitter cold. Last night at 9 O'clock the Mercury was 28° + this morn at 8.A.M. was 20°. This is the most severe cold ever experienced in March. The Peaches and Plums, being in the most tender stage, are every one killed. The worst part of it is that it's so universal. Its nearly cold enough to freeze the seed in the ground. Just at this time it is most disastrous on acct of the dearth of provisions, but it being purely providential it becomes us to submit cheerfully. Lt Gen Kirby Smith has been promoted to be [full] General and Military Dictator of the Trans-Mississippi Dept.[26]

Friday March 18th: Cold and Clear. A million dollars was funded here yesterday.[27] Dr. Clark, of Richmond Co, sat nearly all the afternoon with us. . . . Made 12 envelopes from 10 oclock. The Recognition rumors are again blown over. Gen Grant is comd in chf [commander in chief of] U.S. Armies[28] and Meade is to be relieved soon. Colonel L.Q.C Lamar spoke here last night.[29] All is quiet at Dalton, + Gens Hardee + Hood are outvieing each other in drills + Reviews. Hindman's, Stewart's, Cheatham's, Stevenson's, Bates', Cleburne's, Walker's divisions form the Army, in all 35000 men? This is the common estimate. Ate Sorghum Candy.

Saturday March 19th 1864: Clear and warm again, but alas! Alas! The mischief's done. Mother got a letter from Thomas. Uncle John is in Athens. He + T[homas] leave for Macon Monday A.M. Mrs. Fort sent us some Georgia Syrup + it is very nice indeed.

Sunday March 20th 1864: Cloudy and warm. 1100 more of our prisoners have arrived in Richmond and they are to continue to come as long as there are no further hitches.[30] Rained a little in the evening. Read *Laneton Parsonage*. Grant is marshalling his forces in upper Ga. He is the big man of the Yankees and they laud him to the skies.

26 A tongue-in-cheek reference to the fact that the Trans-Mississippi was so far away and disconnected from Richmond that Gen. Smith could essentially do whatever he pleased.

27 Although not clear, LeRoy is likely referring to the new taxation revenues set by the Confederate Congress.

28 U. S. Grant was promoted to lieutenant general (highest rank in the Union army) and brought east to Washington to command all the Union armies. He now answered only to President Lincoln.

29 Col. Lucius Quintus Cincinnatus Lamar II, James Longstreet's cousin, was sent by President Davis to advocate on behalf of the Confederacy, which was why he was in Macon.

30 The exchange of soldiers was formally arranged in the Dix-Hill Cartel of July 1862. When the Confederates refused to exchange black soldiers who had once been slaves or their white officers, the

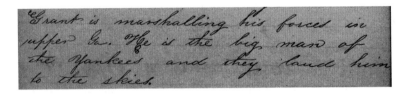

Monday March 21st 1864: A real rainy day. Rained all night and it has rained all day so hard that Minnie did not go College. The [Ga.] Legislature adjourned Sat. after passing resolutions offering peace to the Yankees, and protesting against the suspension of the *Hab[eas] Corp[us]* Act. I received a letter from Aunty enclosing an autograph of Gen J.E.B. Stuart and +c.

Tuesday March 22nd 1864: Rained and sleeted alternately from breakfast till noon, + it is very cold indeed. Thomas arrived at daybreak from Athens + Uncle John came down with him. Gen W[illiam]. F. Smith has been made Comdr [Commander] of the "Army of Potomac" U.S.[31] Grandma sent me some dried plums.

Wednesday March 23d 1864: Clear and very cold. Uncle John came up to see us this morning. My Back on a very very low average, has run 1000 teaspoonsfull since Feb. 11th 1863![32] General Joseph E. Johnston's official report of the "Siege of Vicksburg" is just out and scathes Pemberton just right and shows that he did not obey a single order of General Johnston's. It is very interesting, too. Uncle LeRoy came up on the P.W.R.R. yesterday evening and was back this morning early. His object was to find some money. The press for investing [in the Confederacy] is over. Julia Ann has been in bed since Monday, + Johnston [Johnson, a plantation slave] is reported unfit for duty. Mother has taken fresh cold and is really unwell today. Mrs. Edwards borrowed 3 *Eclectics*.

Thursday March 24th 1864: Clear and cold. Uncle Jno + Mr. Flinn took tea with us and Mr. F[linn] stayed all night with us. Mother went to bed sick with a cold + is in bed this morning. Mr. Flinn left for the Army this morning. Uncle Jno is looking better than I ever saw him. Uncle J[ohn] dined here.

Friday March 25th 1864: Rained all night: cloudy all day. Cousin Ada, Mother + I rode down town but were driven home by the rain. No news. Johnson is very ill indeed: has had a stroke of paralysis and is perfectly helpless. Cousin Ada arrived yesterday

---

Lincoln administration suspended exchanges on July 30, 1863. This burdened the South with tens of thousands of men it could not properly feed, clothe, or otherwise care for.

31 Gen. Meade remained in command of the Army of the Potomac, and would until the end of the war.

32 LeRoy estimates his abscesses have drained 1,000 teaspoons of fluid since February 11, 1863.

evening.[33] . . . Mother is knitting a pair of Gloves for Father + Cousin Ada has started a pair for Thomas. The Exchange of prisoners has stopped again + they are trying to get a place to put some officers here.[34]

Saturday March 26th 1864: Clear and cold. Cousin Ada + Minnie perambulated all over town this morning. Miss Sadie Rowland called + sat an hour + so. Received a letter from Auntie. Everybody gone to Mrs. Whittle's to see the dancing class.

Sunday March 27th 1864: Clear and splendid spring day. Dr. Stiles preaches today in our church on the "State of the Country." Johnson is a hopeless paralytic, so Dr. Fitzgerald says. Thomas has three positions offered him viz: Clerk to [Gen] Gist, Clerk to Maj Gen Walker's inspector, + a position in the Engineer Corps, and is in a quandary not knowing which to accept. Dr. S[tiles'] sermon was 2 hours + 40 minutes.

Monday March 28th 1864: Cloudy and raw. Mother + Cousin Ada are down town. Made 12 envelopes. Since January, I have made 144. No news at all. Commenced to rain after dinner and rained slowly all the P.M. . . .

Tuesday March 29th 1864: Clear and cloudy alternately. It rained hard in the night and to day the sun seems to be undecided whether to shine or not. Mother has a terrible bad cold. She + Cousin Ada have gone to Cousin Eliza's. I am reading *Jean Valjean*, the last of *Les Miserables*. Miss Sue Rowland sent me a piece of poetry, *Anthony to Cleopatra*, which she copied at my request. There is no news but great excitement in financial circles. . . .

Wednesday March 30th 1864: Cold windy disagreeable day. . . . No news at all. We had a big eggnog last night in honor of Uncle John. Mr. Kemp came up last night + went back this morning. I am not well at all: have a bad pain in my breast + back. Thomas has taken cold. *The Savannah Republican* is out + we do not care to renew the subscription.

Thursday March 31st 1864: Clear and cool. Tracy has got the measles. Father bought Tom a knapsack. Finished *Jean Valjean*, the saddest of books. Cousin Ada, Thomas + I rode all around town, out by the government works. Uncle John came round after tea to bid us all goodbye and we sat up past 11 oclock.

Friday March 32nd 1864: Cloudy and damp early in the morn + clear towards 10.A.M. Thomas took a Dover's Powder for his cold last night and today an eruption has appeared making us very uneasy as to its nature, he having had measles. We fear

---

33 Possibly Lucretia Adeline Johnson, a cousin through the Jones side of the family.

34 Union officers were eventually housed once more at the fairgrounds (Camp Oglethorpe).

scarlet fever. What chill, miserable, cold, weather it is for spring! One seems to be less able to bear it so late too.

Saturday April 2nd 1864: Clear windy and cold. Thomas has broke out with what Dr. Fitzgerald says is measles: How strange he should have it Twice![35] We are much relieved to know that it is not Scarlet Fever. No news. Mother, Cousin Ada, + Min are all down town.

Sunday April 3d 1864: Clear and cool. Thomas is broke out very thick. $13,519,600 funded here. Agusta beat Macon some having funded 15,700,000.[36] Forrest has captured + burned Paducah, Ky but rumor says has got licked. . . .

Monday Apr 4th 1864: Cloudy and windy. Rained in the night. Father sleeps upstairs with Thomas. Thomas is some better today. Am Reading *Jane Eyre*. Some one sent me a phamphlet copy of "[Gov.] Brown's Message"! The weather is inexplicable . . . raw and uncomfortable.

Tuesday April 5th 1864: Cloudy and raw. Miserable weather indeed for spring. Thomas is getting along well. . . . Read *Charms and Countercharms* all the P.M. Copied *Antony to Cleopatra* for Cousin Ada. The biggest battle of the war is to be fought in Virginia in May. Grant is marshalling his forces for the fray. All the seed in our garden has perished in the ground, and will have to be replanted. I am very sorry, for I took so much pains to have my cantelope seed well planted.

Major Gen J. Q Squeezliphantum.[37]

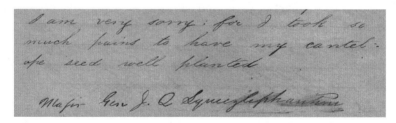

Wednesday April 6th 1864: 1 [2] year today since "Shiloh." Thomas not so well. Cool + clear. No news. . . . Cousin Sallie is afraid to come here on account of the measles.

---

35 Thomas' first case of measles must have been light, and it did not inoculate him from catching measles a second time.

36 Raising money for the Confederate cause.

37 LeRoy is engaging in word play, making up what he thinks is an amusing name for a general.

Thursday April 7th 1864: Rained a little in the morning. Clear from 12 to 4 P.M., then cloudy again. Heard from Uncle Richard through Grandma. He is at Rock Ild. [Island], Ill.[38] + treated kindly. Is pretty well. I copied the letter from Uncle R[ichard] and sent it to Uncle John. Thomas is better: sat up a little. . . . Gen Cobb is assigned to the duty of reorganizing the Reserve Corps C.S. with Head Qrs [Quarters] at this place [Macon].

Friday April 8th 1864: Cloudy, rained a little. This is Confederate Fast day. Thomas down stairs for the first time. Slept badly. Longstreet's Corps is at Petersburg, Va., so Tennessee is abandoned.[39]

Saturday April 9th 1864: Rained in the night. Cleared up after breakfast. Mother sick. . . . Thomas' suit + overcoat came home and fit nicely. No news at all.

Sunday April 10th 1864: Clear and windy. Communion Day. Mother unable to be out. No News. Vegetation is advancing rapidly notwithstanding; we've had no spring as yet.

Monday April 11th 1864: Clear and cool. Thomas and I played Backgammon on the front porch. . . .

Tuesday April 12th 1864: Clear and cool. I coughed very badly all yesterday and took a Dover's Powder last night. I feel most dull and stupid. Layed in the dark, in the Parlor + tried to sleep off the effects of the medicine. I am taking the measles; cough incessantly, took Brown Mixture for it.[40] . . . Mother making Thomas' flannel shirts. My breast is sore from coughing. Cousin Ada + Tom are playing Backgammon.

Wednesday April 13th 1864: Cousin Ada + Sallie went home today. A stone building near Dr. Emerson, and full of cotton, burned down today.[41] Last night took a Dover's Powder for my cough. About 3 oclock in the night was taken with toothache + I have suffered tortures today. Mother very unwell.

---

38 Rock Island was a prison in Illinois built on a swampy, 12-acre island in the Mississippi River. It housed 5,000 Confederates at its peak. Shortly after Uncle Richard arrived, rations were cut in retaliation for the treatment of Union POWs at Andersonville. His capture is described in the Feb. 8, 1864, entry.

39 Gen. James Longstreet returned to Virginia after his failed East Tennessee campaign to rejoin Gen. Lee's Army of Northern Virginia.

40 Another opiate mixture with extract of licorice root, tartar emetic, and spirit of ethyl nitrite glycerol, used as an expectorant.

41 Planters in Georgia were still planting cash crops like cotton instead of much-needed food crops, which exacerbated the food shortage. They hoped to slip the cotton through the blockade while prices were high.

> Tuesday April 12th 1864.
> Clear and cool I coughed very badly all yesterday and took a Dovers Powder last night. I feel most dull and stupid. Layed in the dark, in the Parlor + tried to sleep off the effects of the medicine. I am taking the measles; cough incessantly. took Brown Mixture for it.

Thur. Apr 14th 64: Took a Morphine pill and though I did not sleep well my tooth got easy. Father left for Houston. I broke out thick with measles this morn and have been very sick all day. Dr. came to see me but said I was doing first rate. Coughing a good deal. The Savannah darkies arrived + look well with the exception of Frank who is just getting over measles. Minnie came home after the 1st hour at College with symptoms of measles.

Friday Apr. 15th 1864: Minnie broke out and has been very sick all day. The Negroes went to Houston. Major Scherck called to see Father and Mother invited him to tea. Father came just at supper and mighty glad we were to see him. I have been better today and the eruption is not so thick.

Saturday April 16th 1864: Coughed a good deal in the night + took Brown Mixture for it. Minnie coughed incessantly + is very sick today. Eruption paler on me + cough better.

Sunday Apr 17th 1864: Clear and cool. Took a hot Milk Punch last night at bedtime. Minnie took Laudanum + is better today.[42] I am a good deal better and the eruption is disappearing. Ella "broke out" today. Our forces under Genl Chalmers have captured

---

42 Milk punch was milk mixed with brandy or whiskey. Laudanum contains the opium alkaloids (including morphine and codeine) and was a strong narcotic. It was used mainly to relieve pain and as a cough suppressant.

Fort Pillow[43] and killed nearly all the garrison. The Yankees have met with a disastrous defeat at Shreveport. No particulars.

Monday April 18th 1864: Minnie and I convalescing. It has vacillated between rain and sunshine all day. About dark there was a thunder storm with heavy rain + some hail. Nothing tastes natural to me and I have not a particle of appetite. Polk's forces have gone to Va: all travel stopped beyond So. Ca. Lee is stripping for the fight. Longstreet is in the right place + when the fight come off will be there. Thomas is in a sad quandary as to whether to accept the position as clerk to Major Dearing, Gist's Brig[ade], Or the position in the engineer Corps. It looks like we are to have no spring this year at all. No news I believe. Mary made nondescripts.

Tuesday Apr 19th 1864: Got out of bed and dressed. Rumored that Forrest has whipped the Yanks in 10 miles of Memphis. The extent of the fight at Shreveport, La. is not known, but the repulse of the Yankees is confirmed.[44] Minnie getting well. This is very cool weather for the season. Thomas has decided to accept the appointment in the Engineer Corps. Frost tomorrow.

Wednesday Apr. 20th 1864: Clear and cold. Not quite cold enough for frost. Forrest is stirring up the Yankees in W Tenn. Thomas' order to go to Va. in the Topographical Engineers of the Army Northern Va, came: so the die is cast . . . Minnie sat up today some, but is still troubled with her ear. I slept tolerably and, with the exception of a cold in the head, am well as usual. . . . No news—but all eyes are turned to Virginia where the preparations for the most decisive battle are rapidly going on. Thomas wrote to Uncle Jno. Heard through Cousin Eliza, that Cousin Mollie + Uncle Edmund had gone to Fla to see Cousin Jessie, who was very ill. Maj Harris is to be superceded at Comdr Concpts [Commander of the Conscripts] by a man named Brown. Scip [plantation slave] is dead. My cough troubles me a good deal yet and I am not troubled with appetite.

43 Gen. James R. Chalmers. The Battle of Fort Pillow (April 12, 1864) in Tennessee, where Gen. Nathan Bedford Forrest attacked the Union-held fort on the Mississippi River and killed, wounded, and captured the garrison, much of which consisted of African American troops. It is generally accepted that many were killed after the garrison surrendered.

44 The Red River Campaign (March 10-May 22, 1864). Federal forces under Nathaniel Banks, with a powerful naval armada, moved up the Red River in Louisiana intent on taking Shreveport. Banks' command was defeated by Gen. Richard Taylor's Confederates at Mansfield (Apr. 8), but beat back Southern attacks at Pleasant Hill (Apr. 9). The river fell, trapping his ships. The warships barely escaped by cleverly raising the level of the river with a dam. The entire campaign was a Union disaster.

Thursday April 21st 1864: Bright clear day. Last night at supper was taken sick, threw up and coughed badly. Went to bed + took a dose of Paragoric.[45] About 12 oclock in the night took another dose and I have slept 'till 11 AM + do not feel able to get out of bed. Allen taking measles. . . .

Friday April 22nd 1864: Clear and cool. No news. Slept tolerably and got out of bed again today. . . . Thomas went with Iola Lamar to a party at Mr. Moughan's and danced till 3 oclock. Have coughed a great deal today.

Saturday April 23rd 1864: Slept miserably: kept awake by cough. Took Paragoric at 2 oclock. . . . Went on my wagon for first time. Allen in bed. . . .

Sunday April 24th 1864: Rained in the night and till nearly 10 o'clock today. . . . Gen Hoke has stormed and taken Plymouth, N.C. with 2500 prisoners, large amounts [of] stores, 2 gunboats taken + burned. Victory complete.[46] The fight in Lousiana is beyond comparison muddy. Both sides claim to have taken 2000 prisoners + 20 cannon. All is mystery. Allen quite [incomplete]. Dr. F[itzgerald] called, pronounced him doing well. My cough is better.

Monday April 25th 1864: Clear and windy day. Slept badly: but feel a constant disposition to sleep in the day. Got a letter from Grandma. Miss Kate Rucker is very ill with pleurisy.[47] Minnie went to College.

Tuesday Apr 26th 1864: Clear and cool. Father was sent for to go to Houston + left with Dr. Fitzgerald this morn. The Pneumonia is going the rounds. Father hated to go mightily, especially as we are to have a dining. Cousin Juliet, Cousin Charlie, Aunt Ann, and Miss Ada Reid dined with us and Thomas presided. Every thing passed off well. I like Cousin Juliet mightily + her sister [Miss Ada] too.

Wednesday April 27th 1864: Clear and pleasant. We have been sitting without fires for 3 days. Vegetation has advanced wonderfully. The fig trees are killed nearly to the ground. Dr. Fitzgerald returned in the buggy. Peter [slave] died at 10 oclock last night. Ned down with [pneumonia]; Little Ben better; Martha very ill. . . . Taken with a sort of pain in my back at 4 oclock.

Thursday April 28th 1864: Clear and warm. Suffered with pain in my back till midnight; then took a Morphine pill and got easy about 1 AM. Felt so unwell that I did not get out of bed at all till about 5 oclock. Father arrived on the R.R. from the

45 Another tincture of opium, this time mixed with benzoic acid and anise oil, used to control diarrhea.

46 Gen. Robert F. Hoke led the successful attack on Plymouth, NC (Apr. 17, 1864).

47 Uncle Richard will marry Martha Catherine "Kate" Rucker on Aug. 9, 1865.

plantation. No one but Martha [slave] is dangerously ill. Cousin Annie + Mary left for home at half past 3. Mother sick after supper. Allen well again.

Friday April 29th 1864: Cloudy and a good deal cooler. Feel better today. No news. Stayed on my wagon a long time. The Exchange of prisoners is permanently stopped, it seems, and there is no prospect of its early resumption.[48]

Saturday April 30th 1864: Cloudy and warm. Minnie and Thomas went to hear *Hamlet* acted last night. We do not know whether the big fight is to be at Dalton [Ga.] or in Virginia, but from all appearances it is likely to be at both places.[49] I received a letter from Uncle John. Heard from the sick negroes: Martha, Ned + Chany, and they are no better. Martha worse.

Sunday April May 1st 1864: Cloudy and warm. Rained hard in the P.M. Minnie did not go to Church. Thomas pulled the remains of an Old black cat from under the front steps. Congress meets tomorrow. A battle expected at Dalton in a few days.

Monday May 2nd 1864: Clear and cool. Father went to Houston on the R.R. Yesterday we heard the sad news of Cousin Jesse Green's death in the Lake City hospital, Fla on the 13th of April. Cousin Eliza saw the resolutions of his company about him + sent it to us.[50] Cousin Eliza sent us some goodies, cake, custard, +c. Col W[ilia]m M. Browne has assumed command of the Conscripts. Allen sick with colic. Dr. called.

Tuesday May 3nd 1864: Clear and cold. Miserable weather. Too cold to be without a fire: too hot with one. Out of doors too cool in the shade, too hot in the sun. Heard from Father. Negros about the same.

Wednesday May 4th 1864: Clear and cool. Gen Kirby Smith's [Gen. Richard Taylor's] victory at Mansfield, La. on the 8th and 9th April is confirmed. We took 21 pieces artillery, small arms, stores, +c. Gens [Alfred] Mouton and [Thomas] Green killed on our side. Taylor commanded the centre; Walker and Mouton the wings; E. K. Smith directing all. Price whipped Steele: cut him to pieces! + took 4000 prisoners, 250

---

48 Stopping the exchange of prisoners left Uncle Richard a POW for the rest of the war.

49 This was a perceptive prediction because Gen. Grant intended to strike in several places at once, including Gen. Johnston in north Georgia and Gen. Lee in Virginia.

50 "Resolutions" were positive statements about Jesse from his soldier comrades, written and sent to families to ease their pain over the loss of a loved one.

wagons, +c. Such is the news + we swallow it all.[51] Enemy reported advancing on Lee. Rode down to the Brunswick Depot to meet Father and stayed in town an hour or so. Minnie came home from College with 6 wreaths on: crowned in honor of securing a Junior place. *The Savannah Republican* 3d [issue] came; subscribed to for 3 months.

Thursday May 5th 1864: Clear and pleasant. Julia Ann left for Houston to see her sister Martha, who is at the point of death. Nought news. Grant's whole force is reported on the move and a great battle is anticipated early next week.

Friday May 6th 1864: Clear and pleasant. The Yankees are making a demonstration on Dalton, but whether it is a feint or not is not known. Minnie in bed today. It is supposed that the biggest battle of the war is going on near the Old Chancellorsville battle-ground. Yesterday the enemy attacked us + Gen Lee says "we maintained our position by the blessing of God." Gen Jones + Stafford killed.[52]

Saturday ~~April~~ May 7th: Clear and warm. Minnie sick in bed. We are an anxious beyond measure about the battle in Va. I am afraid that we'll have to fall back to Richmond.

Sunday May 8th 1864: Clear and warm. . . . All day on the 6th, the fight between Lee + Grant raged, and General Lee says: "with God's blessing we were able to maintain our position." Gen Longstreet severely wounded; Gen Benning, Pegram, Stafford also w[ou]nded. General Jenkins killed. The 1st two by our own men in a time when there was a little confusion.[53] The Battle was not decided, both sides maintaining their respective positions, and as far as we know it was not renewed on the 7th. The Capt of the Gresham Rifles, Munch, killed. U.S. Gen Wadsworth is killed. General Lee says: "we mourn the loss of many brave officers + men." I do not think there is anything to discourage us: Grant has received a check, and it is the immense loss of life that we mourn over. The fighting was near the Chancellorsville battle-ground. All quiet at Dalton; but I am of the opinion that a fight will come off there this week. Banks is

---

51 Gen. E. Kirby Smith was the head of the Trans-Mississippi Department and did not command at the battle. Sterling Price defeated a Union effort under Gen. Frederick Steele in Arkansas to reinforce Banks in Louisiana during his Red River Campaign.

52 The Overland Campaign had begun. Gen. Grant attached himself to Gen. Meade's Army of the Potomac (Meade remained in charge of the army) and crossed the Rapidan River. Gen. Lee attacked the Federals in the Wilderness (May 5-7, 1864). The bloody two-day battle left 29,000 Union and Confederates killed, wounded, and captured. Gens. Leroy A. Stafford and John M. Jones were killed. This battle marked the beginning of what would be nearly constant fighting until the end of the war.

53 Gen. James Longstreet was severely wounded and Gen. Micah Jenkins killed in a friendly fire incident. Capt. Lewis Munch of Company A, 45th Georgia Infantry; Federal Gen. James S. Wadsworth was mortally wounded.

whipped out of his boots: has retreated to his starting place; lost 4 of 5 gunboats; a large number of stores, prisoners, and his army is demoralized for the campaign. "Victory! Liberty!" Texas is saved. Price has Gen Steele surrounded in Arkansas, and will whip him badly if he does not capture him.

Monday May 9th 1864: Clear and warm. Thomas and I went to see Aunt Ann soon after breakfast. The News from Va is good, but I have not seen the dispatches. P.W.A.'s telegrams contain nothing new. Thomas was to have left this P.M. but could not get ready. Skirmishing commenced at Dalton Saturday; battle imminent.

Tuesday May 10th 1864: Clear and warm. Grand news today if true. U.S. Gen Steele has surrendered with 9000 men to Gen Price at Camden, Ark. on the 29th April. I reckon the truth of this is that Price has whipped him and taken a greater part, but not all, his army prisoners, and that Steele himself escaped.[54] General Lee telegraphs: "General Gordon with his brigade turned the enemy's right, captured his rifle-pits, and among other prisoners took the 2 Fed[eral] Gens [Truman] Seymour + Shally [Alexander Shaler]." This was on the 7th. On the 8th, Gen R.H. Anderson repulsed the enemy, near Spotsylvania C[our]t House, with heavy slaughter.[55] "I am grateful to the giver of all victories that our loss is small."?? The Yanks attacked the R.R. between Petersburg + Richmond, and were repulsed with a loss of 1000. Beast Butler made a narrow escape from capture by our pickets.[56] [Joe] Hooker's Corps made a strong attack on one of our positions at Dalton, and was repulsed. The Ram *Albemarle* "went down" in N.C. and engaged the Yankee gunboats + sunk one + disabled 2 others![57] Kirby Smith has Banks hemmed in Alexandria. If all is true what a glorious record!

Wednesday May 11th 1864: Rained in the night + again at 11 oclock. Yesterday evening Thomas left for Virginia to join the Topographical Engineers. It was a hard parting, particular hard to each one of us, and to each in a different way. Yet we ought to try and bear it cheerfully and sustain one another. A long and lonely summer is

---

54 Steele's Camden Expedition (March 23–May 22, 1864). Steele escaped, but his thrust was rebuffed.

55 After the Wilderness fighting, Grant continued south rather than retreating as Northern armies had done in the past. Gen. Richard Anderson, who assumed command of Longstreet's corps after Longstreet was wounded by his own men, won the footrace to Spotsylvania Court House. The armies gathered there and waged the horrendously bloody Spotsylvania Campaign (May 8–20, 1864).

56 The Bermuda Hundred Campaign (May 6-20, 1864), a Union attempt under political Gen. Ben Butler to sever the railroad feeding Richmond and perhaps capture the capital from the south while Gen. Lee was battling Grant farther north.

57 The ironclad CSS *Albemarle* steamed down the Roanoke River to assist in the fighting at Plymouth, NC. She beat off the USS *Miami* and sank the USS *Southfield*.

before me. An attempt to cut the R.R. between Dalton and Resaca by the enemy was repulsed and a general engagement may occur at any time, probably today.[58] Gen Lee dispatches: the enemy attacked our forces at Spottsylvania [Spotsylvania] Court House and were "handsomely driven back." This on the 8th. Our entire loss estimated at 6 or 7000; few killed and many slightly w[ou]nded. Little or no artillery used: all musketry. We have had beautiful rains this P.M. and they were much needed too. Father and I took a nice ride yester'eve, out to Vineville [two miles northwest].

Thursday May 12th 1864: Cloudy and cold. The wind blew very hard in the night and today it is comfortable close by the fire. There is not a word from Va, but I suppose the heavy storms have blown down the line. Still all feel uneasy. The enemy attacked our position at Dalton at 3 points and were driven back with heavy loss by [Carter] Stevenson, [A.P.] Stewart, and [Thomas] Hindman each holding one of the positions. Our loss not heavy. Butler continues his efforts to cut the Richmond + Petersburg Road, + a fleet of ironclads threaten Drewry's Bluff. Rode down town in the buggy at 12 oclock and weighed—64 lbs., a gain of 1 lb. since November.

Friday May 13th 1864: Cloudy and cool. Rained in the night. Minnie is in bed with sore throat. Wrote to Uncle John. Grant is entrenching. 4 determined assaults on our works at Dalton were repulsed with heavy loss on the 11th. Father wrote to Thomas.

Saturday May 14th 1864: Clear and cool. Every body is uneasy about Lee. Communication cut between Richmond and Petersburg. Minnie is up. Today we heard through a letter from Sallie B[ird] to Minnie the sad news of Cousin Teedee Hayes' sudden death. She was as well as usual when she fell into a fainting fit, from which she did not rally, and died in 20 minutes.[59] 6 P.M.: latest news! Joe Johnston falling back.[60] Richmond entirely cut off; our cavalry defeated. Where is Thomas? We are most anxious to hear.

Sunday May 15th 1864: Clear + cool. Took 20 drops [of] laudanum to check Diarrhea. Minnie in bed; took oil. Mother in bed; was quite sick all night. My leg ached

---

58 Gen. Sherman's three Union armies (Cumberland, Tennessee, and Ohio) moved out against Joe Johnston's Confederate Army of Tennessee. A Union flanking effort nearly cut the railroad behind Johnston. He withdrew from around Dalton and began the long retreat to the gates of Atlanta.

59 Cousin Sarah C. "Teedee" Hayes was Aunt Sarah Ann Wiley Hayes's daughter. She lived in Athens. Teadee was close to Minnie and Sallie Bird. She died suddenly without any symptoms of an illness.

60 As noted earlier, Gen. Johnston fell back from Dalton. The Battle of Resaca (May 13-15, 1864) ended with another Confederate withdrawal across the Oostanaula River.

all night. The Battlefield Committee leave this morning for the "Front."[61] Mother made biscuits for them. Fighting was going on yesterday and probably again today. The Yanks [Butler] are fortifying between Richmond + Petersburg. We are anxious beyond measure. There was never a more solemn crisis in the world's history. Richmond hangs in the balance. Banks is surrounded [in La.] by General Smith.

Monday May 16th 1864: Clear and cool. Minnie is worse today; has some fever. No news. The Government has possession of the lines and no dispatches are allowed to come. A private telegram came from Richmond; Beauregard's headquarters [are] at Petersburg. No general engagement at Dalton Saturday.[62] We are very anxious to hear from Thomas.

Tuesday May 17th 1864: Clear and warm. Clouded up and rained a little at about noon. No news—Walkers Division had a hard fight at Dalton and heavy engagements on Sunday and Monday, but no General Battle came off. No dispatches are permitted to pass the lines. Dr. Hall is visiting Minnie; she is better today. Am reading *Macaria*, loaned to me by Mrs. Watkins. O! for news from Thomas + Va. . . .

Wednesday May 18th 1864: Clear and cool. Minnie is in bed + about the same. Had a mess of strawberries out of the garden. Gen Joe J[ohnston] falling back from Resaca!

Thursday May 19th 1864: Clear and warm. Minnie sitting up. General Lee has issued an order to prepare his men for the grand trial yet to come. Grant's loss rumored to be 31 gens + 45000 men!!! There's a good one.[63] Our loss at Dalton in the tremendous partial engagements is 4 or 5000; enemy's 12000? General Johnston falling back, back—1400 officers U.S.A. confined at the Fair ground. Col Harris commands a regiment [of] reserves; was elected yesterday. Made 25 (+13=38) envelopes.

Friday May 20th 1864: Clear and warm. Minnie is up + looks very weak. Had strawberries for dinner at 2 doll[ar]s a quart. Rome [Ga.] evacuated and our army [is] at Kingston [NC]. Lee maintaining a strictly defensive policy at Spottsylvania Court House, receiving and repulsing Grant's attacks. Wrote to Thomas. Baked 10 lbs. flour into biscuits for the Battlefield Committee. No letter from Thomas. Made 25 + 38, 63

---

61 A group of 15 men who met that March to coordinate with the Ladies Soldiers Relief Society so materials needed by the troops made it directly to the battlefields.

62 Gen. Beauregard was sent from Charleston to take command below Richmond to counter Union Gen. Ben Butler's thrust at the railroad and Richmond. LeRoy seems not yet to have grasped that Joe Johnston had already given up Dalton and was by now far to the south. His knowledge of the geography of northern Georgia is confused/limited.

63 LeRoy, who has read much on the war, knows the news is often far from the truth.

[envelopes] in all. 2 packs [of 25 each] + 13 over. Rode round in the buggy in the evening to see Johnson [slave]. He is no better [after his stroke] and has a lonely time.

Saturday May 21st 1864: Clear and warm. Gen Johnston's battle order is out. No news. Today is somewhat like summer. The Greensboro + Danville R.R. is completed + we have another route to Richmond.

Sunday May 22nd 1864: Clear and warm. Gen Johnston has crossed the Etowah [River] + burned the bridge. "Fighting Joe" [Hooker] reported killed and his body in our possession. Minnie in bed again. The Yankees claim to have captured a whole division of Lee's army (Johnson's) with Generals Stuart + Johnson + 20 pieces artillery.[64] A rumor of General J.E.B. Stuart's death is afloat, but no positive confirmation.[65] We are all fearfully anxious, this bright beautiful Sunday morning, about affairs in North Georgia. It is quite warm, and I put on a summer coat and thin drawers.

Monday May 23d 1864: Clear and warm. Out for the first time in summer clothes. Minnie sitting up. Last week + today made 75 envelopes, out of old letter-backs: 3 packs. Mother and I went up stairs and put away all Thomas' things. Bought a quart of strawberries at $2. My leg + back pained me all night. One joint of my spine, right between the abscesses is very sore and you can see the matter, as it runs from that joint to the abscess, which proves that, as long as there is any disease there, the sores cannot heal.[66] Father left at 4 P.M. for Agusta, to attend a meeting of the Factory men.[67] We were cheered by the reception of a letter from Thomas, at Petersburg, where he is cut

---

64 Gen. Grant launched a massive pre-dawn assault against the tip of Lee's entrenchments (the "Mule Shoe") on May 12. The breakthrough was eventually contained, but the fighting (much of it hand-to-hand or at very short range) continued all day. Thousands of Confederates were captured, including Gens. Ed Johnson and George Steuart.

65 The rumor was true. Gen. Stuart was mortally wounded on May 11 at Yellow Tavern and died the next day in Richmond.

66 In spinal tuberculosis, mycobacteria spread through the bloodstream to the vertebrae. Usually more than one vertebra is destroyed by the infection, which then spreads into the disk spaces between the vertebrae, allowing the spinal elements to collapse, creating a wedging and angulation of the spine. The infection can also extend into the surrounding soft tissues, including muscle. An abscess cavity forms. The abscess enlarges and burrows along the path of least resistance, eventually rupturing through the skin. Apparently a spinous process (which he refers to as a "joint of my spine") was exposed on LeRoy's back, and he observed pus ("matter") draining ("running") from it into the adjacent soft tissue abscesses.

67 The exact purpose of the meeting is unknown, but as a factory owner and president, John Gresham was probably there to meet with other factory and military production officers to discuss the confiscation of their workers for army use.

off. [He] has been put on temporary provost duty 'till the road to Richmond is opened. News of today shows the fighting around Spottsylvania C[ourt] H[ouse] to have the most bloody and desperate of the war. We have lost in killed, +c 16 Generals + 15000 men. General Ed Johnson [is] a prisoner with 2000 of his men; on the 12th Grant's loss is 45,000 men + 31 General officers. General Jeb Stuart died on the 12th, General [John] Gordon promoted on the field. The "Battle of Spottsylvania" 12th May 1864; thus this great conflict is to be called. No news from Army in Ga.

Tuesday May 24th 1864: Cloudy and war. Mother sent a big pot of coffee to the Hospital. Pasted in my scrap-book. Minnie is busily engaged in writing her Junior composition. Lee fallen back to Hanover Junction, 25 miles [northeast] from Richmond. It is my opinion that the whole movement in Ga. is a feint to keep Johnston employed. I received a letter from Thomas: he left Petersburg for Richmond on the evening of the 18th. Beauregard drove the yankees to their gunboats on the 17th and would have taken half the force prisoners, but for an unfortunate blunder + delay of Gen [William] Whiting's in not making the attack as ordered. Mother got a sad + broken hearted letter from Aunt S[arah] Ann [Wiley] Hayes about [her daughter] Cousin Teedee.

Wednesday May 25th 1864: Clear and warm. Father arrived at breakfast time. Minnie in bed; had considerable fever in the night. No news. Marietta has been opened to the enemy + all stores removed. Forrest reported at work on the enemy's lines of communication. Mother and Father dined at Cousin Jimmie's. I rode down + had my nankin coat and vest cut. The Richmond mail came through today; 4 *Whigs* [papers]. P.W.A.'s letter about the fight of 12th was copied into the *Appeal* from the *Richmond Dispatch* under the signature of "Sallust" + Mother read it aloud after tea. On the 15th of May, at New Market, Va, Gen Breckinridge routed the Yankees under Sigel and run them 30 miles.[68] Gen Joe Johnston's army is in "statu quo." Today is Father and Mothers' 21st Anniversary and it is the first one that ever passed without something to remember it. Bacon + greens composed the dinner.

Thursday 26th May 1864: Clear and cooler. No news. Minnie out of bed, but she is taking Quinine. I Was restless and excited and could not sleep last night 'till towards morning.

---

68 The Battle of New Market (May 15, 1864) in the Shenandoah Valley, where Confederates under Gen. John C. Breckinridge routed Gen. Franz Sigel's Union army. The battle is famous for involving cadets from the Virginia Military Institute.

Friday May 27th 1864: Clear and cool. Letter to Mother from Thomas at Richmond. Had received no letters from home. [He] slept in Mr. Saulsbury's + ate at the Wayside Home. Has not been assigned [to his unit] yet. Also a letter from Grandma saying that Miss Sarah Hunter was paralyzed on one side. No news. A fight is imminent in upper Ga. Thomas says our [ironclad] rams in Va. are going to make a sally [attack] down the James [River]. Bought a "bully" bait of strawberries. Mrs. W.P. Johnston has a baby. 3 weeks old, named Mary Ellen—Know all men by these presents that we the undersigned did partake + eat of a broiled chicken this 27th May. Given under my hand + official seal. . . . [Read] P.W.A.'s account of the "Battles of the Wilderness." It is very fine too. Heavy skirmishing commenced yesterday between Johnston and Sherman. Wheeler took 80 wagons + the gaurd of 204 men in the enemy's rear. Bought 1 qt of strawberries and ate the whole myself. Pemberton has resigned + taken com[man]d near Richmond as Lt Col of Artillery.

Saturday May 28th 1864: Clear and cool. There was heavy fighting between Hood's Corps + Sherman, near Dallas [Ga.] yesterday. Gens [Daniel] Reynolds + [Alfred] Cumming wn'ded [wounded] on our side. Wrote to Thomas + Uncle John. Julia Ann has finished my nankin pants + begun on my vest. Minnie has finished her composition on "Life is real, life is earnest" +c + is copying it off. I rode to B.R.R. Depot to meet Father.

Sunday May 29th 1864: Clear and cool. Minnie got a letter from Thomas. He was to have left Richmond on the 23rd for Salem, Va, to report to a Lt J— Zard. Heavy partial engagements have taken place near Dallas. On the 27th, Cleburn ambuscaded the Yankee attacking column + routed them, killing 6000 with loss of only 400 to 600 himself.[69] A general engagement was imminent. Dick Taylor has been made Lt Gen.

---

69 The Battle of Pickett's Mill (May 27, 1864) was part of the Atlanta Campaign. After the bloody fighting at New Hope Church, Gen. Sherman ordered an attack against the right side of the Confederate army. The Confederates were ready, and Union reinforcements did not show up. Gen. Patrick Cleburne's division repulsed the Union attack easily and in less than one hour, inflicting about 1,500 casualties while suffering about 500 of his own.

Monday May 30th 1864: Clear and cool. Mother gathered a mess of [word scratched out] Raspberries out of the Garden. No news. RRRR

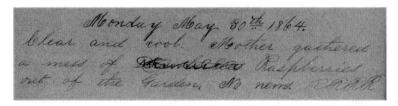

Tuesday May 31st 1864: Clear and cool. No general [major] engagement in upper Ga yet; only very heavy partial engagements. Father is very gloomy and says Sherman will not fight [attack] but fortify + hold upper Ga. Query—Can it be held without fighting. We will see.[70] Grant has worked round to the Pen[insul]a + Butler is embarking to join him.

Wednesday June 1st 1864: Clear and warm. Rained a little in the PM. Could not sleep much on account of pain in my leg. Have suffered a good deal today. Took some medicine for my bowels. Nought news from Dalton. No general fight, only heavy skirmishing. The public stores are being moved from Atlanta. Ewell's corps had a fight yesterday in 9 miles of Richmond. I wrote to Grandma.

Thursday June 2nd 1864: Cloudy and warm. All quiet along the lines. Mother in bed. My leg well. June apples ripe. Grant is on the Old McClellan track: Mechanicsville + Cold Harbor [east of Richmond]. Breckinridge has joined Lee with his forces + all is well.

Friday June 3d 1864: Cloudy and sultry. Minnie is writing to Thomas; Mother in bed. There has been severe fighting around Richmond: Gen Doles + Major Rylander; Gens Kirkland + Lane wounded. Ate the first ripe plums of the season. . . . Had bully bait of raspberries for Dinner.

Saturday June 4th 1864: Cloudy and warm. Rained very hard before breakfast. All is quiet in Upper Georgia. Come out for the first time in my suit of nankin. We have had fine rains today and it has come down slowly, so that it has soaked in thoroughly. The M.+W.R.R. [Macon and Western RR] have just completed a new engine called the "Sunshine."

---

70 LeRoy asks a rather sophisticated question and implies some disagreement with, or at least a challenge to, his father's way of thinking.

Sunday June 5th 1864: Cloudy and cool. Severe fighting around Richmond in the vacinity of Gaines' Mill. Our line on the 3d was 6 miles long and the Yankees assailed it, at different times, along its whole length, gaining a temporary success in General Breckinridge's front, but they were beaten back at all points with "heavy loss." "Under the blessing of God"—says Gen Lee, "our success was all that we could expect." Gen Law[71] + Finegan slightly wn'ded [wounded]. Gen Breckinridge injured by a fall from his horse. All quiet at the front. The hostile lines are in 500 yards of each other and the sharp-shooting is continuous + Fatal.[72] . . . Minnie went to her S.S. school for the 1st time in 6 weeks.

Monday June 6th 1864: Cloudy early in the morning, clearing up towards 10 AM. Am taking 2 iron pills per day. Dr. Hall sent only 6 for me to try. Minnie went to school this morn part of the time. And now, dear Reader, pause one moment and drop one tear over the memory of an honest faithful cat. Poor Kitty had one of her hard fits yesterday PM at 3½ Oclock from which she could not rally + by 6½ PM she died. It was too late to bury her, so with many a sigh we ordered her to be laid out on top of the grape arbor till morning. This morning, [with] Allen acting as grave digger + I as sexton, we laid her in her grave. Nearly all her teeth were gone. Her age was 7 years + 1 month. It was a male cat + its name was "Boy"; but we always called it "she." "Requiescat in pace."[73]

June 7th Tuesday 1864: Clear and very warm. Grant was hugely slaughtered in his assault on our works Thursday (the 3d). Our loss is 1000 and the yanks' 15000!!!! He seems to be preparing for another attack. The Yanks have taken Staunton [Va.]. I hope they won't come to near where Thomas is. Johnston has abandoned Alatoona + back, back, even unto the gates of Atlanta doth he come. Mother sent 9 pr crutches, in behalf of some other ladies, to the "Blind School Hospital." Mother and Minnie sick. . . . Lee has lost 22 Generals, Killed, wounded, + missing, since the 5th of May. 9 P.M.: It is dripping rain. It has been very hot all the P.M. Uncle Tom, so says a letter from Aunt Ellen, passed through to the 29th of April safely without a scratch.[74] LeRoy W Gresham

---

71 Gen. Evander M. Law.

72 Battle of Cold Harbor (May 31 - June 12, 1864). Grant assailed Lee's lines and was repulsed with heavy losses just a few miles east of the Confederate capital. Gen. George Doles was killed June 2.

73 LeRoy's Latin play on words for "Rest in Peace" (for cats).

74 Thomas Wiley Baxter, LeRoy's mother's brother. He married Ellenora Francisca Scott Baxter in 1854.

June 8th 1864 Wednesday: Clear and warm. I received a letter from Thomas in Fincastle, Botetourt Co[unty], Va. Has been marching, carrying the chain,[75] 14 + 15 miles a day; has heard from home but once. Poor fellow. Baked a lot of biscuits for the soldiers today. Johnston is making for the Chattahoochee River [just outside Atlanta] —so rumor says. What is to become of us?! Pasted in my scrapbook, the "Battles Wilderness + Spotsylvania." I wear Mother's watch now all the time. The *Richmond Whig* comes so irregularly that it is of little use to us.

Thursday June 8th 1864: Clear and warm. Grant is quiet since his disaster of the 3d [at Cold Harbor]. The Yankees are only 7 miles from Marietta, [Ga.]. They go just where they please, it seems. Minnie at school. Had a splendid blackberry pie for dinner, the berrys being $1.50 per qt.

Friday June 10th 1864: Clear and warm. Rained in the PM a little. Gen Lee says "all is quiet in front." Gens Gordon + Kershaw[76] have been promoted Maj Gens; R.H. Anderson temporarily assigned to Longstreet's Corp, and Early to Ewell's. Finished *Is the Bible from God* PSS—a very good little book. The enemy are marching on from Staunton, Va toward the Va.+E.T.R.R. Took off undershirts this morning.

Saturday June 11th 1864: Heavy shower at 12M; another at 2½, and a very hard rain at 5½ P.M. and now at 6 oclock it is pouring down with a vim. All quiet; no news. I wrote to Thomas. Julia Ann finished another pair of nankin pants and is at work on a checked nankin vest: so all is nankin "no nothing else."[77] Louis Bates is home; came last night.

Sunday June 12th 1864: Cloudy and warm. Showery weather. Rain before breakfast + again at 2 oclock. Forrest and Lee have routed the foe in North Mississippi.[78] Lee + Johnson quiet. Johnson falling back still: it is rumored to this side of the Chattahoochee. . . . Read a little in *Alexander's Evidences*. A cat bird has built her nest in the laurel + the young ones keep up a continual noise. Day mosquitoes are just beginning to make their appearance. No night ones as yet. This time last year we had

75 Topographical engineers used a chain to measure distance and for surveying purposes. The chains measured 66 feet, and were made up of 100 links each measuring .66 inches. Some property documents and surveys still refer to measurements in "chains and links."

76 Gen. Joseph B. Kershaw.

77 Another example of limited access to a variety of resources, even for the wealthy, as a result of the blockade and the limitations of Southern production.

78 Gen. Stephen D. Lee was in charge of the department, and gave Forrest the discretion to act. At Brice's Crossroads (June 10, 1864), Forrest intercepted a Union column under Gen. Sam Sturgis and completely defeated it, capturing 1,600 men and many guns.

gone up stairs for the summer. Minnie went to church for the first time in 8 weeks. Prayer-meeting for the country instead of church tonight. Raining tremendously all the evening from 2½ 'till 6 oclock. Uncle LeRoy got here at 4.

Monday June 13th 1864: From half past two yesterday 'till 9 oclock, it poured down as hard as I ever saw it, it seemed to me. Rained from day light till 9 this morning. It is bad on the wheat. I hope it will keep Sherman back, though. The yankees report a part of Johnston's army falling back to this place, + another + larger part to Athens!!! It has rained slowly, all day long and it has been so cool that we sat around the fire part of the day. Uncle LeRoy has played backgammon all the evening, first with one + then with the other. . . . Julia Ann finished my checked vest and I like it very much. Lincoln and Andy Johnson is the Republican nomination.[79] Our army is in line of battle 3 miles beyond Marietta; but as to whether there will be a fight no one knows.[80] Uncle LeRoy's foot is a great deal better than when he was here in the latter part of March. I had to put on a winter coat today having taken off my undershirts. All is quiet along the lines ~ How soon will it be broken by the roar + clash of battle in upper Ga? I hope very soon.

Tuesday June 14th 1864: Cloudy and very cool. Sitting with a fire. Uncle LeRoy left at 8 A.M. Mother made me a narrow black silk cravat [tie] yesterday and I like it very much indeed. Grant is moving to cross the James [River].[81] Sherman quiet, but threatening. Affairs in the Va [Shenandoah] Valley look bad. Lexington is occupied + Lynchburg is next. I wish Thomas was away from there. Father has applied to Head Quarters for his transfer to Georgia.

Wednesday June 15th 1864: Cloudy and cool. Father left this morning for Marietta to act as chairman of our Battlefield committee. I wrote a long letter to Thomas. Hampton has given the Yanks under Sheridan[82] a good licking, taking 500 prisoners. Forrest whipped the enemy, 10000 strong, with 3000 men, routing them, killing 1000 + taking 3000 prisoners. Mother very unwell. Minnie wrote a piece on the impressment

---

79 Andrew Johnson, a Southern War Democrat from Tennessee. Lincoln intended to demonstrate he was committed to the reestablishment of the country by including a Southerner on the ticket.

80 Gen. Johnston's Confederate Army of Tennessee was arrayed on several mountains less than 20 miles north of Atlanta in what looked to be an impregnable line.

81 Grant shifted Meade's Army of the Potomac south and began crossing the wide and deep James River on pontoon bridges on June 12, 1864, in an effort to steal a march on Gen. Lee and capture the critically important railroad hub of Petersburg 25 miles south of Richmond.

82 Gen. Philip H. Sheridan was beaten soundly by Gen. Wade Hampton's cavalry at Trevilian Station (June 11-12, 1864). No formal cavalry commander for the Army of Northern Virginia was selected after Stuart's death until Hampton was elevated in August 1864.

of the College for a hospital and published it in the daily + it has created a sensation at school. Gen Polk was killed instantly at Marietta by a stray cannon ball. The whole Confederacy will mourn the loss of this great and Good soldier and Christian patriot. The position of the army is not materially changed.[83]

Thursday June 16th 1864: Cloudy and cool. Nothing new. Wrote to Uncle Edge. Rode down town in the carriage + got some letter paper. While we were gone, Ella + Julia Ann had a fight. The sun has not been out for two days; it seems unable to pierce through the grey canopy of clouds. Grant will cross the James; that's settled.

Friday June 17th 1864: Cloudy: Raining when we got up. The yankees have captured the outworks of Petersburg. No news from Marietta—All's quiet. Hooker's corps attacked Cleburn + (a fabrication) was repulsed with loss. I passed a most miserable night + feel weary and depressed. It has rained slowly all the evening. . . . Bad, bad for the wheat. There is not immediate prospect of a general fight in front. This is Minnie's 15th birthday, + it is marked by her determination to rewrite her Jr Composition.

Saturday June 18th 1864: Rained in unceasing torrents the whole night long. This evening it has rained nearly all the time. I think it is almost without precedent, so much rain in June. I woke up with a pain in my breast and I have hardly been able to sit up at all. We received a letter from Father and he had walked to the top of Kennesaw Mt. + saw the Yankees in their works. Minnie + I sent down + bought a couple of pencils at $2 a piece. Minnie is rewriting her composition today. The first number of the *Examiner* came today dated the 14th. ~~The subscription will be out the 10th day of September, 3 months and 26 days. We lacked a half dollar of sending enough for 8 months.~~[84]

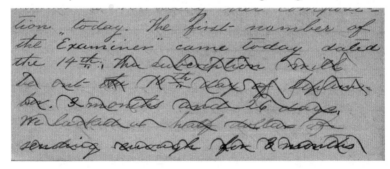

83 Gen. Leonidas Polk was atop Pine Mountain with a group of officers when Sherman spotted the men and ordered one of his artillery batteries to fire. A round struck "The Fighting Bishop" and killed him instantly. Joe Johnston withdrew his lines a short distance to Kennesaw Mountain.

84 The Greshams were part of Macon's high society. To lack 50 cents to purchase a newspaper subscription for as long as they wished is something of an embarrassment to LeRoy, which could explain why he crossed the sentence out in his journal. He relied on newspapers for war news from the fronts.

Sunday June 19th 1864: Cloudy and warm. Rained in the night and drizzled a little this morning. My breast is well. I did not sleep well. Nothing from the front—no prospect of a battle. Grant is transferring his army to the Southside of the James. Morgan "rampagin" all over Ky. when he ought to be at Lynchburg, Va.

Monday June 20th 1864: Cloudy: rained a little. Father arrived at dinnertime to our surprise. Cousin Jones came down with him, hurt by a kick from a horse.[85] He has to report at the Blind Asylum Hospital. A letter from Father to me came this evening after he did.

Tuesday June 21st 1864: Cloudy still. A list of killed + w[ou]nded CS Gens came out in the daily this morn, which I compiled. Heavy fighting around Petersburg. Grant attacked us and was repulsed without difficulty and with heavy loss.[86] His whole army is on the Southside + so is ours. Hunter is whipped + retreating from the Valley. Morgan is whipped and leaving Kentucky. Sherman is quiet. I spent a bad night with pain in my leg + back and O! how glad I was when morning dawned! Cousin Jones has gone to the Hospital to report. He has a bad cough. Rain again at 2½ P.M. On Sunday night at 11 oclock the middle pier of the bridge gave way and the force of the current then broke the bridge in two, the ends swinging round to the bank. I forgot to record it Monday. Father is fearful that Richmond will fall. Grant's new move to the Southside frightens him. My own opinion is that his is to receive the worst defeat of all. P.W.A. is very gloomy too.

Wednesday June 22nd 1864: Clear and warm. The first clear morning in 2 weeks. Rode down in the carriage to see the ruins of the bridge. The impressors run after the carriage to get Howard but we escaped by dint of speed. The impressor, furious at our escape, drew his bayonet and made another warlike demonstration. Cousin Jones is better.

Thursday June 23rd 1864: Clear and warm. The Army of Tenn. is active. The impressing officers are taking nearly every able bodied darkie in town to send to Atlanta

85 John Jones Gresham, one of Uncle Edmund's sons. He served with Marsh's Company , 5th Georgia Cavalry, Joe Wheeler's cavalry.

86 Elements from Meade's Army of the Potomac fought the Second Battle of Petersburg (June 15-18, 1864), the first battle being a bungled affair on June 9 by Gen. Butler's Army of the James. Gen. Beauregard's defensive effort was one of his best performances of the war. Gen. Lee waited until the eleventh hour to send troops south of the James River, unconvinced Grant had crossed in strength. Once the Federals were defeated, both armies began digging entrenchments and the 9-month siege of Petersburg began.

to work on the fortifications.[87] It is supposed that Gen Johnston is preparing to fall back there. I hoped for a letter from Thomas today but none came. I commenced *Eleanor's Victory* by the author of *Aurora Floyd*. Cousin Jones has gone to Vineville to see Mrs. Jerrett.

Friday June 24th 1864: Clear and very warm. . . . Lines cut between Petersburg + Weldon. Had a Blackberry pie. No news. We are beginning to feel anxious to hear from Thomas. Mother had 3 pounds of bread baked for [the] Battlefield Association, and Cousin Jones and I got in the carriage and carried them down. Hood's Corps had a fight with the Yanks on the PM of the 22nd and losing a 1000 men gained nothing.[88] A fight or a footrace for Atlanta is obliged to come off soon.

Saturday June 25th 1864: Clear and warm. The hottest day yet. Nothing from Richmond. Read *Eleanor's Victory* through. Gen Pettus[89] of Ala, the commander of Mr. Phil[omon] Tracy's old Brigade, is killed. Col Cook of the 4th is promoted to fill Doles' place. Minnie is writing to Thomas. Gen Pettus was not killed.

Sunday June 26th 1864: Clear and hot. No news from any point. Richmond is cut off. Let me note two prognostications: Father says Richmond and Atlanta are gone. If R + A are gone, then the C.S.A. are gone. I think that in a month both cities will be safe.[90] The "Macon Light Artillery" lost their battery at Petersburg. They fought well however and more highly complimented.[91]

87 The agent from the entry of the previous day (June 22) was after Howard, an able-bodied black man, in order to impress him into working on the entrenchments going up around Atlanta.

88 The Battle of Kolb's Farm (June 22, 1864). Hood attacked and was sharply repulsed.

89 Gen. Edmund W. Pettus. The bridge in Selma, Ala, known for the famous Civil Rights march in 1965, was named after this Confederate general.

90 Once again LeRoy openly disagrees with his father (who was in fact correct).

91 On June 18, the artillery battery (four 12-pound Napoleons) was overrun after losing most of their artillery horses in the fighting, and thus the means to haul the guns away.

Monday June 27th 1864: Clear and hot. Mother draws ration the hospital and cooks it and carries it to them every other day. I have put on my old white shirts because they are cooler but they are so ragged that I can hardly wear them. I have also put on thin nightshirts. Cousin Jones walked out to Vineville to church yestereve. He is a good deal better. Cousin Jinnie W. Blount's little girl, Mary, is dead. I am very, very sorry for her. As I write, at 20 minutes to 4, we are having a fine shower. Ate a bit bait of onions for dinner. Commenced to read *Redwood, A Novel* by Miss Sedgewick—mighty poor too.

Tuesday June 28th 1864: Clear and warm. The enemy attacked our left at Marietta in 7 lines of battle and were driven back with loss. No telegrams from Va yet. Slept up stairs for the first time this summer. Cousin Jones, Father, + I rode out to Mr. Hickman's and had the measure for my shoes taken + then rode by the Fair ground + saw the dress parade of Cummings' Regiment [of] Reserves + a few Yankee prisoners.

Wednesday June 29th 1864: Cloudy and sultry. Rained a little after supper last night. We killed 5 or 6000 Yankees in the assault on the 27th. Our loss 400. We took some 450 prisoners.[92] Faint uncertain rumors come of a bloody fight in Virginia on the 22nd or 23rd. Tom Collins + Charlie Redding killed.[93] The Danville road is cut. No mail or telegrams are permitted to pass. Poor Mother! The suspense of not hearing from Thomas is very hard on her. It is two weeks since we heard. Cousin Jones succeeded in getting a 25 day furlough this morning. It had to go Atlanta for approval however. Mother on porch with Mrs. Lamar; Minnie and Cousin Jones playing "mumble-the-peg" on the grass.[94]

Thursday June 30th 1864: Cloudy and warm. Father left for the plantation before breakfast. The Situation in Virginia is fearfully critical. Both RR's cut. All quiet on the Ga Front. Pillow is reported in Sherman's rear. The coming week is a terrible crisis with us. Lt Carswell of Company B, 47th Georgia, Jackson's Brigade, Walker's Division dined with us. He is an acquaintance of Cousin Jones. I played two games of chess with him and beat him. He played very well. Mother in bed and not able to see him. Read in Minnie's *Astronomy* all the morning. Mother made 14 qts of berries into Jam. O! how I long to hear from Thomas, more for Dear Mother's sake than my own. Cousin Jones + Minnie playing on the piano reminds me so of him. Poor fellow!

---

92 Battle of Kennesaw Mountain (June 27. 1864). A frustrated Sherman launched a direct attack against Johnston's entrenched lines and was repulsed with the loss of about 3,000 men to 1,000 Confederates. Thereafter, Sherman resorted to another flanking operation.

93 Macon natives Capt. Charles R. Redding, Co. C, and Thomas Collins, Co. B, both 2nd Ga. Battalion, were killed in the fighting in the early fighting at Petersburg.

94 There are variations of this game played with a pocket-knife, and some of then are dangerous.

Friday July 1st 1864: Clear and warm. A slight attempt on the Morning of the 30th at 2 oclock to storm Genl Cheatham's position was easily repulsed with considerable loss to the enemy. Our casualties: 1 killed + two wounded. Gen Pillow went on an expedition to Sherman's rear and got licked.

Saturday July 2nd 1864: Clear and warm. No news. Maj Gen [A. P.] Stewart is assigned to the command of Polk's Corps, so rumor saith. Slept badly; was restless and nervous. Allen was missing when I went on my wagon this morning and on inquiry learned that he was very anxious to be impressed and had gone off doubtless with that hope. About 9 oclock, [he] made his appearance. He had been to the fair-ground and offered his services. On the ground of his leaving without Father's knowledge, they were not accepted. Father "arroved" from Houston at 10½ o'clock with eggs, butter, honey, apples, plums, +c.

Sunday July 3d 1864: Clear and warm. Cousin Jones is reading the *War Trail*.

Monday July 4th 1864: The famous "played out" 4th of yore. This has been a very warm day. I have suffered a good deal with the heat. Commenced reading *The Fortunes of Glencore*. Had apple pie for dinner. There is no news. Hampton has whipped the enemy awfully in Virginia, taking 1500 prisoners, arms, +c, and completely routing the enemy. This is examination week at College.

Tuesday July 5th 1864: Clear and very warm. This day I enter on the fifth year of my confinement to my couch: 5 long and weary years! I am much worse off now than then. Cousin Bella has got another little girl: born Sunday.[95] Gen Johnston has "evacuated" (O! hateful word) Marietta + Kennesaw Mountain. Wheeler has left for Sherman's rear. Finished *The Fortunes of Glencore* and it is a "monsous p. tail." Cousin Jones is reading *Scalp Hunters*. Johnston has fallen back to the Chattahoochee, given up Marietta; and the Yankees have burned the [Ga.] Military Institute.

---

95 Nannie Jones Estes, the last of Bella's children.

Wednesday July 6th '64: Clear and warm. Cousin Jones got a furlough and left for home at 4 P.M. I rode down in the carriage and we picked up Lts Carswelll + Peeler at the transportation office. We have as many cucumbers, squashes, and Irish Potates now as we can eat. Wrote in Miss Clare deG[raffenried]'s Album. Johnston's army is this side of the [Chattahoochee] river.[96]

Thursday July 7th 1864: Clear and warm. Pasted in my scrap-book. All quiet in the "Georgia Front." Am reading *Mabel Vaughan*. The "fowl invaders" have been driven off from the R.R's leading to Va + I do hope we will hear from Thomas before long. Minnie got through her examination this PM.

Friday July 8th 1864: Clear and very warm. Telegrams through from Richmond to day. All is right. Nothing important. All quiet in Ga. The Ga. Militia is doing good service, under Gen [Gustavus] Smith.

Saturday July 9th 1864: Clear and warm. Many sick and wounded are coming down from Atlanta and the impression is gaining ground that Atlanta is to be given up for strategetical purposes! The Yankees say Kirby Smith is crossing the Mississippi + that [Gen. Jubal] Early is in M[arylan]d!! Big lies. I reckon.[97] The Fortifications near Macon are on the Forsythe Road at Singer's Hill. This is the 365th day of the siege of Charleston.

Sunday July 10th 1864: Clear and warm. Rumor hath it that Price has taken Little Rock, Ark [with] Prisoners + stores. The mail communications between Richmond + here will not be resumed for some time, the R.R being damaged so seriously. Father telegraphed to Richmond to know [find out from] Mr. Saulsbury if he had heard ought of Thomas. Refugees are crowding down from Atlanta. Gen Jubal A. Early is at Leesburg for the purpose of arousing the North and quelling the peace parties; at least no other purpose is known. O! for a few of his men at the Ga F[ront]. . . .

Monday 11th July 1864: Clear and rather more pleasant than yesterday. Minnie read at the Junior Exhibition this morning at 22 minutes to 11 oclock. Her Subject was:

"Life is real; life is earnest! And the grave is not it's goal…"

---

96 Johnston withdrew across the Chattahoochee River on June 5—the last barrier between Sherman and Atlanta. Although LeRoy continues to write in a matter-of-fact manner, the stress of the approaching storm of war deep into Georgia must have been palpable inside the Gresham house.

97 Gen. Lee had dispatched a large portion of his army under Gen. Jubal Early to help secure the Shenandoah Valley. Early drove north and crossed the Potomac River into Maryland to threaten Washington and hopefully force Union troops to withdraw from Virginia. He fought the Battle of Monocacy (July 9, 1864) and made it to the outskirts of the Union capital before turning back. Kirby Smith was not crossing the Mississippi River.

The composition was 11½ minutes long. I rode down to Mr. Whittle's corner where I could have the consolation of hearing the subject read out at least.[98] All the darkies went. Mother and Father thought Minnie did as well as any there. Miss Clare deGraffenreid sent me her composition on: "The Mind—that is the man" to read. It was an agreement between us that if I would write an original piece in her Album that she would let me read it. This is indeed a fearful crisis in upper Ga. The enemy are crossing the river in heavy force on both wings to flank us. Our forces to oppose them must uncover Atlanta. Thus the "quid nunes [what nows?]" have it. "We shall see what we shall see." The *Alabama* is reported sunk, off Cherbourg. Captain Semmes + Kell (a 1st Lieutenant) escaped.[99]

Tuesday July 12th 1864: Clear and warm. Gov Brown has called out the militia between 50 + 60; Father is included in that call.[100] Father thinks the C.S.A. are gone, as well as Atlanta. My leg pained me much this evening and I fear I will spend a bad night. Judge Lochrane is "spouting" away at a huge rate, as I write, over at the College. "Personne" (F.G. de Fontaine) is corresponding with the *Savannah Republican* for a short time from the Army of Tennessee under the signature of F.G.de.F.[101]

Wednesday July 13th 1864: Clear and hot. Spent a wakeful night of pain. . . . Every body went to the concert at the College and I read the *Appeal* amd *The Planter's Daughter* 'till ten P.M. We were surprised to see George Beal yesterday. The Yankees are making heavy demonstrations around Charleston, and several hard fights took place. We long inexpressibly to hear from Thomas and Poor Mother sinks under it. All quiet along the Chattahoochee Front, the river dividing the armies. Willis arrived with plantation supplies. Mrs. Johnson, Susie, + Georgia called. Mother was over to Judge Hollis. Many rumors afloat; 0 from Va.

Thursday July 14th 1864: Cloudy and hot. It is getting to be a most serious question with us about Father's going to the war. I do not know what we should do. All the Atlanta papers have "skedadled" except the *Appeal*. Some think Atlanta is to be given up, others do not.

---

98 It is unclear why LeRoy wasn't allowed inside. Perhaps his wagon was considered unsuitable for the surroundings, or his coughing was too distracting. The recitations were the highlight of the academic year, the one time female academic ability and intellectual achievements were celebrated.

99 In one of the most famous sea battles of all time, the USS *Kearsarge* sank the CSS *Alabama* off the coast of Cherbourg, France. Adm. Semmes and his first officer, John Kell, were among the survivors. The wreck was discovered in 1984 and artifacts have been raised and preserved.

100 John Jones Gresham, LeRoy's father, was born in 1812 and was 52 years old in 1864.

101 Many people submitted articles to newspapers under pen names.

Friday July 15th 1864: Clear and warm. Father and I rode out to the cemetery in the buggy. Received a letter at last from Thomas to Minnie dated the 11th June. I hope more will come now, for Mother's sake. Father is ordered to do Gaurd duty tonight. What is to become of us? Early is "rampaging" all over Md; in two miles from Baltimore, stirring up the Yankees to the choice of supporting either the public foe or the government! Gen Bragg is at the Front. Am reading *Vasconcelos*, a novel by Simms. Thomas has, up to the 11th, marched 190 miles.

Saturday July 16th 1864: Clear and warm. Father stood on gaurd at the City-Hall last night.[102] This is volunteer duty. Capt Ross' company hopes to escape going to the front in this way. Gov Brown (I hate him worse than ever) has ordered the arrest of every man who does not leave by the 20th inst. Both overseers are to go. All quiet in Front. Mother Wrote to Thos. For the first time in 2 weeks. Another letter from Thomas which shows how near he came to being captured; in a road forking [like] this:

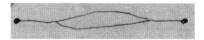

from Liberty to White's Shop. His party took one fork and the Yankees, 400 in Number, took the other, so they met in the parallel roads without knowing it. They run like smoke from Botetourt, but when he wrote on the 22nd alt., were on the way back. I am very thankful for this mercy.

Sunday July 17th 1864: Clear and warm. I have caught a cold + cough and snuffle continually.

Monday July 18th 1864: Cloudy and cool. Took Paragoric last night and slept all this morn. I have caught cold and have a very bad cough. The negroes found a squirrel in the garden and after surrounding him, succeeded in capturing him.

Tuesday July 19th 1864: Clear and rather cool. The news is bad. I was fairly stunned by the announcement that Gen Jos. E. Johnston was relieved from command by General Hood. O! it's enough to make us hate President Davis for his blind + bitter predjudice. Relieved, before the campaign is decided. O! it is *too* mean.[103] The College is filling up with refugees [from Atlanta]. 8½ P.M. Rode out to the labaratory + then

102 This is ironic, since John Gresham had helped pay for and build City Hall.

103 Johnston had by this time retreated all the way to Atlanta and still refused to divulge his plans to President Davis, who finally believed he had no choice but to relieve him, which he did on July 17, 1864. Davis elevated corps commander John Bell Hood to command the Army of Tennessee. LeRoy's reference to Davis's "blind + bitter prejudice" refers to the widely known fact that Davis and Johnston despised one another.

down town via the factory with Mother and Minnie.[104] Gen. [Carter] Stevenson is appointed to the command of Hood's [former] Corps. Had a watermelon, the first of the season, for which Father gave 6 dollars, and we enjoyed it very much. Bought a cantelope and gave 2 dollars for it. Columbus is under arms in order to repel an advancing raid. The Ga RR is cut at Stone Mt.

Wednesday July 20th 1864: Clear and warm. Mother got a long nice letter from Thomas dated Blue Ridge P[ost] O[ffice]: and he had got 6 letters from home. I am so glad. . . . Father sent a box to Thomas with his shoes, 2 shirts, collars, envelopes, sugar, coffee, letter, +c. 6 P.M.: Father has come from down town and could not get off Thomas's box. He went to see Gen Johnston, [who] is staying at Gen Cobb's [house].

Thursday July 21st 1864: Clear and warm. Am reading *Heartsease*. Watermelon in the PM "Huckleberrie" pie. Wounded men pouring down from the front. Heavy fight there yesterday. Col [George A.] Smith, 1st Con[federate] Reg[iment] killed.[105]

Friday July 22nd 1864: Clear and warm; 3000 wounded men expected from Atlanta. Our wagon is gone to help carry them to the Hospitals. A general fight is looked for. There has already been very heavy partial engagements.

Saturday July 23rd 1864: Cloudy and cool. The town is full of wounded + O! the human suffering. Howard was engaged all day yesterday and till 3 oclock this morn, in hauling the wounded to the different hospitals. Mother brought 2 men home with her: one from Missouri + the other from Arkansas. The enemy attacking Gen Stewart, at Atlanta, were driven back two miles, losing heavily in men + 22 pieces Artillery. Their Corps commander, McPherson, was killed. Hardee is in their rear. [106] Father was on gaurd again last night. Col George Smith was not killed. Today is like autumn—a glorious day for army movements and fighting. Briggs Napier lost a leg at the front. Father think Atlanta is gone. Mr. Cox + Mr. Craig are the names of the men staying here.

---

104 Macon hosted an arsenal, armory, and munitions laboratory (C.S. Central Laboratory) run by Capt. John W. Mallet. The laboratory studied problems of metallurgy, the caliber of bullets, etc.

105 Battle of Peachtree Creek (July 20, 1864). Hood assailed part of Sherman's army in an effort to catch it outside of its entrenchments. The attacks were mishandled and defeated. George Augustus Smith III was not killed (he would die at Franklin, Tenn., on Nov. 30 1864), but his brigade commander Gen. C. H. Stevens was mortally wounded.

106 The Battle of Atlanta (July 22, 1864) was a well-conceived attack plan by Hood to sweep Gen. Hardee's Corps around Sherman's vulnerable left flank and roll it up. He was nearly successful. The fighting was long and bloody, and the Confederates defeated, losing about 5,500 to Sherman's 3,600. Gen. James McPherson, commander of the Union Army of the Tennessee, was killed.

Sunday July 24th 1864: Cloudy and quite cool for the season. The Fight at Atlanta was a very heavy one. Gen [W. H. T.] Walker is killed. Gens Gist + Smith wounded. We took 2000 prisoners + 22 pieces artillery. Yankee loss supposed 20000. Ours great in officers. Gen Hood telegraphs that the Militia fought with gallantry. Walker's division must have been cut up badly. Gen Wheeler fought the enemy at Decatur the same day (the 22nd) + took 500 wagons. I got a letter from Thomas giving a description of his companions. Gen Johnston was riding over [through] town yesterday by himself on horseback. I do wish I could see him. . . . Ate a nice watermelon in the P.M.

Monday July 25th 1864: Clear and cold for July. Father got a 4 day furlough from his Capt + left on the R.R. for Houston this A.M. . . . Willie Leconte is wounded. "Personne" writes very fine letters from the front now under "F.G.de F." Bought 2 melons. . . . Ate a cantelope of my own raising and it was very nice.

Tuesday July 26th 1864: Cloudy and cool. Pulled three cantelopes out of the garden. Yankee raids are all the talk. Madison, Covington, Social Circle + other places have been visited, and Athens is threatened 'tis said. No fighting at the Front since Friday's battle. Gen Stevens of S.C. died yesterday at Mr. LeRoy Napier's, from mortal wounds in the head received on the 20th. O! for a soaking rain; in the gardens + the corn. Crops are burning up. The Ga. Mila. [Militia] "won golden opinions" in the late fights and did Gen Hood good service.

Wednesday July 27th 1864: Cloudy and very oppressive. Rained a little at about 2 oclock. Father arrived at 3 P.M. on the R.R. with some Apples, a few peaches, eggs, +c. Rode down [on my wagon] to near the Grave yard, and looked at the Militia. The woods around Mrs. Clarks are full of them.

Thursday July 28th 1864: Cloudy and hot. . . . Had cantelope for breakfast of our own raising. The corn crop is ruined + I wish for rain for the gardens. Mr. Craig, one of the soldiers with us is silent + some what reserved, while the other, Mr. Cox, is as garrulous as a guinea-fowl, "so to speak." Robert Baxter, Uncle John's darkie came down from the front yesterday.[107] Uncle John sent me a piece of the Oak [tree] Grant and Pemberton bargained about Vicksburg under. Walker's Division is broken up + the Brigades divided among other divisions.

Friday July 29th 1864: Clear and warm. Willis came up yesterday with 9 watermelons, a bushel of apples, butter, eggs, flour, +c. Breckinridge + Gordon have routed the yankees, in the Valley of Va., 16000 strong, taking 2000 prisoners, and losing

107 Uncle John's body servant. Slaves often accompanied soldiers to the front to do their cooking, packing, laundry, and other tasks. LeRoy's brother Thomas appears to have gone to the war without one.

only 30 or 60 in all.[108] Sherman has Atlanta completely invested, excepting the place where the M.+.W.R.R. goes in, and we must fight or evacuate soon.[109] Mrs. Nelson sent me 4 beautiful peaches. 6 PM. Reported that the yankees are in 20 miles from here on the Clinton Road. Father is ordered out + the Militia are pouring over the river. Gen Cobb is in command [of the militia at Macon] + Gen Johnston is consulting him. The town is in commotion + the men are arming.[110]

Saturday July 30th 1864: Cloudy and very sultry. All is excitement. The yankee raiders [Stoneman] are within 6 miles of town. Father's company camped in Vineville last night + this morning they marched over the river. Father came by the house. Howard has gone with him [as a body servant]. 11 A.M. Later: Fighting is going on over the river by Fort Hawkins and we hear the cannon firing. Shells have fallen over this side of the river. I went upon top of the house, but could only see the smoke. Every man in town is under arms. Mr. Palmer has gone over. We sit anxiously waiting for news, too excited to read or do anything but think of Father and Cousin Jones + listen to the booming of cannon which are shelling our men. They have cut the Central R.R. at Griswoldville, it is said. A thousand wild rumors are afloat. Cam Tracy reported wounded in the neck. How it stirs my blood to hear the firing. O! how anxious we are about Father! The force of the enemy is estimated from 800 to 30000!! I passed a very bad night: my leg + back pained me so much that I could only toss and roll all night. Mrs. Watkins came over to see us and she was very much frightened. One ball went through Mr. Asa Holt's house.[111] 4 O'clock: Mr. Palmer has just returned and states the enemy left our front at about 1½ oclock. Father is safe. 6 P.M: Father came back. He was in the sharpest fight of the day. Cam Tracy was wounded next to him + his blood splattered on Father. Our men were miserably handled. . . . Strong skirmishing from 9 to 1 was the order of the day. The yanks had one piece of Artillery, a rifled one, and threw shells all the time with it. At one time it was thought the yanks were trying to

108 Battle of Second Kernstown (July 24, 1864), a relatively minor combat outside Winchester, Va.

109 Macon and Western Railroad. The key to Atlanta was cutting her supply lines (road and railroads). Sherman's efforts were geared toward this objective, and Hood was working to block him.

110 Stoneman's Raid (July 27–Aug. 6, 1864). Sherman sent Gen. George Stoneman's 2,100 Union cavalry, supported by Gen. Garrard's cavalry division, to sever the Georgia Railroad. He approached Macon on July 30 and destroyed rail lines and other facilities east of town, but was rebuffed outside Macon by entrenched Georgia militia. He used his artillery to shell the city and retreated. Confederates caught up to Stoneman the next day at Sunshine Church (20 miles northeast of Macon) and he surrendered with about 600 men. The war was now palpably real for Macon and its citizens.

111 Known today as the "Cannonball House," the Holt home was hit by a 3-inch rifled shell (which Leroy mentions later in his entry), and the family barely escaped injury.

cross up by the shoals and forces were sent to oppose them. The Raiders are supposed to have proceeded toward Milledgeville. Walnut Creek Bridge destroyed + Griswoldville burned. The M.+.W.R.R. is torn up beyond Griffin. It is supposed that Hood is fighting. O! it is a critical time with us and Father considers Geo. overrun.

Sunday July 31, 1864: Cloudy and very close + hot. Rained finely at bedtime last night. Our loss yesterday was 9 killed + 30 wounded, and 'tis reported that the enemy acknowledge 8 killed + 30 wounded. Father's company is ordered to report at the W.F. [Wesleyan Female] College at 11 A.M. It is Old Co[mpany] B now. I took a Dover's Powder and I slept better than the night before. It is rumored that the enemy is advancing with our cavalry in pursuit. 11 O'clock. I have been on my wagon all the morning since 10½ looking at the troops, watching the couriers dashing bout. About 12 M. [noon] all was quiet the troops having all been sent to the Vineville front, which is 4 miles off. Co. "B" staid under the shade of the trees just below the college. Other troops were sent up the river to repel any advance, but our cavalry held them in check at Clinton, so at sundown Co. "B" was marched down town and disbanded. At dress parade, speeches were made on the success of the 2 days campaign and the part Co. "B" had taken in repelling the invader + saving Macon from destruction. The raiders were commanded by Genl Stoneman. Some of our men found where they had buried a Lt Col. A cannon was placed in position in front of our house and remained there all night. The neighbors gave them breakfast this morning. Cousin Jones, Mr. Craig + Cox got guns and went down and joined Father's company. Mr. Wills is in "Co. D" but he came out of the fight to carry off a dead man. Mr. Danforth had a ball through his hat. Gen Cobb was in command, Gen [Dan] Ruggles, J.E. Johnston, [Gen. W. W.] Mackall,[112] + Gov Brown were near the field. Tonight I felt so thankful to eat our supper safely and in peace again, and Father with us, covered with the glory of a right severe campaign, if it was short. It has not seemed a bit like Sunday so excited has everybody been. I have been free from pain today. The "dover" cured me.

Monday ~~July~~ August 1st 1864: Clear and warm in the morning; cloudy and sultry in the evening. All is quiet day. They are fighting at Clinton. The M.+.W.R.R. is running again. The fight on the 28th was a bloody one, but no results.[113] The yankees have

---

112 Gen. Daniel Ruggles; Gen. William W. Mackall, who refused to serve under Hood and remained in Macon until March 1865, when he was given command of CSA troops in south Georgia.

113 Battle of Ezra Church (July 28, 1864). In another attempt to several the rail lines feeding Atlanta, Sherman moved around the west side of the city. Hood moved troops to block the effort. The Confederate attacks were poorly delivered and repulsed with heavy losses. Hood had now lost three major battles around Atlanta in just eight days.

burned the Oconee Bridge. Latest news! Glorious Success! Cousin Jones has just come in and announced the capture of Stoneman and 450 of his raiders near Clinton. Stoneman and escort came in this P.M. Iverson was in command on our side, but the fighting was done by Col Crews.[114] Our forces are in pursuit of the remnant of the wretches. Went out in the garden and gathered 6 fine cantelopes. Gen's [W. W.] Loring + [A. P.] Stewart are in town wounded.

Tuesday August 2nd 1864: Clear and hot. Clouded up and rained about 11 Oclock, then turned clear and very hot. Soon after breakfast Father went to the depot and brought home Cousin Samuel Knox who had sent word that he was there wounded. His wound is a painful but not dangerous one, entering on the side and glancing round the body, came out near the spine. His brother Jimmy is with him.[115] The captured raiders were marched into town this morning + at 5½ O'clock; about 1000 of their horses led by our cavalry passed by our house. They look pretty much worn out. Robert Bates came up and played chess with me. The 1st game was won by me, the next very long + drawn. Cousin Jones bade us good-bye and left but returned, the officers having doubts of his being able to find his regiment. [They] told him that he might stay a day or so longer.

Wednesday August 3d 1864: Clear and hot. Grant sprung a mine on Lee's line [in Va] and attempting to enter was driven back, both sides losing heavily. [116] All is quiet at the Georgia Front. . . . I am wonderfully afraid Hood will ruin his army and lose Atlanta to boot with these cruel indecisive battles, that curst so many poor hearts, lose so many brave and gallant men, and accomplish so little. It is said 300 more of Stoneman's robbers have been picked up and brought in to town. Cousin Jones has lost his pocket-book with 120 dollars in it. Minnie went to Miss Lucy McMullan's wedding this P.M. at 7 Oclock. Iverson's men are camped out back of Mr. Bates and they are galloping by at all hours of the day and night.

---

114 Gen. Alfred Iverson and Col. Charles C. Crews led the pursuit. Stoneman was the highest ranking Federal officer captured during the war (exchanged three months later). The Union cavalry was attempting to free Union prisoners at Andersonville. Stoneman's aide, Myles Keogh, was killed in 1876 at the Little Big Horn with George Custer.

115 It is unclear how Samuel and Jimmy Knox were related to the Gresham family. LeRoy later notes that one of the Knox brothers is from Alabama.

116 The Battle of the Crater (July 30, 1864). Pennsylvania troops with mining experience dug a 500-foot tunnel to reach Confederate lines, jammed the end galleries with explosives, and detonated them. The explosion killed and wounded hundreds and the fighting was long and bloody, with nearly 5,000 Union and 1,500 Southern casualties. Lee's lines, however, remained intact.

Thursday August 4th 1864: Clear and warm. All quiet along the lines. A dinner was to have been given to Gen Iverson's command this P.M. but they were peremptorily ordered away at 5 this morning. . . . Father dressed Cousin Sam's wound. Mary Campbell stayed all day with us. Cousin Billie Wiley who is in the Militia and in camp here, came to see us.[117] Cousin Sam went down and made an unsuccessful effort to get off home; but, there having been a collision on the road, no train went out. Cousin Jones has been on provost duty all day arresting every man who could not show his papers. Father was arrested on the streets. The remnant of Stoneman's command passed through Eatonton, on their way to the main army, burning the depot, but being in too great a hurry to do much pillaging.

Friday August 5th 1864: Clear and warm. I have had a pain in my right shoulder and side and it hurts me when I breathe. We have, in the past few days, has a most distressing occurrence in our house, which mortified Mother + Father very much. Cousin Jones thought he had lost his pocket-book, but our suspicions having been directed to Mr. Cox by some remarks of his, his pockets were searched while he was asleep and the pocket-book found. Father talked to him and he said that it was only a joke that he intended returning it: but Father told him that he had carried the joke so far that he must leave, which he did early this A.M. before we were up. It is sad, sad to think of. . . .

Saturday August 6th 1864: Cloudy and warm. Fighting at Mobile. One Yankee ironclad sunk and the *Tennessee*, our best ship, surrendered. The U.S. Fleet has passed Fort Morgan![118] The enemy made a determined assault on our skirmish line at the "Front" + were driven back. The raiders went to Cousin Jinnie Blount's in Jones Co. and pitched all her clothes onto the floor. One of her negroes was hung for insubordination. Several other "contrabands" were "paroled" [freed] for joining the raiders and declaring themselves free.[119] Father stood gaurd last night and it uses him up. These are dull times for news, though there is excitement enough at home there

117 William G. Wiley.

118 The Battle of Mobile Bay (Aug. 5, 1864). A Union fleet under Adm. Farragut engaged a Confederate fleet and three forts for the control of the entrance to Mobile Bay, AL. The ironclad CSS *Tennessee* surrendered after a hard fight, and the forts surrendered within a few days. This is the famous naval battle where, after the ironclad USS *Tecumseh* struck a mine (called a torpedo in those days), turned over, and sank, Farragut is said to have exclaimed to his crew while high in the rigging, "Damn the torpedoes! Full steam ahead!"

119 "Contraband" was a term coined by Union Gen. Ben. Butler early in the war to describe slaves who had made their way into Federal lines. The Union used them for labor, and later armed those who wanted to fight.

being no mails as yet. A negro belonging to Mr. Charles Collins was shot yesterday by Tom Bone while trying his Yankee rifle, which he had bought. It is an outrage, although it is said to have been done accidentally. It is the 3d man he has shot at just for devilment.

Sunday August 7th 1864: Clear and hot. Mercury 82° at 9 A.M. The thermometer has not been above 90° this season certain, and I have not seen it over 89°. I went down yesterday to Mr. Bates' and played 4 games of chess with Bob, beating him every time. Minnie and Cousin Jones played the whole day. Brisk skirmishing on the Ga Front. Affairs must change materially in that all absorbing locality in a day or two whither for better or worse no one can guess. The wildest rumors are afloat. Grant + Lee are mining + countermining. What a contrast is the quiet and peace of today to the bustle, stir, and confusion of last Sabbath! We have some very nice grapes out of the garden now and I enjoy them every morn. Cousin Jenks Jones came up + stayed to tea with us. He is now col. . . .

Monday August 8th 1864: Cloudy and quite sultry. Rained a little in the night. Fine rain at dinner-time, continuing into the P.M. It looks as if Mobile was gone up. I wrote to Aunt Eliza. Played chess against Father and Cousin Jenks consulting, and got beat. Willie Ross is killed.

Tuesday August 9th 1864: Cloudy and cool. Rained beautifully after breakfast. All the forts at Mobile have fallen and the city is probably gone. Bad! Bad! Bad! Miss M. Clare deGraffenreid + Minnie have commenced a course of reading History + Poetry. Cousin Jones left for the front at 6 Oclock this morning. Received two letters from Thomas: one to me, one to Mother. Father got a letter from Gen [Jeremy] Gilmer, chief [of the] Engr. [Engineering] Bureau saying that Thomas' transfer [to Ga.] could not be granted for the present.

Wednesday August 10th 1864: Cloudy and rather cool. Wrote a long letter to Thomas. Robert Bates came up + played 7 games of chess, beating me only once. Commenced *My Novel*. Minnie and Clare de G— are reading Irving's *Washington*. Great anxiety is felt for Mobile.

Thursday August 11th 1864: Cloudy and pleasant-like a fall morning. Rumored that our cavalry have burned Yankee stores in Marietta. Wagon came up from the plantations with 4 negroes to work on the fortifications around [Macon]: also 11 watermelons, a basket of peaches +c +c Have sat up too much today and I reckon on a bad night. If the left hand abscess ceases running one day, it gives me a pain in my back + draws up my leg worse.

> Have sat up too much to-day and I reckon on a bad night. If the left hand abscess ceases running one day it gives me a pain in my back + draws up my leg worse

Friday August 12th 1864: Cloudy and warm. Passed a restless uneasy night. Cut two melons—both green. Our wagon broke down on the road and did not arrive 'till after tea last P.M. 12M. The sun has come out very hot.

Saturday August 13th 1864: Clear and quite warm. Mobile is not taken yet: Atlanta is still ours and Richmond is safe. Grant and Lee in person have gone to the [Shenandoah] Valley and their armies are mostly there. Meade + Beauregard are still at Petersburg keeping up a merely nominal siege.[120] Wheeler is in Sherman's rear. The wagon left for Houston carrying Ella! Our darkies are working out at Singer's hill digging ditches to repel raids. Went down and played 5 games of chess with R. Bates, beating him 4 times + drawing the other.

Sunday August 14th 1864: Clear and very sultry. There is nothing new under the sun. Minnie is suffering with a bad sty upon her Eye! Lt [Robert G.] Burgess of the "Jackson Artillery" was buried today with military honors. . . . It is very sultry today though the Mercury does not show it. . . . Ate the last cantelope of the season. Mr. Craig brought Mr. McCue, a little dumpy Missourian, to dine with us. Today and yesterday we had the first, and I reckon the last, peach pies of the season. The day mosquitoes are so annoying one can hardly sleep or read for them, they bite one's hands so. Rumor hath the Yankee raiders at Eatonton once more and a company went from here this P.M. to Milledgeville.

Monday August 15th 1864: Cloudy and real sultry. Last night was the warmest this summer. Mr. McCue, the dumpy Missourian aforementioned, and Mr. Haines, a burly Arkansian of Mr. Craig's company, stayed all night with us. Both left this morning the latter before "we'uns" get up. Sent out and got my shoes from Mr. Hickman's and they are real nice; low quartered like the old ones I have. . . .

120 None of this was true. The bulk of the armies remained locked in a long siege of Richmond and Petersburg, Va.

Tuesday August 16th 1864: Clear and warm. Father left at daylight for Houston. Milo came for him—trouble among the negroes.[121] There is nothing new. Julia Ann has just finished a pair of homespun pants for me. The day mosquitoes are a torment. I have got a boil on my side and it pains me a good deal.

Wednesday August 17th 1864: Clear and very warm. Minnie received a letter from Thomas. Mr. Craig left on a sixty day furlough to see his relations in So. Ca. All is quiet along the lines. Great Political excitement in the U.S; abuse of Lincoln is the order of the day. Col Cooper Nisbet, supposed killed, is a prisoner. Played 7 games chess with Bob Bates and beat him 4 times.

Thursday August 18th 1864: Clear and Warm. Finished *My Novel* and think it very fine indeed. There has been a severe fight on the Northside approach to Richmond the Yankees being repulsed Gen [Victor] Girardey + [John] Chambliss killed on our side.[122] Minnie went to prayer-meeting and brought home Mary Campbell to spend the night with her. My Boil on the side not well yet.

Friday August 19th 1864: Clear and very hot. Father got home at a quarter to ten last night after we had given him out. He brought a splendid basket of peaches + two fine melons. I have not mentioned my back in a long time. For over a year past it has been dressed twice a day regularly after breakfast and at bedtime. The left hand abscess runs at least 4 times as much as the right hand one. They do not give me much trouble and I have come to think that they will stay open as long as I live. We got a letter from Auntie! Grandma is going back to Athens. Went down and took 4 games of chess with R. Bates, beating him twice + drawing 1. Rained a little while I was there. Mrs. Maj Gen Walthall is boarding at Major Beal's.

Sunday August 21st 1864: Cloudy and pleasant. Rained pretty hard at bedtime; rained again this morning at 11½ A. The raiders have cut the RR at Jonesboro and occupied it; also the P.+.W.R.R.: so there is nothing from Lee or Hood. Read *The Shadow of the Cross*, an allegory. . . . Wore my new shoes for the first time. I had them made for winter use and put them on to try them.

Monday August 22nd 1864: Clear and pleasant. Mr. Palmer and Dr. Airey, Uncle Jno's friend arrived this evening. Was occupied all the morning in cutting out

---

121 With the front lines of the war so close, conflict on plantations was escalating. More slaves were running away in search of freedom, and others were refusing to work or even aiding deserters and straggling Union soldiers in the area. In this case, the "trouble" was caused by a male slave named Bob.

122 Gen. Victor J. B. Girardey; Gen. John R. Chambliss, Jr.

envelopes. I was taken with a pain in my hip after tea last night and I have been very restless all day. A man was killed down town to-day, the 2nd for the past week.

Tuesday Aug. 23rd 1864: Clear and quite warm. Was in so much pain that I took a Dover's Powder and consequently passed a quiet night. Did not get up till 11½ A.M. I am quite easy now. Wheeler is disturbing the Yankee rear considerably, though no reliable accounts are received. The Yankees shell Atlanta fiercely every night and have killed + wounded 5 or 6 women + children. Rumor hath Forrest in Memphis, Morgan in Middle Tennessee. . . . Cousin Jenks sent a big Burke watermelon which he brought up with him. Wagon came up from the plantation bringing 18 melons, butter, eggs, +c +c. Today Thomas' box was committed on it perilous journey.

Wednesday August 24th 1864: Clear and hot. My leg is well again. Rumored that another raid has started from Sherman's army. . . . R. Bates called and played 8 games of chess, getting beat 5 times. I got a letter from Thomas.

Thursday August 25th 1864: Clear and hot. Rumors of a raid prove unfounded. Forrest did not take Memphis but he attacked it and took 500 prisoners. The Yankees in heavy force occupy the Weldon R.R. [in Va.] and are strongly fortified. Our men cannot succeed in dislodging, though there has been some heavy fighting with that object. Wrote to Uncle John a long letter to send by Dr. Airey, when he goes: Fort Morgan has gone up the spout.

Friday August 26th 1864: Clear and warm. Heavy and furious cannonading and shelling of Atlanta. Yankees still hold the Weldon +P.R.R. Mr. Palmer stayed all night with us. Finished off 50 envelopes today.

Saturday August 27th 1864: Clear and hot. Robert came down from Athens this morning bringing us a letter with the sad news of Cousin Geo. Hayes' death.[123] Pasted Geo. Campaign [in my scrapbook]. Sherman is active and a fight or a run is the order of the day, which—the coming week must disclose. 7PM Latest! Gen Lee telegraphed that we have driven off the Yankees from the Weldon R.R. taking 2000 prisoners, 9 pieces artillery, + 7 stands colors. "Our profound gratitude is due to the giver of all victories and to the Brave officers and men engaged."[124]

123 Robert was one of Grandmother's servants. Maj. George E. Hayes was the older brother of Teedee Hayes, Minnie's close cousin who had died suddenly just three months earlier. George, a member of the 3rd Ga. Infantry, was killed in the fighting for the Weldon Railroad outside Petersburg on Aug. 21, 1864.

124 Second Battle of the Weldon Railroad, or Globe Tavern (Aug. 18-21, 1864). Union troops cut the railroad.

Sunday August 28th 1864: Clear and pleasant. Sherman is making some grand strategic move. His forces have disappeared from our front with the exception of the extreme left. I do not think he is retreating, and think a great battle cannot be long delayed. Played 8 7 games of chess with R. Bates yestereve and got beat 4 times. We have a new Kitty, a she kitty too, and that is a strong objection. "Robert" left this morning for the Front.[125]

Monday August 29th 1864: Clear and pleasant. Mother was sent for before breakfast to see little Julia Huguenin who is dying. Evening. Julia died at 11 oclock and her body was carried to Milledgeville to be interred. She died from the effects of Measles.[126]

Tuesday August 30th 1864: Clear and warm. Father left on the R.R. for Houston. Sherman has abandoned his works in front of Atlanta and is making demonstrations toward the M+WRR and I am of the opinion that there will be in a short time, a desperate contest for that line. Had pain in my back yesterday evening and I am not entirely free from it yet. Grant has raised the siege of Petersburg after losing 30000 men in 60 days. 500 per diem [day]!! Triweekly *Republican* came for [after] 6 months.

Wednesday August 31st 1864: Cloudy cool. Rode down yestereve to Mr. Whittle's corner and listened to Cheatham's Brass Band play. They only played 2 tunes and they were beautiful. O! the torment of day mosquitoes. These is no peace from them.

Thursday September 1st 1864: Clear and pleasant. . . . Commenced *St. Ronan's Well*, one of Scott's dry novels. The Yanks are moving toward the M+.W.R.R. at Jonesboro. At 5 PM. Robert Bates + I went down and played Chess with Mrs. Whittle. She beat me once, allowed me to beat her once and I beat her by force once. She beat Bates once. She loaned me a splendid Chess Book: *Proceedings of the American Chess Congress.* I enjoyed myself very much indeed—a great deal more than I expected. Father came back on the RR and brings the news that Bob was hung yesterday and Judy, Ella's sister is dead. Bob was hung by a committee of men—the police of the Company.[127]

---

125 Robert was going to help build entrenchments, work as a body servant, or both.

126 Julia, an orphan, was Col. Huguenin's daughter (see entry Mar. 6, 1863). According to the 1870 Federal Census, the Huguenin children were being raised by their grandmother (Mrs. Fort), who had moved into the home when her daughter, Julia Huguenin, died.

127 On Aug. 13, 1864, Leroy noted Ella was taken to the plantation, and his use of an exclamation point made it obvious this was a rare occurrence. Now we know why: Her sister Judy was dying or had died in childbirth (the baby died a few days later). On Aug. 16, LeRoy had written his father was needed at the plantation because of "trouble among the negroes." The overseer's wife claimed she awoke in the middle of the night to find Bob (who was apparently a teenager) inside her bedroom touching her. Whether Mr. Hill's wife was telling the truth, or something else was taking place, will likely never be known. Mr. Hill had been drafted and was serving in the army at this time.

Friday September 2nd 1864: Clear and warm. Heavy fighting at Jonesboro. Generals Anderson + Cumming wounded and no result. The Situation is fearfully critical, almost desperate. We will be compelled to abandon Atlanta.[128] Attempted to mold some bullets, but failed. Received a letter from Thomas: also one from Grandma to Mother with a copy of one from Uncle Richard. In the fight at Jonesboro Lee's, lately Hood's, Corps broke in disorder. Hardee is at Lovejoy's: Hood, who with Stewart's and Smith's Corps' remained in Atlanta, now in truth the doomed city, evacuated that place last night to join Hardee—Lee's position is not known. Gen Girau[129] of Cleburn's Division is prisoner and say about 2500 of our brave men. The prospect is fearfully gloomy and there is but a slight barrier to keep the Yanks out of this devoted city—that of a badly demoralized army.

Saturday Sept 3d 1864: Clear and pleasant. Col and Mrs. J.B. Thrasher[130] came to see us after tea last evening and stayed 'till bedtime. His views about the Front and the news made us all feel badly. I went to bed at 11 oclock with it determined that the enemy had overwhelmed us and contrary to my expectations went to sleep directly. Mrs. Thrasher brought me a Photograph of Gen [Gabriel] Wharton + his Autograph, also the Autographs of Gen's Hood, Beauregard, Smith, + Polk. Mother and Mrs. Thrasher called on Mrs. Gen Joe Johnston this evening and Mother was very much pleased with her. Mrs. Thrasher sent me a photograph of Gen [Thomas N.] Waul of Texas. Rained a little between 6 and 7 Oclock P.M. Spent all the PM in a vain endeavor to solve a [chess] puzzle viz. The Knights tour over the board.

Sunday September 4th 1864: Cloudy and cool. The abominable dogs of our neighborhood kept us all awake by their howling + Barking, which was kept up all night long. Dr. Airey left us this morning to go to the Front which is about 1½ miles beyond Lovejoy's station M+W.R.R. [Atlanta].

Monday September 5th 1864: Cloudy and warm. Occupied myself all the morning in copying the "Chess Knights Tour." We are seriously thinking of what we will do when the Yankees come, for the present prospect is that Sherman will be in front of Macon

---

128 Gens. Alfred Cumming and Patton Anderson. The Battle of Jonesboro (Aug. 31–Sept. 1, 1864) was Sherman's successful attempt to swing below Atlanta and sever the Macon & Western and the Atlanta & West Point railroads. Confederate attacks to dislodge the Union troops failed, and Hood had no choice but to abandon the city. The major victory, coupled with successes in the Shenandoah Valley, helped secure Lincoln's reelection that November. Leroy demonstrates anew his firm grasp on the how the war was progressing, and realized the loss of the rail lines meant the loss of Atlanta.

129 There is no general with a name remotely similar to this.

130 J. O. Thrasher, Georgia militia.

before a month is out. Our army cannot be more than 25000 strong, while the enemy number at least 80000. Beside this, ours is demoralized and theirs flushed with victory. It is sad, sad. We heard from Mr. Craig today—he had arrived in S.C. safely. Went down and played 3 games of chess with Jim Campbell and beat him twice out of 3. Gave him the "Kts tour" to solve. Father and I solved it this evening and I give the rhyme which it makes:

> The man that hath no love of Chess
> Is truth to say a sorry sight:
> Disloyal to his King and Queen
> A faithless and ungallant knight
>
> He hateth our good mother Church
> And sneereth at the Bishops lawn
> May bad luck force him soon to place
> His castles + estates in pawn.[131]

Wrote to Mr. Craig and enclosed his letters which came after he left. . . .

Tuesday September 6th 1864: Clear and very warm. Rode down to Mr. Bates' and got an elegant bait of Scuppernongs. Gen Jno. H Morgan is killed and most of his staff taken prisoners at Greenville, Tenn. Was occupied from 2 Oclock till nearly 6 with Father, helping him to take the numbers of all his bonds, preparatory to secreting it some time when the enemy come.[132] The only, all-absorbing topic of conversation is the Yankee advance—when they will be in Macon—what will be done in that event—how we will all get along, +c and so on. Sherman is in Atlanta and can take his own time to organize recruit and make that point his permanent base to operate against Macon and Columbus. If something is done to dislodge him, Lincoln is good for

---

131 The Knight's Tour is a famous (and exceedingly complex) mathematical problem, a sequence of moves so that the knight lands on every square only once. The fact that John and LeRoy were able to solve this is rather amazing. The poem, which appeared in *Scientific American* in the 19th century, consists of eight lines of eight syllables each, forming a metaphoric chessboard.

132 There are several important points to consider. John was worried he would be called back into service, and Thomas was away with the Army of Northern Virginia. LeRoy needs to know about the family's wealth and where the investments are located in case he ends up as the only remaining male family member. According to Mary Gresham, "Mr. Gresham says he had fallen into the habit even of advising & consulting with [LeRoy] about many things." See Afterword, Mary Gresham to her sister, 406. Also note that LeRoy did not write "if the enemy come," but "when the enemy come." By this time neither John nor his son believed Macon would escape the hard hand of war.

another 4 years term, and then anarchy desolation and woe to both sides. O! it is fearful thing to look forward at the prospect.

Wednesday September 7th 1864: Cloudy and warm. Sherman has retreated to Atlanta for the present. His losses were very severe in the "Battle of Jonesboro." Mother received a letter from Uncle Richard today dated July 29th and he sent copies to Athens and to Thomas. I got a letter from Mr. Craig. Aunt Sarah, Cousins Eliza and Mary called + the Yankees were discussed. Aunt Sarah looks badly. Mr. Tom Redding, Miss Emma Campbell's husband, is badly wounded and a prisoner. Painted over the black squares of my chess-board today. I have been rubbing and greasing my Pistol but I can't get any balls for it.

Thursday Sept 8th 1864: Cloudy and cool. Mr. Redding is recaptured. Tis said our army is clamoring for Gen Johnston to be reinstated but alas! That can never be.

Friday September 9th 1864: Clear and cool. No news. Mother and Father went down and called on Mrs. Ed. Tracy last night. "Wheeler" howled most dolefully and made one feel wonderfully like one could shoot him. Mr. Tom Redding got home yesterday. Mr. Clisby is out in gloomy colors this morning. Georgia, saith he, lies at Sherman's Mercy. Played two games [of] Chess with Mrs. Whittle, getting badly "wolved" [beaten] both times.

Saturday Sept 10th 1864: Cloudy and warm. Received a letter from Uncle John. The *Examiner* of this morning manifests the greatest indifference about the Fall of Atlanta and the defeat of Hood. Granma, Wilson, and Sallie are still in Athens, but Granma writes that she is going to send them home. I wish she was away from Athens. Mrs. Gen'l Joseph E. Johnston called on Mother this morning, and asked for me.[133] Gen Johnston started, but was met on the way by Gen Cobb and M.L. Smith and with them went out to look at the fortifications. Wagon went back to Houston this A.M. and Father sent two bales [of] Macon Sheeting [cloth] down. It is my opinion that the Yankees will not get to Macon before Spring. If they should I would be mistaken. Mr. James H. Nisbet stayed to tea with us last night and Capt Hazlehurst came after it and told us something about Lieut Izard. I am going to see Cousin Eliza directly. Mr. Tom Redding is dead. Poor Miss Emma! I grieve for her. Rode over to Cousin Eliza's and down town to pick up Father.

Sunday Sept. 11th 1864: Clear and warm. Mr. Redding was buried this A.M. and after the funeral Minnie and Father went on to hear Mr. Markham; but Mother went to

133 The fact that the wife of one of the Confederacy's most prominent generals called upon the Gresham house speaks to the family's social standing.

the grave. Mr. Markham and Mr. Green came home with Father at dinner. Sherman has ordered every white person to leave Atlanta to go North or South as they please. This is unheard of brutality. Hood has granted an armistice of 10 days for the purpose of receiving them into our lines. There are rumors of a change in the Com[man]d of the "Army of Tenn." Read the *Dairyman's Daughter* for the first time. It is a good little book.

Monday September 12th 1864: Clear and warm. Mr. Green left after breakfast for Fort Valley, where he is Post chaplain. No news. The Georgia Militiamen have been furloughed for 30 days. Mr. Bates commences school today.

Tuesday September 13th 1864: Clear and warm. Robert Bates called and I beat him at Chess 3 out of 4. Mother and Mr. Markham and I rode down to the Ocmulgee Hospital. It is exceedingly dry and the dust is terrible. Green with the plantation wagon is hauling wood from beyond the Causeway on the S.W.R.R. crossing and Ned is engaged in cutting it up and piling it away for winter use. I expect we will be pinched for wood this winter and many will suffer. Pasted in the Petersburg Campaign [in the scrapbook].

Wednesday September 14th 1864: Clear and warm. Mr. Markham left at 9½ A.M. He [sang] at Prayers in the morning. He sang finely too. Minnie + I went over to see Cousin Juliet. I received a letter from Thomas.

Thursday September 15th 1864: Clear and warm. Dr. and Mrs. Fort called after tea last night. This is Gov. Brown's fast day. . . . Cousin Sam Knox came home from church with the folks: he is on his way to the Front. Jimmie and Bowie Knox arrived late in the evening. I have been really sick all he evening. Cousin Sam's wound is not entirely well yet. This is the 4th day of Armistice. Hood + Sherman are corresponding on the subject of the exchange of Prisoners.

Friday September 16th 1864: Clear and warm. Cousin Jimmie + Bowie left at 8 A.M. for the Front. I took a dose of Paregoric before going to bed last evening and feel better. Cousin Samuel Knox has just left us (4 P.M.): he goes by the 6 O'clock train. "Hamp" [plantation slave] has come in sick from the fortifications.

Saturday September 17th 1864: Clear and pleasant. A letter to Father from Thomas says that he has been promoted to Rodman of the party with pay of 48$ a month, + that the party was to start into Rockbridge Co. His letters to be directed to Lexington. Went over with Roberts Bates and Lockett and played a long game of chess with Mrs. W[hittle]. It was the Ruy Lopez Kt and I was beat. I played well.[134]

---

134 Robert was the first name of both Bates and Lockett. "Ruy Lopez Kt" is a famous chess move.

Sunday September 18th 1864: Cloudy and damp. We had a very fine rain just before day, which was much needed, and it drizzled slightly 'till church time. Mr. Clisby is completely whipped—and you can see from the tone of his paper [which gives] his adhesion to a reconstruction or submission policy.

Monday September 19th 1864: Cloudy. Rained in the night. The *Telegraph* of this morning announces the retirement of Mr. Clisby. Capt Flash has brought him out and tomorrow will be issued the first number of *The Telegraph + Confederate*. Commenced *The Betrothed*. Rumor foreshadows an important move on the part of the Army of Tennessee on which depends the fate of Geo. and the success of the present campaign.

Tuesday September 20th 1864: Cloudy and damp. Mr. Palmer stayed all night with us and left for Sparta. Allen is sick with fever. Hamp Well. Howard went to market and was conscripted on his way. Father went down and had him released. The armistice on our front was put an end to by Sherman. There is a good deal of sickness in town mostly low fever. Miss Sue Rowland is quite sick with it. The 1st No. of *The Macon Daily Telegraph and Confederate* is much like the old "Daily." Minnie received a letter from Thomas in which he bids a farewell to Botetourt Co. Allen has been quite sick all day. The fever has not once left him since Sunday at dinner time. The Army of Tenn. is entrenched on the West P[oin]t road. Forrest + Wheeler 'tis said have united their forces to move on Sherman's rear.

Wednesday September 21st 1864: Cloudy and cool. Howard left for Houston in the buggy. Allen has been a little out of his head all day and gets out of his bed and walks about. Rained hard in the evening. Mrs. Whittle and I commenced a Game of Chess by correspondence this morning and have made 4 moves forming the K[night]'s gambit. Commenced *Redgauntlet*. I have read all of Scott's novels except this. Among the rumors which fill the air are: that Forrest is to be made Lt. Gen. and put in command of all the cavalry of our army; that the President is to make this department a visit; there is little prospect of the College being opened. 3 of the Professors have left, two of them for good. Father wrote and had the *Republican* changed from Triweekly to daily, so it will be out about the 25th or 26th of November.

Thursday September 22nd 1864: Cloudy and pleasant Maj Gen Rhodes is dead.[135] Allen has to be watched all the time to keep him from leaving his bed. He climbed out the window last night. Nothing of interest from our front, excepting the exchange of 2 or 3000 prisoners. Howard returned with supplies.

---

135 Gen. Robert Rodes, one of Gen. Lee's best division leaders, was killed at Third Winchester (Sept. 19, 1864), a major Union victory by Gen. Phil Sheridan that swept Gen. Early's army from the field.

Friday September 23d 1864: Cloudy and pleasant. Allen about the same; still out of his mind. Howard sat up with him. [Gen.] Early has had a heavy engagement with Sheridan in the Valley and coming off second best + fell back to Strasburg. . . . Gens [Archibald] Godwin, Fitz Lee, and [Zebulon] York wounded. The fight occurred on the 19th (Monday). The *Memphis Appeal* came yesterday. It has resumed publication in Montgomery, Ala. after a suspension of 2 months. I wish it had stopped here for it is the best paper in the South.

A great many people have packed up and are ready to leave these parts on short notice. We have not started yet but expect to soon. Minnie has just finished a new pink net for her hair.

President Davis arrived quite unexpectedly on Yesterday's train and this morning made a speech in the Baptist Church before the meeting to raise money for Refugees. Father characterized it as a defense of himself and not in his usual good taste. He gave poor Gen Johnston a slam, as well as Gov. Brown. I wish he had brought Gen Beauregard along with him. Arch came up from the plantation. Mrs. Whittle and I come alone finely with our Chess and the game we are playing is very interesting. The *Macon Telegraph + Confederate* is not as good a paper as the *Daily* was. It is all advirtisements and Northern news. *Redgauntlet* is a very dry book though not as bad as *St. Ronan's Well*.

Saturday September 24th 1864: Cloudy. Rained hard at noon and cleared up . . . . Allen is much better today. No news. President Davis left yesterday for the Front via Columbus. Wrote to Thomas. Arch carried down the blue couch and a bureau down to Houston in case we should have to go there this winter. . . .

Sunday September 25th 1864: Clear and cool enough early in the morning to wear a winter coat. . . . Nothing at all from Early's fight. All quiet in our front. Allen much better. Hamp convalescing. Mother too unwell to attend service. The Yankees claim a great victory in the Valley and 5000 prisoners stores arms +c +c. Sherman is tearing down the wooden houses in Atlanta to make Barracks for his men. Minnie's palmetto hat came back from the pressers and it is beautiful and tasteful.

Monday September 26th 1864: Clear and beautiful, bracing fall day. Rode over to Mrs. Whittle's and played out our game to see how it would end. I was beat badly. It is so cool this morning that Mother made a little fire in her room. The dogs howled all night and made us mutter maledictions on their heads.

Tuesday September 27 1864: Clear and pleasant. Mr. Wills stayed to tea with us last night. Father left on the R.R. for the plantation. Forrest has taken Athens, Ala: 1300 prisoners, stores, 500 wagons and is pushing for Middle Tennessee. Early has suffered two more defeats and is pushing—backwards.[136] Breckinridge is in E Tenn., and so Early was overpowered with numbers, out flanked by 20000 cavalry and compelled to skedaddle.

Wednesday September 28th 1864: Clear nd warm. No news. Jim Campbell called, and beat me at chess. Mother sick. All is well. Ned quite sick with Dysentery. . . .

Thursday September 29th 1864: Clear and warm Forrest, whose name is the synonym of victory, has taken Sulphur Springs, Ala: 800 prisoners + large amounts of stores cannon +c. The funeral of Sarah, daughter of Judge Powers, is from [at] Whittle's this morning. Gen Beauregard is in Charleston on his way (I hope) to the "Army of Tennessee." Meetings are to be held in our church every night. They began last night Kt.[137] . . . Mother sick with headache. Rode down in the carriage to the B.R.R. depot to meet Father. We have had no authentic acc't of Early's Battle + defeat. Grandma has left Athens for the war, so we learn from a letter dated [in] Sparta.[138]

Friday September 30th 1864: Clear and beautiful day. Mother had made up her mind to go to Sparta next week, but as Grandma says in her letter of yesterday that she is coming to see us, she will postpone her visit for the present at least. Grandma has Candace, Violet, Aunt Peggy, and Frank with her.[139] She scattered valuables among different friends. President Davis reviewed [Gens.] Cheatham's and Bate's divisions and [they] cheered for "Old Joe Johnston." Rumor [is] Hardee [was] relieved but I hope it is not so. Grant is marshalling his legions for the last great trial and On to Richmond of the war. Mother made me a blue plaid silk cravat. Minnie goes to prayermeeting every eve and stays to tea and goes to church with Jim + Mary Campbell. She will join the church on Sunday. The lecture room is crowded every night. . . .

Saturday October 1st 1864: Clear and warm. Gen Hardee is in town, over at the College. Father bought us some shrimps. Bought me a stalk of sugar cane also + gave a dollar for it!

136 The first was Second Winchester (Sept. 19). The second was Fisher's Hill (Sept. 21-22, 1864), where once more Sheridan's Union army routed the Confederates.

137 LeRoy is being clever by spelling "night" the same as the chess piece.

138 Grandma is going live in Sparta, where Aunty lives, for the rest of the war.

139 Grandma's house servants.

Sunday October 2nd 1864: Clear and warm. Mr. Wills, Father, Judge Nisbet, and Mr. Bates came up after service yesterday eve and received me into the Church.[140] Minnie and Kitty Bates join this morning. Two soldiers were admitted yesterday. Hood's army is across [north of] the Chattahoochee!!!!

Monday October 3d 1864: Cloudy and damp. Commenced, at Church time last night, to rain + rained hard in the night. . . . Heavy fighting on the 1st on the Weldon R.R. We charged the enemy to dislodge them from some breastworks which they had taken from us, but failed to do so. Bloody work is anticipated on that line. Grant is determined to outdo Sherman—if he can. Early has checked Sheridan. Hood, it is rumored, has "straddled" the W+A.R.Road.

Tuesday October 4th 1864: Cloudy early in the day; but clear toward noon. Pasted in my scrap-book: Hood's campaign. Forrest is in Tenn moving north toward Sherman's rear. Green came up last night with four more darkies to work on the fortifications. Howard and he are engaged in hauling wood today from the S.W.R.R. crossing on the Houston road. Beauregard has been assigned to the command of the Dept of Ga, Ala, Miss, and E. La—a position where his influence will not be felt.[141] Scholars are coming in slowly at the College. Minnie has gone regularly to work this evening. Gen Hardee has taken command of the Dept [of] So. Ca, S. Ga, Fla. . . .

Wednesday October 5th 1864: Clear and warm. Gen [John] Echols reports the rout of a Yankee cavalry force in E Tenn. Last night we were surprised to see Mr. Smythe ride up to the door. He stayed all night with us and after singing "Larry O'Brien" and playing on the melodeon [accordion], left for Savannah on his horse. Hood's move, he said, was thought in the army to be a desperate one.[142] Father brought home Lieut Jas. Johnson of Tennessee, his own dear cousin on his father's side, whose existence he was hardly aware of until a few days ago when he called at [Father's] office.[143] He was in Cheatham's division but was thrown out by consolidation. He is a very nice little man.

---

140 This took place at home, while his sister Minnie joined in services at the church that same morning. He did not get communion, according to a family letter, because everyone was too busy to bring it.

141 Gen. Beauregard was given command of the new Department of the West, which included Hood's and Taylor's armies. It was mostly an advisory command, with no operational control of the armies unless he joined them in person. Whether his own opinion or his father's, Leroy was right: The former hero of First Manassas would not influence the course of events in any meaningful way.

142 Smythe was Thomas' friend from college. Hood moved his Army of Tennessee north of Sherman in an effort to cut the Western and Atlanta RR and force Sherman to abandon Atlanta and follow him.

143 James Edward Johnson. His grandmother, Elizabeth Walker Jones, and John Gresham's grandmother, Mary Jones Gresham, were sisters.

Mother left this evening for Sparta to make a flying visit and bring Grandma back with her. Frank is cutting wood and piling it away for a rainy day. It has been very sultry all day. Mrs. Whittle has not sent me a move since Thursday last, and our game by correspondence languishes unfinished.

Thursday October 6th 1864: Cloudy and warm. Commenced raining at 1 oclock and rained 'till 3½ PM. . . . Went over to Mrs. Whittle's and played out our game and beat her. [Gen.] Wheeler has captured Rome and 3 negro regiments. Beauregard is in town, consulting with Gov. Brown and others. Minnie has written to Thomas today. It is time we were getting a letter [from him].

Friday October 7th 1864: Cloudy and warm. Howard and Green finished hauling this A.M. Got a letter from Mother in Milledgeville. She has had a hard time getting there: the cars not connecting at Gordon [Ga], she had to wait till 10 Oclock at night and then went down and got to Milledgeville at 2 PM + had to walk to Aunt Eliza's house. Gen Beauregard and Gov. Brown were at Gordon.

Saturday September 8th 1864: Clear, and cool enough for fire. . . . Another heavy attack on Richmond from the northside has been foiled. Gen [John] Gregg killed and [Gen. John] Bratton wounded on our side. Green returned to Houston carrying Hamp and Ned (the two sick ones) and Frank. No letter from Thomas in nearly 3 weeks now.

Sunday September 9th 1864: [date sic] Clear and cold for the season. Mercury at 8 A.M. 50°; Outdoors, it was 42°. The Yellow fever is prevailing in Charleston, S. C., and many die daily. Sherman 'tis said has left Atlanta in pursuit of Gen Hood and the campaign is at a most critical stage. Grant is receiving heavy reinforcements and Richmond is to stand another fiery trial. Read *Bible Truth*, by Dr. Alexander all the evening and some parts aloud to Father and Minnie. Have sat close round the fire all day. . . . Sent to the Post Office with the hope of getting a letter from Thomas but none came. There is no news in the paper this morning.

Monday October 10th 1864: Clear and cold. First frost of the season. Wrote to Thomas. Minnie has a cold and I think she will have sore eyes.

Tuesday October 11th 1864: Clear and moderating. Minnie sick with cold and sore eyes, so she could not go to school. The capture of Rome [Ga] is false. Father brought home two delightful letters, one from Thomas and one from Mother. Thomas in fine health though suffering for a letter from home. Mother gives us a long newsy letter. Uncle Edge has secured a new position of duty in Richmond, Va.[144] Today is splendid—clear and just right not hot or cold. Father received a letter from Mr. Kemp stating that Willis [plantation slave] was dying. Pleurisy is the disease so it is thought.

Wednesday October 12th 1864: Clear and cool. News from Hood states that [Gen.] Stewart was attacked on Alatoona Heights, but the enemy was beaten off. French's Division assaulted the heights and failed to take, but was reinforced and took it with the garrison.[145] Sherman is not in command, having been cut off in Nashville by Forrest.[146] Jim Campbell and I were sitting playing chess, yesterday when he was sent for at home—[his father] Mr. Tom Campbell was dead. We had a visit from old Mrs. Matthews also. I succeeded in working out a problem, which I had been working at a good deal. Rode out in Mrs. Whittle's phaeton [carriage], by her invitation, all around town, first to the trotting track then back through town to Vineville where I saw one glimpse of the fortifications. On the way down we stopped to see the dress parade of the Battalion of the Local troops and saw Father in line for the first time.

Thursday October 13th 1864: Clear and cool. Mother got safely home yesterday at 8½ oclock. The train was behind time and 'twas near nine by the time we got through and halfpast ten before we had settled down sufficiently to retire to bed. She brought us many nice things: apples, popcorn, homespun dresses, but much better news viz: that Grandma + Wilson will spend some time with us this winter. She brought me some nice problems in Chess from the *Spirit of the Times*. Minnie's homespuns are beautiful. Rumors are plentiful enough, but nothing is certainly known of Hood's movements or the position of our army, and a feeling of uneasiness is prevalent. I have commenced wearing my new shoes regularly since last Sunday the 9th day of October 1864. Willis died Tuesday evening.

Friday October 14th 1864: Cloudy and cool. I have had on a winter coat since last Thursday and we've had a fire too. Mr. Hill is here and he thinks Old Uncle Jack is too ill to recover.[147] Father has lost 4 men and two women this season + with 6 or 8 here

144 Uncle Edge had begun work on the Slaves Claims Board, organized in April 1864 to consider compensation claims for slaves contracted into Confederate service (like many of John Gresham's had been) and had either escaped or died of disease.

145 The Battle of Allatoona (Oct. 5, 1864) was a decisive Union victory. Gen. Stewart sent a division under Gen. Sam G. French to capture a Union fort protecting the Western & Atlanta RR at Allatoona Pass in northern Georgia. The attack was beaten back with heavy loss.

146 Sherman was with his armies pursuing Hood in northern Georgia, and not in Tennessee.

147 Old Uncle Jack was another Houston slave. Elderly slaves were often called "Uncle" or "Aunt."

working, he is short of hands. Mrs. Snider sent me word that she had a terrier puppy for me but he was too young to leave his "mammy yet." [148]

Saturday October 15th 1864: Clear and cool. Hood's army is at Dallas [Ga] and I think in a most critical situation. The enemy claim a victory at Allatoona. I was lying on the grass in the front and Gen Johnston came by and bowed to me and I did not know him. O massy, I'm soo sorry. Howard brought home my mould with ladle.[149]

Sunday October 16th 1864: Clear and warmer. Last night Father handed us a letter from Thomas which he had in his pocket nearly two days. Yesterday made my first attempt at moulding bullets and succeeded finely. . . . The northern state elections are going heavily for Lincoln + he is President for another 4 years.[150] Mother did not go to church but was at Mrs Fort's. She (Mrs. Fort) was very sick.

Monday October 17th 1864: Cloudy and cool. Moulded some bullets at the woodpile this morning. Father left on the railroad for Houston. Mr's Kemp and Hill both in service. Mother went down town and bought a dozen apples at 4.00. [Gen.] Price is in front of Jefferson City, Mo. And the whole state is in a blaze of excitement.

Tuesday October 18th 1864: Cloudy half the day. No news. Nothing is known of the position of the Army of Tenn and Gen Hood permits nothing to be told.

Wednesday October 19th 1864: Clear delightful and invigorating day. Pasted in my chess problems this morning and after that went over to Mrs. Whittle's and took a game of chess. . . . Read Bishop Elliott's sermon on Lieutenant General Polk and I think it a splendid thing. Rumor locates Hood's army up in Mill's Valley, like John Brown's spirit, "marching on."

Thursday October 20th 1864: This is Thomas' twentieth birthday. Aunt Eliza and Mary left for Eufaula [Ga] after breakfast and she just did get to the depot in time, for Mother did not know of her intention to leave till it was nearly time to start. . . . Roberts Lockett and Bates came up, and Bates played 4 games of chess, beating once. I have been working at ~ 3 more problems for two weeks and can not solve it. Mother has been suffering with ear-ache all the evening. Father arrived on the railroad this evening and brought me some sugar cane which is a treat to see when it is selling at a dollar a

---

148 Cousin Eliza's mother-in-law.

149 This is equipment LeRoy needed to make bullets for his pistol. The ladle was to pour the molten lead into the mold.

150 LeRoy means all indications were that Lincoln would win a second term; the presidential election was still a few weeks away (Nov. 8, 1864).

stalk in town. Mr. Kemp came up with evening, so our plantations are without any one on them.[151]

Friday October 21st 1864: Clear and cool. Hood has taken Dalton and Ringgold and is pushing on. Commenced *Dr. Antonia*. Father talks of carrying Mother and me to Houston as he'll have to stay a greater part of his time down there.

Saturday October 22nd 1864: Clear and cold. The wind has blown hard all day. I went to Dr. Emerson's with Minnie who had a tooth filled and while there, Father brought me a letter from Thomas. Mother got one from Grandma and she + Auntie are in Athens on a flying visit. Father bought me a nice little copy of *Pollock's Course of Time*. Co. B [of militia] is ordered to the front and we all feel very gloomy at the prospect of Father's going. I hope some means will be provided by a kind Providence to prevent it. Early has got another licking. He attacked Sheridan and then was in turn attacked and routed with the loss of 30 pieces artillery. Maj Gen Ramseur is mort[ally] wounded + Captured. Gens Battle + Conner wounded.[152] Wrote to Thomas. After dinner Father and I went in the garden and shot pistol under difficulties for the balls were too large and we had to cut them down. Mother is sick—has not been well since she came back from Sparta.

Sunday October 23rd 1864: Clear and cold. . . . I read *Pollok's Course of Time* this morning, and our principal occupation was to "charr" sugar cane in the evening. Gen Bragg has been assigned to the temporary command at Wilmington, an attack being expected there.

Monday October 24th 1864: Clear and cold. At a meeting of "Co. B" this morning it was resolved to represent to Gen Cobb that the men over 50 wanted to be relieved from going to the front, and this evening the company was told if they voted to go they might do so, if not they were to be disbanded. The Co. was relieved from gaurd duty. Minnie bought a quart of haws for 1 dollar?[153] No news from any point. Sent for Mr. Whittle's bullet molds and molded some bullet which fit our pistols and shot finely. I am so glad Father is relieved from going to the front, though he will have to go to

---

151 There were no white overseers or white men with authority on the plantations.

152 The Battle of Cedar Creek (Oct. 19, 1864). Gen. Early, whom Sheridan was sure had been completely beaten, launched a daring surprise attack on Sheridan's army camped at Cedar Creek. Sheridan was absent, but made a spectacular return, rallied his nearly beaten troops, and led his men to a complete victory, taking full control of the Shenandoah Valley for the remainder of the war. Gen. Stephen D. Ramseur was killed, and Gens. Cullen A. Battle and James Conner wounded.

153 Small fruit similar to apples coming from the hawthorn tree.

Houston to oversee. All the militia have gone on to Griffin, [Ga]. General Hood does not allow any army news to be sent.

Tuesday October 25th 1864: Clear and cool. Superintended the digging of the Chufas [nuts]. Mother trimmed Minnie's Palmetto hat and 'tis very handsome.[154]

Wednesday October 26th 1864: Cloudy and cool. . . . Father left for Houston in the buggy with Howard. Mother was to have gone but for Mr. Flinn's coming. I rode down to Mrs. Matthews to pay her some money. No news—all is quiet along the lines + it is thought will remain so till after the election. Received a letter from Grandma saying Frank and Aunt Peggy would be here tonight and we are in a box for Howard is in Houston.[155] General Beauregard assumed command of the "Military Div[ision] of the West" Oct. 17th 1864 and his address is fine. . . .

Thursday October 27th 1864: Cloudy until about eleven oclock when it began to rain hard and is still raining. Frank and Aunt Peggy arrived sure enough and had to shift for themselves, for Mary who went down to find them did not see them: so they came on foot. Aunt "Peg" is so blue [upset] that she can hardly speak without crying. Finished *Dr. Antonia* + it is too sad for me and though the tone is exquisite, I am not fond of such novels. Worked out a Chess Problem after tea last night and one this morning. [Gen] Longstreet [has recovered and] assumed command of his Old Corps on the 18th ult: R.H. Anderson takes Beauregard's corps + Dick Taylor and S[tephen] D. Lee exchange positions. Hood is pushing forward to the North is rumored. Howard arrived from the plantation this evening, bringing supplies and some sugar cane for me.

Friday October 28th 1864: Clear and warm. Last night after tea copied *Egypt* for Miss M.C. de G [Clare deGraffenreid]. Heavy skirmishing on the Weldon Railroad. Richard Edwards is home on a 60 day furlough, run down from Chills + fever. Roberts Bates + Lockett called and played Chess with me.

Saturday October 29th 1864: Clear and cool. Several heavy assaults on our lines around Richmond were repulsed Thursday with heavy loss. Heavy fighting on the Southside, also. Rumor has Hood in Tennessee! Father arrived from Houston bringing a quarter of beef. Bates, Lockett, and I went over to Mrs. Whittles and we, all three, played against her and beat her soundly. The Kings Gambit was played both times.

---

154 Ladies' hats could be trimmed with ribbon, laces, real or artificial flowers, and even fabric "curtains" to protect their hair in the back.

155 There was no one to pick up Frank and Aunt Peggy from the train station.

Sunday October 30th 1864: Clear and cool. Lee has whipped Grant on the 28th on the Southside. He attacked us and was repulsed with heavy slaughter and driven to his old position. Our whole loss: 400. Price has whipped the enemy in Missouri.[156] I wrote to Thomas or rather finished my letter of yesterday. Nothing of Gen Hood's position is known. . . .

Monday October 31st 1864: Cloudy and warm. Went down to Dr. Emerson's and he filled + worked for an hour and put cotton in my eye-tooth. I wish it was over. Commenced *Guy Rivers* by Simms, borrowed from Dr. Emerson. Mrs. Matthews called + brought a pair of gloves for Thomas.

Tuesday November 1st 1864: Cloudy, with indications of rain. Frank and Aunt Peggie left for Houston in Aunt Ann's wagon. The Yankees claim to have routed Price with loss of his wagons and cannon. [Gen.] Forrest is at Paris, Tenn, capturing gunboats. Hood is "non inventus [nowhere to be found]." Father brought home news today which makes our heart bleed, in the shape of a dispatch from Thomas in Richmond in these words: "Detail revoked—obliged to join company. Telegraph your wishes—Answer." Father telegraphed him to see Col Lay and endeavor to be reassigned. If compelled—join Capts Wise or Tuft's cavalry or Captains Harris or Massenburg's Battery and try to get a furlough. He also telegraphed Col Lay. It is so hard to bear, after his being so comfortably located to be dragged into a conscript camp + forced to join a strange company.[157]

Wednesday November 2nd 1864: Weather—Raining steadily. Rained hard in the night and in the midst of it there was a fire.

Thursday November 3d 1864: Drizzled rain steadily all day I was to have gone to Dr. Emerson's but it was too damp. Hood's army is away over in Alabama at Tuscambia.[158] Minnie could not go to school. We have received no answer to our telegrams and we feel most uneasy and anxious about Thomas. [Gen.] Early is abused on all sides for the

---

156 Price's Missouri Expedition or Price's Raid (Sept. 18–Dec. 2, 1864) was an overly ambitious Confederate attempt by Gen. Sterling Price to recapture St. Louis and reignite the Confederate cause in the Trans-Mississippi Theater. Leroy could have been referring to one of any number of October battles. Ultimately, Price rode 1,400 miles, fought more than 40 battles and skirmishes, lost thousands of men, and utterly failed. It was the final Southern offensive west of the Mississippi River.

157 John Gresham, who long ago saw the writing on the wall that the Confederacy was doomed, was trying to do everything he could to keep his son out of the front lines.

158 Gen. Hood, with Gen. Beauregard's and Pres. Davis' permission, was operating in Alabama preparatory to moving north into Tennessee. There was little else he could do by this point of the war. Sherman, who had sufficient troops in Tennessee to deal with Hood, was planning his March to the Sea, which would carry his army from Atlanta eastward to Savannah and eventually into the Carolinas.

late disgraceful termination of the "Battle of Cedar Creek" and he ought to be relieved. *Guy Rivers* is [the most] high-wrought overdone affair [that] I have read in a long time. Father and I occupied ourselves tearing off the backs of old letters to make envelopes.

Friday November 4th 1864: Cloudy and cold. The wind blew in the night and the yard is covered with a carpet of yellow China leaves. Rode down to the dentist's and had a huge filling put in my eyetooth + it did not hurt so much as I expected. Got a letter from Thomas stating the facts already telegraphed. Since morning the wind has blown icily though it has not cleared off. I had to wear my overcoat down town. I took a bottle of whiskey along with me from which I took a big drink.[159] The paper made a failure this morning in endeavoring to get off Brown's message which is of huge length and discursive in the extreme. Forrest is capturing transports on the Tennessee River, which he has completely blockaded at Paris.

Saturday November 5th 1864: Clear and cold and it is fine weather to be out. . . . Cousin George's baby is called Mary Eugenia.[160] I put on undershirts last night. Nought from Thomas.

Sunday November 6th 1864: Cloudy and cold. Father went over to Mr. Whittle's last night to see Colonel [Bushrod] Frobel as to Thomas: but nothing can be done. No news except the rumored "Capture" of Decatur, Ala. by Hood with 4000 prisoners, half darkies. A letter from Thomas to Mother brings us sad, sad news. Thomas has been forced to join the infantry of Lee's army and as a privilege was allowed to choose a Geo. Co.: so he chose the Macon Volunteers. O! how it wrings our heart to think of it. All hope of his being reassigned is gone.

Monday November 7th 1864: Clear and warmer again. Father left for Houston in the buggy. Aunt Ann let Major carry me to Dr. Emerson's.[161] He finished the eyetooth and refilled in part the under plug in the left front tooth. Minnie went with me + I borrowed *Woodcraft, or Hawks around the Dovecote*. Went down to Mrs. Lockett's and played 1 game with Rob + got beat. Wrote to Thomas. The weather is most variable. Yesterday morning overcoats were in requisition and I put on my undershirts: today it is warm enough to be without a fire and as I write after tea we have the windows all open + it is hot at that. Gen [Moxely] Sorrell, formerly Longstreet's A.A.G. [staff officer], has been

---

159 Contrary to popular belief, dentists did use painkillers in this era, though what, if anything, Dr. Emerson used on LeRoy is unknown. The whiskey, of course, was to dull the pain.

160 Mary Eugenia, Cousin Kate's daughter, who lived until 1901.

161 Major was one Aunt Ann's house servants.

assigned to the command of Wright's Brigade, so we address Thomas to Co. B, 2nd Ga. Batt[alion], Snell's Brigade, Mahone's Division, Army of N. Va.[162]

Tuesday November 8th 1864: Cloudy and damp. Rained in the night + before breakfast. Forrest has taken 3 Gunboats, 10 transports, + 25 barges at Johnsonville, Tenn. with large amount of stores, freight, + 42 cannon.[163] Since the 31st ult. He has captured 4 gunboats + 14 transports. Congress met yesterday. The message of the Presid[en]t has no important features. The Capture of Decatur is contradicted. The Ram *Albemarle*, the gaurdian of Plymouth, N.C. has been blown up by the Yanks + the town recaptured. So goeth our [ironclad] rams forth to destruction. Today we received two old letters from Thomas, one to Grandma, and one to me dated 22nd Oct. and missent to some other Macon. It only made us sad to read them. Col Lay also writes that there is no chance for Thomas to be got out.

Wednesday November 9th 1864: Clear and warm. Without a fire. No news of interest. The legislature seems to be discussing the smallpox and the propriety of adjourning more than anything else. Rode down and played 2 games of chess + he [unidentified] beat me bad.

Thursday November 10th 1864: Clear and pleasant. Father arrived in the buggy last night. Mrs. Matthews stayed to tea.[164] Yankees report the C.S. Steamer *Florida* sunk.[165] Father bought some splendid white commercial note paper + some fine blue letter paper. Cut out and marked Envelopes all the evening. This evening it has turned a good deal cooler + looks as if it might blow off cold.

Friday November 11th 1864: Clear and cold. This is my 17th birthday and I am old enough to be in the reserve forces of the C.S.A. O! me what a farce! No news. Mr. Mitchell, our neighbor, died this morning at 7. Roberts Bates + Lockett called and I played two games of Chess with Bates, beating him both times, and 3 with Lockett—1

162 Gen. G. Moxley Sorrell assumed command of Gen. A. R. Wright's Georgia brigade (Mahone's division). This would place Thomas on the right, or western, side of Lee's extended lines around Petersburg.

163 Gen. Nathan Forrest was on a 23-day raid in western Tennessee. He disrupted the logistics of Union Gen. George Thomas in Nashville (who was preparing to resist Hood's invasion), but Forrest's efforts had no lasting effect.

164 Neighbor Lucy Dicey Matthews, widow of Isaac Matthews.

165 The raider CSS *Florida* was illegally captured by a Union officer in Brazil on Oct. 7, 1864, and turned over to the Union navy. Brazil, whose territorial rights had been violated, demanded the ship be returned. On Nov. 28, 1864 in Newport News, VA, the *Florida* mysteriously sank after being struck by a Union transport ship.

drawn—the other two got beat. Obviously the reason was my being unaccustomed to the Black Men.[166]

Saturday November 12th 1864: Clear and cool. Father and Mother went to Mr. Mitchell's funeral at 10 A.M. . . . Howard and Allen are hauling wood from the R.R. Lincoln is beyond doubt reelected + 4 years of bloody war are before us! O! for peace, peace.[167]

Sunday November 13th 1864: Weather record: Clear beautiful day. Uncle LeRoy arrived here last night. President Davis' message out—tis 4 columns long. Lincoln is reelected. This is the only news: but it's enough to last a long time.

Monday November 15th 1864: Clear and cold. Uncle LeRoy left after breakfast. Father left at 4 P.M. for Richmond to see after Thomas. We were in a bustle all day trying to get everything ready. Julia Ann + Mother, after working hard, could not quite get his overshirt: so Father left and Howard came back + got it. Father took on his blankets, two overshirts, two undershirts, potatoes and a ham to him. His mess [those accompanying Thomas in his unit include]—Jim Harrison + Price, Coon Conner, Cleve, Franklin, + Ben Smith. Auntie + Uncle Edge leave tomorrow for Va. Grandma will remain behind a while and then come over? We hear today, the somewhat startling news—that, a negro at Mrs. Fort's has the Smallpox! Rather too close for comfort upon honor! It is quite prevalent in town now. Mrs. Dr. Williamson has it and a good many other people have it among the darkeys.

Tuesday November 15th 1864: Cloudy and cold. Many rumors of evacuation of Atlanta, most of which are "bosh." Rode down and played Chess with Robert Lockett and he beat me. Howard went to Houston this morning to get supplies. Commenced *The Caxtons* by Buliver, loaned to me by Miss Sue Rowland and I like it very much as far as I have read. . . . .

Wednesday November 16th 1864: Clear and warmer. Howard returned with supplies. I wrote to Thomas, and received a letter from "Thos. Dated the 8th in the trenches." Rumored that the Yankees are marching out of Atlanta, in this direction, 10,000

166 Leroy means black chess pieces. The player moving the white pieces always moves first, and is considered to have an advantage.

167 It is interesting to note that Leroy (and many Southerners) seemed to believe the war would continue for years because of Lincoln's reelection, when in fact the war was in its final months. It seems obvious to us today only because we know how and when the war ended. It was not so clear in November of 1864.

strong![168] Played Chess with Bates and Lockett after tea last night, beating the first 1 in 3 + the latter 3 "hard running." It had a bad effect on me; I dreamed about it in the night.

Thursday November 17th 1864: Clear and warmer. Rode down to Dr. Emerson's and found the town in an uproar about the approach of the enemy, who are this side of Griffin and "marching on," 10 + some declare 15,000 strong. The trains have been running in all day with the stores. The College will be broken up tis thought. We have about 10 or 11,000 to oppose them + I can't see why Macon should give up. 8 P.M. we have received the following note from Mr. Bowdre which I copy for future reading:

Mrs. Gresham:

The news is bad enough: our forces have been compelled to retreat + were at Barnesville last night (40 miles from Macon) + Gen Toombs tells me they will be some 15 miles from Macon tonight—I mean ours—Sherman's army is coming on as rapidly as they can; his cavalry camped last night, it is said, only 10 miles from Forsythe in Butts Co. He is coming in two columns—it is thought by those who ought to know that Sherman's forces will be here on Sunday or Monday, possibly sooner, unless opposed + we have too small a number to do anything much I fear. We may fight him in this vicinity but I fear not with any chance of success. Gen Toombs advises all ladies + children to get away if they can. He is now at our store I am greatly disturbed myself about my family. PEB Yours in haste P.E. Boudre

We do not know what to do or think. We have no place to run to, where we could be safe, and we feel awfully about it. The town is in a furor of excitement, + I fear little or nothing will be done, to save the town. If Father were only here![169]

---

168 Sherman's March to the Sea (Nov. 15-Dec. 21, 1864). Sherman left Atlanta with 60,000 troops heading generally east by southeast toward Savannah on the coast. The Confederacy had only 10-12,000 troops (many state militia) to oppose him. The march was potentially catastrophic for the Confederacy because many of her most valuable factories and arsenals, including the Augusta Powder Works (the only major producer of gunpowder for the South) were now easily within Sherman's reach.

169 John Gresham left for Richmond, which meant LeRoy was the only male Gresham left in Macon.

Friday November 18th 1864: Clear and warm. After breakfast rode down to see Mr. Bowdre as to what had best be done. Seemed to be greatly perplexed and finally advised us to send Minnie off. Came home via Aunt Sarah's. Mother commenced to pack up Minnie and after an hour or two Mrs. Matthews came up and offered to take her to Thomasville to Aunt Sarah Ann's. Soon we heard the C.R.R. [Central Railroad of Georgia] was cut and they determined to go by Albany. I was never so perplexed, and I determined to do all I could to settle the question of running or staying. Mother and I will stay 'till further developments at least. The yankee advance tis said will be able to reach here by night and I am afraid the S.W.R.R. [Southwestern Railroad] will be cut.[170]

Saturday November 19th 1864: We got up at about half after 4 and had breakfast at 5 and at 6 Oclock Minnie and Mrs. Matthews left. The train did not leave until 8 AM but they were [determined] to get a seat. We hated to see Minnie start, but Providence seemed to open a way for her to go, in the offer of Mrs. Matthews. Howard went along to take charge of their baggage. Rained while they were getting off and so they wrapped up in blankets +c. Minnie hated to go and Mother would not have sent her, but every gentleman consulted advised us to do so. Howard took them in the wagon and Fred went and drove the wagon back. It was hard work to get her off. The last straggling cavalry man + the rear gaurd of Gen G.W. Smith's army entered town this morning and a stand is to be made for the city, tho' we do not think, with any chance of success.[171] I went on the house [roof] to look at the batteries. Last night we could see the gleaming of the campfires. The yankees burnt the business part of Atlanta before leaving and these fires caused the stories about its evacuation. . . . Every man who is able is ordered within the trenches and if they would go, Macon might yet be saved. And if Macon is taken it seems to me Sherman might be greatly damaged, if not entirely defeated, if proper efforts were made for reinforcements. Julia Ann + Mary hid a barrel of sugar + two cans of lard under the house. Judge Holt's folks left in the carriage today. Some of the neighbors are not going to run + I am glad of that.

Later! Rode down and played chess with R. Bates. Heard while there the Yankees had only made a feint on Macon and done off in the direction of Agusta. Thank God! We are safe for a little while longer.[172] Went down to Mrs. W[hittle]'s corner and looked

---

170 The issue of "running or staying" was being debated in the Gresham house. Leroy implies his mother could not make up her mind, and he was determined to convince her of the best course of action.

171 Gen. Gustavus W. Smith was in command of the Georgia state militia, about 3,000 older men and teenagers.

172 Sherman feinted at both Augusta and Macon—two important logistical manufacturing centers—to divide any Confederate opposition and continued southeast between the two cities toward the coast.

at Wheeler's cavalry passing in a steady stream for over an hour. They cheered + yelled when the ladies waved their handkerchiefs at them, and seemed to be in very high spirits.

Sunday Novemeber 20th 1864: Cloudy and warm. It does not seem like Sunday and we can hardly realize that it is so. Wheeler's men have been passing since 10 Oclock steadily + going down to the river and crossing on pontoons. It is now noon. The general opinion is that the enemy have gone in the direction of Agusta to burn the Powder Works.[173] The artillery was sent off on the cars to that place and the horses left. General Beauregard telegraphs from Corinth to the people to stand firm, that he was hastening to them to help them defend their homes. All our congressmen join in an appeal to the people to impede their progress as much as possible and they [Union forces] would be ruined. Yesterday we received a telegram from Father to get Col Frobel to apply for Thomas and I rode down to Mrs. Whittle's to ask where he could be found and then Fred offered to go + look him up which he did and succeeded in finding him. But for his assistance I do not know what we would have done. This morning the ladies gave the soldiers flowers and one man halloed that he would "heap rather have a dodger of bread!"—a very sensible remark—tho' the flowers were only the evidence of our good wishes. Mrs. Beal was quite huge on the subject of folks running off and almost insulted Mother because she sent off Minnie. She was one who came in after the danger was over and always knew it was [a] feint! This explains it. I have done nothing all the morning but ran to the gate to see the cavalry and I feel I have not kept Sunday [the Sabbath] right.[174] [Gens.] Dick Taylor and Hardee are or will be in town—as well as [Gens.] Smith, Johnson, Beauregard, Cobb, Wheeler + others. Sherman seems to have cut loose in Atlanta entirely and is going it blind. It is a glorious opportunity if we had only some men. The Atlanta papers have both "refugeed." The *T+C* is still published and will continue to be as long as possible!

Monday November 21st 1864: Rained steadily all day. We were surprised and delighted to see Cousin Jones walk into the sitting room this morning while we were at breakfast. He brought two men from his regiment along with him named Gordon + King. He has been with the army as scout for the provost marshal general since he left

---

173 The Augusta Powder Works was a massive gunpowder manufacturing facility. It was the only major supplier of gunpowder for the Confederacy, and had been left essentially unprotected the entire war. Its destruction should have been the primary objective of Union operations months earlier; its destruction would have ended the war quickly. Curiously, Sherman would bypass the facility on two occasions: on his way to Savannah, and when he moved north early in 1865 from Savannah into South Carolina.

174 "Ran to the gate to see the cavalry" is, of course, a figure of speech. LeRoy was either carried or was in his wagon. By this time he was almost certainly unable to use crutches.

here + has not heard from home in that time. They left at 3 oclock to hunt their wagon train + try to overtake the regiment. Gen Hardee is pressing every horse and negro on the Streets. Mother got a pass from Gen Hardee for Howard.[175] The latter got home last night and reports Minnie sent off safely. Our artillery fired on the Yankee cavalry yesterday and we could see the firing + hear the shells very plainly. The Yanks have gone to Agusta. Wrote a long letter to Thomas. 6 Oclock: Cousin J[ones] + Mr. Gordon have come back to stay all night. It is clearing off very cold as I write. . . . The yankees are marching on and they seem to aim toward the coast. Gov. Brown has offered pardons to the penitentiary convicts if they would volunteer for the war and 150 accepting it, they were organized, armed, + equipped on the spot.

Tuesday November 22nd 1864: Tremendous freeze and a slight snow. Turned bitter cold in the night. Cousin Jones + Mr. Gordon slept on the floor in the sitting room, preferring it to a bed. Just before dinner we received a telegram from Father conveying the joyful tidings of Thomas having been detailed; that they left yesterday for Macon! Sat down and wrote the good tidings to Minnie. We were so rejoiced we could not eat dinner and every now + then I would look at the dispatch to see if were really so. Cousin Jones and Mr. Gordon left in good earnest. Cousin came back for his saddle-bags and went off + left them and Howard had to carry them to him at last. Cousin Jones had some specie [coins] he took off of a Yankee spy. The yanks are working their way down toward Millen, [Ga]. It has been freezing all day.

Wednesday November 23d 1864: Clear and cold. Thermometer 17° at 8 AM and I think it must have been lower. Went down to Mrs. Whittle's to see if there was any news. Our forces have been licked at Griswoldville and the yankees have a fair chance to take Macon. The authorities have been fooled and have sent off the forces in town. Just as we were beginning to feel a little easy, the yankees come and threaten us again. Griswoldville is burnt and it is rumored that a large number of our men are killed and wounded. Father + Thomas are cut off—all lies about their going to Savannah.[176] . . . Clinton is burned and I have no doubt that this was the light we saw in that direction Monday; indeed there was a lurid glare in all the Northern + Eastern horizons which was wonderfully suggested of ruined homes and desolate firesides. Sherman occupied

---

175 Official passes were necessary in areas of active conflict to control the movement of individuals. This helped regulate espionage.

176 Battle of Griswoldville (Nov. 22, 1864), just twelve miles north of Macon, pitted about 3,000 Union troops against 2,300 Confederate militia. The one-sided battle killed and wounded about 650 Confederates to 62 Union. The family was hearing John and Thomas were making for the coastal city; LeRoy no longer believed it.

Milledgeville + tis supposed that he burned Milledgeville at least the public buildings. Sent 5 dollars to the daily to renew our subscription which was out.

Thursday November 24th 1864: Clear and cold. Mother was sick and we had a fire made in our room upstairs and Julia Ann and I cut out a bag for my pistol. She slept before the fire in the room with us. The fight at Griswoldville was a very severe one. The militia and some other forces attacked the yankees in their intrenchments and were repulsed. Gen W[heeler] had a fight too and drove the Yanks. Their infantry, 'tis said, are steadily moving toward Agusta and it is not thought that Macon will be attacked. Sherman is 40000 strong. Cousin Eliza called—she is at home alone. Am going down town in the buggy to hunt some news. 5 Oclock: Rode down to the river to see the pontoon bridge but found that they have constructed a temporary bridge on the site of the old one, and taken up the pontoons. Came back by Mrs. Bowdre's and delivered her some papers which Mother sent her—some deeds of Uncle LeRoy's. Gen Beauregard is at Gen'l Cobb's. Hardee has gone back to Charleston and Dick Taylor commands here—the enemy are clean gone toward Agusta. Reading Olmsted's *Astronomy*.

Friday November 25th 1864: Weather Record. Clear and cold 34°. The Central Rail-road is torn up for over 20 miles and no trains run. The Yankees are moving down the road. Howard returned on the R.R. from the plantation bringing 2 quarters beef, potatoes, 10 hams, peas +c. The plantations are going to ruin fast. Mr. Griswold was in possession of our lower place [Pinelands]; deserters stole the colt and so they go. Gov. Brown authorizes such scoundrels to be shot down on sight. Alas! what a state of things! Deliver one from "refugeeing" to the country.[177] The M+WRR runs to Griffin! There is not a yank on that road, but there is enough and to spare, on the Central. The Yankees say Sherman will, if necessary, make a forced march and join Grant [in Va]! We are completely cut off now from the other seats of war and not a letter or paper, except a stray *Memphis Appeal*, comes to cheer us. I wish Father + Thomas could slip in, in some way or other.

Saturday November 26th 1864: Clear and cold. . . . Macon is safe for the present. Sherman is pushing toward Savannah. All the militia have gone on the S.W.R.R. marching 40 miles to the Gulf road. Rumor says a portion of Dick Taylor's command has gone, via Ft. Valley, in the same direction. Sherman seems to me in a critical condition, tho' they have been in as bad before and got away. The railroad has been

---

177 Many areas of Georgia were without any sort of law enforcement. Deserters (and Union stragglers) ran rampant. In some cases men trying to enforce the law were found hanging from trees.

ordered to be repaired to Atlanta, and that city will soon be in our hands again. I saw Gens Beauregard + Cobb riding 'round the city yesterday P.M. The former is [a] much older <u>looking</u> man than I imagined.[178] 6 couriers followed in their train. A good many people are coming in from Va via Thomasville + we look for Father that way. Our scouts took, yesterday, in the direction of Gordon, 250 cattle which will be a heavy loss to the Yankee commissiarat.

Sunday November 27th 1864: Clear and warmer. The yankees have left Milledgeville and Gordon and are proceeding down the Central Road thoroughly destroying as they go. The Penitentiary and Arsenal were the only public buildings burned in Milledgeville. Two houses burned in Clinton. Cousin Jinnie and Aunt Ann were here yesterday and gave us an account of the sacking + burning of her house in Jones Co. Received a letter from "Aunt Matthews" announcing their arrival in Thomasville.[179] Min has written but we have not received it. Thanksgiving Union Prayermeeting to be held in our church this P.M. for the safety of Macon from a ruthless foe. Dreamed two or three times last night that Father + Thomas had come.

Monday November 28th 1864: Foggy and warm. You can't see 200 yds. No paper this morn: and no news. All of the troops have gone from here to Savannah. [Gen.] Cumming's Reg[imen]t of Reserves went yesterday.

Tuesday November 29th 1864: Clear and warm. We were rejoiced beyond expression to welcome Father and Thomas home yesterday at four Oclock yesterday evening. They came by way of Charleston, not daring to go by Agusta for fear of getting into the trenches there.[180] Came on the Gulf road to Thomasville where Minnie was but did not know of her being there. Had a variety of adventures on the way up home. Father is completely broken down, with a cold and is nearly ready to go to bed. Thomas and I slept up stairs and talked till midnight. Robert Lockett came up and played Chess with me. I beat him badly. Thomas and I shot pistol after we got through playing. Col Frobel

178 LeRoy finally got to see Gen. Beauregard in person. He appeared "much older looking" because his hair was black in the early-war photos LeRoy had seen, but it was now very white. Although friends attributed the white hair to stress, others claim the blockade had dried up the source of Beauregard's hair dye.

179 Mrs. Matthews, who chaperoned Minnie out of Macon, has acquired "Aunt" status in the Gresham family.

180 Given its overarching importance to the Confederacy, it is odd that Augusta remained almost completely unprotected. Light earthworks had been thrown up around parts of the city, and only a few thousand men (mostly militia) were manning them. John and Thomas avoided Augusta because they were concerned they would have been forced to erect works and/or help defend the city against an attack every Southerner was sure was coming.

is gone to Savannah + I do not know what he'll do. Sherman is marching on to the coast and tis supposed he will convey his army to Grant.[181]

Wednesday November 30th 1864: Clear and warm. Molded some bullets and then Thomas and I rode down back of Mrs. Clark's to find a good place to shoot at, but there was soldiers camped back there. We saw a fort just back of Mrs. Clark's house. Came back to the horse lot and practiced there, though it was hard work on acct of the meanness [poor quality] of the [percussion] caps. Had a bad headache all the P.M.

Thursday December 1st 1864: Clear and warm. Thomas left for Houston with the buggy + two horses. Father continues so unwell that it was impossible for him to go + the deserters and stragglers are tearing things to pieces. Recd two letters from Minnie today giving a graphic and sprightly account of her journey and stay up to the 25th in Thomasville. Had the headache all night, but am well this morning. Milledgeville is completely sacked + we have heard nothing from Aunt E[liza] or Cousin Annie. The U.S.A.'s are beyond the Oconee River—"marching on." Went down and played Chess with R. Bates. Uncle LeRoy arrived from Flint River. We have heard from Aunt Eliza. The Yankees left them without a mouthful of food + all 5 of their negroes left them.

Friday December 2nd 1864: Clear and warm. Uncle LeRoy left again this morning. Slept in the back parlor. No war news. Thomas and Howard came back this evening with some sugar cane, squirrels and butter. Cousin Jinnie W. Blount has a son.[182]

Saturday December 3d 1864: Cloudy and warm. The Yankees are marching on and are about Millen. Father is better. The fire bells were rung with great violence for a good while last night at bedtime, but no fire could be seen. I believe it was in the engine room of the Armory. We received a letter from Minnie asking for Father to come after her. Thomas will have to go if he can get permission. Father is too unwell. Thomas bought a repeater from Mr. Kemp for 100 dollars.[183]

Sunday ~~September~~ December 4th 1864: Clear and cool. . . . No news. Hood is moving on Nashville and [General] Thomas is opposing him. We are anxious to hear

---

181 In fact, that was exactly what the original plan called for. Once Sherman reached Savannah, he was to put his army on ships bound for Virginia. Once there, however, he would convince Grant to let him march north through the Carolinas.

182 Recall how the Yankees had treated Jinnie a few months earlier while pregnant (see entry Aug. 6, 1864). The baby, Joseph G. Blount, was the first of the Blount children to survive infancy and make it into adulthood.

183 It is not precisely clear what Thomas purchased, but it may have been an 1855 Colt Revolving Rifle, an 1860 Henry, or a lever-action Spencer. These weapons, while efficient and deadly, saw limited use during the war.

something from Grandma; we fear the Yankees passed near Sparta. A large force is at work on the Central Road, so as to get through to Milledgeville, then via Sparta, to Agusta + Richmond. Beauregard has gone back West. Gen Mackall is in command of this Post. George Beal is his clerk!

Monday December 5th 1864: Clear and cold. Thomas and I rode down in the buggy and had my measure taken for pants and his for a suit. Saw Gov Brown for the first time.[184] There has been a severe fight with the Yankees in So. Ca, the Ga militia being the principal force engaged. Our loss was 80 or 100. We held our own and the fight; it was thought would be renewed. Hood + Thomas have had a great fight and rumor says we have the best of it. Many of our Generals are killed and wounded.

Tuesday December 6th 1864: Clear and cool. Father left for the plantation and Thomas to go after Minnie. I long to hear more of Hood's fight. Gen Cleburn is reported killed. I am sick today with pain in my back and soreness of the old abscess. [Robert] Lockett came up and played three games of Chess. I beat twice. I could not read and it diverted my mind. Sherman appears to move quite slowly and it is not known certainly which point he will fight. Gen Smith's fight was a very severe one. Over 800 Yankees men killed and it was a victory so far as it goes. Ga. Militia fighting on So. Ca. soil! They ought to be ashamed.[185]

Wednesday December 7th 1864: Cloudy and warm. Suffered all day with pain in the left abscess and I would not put on my clothes at all. I could not move without pain. Had a starch poultice on it so as to make it discharge. I never was so bad off with it since they were made.

---

184 Leroy has criticized Brown many times in his journals. It is unfortunate he did not relate more of what he thought or heard at this time.

185 LeRoy, like many other Georgians, believed they should have remained in Georgia to fight Sherman.

Thursday December 8th 1864: Cloudy + cool. Went to bed very early last night but could not sleep and about 11 Oclock, Mother got up and gave me 20 drops of laudanum, after which I rested better. I have never saw my back run so. When the dressings are off and I strain it runs in a stream. Had a poultice on all P.M. and when it was taken off it ran hugely. Received a long letter from Minnie. The people down in Thomasville are afraid Sherman will turn + come back by Macon!

Friday December 9th 1864: Cloudy and cold. I am much better this morning. The running of my back has relieved me. Wheeler whipped Kilpatrick Sunday and the latter is reported wounded. Hood must have cut up his army from the number of officers killed. Gens Cleburn, Strahl, Granberry, Gist, Adams killed; Maj Gen Brown, Canty, Manigault, Quarles, Cockrell, + Scott wounded + Gordon captured.[186] We took 1000 prisoners + lost as many. The enemy will be reinforced + Hood will skeedadle in a hurry. Put on my clothes today and my new vest which was just finished, for the first time. . . . Rained hard all the evening and it was the coldest sort of rain.

Saturday December 10th 1864: Cold and drizzling rain. It looks as if it would turn to sleet. Father arrived from Houston yestereve. Rained hard after we went to bed and I reckon Minnie and Thomas are out in it all. Richard Edwards called to tell us he saw Minnie Wednesday. Father thinks Hood will be gobbled up by Thomas.[187] We expected Minnie and Thomas home this evening and were disappointed that they did not come.

Sunday December 11th 1864: Cold and windy. "We are fighting no longer for Independence but terms!" Father says. Uncle LeRoy thinks we should submit + Grandma writes that we are gone up! Everybody in the country is demoralized. By the way I forgot to say we received a letter from Grandma giving an account of the Yankees in Hancock, [Ga]. They did not get to Uncle E[dge]'s place, but in running off some valuable provisions, they lost two mules and 4000 dollars in sugar, coffee, cloth,

---

186 The Battle of Franklin (Nov. 30, 1864) in Tennessee. When Hood's army arrived to find Gen. John Schofield's Army of the Ohio pinned against the swollen Harpeth River, Hood quickly launched one of the largest attacks of the war. The fighting was intense and prolonged, with heavy hand-to-hand combat that lasted into the night. Hood's attack was repulsed with heavy loss and Schofield barely escaped. Five Confederate generals were killed outright (Otho F. Strahl, Hiram B. Granbury, John Adams, States Rights Gist, and Patrick Cleburne) and one mortally wounded (John C. Carter). Many others were wounded, as Leroy noted (Gens. John C. Brown, James Cantey, Arthur M. Manigault, William A. Quarles, Francis M. Cockrell, Thomas M. Scott. Union Gen. George W. Gordon was captured). Hood's losses were at least 5,000, while Schofield's ran about 2,300. Hood continued north toward Nashville.

187 John Gresham was often right in his predictions, and this one would come precisely to pass when Gen. Thomas nearly destroyed Hood's army outside Nashville on Dec. 15-16, 1864.

+c. The latter was burned by the woman at whose house the overseer left them because she said the Yankees would burn her house if they found them. She no doubt cabbaged [stole] them. So much for "runageeing." Thomas and Minnie did not come and we begin to feel somewhat uneasy about them, especially as it has blown off very cold and they may be delayed on the road some where. It is rumored that Sherman is moving toward the Atlantic and Gulf railroad + that Darien is to be the effective point of that enterprising Yankee.[188]

Monday December 12th 1864: Clear and hugely cold. The mercury in the passage [hallway] at 8½ was 28° outdoors at 9.45 it was 17°. It must have been at least 10° as it is colder than the cold Tuesday a fortnight ago. . . . Lockett came and played Chess with me, beating me.

Tuesday December 13th 1864: Cloudy and cold. Father and Howard went to the depot at 3½ P.M. for Min + Thomas and waited, until dark and the train did not come, so home they came cold and disappointed. Just as we had finished tea, they came, had to walk from the depot. The train was detained on "acct" of as Thomas says "a sick Engine." They bring the rumor that Sherman has cut the Gulf road at the Altamaha [River]. Thomas got Minnie a seat in a government wagon train and leaving Thomasville Friday, they got to Albany Sunday. Two nights they camped out and the ladies slept in an old church. It was romantic if not very comfortable.[189] The weather has moderated and it is just cold and cloudy enough to snow. The wagon came up with fresh meat. They killed 16 hogs. Rode down and played Chess beating him two in 4 + would have beat him 3 but for a little carelessness. Robt. Lockett that is.

Wednesday December 14th 1864: Cloudy and cool. Rumor hath Fort McAllister taken and Father has given up Savannah as gone if Mass. Sherman deigns to take it.[190] I hope not. Mr. Ralston died yesterday and was buried this evening. Lincoln's message says he will fight as long as we fight him.

Thursday December 15th 1864: Cloudy and warm. . . . Thomas is assigned temporarily to duty in the Top. [Topographical] Eng[inee]rs in this vicinity and is to report to Capt. Renshaw until he can get to Col Frobel. "Swopped" Thomas out of a blank book for a

---

188 The first Sunday entry in which LeRoy did not mention it was the Sabbath or Communion Day.

189 LeRoy means the "romance of adventure" rather than its more common modern usage.

190 The Battle of Fort McAllister (Dec. 13, 1864) was the last phase in the March to the Sea. The large earthen fort was part of the defensive network for Savannah. It fell after a just a 15-minute attack. Gen. William Hardee managed to withdraw the 10,000 men defending Savannah and the city fell without further fighting. Sherman offered Savannah to President Lincoln as a Christmas gift.

diary. Played a game of Chess with Thomas and beat him, giving him 2's Kt. Mother hard at work making her new cloth cloak.

Friday December 16th 1864: Cloudy and warm. Fighting on the Weldon Road again. Hood "squatted" in front of Nashville. Sherman is sure to get to the coast now. Minnie is going to School again. Occupied all the eve looking at Thomas inking over a map.

Saturday December 17th 1864: Clear and warm. Thomas gone off toward Clinton on a Topog[raphical] Expedition. Bob Lockett called and beat me 4 out of 5 games of Chess. I don't know what's got into me. The Yankees marching on Mobile and they are advancing in N. Carolina, too. Savannah completely cut off. Wrote to Grandma.

Sunday December 18th 1864: Clear and warm. It is rumored in town that an attack has been made on Savannah and repulsed. . . . George Beal called this evening. He says his health is fast declining in anticipation of having to go in service.

Monday December 19th 1864: Clear and warm. Father left on the R.R. for Houston. Thomas went off on Prince to Jones Co. for a week's engineering. Robt Lockett called this P.M. and we played three long + interesting games of Chess: 1 drawn, 1 I beat, and 1 he beat. And old letter from Thomas dated Petersburg 12th November came to hand today. So much for C.S. mails. We get nothing from Sherman. Rained a little after tea.

Tuesday December 20th 1864: Cloudy and cool. Pasted Lee's Campaign from September and the Valley campaign in my scrapbook. Drizzled rain some this morning, and on the strength of it, Thomas came home fearing it would rain harder. Ft McAllister has fallen and Savannah is in a most critical state. The Ft was taken last Tuesday by Assault.

Wednesday December 21st 1864: Cloudy and cold. . . . Thomas went off again. Saw in the *Memphis Appeal* a list of the casualties of the Battle of Franklin. Cousin Sam Knox wounded. Col George A. Smith killed. Hood butchered his army and gained nothing. . .

Thursday December 22nd 1864: Cold and windy. Mercury 29° outdoors. Thomas spent the night at home. The river bridge lately built is giving way. Commenced wearing my new pants made out of Athens cloth. We hear nothing from Savannah. 700 men were captured in Fort McAllister. Hood has been whipped at Nashville so the Yankee accounts say. The yanks say Hood is such a fool there is no counting on what he'll do and it is a true estimate of his character. The *Richmond Examiner* blocked up by the interruption of mail communications came through today by the Sparta + Milledgeville route. Also an old letter from Thomas in Petersburg to me. I notice the name of our newfound cousin James Johnson, A.A.G. [staff officer] for General Strahl, among the killed at Franklin; at least I suppose it is him.[191] The only way we hear from Savannah is thro' the Charleston papers. The only Christmas present I expect to have this year is a new diary.

Friday December 23d 1864: Clear and very cold. Mercury 20 in house. We expected Father home this evening but he did not come. Minnie went down town and bought a comb and gave 35 dollars for it.

Saturday December 24th 1864: Clear and cold. Frost as white as snow Christmas eve! I can hardly realize it. We are all invited to dine at Cousin Eliza's Monday. Milo came up with fresh meat last night; returned today carrying Hamp. Uncle LeRoy arrived about 4 oclock and soon after Father. Thomas came about dark.

Sunday December 25th 1864: Cloudy until 10 Oclock. Christmas is always rainy or very cold. Accordingly at the hour above named it rained a little. From dinnertime till night it poured down. The darkies have had no chance to sport their finery and we have all been huddled around the fire and have done nought but mope and discuss the war—a truly delightful Sunday occupation—and that is not a very cheerful theme about now. Many a time have our thoughts wandered back to the good peace times, when all was joy and merriment. . . . My back has not discharged freely in the past week and so I have suffered with pain in it all day. Florence is the only one [of] the lot who seemed to enter into the spirit of Christmas. We received a letter from Grandma today and she promises to come over and make us a visit when the Railroad is opened. Major Gen Price is dead. It is a matter of doubt whether we will be in possession of a home by next Christmas. Hood whipped around Nashville + Sherman investing Savannah completely.[192] The prospect is indeed gloomy.

Monday December 26th 1864: Cloudy and cool. Bad news! Savannah is evacuated by Beauregard + Hardee, and the Yankees entered it Wednesday, the 21st of December.

191 It was not the "new-found cousin" James Edward Johnson that Leroy thought he saw in the casualty list from the Battle of Franklin. This cousin lived until 1912 and had four children during and after the war.

192 The Battle of Nashville (Dec. 15-16 1864). Gen. George Thomas assaulted Hood's lines outside the city, smashed through the second day, and the Confederate army broke apart in abject rout. Confederate losses were at least 6,000, with most of them captured/missing; Union losses were about half that. The victory was one of the most decisive of the war and ended the Army of Tennessee as an effective fighting force. Hood withdrew his survivors into Mississippi and would resign his command on Jan. 13, 1865.

Hood, so the Yankees say, is retreating and has lost Johnson's division, which the enemy have captured entire with a with all its brigade commanders. I slept pretty well last night and I am well today. Thomas is taking holiday today. All the folks went to take dinner at Cousin Eliza's and Uncle LeRoy and I took a frugal meal alone in the sitting room. Cousin Eliza sent me cake, custard, and syllabub, which I enjoyed very much indeed. . . . Sherman has taken Savannah and has the states of Georgia + So/ Ca. at his mercy.

Tuesday December 27th 1864: Cloudy and warm. Uncle LeRoy left before we got up. Rained a little at dark. Done nothing all day. . . . Every one is gloomy on the war, and the wildest rumors are credited. Ever since Saturday it has been rumored that President Davis was dead. Today a dispatch came saying that he had been ill with neuralgia but had recovered. O! gloomy, gloomy, Christmas! Long will it be remembered, tho' 'twere every one's wish that it could be forgotten.

Wednesday December 28th 1864: Cloudy and cool. Wind blew all night. Ate pound-cake and molasses candy today, the first goodies of the Christmas. Went to Mrs. Whittle's and played one game of Chess in which I held out valiantly till I was beat. This satisfies me. Price's death is contradicted. Uncle Edmund writes of his losses by the Yankees and they are very heavy: 125 bales of cotton, large amount of corn, mules, +c. Wheeler's men took 800 bushels of corn and 60 or 70 hogs. It is exasperating to be thus despoiled, by our own side. We had a huge old turkey for dinner. He was to have been the chief dish of a dining, but F[ather] and M[other] concluded not to have it. Rode in the buggy with Thomas out to Mr. Hickman's to carry the leather to have him a pair of shoes made. It was quite a "cold ride" but I enjoyed it. Father had got some splendid paper to make me a diary, if he can get it bound well. Thomas brought home his new suit of Columbus jeans and the tail is a mile long.

Thursday December 29th 1864: Clear and very cold. Thomas gone to work. . . . Masquerade at the Watkin's tonight. Big nigger party at the College.

Friday Dec'r 30th 1864: Clear and cold. Slept down stairs. Whenever Thomas comes home I go up stairs and when he leaves I come down. We are invited to an eggnog at Mrs. Whittle's tonight. Heard that the Mr. Cox who stayed with us was killed at Franklin.[193] Wilmington is threatened with an immense fleet. Hood is rapidly retreating. Sherman has issued orders allowing ingress and egress for 20 days from

---

193 This was the soldier who had stolen the pocket book while staying in the Gresham home and was asked to leave by John Gresham. See entry Aug. 4, 1864.

Savannah and all those who remain after that time will be compelled to take the oath of allegiance to the U.S.

Saturday December 31st 1864: Clear and cold. Rained before day and it has blown off very cold. Mother and Father went to Mrs. W[hittle]'s last night and enjoyed themselves very well. It was a tolerable large supper, mostly neighbors. Minnie + I sat up till ¼ to 11. This morning we were surprised to see Mr. Craig. He was married in So. Ca: looks considerably better.[194] Thomas home again. Comes home like darkies— Saturday. This is the last day of 1864. A year of such sorrow as the world has rarely seen before and the new year dawns on a grief-stricken, gloomy country. O! the homes that have been desolated and the firesides that have been ruined! We began the summer bright and hopeful and end the year sorrowing for the men who have been lost who can never be recovered.

[LeRoy here has a lengthy chart of his chess games. See facing page.]

January 1st 1865: Clear and exceedingly cold. Mercury 20° at 9 O'clock. Mr. Craig all day with us. Had the Communion administered to one tonight. Sherman telegraphs to present Lincoln Savannah as a Christmas gift. Richard Edwards and two French ladies joined the Church today. He came after tea to bid us Good Bye as he leaves for Virginia tomorrow. Judge Nisbet and Mr. Wills came up just after they got through the Communion at the Negro Church. That is Mr. Wills did—Judge N[isbet] came from home. Mars is a conspicuous object in the Heavens now and it is about 3 feet from the Seven Stars.

January 2nd 1865: Clear and cold. Did not sleep well on account of a lurking pain in my hip, which has now grown to a steady ache. Worse than all it is in my right leg. Mr. Craig left for the Army of Tenn, which has arrived this side of the Tennessee once more, with the loss of it morale and artillery.

Tuesday January 3d 1865: Cloudy and raw. Rained slowly nearly all day. The wagon has arrived bringing Laura to see Julia Ann. Mr. Kemp is very ill and Mrs. K[emp] has a baby. Lockett called and I forgot my leg in 4 games of Chess, 3 of which I beat + one drawn. I suffered much last night and all today. I have had a constant aching in my hip which is very annoying and hard to bear. It has drawn up my good leg too. . . . Mother

---

Opposite page: As LeRoy noted at the end of his chess chart, "The number of recorded games is 90, though it would be largely over 100 if I had put down every game." *LOC*

194 Mr. Craig was the other soldier (along with Mr. Cox) the Gresham's had taken into their home.

Aug. 3

Games of Chess played from Sept 1st
1864 till Dec 31st 1864

Date	Opponent	L.N.G	Adv.	Drawn
Aug. 2nd	R. Bates	1	0	1
Aug. 6th	" "	4	0	0
Aug. 10th	" "	6	1	0
Aug. 13th	" "	4	0	1
Aug. 17th	" "	4	3	0
" 19th	" "	2	1	1
" 24th	" "	5	5	0
" 27th	" "	3	4	0
Sept. 1st	Mrs Whittle	2	1	0
" 5th	J. Campbell	2	1	0
" 9th	Mrs Whittle	0	2	0
" 13th	R. Bates	3	1	0
" 17th	Mrs Whittle	0	1	0
Oct. 19th	" "	0	1	0
" 20th	R. Bates	3	1	0
" 24th	Lockett Bates & J. v. 5 Mrs W allies	2	0	0
Nov. 7th	J. W. Lockett	0	1	0
" 11th	R. Bates	2	0	0
" "	J. W. Lockett	0	2	1

Date	Opponent	L.N.G	Adv.	Drawn
Nov. 15th	R. Bates	1	2	0
Dec. 6th	J. W. Lockett	2	1	0
" 13th	" "	2	2	0
" 13th	T. B. Gresham	1	0	0
" 17th	J. W. Lockett	1	4	0
" 19	" "	1	1	1
Dec. 28th	Mrs Whittle	0	1	0
		51	34	5

The number of recorded games is 90
though it would be largely over 100 if
I had put down every game.

brought me an apple and some cakes the size of a dime. The people down town are greatly demoralized about Sherman + exasperated at the government for permitting it. Other circumstances combine to produce this feeling. Gold is 50 for 1 and rising, and Father thinks there is a general breaking down in public sentiment.

Wednesday January 4th 1865: Clear and bracing day. Took twenty drops of laudanum and did not in consequence get to sleep till after midnight. My leg numb and painful when it is moved. My appetite is gone. I ate 3 eggs for my breakfast and a partridge which Father bought down town for my dinner. When I press on a certain spot near the right abscess I can feel a sharp pain shoot down into my hip. The Yankee expedition against Wilmington has returned to Ft Monroe, chagrined at not gaining their object.[195] Mr. Isaac Scott has sold out his stock in and given up the Presidency of the M&W.R.R., preparatory to deserting these parts.

Thursday January 5th 1865: Cloudy and pleasant. I have laid in bed and on my couch all day. I slept badly: took 7 drops of laudanum. Father went to a gentleman's tea party at Dr. Hall's and brought me a cake and apple and Mother gave me her orange for my cake which was all on my side. I got out of bed at 12 Oclock. Father went to Houston in the buggy. Toward night my throat had grown sore and I feel really sick. This is the second spell of pain I have had in my good leg. My back runs profusely.

Friday January 6th 1865: Cloudy and cool. . . . Spent a miserable sleepless night but I am thankful to say I feel a little better today and hope this spell is over. The press, and the people are down on Hood and, declaring him a blunderer, call for a change. He has brought his army out of Tenn with heavy loss and Forrest had to suffer heavily to save him from destruction. Thomas came home at 3½ P.M. He has finished the field work of his district. . . . My new diary is being bound and I hope to get by next Monday.

Saturday January 7th 1865: Windy and cold. . . . Slept pretty well, but there is a slight pain in the hip yet. Mother sick in bed. Rode over and played a game of Chess with Mrs. Whittle and after a very long contest succeeded in winning the first time on record when I was satisfied she played her best. While I was there I became so hoarse that I could not speak even in a common tone. Came home rather uneasy, but it got better toward night. Father arrived from Houston with some partridges +c. Gen Beauregard

---

195 The First Battle of Fort Fisher (Dec. 23-27, 1864). Fort Fisher was a massive sand fort guarding the approaches to the Cape Fear River and the important port of Wilmington. This battle was primarily a Union naval siege. An explosive-laden ship was ineffective, and troops landed to storm the fort were recalled because of bad weather and word of approaching Confederate reinforcements. Gen. Ben Butler, the Union commander, called off the effort and Lincoln happily relieved him of command.

+ his staff are in town on their way to the army. So all the rumors of [Gen.] Johnston's restoration are untrue. It is a sin and a shame on J. Davis.

Sunday January 8th 1865: Clear and cold. Had an eggnog last night. Sherman is acting mildly in Savannah, in comparison and the Mayor + several aldermen have given in their allegiance.

[Added at the end of the journal, fleshing out earlier entries:]

Nov. 18th: Took out of the bundle in tin box marked 1200 dollars, 500 dollars for Minnie to go to Thomasville in 100s 50s 5s + 10s

Thursday Nov 25th: I wonder where Father and Thomas are. I wish they'd try and come home via Savannah + Thomasville + the S.W.R.R.

LeRoy Wiley Gresham

[LeRoy drew the following "Jack the Giant Killer" sketch a the end of his journal. The story of Jack is from an English fairy tale about a young man who killed giants during King Arthur's reign. LeRoy would have read the tale in one of his books, as there were many versions of it in print by the 1860s. It is interesting to note that LeRoy owned a pistol (which he references on several occasions), and that the "giant" he is killing in his drawing sports a stovepipe hat—which may imply he is metaphorically shooting Abraham Lincoln.]

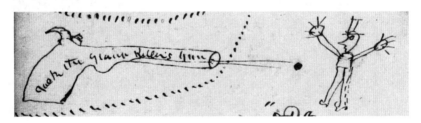

5.D/4

Long may she wave!

"The Flag of the Confederacy
Adopted:
March 1865:
Went up:
Apr. 65.

Above and facing page: The inside covers of Volume 7. *LOC*

DAILY RECORD

BY

Leroy Gresham.

1865.

DAILY RECORD

1865

Volume 7

January 1, 1865 – June 8, 1865

January 1st 1865: Clear and cold. Mr. Wills and Judge Nisbet came up and administered the Communion to me.

[January 2, 1865: No entry]

Tuesday January 3d 1865: Rained slowly nearly all day. Lockett called and played 4 games of Chess. I beat 3 and 1 was drawn. Suffering very much with pain in my right hip.

Wednesday January 4th: Clear and fine. Took 20 drops of laudanum. Did not sleep any and have suffered very much during the day. Father bought me a partridge for my dinner and enjoyed it greatly. It cost one dollar.

January 5th 1865: Laid in bed until 12 noon. Father . . . left for Houston this morning. Throat slightly sore.

January 6th 1865: Did not sleep hardly any, but still am better. Thomas came in from Jones [County]. Has finished his work.

January 7th 1865: Leg better. Rode over and beat Mrs. Whittle one game of Chess.

Sunday Jan. 8th 1865: Clear and cold. Had an eggnog last night the first of our Christmas. Read *Advice to Young Communicants* by Dr. Jas. Alexander of New York City.

Monday, January 9th, 1865: Cloudy and raw. . . . Cousin Howard called and has been here all day. Lurking pain in my hip. Thomas at work surveying or plotting. Got this diary today and it is much nicer bound than I expected.

Tuesday, January 10th 1865: . . . At daylight there was a tremendous storm which lasted 'till nearly 8.A.M. Did not rest well on account of my leg. Jim Campbell, whom we all thought was captured, has turned up. He hid seven days, in the swamp, and thus escaped. Sherman has begun a new campaign, the object of which is to cut the R.R. centre at Branchville, So. Ca.

Wednesday, January 11th, 1865: Clear and blowing very cold. Occupied in the A.M. calling out the bearings for Thomas to plot by. Hood is at Corinth. Forrest is still north of the Tennessee. Macon is a whipped city and many are talking of holding Union meeting. The river is very high. The new bridge is gone. A man was drowned near the bridge yesterday.

Thursday, January 12th, 1864: Clear and cold. Agusta is inundated and the rivers all are very high. 3 bridges washed away, on the R.R. between Montgomery + Opelika. . . . "Wheeler" has been missing all day and I fear someone has killed him. He was never away before in the day.

Friday, January 13th, 1865: Clear and cool. The wagon came up with meat. One of the hogs killed weighed 376 lbs. "Wheeler" is still missing and we have given him up. Poor fellow! he loved us all and we hate losing him very much. . . . Two divisions of Lee's army have come out to defend Branchville. O! if they had been at Savannah six weeks ago! Early's army has joined Lee, excepting one division.[1]

Saturday, January 14th, 1865: Cloudy and cool. George Beal called after tea last night and the various methods of keeping out of the army were fully discussed. My leg is not well yet and every time I go out in the cold, it aches. . . . I miss "Wheeler" so much when I go on my wagon. No trace of him has been discovered. Next to Cuff he was as good as any dog we have ever had.

Sunday, January 15th, 1865: Clear, bright and beautiful day. Collection taken up, amounting to over 5000 dollars, to pay Mr. Wills' [church] salary. Hood is coming to Georgia. [Gen.] Thomas is pushing to Chattanooga, + it is supposed will move via Knoxville into Virginia, there being no force to oppose him. Read Jay's *Morning and Evening Exercises* all the A.M. Finished 1st Kings; am reading the Bible regularly through. My back is running profusely and still my legs ache every night. . . .

Monday, January 16th, 1865: Cloudy and cool. . . . Lockett and Bates called, and I beat the latter twice, and was beat by the former once. . . .

Tuesday, January 17th, 1865: Beautiful, clear, winter day. The enemy on the 14th attacked Hardee at Pocataligo + drove him back.[2] They were under Foster, and 15,000 strong. . . . Gen Cobb + staff have left for So. Ca. . . . Thomas has finished his map and is ordered to survey the 9th District, Jones County. . . . Thomas is engaged in drawing a valentine.

1	After being defeated in the Shenandoah, most of Early's survivors rejoined Lee's army at Petersburg. Early remained in the Valley with a small force. No infantry from Lee's army was sent to South Carolina.

2	A move along the Pocatalico River (Jan. 13-14, 1865), so Sherman's forces to enter South Carolina.

Wednesday, January 18th, 1865: Clear and ~~warm~~ cold. Father and Minnie went to Dr. Green's to a small party. The enemy came back to Wilmington and on the 15th, bombarded Fort Fisher furiously. At two on the morning of the 16th, just after fresh troops had been thrown in the fort, with its garrison, was taken. This _is_ an unexpected disaster. So they go.[3]

Thursday, January 19th, 1865: Cloudy and cool. We are in a stir of preparation for our long delayed supper, and it's going to be done up in the best style. "Nab" [Houston slave] is baking the cakes. Operations grow lively around Charleston. Two [enemy] corps are advancing on it. Drizzled rain very slowly all the evening. It will be a bad night, I fear.

Friday, January 20th, 1865: Rainy, gloomy day. Our supper passed off splendidly, and I enjoyed myself very much. The supper was about a quarter to ten, and the gentlemen seemed to enjoy the whiskey, coffee + eggnog, + after supper, the cigars. I eat a heavy supper, + the novelty of being in company gave a zest to my appetite. I will name the company for future reference: Zeph Conner, Captain Wrenshall, J.T. Nisbet, Mr. J.B. Ross, 2 Johnsons, J. Cowles, Colonels Whittle and deGraffenreid, Dr. Hall, Cousin Charlie, Captain Holt, W. Fort, + Mr. Bloom. The supper looked elegantly. Minnie did not come out, and Mother only for a short time. I liked Captain Wrenshall very well. He, Cousin Charlie, "Coon" Conner, Thomas and I sat in the sitting room till 12 Oclock, at which time everyone took a dram [drink] and left. Mother sick in bed, and Father with a bad headache today. Poor Old "Wheeler's" remains have been found in a gully down by Mr. Wills', shot thro' the side. I am glad to know his fate even tho' it is such a sad one. It has continued raining all the P.M.

Saturday, January 21st, 1865: Rained all night and . . . continues to rain as I write at 10 A.M. Thomas has gone to work. A son of General M[artin]. L. Smith goes to learn with him + they wanted him to start rain or shine. Father's birthday. . . . Richard Taylor is

---

3 Second Battle of Fort Fisher (January 13-15, 1865). Wilmington was the last major port open to the Confederacy. A large combined force of infantry and naval ships attacked Fort Fisher. Troops landed on January 13 and attacked concurrent with a naval bombardment on the 15th. The lengthy fighting eventually captured the fort and its entire garrison of 1,900 and mortally wounded its commander, Gen. W. H. C. Whiting. The loss of Fisher sealed the fate of Wilmington, which fell a month later.

appointed to the Army, Hood being relieved at his own request. O! me! It seems to me the President might appoint Johnston; he is certainly the man to restore the morale.

Sunday, January 22nd, 1865: A rainy day. . . . No one went to church except Father. Thomas went off to work at 12 O'clock. . . . Beast Butler has been relieved of his command. Two Yankee peace commissioners have been to Richmond on their own hook: viz: Singleton + F.P. Blair.[4]

Monday, January 23d, 1865: Drizzling rain in the morning, and blowing cold in the evening. Read *Christie Johnstone* and think it very beautiful. Father bought two gallons of Georgia syrup. My throat is sore a little. We hear nothing from Wilmington; but I wouldn't be surprised to hear of its fall, at any hour. Grandma writes, that "she will come over as soon as she can."

Tuesday, January 24th, 1865: Clear and cold. My throat is so sore I can hardly swallow. Howard went to Houston on the mule Father bought a day or two ago. The town is agog with Recognition rumors which would assure us independence if true; but they have hitherto proved frail supports. Lt. Gen D.H. Hill has assumed command at Augusta. A very poor appointment.[5]

Wednesday January 25th, 1865: Clear and very cold. Gargled with sage tea last night, but my throat is very sore and somewhat swelled. Congress is in a "muss." Foote of Tennessee expelled;[6] quarreling over the currency + consolidation bills; the restoration of Joe Johnston, and the appointment of a Generallissimo recommended; both the last bitter pills for President Davis. There is very much talk of peace on both sides and events seem culminating to a negotiation of some sort. Let it come; O! for peace of almost any kind! My throat becoming ulcerated, we sent for Dr. Hall, who prescribed, Chlo. Potash [Potassium chloride] gargle.

Thursday, January 26th, 1865: . . . Mercury at 26° at 8 A.M. in the passage. Out of doors 17 to 18. Coughed a good deal in the night, and my throat quite sore. Dr. called 5 P.M.; pronounced it better and ordered the gargle to be continued. Pain in my back and

4 James Washington Singleton; Francis Preston Blair, Sr.

5 By this time LeRoy had a fixed opinion of Gen. Daniel H. Hill, whose constant complaining and inability to get along with others had prompted Gen. Lee to send him away from the Army of Northern Virginia in 1862. Hill proved no less irascible (and unreliable) in Georgia under Gen. Bragg with the Army of Tennessee, and would end the war in North Carolina. He carried it on in postwar literature.

6 Henry Stuart Foote tried to cross through Union lines to reach Washington, D.C. but was arrested by Confederates. The Confederate House of Representatives voted to expel him on January 24, 1865, but could not muster the necessary two-thirds majority.

chest. Arch brought up fresh meat. The last of the pork is killed. Received a letter to Mother from Auntie + Fa[ther] one from Uncle Edge.

Friday, January 27th, 1865: Clear and bitter cold. Mercury 15½ 16° outdoors at 8.A.M. We have had frozen milk for three mornings. I enjoyed it very much. Took a Dover's Powder last night and my throat is well. Hood's farewell address is in the daily. [Gen. Stephen] Lee's Corps is passing thro' here on its way to So. Ca.[7] Cheatham's will follow.[8]

Saturday, January 28th, 1865: Clear and cold. We sweetened some cream and it froze finely last night. Peace negotiation is all the "talk" + it is tending to reunion; people talk of reconstruction quite coolly. I am much better this morning, but the cold is hard upon me. Sammy Virgin called on "Min" at 6½ yesterday Oclock and sat till 9! We all got "mighty" hungry, but postponed supper thinking he would go. At 8, all but "Min" went out and eat. It's the best joke I've seen in some time. Thomas came home at dusk. Father bought him a horse for 1550 dollars today. Mr. Charles Collins died very suddenly this evening. He was down town this morning.

Sunday, January 29th, 1865: Clear and 17° at 8.A.M. Vice President Stephens, Senator Hunter, + Judge Campbell, are appointed peace commissioners to go to Washington.[9] O! may it end in peace at last. Nothing else is talked of but negotiation. General Hood is in town. The folks went to Mr. Charles Collins' funeral this evening. It is thought he died of Rheumatism of the heart.

Monday, January 30th, 1865: Clear and cold. Thomas went off on foot, to Jones, to survey the district Lines, preferring to do so, because of the danger of his horse being stolen when he left him. . . . I have been sick with a pain in my back and heart all day. O! for Spring!

Tuesday, January 31st, 1865: Clear and cool. My back ran immensely, and I feel much relieved. Father left for Houston. Sherman is marching up both sides of the Savannah [River] to Augusta. Robert, Uncle John's boy [slave], arrived yesterday, and left this

---

7   Stephen D. Lee.

8   What remained of the Army of Tennessee was moving east to reach the Carolinas in an effort to stop or at least slow down Gen. Sherman's march north.

9   The Hampton Roads Peace Conference would be held aboard the steamboat *River Queen* on Feb. 3, 1865. The Confederate representatives (Vice President Alexander Stevens, Assistant Secretary of War John A. Campbell, and Senator Robert M. T. Hunter) met with President Lincoln and Secretary of State William Seward. Exactly what transpired is still debated, but the conference was unsuccessful.

morning. He left Uncle Jno to bring Major Dunlap home. Susie and Georgia Tracy called and behaved beautifully.

Wednesday, February 1st, 1865: Clear and cool. Howard left for Houston, in the wagon, driving Tom's horse. Breckinridge is appointed Sec'y of War. [Robert E.] Lee nominated General-in-Chief. The commissioners have gone to Washington. They are informal, and go merely to see if peace is attainable. Sherman steadily advancing into So. Ca. Miss Sallie Fort is to be married tonight to Dr. Milton.

Thursday, February 2nd, 1865: Cloudy and warm. Miss Sue Rowland went to the wedding with Mother and stayed all night with us. Mother brought me two hearts [cakes] and "Min" one + I enjoyed them very much. We got a letter from Uncle Richard dated Nov. 14; and 1 from Uncle Jno at Tupelo, Mississippi. Father and Howard arrived from Houston. Father brought me some partridges. Had splendid ice cream for dinner frozen with some ice we found in a tub. It was elegant.

Friday, February 3d, 1865: Rained until ten oclock. Minnie sick in bed. No new rumors. Allen has had one eye sore for two months and now the other eye is affected. Dr. Hall thinks it a serious case + has ordered a blister for his back. He may go blind. Rained steadily from 12.M. till 4 P.M. President Davis refuses to give Joe Johnston a command, though urged by the Government + members of Congress from S. C. to place him over Hardee. Too great obstinacy is a heinous fault, indeed.[10] Gold has fallen from 60 to 40 for 1 on the strength of Peace rumors +c.

Saturday, February 4th, 1865: Cloudy and warm. Minnie out of bed and a little better. Allen in bed, and I am confined to the house. Father is despondent about the country + thinks the peace commission will amount to nothing. Thomas came home at dark. . . . Cheatham's corps is en route to S. Ca. The 2nd [Ga] Batt[alion] is at Branchville.

Sunday, February 5th, 1865: Clear and warm. Our commissioners will not be allowed to go to Washington—Seward is to meet them at Fort Monroe. Recognition rumors still are the talk. Congress has altered the C.S. Flag by changing ½ the white field to red.[11] . . .

---

10 LeRoy believed President Davis' unwillingness to bring Johnston back as a fault. Famous diarist Mary Boykin Chesnut, in her outstanding journal *Diary of Mary Chesnut* (Appleton, 1905), wrote much the same thing: "We thought this was a struggle for independence. Now it seems it is only a fight between Joe Johnston and Jeff Davis." To be fair to Davis, Johnston's way of waging war was, and had always been, different than what Davis demanded and expected. Against his better judgment, Davis placed Johnston in command of the Army of Tennessee in early 1864, and would install him again at army command during the final months of the war in the North Carolina.

11 This version was known as the "Blood Stained Banner."

Monday, February 6th, 1865: Cloudy and raw. . . . Thomas rode his horse, yclept[12] "Old Slow," to Jones for the first time. General Lee calls for supplies: his army is living on corn meal and no meat. Allen's eyes are both affected, and it looks very much like he will go blind.

Tuesday, February 7th, 1865: Rained in the night and it is raining this A.M. Uncle John staid to tea with us last night. Our commissioners have returned. Lincoln + Seward met them and offered terms, viz: unconditional submission + abolition of slavery. They will yet live to rue their arrogance, for the South will be nerved to prosecute the war to the bitter end, + we will surely achieve Independence! Father says, there is no end to the war now.[13] If we will endure, and suffer patiently, all will yet be well. Have had a slight pain in my hip all day: it makes me very restless.

Wednesday, February 8th, 1865: Clear and cold. Slept well, notwithstanding the aching in my leg. Read *Peg Woffington* through today, + enjoyed it very much. My leg aching all day. Branchville is taken or rather the road is cut. So rumor hath it. Thomas came home at dark, to get some clean clothes, having fallen into a bog. The Dr. pronounces Allen's eyes much better. It was a case of Iritis, an acute inflamation of the pupil. The legislature is to meet here next week, and they are trying to get a house here for Governor Brown.

Thursday, February 9th, 1865: Clear and very cold. Fighting on the So. Ca. front. Dr. Airey arrived on his way from Ala. to join his command + we were glad to see him. We were so shocked to hear, this evening, of Mrs. Lou[isa] Fitzgerald's death [Dr. Fitzgerald's wife]. She had been very weak for some time. It is so very sad.

Friday, February 10th, 1865: Clear and cold. Uncle John came up and sat all the morning to talk with Dr. Airey. Mother and Father have gone to Mrs. Fitzgerald's funeral. We have nothing from the march of Sherman. General Beauregard is in command. Mrs. Armstrong has just heard of the drowning of her son (in the navy) at Richmond. Played 11 games of backgammon with Thomas and beat 6 times. We are about equal.

Saturday, February 11th, 1865: Clear and cool. Dr. Airey left at daylight. Uncle John stayed to tea with us last night, and we had a fine time. I have taken a bad snuffling cold, and feeling droopy, did not get up to the matutinal [early morning] meal. Minnie and I, Miss Clare deG[raffenried], + Miss Fannie Payne, went on top of the house and looked

---

12 Yclept is an old term meaning "by the name of," and is not in use today.

13 John Gresham by this time was a realist when it came to the prosecution of the war, and he likely meant there was no "end" other than complete defeat.

at the people who were walking out. Thomas has gone to take tea at Aunt Ann's this evening. No news or rumors.

Sunday, February 12th, 1865: Clear, beautiful day. My cold, better. Delayed press telegrams give us particulars of the interview of the peace commission. Lincoln told a joke which made them roar with laughter. Neither side would yield a hair's breadth; our noble trio stood as firm as rocks. Mr. Stephens will canvass Georgia, in favor of a vigorous war. Heavy fighting on Lee's lines, on the 6th. Pegram's, Gordon's, and Mahone's divisions engaged. Pegram killed and Gen Sorrel severely wounded in hip.[14] Nothing reliable from S. C. At 1½ O'clock, just as we sat down to dinner, Father was taken with colic, and he had a very severe attack, but was eventually relieved by mustard + 100 drops laudanum.[15] This is the first attack he has had in two years, and I sincerely hope he will not have a return of it. . . .

[The following was written on a separate sheet of paper]

Macon, February 12th, 1865

This is a bright and charming day, and it is the Holy Sabbath. A large congregation turned out, today, in the Presbyterian Church, and Mr. Wills preached on Christ's conversation with the woman of Samaria, at the well. I read in *Plantation Sermons* during the morning, and then went out, and layed me down in the sun, to wait for the folks. We hurried dinner, because Thomas was going off. Just as we sat down and commenced eating, Father said he could not straighten himself: seems he was taken violently with colic, and had a hard attack, but was finally relieved by mustard + a dose of 100 drops of laudanum. Thomas was delayed and did not go off at all. Dr. Hall came after Father was relieved.

Three columns of delayed telegraphic news out in the daily. Our commissioners were not allowed to leave the boat at Fortress Monroe. Lincoln and Seward met them there. While Mr. Stephens was making one of his points, Lincoln sprang up and said that "he was reminded of a man in Illinois," and the commissioners were convulsed with laughter, and thus the merry gorilla treated the last effort at negotiation. This commission was sent in good faith and we were willing to give the enemy everything except the only thing they wanted: unconditional submission; and they would give—us nearly all we required excepting Slavery + Recognition! On these points neither side would yield a hairbreadth. Both side will be nerved to renewed exemptions. Vice

---

14 Battle of Hatcher's Run (Feb. 5-7, 1865). Another attempt to cut Lee's supply lines. Gen. John Pegram, married three weeks earlier, was killed.

15 A painful gastrointestinal attack.

President S. is coming home to canvass the state in favor of a vigorous prosecution of the war.

There has been very heavy fighting on the lines around Petersburg. Pegram, Mahone, and Gordon were engaged. Pegram was killed + Gen Sorrel was wounded severely in the hip. Sherman seems to be having his own way in South Carolina. Wheeler is doing gallant service!! Things look dark, but the tide of war may turn at any moment and the skies will be bright, our hearts will be cheered and our Independence achieved.

LeRoy Wiley Gresham

Monday, February 13th, 1865: Clear and cold. Thomas off to work. He killed 3 robins for my dinner. I never saw them so tame + plentiful. I suppose it is because they are shot at so little. Received a long letter from Sallie Bird. Father did not go down town at all today. Robins thick.

Tuesday, February 14th, 1865: Damp raw and sometimes drizzling. St Valentine's day. Minnie sent a valentine to Ellen Ross, and Thomas to I.L. Congress is going to "put in" the darkies to help stop Yankee bullets.[16] Joe Johnston is acting volunteer aid to General Hardee! Tis not settled whether Sherman will take Augusta, Columbia, or Charleston, or all three! Uncle John dined with us. Raining after dinner and freezing on the trees, after it falls. Killed a robin with my bow. I ate my robin for dinner. I stood in the door + killed him in the China tree by the wing. Mother had molasses candy made. Ate lots of ice, from off the leaves.

Wednesday, February 15th, 1865: Cloudy and foggy. Mother and I rode down town. Father bought 10 lead pencils at 3 dollars apiece, on a speculation. Mother had her measure taken for some shoes. On the way back, came to see Cousin Eliza. Tho' very anxious, we hear nothing from So. Ca. . . . The legislature met today, but there was not a quorum in either house. . . .

Thursday, February 16th, 1865: Clear and warm. Uncle John called and bade us "goodbye," last night. Wood is 45 to 50 dollars per load. It is nearly as high as Gold, and I don't see how the poorer classes get along.[17] Father gave 50 dollars . . . for a pocket

---

16 The Confederate Congress was debating the passage of a law to allow the enlistment of blacks in the Confederate Army for the duration of the war in exchange for their freedom. It was not passed until March 13, 1865—far too late to have made any difference.

17 The statement is revelatory. LeRoy still considers the Gresham family to be wealthy, or at least not poor (which was still true). He also realizes that high fixed prices affected the poorest amongst them.

knife for Mother.[18] . . . No quorum yet in the legislature. Auntie is cut off in Richmond. O! how we long to hear something definite from S. C. Refugees are pouring out of Augusta.

Friday, February 17th, 1865: Clear, with the wind blowing a gale. Gen Cobb addressed an immense audience at the City Hall last night on the "state of the Country." Father says the people cheered lustily for Joe Johnston. Hon. Benj. Hill speaks tonight.[19] On my wagon most of the day, basking in the sunshine and drinking in the balmy air.

Saturday, February 18th, 1865: Clear and pleasant. Gov. Brown's message is a tirade against Pres. Davis, and it is a miserable, morose, revolutionary document. Saith he "we are drifting to utter ruin!" Sen[ator] H[ill] scored [beat] him soundly last night. Mother went to see Cousin Jack who is very bad off with carbuncles on his leg. Thomas came in this morning having finished his district. Every one is down on Gov Brown.

Sunday, February 19th, 1865: Clear, bright, beautiful day, and the church was filled. . . . All the amen [front] pews were filled. Mr. E.P. Palmer dined with us. Father wore his new black suit for the first time, and it is elegant. We hear nothing from So. Ca. General Lee has been to Columbia + had a conference.

Monday, February 20th, 1865: Clear and bright. Father went to Houston, taking both horses. Mother sick. I was occupied all the evening in calling out to Thomas the bearings for him to plot by. Mother bought me "marginalia" or anecdotes about the war by [correspondent] "Personne." All the members of Congress, except 6, signed a petition to the President, to make Forrest a Lt Gen, and he refused. O! what obstinacy + prejudice.

Tuesday, February 21st, 1865: Cloudy and cool. On my wagon all the morning looking at Howard working in the garden. Seed are quite hard to find and we can only get supplied by begging them.

Wednesday, February 22nd, 1865: Cloudy and pleasant. Looking at Howard planting peas, beets, turnips, in the A.M. Thomas stays in the office 'till 3 O'clock; does not come home to dinner. He is drawing anew his old map, having discovered a big mistake in it. We have news this evening of the evacuation of Charleston under the supervision

---

18 It is possible John Gresham was using Confederate money to purchase things that would have some lasting or intrinsic value, since he realized the end of the Confederacy was drawing near and the money would soon be worthless.

19 Benjamin H. Hill, Confederate senator from Georgia.

of Beauregard and the fall of Columbia, S. C. Sherman is marching triumphantly on, on till he reaches the rear of Lee.

Thursday, February 23d, 1865: Cloudy. Rained a little between 8 + 9 A.M. Sherman is marching on Charlotte, N. C., tearing up the R.R.'s + destroying everything. He is aiming for Danville. Gen D.H. Hill was relieved from command at Augusta on the 22nd. Poor Lee! how awfully pressed he is. Father returned from Houston with 5 partridges, doves + blackbirds; also "Bill" to pull me. Allen is "played out." Aunt Ann sent me cake, pudding, syllabub, turkey, jellie, pickle, +c.

Friday, February 24th, 1865: Raining slowly when I got up. Bad news is common. Cheatham's corps attempting to flank Sherman was scattered. The Yankees burned a large part of Columbia.[20] They are meeting with no opposition. Our army is scattered and Sherman's in a concentrated column. I confess I feel somewhat demoralized at the prospect. It has rained all day, + very hard all the evening. Had a blackbird + dove pie for dinner. Lockett and Bates called to say "good bye"—they leave to join the Cadets.

Saturday, February 25th, 1865: Drizzling rain in the A.M. Milo came up last night. Green ran away over a month ago + has not been heard from since. Father thinks he is trying to get to the Yankees. Those treated best, leave first. We had a dining today, and Cousins Helen, Zeke, Ira, Cousin Jimmie + Cousin "Liza" came through the pouring rain. Notwithstanding outside gloom we had a nice dinner and pleasant time. From noon till dark it literally poured down and there will be a heavy freshet.

Sunday, February 26th, 1865: Clear and warm. . . . The wagon train of the Army of Tenn. is passing over the river here on pontoons. They are over 1600 in number. Walnut Bridge was partly washed away yesterday, but is repaired now. Enjoying ourselves, "licking 'lasses candy" today.

Monday, February 27th, 1865: Clear and beautiful day. The [state] Militia have been furloughed indefinitely. . . . A letter (brought thro' to Ga. by Vice Prest. Stephens) came from Auntie to Grandma today. She is very anxious to get home. Nothing reliable from Sherman. I have been trying to clothe "Bill" in the garments of civilization today + have improved his appearance wonderfully.[21]

---

20 Gen. Beauregard ordered Confederate forces to evacuate Charleston on Feb. 15, 1865, and the city surrendered three days later. Columbia fell to Sherman's armies on Feb. 17-18. A huge fire destroyed much of the city, the cause of which is still disputed.

21 Vice President Alexander Stephens was acquainted with Grandma. Bill, brought up from one of the Houston plantations to attend to LeRoy, arrived in rough field clothing. LeRoy was dressing him in nicer clothes more suitable to Macon living.

Tuesday, February 28th, 1865: Rained nearly all night and ceased after day. The river is very high. Willie Carhart, Jas. Ralston, Mrs. Pease + Eddie + Mr. Deloache + Mrs. Tucker ("ci devant"), Miss Prentice have gone North. Verily, there is a scampering of the rats from the ship. Thomas and I rode down to the river to look at the pontoon bridge which was, to me a novel sight.[22]

Wednesday, March 1st, 1865: Rained in the night and tis a damp day. The orders of GenLee, on assuming command of all the armies, are in the daily. A great part of Columbia, S.C. is burned. Wilmington is attacked + Mobile threatened. Wade Hampton is Lt Gen. . . . The 1st number of the *Daily Journal + Messenger* greets us this morning. 5½ P.M. . . . Rev. Mr. Palmer of Marietta, dined with us.

Thursday, March 2nd, 1865: Cloudy and humid. Rained in the night, and the tomcats made night hideous, with their caterwaulings under our window. Maugre[23] the latter, I slept well. Minnie + Miss Clare deGraffenried rode with Mother down to see the pontoon bridge, which is the lion of the day. So anxious is every one to hear news that we manufacture it.[24] The town is agog with rumors of the defeat of Sherman. About two thirds of Columbia was burned to the ground. Tis said the fire caught by accident + no one could stop it or no one <u>did</u>.

Friday, March 3d, 1865: Foggy and warm. We have the joyful news this morning that Joe Johnston was appointed to the command of the Army of Tennessee at Charlotte and that our army is massing in Sherman's front. Cousin Jimmie Knox came to see us this evening. Cousin Sam [Knox] was wounded in the lungs + captured, in Tennessee.[25]

Saturday, March 4th, 1865: Cloudy and cool. Rained hard in the night and the wind blew a gale. Father invited Col Frobel to tea yesterday and we made ready for him and waited supper till nearly 9 P.M. + he did not come! What a "cham"! Cousin Jimmie

---

22 A pontoon bridge use floats or more commonly, shallow-draft boats, to support decking to enable wagons and troops to cross rivers.

23 Another old word meaning "in spite of" or "notwithstanding."

24 LeRoy astutely realizes people are simply telling others rumors and gossip as if it were truth to fill the vacuum of reliable news.

25 President Davis relented and elevated Gen. Johnston to command the Department of South Carolina, Georgia, and Florida, and the Department of North Carolina and Southern Virginia. His command was a motley collection from a variety of armies, garrisons, and small posts. The Army of Tennessee comprised a small part of the total because there were few left after the Nashville disaster, and fewer still that made the long trip to the Carolinas. The identity of "Cousin" Knox has not be determined.

called to bid us Good Bye. He leaves with the wagon train of [Gen. A. P.] Stewart's Corps for So. Ca. Sherman is marching on Wilmington + he will take it.

LeRoy W. Gresham

Sunday, March 5th, 1865: Clear, beautiful day: and the pleasant sunshine is welcomed after a week's advance. . . . Cousin Jimmie came back yesterday, the wagon train having moved only 2 miles, and he and Thomas went to the theatre. He left today for good. The Yanks report Wilmington in their hands. Sherman is safe now, + Wilmington will be his new base, for a grand onslaught on Lee! Mother has gone over to see Cousin Helen. Queen "Vic," [Victoria] in opening the British Parliament, declares steadfast neutrality to be the policy of England in reference to this war!

Monday, March 6th, 1865: Cloudy and chilly until 11 A.M., when the sun shone out warm. Thomas went off, after early breakfast, on the cars to Griswoldville, to survey the 6rh District. . . .

Tuesday, March 7th, 1865: Clear and cool. Arch came up with supplies, wheat, butter, a wild turkey, +c. Allen returned to Houston with him, riding "Old Slow"; so Gulielmus, vulgarly termed "Bill," is regularly installed.[26] . . . Gen Jos. E. Johnston's report of the North Ga. campaign is published in the daily and it is a splendid document. Many rumors from the seat of war, but nothing reliable. . . .

Wednesday, March 8th, 1865: We found it pouring down rain this morning + at 9 A.M. 'tis drizzling. Col Jas. Chambers of the Senate took tea with us last evening. We heard, by a letter from Grandma, yesterday of the death of Uncle Eli, on the 3d Jan. in Texas, of congestion of the lungs.[27]

Thursday, March 9th, 1865: Drizzled rain 'till 11A.M. when it began to pour down; and at 2½ P.M. it continues raining steadily. Pasted in Hood's campaign +c and it nearly finishes my scrap book. I begin to doubt whether it is true, that Gen'l Johnston is

26 With Allen returning to work on the plantation, Bill (his real name apparently Gulielmus) was left at the house to assist LeRoy.

27 The identity "Jas. Chambers" has not been determined. Uncle Eli Harris Baxter, Sr. (1798-1865) was Grandmother's brother and lived in Texas. Cousin Eli Leroy Baxter (1834-1862) died in Confederate service in Texas.

restored. The fruit trees are backward. The plums are first in bloom, while only one tree, the honey peach, is beginning to bloom. We augur from this a good fruit year. . . .

Friday, March 10th, 1865: Clear and cool. Confederate Fast day; and everyone is at Church. Lt Col Frobel came in last night and took social tea + it was a slim one at that. Asst. Eng[inee]r Gresham [Thomas] also surprised us with a visit, leaving again early this morning. Genl Johnston's order assuming command at Charlotte it out. Great rejoicing at the North over Sumter, Charleston + Wilmington.

Saturday, March 11th, 1865: Clear and cold. Ice thick as glass. Thomas came in again last night. Bowie Knox arrived this evening on his way to the army. He says reports from Franklin say Cousin Sam is dead. He was a brave true Soldier, and there was something so winning in his manner.

Sunday, March 12th, 1865: Clear and cool. Bowie went off before breakfast. Sherman does'nt seem to get along very fast . . . Johnston, Beauregard + Hardee are concentrating in his front, meanwhile. Read through the Bible to Nehemiah 7th this day. . . .

Monday, March 13th, 1865: Clear and lovely day. Mother and I rode down town this morning. Bought a stick of sealing wax for 10 dollars! Reading *Billy Milton*, a present from Thomas. The legislature adjourned at 12 Oclock Saturday night. Even Father has about given up that we will not see Grandma this winter. If she don't come this week she will have to go to Athens. "Bill" surprised us all today with his skill in knitting on straws.[28]

Tuesday, March 14th, 1865: Cloudy and warm. Thomas went to work on foot again. Sherman is said to be at Cheraw [SC]. A federal force is moving down the Valley to Lynchburg. Lincoln's inaugural is a hypocritical, Praise God Barebone piece of puritanical fanaticism. He actually admits that the Lord of all has purposes of his own in this war. Congress adjourned Saturday. Passed the Negro soldier bill in the Senate by 1 vote. Rained a little about 3 Oclock.

Wednesday, March 15th, 1865: Rained from 7.A.M. to 10 Oclock. Are we never to have sunshine again? Father says Peace can only come now by Reconstruction, or through France! He is not very hopeful of the latter. Thomas came in at 5 P.M.

Thursday, March 16th, 1865: Woke up and found the heavens hung with clouds: soon it began to rain hard, + it continued to drizzle till 11 A.M. Sunshine has deserted

---

28 Slaves had to make use with what they had, and it would not have been unusual for Bill to be adept at kitting straw into various things, including a blanket.

us. General Lee reports a heavy fight at Kinston, N.C. Our men drove the enemy under Schofield, + took 3 guns + 1500 prisoners. Our loss small.[29] We can get nothing reliable in regard to Sherman, tho' there are many rumors of fighting afloat. Mother got a letter from Auntie dated February 19th. She was well + endeavoring to get an escort home. The negro bill is a law. And there is much discussion as to the propriety of giving up the slavery question, as it is unquestionably does. I am in favor of trying it on a small scale at first.[30] "Bill" is learning to wait on me pretty well + can do all that Allen did. Sun came out, and the wind blew hard, in the P.M. My daily occupation, doing nothing, is becoming more irksome to me every day. I do long for health + active employment.

Friday, March 17th, 1865: Clear beautiful spring day. Out on my wagon till 1 Oclock + occupied myself making a trap to catch sparrows. Recognition by Napoleon is completely "squelched." Maximilian is recognized—but alas! poor "Confed."[31] We sent to the Govt steam bakery + got some hard tack [hard bread biscuit] which we find very nice when softened. Thomas off on Prince to work early this morning. Father went to a big gentleman's supper ant Mr. Johnston's (W.B.) last night + came home at 1½ A.M. Painted the new C.S. Flag in my diary. Every one is pleased at the alteration. The fruit trees are in bloom. O! I do long for a good fruit year. Howard is planting potatoes. Mr. Whittle's house was entered last night and a silver pitcher +c stolen. A great many houses have lately been entered + soldiers + negros are at the bottom of it. Our turn must come.

Saturday, March 18th, 1865: Clear beautiful day. Caught two birds + made a trap for "Bill." Hilly Green called and played two games chess last night. I beat. Frank, riding "Old Slow," + Milo, came last night, bringing a wild turkey, +c.

Sunday, March 19th, 1865: Clear beautiful day. . . . Caught 4 birds, two at a time. "P.W.A." is to correspond for the daily. Pres. Davis has sent in a gloomy message in

29 Battle of Wyse Fork, or Kinston (March 7-10, 1865). Part of the Carolinas Campaign and an attempt to halt Sherman's advance through North Carolina. Southern losses totaled about 1,500 men to 1,100 for the Union.

30 This is the first time LeRoy weighs in on the ending of slavery. Given his upbringing and his family's dependence upon slave labor, it is interesting that he is in favor, if slowly, of its abolishment. He may well be repeating what his father is articulating to him, although he is smart enough to realize the institution was doomed (as he implies from the Enlistment Act just passed by the Confederate Congress).

31 France (with Britain and Spain) had invaded Mexico in 1861 and set up Austrian prince Maximilian as emperor. Britain and Spain withdrew shortly thereafter, leaving France to run the country. Several European governments recognized French interests there and Maximilian as emperor, but they did not do the same for the Confederacy—which is LeRoy's point. It would not end well for the Austrian; his regime collapsed in 1867, and he was executed by firing squad.

which he says, "The country is in more peril now that it ever was." Had a wild turkey, and "tater" custard, for dinner. It has been almost warm enough to be comfortable without fire. There are over 100 cases of smallpox in town. The carrier of the daily has it + we have to send for the paper which is very inconvenient.

Monday, March 20th, 1865: Clear and beautiful. Thomas rode his steed "Slow" to work. Frank is engaged in repairing our fence. Some of it was blow down by the winds, and some torn to pieces, by the Collinsvillians, for firewood. Aunt Eliza writes that Grandma is in Milledgeville + will be here tomorrow.

Tuesday, March 21st, 1865: Woke up and found it raining hard. When shall we have fine weather. Every Tuesday or Wednesday it rains. Minnie went out to Mr. Clisby's last night, to tea. Reading *The Old Farm House*. Grandma arrived this evening at 5 O'clock. She had a hard time getting to the depot. The deserters are pouring in under General Lee's amnesty + the appointment of Joe Johnston.[32]

Wednesday, March 22nd, 1865: Clear and cool. Congress adjourned on the 18th. Father went in the wagon with Howard to the plantation. It is rumored that a battle is going on in [North] Carolina. Sherman is in Fayetteville, Schofield in Goldsboro. . . .

Thursday, March 23d, 1865: Clear and pleasant. General Johnston reports that he attacked the enemy at 5 P.M. at Bentonville Carolina and routed him. Our loss small. Enemy's 5000. It is reported the fight was renewed the next day.[33] The wind has been blowing a gale all day and it is real March weather. . . . Our laurels are in full bloom now and they are beautiful.

Friday, March 24th, 1865: Cloudless, windy day. Forrest has been commissioned Lieut. Gen. Cousin Charlie + his wife [Juliet] called, after tea, last night. Father came back riding on top of the fodder in the wagon. He brought a quarter of beef, butter, groundpeas + other supplies.

Saturday, March 25th, 1865: Clear and cool. Hilly Green called and remained all the A.M. + played 6 games of Chess—I beat 4.... . Thomas came home at dark. He has almost finished his district. We get no news from Johnston's fights. Green has written

---

32 Gen. Lee had issued an amnesty, promising to forgive soldiers absent without leave if they would only rejoin their units. It is LeRoy's opinion that Johnston had a great deal of loyalty amongst his troops, which is largely true.

33 The Battle of Bentonville (March 19-21, 1865), one of the final large pitched battles of the war. Johnston struck one wing of Sherman's army as it marched through North Carolina and nearly defeated it. The fighting on the last two days was light compared to March 19. Johnston was able to withdraw. Confederate losses totaled 2,600, and Union 1,500. By this time there was nothing the Southern army could have done to change the course of the war.

to his Mammy that he is hired to the surgeon, 54th Virginia Regiment, which I think is in Reynold's [Palmer's] Brigade [of] Lee's Corps.

Sunday, March 26th, 1865: Clear and bright. Slight frost. . . . In the evening Thomas, Grandma, and Mother went over to Aunt Ann's.

Monday, March 27th, 1865: Clear and bright. Rode down town with Mother and Grandma. Mother brought home her shoes of calf skin. There is no news; and we can get no details of Johnston's fights. It is rumored that he has fallen back to Raleigh. Mr. Sparks has received a telegram giving the casualties in a fight at Petersburg which we had never heard before. I reckon we got whipped, or we would have had some news about it. The enemy have cut the R.R. between Mobile + Montgomery, 70 miles from the latter.

Tuesday, March 28th, 1865: We woke up and found it raining. Cousin Annie arrived at 3 P.M. from Eufaula. Aunt Ann + Cousin Mary called. Nothing from Lee's fight.

Wednesday, March 29th, 1865: Drizzled until 12 noon. All of us but Minnie dined at Aunt Ann's and had a very nice time. Auntie writes from Sparta. She encloses a letter from Uncle Richard. Robert E. Lee attacked Grant on the 25th and Gordon swept his lines for 500 yards taking 600 prisoners. The position was given up on account of a cross fire. Gen. Phil Cook + [William] Terry wounded.[34] Cousin Jinnie Wiley's baby was very ill all day + I feel so much for her. Cousin Annie made a beautiful collar and gave it to Mother + is making one for Minnie

Thursday, March 30th, 1865: Clear and windy. . . . Thomas came home at 9 A.M., having finished his district.

Friday, March 31st, 1865: Windy and cool. Cousin Annie heard of Cousin William's capture in North Carolina. Tracy came up and spent the day with us. Father was taken with colic at 2 P.M. but it was not violent + the Dr. did not come till 5 Oclock. The usual remedies seemed to fail entirely + he suffers still. Henry Ralston + "Bill"[35] were going over to Columbus on a train with 5000 lbs. ammunition on board, when it ran off, igniting the powder + killing them both. Henry instantly. . . . 8 P.M. Father not easy yet. The pain is not violent as tis sometimes.

---

34 The Battle of Fort Stedman (March 25, 1865) outside Petersburg, VA. A desperate Confederate attack designed to break through Gen. Grant's front, force him to contract his lines, and perhaps disrupt any attack he had planned. The pre-dawn assault met with considerable success (as LeRoy noted), but it was not strong enough to do anything lasting, and the Rebels eventually retreated. Confederate losses exceeded 4,000, while Union casualties were perhaps 1,000. It was Lee's last large-scale attack of the war.

35 A different Bill, and not LeRoy's servant.

Saturday, April 1st, 1865: Clear and pleasant. Father was apparently easier when we retired; but the pain returned and was not relieved till nearly day. Gen Lee reports: Grant attacked in Gordon's front + was repulsed. Heavy fighting around Mobile [Ala].

Sunday, April 2nd, 1865: Communion day, and a bright beautiful day it is. . . . Father still in bed and Dr. Hall gave him oil. There has been another fight on [Gen.] Bushrod Johnson's [Petersburg] lines + the yanks were driven back with heavy loss. The fruit crop promises well if it's not killed soon. I did not commune today. I hope ere long to be able to go to church long enough to have that privilege.

Monday, April 3d, 1865: Clear and windy. Father in bed still + tho'weak from the effect of medicine, is better. . . . Reading *Rena, or the Snowbird* by Mrs. Hentz.

Tuesday April 4th, 1865: Clear and warm. Father took Dover's Powder and seems better. He has to stay in bed on acct of soreness in the muscles. Milo came up in the wagon last night with supplies. Alabama is invaded by a column of 5000 from Pensacola + as many from the north. Fighting in front of Selma + Mobile. Everything looks squally in that section. Mrs. [Gen.] Johnston and Mrs. Ed. Tracy called. We have all been sitting in Mother's room with Father today. I have taken slight cold.

Wednesday, April 5th, 1865: Cloudy and windy. Cold indoors and pleasant outside. Bad news! Selma is evacuated. Mobile is to follow. Ala. overrun. Father is still confined to bed with neuralgic pains in his side.

Thursday, April 6th, 1865: Cloudy early in the morning + clear at noon. Father in bed yet and today Mother is sick. A dispatch dated Danville brings us the news that Lee's lines being broken through, after 4 days hard fighting, he was compelled to uncover Richmond. On Sunday the evacuation commenced and only the Gov. officials got out. President Davis + cabinet are at Danville. The Va State archives are lost. After the evacuation the mobs began to plunder the stores. Very few citizens escaped owing to the retreat. Lee's position is unknown.[36]

Friday, April 7th, 1865: Cloudy and warm. President Davis has issued an address calling upon the people to stand firm + meet the crisis "with unconquered + unconquerable hearts." It is a soulstirring appeal. Father up today tho' quite weak.

---

36 On April 1, Lee's far right flank was turned in a defeat at Five Forks, VA, which exposed Lee's only remaining lifeline—the Southside Railroad—to Union capture. Grant launched a large-scale general attack all along the lines the next day, and the Petersburg defenses crumbled. Lee notified President Davis he was evacuating Richmond and Petersburg. Lee escaped with most of his army and marched west in an effort to outrun Union pursuit so he could turn south and unite with Johnston's army in North Carolina. President Davis with members of his cabinet and staff left by train for Danville, Va.

Saturday, April 8th, 1865: Cloudy and cool Thomas went with Minnie and Miss Clare to a tableau at Mr. B.F. Ross'. Father up and dressed. He looks weak + is considerably worsted. Montgomery has not yet fallen. We have nothing from Lee; No further particulars of the Evacuation.

Sunday, April 9th, 1865: Cloudy all day. I believe it is the only cloudy Sunday we've had this year. . . . Minnie and Thomas went [to church].

Monday April 10th, 1865: Clear and cool. Father down town for the first time in ten days. Grandma, Mother and I rode down town in the evening. Maj. Alexander, whose wife is at Granite Farm, called + brought a long letter from Auntie to Grandma. There is much talk of where the Capital is to be. Macon is spoken of and the Commissary Department is already reported ordered here + tis thought the Q.M. Dept. will soon follow.

Tuesday, April 11th, 1865: Clear and warm. Gen Lee is moving toward Lynchburg, followed by Grant and fighting him daily. The fate of the country hangs on the issue. Richmond reported burned by mobs.[37] Montgomery [Ala] has fallen and our army gone toward Miss, leaving Columbus [Ga] open. The "N.Y. Herald" reports that the Confederacy was recognized by France on the 3d March! . . .

Wednesday, April 12th, 1865: Clear and pleasant spring day. The trees are coming out green and beautifully. Lieut. Gresham, Asst. Eng[inee]r, left this A.M. to make a survey of the 1st District, Baldwin Co. We have tremendous reports of the losses in the engagements previous to the fall of Richmond. The yanks made 15 assaults + were repulsed; but finally broke thru' the lines, and they could not be reformed in time to prevent the evacuation. Our loss 15,000! Enemy's 60,000. Lt. Genl. A.P. Hill killed, with other gallant officers.[38] There has been tremendous fighting on the retreat. We do not know whether we have suffered a disaster or gained a victory. Our fate is soon to be decided. The enemy occupy Montgomery, Ala.

Thursday, April 13th, 1865: Cloudy and warm. Rained a little. The gardens are needing rain. No news. The other day Father bought a 4 blade pocket knife and gave 100 dollars for it, and presented it to me. Afterwards we concluded to swap + I took his old one as it suited me better.

---

37 A fire set by the Confederates to destroy supplies and records spread and burned nearly the entire business district. Unfortunately, a large portion of Confederate records perished in the flames.

38 Gen. Ambrose P. Hill, who led a corps in Lee's army, was killed on April 2 when the Yankees broke through his lines.

Friday, April 14th, 1865: Cloudy and pleasant. Wrote to Thomas. Gen Fitzhugh Lee was wounded + taken prisoner in the late Petersburg fights. Many rumors are afloat of how immensely Lee lost. I reckon it was not more than 15000. Mrs. Howell Cobb sent me a nice basket of radishes. Mr. Markham, our friend [and pastor] who was with us last summer, arrived this P.M. on his way to his command in the Army of the Tenn.

Saturday, April 15th, 1865: Cloudy, balmy, spring weather, and just such as I enjoy. Papers full of yankee rejoicings over the fall of Richmond which are galling to one's pride. Since the disgraceful abandonment of Montgomery, we have but few cities to give up. . . .

Sunday, April 16th, 1865: Clear and beautiful day. Mr. Markham preached in the A.M. Mr. Adams is to preach tonight. Mr. Bunting, a chaplain in the Texas Rangers, called last night. Mr. Bryson is a Tennessee chaplain and a very nice man. The yankees are marching on Columbus, Georgia.

Monday, April 17th, 1865: Clear and warm. Have been suffering with Diarrhea for some days.[39] Took paregoric last night and slept nearly all the morning. We have intelligence of the fall of Columbus and there is some uncertainty as to the fate of our army under Gen Cobb. I got a letter from Thomas telling us how he was getting along. Cousin Annie's Baby very ill.

Tuesday, April 18th, 1865: Clear and warm. . . . Quite a handsome fight was made at Columbus but the enemy sent some cavalry to our rear and took possession of the bridge and our men had to uncover the city + cross the Chattahoochee above + below. Gen Cobb's present position is unknown. Many wild and terrible rumors are bruited [spread] about of Lee's condition. I have been very drooping today. Dr. Hall came to see me last night + prescribed camphor + paregoric which relieved my trouble [diarrhea]. I have nausea + no appetite still. The yankees can come here easy enough. Gen Cobb saved only 50 or 100 men of his army and the local troops here cannot repulse 5000 veteran troops.

Wednesday, April 19th, 1865: Clear and beautiful day. Lay on the sofa nearly all day + suffered no little with pain in my back. A day of unceasing pain. Thomas came home yesterday and he and ~~Thomas~~ Father have been very busy hiding all day.[40] Rumor hath the road cut at Barnesville but nothing positive is known.

---

39 This is the first reference LeRoy makes to his health in some time. In fact, he had been very sick, very weak, and was now clearly losing his battle with pulmonary and spinal tuberculosis.

40 LeRoy means they were busy hiding items of value.

Thursday, April 20th, 1865: Clear and warm. Put on a summer coat and it feels fine. I was in much pain when I went to bed last night; took a Dover's Powder and feel relieved from pain. The yanks are on the M+WRR and the Columbus road but it is not known when they will be here. I doubt whether much resistance will be made. Thomas has reported to Capt. Glenn and is galloping around the lines with him. The Corps will go to Augusta if Macon falls. 5 P.M: Great excitement! The yankees are on the outskirts and the town being under an armistice, no resistance will be made.[41] Generals Johnston and Sherman have declared an armistice for the purpose of settling existing difficulties, and great uneasiness exists for fear Lee is captured as Johnston made the truce. Thomas made a dash, on Prince, for the bridge, but when he got there he could not cross; the pontoon being broken. All is excitement + alarm. After Supper Thomas made another attempt on foot and again failed.[42] The city is full of yankees; but everything is quiet now. They came with torches into the horselot and took Prince, so Good Bye Josie.

Friday, April 21st, 1865: Cloudy and warm. Thomas and I slept upstairs, and I slept very well notwithstanding the yanks were passing by all night. This morn, bright and early, sent Howard to Head Quarters for a gaurd [for the house] but did not succeed: so Father went down town, and being introduced to Captain Hinson of [Gen. Kenner] Garrard's division, invited him to the house and he has taken Mother's room with his servant.[43] He is wounded in the leg. The hours of the morning dragged away. At noon a column of 200 blue coats passed the gate with a splendid band and the rear brought up by negroes on horseback. All is quiet and orderly and no one has entered the house. One came + looked at Father's saddle but he would'nt have it. Thomas is upstairs "lying low." Gens [Howell] Cobb + [James] Wilson, the Yankee commander, are trying to settle the status of the man captured here as the enemy entered in time of truce, and General W[ilson] has telegraphed to Sherman for instructions, and is awaiting his answer. Mr. Knox of Ala. sent us word that he was at Gen Wilson's Qr's and Father carried him something to eat. Very soon he was paroled and is here now.[44]

---

41 Federal forces under Union Gen. James H. Wilson were advancing on Macon.

42 Thomas was attempting to avoid being taken prisoner.

43 This is the first time LeRoy had close contact with a Yankee officer—in this case, Capt. Daniel K. Hinson, Co. A, 35th New Jersey Infantry. Hinson, who had been wounded in the leg, and his orderly Peter Muller, took up residence in the Gresham home, where a very quiet and out-of-uniform Thomas Gresham also resided.

44 Mr. Knox, it will be recalled, was one of the two Confederate soldiers who had convalesced in the Gresham home.

Saturday, April 22nd, 1865: When we woke up this morning after a quiet night's rest it was hard to realize that we were under U.S. rule. But the clanking sabre and the tramp of the horses teaches us how stern is the reality. It is cool and cloudy + we had to have some fire. Thomas came to breakfast this morning + wonderfully stiff it was. The Yanks are not going to burn or destroy anything till they hear how the flag of truce turns out. They burnt the prison barracks at the fairground yesterday. There is one camp just below the College and another below Mrs. Mitchell's. The capitulation of Lee is believed to be true: if so Good Bye C.S.A. Gen Wilson is staying in Maj Nelson's house + his Head Qr's are there.

Sunday, April 23d, 1865: Clear and cold for the season. When we went to bed last night a big fire had been burning for over two hours down town. It is said to have been Wards' old carriage shop + the block connected thereto; and afterwards Mr. Burke's, Johnston's + Weed's stores. I would not be surprised if most of the business part of town were destroyed. There was been another fire this morning, but have not heard where it was. We have no idea how long the armistice will last and the enemy seem to have determined to occupy Macon for the present. We have no news at all from Lee of Johnston and many consider the war over and resistance played out. . . .

Monday, April 24th, 1865: Clear and cold. Sitting around the fire all day. Our present condition is the most anomalous ever heard of in the annals of war. Confeds + Feds walking the streets together and still Gen Wilson claims every soldier in the city a prisoner. The S.W.+M.+W.R.R. left this morning with an officer from each side on board. I saw [our horse] Prince with a U.S. officer on him this morning. Gaurds are stationed at every corner and Father is authorized by Gen W[ilson] to call on them for assistance.

Tuesday, April 25th, 1865: Clear and cool. The Gen commanding authorizing it, there is a small daily called the *Evening News* issued from the Confederate office, price two dollars in C.S. money; 5 cents in specie. It has full particulars of Gen Lee's surrender. He had with him only 9000 armsbearing men—23,000 men in all. Officers and men were paroled and permitted to go home. The scene of surrender between Grant and Lee was very affecting and the latter was allowed to retain his glorious sword, Gen Grant returning it to him and complimenting him on his bravery. He, with other high officers, were on parole in Richmond. In my humble judgement the farewell address of Gen Lee to the "Army of Northern Va" closes the war.[45] Lincoln was assassinated on the night of the 11th coming out of the Opera—shot dead; and at the same time Seward was stabbed in his residence, but he will recover. In the struggle Seward's son was mortally wounded.[46] There are three orders from Gen Wilson inviting people to open stores, resume trade, and bring in supplies +c. Commenced to read *John Marchmont's Legacy* loaned to me by Claire deGraffenreid. We have no butter, and can get none, and live on ham gravy instead.

Wednesday, April 26th, 1865: Clear and warmer. Thomas went down on the R.R. to Houston this morning and found no difficulty in getting off at all. There are many rumors of peace having been declared but I think they are somewhat premature. All the prisoners here are to be paroled as soon as possible. Andy Johnson is inaugurated President of the U.S. Just to think of it. The schools and the College have resumed; the Factory has started + everything is quiet. Pete Muller, Captain Hinson's orderly, keeps them off the lot and out of the house.[47]

---

45 Out of food and general supplies, and with the enemy blocking any reasonable means of escape, Lee surrendered his Army of Northern Virginia to Grant at Appomattox Courthouse on April 9, 1865. LeRoy is right: for all intents and purposes, that surrender ended the war. Joe Johnston followed suit in North Carolina on Apr. 26, and Gen. Richard Taylor surrendered the Departments of Alabama, Mississippi, and East Louisiana on May 4. Others followed, including Kirby Smith in the Trans-Mississippi on May 26. The last recognized surrender would not come until Nov. 9, 1865, when the raider CSS *Shenandoah* surrendered in Liverpool, England.

46 As usual, the first rumors of events were untrue. Lincoln was indeed assassinated (on April 14, not the 11th) by John Wilkes Booth, in Ford's Theater. Secretary Seward was stabbed by another conspirator, but his son was not mortally wounded. What is more interesting is the matter-of-fact manner in which LeRoy related the killing of a president. His coverage is cold and detached. Given what they have experienced, this is understandable. It is also possible he is laboring under the ill-effects of opium or some other medicine and "cloudy" or feeling "stupid," as he had noted in past entries.

47 LeRoy means the Union officer was keeping soldiers, newly freed slaves, and others wandering about in Macon off the Gresham property.

Thursday, April 27th, 1865: Cloudy and warm. Cousin Jimmie + Eliza called. Father succeeding in getting Prince back this morn. . . . Suffering with pain in my right leg—a never ceasing ache. A courier is on his way from Johnston and both sides C.S. + U.S. are awaiting his arrival as that will definitely settle the status here. Commenced *Flower of the Flock* by Pierce Egan. A hiafalutin story...

Friday, April 28th, 1865: Cloudy and warm. I was very sick all night threw up and kept awake nearly all night by pain in my right leg and back. Peace rumors are rife; and it is reported that definite terms having been agreed upon; Joe Johnston will disband his army soon. Aunt Ann sent me some delicious strawberries, which I enjoyed greatly. Confederate money is a drug in the market. No one wants it and we have no gold or U.S. funds and so there will be great distress among those who have nothing to barter. We got a nice mess of butter, 4 hams, +c from Houston yesterday + a letter from Thomas. No negroes left + all is well as yet.[48]

Saturday, April 29th, 1865: Recorded as a day spent in dozing on account of Dover's Powder taken last night. In the evening suffered very much with intense pain in my right leg. Was sick and threw up my supper. We get no definite news. There are two big rumors pro + con: 1st that Genl Johnston has disbanded his army + peace will soon be made. 2nd Jeff Davis is going across the Miss. to fight it out, the C.S.A. being recognized by France, +c, +c, +c. Meanwhile we rest quietly under Yankee rule till things are settled.

Sunday, April 30th, 1865: Clear and warm. Father and Minnie walked to church and on coming out found some Yanks had crossed two U.S. flags over the sidewalk coming up our way and were standing by awaiting the effect. Most of the ladies quietly but indignantly walked around. We did not know George Edwards was so ill till this morning. At 11 A.M. Mother went to see him and he died at two of acute Dysentery. Dr. Hall called to see me this morning and examined my back + the abscesses. He is afraid to trouble them but is going to make me some tonic pills and see if he cannot relieve the indigestion + Dyspepsia from which I constantly suffer. I feel very low spirited myself + want to take something.

Monday, May 1st, 1865: Bright and cool. Blew off cool in the night. Father went to Houston on the R.R. I passed a miserable night and today my good leg is drawn up as bad as the left. It is not aching much either. Bought a fine bait of strawberries at 10$ a quart + Min + I reveled in them. General Johnston has surrendered his army + the

---

48 Thomas informed the family the slaves had not yet fled the Houston plantations.

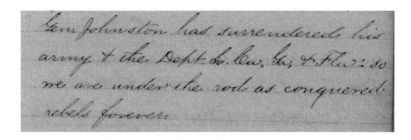

Department [of] So. Car, Ga; + Fla: so we are under the rod as conquered rebels forever.

Tuesday, May 2nd, 1865: Clear and cool. Took a Dover's Powder and passed an easy night but my leg pains me all the time and is badly drawn up. Dr. Hall brought me some iron pills. I never had as tedious a spell before. Capt. Hinson left at daylight this morning to go North. Pete Miller [Muller] is here yet. Father returned today with supplies.

Wednesday, May 3d, 1865: Clear and cool. Took Paregoric last night and today have suffered tortures with my leg. Lay in Grandma's room all the morning and in the back room in the evening. I am perfectly helpless—both legs being drawn up badly. I have no appetite and if I eat it disagrees with me.[49] There is one Yankee camp near Mrs. Mitchell's and another in the woods in Collinsville, and we hear their bands and bugles playing constantly. As I write they are playing the "Starpangled Banner."

Thursday, May 4th, 1865: Took a Dover's Powder but my leg is no better. Went on my wagon and watched them make strawberry preserves. We gave 200 dollars for 8 quarts and I had a most delicious treat. At 1 Oclock today a salute of 200 guns was fired and the bell was toll'd at the same time—out of respect to Lincoln I suppose. A tremendous federal flag was raised in front of the Lanier House. All this in honor of the subjugation of the Confederate States. . . . I am very low-spirited now, I am so completely helpless with both legs contracted and one of them almost paralyzed from pain.

Friday, May 5th, 1865: Clear and warm. We are needing rain sadly. Some of the Yankees have gone to Atlanta from here + more are going. Slept miserably + feel sore and bad leg still aching. Mother made me some baked custard for my dinner. Tracy is here spending the day. Mrs. Johnston called. Anniversary of "Battle of the Wilderness."

---

49 LeRoy is now routinely throwing up most or all of what he eats, which reduces his caloric intake and further weakens his immune system. His mother would later comment upon his his poor wasted, disease-wrecked frame." Mary Gresham's letter to her sister, Sarah Baxter "Sallie" Bird, Afterword, 404.

Saturday, May 6th, 1865: Clear and warm. Took a Dover's Powder last night and woke up feeling a little better; this P.M. I have suffered a good deal. Had strawberries at 30$. There is only one regular division left here now and the streets are thin of yanks to what they were. Most of them have gone to Atlanta. Lee's + Johnston's men are passing thru daily in hundreds.[50]

Sunday, May 7th, 1865: Clear and the warmest day yet. No sign of rain + everything is suffering for it. No one but Father went to church. Had to take Paregoric last night + I had not much rest from pain during the latter part of the night. I long for ease and freedom from pain.

Monday, May 8th, 1865: Cloudy and warm. Rained a very little. Although I took a Dover's Powder, I rested but little and feel weak and sore. O! how much I suffer! No position in which I lie is easy and the days are long and painful + the nights weary. Father went to Houston on the cars this morning. Sent and got a quart of strawberries for 1½ lbs sugar. Father and Thomas both got here this evening, Thomas in the wagon with Milo.

Tuesday, May 9th, 1865: Clear and warm. Cousin Howard Tinsley, and Aunt Eliza arrived late yesterday + left early this morning for Flint River, Uncle LeRoy's place. Took a Dover's Powder and rested very sweetly and feel a little better. Got some more strawberries. A gentleman sent Father two partridges and I enjoyed eating one very much. Father went in the wagon with Milo to Houston. Have just finished *The Scarlet Letter* by Hawthorn + begun *Amaury* by Dumas, both loaned to me by Mrs. deGraffenreid. Confederate money ceases to pass on the R.R.'s today + now tis taken only in payment of a few debts. A great many of the Second Battalion have got home and Thomas finds nearly all his old messmates.

Wednesday, May 10th, 1865: Clear and warm. Slept under [effects of] a "Dover," enjoyed my breakfast and am free from pain almost. Governor Brown has been sent North—left here this morning and was not allowed to communicate with his friends. 100,000 dollars reward is offered for Pres. D[avis], Clem Clay,[51] and others as the instigators of Lincoln's murder. A Yankee trick to hang him. Vice President Stephens is arrested + thus down comes the iron screw on our powerless necks.

---

50 Thousands of men from Virginia and the Carolinas were passing through Macon on their way home. Some were able to catch rides on railroads, others rode horses, and many more simply walked.

51 Clement C. Clay, senator from Alabama. The Union was interested in him because of his role in the Confederate War Department and activities related to espionage.

Thursday, May 11th, 1865: Spent the day in bed. Had an attack similar to Cholera morbus.[52] Vomited freely. Took some paregoric and today have suffered from Diarrhea. I haven't a particle of Appetite.

Friday, May 12th, 1865: Clear and cool. Yesterday we had a fine rain which lasted 3 hours with hard wind. The wind blew hard in the night. I feel about the same today. Suffered all day with nausea and I can't touch anything to eat. Minnie and Clare deGraffenreid have taken the 1st Honor at College and Miss Flora Smith the 2nd. This was announced Wednesday but my brain is so muddled with Opium I forgot to record it.[53] . . . Sent to depot for Father who didn't come. The wildest rumors are afloat concerning the whereabouts of President Davis and bands of cavalry are scouring the state to capture him. He is making for Texas. Clement Clay has come in and delivered himself up to the Yankee Authorities.

Saturday, May 13th, 1865: Clear and cool. Rested tolerably well and feel better this morning. Found out on awaking that Mary [slave] had left with her "duds" and gone to the yanks I reckon. President Davis is captured and will be here today.[54] Poor old fellow! Father got home this evening worried in mind. The Yankees have passed the plantation in crowds and took large amounts of forage. He succeeded in getting a man, by name Roberts, to oversee for him. Allen + Abram have run away to the Yanks. President Davis and his escort of Yankees wretches passed the plantation. He, poor man, is now confined in the Lanier House with 200 mounted men on each side.[55]

Sunday, May 14th, 1865: Slept so badly and felt so weak + sick I did not get up. Dr. Hall prescribed for me and sent me some elegant brandy to take every 4 hrs. I have

52 Acute gastroenteritis marked by cramps, diarrhea, and vomiting.

53 LeRoy is now taking larger doses of opium more often because his pain has increased. His doctor is doing everything he can to make LeRoy's final days as peaceful as possible because his condition is clearly terminal, though he remains unaware of that medical certainty.

54 President Davis was captured along with his wife Varina on May 10 at Irwinville, Ga. Davis was taken to Fortress Monroe in Virginia and indicted for treason. He was held there for two years, never tried, and released.

55 The ending of the war is rapidly changing the way of life LeRoy and his family had known for generations. Slaves were leaving, property was being confiscated or destroyed, and their money and bonds were no longer of value. There was no telling what each new day would bring for them.

never been so weak and . . . low-spirited. Mr. Wills preached to a house two thirds Yankees. Pres. D[avis] left for the North via Atlanta last night, his family with him. . . .

Monday, May 15th, 1865: Clear and warm. Dressed out in full summer clothes and feel some better. Father sent some silver and got me some steak[56] which I relished eating + threw up soon after. My stomach is so weak it cannot digest anything. Dr. H[all] called. Thomas went to Houston. I am so so weak I can hardly write.

Tuesday, May 16th, 1865: Clear and warm. Slept well though I am still sick and my bowels troubling me. Father borrowed 5 dollars in U.S. funds and subscribed for the Daily under the new regime. I have eat nothing today but beef tea and a few raspberries and have no appetite. Recd a letter by private hand from Auntie announcing Grandma's arrival. By the way J.H.R. Washington has been made Post M[aster] here and the U.S. mail is to start soon.

Wednesday, May 17th, 1865: Clear and warm. Dr. Hall came and prescribed calomel + opium. He thinks it is my liver which is disordered. Ate beef tea for breakfast + dinner. Mrs. Judge Nisbet died this morning. She has been very sick for a week with Dysentery and yesterday sunk so rapidly she could not be rallied. I am so sorry. Every one who knew her loved her so well. Thomas came home bringing 3 squirrels + 2 doves. 3 more darkies have gone. Frank Jones, Elbert, + Sam. Dr. Hall called + prescribed a mixture for my trouble which I hope will cure me.

Thursday, May 18th, 1865: Clear and warm. Am a little better. Enjoyed my squirrel + dove hugely. This is the day appointed for our Gen Assembly to meet here but I reckon no one will come. Mrs. Nisbet's funeral is this evening at 5 Oclock and all our folks have gone. Father saw Elbert + Frank. Rained heavily this evening during the funeral, and Father got very wet.

Friday, May 19th, 1865: Clear and pleasant. Mr. Cha[rle]s Whitehead, his son Amos, and Frank Burnett Esq. stayed all night here last night. The two latter left this morning.

Saturday, May 20th, 1865: Dr. Hall thinks best that I should remain in bed today and so here I am. I enjoyed very much a piece of mackeral sent to me by the above doctor for my breakfast. Father bought two quarts of cherries which as they were forbidden fruit troubled me the more sorely. Plums are ripening slowly and we have gotten a nice mess of Raspberries from the garden daily—

---

56 With the collapse of Confederate currency, silver and gold were especially precious. John Gresham was more than willing to use silver for a steak in the hope the meat would help his son.

Sunday, May 21st, 1865: Clear and the warmest day of the season. Laid in Thomas' Room all day. Eat ½ broiled chicken for breakfast and the same for dinner—a present from Mrs. Edwards. Mr. Wills preached to a house half full of Yankees and Father says it is very little pleasure for him to go to church. Thomas went to the Episcopal church in the afternoon.

Monday, May 22nd, 1865: Clear and very pleasant. Had a fine shower before breakfast. My bowels still trouble me and it does not seem to matter what I eat. I am taking Bismuth every three hrs.[57] I am in bed in the wing today. I change every day for variety. We get no news from the outside world but it is supposed all the negroes will be declared free in a day or two. Last night a Yankee Sergeant harangued them at Church and told them of the priceless blessing of freedom which the federal authorities had given them.

Tuesday, May 23d, 1865: Clear and beautiful. Slept well, enjoyed my breakfast—a broiled chicken and feel better today. Have just dressed and come down into Mother's room. A brigade of Yanks left here this morning for the North and there is not more than an ordinary garrison left. The yankees are discharging immense numbers of men + reducing their army to 150000 men. Father left in the buggy before breakfast for the plantation. Dr. Hall pronounces me so much better today that I can eat raspberries in a week. I am to continue the Bismuth 3 times a day. I keep a lovely June Apple to smell which is delicious torture. Mrs. Robert Lanier's funeral is this P.M. at 5 Oclock. Thomas heard today that Jerry and Duke, Old Slow, + a mule had been stolen from the plantation, but Mr. Kemp followed the rogues + recovered the two last.

Wednesday, May 24th, 1865: Clear and delightful. Feel a great deal better and have a good appetite. Our old friends Messers Markham and Bryson rode up to our gate last night. They are on their way home, one in Louisiana + the other in Tennessee. I rode out in the garden this morning and everything has grown out so green and beautiful.

Thursday, May 25th, 1865: The 22nd Anniversary of Father and Mother's ~~anniversary~~ marriage and we killed a fat pig in honor thereof. Mr. Markham left at daylight on horseback for Columbus. It is rumored that some man from private motives has killed Forrest. Howard got me yesterday from Mr. Winship's a nice little bulldog looking pup which will afford me great amusement. Father returned at dinner time so as to be here and eat the anniversary dinner. He brought me some young chickens.

---

57 Bismuth, an anti-diarrheal, is found in Pepto-Bismol and Kaopectate, two modern medicines that treat the same problem.

Friday, May 26th, 1865: Clear and the wind blowing a gale. Ate too much pig and am sick today. Mr. Bryson left for Columbus. We were all delighted with him + very sorry to see him go. I have named my dog "Fosco." He behaves very well and does not cry much. Howard got me another little white bull terrier today for a pet and so I am well supplied. They stay under the back steps. Walter Harris, Uncle Edmund's nephew, came to stay all night with us.[58] Dr. Hall called. He did nothing but caution me against imprudences in eating. . . .

Saturday, May 27th, 1865: Cloudy and cool. Walter Harris left after breakfast. Thomas stayed all night with Mrs. Moughan; there being no gentleman there she requested him to act as their protector. Minnie stayed with Clare. I feel better again this morn and hope I'll get well. My appetite is ravenous. Named my terrier "Guy Darrell."

Sunday, May 28th, 1865: Clear and cool. We had a fine shower yestereve and it so cooled the air that fires would not be uncomfortable. Father left for Uncle LeRoy's Flint River place this morning. . . . I am quite unwell today + feel very despondent. Dr. Hall came to see me and says the whole thing is from eating that pig.

Monday, May 29th, 1865: Cloudy and cool. Julia Ann came + left telling Mother Farewell. She announced her intention to leave because Mother slapped Florence: Joy go with her! She will repent it to the day of her death. After every meal I suffer pain no matter how little I eat. My back runs a great deal.

Tuesday May 30th 1865: [The remainder of the entries are in Mary Gresham's handwriting, with LeRoy dictating to his mother.] Father returned yesterday from Flint River and says he thinks Uncle LeRoy will go to New York before very long. Howard + Evelina being our only servants now, do all the work. My "valet" Bill left this morning. I suppose Julia Ann induced him to go. Very unwell to-day and being so will miss Bill the more.

Wednesday May 31st 1865: Still in bed. Dr. Hall sees me daily. Father is also sick to-day—threatened with one of his old attacks of colic. The weather is quite warm during the day but the nights are so far pleasant. Thomas was to go to the plantation today but put it off on account of sickness of self and Father.

Thursday June 1st 1865: This is the day of fasting and prayer for Lincoln's death—A Yankee chaplain preached in our church, but none of the family went—neither was

---

58 Son of Elisha Harris, who married Edmund's sister-in-law, Rosa Anderson. No further information has been found about either.

LeRoy's last entry in his own hand was May 29, 1865. His mother, Mary Gresham, continued recording his observations and thoughts as he dictated them to her. *LOC*

there much fasting among the Southern portion of the Community. No better to-day myself—Father improving.

Friday June 2d 1865: I am worse this morning than I was yesterday—the Doctor says that my case has assumed the form of Dysentery which he said does not dread so much as the Diarrhea I was having before. They say that the Yankee chaplain who preached yesterday used all the insulting language he could think of to the Southern people—what a low order of animal he must be!

Saturday June 3d 1865: No material change in my condition since yesterday. The wagon came from the Plantation yesterday bringing "Aunt Peggy" to be our cook, and Julia, a small Darky, to supply in some measure Bill's place. By the way it seems that the latter youth ran away on his own responsibility and not at Julia-Ann's instigation as was at first supposed. Father is quite sick again to-day, and will have to be very careful in his diet: very warm—

Sabbath June 4 1865: I have the same report to make to day of my health—no better. Mr. Bates called to see Father this morning. Minnie and Thomas alone attended church today. . . .

Monday June 5th 1865: Col O'Neal called to-day bringing a <u>short</u> letter from Aunty and a Photograph of Uncle Edge. . . . The Doctor comes to see me now twice daily and will continue to do so until I am better. My appetite is Vocative—wanting.[59]

Tuesday June 6th 1865: Thomas went to Market to get some beef to make tea for me which I did not I am sorry to say relish very much. Dr. Hall has prescribed a preparation of Creosote for me to take which he says is one of the best remedies known to the profession.[60] I am continually under the influence of opium which I am taking every three hours in larger quantities than I ever did before.

Wednesday June 7th 1865: Clear and hot—Lay in Thomas' room in the daytime for a change. Thomas has been to-day delivering some flour which father had sold to the Factory for cloth. Miss Julia Beal sent me some Jelly and squabs which I could not eat. George Beal is here looking badly and suffering from Rheumatism. Mother has hired an unsophisticated country girl to do the house-work. Howard + Evelina have set up for themselves—but we have hired them to do the same work they did before.

Thursday June 8th 1865: I have slept pretty well for the last two nights under the influence of a quarter grain of Morphia. Nothing definite from Bill as yet—doubtful whether I will ever see him again. I have read nothing at all for the last ten days and consequently know little of the outside world. My Puppies Fosco + Guy have grown to double their former sizes so that I scarcely knew them. I eat very little and even this nauseates me. My back runs very little now and I only dress once in two days. Thomas

---

59 The fact that the doctor is now coming twice a day is a good indication of just how fast LeRoy is now declining. He remains unaware that he has a terminal disease.

60 Creosote was used to treat skin wounds and as an antiseptic. Guaiacol, a natural organic compound derived from raw creosote, was used in Europe as early as the 1830s as a treatment for tuberculosis (consumption). Its cough suppressant properties convinced doctors it was doing something useful. The remedy fell out of favor by the turn of the century. An expectorant, today known as guaifenesin, was made from creosote.

has started to read Blackstone's *Commentaries*.[61] Mr. Goulding called to see me this afternoon. Mr. Burke was robbed the other night of his watch and chain.

Friday June 9th 1865:

I am perhaps[62]

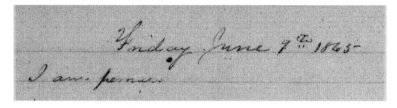

(LeRoy Wiley Gresham, author of this diary, died in Macon, Ga. June 18th 1865)[63]

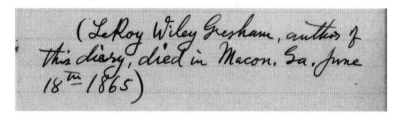

61 William Blackstone, *Commentaries on the Laws of England* (London, 1765-1769) was commonly read by those interested in the law. Thomas later became a lawyer and practiced with his father after the war.

62 When all available source materials—including private Gresham letters—are read together, it is clear LeRoy did not know he was dying until his final hours. When everything is put in context, the last three words in the June 9 entry make sense. His mother was writing as he dictated, and LeRoy calmly told her, "I am perhaps *dying*," or something along those lines. He would have kept talking, but the accuracy of his announcement would have stunned and hurt his mother, who simply could not bring herself to write the horrible truth he had just spoken. LeRoy's use of the word "perhaps" suggests he was speculating about what was happening to him. We know from the long letter Mary wrote to her sister shortly after LeRoy's death (reproduced in Addendum: Parental Grief, page 403) that her son did not know with *certainty* that he was dying until the day *before* he passed, when he asked her directly, "I am dying, ain't I?"

63 This final entry in LeRoy's journal was written by his father in bright blue ink.

Obituary

[This obituary ran in the *Macon Telegraph*]

Le Roy Wiley Gresham, the son of John J. and Mary B. Gresham, departed this life on the 18th ult., in the eighteenth [seventeenth] year of his age.

Endowed by nature with a superior intellect, he had added the charms of refined cultivation until there was scarcely a subject in ancient or modern history, or within the range of polite literature, with which he was not perfectly familiar. Confined to his couch by disease for many years, he read much and conversed with an ease and fluency which were the admiration of all who knew him. In fact, with the voice and body of a boy, he had the head and culture of mature manhood. From the nature of his disease he was deprived of the ordinary pleasures of boyhood, yet he bore this without a murmur, and would cheerfully look-on and empathize in the sports his joyous spirit would have so keenly relished had God given him physical strength. Within himself, however, he found many sources of happiness, and his ringing laugh, his merry voice, and his sweet songs were the joy and delight of the whole household.

He had long thought seriously on the subject of religion, and had studied closely and with great profit the history and doctrines of the Bible. His whole life and conversation gave evidence to the change which had been wrought within; and in October last he felt it to be his duty to give public testimony to his faith in Christ. He then united with the Presbyterian church, and was enabled in his last hours to say, with perfect composure and a smile of heavenly serenity, and while his friends stood weeping around, "I know that my Redeemer liveth." "I know in whom I have believed, and am persuaded that He is able to keep that which I have committed to Him." He sank to his rest so sweetly, so calmly, that it could scarcely be discerned when the spirit winged its flight from his frail earthly tenement to rejoice around the throne forever. Those who mourn for the blessing taken away and for the light gone out of their dwelling cannot sorrow as those without hope, with the remembrance of his pure life so fresh in their memories, and his last words of counsel sent to absent friends to "trust in Jesus," yet sounding in their ears.

"We shall go to him, but he shall not return to us."

Addendum:

Parental Grief

Mary Eliza Baxter Gresham wrote the following letter to her sister, Sarah Catherine Julia Baxter "Sallie" Bird, just a few weeks after LeRoy's death. Her letter— filled with deeply personal thoughts and evincing tremendous personal pain— also fills in many important pieces of the puzzle that was LeRoy Wiley Gresham's short life.

*   *   *

Macon July 12th 1865

Thinking that I might send a letter by Bishop Pierce, I will try & write you my dearest Sister, though when I attempt to put on paper anything of my departed treasure's last days I feel it so poor & cold compared with the emotions of my aching heart, that but for a sense of duty I would not write at all. But you all loved my precious boy, & there is so much of tender touching interest to tell, such gracious dealing from the Heavenly Shepherd with my [treasured] lamb to recount that I feel it is good to be heard…

I had for some days lost hope, but would nigh give way for fear of trying him, for watchful to the last, he was quick to see any sign of grief upon my face & racked with suffering as he was, his ready sympathy was for me and for us all. Oh Sister dear! God has tried me often, & in many ways but never has my heart been so wrung as now & yet the trial has so much mercy mixed with it that my soul melts within me when I think it all over.

The day before he left us, while Mr. G & the children were at dinner, he suddenly said to me, "Well, Mother, this is the end." I said, "What do mean, my Son?" "I am dying, ain't I?" was his reply. Oh my God, I thank Thee for the strength given me then, but with streaming tears and choking voice I asked him, "If you are, my darling, you are willing to trust your Savior?" and the smile which beamed over his poor wasted features will be with me to my dying day as he said, "Oh yes – I know in whom I have believed, I know that my Redeemer lives. Call them all, & ask Father to read the 24th Psl. & part [of Romans 8]." He exhorted Thomas to give himself to Christ, sent messages to many absent friends – attempted to dispose of his treasures, but found that he was too weary to go through & said give something of mine to those he named. "I wish you had told me sooner that I was dying," he said that I might have done all these things, but for my soul I can trust that to Jesus."[1]

He had suffered so much from nausea during the last week that his countenance had a look of distress upon it, which I never saw it wear before & his tongue was so sore & stiff that it was painful to speak, but his mind was clear to the last, & not two minutes before he breathed his last, opened his eyes, looked brightly & lovingly at us & pressed my hand. He called John's name in [illegible] with mine again & again, but in no distinct sentence for it was a few minutes before he was gone.

Though I know well what he was thinking about 10 minutes before he went away from us he said "don't forget to do all I told you" and drew his hand out of mine. Then said, "I took my hand away, Mother, because yours felt too hot" thus showing his thoughtfulness for others so remarkable during his life. He feared to hurt any one.

It had been our dread to see him struggle or strangle in coughing, but God dealt mercifully with him & with us for his departure was so quiet that we watched to see him breathe again, & his face assumed in death the quiet serenity habitual to it & I could scarcely tear myself away from his precious body, it was so sweet, so peaceful – I cannot tell you one half of the precious things we have to comfort us now & you knew his virtues, his generous unselfishness, his cheerful uncomplaining patience under suffering, his bright buoyant spirit, his sympathizing heart which felt for every body's joys or sorrows.

Oh my heart, how am I to live without him, who has been the star of my life, my "heart's delight" for 17 years. He was always in the house, & whenever any of us went out, he met us & to him was told everything. Not a room but is full of

---

1   This is further evidence that the Greshams had never informed their son that he was fatally ill, or the fact that he was suffering from tuberculosis (consumption).

associations now sad but precious. In the morning when we all sit on the back stoop, we miss his wagon at the foot of the steps with the happy face upon it.

What a blessing from above such a spirit as he had, but particularly for one deprived of the ordinary pleasures of childhood, for he had the rare faculty of extracting pleasure from even the most trivial sources. When our [family] circle assembles at evening here my eyes grow dim whenever they rest upon the [couch] where his mattress used to lie. My heart feels like breaking whenever the cantelopes are brought in, for he superintended Howard's planting of them & now both are gone. There are so many jokes – so many things which are not needed to keep his memory green. The first time poor Mr. G. carved a chicken was overcome at the remembrance of dear Loy's saying so often that "Father was the one he knew who could make 5 quarters of a chicken."

Oh pardon me dear Sister that I write these seemingly trifling things, but my heart is so full & I have so longed for Mother or Sister. Time when alone we talk of little else but our lost darling but I have been peculiarly tried in many ways. When Mr. G. went to see about the last resting place of our dear boy, he found to his horror the graves of both our children had been desecrated, the slab thrown down on one & the bricks picked out for a foot or more of the other.[2] God forgive me if I do her wrong, but I believe J. Ann directed the wretches there, for Mother may have told you of the point made of carrying our silver off & Mr. G. & T. drove in that direction. It was at night & care was taken that she should see them go.

Oh I do thank God that no menial [former slave] came near him in his last illness, that the most humble offices were performed by the loving hands of Father, Mother, Brother, & Sister. I remembered how sensitive he was, and could not bear to have a stranger touch or comment on his poor wasted, disease-wrecked frame, and Father, Mother & Brother washed & dressed him for the grave and I am thankful to Him who have me strength for the duty. Never did a servant dress his back one time, and the same loving hands that ministered to him in life performed the last duties we could & even those who bore him away from the house consecrated by his birth, life & death, were just such as he would have preferred – not one of the servants who professed to love him at least came

2   Edmund Gresham (1845-1846) and Edward Tracy Gresham (1851-1853).

near him or us & may God forgive them, but I humbly hope that I may never see them again.[3]

How painfully I felt dear Richard's return.[4] How I groaned in Spirit when I thought of "Loy" who would have welcomed him back so cordially & I thought in agony of Spirit how much he would be missed by those who visited us, for he was the "sun" in our little system. Mr. Gresham is completely broken down – his health is not good & in bitterness of heart grieves for his little Comforter. He was the confidant of us all – to "Loy" every thing was carried & Mr. Gresham says he had fallen into the habit even of advising & consulting with him about many things. The contemplative life he led & the holy instincts of a pure nature unsoiled by contact with the world had ripened his judgment & he was capable of advising many older than himself.

The tie between Loy & Thomas was unusually strong & very peculiar too. It was beautiful to see them together & they used to talk to each other in a sort of baby talk which they alone understood, but touching to the looker on, from the loving tones & caressing actions. Poor boy, he says his heart aches for the sound from those precious lips of one of the many pet names Loy used to give him. And Minnie pines for the dear Brother, who took such pride & interest in her success & studies & to-day is the Commencement Day, of which he so often talked with brotherly pride. But it is a sad day to her spent in tearful solitude consecrated doubly to his memory.

Oh! we are a bereaved household & cling with closer love to each other. It has been & is still a sore trial to me to be obliged to "labor with my hands" when I would give worlds to sit down in quiet with my sorrow. I need not of body as well as of mind & when the work of the day is done – the dishes washed up & put away at night, I feel thankful that I can then sit down & continue with my own heart & be still. I have often pitied men who in the midst of great sorrow have been compelled to mingle with the world & attend to business, but I never knew till now how severe the trial.

---

3 Mary's bitterness is understandable, though perhaps misplaced. The former slaves would not have been told of the specific nature of LeRoy's illness, but his coughing, spinal abscesses, and wasting would have been enough to keep them away for fear of contagion. While they were slaves, they had no choice but to work in the house and be in proximity to LeRoy. Once free, it is understandable that, even if they felt affinity for the young man, they kept their distance.

4 From **Rock Island prisoner of war camp in Illinois.**

Mr. Gresham wanted me & Minnie to go to Indian Springs for ten days, but I felt it almost impossible, first from want of a servant capable & reliable to take care of things in the house & 2nd the want of money, though Mr. G. said he could try & get sufficient for this trip. But if any money is spent in traveling I want him to go & see his Brother. I have not even had the solace of sympathizing letters from friends. Your dear letter, my gracious Sister, is all I have had save one from Judge Nisbet who is at the Springs & whose own spirit is bleeding from the loss of as true a wife as man ever had. True I have had notes from friends in town, but oh my heart yearned towards my own flesh & blood.

I was shocked to see from Mother's letter by John how unconscious she was of my bereavement, for in both of my letters sent by Gen. Cobb, I gave her his true state & he was then very low & we disparaging, indeed his Father had then lost all hope & had written by Express previously, saying that without a speedy change "this light would soon go out of our dwelling" – as we got no answers, we concluded that the Express was not to be depended on & so I heard of private opportunity till Richard went & by him I wrote. I think Minnie wrote to Sallie yesterday – my love to her – & tell her how I could tell her of many tender things that her sainted Cousin said about her at various times.

It seems at times, dear Sister, as though I were stunned – than that my darling will return again & then again a full realization of my loss comes over me, & it seems but for the relief of tears that I could not bear it. Sometimes for a whole day I cannot shed a tear and my brain seems on fire – at last the remembrance of some sweet way, or loving word melts the rock & my eyes are wearied with the tears, which cools my aching brain as seems to relieve the tension around my heart I can then dwell upon the sweet memories stored up in my heart & pray that I may be enabled to watch & not weary – to patiently wait till I be permitted to "go to Him" – When I lost my babies, death seemed very terrible to me but when I saw my timid darling go with unfaltering steps & bright beaming eyes "down into the river" while we stood weeping to see him go, Oh Sall dearest, I realized as I never did before from beyond all praise was the assurance that "thy rod & staff, shall comfort me." The Savior took him from our arms & now no more pain, no days of weariness & nights of wakefulness – no more sighing & longing for rest.

One day he said, "Oh Father, if God would only give me a little freedom from pain, a little rest before I die!!" & so it was. Save an occasional fit of coughing he suffered but little the last two days & the last 12 hours were truly peaceful. I have seen many deaths, but none so sweet, so peaceful as Loy's. Now where the [ruined] was so perfectly clear to the very last, and oh the unspeakable blessedness to go thus and redeemed into the presence of Him who made us… "May my end be like his."

For fear that I may not have another opportunity – I want to write a few lines to Wilson, knowing how long the time seems to children when they wait for answers to their letters. My love to all who remember me in my sorrow – Tell Mrs. Whitehead I have thought often of her and the dear boy she lost. Love to Mr. Bird & thanks for his kind message. Never let an opportunity pass without writing; I am so cut off.

Your own loving, sorrowing Sister

Postscript

The Gresham Family after the Civil War

The death of his son, to whom he was very close, was a double blow to John Gresham and the surviving members of the family. The defeat of the Confederacy had turned their cultural world upside down and left the Greshams financially strapped. The elimination of slavery made it impossible for John to run his plantations, and Reconstruction only promised further uncertainties. Apparently, much of the land was broken apart into tenant farms, but they would not generate any sustainable income for some time.

In search of a reliable source of income, John returned to the practice of law and formed a partnership with his son Thomas. John had not enjoyed the law in the 1830s, and he liked it even less in the late 1860s. After a brief time he retired to pursue other interests, including managing the tenant farms, which were finally generating steady income, and other business interests.

Education was always important to the elder Gresham, who was a strong proponent of good schools. In 1872, he and several other men from Macon were appointed to serve as the Board of Education and Orphanages for Bibb County, a position he held for many years. He also spent many years as the treasurer of the Macon Free School and was chairman of its board until his death, as well as the president of the Alexander Free School in Macon. He served on the board of the University of Georgia for more than two decades, and as a trustee and treasurer of Oglethorpe University. The Central High School in Macon was renamed Gresham High School in honor of his many contributions to education.

John J. Gresham was visiting his daughter Minnie in Baltimore, Maryland, when he died unexpectedly at 9:00 p.m. on October 16, 1891. His daughter and her husband, Arthur Machen, accompanied his body back to Macon, where following a showing in the Gresham home he was buried next to his beloved wife Mary in Macon's Rose Hill Cemetery. Eight years later, Thomas and Minnie donated money for the John J. Gresham Memorial Hospital building in Macon.

Little is known of Mary Gresham's life before or after the Civil War. Other than a handful of letters, she lives on almost exclusively through LeRoy's pen and a single photo of her taken later in life in a rocking chair on the front porch of the Gresham house. The loss of three of her children (and at least one miscarriage) took its toll on Mary. She died in 1889, three years before her beloved husband, and is buried in Rose Hill Cemetery.

Thomas Gresham moved north after the Civil War and studied law at the University of Virginia. He returned to Macon in the late 1860s to partner with his father, who retired a short time later. Unlike John Gresham, Thomas enjoyed the profession and formed Lyton & Gresham, a legal partnership with Richard F. Lyon. In 1887, Thomas moved to Baltimore in 1887 where, like his parents he took an active role in the Presbyterian Church.

The eldest Gresham son married Tallulah "Lula" Billups (1848-1879), a native of Madison, Georgia, on October 15, 1869. Their only child—a son—was named LeRoy Gresham (1871-1955) after Thomas' brother. And like his brother, Thomas lost his wife to tuberculosis in 1879. He married again eight years later to Bessie E. Johnston (1848-1926) of Baltimore. Thomas died in 1933 in Roanoke, Virginia. He is buried in Green Mount Cemetery in Baltimore.

Mary Jones ("Minnie") Gresham was the first of the Gresham children to move north after the war. She attended Wesleyan Female College in Macon, from which she graduated in 1865. On February 13, 1873, Minnie married prominent Baltimore attorney Arthur W. Machen. The couple had three sons. Minnie's middle son was named after her father, John Gresham Machen, who became a a well-known Presbyterian theologian. A devout Presbyterian, Minnie wrote The Bible in Browning (1903), a book tracing the influence of the Bible on Robert Browning's poetry. She died on October 13, 1931, and is buried in Green Mount Cemetery in Baltimore.

A Medical Afterword

Parallel Struggles

LeRoy Wiley Gresham's diary is a tale of two conflicts. In the background, far away, a momentous struggle rages to decide the political destiny of a people. Although the actual fighting remained remote for most of its duration, the clashing of the armies generates shockwaves of hardship and uncertainty that reverberate back home. The journals provide rich insight into the thoughts and fears of Confederate civilians on the fringes of the fighting, but military conflict is only a part of the story, and perhaps a minor one at that.

From page one, Gresham is an invalid. As the war grinds on, his health deteriorates and he finds himself increasingly preoccupied with his own struggle against an invisible enemy that will ultimately claim his life. In the end, it is not his youthful reflections on the politics of the day, or his observations about the maneuvering of the armies that rend our hearts. Rather, it is Gresham's intimate sharing of his own physical suffering, and our appreciation of his personal bravery and good-natured patience, that pack these journals with poignancy and power.

Medical Care during the Civil War

The world of medicine in the mid-nineteenth century was far different from the sophisticated technology-driven system that we take for granted today. Back then there were no prerequisites for entry into medical schools. The medical curriculum consisted of only two years of study, with lectures conducted only four or five months of each year; the curriculum for the second year merely repeated the coursework of the first semester. Clinical experience was not part of the program. There were no licensing boards. The germ theory of disease was unknown. There was no real concept of sterility or antisepsis. Sanitation was not a major concern. Intravenous fluids did not exist. Anesthesia was primitive, consisting of chloroform or ether inhalation. Medicines were largely plant-based, and most physicians compounded their own medicines.

LeRoy Gresham's Doctors

We do not have the benefit of a detailed description of the injury that precipitated LeRoy's troubles, or of the treatment administered by local physicians during the first four years of his disability. All we know is that the outcome was less than satisfactory. As the journals open, LeRoy's suffering has prompted his father to plan a journey of more than 800 miles to consult with a nationally recognized medical expert.

During the Civil War years, the American South was largely rural, especially in comparison with major population centers of the North. With slightly more than one million inhabitants, the entire state of Georgia had fewer residents than the Union's two leading cities, New York and Philadelphia.

LeRoy's hometown of Macon (pop. 8,247) ranked fifth among the Georgia municipalities, behind Savannah (22,292), Augusta (14,493), Columbus (9,621) and Atlanta (9,554). The state capital in Milledgeville, 30 miles northeast of Macon, had a mere 2,480 residents.

In 1860, the state of Georgia could claim four medical schools—the Medical College of Georgia, established in 1829, and three rival institutions that had only recently sprung into existence: Savannah Medical College (1853), Atlanta Medical College (1855), and Oglethorpe Medical College (1856).

While there is no indication the Greshams lacked confidence in their local physicians, they apparently thought the time had come to use their considerable means to seek out the best available medical care for their ailing son. The moment must have been filled with anticipation and hope. It was at this time LeRoy's mother presented him with a blank journal in which to record the details of the trip north.

The purpose of the journey to Philadelphia was to consult with Dr. Joseph Pancoast, a distinguished general and plastic surgeon who held the chair of General, Descriptive and Surgical Anatomy at Jefferson Medical College. He was the author of *A Treatise on Operative Surgery* (1844), as well as of numerous other scholarly articles and books, and was famous for his lectures and clinics in anatomy and surgery. Surely if anyone could provide the miracle LeRoy needed, it was this renowned specialist.

Sadly, the initial entries in LeRoy's journal reveal that, after less than a week in Philadelphia, the young patient and his father were returning from the northern medical Mecca with little more than a few encouraging words, a new prescription, and, to LeRoy's dismay, instructions to rest. The secession of the Southern states and initiation of hostilities between the North and the South, made the logistics of continued contact between the Georgia youth and his Pennsylvania specialist significantly more difficult, and in practical fact, impossible. After January 1861, when Dr. Pancoast dispatched two bottles of medicine to LeRoy via express mail, there is no further mention of Dr. Pancoast in the journals.

Fortunately, a group of competent Philadelphia-trained physicians was available in Macon and its environs. Dr. Edmund Fitzgerald enters the narrative in April 1862. Having graduated from the Jefferson Medical College in 1848, he had spent the first six years of his professional life in Houston County, Georgia, relocating to Macon in 1854. According to his 1886 obituary, "he enjoyed the full confidence and respect of the community, and did a large and extensive practice among the best people of Macon."

In May 1862, LeRoy was being attended by a Dr. White of Milledgeville, then the state capital of Georgia. Several prominent physicians named White were living in Milledgeville at the time. Dr. Benjamin Aspinwall White (1793-1866), a graduate of Harvard, had done his medical training in Philadelphia. He was president of the Georgia State Board of Physicians for most of his career, and had been appointed Surgeon General of the Georgia State Troops in 1861. His son, Dr. Samuel Gore White (1824-1877), a graduate of the 1845 class of Jefferson Medical College in Philadelphia, served as Assistant Surgeon in the U. S. Navy until the close of the Mexican War, was mayor of Milledgeville in 1853-54, and served as a surgeon in Cobb's Legion, 64th Georgia Infantry, during the Civil War.

Dr. William Scherzer, who treated Leroy in September 1862, had emigrated from Bavaria to Savannah, Georgia. He went on to study medicine at Hahnemann Medical College of Philadelphia, graduating in 1857, and continued his training abroad in Vienna, Prague, and Leipzig. Upon returning to the United States, Scherzer set up a medical practice in Macon, where he stayed for several years before moving back to Savannah in 1866, and then on to New York two years later.

Based on the credentials and experience of these physicians, it appears that young Gresham had access to state-of-the-art medicine as it was practiced in both North and the South during the Civil War era.

From Symptoms to a Diagnosis

In medicine, a symptom is something an individual notices as a departure from his normal state of feeling or function—pain or nausea, for instance. It is subjective. A sign is objective evidence of disease that is observable by others—a temperature elevation, jaundice, or a palpable tumor. Gresham's journals deal exclusively with symptoms and signs of his infirmity.

Diagnosis involves the gathering of information and then applying clinical reasoning with the goal of identifying the underlying nature or cause of an illness. Whereas treatments can be prescribed on the basis of symptoms alone (an analgesic to mask pain, for instance), diagnosing the root cause of an illness is necessary for precise and effective treatment. This is especially true when multiple symptoms coexist. Knowing the cause of a disease is also a prerequisite to finding a cure.

Medical doctors of earlier eras categorized diseases almost exclusively on the basis of patterns of symptoms and physical findings. They did not have the luxury of x-rays or ultrasound with which to peer beneath the skin, and there were no laboratory tests to detect abnormal pathology or altered physiology at a cellular or molecular level.

In reading the medical portions of LeRoy's diary, we are handicapped by the lack of a unifying diagnostic label for his condition. His doctors most likely had one, but they failed to share it with him. Fortunately, there are enough clues in the writing to allow us to pronounce an accurate twenty-first century diagnosis. First, however, we must engage in a bit of medical detective work.

Past medical history is always an important part of the diagnostic process. In this case, the pertinent element is the history of a major traumatic injury during childhood. LeRoy was only eight years old when a brick chimney collapsed on him, crushing his left leg. To him and to his family, it seemed that this accident was the beginning of his many troubles. That may be true, but we should be careful not to jump to hasty conclusions in the diagnostic process—especially when the progression of symptoms seems to far outpace the suffering one would normally expect from a broken leg. A good diagnostician must hold open the possibility that the accident was merely a coincidence—a red herring in the chain of events that led to this patient's untimely demise.

As the diary opens, the lad is twelve and a half years old, and on the threshold of a trip to Philadelphia to meet with a specialist, presumably concerning his broken leg and some accompanying back pain. Surprisingly, Doctor Pancoast pronounces his condition better than expected, and prescribes only some medicine and a summer of rest.

What follows confounds our expectations of the course of a boy with a gimpy leg. It is not surprising that there would be some pain, but LeRoy's complaints are centered more in his back than in his injured leg. Belladonna plasters and Jimson weed salves are employed, along with opium-derived drugs to quell the discomfort. A wagon is constructed to provide mobility, and to enable the invalid to avoid becoming completely bed-ridden. But the lad's troubles only multiply and intensify.

Despite the fact the injury was to his leg, LeRoy's most vexing symptom turns out to be a chronic cough. First mentioned in January 1861, it quickly becomes "incessant," "troublesome," "exhausting," "annoying beyond measure," "a continual hacking." It persists as a central feature throughout the five-year narrative. The cough is especially bothersome at night—as soon as he lies down, sometimes all through the night. Later, it becomes diurnal and productive of phlegm. Headache and sleeplessness often accompany the coughing. Who can sleep with constant hacking and a headache? Fevers begin to punctuate the narrative, at first intermittently. In early 1863 they occur frequently in the evenings, along with night sweats.

The young man becomes consumed by a general wasting and debility. In November 1863 he weighs only 63 pounds, which is well below the CDC's 5th percentile (105 pounds) and less than half of the weight at the 50th percentile (135 pounds) for a sixteen-year-old boy today.

LeRoy early on develops an open sore on his back. We could postulate that it might have been a pressure sore—a decubitus ulcer from his confinement to bed and wagon that today we call a bedsore. Could it have been something more? Plasters and salves and liniments are employed to treat the back pain and the sores, but the young patient goes on to develop abscesses, first on the left side of his back, and later on both sides. His father paints them with iodine. Dr. Fitzgerald lances and drains them. In 1863 (and perhaps earlier) they are "running freely," discharging large quantities of pus continually, suggesting the presence of a large, deep, and incompletely evacuated source of infection.

As the pain intensifies, LeRoy's back becomes so weak he cannot sit up without pain. By February 1863, his grandmother has devised a corset-like bandage for his torso that laces up, giving him support for his spine and thus improved comfort. Nevertheless, his hips ache all night long, and he develops new pain in his breast and shoulder.

On May 23, 1864, he writes, "One joint of my spine, right between the abscesses is very sore and you can see the matter, as it runs from the joint to the abscess."

In early 1865, LeRoy's throat is sore and swollen. Indigestion, anorexia, nausea, vomiting, cholera-like diarrhea, and finally bloody dysentery follow. His right (good) leg had begun showing signs of contraction by late 1862, and by January 1865, the previously uninjured right leg "has drawn up," just as the left leg had been years earlier. Eventually the pain-wracked, emaciated and exhausted body of LeRoy Wiley Gresham can endure no more. The courageous young man succumbs on June 18, 1865, at the age of seventeen.

What was the ultimate cause of this death? Was it the fallen chimney that broke the boy's leg eight years previously? That seems unlikely. The most plausible explanation, based on the medical evidence found in these journals, is that LeRoy Wiley Gresham suffered from the scourge of tuberculosis.

Statistical probability is solidly on our side. Tuberculosis was the leading cause of death in the latter half of the nineteenth century, and the killer of nearly one-half of the young Americans who died between the ages of 15 and 35. Also known as "consumption," tuberculosis was characterized by fatigue, night sweats, and a general "wasting away" of the victim, along with persistent coughing-up of thick white phlegm. LeRoy's chronic cough and classic constitutional symptoms of fever, night sweats and weight loss fit the picture well.

The progression of the disease in this particular case, however, suggests more than just pulmonary manifestations of tuberculosis. Gresham's back ulcers, progressing to chronically draining abscesses, and the progressive pain and weakness in his spine, suggest that he suffered from Pott's Disease—extrapulmonary tuberculosis of the spine, extending into the paraspinal or psoas muscles and causing the chronic drainage there. As LeRoy so perceptively noted, "as long as there is any disease there [in what he terms a "joint of the spine," i.e., a vertebra], the sores cannot heal." This natural evolution of spinal tuberculosis is summarized nicely in the following descriptions from medical journals in our current era:

> The natural course of skeletal tuberculosis without chemotherapy passed through three stages spanning 3–5 years. In the "stage of onset," lasting from one month to one year, the localized disease developed into a warm tender swelling with marked localized osteoporosis and minimal destruction. In the "stage of destruction," lasting one to three years, the disease progressed until there was gross destruction of the vertebrae with deformity, subluxation, contractures, and abscess formation. The abscesses finally ruptured and drained as ulcers and sinuses developed frequent secondary pyogenic [pus] infection. With superimposed pyogenic infection, the general defense mechanism of the a patient became markedly lowered, with severe cachexia [wasting of the body], frequent tuberculous dissemination [miliary tuberculosis, tuberculous meningitis], and death in nearly 1/3 of the patients.[1]

> Extension of tuberculosis from vertebral and discal sites to the ligaments and soft tissues is frequent. Paravertebral (next to the spinal column) abscesses occur at all levels and may be on one side only, on both sides symmetrically or asymmetrically, or may occur only in front

---

1 Surendar M. Tuli, "Historical aspects of Pott's disease (spinal tuberculosis) management," www.ncbi.nlm.nih.gov/pmc/articles/PMC3691412/, *European Spine Journal* (June 22, 2013) Suppl.4, 529-538. It is easy to understand why early writers used the term "consumption."

of the spine. The paravertebral abscess may remain localised or extend for a considerable distance.[2]

Not only the drainage, but also the drawing up of his legs can be explained by spinal tuberculosis, which causes a sharp angulation, or "gibbus" deformity of the spine, with impingement on the nervous tissue of the spinal cord, leading to paralysis. LeRoy described, near the end of his account, contractures of his good right leg, as well as of the previously injured left one.

The sore throat and terminal gastrointestinal manifestations are also potentially tubercular in their etiology. Ulcers in the mouth, larynx, or gastrointestinal tract might well have been the result of chronic expectoration and swallowing of the patient's own highly infectious pulmonary secretions.

It appears that LeRoy's doctors suspected this diagnosis. It is revealing that, on January 22, 1863, they prescribed "Syrup of the Hypophosphite of Soda, Lime + Potassa." An 1870 newspaper would later advertise Grimault's Syrup of Hypophosphite of Lime as "the best and the most rational of all remedies against consumption (tuberculosis). The ad claimed the concoction was curative. In this case, unfortunately, it was not. Alum water, creosote and mercury preparations are other remedies used by LeRoy that were recommended specifically for the treatment of symptoms of tuberculosis in the medical lore of the time.

The evidence argues very strongly in favor of the hypothesis that LeRoy Gresham's life was consumed by the "white plague"—tuberculosis. As a result, his journal serves not only as a window into a Southern teenager's perspective on the politics and execution of the Civil War, but as an in-depth chronicle of the suffering, treatment, and death of one afflicted by the most pervasive pestilence of the day.

Natural History of Tuberculosis

Exposure to tuberculosis was widespread in nineteenth-century America. As much as 80% of the population may have been infected, most commonly in childhood.

Primary tuberculosis refers to a new infection in an individual whose immune system has never before encountered the mycobacterium. Typically, the only symptom is a low-grade fever lasting for 2-3 weeks. The immune systems of 90 percent of patients gain control of the replication of the bacillus, which then enters a dormant or latent phase. Only ten percent of individuals develop active tuberculosis pneumonia or

2   https://pdfs.semanticscholar.org/0645/29ac5aa41376c2a738b3fa4e4ecb90f6ce5e.pdf.

distant dissemination from the primary exposure. Today, in this country, 10-15 million residents are thought to harbor latent tuberculosis.

Reactivation occurs when there is a compromise of the immune system that allows latent bacilli in previously exposed individuals to begin to multiply. Symptoms are progressive. Low-grade fever becomes more pronounced over time. It is classically diurnal. A nonproductive cough becomes more continuous and more productive over time. Nocturnal coughing, anorexia, wasting (consumption), and malaise are commonly seen with advanced disease.

In modern times, we know that antimicrobial drug therapy is the only effective remedy for tuberculosis. Typically, patients with active tuberculosis receive at least three drugs as their initial treatment. Using fewer than three drugs can result in development of resistant strains of the mycobacterium. The most common and effective agents include Isoniazide, Rifampin, Pyrazinamide, Ethambutol and Streptomycin. The course of treatment may last six months or more.

Medicines Used in
the Treatment of LeRoy Gresham' Symptoms

Most of the pharmaceuticals of the nineteenth century were plant- and mineral-based, and many were used to treat multiple symptoms. In this case, it is interesting and instructive to note how many of LeRoy's medicines were specifically prescribed in his era for the treatment of tuberculosis.

Alcohol (brandy, porter, whiskey, catawba wine) was used medicinally in the nineteenth century as a stimulant to increase the cardiac output and blood pressure and as a depressant and sedative. Because it could supply up to 40% of a patient's required calories and was easily absorbed, alcohol was also used as a calorie source for invalids.

Although alcohol abuse is now considered a risk factor for tuberculosis, there was a belief among some physicians during the nineteenth century that alcohol was specifically antagonistic to tuberculosis:

> Dr. Austin Flint . . . sings its [alcohol's] praise in season and out of season; and from reading some of his elaborate articles on phthisis [pulmonary tuberculosis], especially his book-reviews in the American Journal of the Medical Sciences, one would conclude that alcohol was the only medicine for the disease.[3]

---

3 Addison Porter Dutcher, *Pulmonary Tuberculosis: Its Pathology, Nature, Symptoms, Diagnosis, Prognosis, Causes, Hygiene, and Medical Treatment* (J. B. Lippincott & Company, 1875), 360.

In this light, one can better understand the provision of regular portions of brandy, porter, whiskey, and Catawba wine to an adolescent.

Alum Water was obtained from a mineral spring near Lexington, Virginia. In 1883, The Medical Association of Virginia endorsed the water for people afflicted with scrofula (tuberculous infection of the lymph nodes of the neck), incipient consumption (early stages of tuberculosis) and other pulmonary disorders including chronic forms of bronchitis, laryngitis, and pneumonia. LeRoy's father obtained some of the mineral water for his thirteen-year-old son in the spring of 1861, when the lad was complaining of a troublesome cough. The taste was not to his liking.

Belladonna, also known as Deadly Nightshade, is a perennial plant in the same family as the tomato, potato, and eggplant. Atropine, scopolamine, and hyoscyamine can be extracted from its foliage and berries. LeRoy would have used the drug as a plaster (medicine-filled gauze applied to the skin) for local pain relief and muscle relaxation.

Belladonna disrupts the parasympathetic nervous system. The window between therapeutic and toxic levels of the drug is quite narrow, and LeRoy may well have experienced significant side effects, including dilatation of the pupils (with associated light sensitivity and blurred vision), rapid pulse, loss of balance, headache, flushing, urinary retention, dry mouth, constipation, confusion, hallucinations, delirium, and/or convulsions.

In modern times, Belladonna can be obtained without a prescription at local pharmacies in ointments and plasters for use in the treatment of rheumatism, sciatica, and neuralgias. Atropine is used in eye drops to produce pupil dilatation for ophthalmologic examinations, and to accelerate an abnormally slow heart rhythm. Scopolamine patches are used to prevent nausea and motion sickness. The combination of belladonna and opium has been used for the treatment of diarrhea and some forms of visceral pain, including bladder spasm. The combination is still available for use primarily in urologic practices as B&O suppositories.

Bismuth is an anti-diarrheal agent, and even today is an active ingredient in Pepto-Bismol.

Black Pepper Tea was utilized to stimulate mucous production and to loosen phlegm in patients like LeRoy who suffered with a cough, sore throat, or severe nasal congestion.

Calomel (mercury chloride) was commonly used as a laxative. Black wash referred to a lotion of calomel and limewater that was applied to syphilitic and other sores, and was tried on LeRoy's back.

Creosote was obtained by the distillation of coal and wood tar. It was suggested as a treatment for tuberculosis as early as 1833, and was recommended specifically for the control of coughing.[4]

Dover's Powder was a traditional medicine against cold and fever developed by Thomas Dover, an eighteenth century English physician whose privateering voyage to the South Seas in the early 1700's provided the storyline for the novel *Robinson Crusoe*. The powder was a combination of ipecac (an agent to produce vomiting and expectoration), opium and potassium sulfate that was intended to induce sweating and prevent the development of a "cold" at the beginning of any attack of fever. It was also employed as a cough suppressant, antidiarrheal, and pain reliever, due to its opium component.

Le Roy mentions Dover's powder at least 42 times. He typically took it at bedtime, often for pain, as did his father on occasion and perhaps his mother as well.

Dover's powder was specifically recommended to suppress nocturnal coughing in tuberculosis: "In many cases nothing but opiates gives relief [of coughing]. . . . A dose of Dover's powder may be given in the evening now and then with a view of controlling the cough during the night, but to continue the administration of opium in any form for any length of time is dangerous." Dover's powder was also used for the treatment of diarrhea in tuberculosis.[5]

Hypophosphite of Lime was made by boiling phosphorus with lime, a calcium-containing mineral. The solution was then filtered and evaporated over sulphuric acid. "Alkaline sulphites" were used to treat various fevers, stomach disturbances, nervous disorders and anemia, sometimes in combination with iron or quinine. Hypophosphite of lime was specifically hyped as "the best and the most rational of all remedies against consumption (tuberculosis)," and advertised as a cure for tuberculosis in a nineteenth century newspaper.

Iodine was used as a disinfectant, but also for the relief of the chest pain of tuberculosis. (See Mustard Plaster, below).

Jimson Weed, or Devil's snare, is another plant in the nightshade family, similar to Belladonna. It was used as a sedative, as a treatment for cough, intestinal cramps, and diarrhea, and as a pain killer for arthritis, rheumatism, and headache.

Laudanum, introduced to the Western world during the Renaissance, was a "tincture of opium," a solution in ethanol, containing almost all of the opium alkaloids, including morphine and codeine.

---

4   Maurice Fishberg, *Pulmonary Tuberculosis* (Lea & Febiger, 1919), 646.

5   Ibid.

Lavender, an aromatic herb, is thought to relax the nervous system, reduce stress, and encourage a good night's sleep.

Lettuce Opium, a milky fluid, or latex, secreted from the base of the stems of several species of lettuce was used as a sedative for irritable cough and as a sleeping aid for insomnia.

Mercury (given to LeRoy as *Blue Mass*), was a mercury-based medicine in pill form used in the nineteenth century as a treatment for syphilis, and as a remedy for tuberculosis, constipation, toothache, parasitic infections, and the pains of childbirth. Mercury is very toxic. Symptoms of mercury poisoning could include muscle weakness, poor coordination, paresthesias (numbness in the hands and feet), rashes of the skin, anxiety, memory problems, trouble speaking, or difficulty with vision or hearing.

Magnesium Citrate is a saline laxative. Le Roy may have used it to treat constipation resulting from the use of belladonna derivatives and narcotic agents such as opium (including Dover's powder), and morphine.

Mustard plasters were made by spreading mustard seed or powder inside a wet dressing. An enzymatic reaction in the wet mustard powder produced a chemical that was absorbed through the skin, providing warmth and stimulating nerve endings to distract the pain-sensing mechanism of the body. The warm dressing was used to treat rheumatism, arthritis and aching muscles. It was also prescribed for chest congestion. If left in place for too long, a mustard plaster could produce first-degree burns. During the nineteenth century, this remedy was specifically recommended in the treatment of the chest pain of tuberculosis.[6]

Opium, obtained from the opium poppy, contains the powerful pain-reliever, morphine, as well as the closely-related opiates codeine and thebaine (a precursor to synthetic opioids hydrocodone and hydromorphone).

While opium was used primarily as an analgesic, it had multiple roles in the pharmacopeia of the Civil War era. Due to its constipating effect, it became one of the most effective treatments for cholera, dysentery, and diarrhea. As a cough suppressant, opium was used to treat tuberculosis, bronchitis, and other respiratory illnesses. Opium was additionally prescribed for insomnia. Compared with other drugs of the day, including mercury, arsenic and emetics, it was relatively benign, but had the potential for addiction.

6   Ibid., 661.

Paregoric was a 4% opium tincture, also containing benzoic acid, camphor, and anise oil. It was a household remedy in the 19th century, used to control diarrhea and as an expectorant and as a cough medicine.

Quinine, an alkaloid drug extracted from the bark of the cinchona tree, was specifically indicated for the treatment of malaria, but was used for the treatment of chills and fever of all kinds. Common side effects that LeRoy might have experienced from quinine were headache, ringing in the ears, and visual disturbances. More severe side effects could include deafness, low blood platelets, and an irregular heartbeat.

Sage Tea, which was sage juice in warm water has been recommended since ancient times for treatment of hoarseness and coughs. Sage was officially listed in the United States Pharmacopoeia from 1840 to 1900.

Dennis A. Rasbach, MD, FACS

Note on Sources

A wide variety of sources were used to footnote LeRoy's entries. The following are among the most important:

Books

Mark Boatner, *The Civil War Dictionary* (Vintage, 1991), has thousands of entries on nearly ever prominent officer, battle, campaign, ship, and event of the war.

Harriet F. Comer, ed., *History of Macon: The First One Hundred Years, 1823-1923* (The Macon Telegraph, 1996) is a reprint of a circular published for subscribers to the paper, which put some of Macon's civic institutions (church denominations, schools, etc.) into a wider context.

Richard William Iobst, *Civil War Macon* (Mercer Univ. Press, 2009) was one of the most pivotal sources in working with LeRoy's journals. Iobst verifies many of the events mentioned by LeRoy, usually provided more depth, and often added important information on other issues LeRoy either did not know about or may have avoided, such as the scandal and solution regarding the pricing of Macon Manufacturing Company fabric. Iobst also included chapters on the arsenal, armory, hospitals, and munitions laboratory, all of which were critical in the role Macon played in the Civil War.

John Rozier, ed., *The Granite Farm Letters: The Civil War Correspondence of Edgeworth & Sallie Bird* (Univ. of Georgia Press, 1988) made available invaluable letters between LeRoy's Auntie and Uncle Edge. These provided insight into their relationship and the close relationship between the Gresham and Bird families. The letters between husband, wife, and children verified and expanded upon information LeRoy wrote about in his journals, such as the capture and imprisonment of Uncle Richard, the relationships of various family members (such as Cousin Teadee), and how the Bird family viewed their relationship with and responsibility towards their slaves.

Iris Margaret Ayres Smale, *Albert Martin Ayres I Memoirs* (LuLu, 2004) A contemporary of LeRoy's, Albert Ayres describes decades after the event the accident that crushed LeRoy's left leg (he was also injured, only slightly). While he does not mention LeRoy by name, Ayres places him as a student at Sylvan Bates' school at the time of the collapsing chimney.

David Williams, *Georgia's Civil War* (Mercer Univ. Press, 2017) offered a wider focus on issues Georgians dealt with during the Civil War, like maintaining sufficient troop levels, regulations regarding the planting of cotton, problems with deserters, layabouts, and rebellious slaves, and the overall political and economic atmosphere as the war progressed. This book explained the seizure or "conscription" of slaves to work on fortifications, draft animals for military use, and discussed taxation (which was often more than the legally prescribed 10%).

The War of the Rebellion: A Compilation of the Official Records of the Union and Confederate Armies, 128 vols. Washington, D.C.: Government Printing Office, 1880-1901, is absolutely required when researching events of the Civil War.

Internet

Ancestry.com was and remains invaluable resource and was indispensable in putting together LeRoy's family tree which includes 1,700 identified related individuals. Ancestry includes the 1860 Federal Census, 1860 Federal Slave Schedule, various Confederate military records, taxation records, and much more.

INDEX

Adams, John: 357, 357n

Aiken, David Wyatt: 248, 248n

Aiken, Warren Sr.: 80, 80n

Albert, Prince Consort: 97, 97n

Alexander, Peter Wellington ("P.W.A."): 154, 154n, 211, 219, 228, 241, 256, 267, 268, 269, 270, 272, 303, 307, 308, 314

Allatoona, Battle of: 341, 341n, 342

Allen (slave): 64, 64n, 65, 65n, 66, 69, 70, 71, 81, 88, 91, 93, 95, 96, 101, 190, 199, 206, 206n, 208, 208n, 227, 262, 265, 283, 290, 300, 301, 310, 317, 336, 337, 348, 374, 379, 381, 381n, 395

Anderson, George Burgwyn: 167, 167n

Anderson, James Patton: 290, 290n, 331, 331n

Anderson, Richard Heron: 58, 58n, 72, 72n, 133, 134n, 167, 167n, 236, 239, 262, 303, 303n, 311, 344

Anderson, Robert: 20, 20n

Andersonville: 292n, 297n, 325n

Andrews, James J.: 127n

Antietam/Sharpsburg, Battle of: 70, 152n, 166, 166n, 167n, 168n, 169, 170, 171,177, 178n, 215n, 237, 248, 249n

Arch (slave): 84, 101, 177, 195, 201, 246, 247, 249, 251, 252, 271, 274, 274n, 284, 337, 373, 381

Arkansas Post/Fort Hindman, Battle of: 201, 201n

Armistead, Lewis Addison: 167, 167n, 236, 237n, 239

Arthur (slave): 4, 4n, 45, 186, 275

Ashby, Turner: 141, 141n

Atlanta Campaign: 308n

Atlanta, Battle of: 320n

Aunt Peggie/Peggy (slave): 11, 11n, 19, 338, 344, 344n, 345, 400

Axson, Ellen Louise: 124n

Axson, Rev. Isaac Stockton Keith: 124, 124n

Bagby, George William: 245n

Baker, Edward Dickinson: 78, 78n

Ball's Bluff, Battle: 76n

Banks, Nathaniel Prentice: 50, 50n, 137, 137n, 155n, 192, 196, 227, 229, 229n, 236, 240n, 287, 299n, 302, 302n, 303, 305

Barksdale, William: 236, 237n, 239

Barlow, Francis Channing: 238

Bartow, Francis Stebbins: 42, 42n, 44

Bates, Bob/Robert: 9, 9n, 28, 30, 31, 66, 81, 81n, 218n, 325, 326, 327, 328, 329, 330, 331, 335, 343, 344, 347, 349, 350, 355, 370, 379

Bates, Mr. Sylvan: 8, 9n, 13, 18, 23, 26, 34, 36, 63, 68, 70, 70n, 75, 77, 79, 84n, 87, 100, 101, 104, 107, 108, 123, 131, 132, 145, 162, 178, 182, 186n, 190n, 219, 220, 227, 252, 285, 325, 326, 333, 335, 339, 400

Bates, Olivia: 99, 218, 218n, 219

Bates, William: 290, 293

Baxter, Alice: 24, 24n, 47, 51, 52, 54, 56, 58, 59, 60, 66, 67, 89, 91, 100

Baxter, Andrew (Uncle Andrew): 10, 24, 24n

Baxter, Caroline Tracy (Aunt Carrie): 8, 10, 10n, 15, 23, 24, 37, 38, 39, 39n, 45n, 89n, 202n

Baxter, Dr. John Springs (Uncle John): 10, 11, 13, 15, 21, 23, 25, 39, 41, 42, 43, 49, 50, 52, 52n, 53, 56, 57, 58, 59, 60, 70, 71, 73, 74, 75, 76, 77, 83, 84, 86, 89, 93, 94, 96, 99, 100, 101, 117, 119, 128, 130, 131, 132, 136, 141, 148, 159, 168, 181, 183, 192, 197, 198, 201, 204, 207, 219, 223, 292, 293, 294, 295, 297, 299, 301, 304. 308, 322, 322n, 329, 330, 334, 373, 374, 375, 377

Baxter, Edwin Gilmer (Uncle Ed): 25, 25n, 60n, 74, 217, 254

Baxter, Eli Harris, Sr. (Uncle Eli): 158, 158n, 381, 381n

Baxter, Eli Leroy (Uncle Link): 50, 50n, 74, 113, 153, 153n, 179, 183n, 220

Baxter, Ellenora Francisca Scott (Aunt Ellen): 74n, 310, 310n

Baxter, Frank (slave): 36, 36n, 45, 100, 101, 101n, 134, 163, 176, 181, 186, 212, 213, 279, 283, 298, 340, 344, 344n, 345, 383, 384

Acknowledgments

As it is with any book, many people assisted along the way. If you do not find your name here, please know it was an oversight, and that I deeply thankful for your help.

Theodore P. Savas, managing director of Savas Beatie, brought me into this project and worked "shoulder-to-shoulder" with me from beginning to end as its developmental editor, advisor, and confidant. Ted helped with the military aspects, secured many of the images, oversaw the production of maps, and suggested a number of research leads. His interest in LeRoy and his journals is as deep and heartfelt as my own. His staff has also been very helpful, including marketing director Sarah Keeney, and media specialist Renee Morehouse.

The nature of LeRoy's medical condition remained something of a mystery until Ted asked one of his authors, Dr. Dennis Rasbach, for his considered opinion. He jumped in and worked tirelessly to determine that LeRoy was suffering from spinal tuberculosis. Dr. Rasbach also graciously wrote A Medical Foreword, and A Medical Afterword, which provide context and fascinating information on LeRoy's doctors, treatments, medicines, and much more. *The War Outside My Window* would not be nearly as valuable were it not for his selfless contributions. Thank you, Dennis.

Many others provided tireless assistance, including: Civil War cavalry expert Eric Wittenberg on various Confederate cavalry and horse-related issues; former teaching colleague Tonya Curtis, for her help with LeRoy's Latin words and phrases; Jay Foulk for information on the practices involved in nineteenth century surveying that helped me make sense of some of the information LeRoy conveyed about his brother's work as an army surveyor; Lamar Williams graciously provided photos of Mary Gresham's brothers and other helpful materials; Dr. Mark Newell, an archaeologist and Ted Savas's close friend, was a source of terrific information about the era and was always available for questions or to bounce around ideas; Samantha McLaughlin helped educate me on the finer points of life in this era and answered questions that I had; Hal Jesperson for the outstanding maps.

E. J. Noble and Keith Bryan, the magnificent 1842 Inn in Macon, Georgia, have been especially helpful and gracious. The lovely bed and breakfast is the mansion built by John Gresham in 1842, and in which LeRoy was born, wrote his journals, suffered, and died. E. J. and Keith provided previously unpublished photos, answered my many questions, and were helpful from beginning to end. Thank you!

There are so many friends in my different support networks, as well as my family—especially my daughters Allison and Lauren—who provided unending encouragement. A special thank you to Carolyn Berry and Randy Silvers, who have given me more than they know. They look forward to getting to know LeRoy Wiley Gresham, and I look forward to sharing him and his story with them.

I hope everyone finds LeRoy and his story as remarkable as I do.

About the Editor

Janet Elizabeth Croon holds a Bachelor's Degree in Political Science, Modern European History, and Russian Language and Area Studies from the University of Illinois at Urbana-Champaign (1983), and a Master's Degree in International Studies from the University of Dayton (1985). She taught International Baccalaureate History for Fairfax County Public Schools for nearly two decades, and developed a deep interest in the Civil War by living in northern Virginia. *The War Outside My Window* is her first book.